THE ROYAL HORTICULTURAL SOCIETY

A History 1804-2004

THE ROYAL HORTICULTURAL SOCIETY

A History 1804-2004

BRENT ELLIOTT

PHILLIMORE

2004

Published by
PHILLIMORE & CO. LTD
Shopwyke Manor Barn, Chichester, West Sussex, England

ISBN 1 86077 272 2

Printed and bound in Great Britain by
CAMBRIDGE PRINTING

Contents

Acknowledgements

David Banks/*The Garden*, 178; Lady Anne Berry, 97, 98; Dave Chancellor, 266; Trevor Nicholson Christie, 96, 101 (left), 108 (both), 298, 301; Dr Frances Clegg, 170 (bottom); Private Collection of Mr Rene Dee, 159; Brent Elliott, 86, 346, 356; *The Garden*, 113, 149, 225; John Glover, 89, 94 (top and right); Jerry Harpur, 137, 276; Marcus Harpur, 107; Dorothy Irvin/NAFAS, 304; Greg King, 95 (bottom); London Borough of Hounslow, Local Studies Collection, Chiswick Public Library, 13, 18 (bottom), 61; Elspeth Napier, 191 (below left); Martin Page/*The Garden*, 76; RHS/M.C. Sleigh, 261, 349; RHS Estate Office/Martin Harvey, 162 (both), 163; RHS Garden Harlow Carr, 109 (below left); RHS Garden Harlow Carr/C. Bower, 109 (right), 110; RHS Garden Rosemoor, 99, 100, 101 (right), 102; RHS Garden Wisley/M.C. Sleigh, 83 (right), 92, 226, 227, 246, 267, 282, 310; RHS Press Office, 128 (top), 134 (bottom), 322, 334; Paul Richardson, 90; Mrs Helen Robinson, 103, 104; Jane Sebire/*The Garden*, 137 (top), 268, 347; Tim Sandall/*The Garden*, 105, 145, 146, 280, 293 (bottom); Martin Slocock, 148 (top); Ticketmaster, 139; Jennifer Vine, 176; Greg Wise, 94 (left), 279; Steve Wooster, 106; all other illustrations RHS Lindley Library.

Every effort has been made to trace and acknowledge the copyright of illustrations. If any have been overlooked the RHS would be pleased to hear from the copyright holder.

Preface

The history of the Royal Horticultural Society has been written several times before, in differing degrees of detail. The first substantial history was compiled by the then Assistant Secretary, Andrew Murray, and published in 1863 as *The Book of the Royal Horticultural Society*. The Society, originally founded as the Horticultural Society of London, had received a new Charter and changed its name only two years previously; the book's tone was celebratory, its pages decorated with steel-engraved borders and pasted-in photographs, and it remains a source of useful information. Thereafter, officers of the Society tried their hand at compact accounts: William Wilks, the Secretary, in 1890, and Sir Trevor Lawrence, the President, in 1896. During the 1940s, Arthur Simmonds, the Assistant Secretary, wrote a series of well-researched biographical studies of the Society's founders, followed by a capsule history of the Society for the sesquicentenary edition of its *Journal*. By the time he retired in 1961, he was already working on a larger-scale history, and Council formally requested him to write it.[1]

Simmonds worked on the project for a further three years, and submitted a typescript that was pronounced 'remarkable', then subjected to the scrutiny of a committee which decided that it needed revision and editing. Simmonds was by now failing in health, and Harold Fletcher, formerly Superintendent of Wisley, was asked to undertake the revision. In fact, as a comparison of the typescripts shows, Fletcher made few substantial alterations to Simmonds's text, apart from in the closing chapters; his major addition was a series of 'interludes' intended to give the garden-historical background to the Society's activities—a task, it must be said, for which he was not gifted. Fletcher expected the book to be published under the names of Simmonds and Fletcher jointly, but in 1968 Council took the decision that Fletcher's name alone should appear on it. Fletcher wrote a letter of remonstration, but Simmonds—sick, a month away from death, probably unaware how little Fletcher had altered his text—gave his approval, and the book duly appeared under Fletcher's name in 1969 as *The Story of the Royal Horticultural Society*. The following year Fletcher was officially appointed Historian to the Society.[2]

The book was well received; Joseph Ewan reviewed it for the Society's *Journal*, and declared that it would 'become a family word in the garden circle'.[3] He concluded with some unanswered questions (I hope I have answered them, but alas! he is no longer around to comment), but many more could have been found. The Fletcher-Simmonds history ignores past scandals whenever possible, skates lightly over the Kensington years in general, barely notices the series of provincial shows, virtually ignores the histories of the Society's numerous committees, which have been its effective life-blood. Above all, perhaps, it is deficient in reference notes, so that the reader simply has to take the authors' word for things, and its index falls some degrees short of user-friendliness. Accordingly, when the decision was taken to commission a new history for the Society's bicentennial, it was to be not a revision of Fletcher-Simmonds, but a completely new book. Unlike its predecessor, it is largely organised by subject rather than by overall chronology, at the risk of a certain degree of repetition. The first three chapters offer an overview of the Society's establishment and administrative history; then the various gardens, shows, halls, research programmes, and other activities are dealt with in separate chapters.

I have tried to provide fairly comprehensive documentation for my statements, so that future researchers do not have to take my word for anything. The single most important source for the Society's history is its own archives, but these are both intermittent and in need of supplementing from other sources. The intermittence is the consequence partly of attrition predictable in an organisation which has changed address several times, and partly of a deliberate instruction from John Hamer, the Society's Secretary from 1962 to 1975, to clear out the mass of old documents that had accumulated in the offices. (Hamer's catchphrase has been quoted to me as 'What's the good of history?') Peter Stageman, the Librarian, and Eva Weise, the head of the typing pool, hid various volumes of minutes in the backs of cupboards, so that Hamer would not realise they had not been destroyed; but nonetheless a large mass of material disappeared, and apart from the minutes of Council there is hardly a longstanding committee whose paperwork survives in unbroken sequence.

This is not to say that the surviving minutes are necessarily models of informative clarity. They tend to be records of decisions, rather than of discussions. George Glenny accused the Council of the 1840s of falsifying the records of its meetings, by recording absentees as present; and certainly, at times of crisis, a reticence can be discerned, as when the minutes state that 'A communication was made to the Council by one of the Members present, and certain resolutions taken thereupon'.[+] There are clearly gaps in the record other than those induced by 20th-century clearance.

My gratitude, therefore, to those libraries to which I have had recourse for additional information: most notably those of the Royal Botanic Gardens, Kew; the Natural History Museum; the Linnean Society; the local history collections of the Westminster, Chiswick, and Kensington and Chelsea libraries; the British Library and the British Newspaper Library at Colindale; and the Aberdeen University special collections. And here I may slip in the names of the Library staff of the Royal Horticultural Society during the period on which I have worked on this book: John Fisher, Rita Flain, Liz Gilbert, Mark Handley, Menai Jones, Debbie Lane, Paula Lavis, Kathy Lazenbatt, Wendy Payne, Michael Rudd, Carole Sharp, Natasha Spencer, Jennifer Vine, Phanis Vrettos, Helen Ward, Carol Westaway, and Chris Wisdom. Without their assistance and load-bearing capacities I would undoubtedly have foundered. Special thanks are due to my wife, Frances Clegg, for tolerating all the disruption this book has brought into our life.

A problem, of course, arises with the treatment of the recent past. In common with many institutions, we maintain an effective 30-year rule on the accessibility of archives; we do not refuse access to recent archives in principle, but we require readers to submit written notice, so that we may vet the materials that are asked for, and ensure that potentially libellous or sensitive documents are kept back. Accordingly, I have tended to cite published accounts only for the more recent events. This is also the place to mention an editorial decision rarely to mention the names of current staff members below the level of Director unless they have been very long-standing.

Portions of this book have appeared previously. The account of the building of the New (Lawrence) Hall is taken with little alteration from an article I wrote for what was then the *Thirties Society Journal* (1991). In 1988 I compiled an appendix to the report of the Review Committee on Committee Structure, giving the history of the Society's various committees; portions of that text have been re-used. And various articles, biographical or otherwise, that I have contributed over the years to *The Garden* have also yielded paragraphs here and there.

An institutional history like this is inevitably a collaborative undertaking. Everyone I have worked with at the RHS has contributed to it in some way or other, if only by being part of the history. I will limit myself here to acknowledging those who have helped by reading portions of the text while it was being revised, or being interviewed on points of amendment: Barry Ambrose, Jim Arbury, Christopher Bailes, Stephen Bennett, Rebecca Bowen, Barbara Collecott, Rene Dee, Malcolm Duncan, Colin Ellis, Jim Gardiner, Paul Griffiths, Liz Hughes, Linda Jones, Sally Kington, Lucinda Lachelin, Don Lamberth, Alan Leslie, Diana Miller, Lynn Palmer, Michael Pollock, Mary Shirville, Bob Sweet, Mavis Sweetingham, Lindsay Thomas, Will Tjaden, Simon Thornton-Wood. And of course, Susanne Mitchell and Barbara Haynes of our Publications Department, who have read the thing innumerable times, hunted out illustrations and whittled down my proposed selections, rung alarm bells, tried to avert stampeding footnotes, bolted the door against a proliferation of appendices and tables, and in general been constantly encouraging and supportive.

BRENT ELLIOTT
July 2003

List of Subscribers

Linda Frances Aaronson
Ann Lady Aberconway
A M E Adams
Andrew Adams
Miss Sylvia Adams
Gabriele Ahlemeyer
Mr Mumtaz Ahmad Sudullah
Peter Alder
Mr & Mrs V N Alexander
Patricia Spence Allan
Diana Allen
Paul Alan Allen
T M Allen
Jane Wallace Alling
Mrs B Alsop
Barry Ambrose AHRHS
Valerie Ames
Mrs Barbara Anderson
Dorothy Anderson
Warren David Anderson
Des & Elizabeth Andersson
Marguerite Andrieux
Roger Angerson
Richard Ansell
Linda Antell
Marian Armstrong
Mr & Mrs R G Armstrong
John A R Arnold (Mr)
Raymond Ash
Mrs Annette Asteraki
Mr Brian Atkinson
Patricia Atkinson
Maria Cecilia Barbuto Attie 1904/
    1954/2004
Mr A R J Bailey
Mrs Beatrice I Bainbridge
Jannie Baker
Mrs Jean M Baker
Joy Baker
Mrs Jane Balfour
Mr & Mrs Roy B Band
Margaret Bankier
Lawrence Banks
Mrs Joan M Barclay
Dr Peter M Barham
J M Barlow
Richard E Barnes
Susan Barrance
Paul Barrow
Mrs S Barrows
Anthea M Barry
John D Barry
Lester G Batchelor
J D Bates
Nick and Anne Bates
Gwendoline Batham
David Bathurst
Daniel Luke Batie
Jean B Bavister
Joan M Baylis
Elisabeth Bayliss (Mrs)
Carolyn I Bazeley
John E Beales
Anne E Beall
Christopher N Beard
Jenni Beard
Ruth Lydia Beard
Dr Roger D Beauchamp
Anne Beaumont
Mrs Rosemary Beer
Headley T Beeson
Douglas M Begg
Ruth C Bell
Colin and Margaret Benfield
David M Bennett
Dennis G Bennett
Stephen Bennett
Janice Bennetts
Susanne Benton
Mary Bickerton
Jean Bigger
Mr & Mrs W Biggs
Dr Margaret Billinghurst
Victor H Biraben
Alan J Bird
Jane Bird
I D Bisset
Elizabeth Black ·
C F Blackman
Barbara H Blagg
Glenys Catherine Blake
Mrs Norma J Blakey
Brian J Blaylock
Mary Blears
Linda Blenkinship
Shirley Blick
Gladys Mary Blizzard
Geoffrey Bloomfield
Blue Mountains Rhododendron
    Society of New South Wales Inc.
Shirley Blyth
Sylvia Bodle
Caroline Boisset
Mrs S D Bolton

Alan Edward Bond
Mrs C M Bond
Joan Booker
Joanne M Booth
Pauline Booth
Mrs Moira E Borthwick
Rt Hon Robert Boscawen MC
Alan Boswell ACII
Val Bott
Miss G M Boughton
R E Boughton
Andrew Parker Bowles
Eddis C Box
Stephen Boys Smith
Anita Bracalente
Howard Bradley
Jane Bradley
Christine M Bradshaw
Rebecca Brain
Peter D Brant
Clare & Ron Brazier
Margaret Breakell
D Brehaut
C D Brickell
Michael John Brill
Elaine Brooke
Ann Brooks
Audrey V Brooks
Roy Brooks
Carole Brown
David H Brown
Elizabeth Brown
Mrs Joanna G M Brown
Julie Brown
Lesley Brown
Peter William Brown
Miss Rosalie Brown
Sandra V Brown
Mrs Susan Brown
Sybil Brown
William Brown
Rosemary Brownlow-Smith
Cedric D Bryant
Brian Daniel Buckley
Peter Buckley
Pamela M Bucknall
Antonia J Bunch
Nigel Bunning
W F Burman
Graeme N Burn
Richard S Burnell
Erica Dale Burnett
Roger Burnett
Jane Burnley
Brian J Burton
Lt Col and Mrs G J Buss
Alan H Butler
Henry Butterfield
Ellen Joice Butterworth
Susan Buttery
Sara Byrne
John W Cairns
Frances Mary Cameron (Miss)
Jane Camp
Paul Campbell
Theresa Candler
R Cann and R Bradford
Barbara Ann Cantelo
Peter & Eileen Cantillon
James David Care
Sir Kenneth Carlisle
Lynne Carruthers
Roger Carsley
Robert Spencer Carson
Mr D J Carter
Jim Carter
Muriel Carter
Stephen Carter
Robert P Case
Lori Anne Cates
Maureen Catlin
Mrs Jane L Causebrook
Mr N E Cave
Barbara M Challenor
Anne Chapman
Michael Charlesworth
Margaret Charlton
Albie F Cheeseman
Mrs Henrietta Cheshire
Ivor Chinman
Palle Christensen
Leslie A Clack
Helen M Clancy
R W Clargo
Alastair & Ruth Clark
Judith M Clark
Paul Clark
Mr V C Clark
Valerie Clark
Dr D D Clarke
Jean E Clarke
John V Clarke
Mary Clarke
Paul Clarke

Tricia Clarke
R M Claxson
Brenda Mary Clayton
Maureen Cliff
Penelope Clive
Mrs H P Coates
John C Coker
Roger and Pam Coldham
Dr Martin Cole
Barbara Collecott
Mrs J S Collier
Richard M Collier
Michael J Collins
Sheila M Collins
David Collyer
Ivan Colover
Martin Colyer
June Condy
Janet Cone
Conservatoire Botanique de la Ville de
    Genève
Dennis Cooke
Eileen Cooke
Gary Cooles
Michael Cooling
Gillian Coombs
David Cooper
Mr William Nigel Cooper
Mrs Kathleen Copland
Joy Copling
Ray Coppack
Wendy Corben
Peter James Corns
Valerie J Coster (Mrs)
Hazel G Cotgrove
Phil Cottingham
Joan Ellen Coules
Dr Hilary Coutts
Fiona Cownie
Mrs Dorothy Cox
Joan Crane
Alan Douglas Crawford
Susan Crawford
Mrs Theresa L Creed
Peter John Criddle
Mr Christopher Cripps
Audrey A Croom
Ted Croot
Alan S Cross
J Cubey
Jane Cummings
Robert H Cummins
Peggy S Cunningham
John Currie
Peter & Janet Daborn
M R Dace
P J R Dale
Prof R P Dales
Mrs C A Daniels
Mr & Mrs J F R Danks
Paul Darlington
G A J Dash
Mrs Ann Davies
Mrs Josephine Davies
Margaret Anne Davies
Ronald Davies
John Davis
Julie Davis
William A Davis
Susan Davison
Nigel Peter Dawson
Peter Dean
L Debersaques
Fr Jacob Deckwitz
Ann Frith Cartwright DeCouto
Mr Graham F Deeprose
Robert J Dell'Angelo MD
Sheilah M Dellow
Harvey D F Dennett
Charlotte Derry
G L Devereux
Jill Dewar
Jacqueline A Dewdney
Jean & Alan Dietz
Linda Diggins
Hanneke van Dijk
Veronica Dillon
Celia Dinsdale
Mr Geoff Dipple
Mrs Elaine Dixon
Pamela Dixson
Val Dolman
D M Donovan
Anthony C Dorman
M W Dornan
Sharon Lesley Dowie
Mrs C E Downing
Ivan Downs
Dr John J Drew III
R Dromard
I S Drury
Kath Dryden VMH
John H Dryfhout
Steve Duckworth

Mrs Glennis Dudeney
R G Dukes
Brenda Dulake
Allan Robert Duncan
Malcolm Duncan
Mrs Morag Duncan
G W Dunham
Piers Dunn
Zoe Dunsiger
Daphne Dunster
Christine Dunwell
Miss A E Durham
Vivienne Durne
Mr T H Eaton
Ronald J Eddey
Elizabeth I Edgeler
Derek J Edis
Margaret Edis
John Edmondson
Gerald M Edwards
Dr Peter Edwards
Ronald Glyn Edwards
Simon J Edwards
Susan Diane Edwards
Diane Eldridge
Jacqueline L K Eldridge
Ann Patricia Eley
Brian & Olwyn Ellerby
Gwyneth Ellery
Baroness Elles
Michael Elles
Margaret G A Elliott
Charles Ellis
Colin P Ellis
Mrs Patricia Ellis
Graham John Elvidge
Angela Emery
Gillian Emery
Mrs Susan Emsley
Pat English
Colin Ennis
Elizabeth Ellen Erskine-Black
Lorna Anne Espenhahn
Mrs Zenaida Etheridge
Mrs Jose Aline Evans
Mrs Phyllis V Evans
Mrs Adrian Eve
M A E Everett
Barbara R Faithfull
Gabrielle Falkiner
Mark John Farley
Margaret Farndon
Dr P J Faulkner
Simon Fawcus
C D Fears
Nini C Feddersen
Jean Frances Fellowes-Prynne
Simon P Fenelon
Miss M G Fenner
J Barry Ferguson
Dr John A Ferguson
Colin Ferries
Marjorie Field
Anne Fielder
K G Fisher
Margaret & Alan Fisher
Brian Fishpool
Jo Fitz-Henry
David A Fitzjohn
Peter James Flannery
Laurence Flatman
Margaret A Fletcher
Sibylla Jane Flower
Mrs P M A Fogg
Betty Foley
Raymond Foord-Brown
Ancia & Tony Ford
Dr Thomas W Ford
Mrs Hilary Forder
Barbara R Forshaw
Roy Forward
Suzanne Foster
Debra Fowler
Dorothy Fox
Martin and Bridget Fox
Mrs Pamela S Fox
Miss Pat Fox-Matthews
Mrs Robert L Frackelton
Arthur Freeborn
Michaela Freed
Nicholas Freed
Anne French
Mrs & Mrs John French
Frenchay & Hambrook Hort. Society
    1943-2003
Monika Frey
Luke Fromant
Peter Frost
Helga Fryars
D J Fuller
Anita Fursey
Araceli Fyfe
Victor R Gainey
Jim Gardiner

Arthur Gardner
Dr Harry W Gardner
Jean E Gatcombe
Diane Gauld
Brenda Geeson
Mr G J George
Christine Gibbs
Arthur & Margaret Gibson
Kenneth John Gibson
John Gilbert
Richard Gilbert
Mr Malcolm Giles
R Gilkerson
Gordon Gill
Joanna Gilliat
Kathleen Gilman
Mrs Jean M Gilmartin
Andrew J Gladwell
Brian W Glover
Michael Godbee
Olive Godden
James & Fiona Gold
Barbara Golden
Joan Gollins
Nigel Goodman
G Goodship-Patience
Jillian Goodwin
Christopher Gore
Mrs Janet Gotch
Gillian Goudge
Connie J Gover
Graham D Grace
Jennifer Grant
Angela Margery Gray
Ian Charles Gray
Mrs Ivy Grayshon
Mr R Å Greatorex
Diana Withers Green
Mrs Laura Ann Green
Louise Green
Richard Green
Nancy E E Greenway
Mrs Betty Greenwood
Sue Gregory
Mary Grevatt
Margaret Grey
Gary Grief
A Griffin
Claire M G Griffiths
John Grimshaw
Viv and George Grinbergs
Joan B M Grinsted
Joseph G W Grist
Anne Grocock
Janet Margaret Groom
Peter Gross
Robert Gunnett
W S A Gunter
Mr Carol Gurney
Mr N Gwilt
Carole Hack
Patricia Hadland
Mrs Vera Haigh
Mrs Gladys Hakansson
Pamela H Hales
Mrs Caroline S Hall
Margaret Hall
Nigel Hall
Valerie Hall
Peter Hallam
Jan Hallett
F M Halliwell
Valerie J Hamill
Dorothy Hamilton
Mary Ann Hanbury
Martin Hancock
Mr & Mrs Martin Hancox
Hartha Johnson Hanerfeld
Anne Stine Hansen
George Hanson
Miss Janice Hardern
John Harding
Miss P Harding
Mervyn E Hardman
Mrs Wendy B Hardwick
Carolyn Hardy
Leslie A Hardy
Michael & Betty Hardy
John Harford
Derek Hargreaves M Hort (RHS)
Marion Hargreaves
Mr Ralph Hargreaves
Hilary Harmer
Miss Anne Harris
Edward H V Harris
Ingrid Harris
Richard Guy Harris
Sheila Harris
Mrs Diane L Harrison
John Harrison
Wendell and Sandra Harsh
Avis Hart
Mrs M M Hart
C den Hartog
Joan E Hartwell
Anthony P Harvey
Brian R Harvey
Mary Harvey
Peter Harvey
Michael George Haslam
June Hawkins
Patricia Hayes

Jane E Hayter
Brian Hayward
Mrs Nicolin Hayward
Ann Hearn
Donald Hearn
Trevor J Hearn
Nancy D Hedley-Dent
Jane Hellman
Ann E Hemingway
Malcolm Hemming
Mark Hemming
S C Hemming-Clark
Peter Hemsley
Reinier Hendriksen
Yolanda Henneberry-Lazaro
Barbara Hertzell
David G Hewett
Maureen Hewitson
Hilda Hewitt
Andy Hibbard
Nicole Hickey
Allen Winston Hickson
Margaret Higginbottom
Mrs J Hill
Nora M Hill
Maureen Hilling
Mrs Vicci Hine
Ian and Judith Hodgson
Mr Hildo Hoek
Liz Hogfress
Vic & Issy Hogg
Isla Holden
Jackie Holloway
Moyra Holm
Carole Holme
Dave Holmes
Michael Holmes
Mrs M E Telford Holroyd
Pat Holt
R G Honnor
Mr D L Hooke
C R Hooper
Keith Hopkinson
James Horgan
Margaret Horn
Mr J J Hornby
Fiona S D Horner
George H Horrocks
June F E Hoskins
Gerald Leslie Hougham
Mrs R J Howell
Caroline Howells
Martin A Howells
Frances Howie
Kenneth Hudson
Liz Hughes
Jean Humphries
Patsy Hunt
Peter F Hunt
Martyn J Hunter
Maurice Milburn Hunter
Arthur Hurran
Ian Huxley
Janice Imrie
Mrs Ruth Ingham
Sally Anne Ingram
Ipswich Horticultural Society Inc
Jeffrey Ireland
Ralph & Maureen Ireland
Mrs Valerie Irving
Alan Jackson
Annette Jackson
Derek & Rachel Jackson
Elizabeth Jackson
C M Jacobson
Sharon Jager
Robin J James
Ann and Paul Jansz
K Jaruthavee
Pauline Jayes
R S Jeeps
Paula Jefferson
J D Jeffery
Mr H R Jeffs
Mrs Ruth Helen Jenkins
Carole Jennings
Judith Jepson
Christine Jessop
Erling Ove Johansen
Alexander Philip Johnson
Anthony Johnson
Clive B Johnson
Helen Johnson
P B Johnson
Peter Ewen Johnson
Phyllis Mary Johnson
R H W Johnson
Marie Johnston
Lynne Johnstone
Sylvia Johnstone
Sandra & Ed Joinson
Angela Jones
Brian Jones
Colin Jones and Donna Ford
David Geoffrey Jones
Dr Mary Jones
Sally I Jones
Mrs Sylvia Jones
Michael Jordan & Linda Henry
Dawn Judd
Dr A S Judge
Betty Judson

Yu Kawai
Mrs R W Keating
David P Keep
Kay Keeton
Dr Siegfried Kehl
Joe and Pauline Kellett
Charles Julian John Kember
Michael Kember
Paul Kempster
Richard G Kenworthy
J A Ross Kerby
Marjorie L Kevlahan
Sigrun Khan
Rachel Kilner
David Gilbert King
Derrell King
Mark A King
Mrs Pamela Helen King
Sally Kington
S E Kinsey
Mrs Joan Kirby
Jenny Kirkman
Mrs Wils Klaver
Albert Klein
Mr Renatus W Klüver
A M Knott
Maria Koehl
Lilian A Koss
Dorothy and Eddie Kreeger
Patricia M Kuegler
Bala Kylassum
Lucinda Lachelin
Mrs Jenny Lamb
Mr Don Lamberth
Norman G Lamdin
Yvette Lamidey
Roy Lancaster
Graham and Carol Lane
E M Langford
Rita and Kerry Langler
Joanne Langley
Bernard A Langworthy
Mr S Lansdell
Constance B Latzko
David S Law
Derek Lawrence
Graham Lawson
Frederick Lawton
Miss A J Lee
David J Lee
Linda Lee
Margaret A Lee
Mrs Ann Lees
Dorothy Lees
Thelma Legge
Suzanne Leggett (Mrs)
Vivien Leigh
Shona Leith
Wim Lemmers
Valerie Lenthall
Dr A C Leslie
Alan Lettin
Alison Levey
Audrey Levy
Jocelyn P Lewis
Mrs Linda H Lewis
Pamela Lewsen
Mrs Ida Leyland
Maureen Liepins
Sarah Jane Hunt Lightman
Hannah Lilien-Kipnis
Harry Lill
The Lindley Library
P J Lindley
Helen Lines
David I M Linklater
Elizabeth Liptrot
R W Littlechild
David Livermore
John Living
Arnold Lloyd
Pauline Lloyd-Thomas
Mrs Marina Long
W Anthony Lord
Mrs Helen Lorimer
Fiona Lott
Wayne Loveday
David K Low
Joyce M Low
Geoffrey Lowden
Heather P Lowe
Ann Lowther
H Luddington
Mrs Ann Ludford BA AMA
Marian Lund
Dr Ian J MacBean
Maria T L I Machado da Cruz
Mary A Mackay
C Mackechnie Jarvis
Joyce Collins MacLaren
Mr Iain Maclean
John Macleod
Denis M Magee
P A Maguire
John D Main
Beryl L Maltby
T T Mantel
Joseph G Marano
Tony Margel
Norman D Marrett
Jan Marsh

Sue Marshall
Juliet Marsham
Juergen Mart
Olive Martin
Mrs Stella Martin
Julia Matheson
Brian Mathew
Victoria Matthews
Tom and Heather Matthissen
Mr J W Mattingley
John Mattock VMH DHM
Janet Vivien Maughan
Simon Maughan
J O May
Penelope A McCartney
WL & JP McConnell
William McCutcheon
Mr J E McGahan
Linda McGowan
Paul McHarry
Terence J McKenna
Virginia McLaughlin
Brenda J McLean
Elizabeth P McLean
Margaret McOnie
Mrs Emid Measures
Cyril Leslie William Meen
Jean Megson
Monika Meier
Susan Mensforth
Yve Menzies
Vera J Mercer
Alec L Merrifield
Mrs Erica Metcalfe
R D Micklem
Yuki Mikanagi (Ms PhD)
Mrs C M Miles
Margaret Miles
Paul Miles
Anne Millar
Mrs Kitty Millbank
Daniel James Praed Miller
Diana M Miller
Gloria Miller
Mary Miller
M E Mills
Richard Mills
Bertha Mills-Hicks
John C Milner
Bernard Minter
Missouri Botanical Garden Library
C H Mitchell
Grayham Mitchell
Peter B Mitchell
Jane Mitson
Miss Josephine Mitson
Kimio Mitsuno
Eberhard Mohs
Leonard George Monk
Joan Monroe
Dennis Moorcraft
Alasdair Moore
Ann Moore
Joan Morgan
M W Moriarty
Angela Morris
Robert Morris
Sir Charles Morrison
Robin Morrison
Mrs Louise Mosey L.C.S.F.
Paul Moxey
Jeremy H L Mudditt
Jim Muil
Leslie A Mulford
Francis Allan Mullins
Alys Munden
Joanne Munro
Mrs Anne Elizabeth Murray
Mrs Julia Murray
The Museum of Garden History
Mr R B Musk
Dr Murray Mylechreest
Dr G P Nagel
Betty D Naish
Allison Napier
Lesley Naylor
Sylvia A Neale
Felicity Nelson
Danielle Neuman
Reginald Neuman
June T E Nevin
J E Newcomb Esq
J A Newton
John Nichol
Eileen Nicholson
Hugh L Nicholson MBE FLS FRICS
Bob and Maureen Niddrie
William Charles Noble
Jeremy Nolan
Barbara Eugenie Normanton
Trevor Nottle
H Nouwen-Kolthoff
Milton Nurse
Martin Oake and Liz Pieksma
Diane M Odell
Makiko Odori
Mary-Agatha O'Grady-Savage
Léonie Hazel Oldfield
Olive M Oldham
Mrs S Oliver
Susan Oliver
Brian & Christine Olivey

David A Orcutt
John E O'Reilly
Margaret Ruth Orr
Sheena and George Orr
Mary Osborn
Mrs C J Osborne
Tsue Asami Ostermann
Chris Owen
Lynda Padmore
Martin Page
David Palmer
John Palmer
Lynn Palmer
Richard Palmer
Jack & Rosemary Anne Pamment
Jan Park
Patricia Parker
Susan Parker
Eric Parkinson
Mrs Pauline Parkinson
Elma Parr
A du Gard Pasley
Sheila Passant
Karen Passey
Joy Frances Paton
Valentine Paton
Mrs J A S Pattullo
Royston Pavelin
Susan Pay
Mr Maurice G Payn
Irene Payne
Michael Payne
Peter Payne
Mrs Roger Peach
David & Barbara Peacock
J A Peacock
Gerry & Maggie Pearse
Margaret Penny
Ms Miriam Perrin
Jean Perry
Clara Perryman
Jean Petre
Pettet's Nursery
Mrs Dawn Pettit
Mr H W Pettit
Stephanie Pettit
Joanne Phillips
Nicky Pickett
Mary & Alan Pickles
Mary G Pinciotti
Susan Pinder
Peter and Jill Pitman
Mr John Plumpton
Julie Ann Pokrzywnicki
Sir Richard Carew Pole
Mrs J P Pollard
Nick Pollard
Mrs Evelyn M Pond
Madame Sara Pons
Dorothy J M Pope
Graham S Porter
Norma Postles
Richard J Potten
Gill Pratt
Joan Price
Sue Price
Jeanette Propert
Mr A J Proud
Ann Proudfoot
Gill Purkiss
Hazel Putland
Dr Roger Pyrah
Barbara Quiggin
James Quin
Rachel Quinlan
Mrs M Radford
Gordon H Rae
Mrs Arnold Rakusen
K C Ralph
Agnes Ramsdale
Rosemary Rankilor
Sandra Raphael
C H G Rasch
Madge Audrey Rayner
Mrs J Rosemary Read
AR & BJ Read
Karen Read
Stephen Record
Alan D Reder
Philip Armiston Redman
B C Redwood
June Redwood
Malcolm Redwood
Mrs Patricia Reed
Paul A J Reed
Mrs Muriel E Rees
Barbara Reid
Arthur Charles Rendell
John Rennie
Verena Rentzel
RHS Product Licensing Team
Lesley Ribeiro
Anne Richards
Mr Clive Richards OBE
F Stephen J Richards
Joyce Richards
Alex Richardson
Ann Richardson
Cynthia Richardson
Peter T Richmond
Mr Nicholas Riddell
Christine and John Ridge

David Ridgeway
G W Ridley
The Viscount Ridley
David & Susan Rigby
Brian Roberts
Michael Roberts
Susan Christina Roberts
Mrs Una A Robertson
Dr & Mrs C Robinson
Mrs Ellen Robinson
G Robinson
Helen Robinson
Margaret Robinson
Peter W Robinson
Dermot Rochford
William D Roe
Heidi Rogers
Trevor Rogers
Virginia Rolls
Naomi Rose
Martha Rosney
George Ross
Graham Alastair Ross
Ann Rossiter
Royal Botanic Gardens, Kew, Library
Keith Roylance
Mrs Joan C Russam
Joyce Russell
Mrs Barbara Sadler
Mrs H J Salter
Philip & Susan Sambrook
Vyvyan Sanson
Barbara Sargeaunt
Edwina Sass
Margaret Satterly
J Saunders
Dr Michael Saunders
Miss P A T Saunders BSc
Peter Saunders
Sheelagh M Savage
B C Savill-Daw
Allan Sawyer
Stella Saywell (Miss)
Andrew Walter Scales
Di Scammell
Mark C Scanlon
Prunella Scarlett
Sarah Scarlett
H Scherer-Flores
Maria Schofield
Lynnda Jean Scott
Patricia Scott
Peter Scott OBE
Timothy Scott-Saunders FRHS
Mr Alan Secrett
Catherine Sedgwick
Elizabeth Seel
Rob Senior
Elizabeth Mills Sesselberg
Carole Sharp
Reginald W Sharpington
Rose Sheldon
Shirley Anita Sheldon
Jannene Sheppard
Peter B Sheppard
Jacqueline Shepstone
Stan Sheriff
Paddy Sherrard
John Shinner
Mary Shirville
Colin Shorter
Tina Shrimpton
Theodora G Sibley
Tony Simkins
Bill Simpson
Mr & Mrs D J Simpson
Lelia Simpson
Mr Peter James Simpson
Mr & Mrs R J Simpson
Colin Simson
Timothy W Sineath PhD
Susan Janet Skevington
F E Skinner
Carol A Slater
Kaaren Slawson
Martin Slocock
Brett C Sloman
Dr Terry Smale
A R Smith AH
Anthony N Smith
D W Smith
Jane M Smith
Janet L Smith
Mary Smith
Mrs P J Smith SRN
Mr J Raymond Smith
Tracey D Smith
Mrs U L Smith
Dr Michael Sneary
Tricia Sneath
Maxim de Soissons
Grahame Mark Sole
Lilian Sommerfeld
Pamela South
Pamela M Southwell
Sir John Sparrow
G R Speed
Duncan Spence
Bernard R Spencer
John C Spencer
Hilda Spensley
Jenny Spivey

Douglas Stacey
Pip and Adam Stacey
O R Staples
Chris Starnes
Mrs Valerie Stearns
O E Steele
Mr M Stefanyszyn
Mrs M P Stenning
Douglas Stevens
Jacqueline Stewart
Joyce and Donald Stewart
K P Stinson
Shirley Stirling
Lady Stoddart of Swindon
Henry Arthur Stokes
Val Stone
Louise Storer
Peter J Storey
Mrs Angela Stray
K A Stroud
Anne Strover
Jean F Strutt
James A C Stuart
Jessie Stuart
Mrs Jane Stubbs
William W Stump
Shintaro Sugio
Hansi Summers
Patricia Sutcliffe
Stuart W Swan
Eileen Sworder
Amoret Tanner
Lesley Tanner
Mrs Maureen Taphouse
W Taplin
Noel Tappenden
Tatton Garden Society
Bernard Taylor Esq
J F Taylor
Jean A Taylor
Jean L Taylor
Patricia Taylor
William Taylor
Glenys Ruth Taylour
James F Tearle
Saina Tebble
J Tempest
Marjorie Theobald
A M Thomas
Brian Thomas
Glyn & Gill Thomas
Mr Graham R Thomas
Helen Thomas
Mary Persis Thomas
Ronald S Thomas
Michelle Thomasson
Brenda Thompson
Jane Louise Thompson
Margaret Thorley
Sally Thornton
Stephen Peter Thorpe
Keith Tilbury
Robert Tindall
Will Tjaden
Paddy & Mary Tobin
Dr P F Todd
D L Tombs
M R Tombs
Catherine Toms
Phyllis Toms
Tommy Tonsberg
Mr Christopher Toop
Hanne og Torben Skov
Toronto Botanical Garden Library
Peter Torrent
Mrs P S Towers-Clark
Sarah Catherine Treays
Dr Kenneth H Trigg
Joanna Truman
R E Truss
Eric G Turner
Frank Turner
Frederick S C Turner
Gerald B Turner
Mr & Mrs John G Turner
Nancy R Turner
Zena Tutt
Sheila Tutty
MD Majir Uddin
Pat Udy
Michael Upward
Marion Ure
Donna & Stephen Urquhart
Julie Uttridge
Paul Anthony Vacher
Geoffrey L Vandervelde
Sheila M Varo
Barbara Vaughan
Lily Ventom
Dennis Vernon
John Vickers
Daphne Vise
Alan Volke
Jean-Robert de Vooght
Charles Wace
Derrick Waddington
John H Waine
Bret Walker
Claire Walker
Miss Jane W Walker
Jennifer A Walker
Derek W Wallace

Paula Wallen
Chloe Waller
Ann Walters
Mrs Joan H Walters
Dr S Max Walters
Felicity Ward
Larry Ward
Raymond Ward
M Wardhaugh
Madeleine Wardle
Malcolm Warner
Josephine Warren
Roger S Warren
Annette Waterhouse
Christine & Stuart Waters
Mrs I D C Waterworth
B G Watson
Mr E Seymour Watson
Steven Watson
W Malcolm Watson
Edward Wawrzynczak
Brenda A Way
Emma Way
Brian E Waygood
Daphne Wayman
Gillian Weatherstone
Pauline Weaver
Amanda Webb
Harold A Webb
Mrs P L Webb & Mr M R Webb
Richard Webb
Michael Webley
Sir Martin & Lady Wedgwood
Brenda and Dennis Weeks
Dr David Weir
Sarah Weld
Margaret K Wesley
Anthony J W West
Mr G J West
Maureen West
Dr Pamela G West
Jane Wethered
Mr K Wetherell
Patricia & Brian Whalley
Claralouise Wheeler
Eileen Wheeler
Maggie Whitaker
Audrey M White
Dr David White
Graham White
Dr James White
Raymond White
Mrs Jane Whitehead
Morag G Whitehead
Catherine L Whitehorn
R T Whiteley
David B D Whitworth
Ronald C Wigley
John B Wilcox
Jean P Wildi
Anthony Wilkie
Debbie Wilkinson
Frederick Wilkinson
Mr John A Willard
Helen Margaret Welcome Willcock
Dennis Williams
Haden Williams
Lise Williams
R C Williams
John A Williamson
Susan Willis
Ursula Wilms
Mrs V E Wilshaw
Brian J Wilson
Cecilia Wilson
Christine Wilson
Mr David Wilson
G H Wilson
Gillian Winsey
Elaine Winter
Didier Wirth
C J Wisdom
S A Wise
Mrs Graeme Witts
Jeremy Wong Esq
Ian Wood
James Wood
Michael and Ruth Wood
Rob and Janet Wood
Sylvia Wood
Maurice John George Woodfield VMM
Mrs Judith P Woodman
Jennifer Woods
Dr Jenny Woods
Eileen Woodward
Drs Gerritje H Woudenberg-Bogerd
Jan Woudstra
Dr A Peter Wright
Norman Wright
Olive Wright
Lady Sarah Wright
Gail Marie B Yanchunas
Michael Yeatts
Brian Young
Elizabeth Young
Ian Young
Lorenzo H Zambrano
Nikita Zharinov
Zoffany

The Formation of a Horticultural Society

I

ON 7 March 1804, a group of seven men met at James Hatchard's bookshop on Piccadilly, to plan the creation of a new society devoted to the improvement of horticulture. (Hatchard had opened his bookshop seven years before, and it had become a well-established meeting place, especially for men of an Evangelical persuasion.)[1] The seven men were Sir Joseph Banks, the President of the Royal Society and Britain's effective scientific dictator; John Wedgwood, a member of the famous pottery family but currently working as a banker; two gentleman amateurs, Charles Francis Greville and Richard Anthony Salisbury; two royal gardeners, William Forsyth of Kensington and St James's Palaces and William Townsend Aiton of Kew; and the nurseryman James Dickson.

Banks had organised the meeting, but Wedgwood chaired it, for it had been he who first proposed the creation of the Society, and most of this first meeting was devoted to considering a paper he had circulated. The following version of Wedgwood's proposal, and of the proposed rules for the Society, was written in the first volume of the Society's minutes:

Letter from Sir Joseph Banks to William Forsyth, 31 July 1801, expressing his interest in Wedgwood's idea for a horticultural society.

FACING PAGE
Hatchards, the Piccadilly bookshop where the Society was founded, a date commemorated in a plaque at first-floor level.

> In almost all the Counties of Great Britain, there are now established Societies for the Improvement of Agriculture, which have been all attended with more or less success, by the introduction of new breeds of Cattle, or new Implements of Husbandry &c. Some of these Societies have considered Orchards as a branch of Agriculture which deserved peculiar attention, and have given Premiums accordingly: For example, the Society for the encouragement of Arts &c. in the Adelphi, and the Bath Agricultural Society. This last Society particularly has held out a premium for the raising new sorts of Apples from the Pippin. These appear to be the only instances where any branch of Gardening, has been encouraged by the Agricultural Societies, and these instances only apply to Orchards as a branch of Agriculture, and not as a part of Gardening. It is now proposed to institute a Society, for the sole purpose of encouraging Horticulture in its different branches. To form a Repository for all the knowledge, which can be collected on this subject, and to give a stimulus to the exertions of individuals for its farther improvement. It is well known to all persons who have made inquiries on this subject, that there are various facts relative to Gardening, confined to small districts, which would be of general utility. These facts will be collected by the Society, and the knowledge of them dispersed generally over the Country. The following Rules and Regulations have been drawn up as the basis of the Society, by which it will be clearly seen, that they most earnestly desire, not to interfere with the Plans of any other

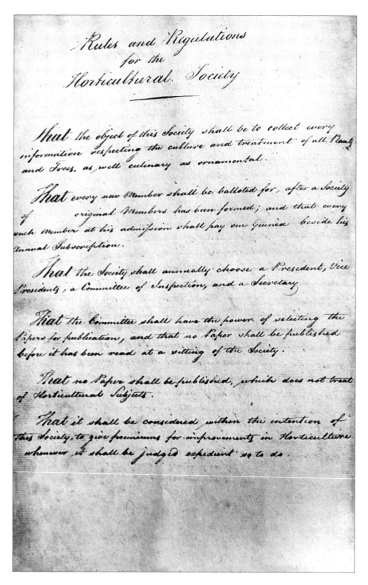

Paper shall be published before it has been read at a sitting of the Society.

That no Paper shall be published, which does not treat of Horticultural Subjects.

That it shall be considered within the intention of this Society, to give premiums for improvements in Horticulture whenever it shall be judged expedient so to do.[2]

Wedgwood was asked to have his paper printed, and to send ten copies to each of the others, for distribution to possible members; the group agreed to meet a week later to discuss membership recruitment, and thus the Horticultural Society was started on its long career.

The idea of a horticultural society

The first meeting provisionally agreed to Wedgwood's rules, but resolved that they should not be 'considered as confirmed until the Society has actually met'. The statement of objectives that was eventually published in the first part of the Society's *Transactions* was augmented beyond Wedgwood's brief proposal, and by another and a rival hand; so to elucidate Wedgwood's purpose, and find out what needs the Society was intended to meet, let us restrict ourselves to his initial document.

First of all, let us note what it was not intended to be. It was not proposed as a scientific society: Wedgwood probably thought that there were enough organisations already devoted to botany. The Royal Society, founded in 1665, had published much on the subject; there had been a Botanical Society, founded by Dillenius and John Martyn in 1721, which had fizzled out later in the century; by the beginning of the 19th century, there were the Linnean Society, founded by Sir James Edward Smith in 1788 (with James Dickson as another founder member) and devoted to both botany and zoology, and the Society for Promoting Natural History, founded by William Forsyth in 1782. (This latter society would wind itself up in 1822 and donate its collections to the Linnean Society.) So taxonomy and physiological botany did not form part of the remit for Wedgwood's intended organisation.[3]

Wedgwood took his starting point from the deficiencies of the existing agricultural societies. The Bath and West of England Society (founded

Wedgwood's rules and regulations, from the first volume of the Society's minutes.

Society whatsoever, but wish to concur with them, in the general improvement of the Country.

That the object of this Society shall be to collect every information respecting the culture and treatment of all Plants and Trees, as well culinary as ornamental.

That every new Member shall be balloted for, after a Society of [blank] original Members has been formed; and that every such Member at his admission shall pay one Guinea beside his annual Subscription.

That the Society shall annually choose a President, Vice Presidents, a Committee of Inspection, and a Secretary[.]

That the Committee shall have the power of selecting the Papers for publication, and that no

1777) and the Highland Society (1784) were only the most powerful and prestigious of an increasing number of local societies devoted to spreading news of new developments in agriculture. Collectively, through the agencies of shows, journals, and meetings, these societies transformed British agriculture throughout the course of the late 18th and early 19th centuries, and the improvement of cattle and sheep breeding, the introduction of agricultural machinery, and experiments with tillage systems were all encouraged by them. The pioneering organisation, the Dublin Society, founded in 1731, had even established a nursery and botanical garden, but was alone in extending its activities into horticulture on such a scale. (There had been a short-lived Society of Gardeners in the 1720s, with Philip Miller and Thomas Fairchild among its leading figures, and an interest in the standardisation of the nomenclature of garden plants, but it had faded away before long, leaving the rare *Catalogus plantarum* of 1730 as its legacy.)[4]

The Society for the Encouragement of Arts, Manufactures, and Commerce (later the Royal Society of Arts), had been founded in 1754; soon it was offering prizes for essays on soils and fertilisers, then for afforestation, and in the 1790s it offered premiums of from 30 to 50 guineas (plus medals) for orchard planting. One of the winners, Thomas Skip Dyot Bucknall, published a monograph on his orchard practice.[5] This was the sort of activity that Wedgwood especially wanted to encourage: practical improvement, and the pooling of regional information. His proposal gave no indication that he expected the Society to conduct or finance its own researches, let alone develop an experimental garden.

This, then, was the modest goal that Wedgwood's society was to pursue. Little could he have imagined that two centuries later his brainchild would have developed into an organisation with a third of a million members, four gardens and possibly more to come, a laboratory providing advisory services to members and conducting experimental research on plant pests, the world's greatest horticultural library (with branches at all its gardens), three or more periodicals and a

The minute of the first meeting, 7 March 1804.

publishing programme directed at every level of the gardening market from the beginner to the academic, a programme of examinations in gardening which (though declined from its zenith) had similarly targeted every level from the beginner to the teacher, two exhibition halls and a network of flower shows around the country that regularly drew attendances in the tens of thousands.

The founders, and their feuds

The seven men who met at Hatchard's on 7 March 1804 were in many ways a remarkably disparate group. The number could easily have been greater: John Hawkins, another wealthy amateur, attended the second meeting a week later, saying

Continued on p.6

THE FOUNDERS

William Townsend Aiton
(1766-1849)
Son of William Aiton (1731-93), whom he succeeded as Superintendent of Kew, having practised in his 20s as a garden designer. Worked closely with Banks on the administration of Kew. The elder Aiton had published *Hortus Kewensis* (1789), a catalogue of the plants at Kew, with great assistance from Banks's librarian Jonas Dryander; W. T. Aiton, again with Dryander's help, published a revised edition in five volumes (1810-13), with much historical research into the introduction dates of the plants cited. Also published *Delineations of Exotick Plants ... at Kew* (1796-1803), with illustrations by Ferdinand Bauer. After the death of William Forsyth, the gardens of Kensington and St James's Palaces came under his control; in the 1820s, George IV added Windsor Great Park to his responsibilities. By that time Banks had died, and the botanic garden at Kew began to fall into neglect as Aiton's duties focused his attention elsewhere. In 1838 Aiton was interrogated by John Lindley about his management of Kew, and Lindley's report led to his having to relinquish control of the botanic garden in 1841; he finally retired in 1845. Buried in his father's tomb in Kew churchyard.

Carl Peter Thunberg named the South African shrub genus *Aitonia* after the elder Aiton, but it has since been absorbed into the genus *Nymania*.

Sir Joseph Banks
(1743-1820)
An explorer from an early age, Banks took part in an expedition to Newfoundland in 1766-7, circumnavigated the world with Captain Cook on the *Endeavour* in 1768-71, and in 1772 travelled to Iceland with Daniel Solander (bringing back a quantity of lava which he used in making a rock garden at the Chelsea Physic Garden). In 1778 he became President of the Royal Society, a position he held until he died. In this capacity he exercised an enormous influence on the organisation of scientific projects in Britain, including the settlement of Australia and the early exploration of Africa. Made a Baronet in 1781.

From some point in the 1770s he became increasingly involved in the administration of the royal gardens at Kew, until by the end of the century Aiton was working under his direction. He maintained a vast library, which became the core of the Natural History Museum's; various scholars were allowed to use it, but Banks was criticised for being stingy with plants from Kew.

At his house at Spring Grove, Isleworth, he experimented in growing American cranberries and had a greenhouse which was depicted on the reverse of the Horticultural Society's medal.

The younger Linnaeus named the Australian genus *Banksia* in his honour; R. A. Salisbury also coined a genus *Josephia*, which has been absorbed into *Dryandra*.

James Dickson
(1738-1822)
Amateur botanist and seedsman, born at Kirke House, Traquhair, but moved to London when in his 20s, working for the nursery of Jeffery and Company at Kensington Gore (the site of the future RHS Garden).

In 1772 he established a seed shop in Covent Garden. One of his clients was the young Joseph Banks, who in 1781 arranged for Dickson to take over the maintenance of the British Museum's garden. Forsyth, at Kensington, was another client. Between 1785 and 1791 travelled extensively in Scotland and the Hebrides, collecting plants. He was a particular authority on mosses and other cryptogamic plants; between 1785 and 1801 he published in parts a major work on the flowerless plants of Great Britain, *Fasciculus Plantarum Cryptogamicarum Britanniae*, with the (unacknowledged) assistance of John Zier. One of the founders of the Linnean Society in 1788, Dickson was instrumental in promoting the career of the explorer Mungo Park.

By 1817 he owned a house and garden in Croydon, where he died in 1822, and was buried in the churchyard of All Saints, Sanderstead, where he had collected mosses.

L'Héritier de Brutelle named the tree fern genus *Dicksonia* in his honour in 1788.

William Forsyth
(1737-1804)
Born near Aberdeen, Forsyth moved to London in his 20s, and became gardener at Syon Park in 1763. In 1771 succeeded the famous Philip Miller as superintendent of the Chelsea Physic Garden. In 1784 appointed Superintendent of the gardens of St James's and Kensington Palaces (i.e. the Central Royal Parks, as we now think of them); held that post until he died.

Published *Observations on Diseases, Defects and Injuries in all Kinds of Fruit and Forest Trees* (1791), and *Treatise on the Culture and Management of Fruit-trees* (1802 – reaching its 7th edition in 1824). In 1791 he was paid £1,500 by the Treasury for his treatment of diseased fruit trees, but was fiercely attacked by Thomas Andrew Knight for his theories on the subject, and effectively accused of fraud.

Vahl named the genus *Forsythia* in his honour; the plant was not introduced into England until the 1840s, when Robert Fortune brought specimens back from China.

His son, William Forsyth Jr, went into partnership with James Gordon, the Fenchurch Street nurseryman; he compiled an immense library on the history of gardening, which was used by J. C. Loudon and others for their historical researches, but was dispersed by auction after his death in 1835.

Charles Francis Greville
(1749-1809)
The younger brother of the 2nd Earl of Warwick, Greville had a career in Parliament as MP for Warwick and, successively, a Lord of Trade and of the Admiralty. More famously, he was the nephew of Sir William Hamilton, the Ambassador at the court of Naples, with whom he collaborated on purchases of antique art, and whose heir he hoped to become. In 1782 he took the young Emma Hart as his mistress, tutored her in the arts, and introduced her to Romney, who made several portraits of her. On being advised by Hamilton that he ought to marry an heiress, he arranged to send Emma to Naples in the expectation that he would follow. Emma eventually became Lady Hamilton, and later Lord Nelson's mistress; Greville's attempt to court an heiress ended in failure. In compensation, Hamilton made him the proprietor of his Milford Haven estate, which Greville developed as an important port. In 1794 he was made Vice-Chamberlain of the Royal Household, and on Hamilton's death in 1803 inherited his estate.

Collected minerals; read paper on meteorites to the Royal Society. FRS 1772; later Vice-President of the Royal Society. Friend of Banks and Wedgwood, and at his garden on Paddington Green experimented with growing exotic plants and methods of treating insect infestations. Fourteen of the plants in Curtis's *Botanical Magazine* were illustrated from his specimens. First in England to flower the vanilla orchid.

In 1810, Robert Brown named the genus *Grevillea* in his honour.

Richard Anthony Salisbury
(1761-1829)
Son of Richard Markham, a Leeds clothmaker; took the name Salisbury as the condition of a legacy. Studied at Edinburgh University, where he became a close friend of James Edward Smith, the future founder of the Linnean Society. In 1791 he published his first book, *Icones Stirpium Rariorum Descriptionibus Illustratae*. Salisbury had a garden at Chapel Allerton near Leeds, and in 1796 issued a catalogue of the plant collection, *Prodromus Stirpium in Horti ad Chapel Allerton Vigentium*; in this he published many new names to replace ones of which he disapproved, and throughout his life was to pick rather pointless quarrels over nomenclature.

1796 also saw his marriage, to Caroline Staniforth; two years later, she left him, taking her infant daughter, and Salisbury appears to have fraudulently presented himself as a bankrupt in order to evade claims for maintenance. At any rate, he moved to London, and acquired the famous garden of Peter Collinson at Mill Hill, where he lived from 1800 to 1806, when he moved to a house in Edgware Road, and thereafter gardened 'in my smoky court'. Later works: *Paradisus Londinensis* (1805-8), illustrated by the artist William Hooker, who (probably through Salisbury) became the Horticultural Society's first artist; at least the co-author of Joseph Knight's work on *Proteae* (1809).

In happier times, Smith named the genus *Salisburia* in his honour – as an attempt to find a more euphonious name than the 'barbarous' *Ginkgo*. Neither man had much respect for the rules of priority: *Ginkgo* was used by Linnaeus, and *Salisburia* is now a distant memory.

John Wedgwood (1766-1844)
Son of the celebrated potter Josiah Wedgwood; born at his father's pottery works at Etruria, Staffordshire. Worked for the family firm intermittently, but at the time of founding the Horticultural Society was working as a banker with the London and Middlesex Bank, and lived at Devonshire Place. In 1816 the London and Middlesex was taken over by Coutts' Bank, and he retired, travelled extensively, then settled at Cote House near Clifton, then at Kingscote, Gloucestershire, where he experimented with growing T. A. Knight's new fruit varieties, alpines from Seringe of Geneva, peonies from Lee's Hammersmith Nursery, chrysanthemums and dahlias (on which he wrote for the Society's *Transactions*). His Kingscote garden book is now in the Lindley Library; E. A. Bunyard wrote of it: 'from these faded pages there comes to life a very charming picture of a man and his garden – a garden essentially English in that the fancier's and collector's spirit predominates'.

that he would have attended the first meeting had he known of it; there were others who had already been active in discussions with Wedgwood and Banks but who for one reason or another did not turn up until a few meetings later. The first meeting agreed that 28 should be the initial number of members—each of the initial seven nominating three others; with Hawkins and his three nominees, and discrepancies between different lists, there seem to have been 34 'original members' in all; but the news spread quickly, and several men applied for membership within the first month. By the time of the meeting of 28 March, there were 61 names on the potential membership list, whether or not they had yet paid the required guinea. Taking this total number into consideration, anyone could be forgiven for predicting that the venture was doomed from the start, because of the bitter quarrels that were running between some of them.[6]

The very composition of the initial meeting reveals the tensions. Wedgwood had first proposed a horticultural society back in 1801, in a letter to William Forsyth:

I have been turning my attention to the formation of a Horticultural Society, and have drawn up such heads as have appeared to me necessary for the first formation of the Society. It would be proper to add a preamble, just stating the ideas of the first founders of the Society, and intimating that we wish to clash with no society at present instituted whose plans are different from ours. By this means we shall give no offence to any party. By not binding ourselves to publish annually we shall not be obliged to expose ourselves to the world in an imperfect state by publishing papers not worth making public. When you have read the enclosed, I shall be happy to have your opinion on it. ... If you should see Sir Joseph Banks, will you be so good as to ask him his opinion of the plan, and learn how far we might have a chance of having his patronage of the scheme.[7]

He had also, the next year, sent Forsyth the first draft of his paper, which differed little from the version provisionally adopted at the 7 March meeting. Forsyth evidently interested others in the idea, notably John Hawkins and the economist and agricultural writer James Anderson. There is no obvious reason why the Society could not have been inaugurated two years earlier than it was—except that Forsyth was busy publishing his book on fruit trees, and involved in an acrimonious dispute with one of the three men Sir Joseph Banks was to propose: Thomas Andrew Knight. Forsyth had received a government grant for publishing his formula for a curative plaster for tree injuries; Knight had

attacked the formula as fraudulent, condemning Forsyth's ideas about plant disease, and challenging him to answer various pointed questions about his practice. Knight had heard of the proposed society, probably in 1802, from John Hawkins, but on learning that Forsyth was involved (and Anderson, whom he saw as Forsyth's publicist), he declined to have anything to do with it. Banks, however, proposed Knight for membership at the meeting of 14 March, and he was formally accepted on 11 April.[8]

So here was a potentially explosive situation, with a Wedgwood-Forsyth alliance at odds with a Banks-Knight alliance. The matter was resolved quickly but unsatisfactorily: Forsyth died in July 1804, and Anderson resigned from the new Society at the next meeting. Thereafter the way was open for Knight to play a larger role in the Society; Banks put him to work drafting the 'Introductory remarks relative to the objects', and Knight, no doubt uneasy about relations with Wedgwood, insisted that his prospectus carry a declaration that he had been asked to compile it by Council. It also carried an implied dig at Forsyth:

The establishment of a national society for the improvement of Horticulture has therefore long been wanted; and if such an institution met with a degree of support proportionate to the importance of its object: if it proceed with cautious circumspection to publish well ascertained facts only, to detect the errors of ignorance, and to expose the misrepresentations of fraud; the advantages which the public may ultimately derive from the establishment, will probably exceed the most sanguine hopes of its founders.

With that, the Banks-Knight alliance could be said to have won the day. There is no documentation to tell us how Wedgwood and Hawkins got on with Knight over the ensuing years, but in February 1809 'A letter from Mr Wedgwood declining to remain a Member of the Society was read'. Wedgwood's resignation from the Society he had created has been attributed to his difficulty in attending meetings, though the wording of the minute suggests that tensions with Knight contributed to it. Knight's final triumph was to become President two years later.[9]

The second simmering quarrel was less likely to tear the Society apart, though still productive of sparks. R.A. Salisbury proposed Sir James Edward Smith, the founder of the Linnean Society, as one of his three nominees. The two had been bosom friends since the 1780s, but had since then fallen out over questions of taxonomy: Smith was, of course, a loyal upholder of Linnaeus's system of classification, while Salisbury in the 1790s adopted

Thomas Andrew Knight (1759-1838), second President 1811-38. Younger brother of the aesthete and antiquary Richard Payne Knight, who gave him his estate at Downton Castle, Herefordshire, where he conducted experiments on plant physiology and breeding.

the new natural classification proposed by Jussieu. Salisbury's proposal of Smith as a member may have been a peace offering: if so, it didn't work. Neither man was prepared to be temperate in publication; each of the two slandered, plagiarised from, and tried to invalidate the botanical names proposed by the other. The peak of resentment was to be reached in 1808-9. An article in the *Monthly Magazine* in 1808 accused Salisbury of turning against the Linnaean classification for personal reasons, in order to have an excuse for attacking Smith; Smith seemed to endorse the idea in a later issue; Salisbury replied with a pamphlet, attacking Smith, among other things, for 'lending his name to the miracles of Forsyth'. While these hostilities were being exchanged, Robert Brown, the Librarian of the Linnean Society, read a paper on Proteaceae to that Society in January 1809; Salisbury, who had been working on the Proteaceae for years, was in the audience, and heard himself criticised. Brown, a slow, painstaking perfectionist, did not publish his paper until the following year, giving Salisbury time to defend his priority. Late in 1809 a book on Proteaceae appeared under the name of Joseph Knight, including several of the plants Brown had described, but under different names. Knight had recently started a nursery in Chelsea, and was expert in the cultivation of the plants, but was not a botanist, and Salisbury was immediately recognised as his unattributed co-author—and therefore stigmatised as the plagiarist of Brown's descriptions, underhandedly trying to get priority for his own names. Brown resignedly adopted his rival's coinages—'as Mr. Salisbury's generic names have the unquestionable right of priority of publication, I have in most cases adopted them, though I wish some of them had been differently constructed.' Knight's preface, however (in addition to protesting too much: 'Perhaps few works have greater claims to originality than the present, not a single line being copied from any other'), implicated the Horticultural Society, of which Salisbury was the Secretary, in the business:

> That the work will be candidly received, he presumes to flatter himself, from the circumstance of a great portion of it, having been unanimously voted to be printed by the *Council* of the *Horticultural Society*, but the latter part having excited some jealousy in a quarter, which it is now unnecessary to mention, the author's pacific sentiments did not allow him to hesitate one instant, about withdrawing the whole.

During all this fuss, the Horticultural Society was renting rooms from the Linnean Society: it is a tribute to everybody's forebearance that the explosions were largely confined to print.[10]

George Legge (1755-1810), 3rd Earl of Dartmouth. President 1804-10; also Lord Chamberlain, and President of the Society for Promoting Natural History.

That such a volatile company managed to form a stable society was owing partly to a determination to overlook personalities, and partly to the dominance of Sir Joseph Banks. He was closely connected to all the founding members except Wedgwood himself, who used Forsyth as his intermediary for approaching him: he was the effective employer of Aiton at Kew, had got Dickson the contract for maintaining the British Museum's garden, had dealt with Forsyth at the Chelsea Physic Garden in the days before he had become the Royal Gardener at Kensington, and was a regular correspondent and adviser of Salisbury and Greville. And, of course, he was responsible for Thomas Andrew Knight's entrance into the Society, and for getting him to write the Society's prospectus even before he had become a Council member.[11]

The development of an administration

The first meetings of the Society were largely devoted to the process of signing up new members. By May 1804 an administrative structure had been agreed, with the Earl of Dartmouth as the first President, Wedgwood as Treasurer, and the Revd Alexander Cleeve as Secretary. (Forsyth had been keen on getting James Anderson to be the first Secretary, but abandoned the effort when Wedgwood told him that he found 'so strong a prejudice against Dr. Anderson that I should advise his friends not to propose him'.) Hatchard recommended a man named Bartholomew Peacock to act as clerk: the Society's first employee. Banks, Dickson, Greville, Salisbury, and Wedgwood, along with James Sims, the President of the Medical Society, were appointed Vice-Presidents. A Council of 21 members was chosen by ballot, including all seven founders; before the year was out, Forsyth had died, and the botanist Aylmer Bourke Lambert was balloted to replace him. The year ended with the first donation to the Society: five pounds from the medical botanist John Coakley Lettsom.[12]

The meetings were held at Hatchard's bookshop, in a room that Hatchard rented to the Society for Bettering the Condition of the Poor, until February 1805, when Hatchard raised the question of some remuneration for the use of the room. Peacock began asking about a salary at the same time, and the response to both requests was: how much? The result was £20 for Hatchard, £30 for Peacock, and negotiations to secure new rooms and new staff. Salisbury offered his services gratis as Secretary, and Cleeve, though stepping down as Secretary, agreed to serve as Assistant Secretary, also gratis; the Revd George Glasse,

Continued on p.10

George Cruikshank's cartoon of a Society Meeting

Listed left to right, top to bottom

- 'An Irish Potatoe Plant with young ones dress'd in their Jackets after the fashion of the Country', imaginary picture.
- Portrait of Sir Joseph Banks (the Phillips portrait which hangs in the RHS Council Room today), labelled 'Hortus siccus', i.e. a collection of dried plants: Banks had died in 1820.
- Bust of the Prince Regent, later George IV, labelled 'Penny Royal'.
- Portrait, allegedly of Lady Monson: text based on R.A. Salisbury's description of *Arethusa bulbosa* in *Transactions*.
- Joseph Sabine, Secretary: 'The Friend of Mæcenas—"arvum coelumq[ue] Sabinum non cessat laudare"—Hor. Epi.'.
- John Elliot, Treasurer and Vice-President: 'A most respectable Cauliflower always in order'.
- John Turner, Assistant Secretary: 'An highly cultivated Specimen—requires glass'.
- 'The Pink of Fashion or Dandy Lion'.
- 'A variety of Horn-beam—a double bearer'—Robert Albion Cox, Alderman, who the previous year had obtained damages from the actor Edmund Kean for adultery; he is looking at a basket containing a baby labelled 'Keen's Seedling, a Hot Bed Plant'—almost the name of the new strawberry 'Keens' Seedling' which had been distributed through the Society.
- 'A Passion-flower in full bloom'—Samuel Rogers, the poet of *Italy* and *The Pleasures of Memory*.
- 'A species of Mistletoe'—probably R.A. Salisbury.
- 'A Bulb from Holland with Offset'.
- 'A monstrous Medler in full bearing'—probably Roger Wilbraham MP.
- 'A sprig of Nobility running to seed—mem. While in this state not to be trusted out of doors—if kept under lock & key it will receive the benefit of the Act'—possibly Lord Verulam?
- 'A Scarlet Runner'—dressed as an officer of the Life Guards: identity uncertain: James Scarlett of Abinger Hall, Dorking (later Lord Abinger, Attorney-General), a Fellow at the time, has been suggested.
- 'An English Crab—a native of the Country'—possibly Lord Verulam?
- 'Heart of Oak, with timber lopp'd—little cultivated at present, the old plants vegetate in the background'—who knows? There were 21 naval officers among the members at the time.
- 'Hortus Cantab—propagated at Newmarket'.
- Exhibit: 'the new Golden Drop or Marvel of Peru—a native of Nomans land To be bought in the City—only. £500 per leaf!! Cheap as dirt & productive beyond belief'.
- 'Rye Coffee by act of Parliament / Almighty Roasters!! / H H Radical Corn Doctor'.
- 'Perkins's new grape house forced by steam—NB warrented not to end in Smoke'.
- 'Specimens—American Acacia. NB. These Trees must not be too much exposed they require warmth & thrive best in a Register'—William Cobbett, the radical journalist, ran a nursery and tried to promote the cultivation of robinia as a useful tree. A register meant a heated case (the term was still used as a synonym for radiator into the 20th century), but also refers to Cobbett's newspaper, the *Weekly Political Register*.
- Fruit specimens with punning labels: 'Sure such a Pear was never seen'; '"A most prodigious Pippin" – Byron'; 'Sundry Specimens of forbidden Fruit – Note Meilleur de son Espéce'; 'A clutch of grapes from Lady Bacchus [...] NB Beware of drunkenness & apoplexy'.

ORDINARY in the HORTICULTURAL ROOM

Street, Soho. And there they stayed until 1817, when, having been refused permission by the Linnean to take over an additional room, the Society rented the first floor of a building at 21 Church Street to accommodate its growing library and other business. In 1819, the Society finally purchased a house in Regent Street (actually Waterloo Street, just off Lower Regent Street), and, 'to the relief of the Linnean Society', moved out.[13]

The Society's activities gathered pace, with the first exhibit at a meeting taking place in 1805 (a potato, exhibited by Charles Minier), the first donation of books being made in 1806 (from Dr Sims), the first part of the *Transactions* appearing in 1807, and the first medal being struck in 1808. In that year also negotiations began to obtain a royal charter, with Salisbury acting as the go-between with the Crown; the charter was duly issued in 1809, and established the name of the organisation as the Horticultural Society of London. All those members not in arrears were duly inscribed as members of the renamed Society, and there was a sudden flurry of payments by those who were in arrears. The Society's Council was fixed at 15 members, including the officers of the Society and Vice-Presidents, with a quorum of five; three Council members, chosen by ballot of their fellows, were to retire each year. Elections for Council were to take place at the 'Anniversary Meeting' on the first of May (or second, if the first was a Sunday); from 1810 a hundred tickets were printed for each anniversary dinner, and by the 1820s these dinners had developed such a reputation that the porters were given discretionary tickets to admit ladies,

The building in Regent Street (actually Waterloo Place), where the Society's offices were located from 1819 to 1859.

who had also offered his services, was kept as third in line. The early administration was very con-scious of 'the necessity of Oeconomy in the infancy of an Institution, which must look forward to great expenses to form a permanent Establish-ment, viz. the purchase of a House, a Charter &c.' New rooms were found at the offices of the Linnean Society, at 10 Panton Square; the Linnean Society's clerk, Benjamin Price, was hired to be the Horticultural Society's clerk as well, at a salary of 25 guineas; in the autumn of 1805, both societies moved together to new premises at 9 Gerrard

who were not yet eligible for membership. There would be four Vice-Presidents on Council, elected annually.

New faces were appearing. Thomas Andrew Knight became more active in the Society after Forsyth's death and Anderson's departure; when the Earl of Dartmouth, the first President, died in 1810, Knight was elected to succeed him. Wedg-wood, having retired as Treasurer in 1806, was replaced by Greville until the latter's death in 1809; the new Treasurer was the noted brewer Colonel John Elliot, Lettsom's son-in-law, who maintained a 20-acre garden at Pimlico Lodge. Council was augmented by a group of active newcomers: Roger Wilbraham, who instigated a committee to report on the best varieties of fruits for different regions; George Heinrich Noehden, the Assistant Librarian of the British Museum; Alexander Seton, a future Treasurer; and above all, Joseph Sabine, an Inspector-General of Taxes with a keen interest in novel plants. Sabine became a Council member in 1812, and a Vice-President in 1815; in that year his financial skills were put to the test, in a controversy that was to see the last of the founders removed from office. Benjamin Price, the Assistant Secretary, was dismissed with a gratuity, so that he could be replaced by someone with horticultural knowledge, who was capable of dealing with enquiries. Price took legal advice, and threatened proceedings for unjust dismissal, but eventually resigned. Thomas Hare was chosen as the new Assistant Secretary, and found that he could not make sense of the accounts. Sabine led a committee of enquiry, and produced a damning report: the list of medals was deficient, there was no trace of the register book, there were so many arrears that Sabine rescinded a number of orders in order to keep expenditure under control. Nowhere in the report did he criticise Salisbury's actions as Secretary; indeed, in 1814 he had moved that Salisbury be given a Gold Medal for his services; but Salisbury evidently felt that his management had been called into question, and resigned as from the anniversary meeting for 1816. Banks retired from Council at the same meeting. The new Secretary was Joseph Sabine; and two years later there was a new Assistant Secretary, Sabine's protégé John Turner. The triumvirate of

Sabine, Turner, and Elliot was depicted by George Cruikshank in 1826, in a cartoon which provides our first visual evidence of the Society's meetings.[14]

And so, 12 years after the founding of the Society, its founders had effectively passed from the scene, and the team of Knight, Sabine, and Elliot had been established, which would conduct its affairs until the 1830s. The character of the Society had changed from the simple organisation that Wedgwood had envisaged. Already in 1805, when Thomas Andrew Knight's 'Introductory remarks relative to the objects which the Horticultural Society have in view' was published as the first article in the *Transactions*, the focus had sharpened, and Knight specified a number of specific research programmes: tracing the origins of cultivated plants, learning the limits of acclimatisation of exotics, breeding new fruit varieties, improving the construction of green-houses, and researching the properties of soils and fertilisers. Up to the late 1810s, it had relied on meetings and publishing to encourage such activities, but increasingly the need for more directed research was making itself felt: even though the Society did not have a garden, it was receiving gifts of plants, and finding somewhere to keep them was becoming a matter of some urgency. In 1818 Sabine found a small garden site in Kensington which would serve for the time being as a repository for plants, while continuing to look for something more substantial. Several sites were offered and examined over the next few years, and in 1822 an offer from the Duke of Devonshire of a 33-acre site in Chiswick was accepted. With this garden would begin a new and more active phase of the Society's existence.

2 *From Crisis to Crisis*

THE year 1822 began with a sunburst of promise for the future. A committee consisting of Sabine, Seton, and Noehden had been charged with finding a better garden than the little Kensington ground, on the grounds that:

> However promising the efforts made by the Horticultural Society to effect the objects of its institution may have hitherto been, it was at an early period evident that the success of its exertions must be very limited unless aided by the establishment of an extensive garden, in which the new plants acquired might be placed, their peculiarities correctly remarked and the necessary experiments carried on under the immediate superintendance [*sic*] of its Officers.

The Committee had found a site at Chiswick: 33 acres belonging to the Duke of Devonshire, lying between the grounds of Chiswick House and Turnham Green on the north, which were available on a 60-year lease. Now the Society would have the chance to build up a publicly accessible fruit collection, and get the nomenclature of fruit varieties sorted out once and for all. The garden could be staffed largely with young gardeners who would improve their knowledge of the art, and become eligible for prestigious posts at other establishments. Plants of interest could be exhibited at meetings, which would become more interesting than ever before.[1]

The maintenance of this garden would require an administrative reorganisation. A separate account would have to be established for its creation, distinct from maintenance expenditures later; George IV had offered £500 toward this purpose, and if all new members paid an extra guinea, those already enrolled would not need to have a compulsory charge levied on them, though voluntary additions were encouraged. The garden would need to be stocked so well that if a later decline in funds meant that it had to be abandoned, its condition at the time of disposal would not be an embarrassment to the Society.

A minor storm attended the announcement of the proposals to Council. The Committee had proposed that seeds and cuttings could be distributed, but that there would be no attempt to distribute plants already available through the nursery trade; there was to be no thought of competing with nurseries, only of introducing new plants and, by stimulating the public taste for horticulture, causing 'an increase of demand on the nurseries'. Approved fruits could be distributed to 'all the nurserymen connected with the Society'. One Council member, John Motteux, objected to such proposed favouritism, and got that proposal deleted; he also raised objections to the procedures for making byelaws for the garden, which Sabine was only able to quash by offering his resignation (he received a vote of confidence instead).[2]

John Lindley, who had been hired as an artist the year before, was appointed Assistant Secretary for the Garden, at a salary of £120; the ornamental garden was put in the command of Donald Munro, the fruit and kitchen garden of William Morgan, both with salaries of £105. (Morgan was soon to be succeeded by William Christie.) £1,200-worth of Consols were sold, and £400 in exchequer bills purchased, in order to meet the initial costs of work. The plants from the garden in Kensington were transferred, not without a dispute with the landlord over its winding-up. The lease of the completed garden was finalised in June 1823, at which time £1,200 was hopefully estimated as the garden's annual cost. And throughout the 1820s, a brilliant staff was assembled (including such soon-to-be-eminent gardeners as Robert Thompson, George Gordon, and William Beattie Booth, and others like the young Joseph Paxton passing through on their way to bigger things), and the publication of a *Catalogue of Fruits* accelerated the hoped-for reform of nomenclature.

Everything seemed to be going well. The *Transactions* continued to be handsomely printed and well received. Throughout the 1820s the Society sent young gardeners abroad to collect new plants, sometimes with extraordinary success. In 1827 the experiment was made of holding what was at first called a public breakfast, and then renamed a fête: its first attempt at a flower show. In the first year, nearly 3,000 people bought tickets at prices of more than a guinea, and not a single plant was injured by the crowds. John Claudius Loudon could describe the Society in 1826 as 'the most remarkable feature in the modern history of gardening', and note that its membership 'in the short space of a very few years increased from three or four hundred to about two thousand members, among whom is now ranked nearly all the nobility and science of the land ... This society has established one of the most extensive gardens in the world, in the vicinity of the metropolis, and has spared neither cost, nor influence, nor exertions, to accumulate within its bounds all the most rare and valuable productions of the vegetable world.'[3]

The decline and fall of Sabine

But beneath the surface, all was not well. Some of the problems that were afflicting the Society were common to other institutions of the day: the Zoological Society was also criticised for reckless expenditure triggered by too great an initial wealth; more than one organisation of the period became riven with factions in response to a haughty and dictatorial secretariat modelling itself on the aristocratic manners of what was still an *ancien régime* society; and none exceeded the Medico-Botanical Society in assiduously courting the favours of royalty and nobility, to the apparent exclusion of useful work. (That unhappy society eventually expelled its founder-secretary, who fled to Germany and spent his last years in obscurity.) Under Sabine, the Horticultural Society fell into line with these models. There was more rejoicing over the enrolment of a Duke or a foreign monarch than over a few score ordinary gardeners, and both plants and costly sets of the *Transactions* were sent as gifts to titled newcomers. The subscription was high: a three-guinea joining fee, with two guineas thereafter per annum for ordinary members; a composition of 20 guineas could make one a Life Fellow (as against 10 guineas for the Linnean Society).[4] And there were additional sources of expenditure.

The new offices in Regent Street provided a regular litany of grumbles, minor crises, and alter-cations with neighbours. Redecoration always seemed to take place at financially delicate moments. A variety of societies, ranging over the years from the Gardeners' Benevolent Institution to the newly-founded Royal Geographical Society and the Society for Bettering the Irish Poor, rented the rooms for their own meetings; and naturally, there were arrears of rent. In 1824 the London headquarters (salaries and upkeep) cost £4,000—£1,000 more than the cost of the garden. There were everlasting struggles over tithes and poor rates, and to reclaim arrears of subscription from defaulting members. After 1826, one of the Society's most active and harassed staff members was the 'collector', whose job it was to recover debts: sometimes a separate staff member, sometimes an additional job title for one of the clerks. The number of clerks grew—the correspondence clerk could not keep up with the work, a junior clerk was added, the garden required separate clerks.

The garden saw a continuous turnover in staff. William Christie, the longest-serving so far of the Society's gardeners, resigned at the end of 1824, despite an attempt to hold him until he had completed a catalogue of the garden's potato collection. Two staff were caught stealing seeds in 1828, prosecuted, and sent to prison for three months; the Society paid the court costs. A house on Turnham Green, a short distance from the garden, was leased for staff accommodation: an unanticipated expense of £84 per annum. A sinking fund of £1,000 was established, and already by the end of 1824 came the first proposals for cutting expenses at the garden 'by keeping down and avoiding several heads of expenditure, the incurring which would be very desirable and very beneficial to the objects of the Society'. The King's promised £500 never appeared, despite many attempts at backstairs negotiation, nor did a loan of £5,000 promised by the government. By the beginning of 1826, the Society was borrowing £3,000 on bonds of £1,000 each, so as to boost the garden account.[5]

The fêtes, which had begun so full of promise for the Society's exchequer, soon dwindled into a nuisance. The first fête had brought in a profit of £500, the second of £1,000—but this was marred by the costs of a lawsuit with a caterer. The third fête was disastrously rained out, and led to embarrassing questions in the *Sunday Times* over the costs of catering. The fêtes can be seen as a pioneering attempt at staging flower shows, but after this debacle they were discontinued.[6]

And on top of, or perhaps underneath, all this was the behaviour of Sabine himself. Apparently not having learned from the Price incident in 1816,

John Claudius Loudon (1783-1843), garden designer and journalist, author of the Encyclopaedia of Gardening, Arboretum et Fruticetum Britannicum, *and many other works. Pioneer of curvilinear glasshouse construction, promoter of municipal parks. Editor of* The Gardener's Magazine, *1826-43.*

Joseph Sabine (1770-1837), lawyer, and Inspector-General of Assessed Taxes throughout his career with the Society. Secretary, 1816-1830. A pioneer of horticultural taxonomy, contributing papers to the Transactions *on cultivars of crocus and chrysanthemum. After his removal as Secretary, he devoted himself to the Zoological Society, which he served as Treasurer and Vice-President.*

he allowed the accounts to become tangled and insoluble, taking financial documents home and, sometimes, getting them lost. He became increasingly dictatorial, insisting that the gardeners obey his instructions, and arbitrarily issuing his own directives without reference to Council or Committee. Donald Munro later testified that Sabine's interference, and refusal to let the gardeners act without his personal orders, resulted in mismanagement in the garden, and Atkinson, the architect for the Chiswick buildings, recalled Lindley remonstrating with Sabine over meddling with plans:

> Mr. Lindley went to him, and said, 'Now, Sir, is it to be done according to your plan or Mr. Atkinson's?' He said, 'Mine, certainly.' Mr. Lindley said, 'You know what the consequences may be; will you be answerable for the building if it should be burnt down?' 'No,' said he, 'I will not be answerable for any thing.'[7]

He obtained favours for family and friends; his brother Edward Sabine (later to become President of the Royal Society) was given accommodation at Turnham Green and a private key to the garden; gifts of plants were regularly sent to the Zoological Society, in which Sabine also had an interest. For many, the final straw was his demand for the continual writing of reports, which most of the staff found a waste of paper, to a 'perfectly absurd degree', and especially for the reporting to him of any remarks made by visitors about the garden or the staff, which Lindley later described as a 'system of espionage'.[8]

> The greatest benefit and the greatest evil to the concern is the secretary; benefit, because he is indefatigable in the establishment and management; his whole time, care, and attention is devoted to the furtherance of it; but then comes the evil—the society receives the benefit of his care, time, and attention for nothing—and this to me is a great evil. Shall we not fall into the same error as other societies who have been patronized by honorary secretaries? Is not the society accepting too much? Seeing how rich it is, would it not be much wiser if all its officers were paid?[9]

(At least the Society never sank to the level of the Medico-Botanical Society, of which Charles Babbage remarked that it 'contrived to render EXPULSION the highest HONOUR it could confer'.)[10]

The first major sign of financial difficulty came in February 1826, when Joseph Davis, the accounts clerk, reported that the Assistant Secretary, John Turner, had embezzled some of the Society's money. Turner admitted the offence, claiming that he had misappropriated small sums as loans to tradesmen, and offered to correct the accounts.

Edward Barnard, the Vice-Secretary, examined his new accounts critically and found them full of inconsistencies. Turner fled to France, but offered to repay the £764 he acknowledged as his debt, so long as he was not dismissed; Sabine and his colleagues agreed, Turner's family repaid the amount, and Turner returned to his position. Knight was informed of the affair at the AGM in May, and, assured that the matter was closed, gave his consent to the actions. Then in the autumn Davis once again caught Turner submitting incomplete accounts; on 7 October Council were finally informed about his defalcations, and presented with a letter of confession, and a bill of sale on Turner's house in the Society's favour. Once again Turner fled to France.

Turner was officially dismissed by Council on 11 November; Lindley took over his duties until a replacement could be found, and that replacement turned out to be Lindley himself—so long as he gave a hefty security. He officially became Assistant Secretary on 9 April 1827. But meanwhile the news of Turner's embezzlement leaked out; Loudon published details in the *Gardener's Magazine*; 16 Fellows immediately resigned, with others following, and another demanded the repayment of a £1,300 loan. John Elliot negotiated an overdraft, but the full extent of Turner's embezzlement had yet to be revealed: it eventually stood at over £1,200, reduced after allowances to £960 1s. 2d. Elliot resigned as Treasurer at the end of 1828, from reasons of health, no doubt exacerbated by the last year's stress; he was succeeded by Robert Henry Jenkinson. And the practical impact of Turner was being felt at Chiswick. Labourers' wages were reduced from 14 to 12 shillings per week, their number reduced by eight by not filling vacancies.[11]

Sabine's response to the Turner debacle was one of concealment. Joseph Davis, the accountant, later reported that he had been specifically told in 1827 not to include debts in the Society's accounts any more; the last published statement of debt (1826) was £3,350. But the debt did not go away, and everything the Society did seemed to excavate the pit further. By 1830 it was secretly in debt to the sum of £18,000.

At the Council meeting of 10 November 1829, an anonymous pamphlet was placed before the meeting, entitled *A Letter to Thomas Andrew Knight*, and containing an attack on the Society's conduct, first in confusing botany and horticulture by spending its money on collecting rare plants, then in its standards of garden design and maintenance, and thirdly in its secrecy over its accounts. The pamphlet was addressed to Knight instead of Sabine on the grounds that, as

President, he bore the ultimate responsibility if the Society's staff misconducted themselves. Knight was 'a very King Log': 'you are sorely guilty of misprision of treason, if not of actual commission—you stand by—'. The author of the pamphlet, and also of letters in *The Times* and the *Gardener's Magazine*, signed by the initial 'B.', in the two months following, was probably the botanist Charles Henry Bellenden Ker.[12]

These letters, especially the one in *The Times*, precipitated the crisis. 'B.' announced that the Society was now in debt to a figure of over £19,000, and that arrears of membership subscriptions alone amounted to £3,000-£4,000. He also revealed that Nicol, the printer of the *Transactions*, had been given interest-bearing bonds in lieu of payment; that Sabine encouraged spying on staff and members; and, most momentously, that Turner had embezzled funds and escaped the courts:

> A friend of mind having heard that the Society were not very punctual in their payments ... discovered some curious facts regarding a bill which was never delivered to the council, and that some tradespeople had been put off with bonds. The recollection that only a few years ago an officer of the Society had levanted with a large sum of money, and that there was apparently some very singular negligence in the way in which he had been allowed to escape, all tended to excite suspicion ...[13]

The letter was cited at the meeting of 22 January 1830, when one of the Fellows, Robert Gordon, MP, gave notice of a petition for a committee to enquire into the Society's expenditure and management. A letter from Knight was read out, in which the President apologised for his lack of day-to-day involvement with the management of the Society:

> When the honour of being made president of this Society was first proposed to me ... I stated in answer, that, if I became president, the distance of my residence, and the nature of my pursuits, must preclude the possibility of my being present in London to attend to the local management of the affairs of the Society; and I only assented to be nominated on the condition that no other person was proposed; and, subsequently, when the wealth and number of the members of the Society had greatly increased, I addressed a similar declaration from the chair, and expressed my willingness to resign my office. I had their reasons, which were very flattering to me, to believe that the Society did not wish me to resign my office; and I retained it, requesting, however, that the members of the Society would not, through 'any tenderness of feeling towards me, retain me in office a single hour to the injury of

the Society'. I therefore trust that the local management of the official business of the Society was not amongst the duties which the members who did me the honour to elect me expected me to perform.

> In thus exculpating myself, I do not mean to shift or cast any blame upon the other officers of the Society. They were misled by apparently well founded expectations of assistance, which subsequently proved fallacious, to take too large a garden, with too great a consequent establishment, and from that source all our subsequent difficulties appear to me to have sprung.[14]

Gordon's committee was instituted, and did at least get access to the Council minutes straightaway. At the meeting of 2 February 1830, 'Mr. Sabine was rather roughly handled', as Loudon put it. While acquitting everyone of deliberate fraud, the Committee complained 'of want of courtesy to the Fellows, of negligent management, of profuse expenditure, and of injudicious engagements contracted without due consideration of the means by which they were to be fulfilled'. Henceforth, the committee ruled, auditors must not be members of Council or the Garden Committee. But then came the question of fixing blame, and Sabine appeared to shuffle off responsibility onto his underlings. Lindley responded with an open letter:

> It has been impossible for me to misunderstand what occurred in the Council to-day [12 Feb.]. Upon being called into their presence, I found that an impression had been made upon them, that certain estimates, prepared by the last Council, and sent to the Committee, had been first assented to by me before the Council, and then dissented from by me before the Committee. It is possible that this impression may have ceased with my disavowal of the charge, and that the Council see that no such stigma attaches to me; but this does not satisfy me. I conceive that you, as a gentleman, and professing to be my friend, were bound not to have allowed any such impression to have existed, as you must have known that I was above suspicion upon such a point. You know perfectly well that I have always protested against the statements by which the Council have frequently been deluded into sanctioning measures and expenditure, which, had they known the real state of the Society's affairs, they could not have countenanced; and that I was entirely opposed in opinion to the very heads of estimate objected to by the Committee ... I think I have a right to enquire why you allowed the Council to suppose that I had assented to their estimates. You may perhaps say that you can explain this to my satisfaction; but I have both seen and heard lately too much of explanations to take them against the evidence of my senses. I see clearly that an

John Lindley (1799-1865), who during his 42 years with the Society did the work now carried out by five departments: Secretariat, Botany, Publications, Shows, and Education. The son of a Norwich nurseryman, he rashly undertook responsibility for his father's debts, and never succeeded in paying them off. In addition to his work for the Society, he was also Professor of Botany at University College London, 1827-61; Professor of Botany at the Chelsea Physic Garden, 1835-53; and editor of the Gardeners' Chronicle, 1841-63, thus effectively holding down four full-time jobs simultaneously for much of his career.

intrigue is going on for the purpose of making it appear that I am at one time allowing myself to be identified with those miserable proceedings which have brought the Society to its present state, and to which I have been constantly and openly opposed, and at another disavowing those proceedings before the Committee. I have never been a party to the exaggerations of the Society's means, and concealment of the Society's debts, by means of which many honourable and excellent men in the Council have been unfortunately induced to believe a ruined Society to be in a state of prosperity. I have been steadily opposed to the measures by which that ruin has been brought about; and I do not choose now, at the eleventh hour, either to be cajoled into a suppression of my opinions, or to allow you to make the world believe that I now, for the first time, entertain sentiments adverse to your proceedings. That there may be no farther misconception upon this and other points, I have written you this letter, a copy of which I shall give to all persons whom it is likely to interest.

I am, Sir, &c., John Lindley[15]

Lindley's conduct in writing and circulating this letter seems to have been admired at the time, and used against him later. The *Cottage Gardener* said in 1856, on publishing it in a biographical notice of Lindley, 'To this letter the only objection is—and it is a strong objection—it ought to have been written years before, and addressed to the Society's Council. Mr. Lindley admitted that he knew of the mismanagement, extravagance, and deceit for years, yet it never seems to have struck him that it was his imperative duty, as the Society's servant, to make known to it what he knew was tending to its ruin.' Loudon's remark that Sabine had 'been the means of bringing forward Mr. Lindley' provided an explanation for his disinclination to whistle-blowing, but the *Cottage Gardener* dismissed that claim 'when we have before us the unmitigated outpouring of revelations against Mr. Sabine, which Mr. Lindley made to the Committee of Inquiry. There was no consideration then for his falling friend; the only anxiety was to escape from being involved in his fall, and to mount upon his ruin.' It has to be said that by 1856 Lindley had managed to irritate the horticultural community in several ways. In fact, the published extracts from his and his colleagues' testimony to the Committee confirmed that he had written letters of remonstrance to Sabine, which the latter had destroyed.[16]

At the next meeting, on 17 February, Sabine offered to retire from the position of Secretary, in the hope that this 'would much facilitate the adjustment of the future arrangement of the

Societys [*sic*] concerns'. Sabine vacated his seat on Council on 2 March, and finalised his resignation on 15 March, delivering up his papers. Some Council members resigned; Jenkinson resigned as Treasurer; Edward Barnard resigned as Vice-Secretary, but carried out the duties of Secretary until a new one was chosen. Thomas Goode, senior clerk for eleven years, offered to resign in order to save the Society the burden of paying his salary. Sabine, in what was probably a penitential gesture, offered to arrange and classify the Society's collections of peonies and rheums, jobs which were eventually abandoned unfinished, as Sabine became involved with the Zoological Society instead.

Assignations of blame were one thing; financial recovery quite another. Gordon's committee noted that 'many objects of the Society have been substantially fulfilled; that the foreign missions for collecting plants, and more especially that of Mr. Douglas, have been eminently beneficial; that the Transactions contain a body of valuable information upon various subjects of horticultural interest, and have been published and distributed to the members without exhausting in any material degree the funds of the Society; that on the merits of the orchard, as an important and useful experiment, there is not the smallest doubt.' They recommended the disposal of plants that were mere botanical curiosities; savings on tools, uneconomically purchased in the past; the production of marketable crops at Chiswick, in order to bring in more revenue. Above all, there should be a reform of accounting. Council responded with proposals that the building in Regent Street be disposed of or let, and the office staff reduced; the house in Turnham Green disposed of; the *Transactions* discontinued, and some of the stock sold; the students at Chiswick to be replaced by ordinary labourers, with the option of students continuing unpaid; visitors to the Garden to pay for admission henceforth.

The assets of the Society were stated to be £14,200, including the suppositious figures of £3,700 for money recoverable from arrears, £5,000 from the sale of the house in Regent Street, and £2,000 from the sale of books and drawings. The Society sold its horses, and held an auction of its back stock of the *Transactions*, but still felt able to send gifts of plants to the London Zoo. The Council minutes for 19 April included an eight-page list of debts, the final figure being £19,768 19s. 7d., all but £5,000 of which were garden debts.[17]

A new Garden Committee was set up, and a Committee of Accounts. Loudon campaigned for Lindley to be appointed the new Secretary, but in the event he was re-confirmed as Assistant

Secretary, with George Bentham appointed as Secretary over his head. The number of clerks was cut back to two. John Reeves was asked to discontinue sending plants and drawings from China, and 90 duplicate Chinese drawings were sold, as were surplus plants and the mineralogical specimens brought back by the Society's collectors; duplicate herbarium specimens were distributed to other institutions, and a number of Library books sold. (The net proceeds of these sales amounted to £337 17s. 6d.) The stock of the *Transactions* was recovered from the warehouse and moved to Regent Street to save on rental and insurance, but the publication itself was revived in a second series. Parts of both the Regent Street and Turnham Green buildings were sublet, and the Turnham Green house finally sold in 1832.

These measures won a degree of public approval; the Society was seen to be responding intelligently to the revelation of its faults. Charles Babbage, in his polemic on the decline of science in England, was cautiously hopeful about its future:

> The Horticultural Society has been ridden almost to death, and is now rousing itself; but its constitution seems to have been somewhat impaired. There are hopes of its purgation, and ultimate restoration, notwithstanding a debt of 19,000L., which the Committee of Inquiry have ascertained to exist. This, after all, will not be without its advantage to science, if it puts a stop to HOUSE-LISTS, NAMED BY ONE OR TWO PERSONS,— to making COMPLIMENTARY councillors,— and to auditing the accounts WITHOUT EXAMINING EVERY ITEM, or to omitting even that form altogether.[18]

The years of rivalry

The crawl back to solvency, however, was slow and interrupted. Bentham lent the Society £700 of his own money to help it carry on; in the autumn of 1832 it was still raising money with bonds to pay off simple contract debts. The Department of Woods and Forests, the landlords for the Regent Street house, claimed arrears of payments; the Society had a similar problem with Layton Cooke, one of its tenants; in both cases the legal negotiations took years to resolve. As of 1834 the gifts of plants to the Zoo were finally suspended. But some initiatives succeeded. In 1833 Lindley started a new

series of flower shows at Chiswick, and by the end of the decade annual ticket sales had reached 12,000. By 1836 the Society felt sufficiently confident again to send a new plant collector to Mexico, and to institute new medals; within a few years it would commission a great conservatory for the Chiswick garden. The 1830s and early 1840s also saw the creation of a Chemical Committee to investigate fertilisers, the first system of examinations for student gardeners, and the tentative beginnings of a scheme for affiliated societies.

Knight died in the summer of 1838, and the Duke of Devonshire was elected as the new President. Lindley's job title was changed from Assistant Secretary to Vice-Secretary; in 1840 his salary was raised to £450, with £50 compensation for travel expenses. Soon afterward, the salaries of the accountants, Davis and Scott, were raised to £150. In 1841 George Bentham resigned as Secretary, and was succeeded by Dr Alexander Henderson, himself to be succeeded four years later by J. R. Gowen of Highclere.

Bellenden Ker no longer played an active part in the Society's affairs, but there was a new claimant for the role of gadfly: George Glenny. Glenny was a journalist of initiative and versatility; he had founded the first weekly gardening newspaper, the *Gardeners' Gazette*; he was skilled at securing the favours of the nobility, as the founder of a *Royal Lady's Magazine*, which he later amalgamated into his *Horticultural Journal*. His great enthusiasm was florists' flowers—tulips,

William George Spencer Cavendish (1790-1858), 6th Duke of Devonshire, the 'Bachelor Duke'. Privy Councillor, KG, Lord Chamberlain of the Household to George IV and William IV. Landlord of the Society at Chiswick, and President 1838-58. From the Society's garden he plucked the young Joseph Paxton to be his head gardener at Chatsworth.

'The flower showe at Chysyk Gardens', by Richard Doyle, from Punch *(1849).*

carnations, auriculas, and the other traditional categories of flowers grown for competition—and in 1832 he had founded the Metropolitan Society of Florists and Amateurs to promote them. Once the Horticultural Society began holding its exhibitions the following year, Glenny joined, exhibited, received prizes, and began to complain when he did not get the prizes he expected. Unlike other disappointed exhibitors, he had magazines in which he could publish his complaints, and he also had a style of personal vituperation designed to draw attention to his anger.[19]

In 1837 Glenny proposed the creation of a new society, the Royal Society and Central School of Horticulture and Agriculture, for which he obtained the lease of rooms in the Egyptian Hall, Piccadilly, and also made an abortive attempt to secure a site in nearby Belgravia for a horticultural hall. He continued to exhibit at Chiswick and, at an exhibitors' meeting after the last show of the year, he proposed the presentation of a piece of plate to Lindley, to show that his hard work on the shows was appreciated, despite the altercations. After an advertisement in the *Gardeners' Gazette* had brought in the necessary subscriptions, one of his employees wrote to Lindley asking him if he would accept the plate. Lindley's reply—published in the *Gazette*—did nothing to cool tempers:

> Your letter is dated from 21 Catherine Street, in the Strand, an office closely connected with that of the Gardeners' Gazette, one of those unprincipled newspapers which are a disgrace of a civilised people and, moreover, a notorious vehicle for the basest calumnies concerning the Horticultural Society of London. Its seal bears the mark 'Royal and Central School of Horticulture and Agriculture', a name by which it has pleased the reputed editor of that newspaper to designate his show-rooms in Piccadilly, and I have reason to believe that the subscription you speak of has been got up by the same individual, for purposes best known to himself. It is most repugnant to my feelings even to appear to treat with discourtesy what may have been intended for civility, but I cannot consent, either as a private gentleman, or as an officer of the Horticultural Society, to receive any communication from places or persons of such a description.

Glenny used Lindley's letter for maximum publicity, and made the *Gazette* a forum for attacks on 'the inflated and infuriated sub-secretary', accusing him, among other things, of using the Chiswick staff to maintain his own garden at the nearby Bedford House, and of helping himself to choice trees from the Chiswick collection.[20] After an abortive campaign to create yet another rival

George Glenny (1793-1874), founder-editor of the Gardeners' Gazette, *the first weekly horticultural newspaper, from whose editorship he was later evicted by the publishers because of the constant risk of libel suits. In later years a columnist for the* Cottage Gardener.

society, he settled for finding a new venue for flower shows: Stafford House, a two-acre garden in Chiswick, needlingly close to the Horticultural Society's garden. He succeeded in getting Council's back up: in March 1839 Council ruled that no further prizes would be awarded to him at shows; but the Stafford House shows were only held for one year, as Glenny began to slip into insolvency. As manager of the Royal Union Association he had failed to control its finances, and before the end of 1839 he had to sell the *Gardeners' Gazette*, while continuing as editor; but the risk of libel suits led the new owners first to alter his editorials and eventually to oust him altogether. He was summonsed for non-payment of duty over advertisements in his newspapers, and his possessions were seized by Crown officers. Glenny eventually was reduced to the role of columnist in various magazines and newspapers, but he still had some years of sting remaining to him.

The first Glenny episode is emblematic of the Society's problems for the next twenty years or more. The shows at Chiswick proved highly successful during the 1830s, the Society's best source of revenue apart from membership subscriptions. But this success depended on the absence of competition, for Chiswick was then outside London, and not yet accessible by rail. Once rival flower shows began to take place nearer central London, the gate receipts at Chiswick began to decline. Glenny's shows at the Egyptian Hall were the first serious rival. Loudon praised the accommodation as the best site for flower shows near London, and urged the Society to use it; but there was little chance of that while Glenny was involved. His flower shows faded out after 1839, but just as a larger and more potent rival was developing: the Royal Botanic Society.

That society, founded in 1838, soon acquired the lease of a site Glenny had himself been interested in: the inner circle of Regent's Park, vacated in 1838 by the nursery firm that had then occupied it. With Robert Marnock, formerly the designer and superintendent of the Sheffield Botanic Garden, as its designer and curator, it opened to the public in 1841, and began to hold its flower shows the following year. The Society's prospectus had been calculated to nettle the Horticultural Society: 'Notwithstanding the manifest importance of a proper acquaintance with the productions of the vegetable kingdom, there is not, to this day, in the metropolis of the commercial world, a public establishment devoted to their study.' The Royal Botanic Society was never to engage in significant scientific work, nor to produce a decent journal, but it developed a public garden of great importance, and Marnock quickly distinguished himself in the management of flower shows. While these shows were badly timed, generally taking place one week after those at Chiswick, they began to attract large numbers, and the crowds attending Chiswick began to thin. In 1845 the Horticultural Society's shows brought in less than £600, a fall of over £1,000 from the previous year.[21]

Meanwhile, Council's brief periods of complacency induced by a successful issue of bonds always gave way to nailbiting and floundering attempts at averting minor financial crises. In 1842 the Society asked its bankers to deduct its income tax from the interest payable on the outstanding bonds; in 1843 it debated an issue of debentures at 4 per cent per annum, only to fall back instead on an issue of promissory notes to the value of £10,000. By 1845 the situation was exacerbated by the falling gate receipts. The idea of investing the salary owed to Robert Fortune, the plant collector currently overseas, was toyed with (it had been tried with his predecessor Hartweg, with acrimonious results), but it was decided his return was too imminent. In the event, the *Transactions* were discontinued, to be replaced by a cheaper *Journal*.

Friction had existed for years between Lindley and Joseph Davis, the accountant, who appears to have had a pugnacious temper.[22] Both had been hired in 1821, and their services rewarded by continual rises in salary, though Lindley's eventually stood at three times Davis's. In 1832 Davis had accused Lindley of financial irregularities; Council had investigated, and decided that while Lindley's accounting skills could use some improvement, he was innocent of wrongdoing. Late in 1845, Davis once again accused Lindley of embezzlement, the key issue being his failure to bank money received from subscriptions; Council investigated, with the same result as 13 years earlier. Davis simmered, and apparently more. As 1846 slid into 1847, the Society's arrears and list of defaulters both grew; *ad hoc* committees were set up to investigate, which grew into the Society's first Finance Committee. Eventually the accountants were ordered to pay all Life Fellows' compositions into a special fund for liquidating the outstanding debt. Davis and his assistant Scott refused, and Davis renewed his allegations of irregularities, pointing out that he'd raised the matter in 1845 but that nothing had been done, and attacking the Finance Committee's handling of matters. Scott resigned; Davis was sacked, and offered either three months' notice or three months' pay; he was not seen again in the offices. Within weeks, unprocessed invoices were found in his desk, and complaints about his behaviour surfaced from other staff, prompting the usual plaint: why hadn't anyone spoken up earlier?[23]

Davis, meanwhile, was writing letters to prominent Fellows, accusing the Society of malfeasance. More importantly, he had taken his version of the story to George Glenny, who was now running a gardening column in the *Edinburgh Weekly Journal*—possibly the first such column in a non-specialist newspaper; Glenny happily published his allegations in January 1848, and they were soon picked up in the London weekly *Gardener, Florist, and Agriculturist*. Davis, with credentials as the whistle-blower who had overthrown Sabine, was said to have been dismissed on the spot, without notice or pay, after making insulting remarks about Lindley; Council was accused of hypocrisy for having participated in the prosecution of a young man for embezzling a Fellow's subscription fee with which he had been entrusted, while hushing up the embezzlement of an unnamed associate.

> A schism has sprung up in the Horticultural Society, and the indefatigable accountant, after many years of service, and good service too, has been dismissed in a most unwarrantable manner, for endeavouring, single handed, to protect the Society at large against certain improper doings in the finances department. He was coaxed by the payment of half a year's salary for doing nothing; but we learn from a party on whom we can rely, that this was suddenly withdrawn, and the dismissal made altogether unqualified, for addressing one of the parties by a name that he richly earned, but which was not altogether so polite as it was true. [Clarified in a later issue: he called Lindley an 'atrocious scoundrel'.]
>   ... gross cases of embezzlement by a salaried servant, have been reported to the Council, who, instead of prosecuting and dismissing the delinquent, have hushed the matter up, and allowed him to make the money up, he being an essential manager of the system of abuses kept up.

(Scott, the under-accountant who had resigned, wrote to Council disavowing any knowledge of Davis's allegations.) The Society threatened the *Weekly Journal* with a lawsuit, which never reached the courts; the paper had been in decline for some time, and closed down abruptly at the end of March 1848, referring in its last issue to unnamed circumstances which made it impossible to continue. Possibly it was the threatened lawsuit that finished it off; that would at least be consistent with Glenny's career.[24] Glenny popped up at a meeting in early March to make his allegations publicly, only to be shouted down and told that, as he hadn't paid his subscription for years, he was not entitled to speak. He promised 'to agitate the question' at the next AGM; but by that time he had apparently become disillusioned with Davis's story, for he disavowed any accusation of embezzlement, and, saying that 'he would not be made a cat's-paw by any one', sat down and let the issue drop. The following year he settled his arrears.[25]

Thus ended Davis's career of 26 years with the Society. (Three years later he reappeared with a demand for the three months' back pay he had been promised; Council deemed that he was not entitled to it, but paid up anyway.) There was an office reorganisation after his departure, leaving the London office with six paid staff: the Vice-Secretary; the Librarian and Sub-accountant; the Professional Accountant; the Office Keeper; the Out-door Porter; and the Collector of Money, or dun. Lindley was authorised to countersign all bills, and all staff had thenceforth to keep absence records.

The annual report for 1848 kept quiet on the subject of debt; but the debts did not go away. In October, the Treasurer reported that the loan notes issued in 1843 had fallen due for payment, and that the Society did not have the money to pay them; half the holders of the notes agreed to renew them at a higher rate of interest (5 per cent instead of 4 per cent), and half (including the plant collector Hartweg) demanded payment, so £2,200 was repaid out of the sale of exchequer bills. Five years later the Society was still floundering, and the holders were asked if they would allow the interest rate to drop back to 4 per cent. And so life continued, with new issues of loan notes, requests for deferral of payments, increased dunning of defaulters, miscellaneous cutbacks. The dunning was not a major success; a committee reported that from those defaulters who could legitimately be pursued and had means to pay, only £700 was recoverable, so the Society had to write off £3,800 as irrecoverable debts. The *Journal* was sent only to members specifically requesting it; the number of meetings per year was cut back; admission fees to Chiswick were reduced in the hope of attracting more custom. The possibility of introducing a class of cheaper memberships was proposed (and eventually, in 1856, acted on, with a two-guinea rate).[26]

The year 1851 brought the announcement of a new society being formed to promote florists' flowers: a successor to Glenny's Metropolitan Society, but conducted under the auspices of nurserymen like William Paul, Thomas Rivers, Charles Turner, and James Veitch; Edmund Foster of Clewer Manor was the chairman. The National Floricultural Society, as it was titled, strove earnestly to maintain good relations with the Horticultural Society, using its constitution as a model, renting rooms at the Regent Street house for its own offices, and holding its exhibitions there. William Brailsford, the Society's former librarian and sub-accountant, joined as Assistant Secretary for the new organisation; and in a delightfully even-handed gesture, both Lindley and Marnock were invited to become vice-presidents. The National Floricultural shows were never exactly a threat to the Horticultural Society's, as they were dedicated to a restricted subject matter that had notoriously been under-valued at Chiswick; but they still constituted rivalry of a sort.[27]

The Annual General Meeting for 1851 brought an upset to Council. The year before, Gowen had resigned as Secretary in order to become Treasurer, and a now obscure figure, Dr Daniel, had become the new Secretary. For whatever reasons, he had not endeared himself to the Fellows. When it was proposed to the AGM that Lord Ashburton retire from Council under the usual rules, the meeting voted him back in and demanded Daniel's retirement instead. The new Secretary, elected by the majority of the meeting without Council's backing, the botanist John Forbes Royle, currently Professor of Materia Medica at King's College London. So spontaneous was the whole affair that, until he was informed of his election, Royle did not even know that he had been nominated. Lindley, who might have seemed an obvious candidate, was passed over. He had long since developed a reputation for officiousness and short temper; as co-founder and editor from 1841 of the weekly *Gardeners' Chronicle*, he was admired and influential, but also frequently resented for his high-handed condemnations and acerbic criticisms. He was shortly to nettle the horticultural community even further when, largely for financial reasons, there was a cut-back in the number of medals awarded. Bellenden Ker and Louisa Lawrence mounted an attack, and threatened to withdraw from exhibitions. By 1856, the *Cottage Gardener* could remark that 'Dr. Lindley neither in temperament nor in habits is calculated to win golden opinions from the men of the spade. We have very abundant evidence of this ...'[28]

In 1854 another venue for rival flower shows opened: Crystal Palace Park, on Sydenham Hill, south of the Thames, but easily reached by the new railway. Although later a municipal park, all through the 19th century the Crystal Palace was run by a company and charged admission fees. Sir Joseph Paxton, the former Chiswick gardener, co-founder with Lindley of the *Gardeners' Chronicle*, and a vice-president of the Society, was the principal director of the new establishment, but was understandably keen for it to succeed, and happy to compete with the Society in its shows administration. Exhibitors definitely preferred the easy-going ways of the Crystal Palace to Lindley's commandeering ways.[29] The combined effect of Regent's Park and the Crystal Palace made a crippling dent in the Society's income from shows. Ticket sales, between 1851 and 1855, declined from £5,046 to £1,681.

April 1854 also saw what some probably regarded as the last straw: the creation of the British Pomological Society, to be devoted to the study and exhibit of fruit. A rival society devoted to florists' flowers, in which the Society had never expressed much interest, was one thing; a society claiming the high ground in what had long been the Horticultural Society's greatest claim to fame, fruit, was quite another. Despite its worsening financial situation, the Society managed to recruit its energies and deal with the opposition. In 1856, it called John Spencer, the Pomological Society's Secretary, into consultation on the improvement of its garden at Chiswick; in 1858, it finally instituted a Fruit Committee, to judge fruits at shows, oversee fruit trials, and advise on all matters relating to fruit. The move was widely welcomed in the press; by the summer of 1860 the British Pomological Society was in debt; that autumn its affairs were wound up, and it was merged with the Fruit Committee.

The Fruit Committee was followed in 1859 by a Floral Committee on similar lines. The National Floricultural Society went the same way as the Pomological: most of its executive joined the new committee. 1858 was the year of that society's last annual report; it was already encountering difficulties with exhibition venues, when the use of the Regent Street house was terminated because of its impending sale. While the reform of the Horticultural Society was not obviously part of the intention underlying either of its rival organisations, that is in effect what they accomplished: together, they gave the Society a committee structure that was representative of national opinion and achievement in horticulture. What they did not accomplish was any significant influx of money into the Society's depleted coffers, and these same years saw the Society sliding towards the abyss with increasing speed.

The verge of collapse

Lindley, in 1854, offered to carry on his work without pay, as an attempt to ease the Society's financial problems. Council could not bring themselves to accept the offer. The *Journal* was discontinued; the Duke of Devonshire agreed to reduce the rental for the Chiswick garden to £200 per annum; alternatives to the house in Regent Street were canvassed, and an unsuccessful attempt was made to secure rooms in the newly built Burlington House on Piccadilly. Robert Glendinning, the landscape gardener who had designed the Chiswick arboretum, valued the Society's property at £15,656; but when asked how to realise £8,000-£9,000 from it quickly, he was forced to admit that his valuation was notional.[30] The costs of staging the shows were exceeding the revenue; special sales of fruit trees and greenhouse plants failed to bring in the anticipated profits. Lindley told Council in July 1855 that the shows would have to be discontinued unless they could be revised in some way, because people were unwilling to travel out to Chiswick: 'The absence of any Railway to Turnham Green, and the proximity to Kew prevent the Society's Garden continuing to be the attraction it once was. It is beaten by distance'.[31]

Gowen had resigned as Treasurer in 1855; his successor, Dr A. R. Jackson, died a year later. The new Treasurer was William Wilson Saunders, an amateur botanist of considerable skill, and also an underwriter at Lloyds'. He entered on his duties to the happy news that neither bank nor insurance companies were prepared to advance any further money to the Society.

> The facts are these. The Secretary of the Horticultural Society has at last openly acknowledged that it cannot go on ... The present condition is a debt of somewhere between £10,000 and £12,000; the income of last year was about £1,700, and the expenditure about £4,000, by which some £2,000 was added to the already enormous debt. The assets are valued at some fabulous sum, of which we do not exactly know the amount, but practical men put them down at less than £5,000. The future prospects are far from bright; the garden clerk and the librarian have been discharged; the necessary working staff in the garden has been reduced; the Quarterly Journal has lapsed, and there is no announcement of shows for the coming year.[32]

Saunders's first approach to the problem was to sell whatever could be lifted without difficulty. November 1855 saw a sale of orchids (£569), and another of exotic plants from the Society's conservatory (£512); this was followed in January by the sale of the Society's herbarium (£225), and an auction of the back stock of the *Transactions* (£250). Still, in March 1856, the standing debt was £9,300. Subscription losses from deaths and resignations were exceeding new memberships. Older hands looked back to the glory days of 1821,

William Wilson Saunders (1809-1879), insurance underwriter, botanist, and entomologist. Successively Treasurer and Secretary of the Society. At his garden at Hallfield, near Reigate, the most important mid-century grower of cacti and succulents. In his prime he was able to finance his own plant collectors; but in 1873 financial reverses forced him to sell Hallfield and retire to Worthing.

before the Society had been lumbered with Chiswick; perhaps the garden could be sold? The accountant pointed out that if the garden were abandoned, the Society would have to pay back the subscriptions of its Life Fellows, whose use of the garden was a stated benefit of their Fellowship, and 'An Actuary is the only person who can ascertain the amount claimable by these Fellows'.[33] A committee under the chairmanship of S.H. Godson opposed the sale, but Council was not convinced, and resolved to terminate the tenancy unless a sum of at least £5,000 could be raised. The news was greeted with shock internationally; a subscription was started for preserving the garden, and support began to pour in. The German botanist Heinrich Behrens, sending £100, said, 'there is no institution in Europe, the discontinuance of which would be in a higher degree deplorable for all friends of gardening than the London Horticultural Society in its full and unabated efficiency'.[34] Only a little over £3,000 was actually raised, but it was enough to persuade Council to look elsewhere than the sale of Chiswick for its rescue package.

Economy measure followed economy measure for the next few years. The great conservatory at Chiswick was converted into a vinery, allowing some income to be generated by the sale of grapes. The shows at Chiswick were discontinued, and alternative premises sought in London: Paxton offered Crystal Palace Park, but the grounds of Gore House in Kensington were rented for the purpose instead. The Godson Committee had recommended staff cutbacks; the two superintending posts were to be amalgamated (George Gordon, after 30 years of service, was given three months' notice). George M'Ewen, the head gardener of Arundel Castle, was appointed the new Superintendent, only to die within little more than a year; his successor, Archibald Henderson, soon left for a more lucrative position at Trentham. An attempt was made to sell the Regent Street house, but it failed to reach the proposed reserve of £3,990. An attempt was made to introduce a cut-rate two-guinea membership, but after the first year it failed to bring in the desired influx of new members.

The year 1858 began with the deaths of the Secretary, Dr Royle, and of the President, the Duke of Devonshire. Lindley proposed that the posts of Secretary and Vice-Secretary be amalgamated, and offered to resign his paid position as Vice-Secretary if he were elected to the new post. His proposal was accepted, so after 37 years with the Society he was finally its chief administrator. A new and powerful Council member, Sir Charles Wentworth Dilke, approached Prince Albert to

Sir Charles Wentworth Dilke (1810-1869), father of the rather more famous politician of the same name. One of the organisers of the Great Exhibition of 1862. Died in St Petersburg while representing the RHS at an international exhibition.

Albert, the Prince Consort (1819-1861). President 1858-61. The opening of the Society's garden in Kensington was his last public appearance in London before his death.

ask if he would undertake the role of President, and the Prince Consort accepted.

This new executive partnership made no initial difference to the Society's desperate financial straits. The bank still refused to advance any money, so Saunders, the Treasurer, advanced £900 of his own money to help meet the Society's bills—with little enough hope of getting it back, one might imagine. A new Finance Committee was established in July, with the purpose of 'examining all Tradesmen's bills, considering all heads of expenditure and all sources of Income'. It was not originally a committee of Council, but after a meeting proved inquorate at a critical time, every Council member was made a Finance Committee member, and summoned as such. Nonetheless, by the end of the year one of the Society's Council members, the great nurseryman James Veitch, was suggesting that the Society be wound up and replaced with something new.

A further financial debacle was threatened by two women named Wainhouse, whose notes for £2,000 were due for payment in January 1859, and who refused to allow a postponement. They were persuaded to take personal guarantees as promissory notes, and eventually paid off by the summer of 1860, but the threatened loss of £2,000, coming at such a moment, seemed to panic Council into radical measures. Every head of expenditure, they ruled at the beginning of 1859, must be reduced to the lowest possible point consistent with the continued existence of the Society: the house in Regent Street must be sold for any price, the Library must be sold, as must any surplus from Chiswick, and perhaps even the Garden itself. As a later historian observed, 'in the winter of 1858-1859 Council lost its nerve after years of struggling with deteriorating finances'. The Society's bankers finally agreed to advance £500 on the surety of the sale. The Regent Street house was auctioned in March for £2,960, much less than the old anticipated reserve, and new rooms were taken in St Martin's Place; the old membership lists were sold for scrap paper. The Library was sold in a four-day sale at Sotheby's in May, and after auctioneer's commission netted less than £1,000. Ironically, by the time that sale took place, the Society had 'turned the corner', and money was already pouring in to establish it on a new footing.[35]

Albertopolis

On 17 November 1858, Sir Charles Dilke called a special Council meeting to discuss an idea he had had, and the result was a motion 'That a letter be addressed to Her Majesty's Commissioners for

Henry Cole, Lyon Playfair, Edgar Bowring, and a young engineer, Henry Young Darracott Scott. Doomed to frustration in some matters—the National Gallery, which Albert had hoped to move into the proposed complex, remained in Trafalgar Square—the project left the long-term legacy of the Victoria and Albert Museum and the attendant royal colleges, soon collectively nicknamed Albertopolis; and for its first quarter-century the Horticultural Society was its centrepiece.[36]

Negotiations moved tentatively, but with sufficient speed that, ten days after the sale of the library, the *Gardeners' Chronicle* could praise the progress toward finding the Society a new home. The Royal Commissioners' terms, approved at a General Meeting on 7 July, were as follows:

(1) That the Commissioners will surround the whole ground with beautiful Italian Arcades open to the Garden, and execute extensive ground works at a cost of Fifty thousand pounds, granting the Society a lease of the ground for 31 years, provided that the Society would at an equal cost lay out the Gardens and erect a Winter Garden at the north end.

(2) That the Commissioners are willing to accept a rental entirely contingent on profits, first providing for the necessary expenditure in keeping up the Gardens at Chiswick as well as Kensington Gore, and next for the payment of interest on any money borrowed by the Horticultural Society, and afterwards for payment of interest on the Fifty thousand pounds to be borrowed by the Commissioners for the Arcades and ground work. All surplus to be then divided between the Commissioners and the Horticultural Society.

(3) The Council being anxious to be placed as soon as possible in a position to confer further with Her Majesty's Commissioners, and to know whether sufficient means will be placed at their disposal, I am to inform the Fellows of the Society that it is proposed to raise the money by Donation, by Life Memberships of 40 Guineas and 20 Guineas, and by Debentures carrying 5 per cent interest with probably contingent adjustment at the expiration of the lease.

(4) That Queen Victoria had promised a donation of £1,000, and that the Prince Consort would contribute £500 and, if necessary, take Debentures to the value of £1,000.

The building at St Martin's Place, where the Society's offices were located from 1859 to 1861.

1851 enquiring whether the Horticultural Society can have about 20 acres of land in the middle of the block of ground lying between Kensington, Cromwell, Exhibition and Prince Albert roads— and if so, on what terms'.

The Society had been using the grounds of Gore House, immediately across the road from Kensington gardens, for flower shows since 1855. Gore House, and a large chunk of adjacent property, had been purchased by the Royal Commissioners for the Great Exhibition of 1851 out of that exhibition's profits. Prince Albert, as President of the Royal Commission, saw this purchase as the opportunity to create a great cultural centre for London, which would contain museums and schools of the arts and industries, bringing together all the resources necessary to improve the standards of design in England. For this purpose he built up a team comprising, to name only those who would play an important role in the negotiations with the Society, Dilke,

Prince Albert viewing the model for the proposed Memorial to the Exhibition of 1851: watercolour sketch by Anthony Stannus.

(5) That several Members of Council had intimated that in addition to taking Debentures they would arrange for members of their families to become Life Fellows.

The appeal was entirely successful. The necessary £50,000 was raised by November, and the debenture list closed. A separate Kensington account was created, which in January 1860 stood at nearly £4,000 while the General account stood at £114. (£3,000 was invested in India bonds, and the remainder kept as a floating account.) Applications for Fellowship flowed in at a rate that filled page after page of the Council minutes, over 300 being elected at a single meeting. Queen Victoria recruited most of the royal family as Fellows, and badgered her continental connections, including the entire exiled royal family of France, into joining.

Not everything proceeded smoothly with the administrative arrangements for the new Garden. The Commissioners' lawyers objected to the form of the debenture. The Society's lawyer Tatham argued that the Society could not legally enter into the agreement with the Commissioners, because the Society's money ought to be under its own sole control, and the Charter allowed no power to make such an agreement, nor indeed to confer privileges on debenture holders. Concluding that 'There is a want of identity between the projected scheme and the legitimate purposes of the Horticultural Society', Tatham urged the Society to secure an Act of Parliament to regularise matters; but the costs of petitioning Parliament for an uncertain result ruled out that course of action. In the end a new Charter was arranged, which filled pages with the details of the Kensington agreement; it was given royal consent in May 1861, and changed the name of the Society to the Royal Horticultural Society.[37]

The lease was arranged for 22½ acres, between the future site of the Royal Albert Hall and that of the Natural History Museum, bounded on the east by Exhibition Road. Already by September 1859, trees were being prepared for transplanting to the new garden. On 25 October, Prince Albert convened a Council meeting at Windsor Castle to discuss plans and staffing. A superlative team was assembled: Francis Fowke and Sydney Smirke as architects, with Godfrey Sykes as a contributory designer, John Kelk as builder, and William

Andrews Nesfield as landscape designer. Nesfield's plans for Kensington were exhibited to the Society on 1 May 1860, and work began soon after on the garden. The structure of the surrounding arcades was completed, though much of the intended decoration had to wait; but in February 1861 the Society was able to move from its little rooms in St Martin's Place to the new offices. The garden was opened on 5 June 1861; there was a private visit in the morning for the royal family and the King of the Belgians, followed in the afternoon by the official ceremony, with the royal family planting a wellingtonia. The first organised competition of flower arranging was staged as part of the event. The press, national and horticultural, exulted in the glories of the garden, undoubtedly the grandest formal garden that had ever been created in London.

The opening of the Garden was Prince Albert's last public appearance in London. On 14 December, he died at Windsor Castle; the cause of death was declared to be typhoid fever. Queen Victoria announced her wish to succeed Albert as President, but within a month her advisers had persuaded her to relinquish the idea, and the Duke of Buccleuch was put forward in her place.[38]

The Kensington years

The Royal Commissioners had also hoped that the Great Exhibition would become the first of a series, and so set up a committee to organise a successor exhibition in 1862; Dilke was one of the committee. The RHS in turn set up a committee to negotiate with the Commissioners, consisting of Saunders, John Clutton, and Henry Pownall. A new building, designed by Fowke, was erected to the south of the garden, with access points into the southern arcade. In October 1861, Lindley offered to resign as Secretary at the next anniversary meeting, at which he would complete forty years as an officer of the Society. In view of the forthcoming exhibition, Council begged him to continue for another year, to cope with 'the influx of scientific foreigners which may be expected', and Lindley, with 'mingled feelings of regret and satisfaction', found it 'impossible to refuse a request thus conveyed'.[39] In March 1862 Lindley was appointed Superintendent of the Colonial Section of the Exhibition, and the extra burden of work it entailed wore down his health. The Exhibition was better attended than its predecessor, but not to the expected degree—a 25 per cent increase had been anticipated—so it was judged to be a failure. In the end the Exhibition made a loss of £11,000, which was made good out of his own pocket by John Kelk. The building was

demolished, and the iron and glass acquired for the making of Alexandra Palace. But the Society had profited, with total receipts of £30,000, and it was actually able to pay the Commissioners £1,000 in rent, an achievement not to be repeated for over a decade.

Once the Exhibition was over and its detritus cleared away, Lindley again offered his resignation as Secretary ('I have become physically incapable of continuing to execute its duties'). (He had to badger Council into accepting it, and by March of the following year was becoming too feeble to attend committee meetings.) He had some advice to offer his successor. 'The danger which he will run,' he said, 'consists in being misled by too much prosperity, out of which sometimes grow financial neglect and administrative supineness.' He then listed the ten salaried staff positions and concluded, 'So much power to move so small a machine, cannot be necessary, except in an exceptional year like the present'.[40] Wilson Saunders gave up his role as Treasurer to succeed Lindley; John Clutton, the builder, became the new Treasurer for two years, before he was in turn succeeded by John Kelk. Lindley died at the end of 1865, after a rapid physical decline exacerbated by his labours on the 1862 Exhibition.

The Estimates Committee behaved as though it took Lindley's words to heart. In January 1863, it proposed recalling the plant collector from Brazil, taking advertisements in the *Proceedings*, cutting back on office staff and making the Council Room a Reading Room, consulting Nesfield about diminishing the flower beds, and, once again, surrendering part of the Chiswick garden. Then in June the *Journal of Horticulture* reported a rumour that Dilke had met Robert Marnock of the Royal Botanic Society to suggest that the two societies should collaborate on cutting back the cost of prizes, as a mutual money-saving venture. While not committing itself to the truth of the rumour, the *Journal* warned that 'if the Council of any Society allows one of its members to become dictator, no one fitting to belong to that Council will remain'.[41]

The first decade or so of the Society's residence in Kensington was, on the face of it, one of its most glorious periods. It had, initially at least, an innovative and fashionable garden, once again a key locus for the London season; it was integrated into a cultural programme that included Music and Fine Arts Committees. To counterbalance this, it still had its trials and its fruit collection at Chiswick, even if Chiswick suffered financial cutbacks and a heavy reduction in size; it also made great efforts to improve its scientific character, and to extend the spread of horticultural

Walter Francis Montagu-Douglas-Scott (1806-1884), 5th Duke of Buccleuch. President 1862-73. Former Privy Councillor and Lord Privy Seal. Became President of the Highland Agricultural Society while still in his twenties. Later President of the British Association.

A cartoon of 1879 by J. Dower Wilson, of social types observed at the Kensington garden.

gardeners, of the establishment of the Scientific Committee, and the investigation into fraud in the seedsmen's trade. A new *Journal* was started under the editorship of Miles J. Berkeley, and a celebratory *Book of the Royal Horticultural Society*, with detailed descriptions of the Kensington garden, published by the Assistant Secretary Andrew Murray.

But Lindley's warning about wealth-induced complacency and administrative supineness was to prove an accurate prophecy. It was not long before the disparity of expenditure on the gardens at Kensington and Chiswick proved contentious; the amount of money spent on statuary for the former would prove a special irritation. As early as 1864 the matter erupted publicly. The arcades had never been completed to their intended degree of decoration, and Henry Cole, who had been elected to Council not long before, demanded that the Commissioners spend some £13,000 on completing the work. Initial works to an approximate sum of £2,300 were begun under the Society's auspices—an exhibition tent for rhododendrons, additional planting—in the hope that the Commissioners would step in to complete the architectural works. This burst of extra expenditure was the signal for the first shot in a 20-year war between Chiswick and Kensington. Robert Hogg addressed an open letter to Andrew Murray, denouncing the waste of funds on the merely decorative:

> When I accepted the office of Secretary to the Fruit Committee of the Horticultural Society it was under the impression that the Council intended to maintain and develop the horticultural character of the Society. For a long time I believed the Council were in earnest in this matter, and so long as I believed they were so I

knowledge. In these years the Society held its first shows outside London, became involved in foreign horticultural congresses and exhibitions, and helped stage the first International Botanical Congress and Horticultural Exhibition in 1866, using its profits to buy John Lindley's library as a partial replacement for what it had lost. (Dilke was to get into trouble once again for apparent bullying tactics in arranging the purchase.) These were also the years of the first schemes for affiliated societies, of national examinations for continued to fill that office. Recent events, however, have convinced me that some other object than the advancement of Horticulture is that which a ruling majority of the late and present Councils have in view.

Murray defended the Council's decisions by making a comparison with the Society's enfeebled state a few years before:

> in the year just before the establishment of the gardens at South Kensington the Society had given up its shows at Chiswick; had ceased to employ a collector abroad; had abandoned the publication of any Journal or Proceedings; held no ballot for plants or seeds; had sold its herbarium and library; had also sold its premises in Regent Street, and located itself in two small rooms in St. Martin's Lane, whilst the Fellows had diminished in number to 985. Whereas, after the establishment of the garden at South Kensington, the flower shows have been re-established; collectors have been and are employed abroad; their horticultural publications have been resumed; Fruit and Floral Committees organised; ballots for plants have been instituted; and the Fellows have increased in number from 985 to 3336.

Hogg replied: 'and all with results so unproductive and disastrous to the interests of the Society as to leave it with a debt of upwards of £50,000.'[42] He resigned his chairmanship of the Fruit Committee, but returned to it a few months later.

Meanwhile, what about Chiswick? The Duke of Devonshire had declined to repossess the garden back in 1858, but was happy to consider the Society sub-letting the grounds. Council decided that at least part of Chiswick was worth retaining as an experimental garden, but its area would have to be reduced. Shortly after the opening of the Kensington garden, Lindley asked George Eyles, the superintendent, to find ways of keeping Chiswick's annual expenditure within £1,000 (except for the costs of supplying plants to Kensington and distributing them to members). Dilke could propose a grandiose scheme for making Chiswick a school of horticulture for the whole empire, but this was difficult to envisage on £1,000 a year.[43] In 1870, the possibility of abandoning Chiswick once again raised its head, and the former Treasurer, George Fergusson Wilson, tried to interest Council in a garden near Weybridge (possibly his own) without any success.[44] Instead, a new boundary was negotiated with the Duke of Devonshire's agents, and the garden at Chiswick was reduced in size by two-thirds, from 33 acres to a little over ten.

Economies had already been made at Kensington in 1866, with Eyles's salary being reduced on the grounds that his additional income from landscape design would compensate him for the loss. Chiswick was removed from his authority, and the senior foreman, Archibald Barron, was made superintendent. When Chiswick was truncated, Barron decided to leave the Society, and was offered the post of Superintendent of Victoria and Greenwich Parks. Council hastily told him he could not resign at less than three months' notice, and offered him Eyles's former post as Superintendent of both Chiswick and Kensington. Barron accepted, and Eyles found his role reduced. He hung on for another four years, increasingly relying on outside commissions for his living, and eventually working without salary on condition that he could continue to occupy his house.[45]

Meanwhile, the Royal Commissioners were busy with the continued redevelopment of South Kensington. The garden was administered by an Expenses Committee, composed equally of Commissioners and representatives of the Society; but the interpenetration of the two organisations extended beyond the joint committee. Four of the Commissioners—Dilke, Cole, Kelk, and Scott—served terms as members of Council, and in 1866 Scott—who was by then acting as the architect of the Royal Albert Hall, having taken over the project on Fowke's death—was elected Secretary of the Society. The Commissioners had been disappointed by the Second Great Exhibition, but within a few years had decided to continue to hold International Exhibitions on a smaller scale, so as to keep the flame of 1851 alive; and the Society, which had profited from the increased attendance in 1862, was happy to co-operate. Sacrifices were, however, required, most notably the loss of control over the arcades. Edgar Bowring, on behalf of the Commissioners, had asked the Society back in 1863 to relinquish their rights over the southern arcade, and after initial resistance the Society had acquiesced. Now further portions of arcade were surrendered to allow exhibition space; Scott completed a new building south of the garden, connected to the south arcade. The first of the smaller international exhibitions was held in 1871, and deemed a rousing success; with each successive year the success was less, and after 1875 they were discontinued.

Scott, in his role as Secretary, won the Society new financial concessions in its relations with the Commissioners, and in 1871, for the second time, the Society was able to pay them a year's rent (£2,400)—and a further half-year's rent six months later. This was not entirely out of profits, however; a little financial chicanery was resorted to. The Society had a reserve fund which it had built up and ring-fenced for the costs of its provincial shows; £1,800 was transferred from the provincial shows fund into the main revenue fund, and the way to paying the rent was eased. Any hopes for continued solvency were quickly eroded, however, as the Society's membership began to complain bitterly about the infringements on the garden. A large number of the newly expanded membership were local residents in the Kensington area, and while no one objected to an apparently unique event like the 1862 (Second) Great Exhibition, the prospect of a continuing series of exhibitions brought protests. Here were people paying a large subscription fee for the use of the garden, and at the right time of year anyone could walk off the street to see the exhibition, and get access into the garden with no additional payment. And to add insult to injury, the Commissioners had ruled that Fellows' tickets to the exhibitions were not transferable.

Matters came to a head at the Annual General Meeting for 1873. For the first time there was a seriously contested election for Council, with opposing delegates named in advance. The rosarian Samuel Reynolds Hole and the nurseryman Benjamin S. Williams were named in the *Gardeners' Chronicle* as candidates to oppose two Kensington worthies, Lord Alfred Churchill and Lord Londesborough. A few weeks later the opposing faction declared itself in *The Times*, calling for a special general meeting to elect a new Council; Sir Alfred Slade, W.A. Lindsay, Sir Coutts Lindsay, S.H. Godson, and ten others, including a former Director of the Bank of England.[46] And just to stir the brew up further came the question of proxy votes. After the AGM was adjourned, George Fergusson Wilson canvassed the Lady Fellows of the Society, asking them to send him their proxies for use on behalf of the beleaguered Council, an action which led to this exchange at the next meeting: 'Wilson: "I shall most assuredly use all the proxies I have been entrusted with." A Fellow: "A most dishonourable transaction."'[47]

The AGM, which eventually stretched into a string of four meetings, frequently degenerated into shouting matches. Scott was denounced as a paid lackey of the Commissioners, though he pointed out that his role as Secretary was unpaid, and 'the only salary I got was abuse'. Shirley Hibberd attacked the Council over its finances. The meeting declared that Council's policy had failed, and refused to accept its Report. Council announced its collective determination to resign, but then discovered that the bye-laws prohibited such a mass resignation. The Society's legal adviser, Nathaniel Lindley (John Lindley's son),

advised Council to call a special general meeting in order to repeal the relevant bye-law, which they did on 26 March. (One Council member, Andrew Murray, was on his way to America at the time of the meetings, and could not take part in the proceedings; he resigned independently on 3 November.) The Solicitor-General, on the other hand, gave his opinion that no such resignation would have been valid until the next AGM, and as a result the Royal Commissioners refused to recognise the legality of the new Council.

The new administration consisted of Lord Bury as President, W.A. Lindsay as Secretary, and Bonamy Dobrée as Treasurer. They were soon confronted with an ultimatum from the membership, in a petition led by the former interim Treasurer Sir Daniel Cooper, with Wilson, Hogg, Thomas Moore, Maxwell T. Masters, William Paul, William Robinson, and Harry Veitch among the signatories, calling on them to terminate the lease of Kensington; they refused, provoking another special general meeting in January 1874.[48] In February 1874, George Fergusson Wilson published his past year's correspondence in the *Gardeners' Chronicle* under the title *The Royal Horticultural Society, as it is, and as it might be*. His proposal was that, as the Society was divided into two factions, one faction ought to keep Kensington and the other Chiswick. By this time the Royal Commissioners themselves were changing, as the original generation, full of the idealism of the Great Exhibition, began to modulate into or make way for more pragmatic men with a sharper concern for finances. Sir Henry Cole had attacked the Chancellor of the Exchequer, Robert Lowe, the previous year for the budget cuts he was imposing, and as a result found himself squeezed into retirement. (His last proposal was that the government should buy the gardens from the Society at half value, pay off the debentures, and remodel the garden as a backdrop for the Albert Hall.)[49] Lord Bury delivered his summary of Cole's involvement with the Society at the 1875 AGM: 'I believe the result of that man's remarkable and magnificent scheme ... will remain an everlasting monument to his genius, but parents are rather fonder of their own children than of other people's bantlings, and Sir Henry Cole, I think, treated the Royal Horticultural Society rather hardly.'[50]

The new Council attempted to make peace with the Royal Commissioners by proposing new fund-raising devices, most notably a skating rink which was offered by a Mr Prince for an estimated annual rental of £1,100, but they initially laboured under the Commissioners' disinclination to conduct business with a body of dubious legality.

William Coutts Keppel (1832-1894), Lord Bury, later 7th Earl of Albemarle. Shortest-serving President, 1873-75. Formerly Commissioner for Indian Affairs in Canada, 1854-57; author of The Exodus of the Western Nations *(1865). MP for Norwich. Later Under-Secretary for War under Disraeli and Salisbury.*

A view of the garden in Kensington in its later years, with the Royal Albert Hall in the distance; from the Journal of Horticulture *(1877).*

In any case, said the Commissioners, 'the Society had no power to divert or deface any portion of the Gardens for a purpose foreign to their objects, and that the act of doing so was a violation of the conditions of the lease'. In the summer of 1874 there were, in addition to the Society's normal management committees, committees on Fellows' arrears, provincial shows, a proposed fête, a proposed dinner, works and finances, and on the future of the orchard houses in the Kensington garden. There was also a controversy being aired in the press that embarrassed the Council further: the case of D.T. Fish's membership. Fish, the famous head gardener at Hardwicke in Suffolk, had been given an honorary 40-guinea Life Fellowship in 1867, for helping the Society with organising its Bury St Edmunds show. In 1874, however, he was told that his Life Fellowship was invalid, and prevented from speaking at a meeting. Council quickly offered him an honorary Fellowship, but Fish, who plainly thought the procedural argument a ruse to stop him from expressing his opposition, refused, and for years to follow garnered good publicity from the Society's treatment of him.[51]

In 1875, once again, there was a stormy meeting, at which Council acknowledged its failure in negotiations. 'As for the charge brought against the Council of not having fostered horticulture', said Sir Coutts Lindsay, 'the answer was that the Council had neither money nor means.' (The Society was refusing to pay for prizes awarded at its shows until its finances improved.) Council was now seen as divided between the horticulturists and the compromisers, Lord Bury being denounced as 'the catspaw of a certain party'. Said William Haughton, the future Treasurer: 'at the last moment, the Council had ceased to wage war against the Royal Commissioners, and ... a treaty of peace had been entered into.'

Frequently in the debate a contrast was made between the horticultural needs of the nation and the narrow interests of those who became Members in order to use the Kensington garden. G.E. Blenkins (Deputy Commissioner of Hospitals), speaking at a special general meeting on 26 March 1873, said that 'His reason for supporting vote by proxy was that he did not think the management of the gardens should be carried on solely by those who lived in the neighbourhood of the gardens—a system which would make the Horticultural Gardens similar to the London squares—the home and residence of nurserymaids. In the country they knew well the meaning of what was going on. He did not see why a clique should be allowed to conduct the affairs of a great national Society like this.' Lord Bury and his colleagues, for their attempts to come to terms with the Commissioners, became known as the 'Kensington clique', and Lord Bury replied by referring to a 'clique of horticulturists' trying to gain control of the Society. The *Gardeners'*

Chronicle summarised matters: 'The fortunes of the Royal Horticultural Society must surely have arrived at their lowest ebb. It is scarcely possible to imagine that they can sink lower.'[52]

The Kensington party accordingly offered to resign at a specially convened meeting, but continued to try to soften the Commissioners in the meantime; this continuation of activity drew a furious rebuke from the next meeting, and it ended with Lord Bury angrily refusing to accept a vote of thanks for his efforts while President. The *Gardeners' Chronicle* expressed horror at this deterioration in manners: 'when the President and Treasurer ... not only refused to pay what we consider "debts of honour", but went out of their way to insult and abuse the men of all others whom it was their duty, as officers of the Society, to conciliate and encourage ... It is not easy at first to see what the motives are which can induce men of position and character to endanger their reputation in this way ...' The fact that the meeting had ended without the proffered resignations, said the *Chronicle*, 'adds another disgrace to the Society, and intensifies the sense of weariness and disgust with everything connected with it, in its present state, that loyal horticulturists must feel.'[53] Such little details as W.A. Lindsay, who had offered his resignation even before the meeting, refusing to hand back his master key to the garden did nothing to smooth feelings. Fifteen Fellows signed a petition calling for a special general meeting; the *Gardeners' Chronicle* anticipated the event with a spoof proposal for a new Council, which envisaged Henry Cole and Shirley Hibberd as joint Secretaries, and Barron as General Superintendent ('with unlimited and irresponsible power').[54] The result of the meeting was that Lord Bury, Coutts Lindsay, and Dobrée all resigned.

Once again a new administration, this time with Lord Aberdare as President, Robert Hogg as Secretary, and Henry Webb as Treasurer. Aberdare wrote that autumn to Sir Henry Ponsonby, the Queen's Secretary: 'You are perhaps aware that I have joined the Council of the Royal Horticultural Society as its President in the hopes of uniting all parties for parties there are in Horticulture as in other matters in a hearty effort to save them from destruction.'[55] The immediate issues facing the Council were the questions of proxy voting[56] and transferability of tickets, both hangovers from the previous administration; the substitution of lawn tennis for the skating rink as an immediate source of income; and a precarious bank balance, which had meant that most of the prizes awarded at shows the previous year were as yet unpaid. In such circumstances, no one was prepared to consider such matters of honour as

paying back the misappropriated Provincial Show funds.[57]

The year 1876 saw the debenture holders take action, calling for the first of many meetings with the Council to put their case. Council had reason to worry 'whether if [they] were to surrender their lease to the Commissioners, the members of the Council would, in the event of the surrender being declared illegal by a Court of Law, be personally liable for damages to the Debenture-holders'. On the other side, the recently-founded Horticultural Club, with members such as Robert Hogg, Thomas Moore, Maxwell T. Masters and Samuel Reynolds Hole, was becoming a focus for the horticultural opposition.[58]

At this point Hogg, in his role as Secretary, published a letter in the 'universally-read columns' of the *Daily News* (26 January 1877), which included the statements that the Society's 'debentures are a charge on the surplus income after payment of its expenses only, do not attach upon any of its property, and do not constitute a debt'; that the Society had no debts, 'and it has long since met all its engagements in respect of prizes and medals'; and that 'The Council have determined to continue the South Kensington gardens on their former footing, and to make them so attractive to the residents in their neighbourhood and of London generally as the means and nature of the society will permit.' The gardening press erupted. 'Is our Council in earnest, or is it a joke?' asked Robert Pince Glendinning (son of the Glendinning who had designed the Chiswick arboretum) in the pages of the *Gardeners' Chronicle*, which moved to the attack in a leader:

> The horticultural expenses have been reduced to a minimum. Such men as BERKELEY, DYER, HEMSLEY, and others have been with scant ceremony dismissed from their offices, on account of insufficient funds; even the salary of the librarian has been cut off. The work at Chiswick has been reduced to a point lower than which it can hardly go. We have acquiesced in all this because we were told it was essential; we assented to it because we saw the Council bravely struggling to pay its debts ... But no: will it be believed that the 'gardens are to be continued on their former footing'? Bands and promenades, and all the worn-out machinery that have proved the downfall of the Society, are to be restored.

(Dyer, who had been Professor of Botany and Librarian, quickly pointed out that he had left voluntarily, while adding his reflection 'that a great society in its last stage of decay should consume itself in the wearisome attempt to maintain a stately but uninteresting garden as the summer lounge of a fashionable quarter, and should be

Henry Austin Bruce (1815–1895), 1st Baron Aberdare. President 1875–8s. Formerly Home Secretary and Lord President of Council; later chairman of the National African Company, which administered the Niger Territory. Chaired commission on noxious vapours, 1876; mocked by the gardening press for his attempts to grow conifers in smoky London.

complacently satisfied with the imperfect achievement of its undignified task, is most deplorable.')[59] George Fergusson Wilson was by now reduced to suggesting that it was time to wind up the RHS, and form a new society.[60]

The question of debts was loudly raised at the AGM that year by Shirley Hibberd, who pointed out the unethical diversion of the money intended for provincial exhibitions into paying off debentures, 'which should have been paid out of the surplus profits of the Society'. The new Treasurer Webb acknowledged the impropriety, but pointed out it had been committed before his time. No positive result emerged from the meeting: the *Chronicle* remarked that it 'passed off in the quietest and tamest of manners, reflecting, perhaps, the paralysis which seems to have temporarily affected the Council.'[61]

Exodus from Kensington

On 6 March 1879, the Royal Commissioners gave notice that their agreement with the Society was terminated, and that they would exercise their power of re-entry. Council replied that their obligations to the debenture holders prevented them from surrendering any part of the garden unless under legal process, and the result was a formal writ of ejectment. The Society engaged counsel to appear in court on their behalf, even though it was noted that the debenture holders could accept no financial responsibility for the court case. The lawyers thought that the Commissioners' right of re-entry was doubtful, and in October the President confidently asserted that the Commissioners didn't really want the garden, so the RHS would probably still occupy it for several years. In 1881 judgment was given in favour of the Society and the debenture holders. The Commissioners took the case to the Court of Appeal, and in March 1882 got the verdict overturned, on the grounds that the relationship between them and the Society was not one of equal partners, but of landlord and tenant. The rights of the debenture holders were now extinguished; Council issued a proclamation that they would be granted the privileges of four-guinea Fellows for the year 1883, but after that they had no further standing with the Society.[62] And this was the situation in 1885, when Lord Aberdare resigned from the Presidency.

The new President was Sir Trevor Lawrence. He was the son of Louisa Lawrence, who had been one of the major competitors at the Society's shows in the 1840s. He entered his new post determined to cut the Society's ties with Kensington; now that the lease had been officially

terminated, and the rights of the debenture holders extinguished, the only obstacles to the move were the immediate lack of alternative premises, and a still shaky financial structure.

Sir Trevor conferred with the government about finding another site; when this failed, he sought the help of the Prince of Wales; meanwhile he set up a subcommittee on improving the Society's public image. All through the spring of 1886 multiple sites, from Primrose Hill to the Thames Embankment, were examined for suitability, without obvious results. Council even contemplated trying to take over the Chelsea Physic Garden. In February 1887, Council addressed a petition to the Queen, asking to be allowed to remain in Kensington. Sir Lyon Playfair, now the doyen of the Royal Commissioners, offered tenancy of a reduced portion of the garden, but insufficient space for the Society's perceived needs. By November Council had effectively broken off communication with the Commissioners.

The Society's finances remained unstable. A large Colonial and India Exhibition had been planned by the Commissioners for 1886, the fourth in its series, and the Society undertook responsibility for the care of all the plants exhibited: another responsibility for Barron. The Commissioners, however, refused to allow Fellows of the Society to have transferable tickets to the Exhibition; Council met complaints of breach of faith by professing helplessness, but there were over 100 resignations. The Society dropped any pretence of good relations, censuring Barron when he missed a meeting of the Chiswick board in order to attend an Exhibition meeting, and instructing him that henceforth he was not to work for other organisations. The Liverpool Show, the last of the provincial shows (1887), left a deficit of £2,100, so the Society had to call on the show's guarantors for the full amount, reneged once again on issuing prizes until that amount had been collected, and arranged a £1,000 overdraft. (Membership now stood at a low of 733.) Another committee was appointed to examine ways of reducing expenditure at Chiswick, including plant sales; staff reductions were mooted, but when Barron pointed out that these would mean abandoning agreed trials, they were shelved.

As the Annual General Meeting for 1888 approached, D.T. Fish proposed that the Society abandon gardens altogether: 'the Royal Agricultural Society of England has virtually revolutionised our national agriculture without either hiring or owning an acre of land, either for experiment or illustration.'[63] At that meeting, Sir Trevor proposed that the Society finally abandon

Sir John James Trevor Lawrence (1831-1913), President 1885-1913. Son of Louisa Lawrence, and father of Sir William. Doctor in the Indian Medical Service; after returning to England, became an MP. Lived at Burford Lodge, Surrey, where he built up a great collection of orchids; hired various botanical artists to paint them.

the garden at Kensington, and fall back on Chiswick, using rented accommodation in central London for offices and shows. Three Council members—Trevor Clarke, Major Mason, Haughton—had already offered their resignations rather than countenance the abandonment of Kensington. Lawrence had the names of Daniel Morris and William Wilks to offer in their place, but, no doubt remembering the enforced resignations of the 1870s, used a good publicity gimmick to signal the parting of the ways: Council offered its resignation *en masse*, with the immediate offer that most of the members were willing to form a new Council. Said Wilks: 'a certain amount of blame had been passed upon the Council for the action they had taken in resigning in a body, and then, as it were, with the same hand proposing the re-election of the greater number of themselves. [Council] had, in fact, utterly declined to act like the proverbial rats, deserting a sinking ship.' Wilks, and the nurseryman Harry Veitch, proposed that the resignation be refused, and the meeting endorsed the proposal unanimously.[64] The *Gardeners' Chronicle* had already remarked how placid the Society's meetings had become, by comparison with the fireworks a decade before.

Lawrence now had the Council he wanted: Wilks, Morris, George Fergusson Wilson, William Paul, Thiselton-Dyer, Edmund Loder, Alfred Smee, Robert Hogg, and Henry Schröder. These were the men who would build a new future, 'no longer trammelled by a connection with South Kensington'. All the Kensington staff except for Barron and J. Douglas Dick, the chief clerk, were given notice that their jobs would end on 25 March 1888—less than a month from the time of notice. On 25 March, the Society moved its offices from Kensington to a building at 111 Victoria Street. Two days later the first fortnightly meeting was held in the London Scottish Royal Volunteers' Drill Hall in Buckingham Gate. The Great Spring Show, which had not been held for years, was held in the grounds of the Inner Temple that May. The garden, already bordered on the south by the new Natural History Museum, was razed over the next few years under Sir Lyon Playfair's programme of redevelopment, and the Imperial Institute (later Imperial College) built on the site.

The building at 111 Victoria Street, where the Society's offices were located from 1888 to 1904. Today, after postwar redevelopment, this site is occupied by the Abbey National Bank.

How to celebrate the centenary

At the beginning of the year, the Society had had a deficit of £1,152; by its end, it was £200 in credit. There was still a shaky ride to come over finances. In 1890, the *Journal of Horticulture* criticised the presentation of the Society's accounts, accusing Morris, the Treasurer, of making Drill Hall expenses appear as Chiswick Garden expenses, the implication being that a covert attempt was being made to prepare for the disposal of the garden by making it appear falsely expensive. Since Robert Hogg, who had so often got into conflict with Council by defending Chiswick, was the editor at the time, the attack was probably motivated by an ingrained defensiveness over his beloved garden.[65]

The early 1890s saw a complete turnover in the Society's business staff. At the end of 1890 Philip Crowley, a wealthy brewer, succeeded Daniel Morris as Treasurer. J.D. Dick, the chief clerk, did not last long; in January 1890 it was found that he had absconded with £349, and the deficiency was made up privately to keep the fact from becoming public. He was replaced in the role of Assistant Secretary by John Weathers. In January 1892, the Chiswick account book was destroyed in a fire; it was concluded that the fire was accidental, but nevertheless John Barry, the long-serving clerk, was dismissed. The Society was taking no chances over its probity. In April of that year, the Society could report for the first time in decades that it had no liabilities. A major change in expenditure was about to take place, however. In May of that year William Wilks offered his resignation as Secretary, and Council, desperate to keep his services, decided to pay him a salary of £250 to continue in that role. For the first time, one of the Society's three major offices had become a paid position. In the same year, the Society for the first time employed a firm of accountants (Harper Brothers) as its auditors, instead of appointing volunteers, at an initial fee of £21 per annum.

Further small increments developed into a major change of orientation. In 1894, advertising was brought under Council's direct control, with the Assistant Secretary paid 7½ per cent commission on advertising revenues. In 1896, the Society acquired a registered telegraphic address (Hortensia, London—later Hortensia Sowest); Council members were issued with badges for the first time. As the 1860 Charter had been so heavily weighted towards the establishment of the Kensington garden, the revision of the Charter and Bye-laws became a priority, and the Society's third Charter was granted in November 1899.[66] These were the years of the first codification of rules for judging flower shows; of a series of small but influential conferences held for the most part at Chiswick; and of the institution of the Society's first award to people rather than to plants or exhibits—the Victoria Medal of Honour. (This last brought about the dismissal of John Weathers as

Assistant Secretary, for having issued the wrong list of names in the press release.)

In April 1895, Council instigated a Committee of Inquiry into the management of Chiswick; Archibald Barron complained about being interrogated, and was assured by Council that there was nothing personal; but the report criticised Barron's management, and recommended that he be made to retire, so that a new scheme of management could be introduced. Barron reluctantly agreed to retire as of the end of December, but the news of his compulsory departure did not take long to transpire to the press, which cried out in horror, demanded the names of the Committee that had dismissed him, and called for a public subscription on his behalf. Council made Barron a Life Fellow, and gave him an £80 pension, but not before the storm had broken; the public subscription raised £500 for him. Barron's successor, S.T. Wright, was the last superintendent of Chiswick.[67]

For Chiswick was suffering from air pollution. The once quasi-rural surroundings of the garden had been built up over the previous half-century: the creation of the Bedford Park Garden Suburb on the site of Lindley's garden, and the extension of the District Railway, had prompted much adjacent development. The familiar cloud of London smoke now hung over Chiswick, and the plants suffered. In 1900, the annual report announced that 'The subject of the approaching Centenary of the Society in March 1904, is naturally attracting considerable attention. After consideration of various excellent projects ... the Council have decided to recommend the acquisition of a new Garden ... as being, under all the circumstances, the best and most practical method of celebrating the Centenary.' In April 1901 a printed scheme for the development of new gardens was issued. But not all thought that a new garden was the highest priority: the Society had no premises of its own in central London, and was holding its flower shows in rented accommodation. The *Gardeners' Chronicle* protested that the garden scheme had not been properly put to the members: 'How can the Fellows acquiesce in anything which is unknown to them?'[68] The Prince of Wales, opening the Temple Show in 1890, had referred to the need for an exhibition hall, and a group of influential Council members, chief among them Baron Henry Schröder, offered substantial contributions toward its cost. In 1902, when Schröder seemed to be manipulating the Society into acquiring a site on Vincent Square, two Council members resigned in protest; then the news came that Fergusson Wilson, the firebrand of the 1870s, had died, and the immediate question in Council's mind was, Was his garden at Wisley for sale?

The RHS Council Badge, instituted in 1896, and incorporating the device of an oak tree. It was not until 1928 that it was eventually decided that the Society's arms should represent an apple tree; but the Council Badge has continued unchanged.

King Edward VII opening the Society's New Hall (now the Lindley Hall) on 22 July 1904.

Eventually it was, and on 4 August 1903, Council received a proposal from Sir Thomas Hanbury: he would purchase Wilson's estate and present it to the RHS as an experimental garden. Council embraced the idea with enthusiasm: now the Society could celebrate its centenary with both an exhibition hall and a garden. S.T. Wright supervised the move to Wisley in the autumn of 1903; in August 1904, the garden site at Chiswick was sold, for a sum of £12,500.[69]

Schröder, meanwhile, had personally taken out the lease on the Vincent Square site to ensure that the opportunity wouldn't be lost. The lease was transferred to the Society in July 1902; work began in May 1903; the Hall was opened by Edward VII on 22 July 1904, and the first show took place four days later. (The Society's other proposal for celebrating the centenary—a grand dinner presided over by Joseph Chamberlain—came to nothing.)

Nearly seventy years were to pass before another serious financial crisis; eighty years, before any major reorganisation; ninety, before there was another stormy AGM. The 20th century would see the Society's activities disrupted by two world wars, but it had weathered its internal storms, and was ready to pursue a course of calm and measured achievement.

Sir Trevor Lawrence, Bart., K.C.V.O., and a Knight of Grace of the Order of St. John of Jerusalem succeeeded Lord Aberdare as President of the Royal Horticultural Society in 1885. The Society was at the time passing through a period of great financial difficulty At the new President's instance the Council devoted the first two or three years of his tenure of office to a thorough investigation of the Society's position and in forming a well-reasoned judgment on the necessary steps to be taken to improve it. After anxious and careful examination the Council convinced themselves that nothing could save the Society but entire abandonment of the pleasure garden policy which he had inherited from his immediate predecessors and a whole-hearted return to the original intention

3 *The Twentieth Century*

I N 1906, Council instituted the Lawrence Medal to celebrate Sir Trevor Lawrence's 21 years as President, in which he had overseen the 'almost phenomenal prosperity of our Society'. The medal was to be awarded 'for exhibits of a specially meritorious character', later clarified as the year's best exhibit at any of the Society's shows. The design brief was taken through the ranks of the most esteemed sculptors of the period, starting with Rodin, moving through George Frampton and Alfred Gilbert, before coming to rest with Bertram MacKennal, whose design was finally struck in 1909.[1]

The early years of the 20th century saw the establishment of Wisley as a major centre of horticultural experiment, with trials of different genera taking place each year, research programmes into pests and diseases, conferences under the Society's aegis and contributions to others. The RHS was able to claim exemption from various taxes as a scientific institution. The property at Wisley grew steadily as adjoining parcels of land came on the market and were acquired; a massive rock garden was created, which required its own skilled foreman; a new Laboratory was built, and enlarged a decade later. The first Director of the Laboratory, in 1907, was a young man named Frederick Chittenden, who thus began a forty-years' career with the Society. Two years later the even younger Arthur Simmonds became Assistant Demonstrator, beginning a career of more than fifty years.

All the old services run from Chiswick were reinstated at Wisley; in 1905, the distribution of surplus reached the record level of 50,000 plants. The old educational programmes at Chiswick were redeveloped into a School of Horticulture under Chittenden's direction, and the Society's General Examination was supplemented by a National Diploma in Horticulture. In 1913 a committee was convened to find ways of augmenting the scientific research programme: the manage-ment structure was re-organised, new posts created for entomologist, mycologist, chemist, and trials officer, and Frederick Keeble, Professor of Botany at Reading University, was appointed Director of the Garden.

In 1909 Maxwell T. Masters died, and the Society instituted the Masters Memorial Lectures in his honour, to help explain horticultural science to the public. Masters was also the last of the original Lindley Library Trustees, and in 1910 an amendment to the Trust Deed made the Society's Council the sole Trustee. The *Journal* became a regular twice-yearly publication instead of an occasional series of conference proceedings; pamphlets and one-off works like an edition of David Douglas' journals appeared under the Society's imprint. Daffodils and orchids became the subjects of the Society's first attempts at plant name registration, and the first checklists of varietal names appeared.

The Society's shows in its new Hall on Vincent Square became fortnightly fixtures; by the time Sir Trevor retired in 1913, there was much talk of extending them from single- to two-day events. The Great Spring Show continued at the Temple Gardens in May, followed by a Summer Show in the grounds of either Holland House or the Chelsea Hospital. In addition to its own shows, the Society contributed to the organisation of the Franco-British Exhibition of 1908, and the Royal International Horticultural Exhibition of 1912, cancelling its own Temple Show to make way for the latter. That exhibition was held at the Chelsea Hospital, and the following year the Great Spring Show was moved there, where it has been held ever since.

Increasingly, other organisations were coming to rely on the RHS, to assume its central standing, to call on it for assistance. In 1909 the Royal Botanic Society made an abortive attempt to offer its garden in Regent's Park to its old rival. No more provincial shows were being held, but deputations of judges were being sent on a regular basis to the larger shows around the country, from Cornwall to Glasgow; increasing numbers of local societies were affiliating. Specialist plant societies were encouraged to hold their shows in the Vincent Square Hall, or to stage their competitions as part of the Society's regular shows. The first joint committees were instituted with other floral societies for the judging of particular categories of plants. The RHS took over the administration of the Williams Memorial Trust in 1907, its Medal becoming one of the Society's; the Veitch Memorial Trust was increasingly relying on the RHS in making its awards, eventually to follow the Williams example in 1922.

With floral committees increasing, and administrative committees for Library and Publications instituted, the Society was beginning to establish a stable bureaucratic structure. It was also beginning to get involved with central government, which, as the age of Chamberlain modulated into that of Asquith, was steadily augmenting the range of public activities it attempted to influence. The Board of Agriculture started to seek co-operation over fruit trials from 1906; a government grant for research work was obtained in 1910; the Chamber of Horticulture was formed in 1912, and a Parliamentary Committee on Horticulture proposed.[2] How the Society would respond to such ventures became a determining question for the 20th century.

In January 1913, Sir Trevor announced his wish to retire. He proposed as his successor Field-Marshal Lord Grenfell, who at first declined; but when his second choice, the Duke of Bedford, also refused, Grenfell relented. There was one problem: he was not a member of Council, and the President had to be chosen from among existing Council members. George Bunyard, the Maidstone fruit nurseryman, was persuaded to resign so that Grenfell could take over his seat a fortnight later; and behold, two weeks more and he was elected President. Sir Trevor had begun his presidency with an ingenious resignation ploy, and ended it the same way. He died before the year was out.[3]

The First World War

The declaration of war against Germany in August 1914 was greeted with rapturous enthusiasm by the best part of a generation, and the staff at Wisley were not exceptions. By the beginning of September the majority of staff who were fit for duty were eager to enlist. The RHS applied for a certificate to retain certain staff, but bowed to the wishes of the majority, and offered to add to their (not lavish) army pay in order to make it equal half their normal wages; the staff who were too old or unfit to volunteer immediately drafted a letter to Council, contributing money from their own salaries to help make up those of their colleagues. Altogether, 63 Wisley staff enlisted. But as the War was prolonged, and conscription introduced, the Society found itself desperately begging for exemptions in order to keep sufficient staff to run the garden. By February 1917, Wisley was reduced to hiring women gardeners for the first time, if only for nine months. During the course of 1919 staff gradually returned to Wisley—or not, as some moved into other positions; once again, other staff voluntarily offered contributions to their war allowances. Twenty Wisley staff had been killed in the War, their names recorded on a memorial in the Laboratory foyer.[4]

As propaganda forces both private and public orchestrated a hate campaign against Germany, the RHS came under pressure to abjure all things German. One of its Council members, Mark Lockwood (later Lord Lambourne), had been mocked six years earlier when he raised an alarm about German spies operating in Epping Forest, who had turned out to be tourists;[5] but in 1914 no one was laughing. The demands, whether from the government, the public, or even Council

Field Marshal Francis Wallace Grenfell (1841-1925), 1st Baron Grenfell, President 1913-19. After a long career of military service in India and Egypt, became Governor of Malta in 1898, and Commander-in-Chief for Ireland, 1904-8.

Punch's view of the Society's future president, Lord Lambourne, in 1908 shadowing German tourists on the assumption they were spies.

MARK LOCKWOOD STALKS THE ALIEN IN EPPING FOREST.

members, augmented from ceasing to trade with the enemy, to expelling enemy aliens from membership, to renaming plants with German names. Council responded by pointing out that nurserymen with suspicious names like Reuthe and Engelmann were in fact naturalised British subjects, and when after the War other learned societies launched a proposal to clear the defeated enemy from their membership lists, by remarking that enemy Fellows ceased to be Fellows as soon as they could no longer send their annual fee payments to England.[6] The Society itself both lost and gained. It lost a Library Committee member when J.R. Loewe, who had been a partner in Wheldon and Wesley, the antiquarian booksellers, for 25 years, was expelled from the country (later to become managing director of Friedländer & Sohn in Berlin). On the other hand, an interned alien, the Danish nurseryman Walter Ingwersen, was paroled into the Society's custody in 1917 in order to look after the rock garden; released from internment in 1919, he joined the staff of Notcutt's and later opened his own nursery at East Grinstead, creating the 20th century's greatest rock garden dynasty.[7]

The Society began the War with wishes for success to the Société National d'Horticulture de

The early days of fundraising. Campaigning for war loans at the 1915 Chelsea Flower Show.

France; by November 1914 it was involved with a relief fund for Belgian horticulturists, soon expanded to include their French and Serbian counterparts; by February 1915, the duration of the War still unanticipated, it had set up a subcommittee on the restoration of horticulture in France and Belgium. For most of the War, the Society maintained two aid programmes, one practical and one financial. Flowers and plants

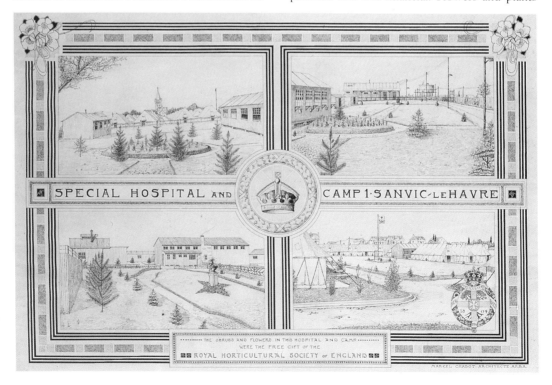

Views in the grounds of the special hospital, Camp 1, Sanvic-Le Havre, drawn by the architect Marcel Chabot in 1916, and sent to the Society to acknowledge its gift of plants and seeds.

were sent to field hospitals (this gradually becoming one of the main jobs at Wisley) and army camps, though as RHS representatives were not allowed to visit the camps, the latter provision was haphazard. Financial aid ranged from fundraising at Chelsea Shows (using, in those early days of the discipline, a boy with a Shetland pony), through Red Cross sales and gala events, to the organisation of a horticultural War Relief Fund, which bickered on through various shifts of responsibility before it became solely an RHS Committee, and which gathered a large sum of donations for replanting devastated towns, as well as paying Wisley's costs for training Serbian student gardeners. Over fifty French mayors later gave thanks to the relief fund for help in civic replanting, and Harry Veitch, the Society's Treasurer, was made a Chevalier d'Honneur for his work on behalf of French horticulturists.[8]

The most curious of the Society's aid programmes was directed at prisoners of war. At the beginning of the war, the German government had set up a civilian internment camp on the Ruhleben racecourse grounds for British

Ruhleben Horticultural Society Nursery. Interior of Pit with Staff.
MARCH 1918

nationals who had been unable to leave Berlin; and in 1916 the internees decided to set up their own horticultural society, in part to improve the quality of their food rations. The RHS arranged for gifts of seeds to be sent to them, along with rules for flower shows, and the Ruhleben Horticultural Society became a thriving organisation, with nearly a thousand members (about 20 per cent of the inmates). They sold their produce to the camp canteen, held competitions for best

barrack garden, and even sent dahlias and chrysanthemums back to England.[9]

As early as 1907, as invasion scares were mooted in the press and the tenor of life became more militaristic, the War Office sought the Society's acquiescence over the use of the Hall if mobilisation took place. Within a few weeks of the declaration of war, the War Office requisitioned the Hall as a bivouac for soldiers on their way to the front. By October, the initial rush had subsided, the Society was allowed to restore its meetings, and it began negotiating for compensation. But in the darker days of 1916 it was once again commandeered, despite frantic attempts to avert 'this menace to the Society' (in Lord Grenfell's phrase), and the final result was its use for the billeting of the Australian army. The Hall was not finally returned to the Society's use until October 1919, during which time the Drill Hall had once again hosted its shows. The War Office at first asserted its right to take buildings without compensation in national emergencies, but in the spring of 1920 the House of Lords ruled that it was not above the law, and the Society eventually got over £9,000 in reparations.[10] After 1916 the Chelsea Show was abandoned for the duration of the War, after increasing press criticism for wasteful expenditure at a time of crisis.

The RHS began the war in such good financial condition that it was able to invest £10,000 in war loan stock. But the Board of Agriculture withdrew its annual grant to Wisley in 1915, Wisley was becoming increasingly difficult to maintain with reduced and untrained staff, and by the summer of 1916 membership figures were in significant decline. In August of that year a Finance Committee was set up for the first time since the Kensington days. In September 1917 W.A. Bilney warned that the Society was beginning to eat into its capital.[11] By that time the Society's work had been in great part redirected to encouraging domestic food production, with lecture programmes, the creation of model allotments, demonstrations of preserve-making and fruit-bottling, and a committee to lobby the government to release sugar supplies to assist families with jam-making.

A photograph from the civilian internment camp at Ruhleben, outside Berlin, showing the nursery that had been established with the seeds sent by the RHS.

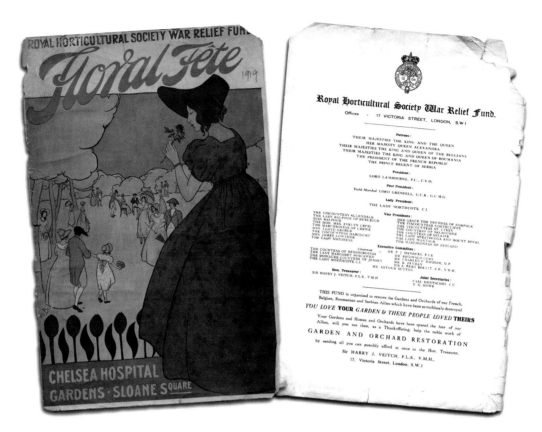

The brochure for a fundraising fête at the Chelsea Hospital, in aid of the War Relief Fund.

Early in 1917 Sir Arthur Lee, the Director of Food Production, requisitioned Keeble's services, and thereafter his time was progressively taken from the Society.

Despite its increasing concentration on food production, the Society tried to ensure that normal horticultural life continued as far as possible. The government started cancelling nursery orders in the summer of 1915, and a press controversy broke out over the propriety of local authorities spending money on flowers for municipal parks, some saying that all cultivation other than food production was wasted, others insisting on the need to keep life normal and spirits up as far as possible. The RHS issued a press statement, and lobbied the government, on the importance of keeping the nursery trade solvent. As the war dragged on, the pressure to abandon ornamental horticulture increased. The Society lobbied the Board of Agriculture, whose spokesman, R.E. Prothero (later Lord Ernle), saw no need for nurserymen to sacrifice their stocks. But the connection with the government reduced the Society's freedom of action, and on 16 November 1917, Sir Arthur Lee issued a press statement under the Society's auspices calling on gardeners to devote all their effort to food production. C.G.A. Nix, the Society's Treasurer, resigned in protest at the RHS letting itself be associated with a call to

abandon ornamental horticulture. (He resumed his post a year later, Sir Harry Veitch having held the financial reins in the meantime.) The media vied to promote Lee's demand; the *Daily Mirror* announced a potato competition, with £500 for the five best potatoes exhibited by a private grower (the Society declined to be associated once it became apparent that its rules of judging would be disregarded), and proclaimed in a leader, 'Every person in the country who has a patch of garden should use it to cultivate potatoes'.[12] The RHS tried to gain exemption from fuel restrictions for important plant collections, but with little success. The most tragic consequence was the death, in the winter of 1917-18, of most of the contents of Chatsworth's Great Stove; in 1920, this pioneering glasshouse was demolished, to spare the expense of restocking it.[13]

By the war's end, the RHS had been turned into a campaigning organisation, one which was increasingly seen to play an important role even in the commercial sector. It had, after all, supported the nursery trade when public spokesmen wanted it sidelined; it had supported the trade's attempt to secure exemption from service for skilled orchid growers and glasshouse workers; and it had tried to ensure that Japanese bulbs for the florists' industry were not subject to import restrictions. The fact that these efforts seldom succeeded was less important than its visibility as a lobbyist.[14] During the dark days of 1916, the question of the post-war economy was under earnest discussion, and the RHS took part in a Parliamentary committee on the imposition of protective tariffs on imports. One might be amused at the way the Society, which had begun its career boasting that it would show how private enterprise in Britain could accomplish what was done in other countries by the state, had slid into recommending increased government control of economic life; but it was following a wider cultural trend, as the free enterprise policies of the Gladstone years gave way to an increasing acceptance of protectionism—a trend associated in great part with the Society's own Vice-President Joseph Chamberlain. In the autumn of 1917, the majority of Council voted that after the war, all the Society's 'energies should be devoted to the reorganisation and development of British Horticulture and our Horticultural Trade'.[15]

Inter-war initiatives

On 25 March 1919, Lord Grenfell announced his resignation. Having a Field-Marshal as President had been very advantageous to the Society in wartime, even if it meant he was sometimes absent at the front, but his chosen successor, Mark Lockwood (now Lord Lambourne), was greeted with cheers by Council. A Grenfell Medal was struck in the outgoing President's honour, which after a few years of general use was restricted to exhibits (including paintings) of scientific interest. As on the previous occasion when a new President was chosen, a problem with Council elections resulted. Robert Wallace was nominated to replace the retiring Herbert Sutton as a representative of the nursery trade, but George Loder had previously been nominated for the next vacancy; the matter was resolved, over some protests, by an *ad hoc* resolution that Council members (other than President and Treasurer) should not allow themselves to be re-nominated after five years of office until at least a year had passed; Lord Balfour of Burleigh and Sir George Holford duly resigned, both Wallace and Loder were elected. Lord Lambourne served as President until 1929, when the first commoner in generations, George W.E. Loder, the creator of a celebrated garden at Wakehurst Place, became President; he was later raised to the peerage as Lord Wakehurst, but not until after he had resigned the Presidency in favour of the second Baron Aberconway, who held office from 1931 until 1953.

Lord Grenfell's departure was not the only administrative change in 1919. William Wilks

resigned after 33 years as Secretary, giving as his reason the number of planned new initiatives that required a younger and more vigorous man to introduce. The new Secretary was William Rickatson Dykes, a former schoolmaster who had become the greatest authority of his generation on irises (and who was to conduct the negotiations for founding the British Iris Society on RHS letterhead). Dykes proved an active and enthusiastic Secretary, but his career was cut short by an automobile accident in 1925. (His wife was hired as a botanical artist, as a form of widow's pension.) Dykes was succeeded by Colonel F.R. Durham, an army engineer who had been Director of Works for the War Graves Commission, and who held the post of Secretary for 21 years.

The administration of the Wisley garden also changed. Keeble had spent the latter part of the war working for the Ministry of Agriculture, and when the war ended was uncertain where his future lay. In 1919 Frederick Chittenden was appointed Assistant Director *pro tem.*, and when Keeble soon after finally resigned to take up an appointment as Professor of Botany at Oxford, Chittenden succeeded him, and soon had an excellent scientific team working under him.[16] Among his tasks was the administration of the School of Horticulture, and the Society hoped that it would prove possible to establish a Professorship for him at Wisley. Arthur Simmonds was appointed Assistant Director under Chittenden, but in a few years was moved to London to serve nearly thirty years as Assistant Secretary. Samuel T. Wright, the first Superintendent of Wisley, died in 1922, having been with the Society for 26 years; no new head gardener was chosen in his place, to the dismay both of garden staff who had hoped to be in the running, and of some Council members.[17] In 1930, a new post of Technical Adviser and Keeper of the Library was created for Chittenden; he was transferred to Vincent Square, and soon relieved of other duties in order to concentrate on the compilation of the *Dictionary of Gardening*.

Wisley began to expand, with the purchase of adjoining lands from Lady Lovelace, and eventually, in 1937, with the acquisition of Battleston Hill, which shortly before the outbreak of war was earmarked as the permanent home of the rhododendron trials. The Laboratory building had been expanded during the First World War; a new range of glasshouses was built; and the Society acquired ever more of the buildings in Wisley Village to serve as staff accommodation.

The national reputation of the Society now stood so high that it began to receive offers of other gardens, accompanied by expressions of

Amelius Richard Mark Lockwood (1847-1928), 1st Baron Lambourne, President 1919-28. MP for Epping Forest. For many years Chairman of the House of Commons Kitchen Committee; very popular with his colleagues as a result.

George Walter Erskine Loder (1861-1936), President 1928-31; later 1st Baron Wakehurst. Developed the garden at Wakehurst Place, which he bequeathed to the Royal Botanic Gardens Kew.

Frederick James Chittenden (1873-1950), lecturer in biology at the East Anglia Institute of Agriculture before he joined the RHS as Director of the Wisley Laboratory in 1907. Director of Wisley Garden, 1919-31; editor of the RHS Journal, 1908-39; editor of the RHS Dictionary of Gardening.

public pressure. The Duke of Bedford tried to persuade the RHS to take over his Woburn Experimental Fruit Farm in 1918, without success.[18] More tempting, as a central London exhibition site, was the garden of the Royal Botanic Society in Regent's Park, but this also was refused, and was redeveloped as Queen Mary's Rose Garden. And not only gardens: in 1919 the North of England Horticultural Society proposed the creation of a northern branch of the RHS.[19]

The stable prices of the prewar world had vanished. Inflation settled in permanently: wages, paper and printing prices, building costs, transport costs, all moved steadily upwards, and led to reviews of expenditure every few years. New legal protections for staff were imposed; unemployment insurance, state pensions required new arrangements; legislation on minimum wages for agricultural workers led to demands for similar rights in horticulture, and the RHS was urged to arbitrate. Difficulties in preparing the accounts in time for the Annual General Meeting led to a series of gradual shifts in the Society's financial year, a process which was to carry on to the end of the century. Technology was changing also: from 1921 it became customary for minutes to be typed,[20] and the provision of telephones and electric cables became part of life. The Society's membership had climbed from 5000 at the turn of the century to over 25,000, and the burden of correspondence, much of it advisory, increased steadily. Another new fact of life was the radio: Chittenden was busy from 1924 in providing texts for gardening broadcasts. The first glimmerings of the concept of branding also made themselves felt: in 1929 the Society obtained an official Grant of Arms ('vert within a bordure, an apple tree eradicated or fructed gules'), thus putting an end to generations of inconsistent logos and badges.

The Finance Committee created in 1916 had been succeeded the following year, on Sir Albert Rollitt's proposal, by a Finance and General Purposes Committee with the duty of 'assisting the Treasurer and advising the Council on financial subjects and on any other matters which the Council may from time to time submit for their opinion'. In 1919 its remit was expanded, and it no longer had to have matters referred to it by Council. In 1926 a subcommittee specified its functions as to 'accept estimates ... and to authorise the payment of all accounts for normal and approved expenditure', to 'sanction, on the Society's Surveyor's report, repairs involving an expenditure not exceeding £100 on any one building', to 'deal with the letting of the Hall', and to 'consider references from the Secretary on the organisation of the Society's office'. The

following year, on the suggestion of Sir William Lawrence, F&GP was dissolved, and Council began meeting weekly. After three months of this, F&GP was reconstituted, with the Treasurer as its official Chairman.[21]

F&GP was not the only administrative committee to begin the development of an internal bureaucracy: a Publications Committee had also been set up in 1917 as a result of the proliferation of pamphlets the Society was producing. During the interwar years it supervised four remarkable projects: the takeover of *Curtis's Botanical Magazine* to prevent it from falling into American hands; the resumption and successful completion of a prewar project, the revision of Pritzel's *Icones* (published as the *Index Londinensis*); the collaboration with the British Colour Council on a Colour Chart for purposes of plant description; and the inception of the immense four-volume *Dictionary of Gardening*. These were also the years of an International Horticultural Congress (1930), a series of successful conferences on subjects ranging from soft fruit to ornamental trees, and the beginnings of a programme of publishing monographs on important genera.

The Chelsea Flower Show was reinstated in 1919, despite attempts to commandeer the Hospital grounds for other purposes, and held consistently until the next war broke out. An abortive attempt at reviving the provincial shows of fifty years before took place, with a show at Cardiff in 1920, but it made a significant loss, and there would be no further provincial shows until after the mid-century. The summer show at Holland House was also reinstated in the early 1920s, but, after Holland House was gutted by fire, it was succeeded by a Great Autumn Show.

By the early 1920s, grumbles could be heard about the adequacy of the Vincent Square Hall for large shows, and the Society obtained the lease of a property on Greycoat Street, behind Vincent Square. (This required a further revision of the Charter, in order to increase the amount of property the Society was allowed to own.) The New Hall (later renamed the Lawrence Hall) was opened in 1928, and became one of the architectural wonders of its age for its introduction into England of parabolic roof arches. (The first show to take place in it was a display of garden sculpture, to accompany an international conference on garden planning, which led to the creation of the Institute of Landscape Architects.) A new floor was added to the now Old Hall (later the Lindley Hall) to accommodate the expanding Library. Despite all this, by the end of the 1930s the RHS was negotiating for the site adjoining its New Hall, in an attempt to increase its office accommodation: that project was shelved on the outbreak of war in 1939, and was never to be achieved.

Specialist societies, devoted to particular kinds of flowers, had begun to appear in the 19th century, but now began to proliferate. The first joint committees, set up with such societies for the purpose of judging plants at shows, had appeared before the First World War; but in the post-war years their numbers increased, and after 1930 had a rationale supplied by the International Commission on Botanical Nomenclature: that in any given country there should be only one organisation making awards to any given category of plant. The RHS was not overly enthusiastic about the proliferation of specialist societies, however, and in 1932 created a Lily Group as a subgroup of its own membership rather than see a separate Lily Society created.

Some of the heady aspirations announced at the end of the First World War had dissipated as normal life returned. The ambitious schemes for spreading allotments throughout the country under the auspices of the Cultivation of Land Order faded away.[22] Trade unionism, agitation over gardeners' wages, and political unrest loomed darkly over life at the beginning of the 1920s, as did economic depression over the beginning of the 1930s. In 1932 Lord Aberconway, little more than a year into his Presidency, wrote to *The Times* to encourage the public not to cut back on expenditure in their gardens:

> Now, the producer of most articles can at any rate stop production to the extent that he is unable to sell his goods, and he can by this means confine his losses to a proportion of his overhead charges. The nurseryman, however, produces his goods for sale many years ahead. His stock thus requires several years' work spent upon it before it is saleable, and that work has to be done without a break—transplanting, weeding, watering, propagation, cannot be abandoned or even severely curtailed without the destruction of the business.

The Society itself was not unaffected by the economic crisis, and in 1929 started a sinking fund on a 40-years' basis. In 1931, the one-guinea membership rate was abolished.[23]

The Society's profile as a campaigning organisation was sustained throughout the interwar period, with representations over trade descriptions on insecticides, the extermination of grey squirrels, and the marketing of pesticides. The Society's hopes for its role in public life were still high, and its aspirations were revealed in a 1932 memorandum on the co-ordination of research stations: 'The R.H.S. of to-day represents the hub of everything appertaining to horticulture ... the existing research station at Wisley should be appointed to act as the Central Horticultural Research & Distributing Station of the U.K.'[24]

The Second World War

Britain's entry into war in September 1939 did not take the Society by surprise. A year before, in the weeks of panicked anticipation before the Munich agreement, the War Office had approached the Society about once again requisitioning the Hall, and leases, staff hirings, and other financial commitments during the ensuing year were all fitted with let-out clauses in the event of hostilities. The lessons of the Great War had been learnt, and the Society swung into action, first to protect itself and then to resume the emergency functions which had been interrupted by peacetime.[25]

Plans for the evacuation of the staff to Wisley were drawn up, but in the event did not need to be used. The Library's rare books were transferred to comparative safety in Aberystwyth, the arrangements having been made the year before; as the War proceeded, more were moved to Wisley, which was already housing the rare books collection from the John Innes Research Institution. Applications were quickly made for the exemption of key staff from military service; staff were trained as air-raid wardens. Once again the Society offered to top up the salaries of any staff who enlisted or were called up; and once again the staff numbers at Wisley dwindled through enlistment, to be replaced by both older and younger men, including War Graves Commission gardeners on secondment.[26]

The Hall was not requisitioned as predicted, but was let to the Territorial Army for training. Three times it incurred enemy damage. A different sort of threat was supplied by the government, which declared that the Society could not be exempted from taxes for the Hall, because the miscellaneous lettings were not a scientific function; it was resolved not to let to anyone other than educational, charitable, or war-oriented groups for the duration of the war.

By the end of December 1938, E.A. Bunyard had produced a report on the organisation of emergency food growing for wartime. A programme of lectures and demonstrations, comparable with that of the previous war, was set in motion. The RHS became a member of the Allotments Co-ordinating Council, and a collaborator in the 'Dig for Victory' campaign; in 1941 it issued what was to become its most successful publication ever, *The Vegetable Garden Displayed*—which was even to be translated into German at

Henry Duncan McLaren, 2nd Baron Aberconway (1879-1953), President 1931-53. Chairman of the John Brown Shipyard in Glasgow, and author of The Basic Industries of Great Britain *(1927). Developed the garden at Bodnant, which he gave to the National Trust in 1949.*

the end of the war, to help with the reconstruction of the German domestic economy.

Apart from the agreed permanent trials and seed tests for the government (including seeds supplied from America under the Lend-Lease plan), most of the Wisley trials effort was shifted to vegetable varieties; the new ground at Battleston Hill was employed for growing potatoes; the distribution of surplus plants to Fellows was abandoned in order to free up staff for cropping. Eventually several acres were devoted to raising plants for two nurseries, Carters and Watkins & Simpson.[27] Training programmes were gradually set up for soldiers, and later for ex-servicemen; courses and demonstrations were carried out for the Royal Air Force, and examinations in horticulture conducted by correspondence with prisoners in POW camps. Of greater significance for the future was the training of women gardeners, begun with donations to the Women's Farm and Garden Association, and developing into more practical instruction with the establishment of the Women's Land Army. When Swanley College was damaged by bombing in 1944, the students were transferred to Wisley. By 1944 the *Gardeners' Chronicle* was calling for Wisley to take women as student gardeners after the War, a decision on which Council procrastinated.[28]

During the First World War, sales of donated items had been held on behalf of the Red Cross; the process was resumed, along with special fund-raising flower shows, although the threat of air raids soon meant that the sales were conducted by postal ballot. (One of these Red Cross sales resulted in the papers of Gertrude Jekyll being acquired for an American library.) Memories of Ruhleben prompted the creation of a committee with the Horticultural Trades Association to organise the sending of seeds to prisoners of war; 33 firms contributed seed, and numerous letters of thanks from prisoners were transcribed into the Council minutes.[29]

Chelsea was cancelled for the duration of the war, as were the Year Books, plant-collecting subsidies, property acquisition negotiations, and progressively the fortnightly shows. But, mindful also of the problems that nurseries had faced in the previous war, the Society tried earnestly to maintain the floral side of its endeavours. The *Journal* was continued, in accordance with the President's comment: 'It is, I think, most important to combat the idea that the Society's main activity is its exhibitions and that the suspension of these ends the major part of its work.' In September 1939 the RHS issued a call for people to continue buying from nurserymen so as to maintain the horticultural industry, and kept its floral competitions going as much as possible.[30] Memories of coal rationing and its deleterious consequences prompted the formation, first, of a joint committee on the preservation of plants of national importance, and then, when fuel rationing was imposed in 1942, of a campaign to get exemptions for significant collections. When the government announced that fuel could no longer be used except for food production,

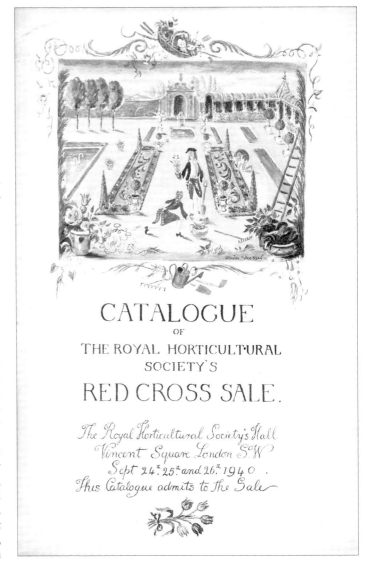

Another war, another cycle of fundraising. Brochure, with a cover design by Oliver Messel, for a Red Cross sale, 24-26 September 1940; in the event the sale was held by post.

CATALOGUE
OF
THE ROYAL HORTICULTURAL
SOCIETY'S
RED CROSS SALE.

*The Royal Horticultural Society's Hall
Vincent Square London S.W
Sept 24ᵗ 25ᵗ and 26ᵗ 1940.
This Catalogue admits to the Sale*

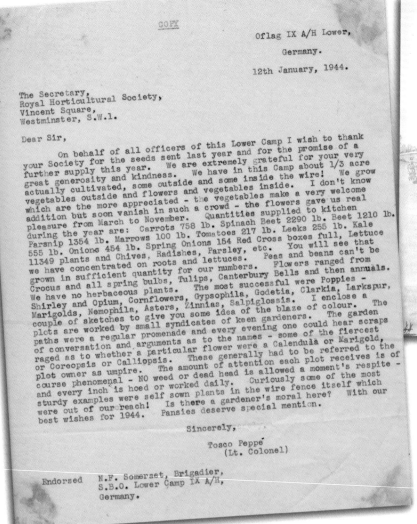

COPY

Oflag IX A/H Lower,

Germany.

12th January, 1944.

The Secretary,
Royal Horticultural Society,
Vincent Square,
Westminster, S.W.1.

Dear Sir,

On behalf of all officers of this Lower Camp I wish to thank your Society for the seeds sent last year and for the promise of a further supply this year. We are extremely grateful for your very great generosity and kindness. We have in this Camp about 1/3 acre actually cultivated, some outside and some inside the wire! We grow vegetables outside and flowers and vegetables inside. I don't know which are the more appreciated - the vegetables make a very welcome addition but soon vanish in such a crowd - the flowers gave us real pleasure from March to November. Quantities supplied to kitchen during the year are: Carrots 758 lb. Spinach Beet 2290 lb. Beet 1210 lb. Parsnip 1354 lb. Marrows 100 lb. Tomatoes 217 lb. Leeks 255 lb. Kale 555 lb. Onions 454 lb. Spring Onions 154 Red Cross boxes full, Lettuce 11349 plants and Chives, Radishes, Parsley, etc. You will see that we have concentrated on roots and lettuces. Peas and beans can't be grown in sufficient quantity for our numbers. Flowers ranged from Crocus and all spring bulbs, Tulips, Canterbury Bells and then annuals. We have no herbaceous plants. The most successful were Poppies - Shirley and Opium, Cornflowers, Gypsophila, Godetia, Clarkia, Larkspur, Marigolds, Nemophila, Asters, Zinnias, Salpiglossis. I enclose a couple of sketches to give you some idea of the blaze of colour. The garden plots are worked by small syndicates of keen gardeners. The paths were a regular promenade and every evening one could hear scraps of conversation and arguments as to the names - some of the fiercest raged as to whether a particular flower were a Calendula or Marigold, or Coreopsis or Calliopsis. These generally had to be referred to the plot owner as umpire. The amount of attention each plot receives is of course phenomenal - NO weed or dead head is allowed a moment's respite - and every inch is hoed or worked daily. Curiously some of the most sturdy examples were self sown plants in the wire fence itself which were out of our reach! Is there a gardener's moral here? With our best wishes for 1944. Pansies deserve special mention.

Sincerely,

Tosco Peppé
(Lt. Colonel)

Endorsed N.F. Somerset, Brigadier,
S.B.O. Lower Camp IX A/H,
Germany.

Seeds for prisoners of war. A letter from a prison camp expressing gratitude for seeds sent, and a watercolour sketch showing how they had been put to use.

though people were still allowed to burn their own wood and rubbish supplies, Lord Aberconway wrote in reply: 'I also feel that when the Government asks people to put fuel into stock, as your Department has repeatedly done, and then prohibits them from using it, they are acting in a manner to which great exception can be taken.' When in December a new order made it an offence to use fuel to heat a greenhouse, Aberconway wrote once again:

Many people, with the aid of rubbish, odd branches of wood and slack from domestic coal which cannot be burnt even in a kitchen range, would manage to keep the frost out of perhaps one little house in which they could store their favourites ... very little would be gained from the national point of view by proceeding with this Order, and it would be greatly resented by tens of thousands of people ... May I put the plea on

somewhat the same footing as would apply if the Government were to make a regulation that all dogs, which could not be proved to be of national importance, were forthwith destroyed? It could be argued that they eat food and take up people's time, but such action would be bitterly resented, as we well know ...

The government relaxed so far as to allow the continued use of non-purchased wood as fuel. The RHS had already set up a Non-edible Plants (Fuel) Committee to advise on exemptions from the rationing. Botanic gardens, first of all, but also municipal parks, cemeteries, and, increasingly, private gardens with significant collections, were assessed by a group of inspectors including the orchid grower Gurney Wilson, John Coutts of Kew, and J. Macqueen Cowan of Edinburgh. The work continued past the end of the War, into the years of post-war austerity, and the Committee was only dissolved in 1949.[31] When petrol for motor mowers was rationed, however, a probably rather weary Council decided that they could not intervene.[32]

Brave new world

With the end of the war, a process of normalisation took place similar to that of thirty years before. The gardeners came home from the front, the land girls left the land, and the School of Horticulture resumed its normal course—with a new hostel, Aberconway House, opened in 1954. The Halls were recovered, fortnightly shows begun again, and the first post-war Chelsea was held in 1947. Municipal parks returned to summer bedding—though troubled now by the lingering problem of vandalism, which prompted some superintendents to query whether ornamental horticulture had a place in modern life.[33] Once again, the great campaign to encourage allotments wound down, to the disappointment of those who had seen in them the channel to a regeneration of national life.[34] Instead, the Royal Society of Arts offered a new vision of the future in the form of the Festival of Britain, a celebration of the centenary of the 1851 Great Exhibition, and the Society integrated the Chelsea Show for 1951 into the event.[35]

But some profound changes had taken place, and were to be consolidated during the immediate post-war years. The great country house had now ceased to be the driving force of horticulture. Rising labour and maintenance costs made the great parterres increasingly difficult to maintain; during the war, the Society had offered a service of helping country house owners to disguise their parterres, so that they would not serve as handy guideposts to enemy aircraft, but many landowners took advantage of the situation to grass theirs over; those that were reinstated after the War were generally replanted in a labour-saving manner. Roy Hay was to publish a book on labour-saving gardening in association with the RHS, significantly titled *Gardening the Modern Way*. The country-house kitchen garden, that traditional training forum for young gardeners, was also disappearing, as the automobile, the heavy goods lorry, the supermarket, and the other forms of modern food provision relegated it to the limbo of inefficient practices. Young gardeners returning from the War, finding no employment at the country houses where they had been trained, increasingly went into the public sector. The students at the Wisley School of Horticulture seldom went into private employment in the post-war years, taking jobs in parks, nurseries, or the Ministry of Agriculture instead.

Back to normal: crowds at the Chelsea Flower Show, 1950, with Prime Minister Clement Attlee and his wife on the left.

For the government's involvement in gardening was growing steadily, as county horticultural stations both carried out experimental work and advised the public. The older experimental stations such as Rothamsted, Long Ashton, and East Malling were supplemented by the Glasshouse Crops Research Institute at Littlehampton, the National Vegetable Research Station at Wellesbourne, and a far-flung range of Ministry stations, of which Kirton, Lea Valley, Stockbridge, Efford, and Rosewarne were of particular importance to horticulture. Add to these the establishment of the Arboricultural Association, the British Weed Control Council, the British Insecticide and Fungicide Council, and it will be apparent that the Society's scientific programmes were successfully rivalled elsewhere.

In the early post-war years this was not yet apparent. With the taxonomist John Gilmour as Director of Wisley, the RHS enlarged its scientific research base, adding to its staff a cytologist (Dr Janaki Ammal, its first female senior staff member) to carry out chromosome counts; it continued to carry out important investigations on plant pests and diseases, and the effects of pesticides. The *Dictionary of Gardening*, the Society's *magnum opus*, was completed and seen through the press in 1951, with a second edition in 1956. The Society also convened another International Horticultural Conference in 1952, and the Third World Orchid Conference in 1960, though the frequency of its former series of horticultural conferences declined. A revised Colour Chart was issued in 1966.

At the International Botanical Congress of 1952, the Society, in the person of its Librarian W.T. Stearn, lobbied for the creation of a Code of Nomenclature for Cultivated Plants, of which Stearn wrote the first draft. Work on horticultural taxonomy and nomenclature augmented steadily. At the end of the 1950s the Society helped to found the International Society for Horticultural Science, one of whose first projects (which the Society grant-aided) was work on the stabilisation of botanical names, and a few years later the International Association for Plant Taxonomy. One significant result of these efforts was the establishment of a network of International Registration Authorities for different categories of cultivated plants, which would compile registers of varietal names (or, to use the new terminology Stearn had introduced, cultivar names) in an attempt to stabilise the names of plants in commerce. The RHS had already been issuing checklists of daffodil and delphinium names, and had offered financial assistance for the compilation of Sander's orchid stud book; during the 1960s it became the International Registrar of

daffodils, orchids, dahlias, delphiniums, lilies, and rhododendrons, with dianthus, conifers and clematis to follow eventually.

In the wake of registering names came the conservation of cultivars. The idea of national collections made a faltering start in the late 1940s as a purely commercial proposal, but in the 1970s the increasing popularity of horticultural revivalism (old roses, auriculas), and the fears that garden centres would have the same corrosive effect on nurseries as supermarkets had had on corner groceries, led to practical proposals for the rescue of endangered cultivars. In 1978 the RHS convened a conference on the subject, which resulted in the formation of the National Council for the Conservation of Plants and Gardens, which launched and successfully popularised a scheme of national collections.

But gradually the programme of scientific work was eroded. The Society had collaborated with the Ministry of Agriculture on the National Fruit Trials since 1922; in 1956 the reference collections of fruit were finally moved to a new site at Brogdale in Kent, where it was generally agreed the growing conditions were preferable to Wisley's; the trial field was turned over to other purposes, and fruit research, which had been one of the most important of the Society's purposes since its inception, wound down until the identification of fruit varieties for Fellows was all that remained. In the early 1950s the impressive scientific team that had been built up was disintegrating: Chittenden and the entomologist Fox Wilson both died in 1950, Gilmour left for the Cambridge Botanic Garden the same year, and two years later Stearn moved to the Natural History Museum. Francis Hanger, who succeeded to the title of Curator in 1950, was a great cultivator, and his Wisley displays at flower shows, domestic and foreign, kept the Society's reputation for horticultural excellence high; but the consequence was that horticulture was granted precedence over research. As early as 1949 Council debated whether the Society should confine its scientific activities to advisory work; the question resurfaced in 1956, in 1964, and in 1966, and each time the bias had shifted further towards the primacy of advisory work.[36]

The Society had emerged from the War with a £3,000 reduction in its general reserve, but during the Treasurerships of Sir David Bowes Lyon (1948-53) and Lewis Palmer (1954-65), a policy of high-interest-yielding investments had brought finances back to a healthy vitality. Lord Aberconway, who had so successfully held the reins of the Society during the War, continued as its President in the post-war years. He died suddenly

Sir David Bowes Lyon (1902-1961), Treasurer 1848-53, then President 1953-61. The younger brother of Queen Elizabeth the Queen Mother. Restored the garden at St Paul's Walden Bury in Hertfordshire.

Arthur Simmonds (1892-1968), Assistant Director of Wisley 1923-25; Assistant Secretary, RHS, 1925-56; Secretary 1956-62. Researcher into the Society's history, and author of A Horticultural Who was Who *(1948).*

in 1953, and the Treasurer, Sir David Bowes Lyon, succeeded him; he too died in harness in 1961, and the 3rd Baron Aberconway was elected to follow in his father's footsteps, a position he held for 23 years. The London administration similarly passed through the hands of a series of dominating personalities. Colonel Durham retired as Secretary in 1946, to be succeeded by another military man, Brigadier C.V. Lycett, whose term of office lasted for ten years. It was then finally the turn of Arthur Simmonds, who, like Lindley, had languished for decades as Assistant and then Deputy Secretary; his term as Secretary lasted from 1956 to 1962, when he retired to work on writing the Society's history. (The analogy with Lindley stuck forcibly in people's minds; when he died in 1968, Lord Aberconway described him as 'the Society's greatest servant this century'.) For his successor, Council once again turned to a military figure, John Hamer (although his horticultural knowledge was derided by his staff, in the same measure as his explosive temper was feared). He was succeeded in 1975 by the easier-going John Cowell, whose horticultural experience was greater, and who had been involved in plant registration.

As the 1940s passed into the '50s and '60s, the programme of flower shows consolidated itself: Chelsea as the flagship, increasing steadily in esteem and attendance to the point where every decade brought changes to layout in order to cope with overcrowding (and, eventually, the problem of access for the disabled); the Great Autumn Show, peripatetic until the late 1960s, when it finally settled irrevocably into the Westminster Halls; and fortnightly shows throughout most of the year. Flower arranging became a regular part of the show season by the early 1950s, as did

The Great Autumn Show, held in the Lawrence Hall in the early 1990s.

exhibits of bedding by the Royal Parks and other local authorities. Display gardens formed an increasing part of the attraction at Chelsea; the Society, always uneasy at making pronouncements about aesthetics and taste, dealt gingerly with proposals for garden design awards and judging. Nonetheless, it exercised an important role in the increasing movement towards the conservation of historic gardens. In 1944, the National Trust, contemplating the purchase of Montacute, asked the RHS for advice on the maintenance of its gardens and, in 1947, the two organisations formed a committee to advise the Trust on purchases and subsequent maintenance of important gardens: Hidcote was the first acquisition under this scheme.

In other respects, the Society found itself in an unfamiliar world. During the interwar years it had adopted civil service pay scales for its salaried staff, and agricultural wage scales for its gardeners; with their attention fixed on other matters, Council kept waking with a start to the realisation that it had failed to keep pace with rising standards, and hastily topping up senior staff's emoluments in order to keep them from straying. Holiday entitlement, pension rights, and health insurance were new and puzzling concepts to adapt to. Militant trade unionism raised its head at Chelsea in the early 1950s, with a new surge every generation. Standards of media presentation were changing, in a process generally seen as one of decline. Council shuddered at the arrival of demotic journalism, whether in the press (the weekly newspaper *Garden News*, described by Arthur Simmonds as 'the underworld of horticulture'), the radio (Sir David Bowes Lyon at first refused to take part in Roy Hay's broadcast series *Home Grown*, saying that it was undignified, but a year later was persuaded by Council to lower himself to the task), or television.[37] Those who adapted successfully to the new media ambience, like Percy Thrower and, after him, Geoff Hamilton, found that the RHS had large reserves of cold shoulder to offer them; and by the 1970s the Society was widely perceived as aristocratic and aloof.

On the other hand, membership kept expanding, and the Society had to adjust. A publicity committee was founded in 1952, as an advertising subcommittee of the Shows Committee; by 1955 it had become a full Committee. The rationale for its existence was provided in January 1956, when, with the subscription of the Society's 50,000th member approaching, the Secretary said, 'Our Society is probably the biggest learned Society in the world, and a good opportunity exists for publicity and propaganda about the Society's activities'.[38] In 1963, a Publicity Officer was appointed for the first time; in the same year, the Society was registered as a charity.[39] But as the membership kept increasing, there came doubt as to whether the concept of the RHS as a learned society was still valid. A student membership rate had been instituted in 1947, a junior membership in 1959. Special interest groups had been set up, on the model of the Lily Group: a Fruit Group, and a Rhododendron Group (which absorbed the older independent Rhododendron Association), both in 1945. Finally, in 1978, after years of debate, the term 'Fellow' was officially replaced by 'Member', since, as Lord Aberconway said, 'no qualification is needed to join the Society except the ability to write a valid cheque for £7.50 or hand over that sum in cash', and the Society had been kept busy for years trying to prevent people from using the initials FRHS in advertisements.[40]

Wisley flourished in the second half of the century. Battleston Hill was developed into a major rhododendron garden in the post-war years, and a series of model gardens gradually unfolded, instructing the public in various aspects of garden-making. The interwar glasshouse range in front of the Laboratory was replaced by a larger and more modernised range at the top of Weather Hill, and a new formal water garden laid out on the site at the beginning of the 1970s. As attendance rose, car parking and refreshments became issues; experiments were made with different caterers, leading eventually to the creation of a substantial restaurant. Less triumphantly surmounted were the Ministry of Transport, which provoked twenty years of anxiety, wrangle, and arbitration as two intersecting motorways encroached on Wisley's boundaries, and the nearby Wisley Airfield site, which successive owners attempted to use for revived air travel and for a rubbish incinerator, all of which the Society had to spend large sums opposing.

By the 1970s, the Society saw itself increasingly in terms of a membership largely concentrated in the south-east of England, for which Wisley and advisory services were the focal point. In 1946 the Northern Horticultural Society was founded, and soon established a garden at Harlow Carr on the outskirts of Harrogate, to provide advisory services for those in a climatic region halfway between Wisley and Edinburgh; soon after there were noises, in the event inconclusive, about the establishment of a Midland Horticultural Society, and of a more active Scottish one. The RHS, long accustomed to co-operation with other societies, welcomed the initiatives, worked out a joint trials programme with the NHS, and hoped merely that the other societies would not try to make awards

Wisley in the 1970s: a view of the Laboratory with the new canal by Geoffrey Jellicoe and Lanning Roper.

to plants.[41] But despite the complacency, it was becoming apparent that the Society was relinquishing parts of the national role it had once claimed.

Complacency challenged

In 1969 Harold Fletcher's *Story of the Royal Horticultural Society* was published. Its final chapter drew a picture of the Society's smooth and efficient functioning throughout its varied activities; and it closed with the words: 'The young Horticultural Society did indeed have many difficulties to encounter and many prejudices to contend with. And this must be the future lot of the Royal Horticultural Society, which, in the meantime, most triumphantly rides the crest of the wave.'[42]

The following year the wave crashed, as falling Chelsea profits and increased spending on Wisley suddenly revealed a deficit. Oliver Wyatt, the Treasurer, forced through a programme of expenditure cuts before his retirement the following spring. Savings were made on prizes and medals; the Wisley Diploma course was discontinued, as irrelevant to modern needs; and, most controversially, the three Year Books were discontinued. This decision was greeted with furious opposition from the relevant committees, especially because

they had not been consulted; smaller paperback successors to the Year Books were eventually issued and partially subsidised by the Society, but there would be no return to the former standard of publishing. *Curtis's Botanical Magazine*, whose subscription level had been declining, was transferred to the Bentham-Moxon Trust in 1971, after fifty years under the Society's direction.

Wyatt's cutbacks helped to restore the exchequer for the moment. In 1971 Chelsea made a loss of £7,000, but turned a surplus of £10,000 the following year. Nonetheless, every succeeding change in the financial world, from increased postal rates to the arrival of Value Added Tax, arrived as a blow to the Society's financial stability. The prospect that VAT would be levied on subscriptions was particularly frightening; Lord Blakenham, the new Treasurer, presented three options: (a) curtailing activities, (b) increasing subscription rates, or (c) running down reserves. Rising membership fees soon became a predictable annual feature, with entrance fees to Wisley running not far behind; but as partial compensation, the Examinations Officer Don Lamberth persuaded Council to introduce concessionary rates for pensioners in the mid-1970s. Learned societies, it was discovered, were exempt from VAT in four EEC countries: 'It would be unjust if the United Kingdom Government was the only one to discriminate against them by imposing the tax.' As the Treasury gradually learned how to manipulate the new stealth tax, the proportion of subscription income liable to VAT moved from 41 per cent to about 70 per cent, and the Society tried various strategies to gain exemption or recover some portion of the tax.[43]

Lord Blakenham's Treasurership saw a variety of initiatives designed to boost the Society's exchequer and end the drain on reserves: royalty-yielding collaborative ventures on flower plates, spoons, and first-day covers;[44] the transfer of the *Journal*, renamed in the process *The Garden*, to a commercial publisher, New Perspectives; the initiation of retail sales at Wisley; and lastly, an abortive proposal to sell or lease the Old Hall, contracting the Society's offices into the New Hall and moving the Library to Wisley. Abortive, because after a year of secret planning, the proposal was defeated by a show of hands at the 1977 Annual General Meeting.[45]

In 1971, the Society faced a deficit of £20,000, and deducted £43,000 from its general reserve; in 1973, it had a balance of £39,000, and budgeted hopefully for a surplus of £24,000 the following year. It was not to be. Instead, it faced a £13,000 deficit, and two years later was forecasting a deficit of £100,000. While the bank balance bounced, Lord Blakenham slashed at the reserves: out went the Hall Rebuilding reserve (completely insufficient anyway) and the Chelsea Contingency reserve (not needed). An appeal to Life Fellows brought in over £5,000; arrangements for interest-free loans were set up, and a special trust founded to receive the proceeds. In 1976 Chelsea turned a profit of £20,000—which helped to offset the £43,000 loss on the London shows. But the financial position was improving, and a new accountant, Tenison-Collins, who was capable of making accurate predictions, inspired confidence. By 1978 the Society's accounts had begun showing consistent surpluses once again.

Adaptation to the modern business world became the order of the day. Computerisation first reared its head in 1972, with proposals for subscription systems; the cost rapidly rose from £5,000 to £12,000. Where the Society had once favoured military personnel for its administrators, it now began looking to the business community: Lord Blakenham's successor as Treasurer was to be a merchant banker, as was Lord Aberconway's successor as President; and this trend was to continue into the 1990s.

Meanwhile, the structure of the Lawrence Hall was deteriorating, its boiler dying, the Library outgrowing its home, and the Wisley water feature leaking. All of these problems called urgently for thousands of pounds to be spent on them, and none of them accepted the money gratefully when it was provided. Few of the Society's building projects undertaken since Aberconway House in the 1950s have run to schedule or kept within budget, and life with the builders has usually ended up in a tangle of compensation payments, arbitration, or litigation threatened or actual. At the beginning of the 1980s, the greatest problem was the Lawrence Hall roof, its urgency signalled when a pane fell to the floor during an examination. An estimated £140,000 was needed quickly. The new Treasurer, Lawrence Banks, solved the problem aggressively, by imposing a compulsory levy on the members; and despite initial controversy, Inland Revenue acceded, the membership paid up, and after six months' closure, the Hall was reopened, almost within the estimated time if not within the estimated budget.[46]

The compulsory levy was an outwardly visible shock to the Society's normally staid public image. More were to come. The Society had emerged from a decade of financial instability to the realisation that its role and its activities needed to be re-examined, and its internal structure made more efficient. From 1984, it was to enter a world of contested elections, review committees and working parties, and public controversy.

The age of the review committee

The last years of Lord Aberconway's Presidency saw a fitful press campaign attacking the Society as an elitist organisation, out of touch with the broad gardening public. Geoff Hamilton used his column in *Garden News* to call for a reform of the Society, on the one hand praising it as 'Our Society, for that is what it is, [with] no equal anywhere in the world', but on the other condemning it for being sunk in the south-east and inaccessible to gardeners elsewhere in the country: 'The days when the RHS was an august body of mainly wealthy people are over. ... Now it is a Society for the ordinary chap who loves gardening. ... So what I want to suggest is that we move into the 20th century and cater for a much wider taste.' After Council sought him out for discussions, Hamilton modified his tone: 'I'm pleased to report that the place is not peopled by retired brigadiers or the recently impoverished gentry. The "powers that be" are in fact as earthy as you and me, and quite determined that the Society should serve the needs of the ordinary as well as the extraordinary gardener.'[47] This little debate prefigured the forthcoming campaigns for regionalisation and restructuring within the RHS.

Charles Melville McLaren, 3rd Baron Aberconway (1913-2003), President 1961-84. Succeeded his father as Chairman of the John Brown Shipyard in Glasgow. Continued to develop the garden at Bodnant; remarking once at an AGM that Wisley was as beautiful as any garden in England, he added that he couldn't quite bring himself to say 'in Britain'.

In 1980 the *Sunday Telegraph* quipped that people interested in betting certainties could try the RHS presidential election: Lord Aberconway, 'as leader in a field of one, should walk it'. This was the last time such a quip could reasonably be made, for the contested election was about to return for the first time since the 19th century. In 1982 an ex-Council member reported that he had been canvassed by various people about the possibility of running as an opposition candidate; and after the 1983 AGM Roderick Cameron, the proprietor of Great Comp Garden in Kent, about which he had written a book, announced his intention of standing for President the next year. He eventually decided to stand for a place on Council instead, and submitted a manifesto which was published in the November issue of *The Garden*, calling for elected regional committees, postal votes, stability of plant nomenclature, and the amalgamation of regional societies. He was not elected, nor in the two following years, but was finally voted onto Council in 1987.

1984 was the year in which Lord Aberconway retired, having hinted to Council for years that it was time to consider finding a successor, and pointedly remarking at the previous AGM that 'I look forward to enjoying the distinction, rather unusual in this Society, of being a Past President'. He was awarded on his departure with the title of Past President Emeritus (to which he replied that it reminded him of 'my Oxford days—Politics, Philosophy and Economics—where I took a distinguished third or fourth, I forget which').[48] He was succeeded by Robin Herbert, a merchant banker who in 1983 had become Vice-chairman of Council, and who promptly announced his intentions for reform, most notably his desire that all members should vote, not just those who attended the AGM. Within a few months of his election, he had convened a review committee, under the chairmanship of Viscount Ridley, to examine the administration and structure of the Society. The Committee submitted its completed report at the end of 1985, having carried out the largest survey of the Society's membership ever undertaken.[49]

The survey revealed that Geoff Hamilton's grumbles two years earlier had corresponded to the public's impression of the Society:

> There was a general feeling that Council is a remote elitist self-perpetuating oligarchy, and that ordinary gardeners, amateurs, and non-specialists were discouraged. In particular, the way in which Council's nominees for election to Council were publicly supported by Council, whereas an outside candidate was not, was felt to be invidious and wrong.

Much of the membership did not understand the voting procedures, and was effectively debarred from voting because of inability to attend the annual general meetings. In 1967 Maurice Mason had proposed election by ballot, and a mandatory retirement age of 75 for Council members, but his proposals were rejected;[50] now the Review Committee made it a major point that either postal or proxy voting be introduced (preferably the former, to avoid complexities). The election of President and Treasurer at the AGM was discontinued, Council electing each officer annually along with up to two vice-chairmen; neither President nor Treasurer would henceforth serve for more than ten years, and Council members would retire after their 70th birthdays (a policy later extended to committee chairmen as well). A *Newsletter* was begun, circulated with *The Garden*, for the purpose of keeping members up to date with events; it ran from September 1986 to December 1988, and was then replaced by a news section in *The Garden*.

In 1984, there was a complicated hierarchy of six categories of membership.[51] Of the nearly 82,000 members at that time, a quarter lived in Surrey, and an eighth in London; the home counties accounted for another 16,000; six northern counties had fewer than 300 members each; there were more American than Scottish members. The Review Committee specified the reduction of this disparity in membership distribution as an urgent priority. Thus the great effort at extending the Society's activities into the regions was kick-started, and pursued with difficulty, enthusiasm, hesitation, and confusion in varying degrees over the next decade and a half. In the heat of enthusiasm, the gardens at Rosemoor and Hyde Hall were accepted, the first regional centres established, and alliances on regional flower shows entered into; but finances did not always keep pace with the extent of these regional commitments, and retrenchments were occasionally enforced. Nonetheless, despite stumbles and setbacks, the RHS programme of regional development grew wider and deeper over the years.

The most far-reaching consequence of the Ridley Committee was less its immediate recommendations than its precedent: in its wake, separate working parties were set up for nearly every individual aspect of the Society's management that it had examined. Apart from the acquisition of Rosemoor and Hyde Hall, these working parties and the changes they instituted were the dominant features of life in the 1980s and early 1990s, investigating in turn senior staff structure (1987), awards (1988), the library (1989), commercial strategy (1990), committee structure (1991), membership (1992), science (1993), special awards (1993), Wisley development (1994), and judging (1996).

The Ridley Committee reported a dissatisfaction among various Council members, that too much time in Council meetings was spent on the fine detail of administrative matters and awards, and that major policy questions were insufficiently discussed. The next decade and a half, as a result, saw a gradual redirection of Council's attention, as a new structure was evolved to deal with administrative issues at lower levels of the hierarchy, leaving Council progressively freer to direct its attention to strategy. Directorates emerged where once there had only been departments, and the regular meetings of Directors took over a large portion of what had formerly been Council's remit.

The Society's chief official, and highest salaried staff member, had for a century been the Secretary. There had been a proposal in the 1970s that John Hamer be given the title of Director, but Lord Aberconway had opposed the idea: 'Secretary' seemed to him the appropriate title for an official of a learned society, while 'Director' suggested the head of a financial or industrial concern.[52] The Ridley Committee, however, finding that there was little communication between London and Wisley, that the respective staffs behaved as if they belonged to separate organisations, proposed the appointment of a Director-General, and a new staff structure 'based on the principle that staff need to be grouped according to their areas of work, and led by a strong head of department with a clear role for developing and supervising the work and personnel involved'. So persuaded were Council of the need for this change that they jumped the gun, and appointed a Director-General before the Ridley Committee had finalised its report. Christopher Brickell, for 15 years the Director of Wisley, was promoted to the new position, and moved from Wisley to London.[53]

The seductions of commerce

The development of commercial enterprise at Wisley began during Lord Blakenham's term as Treasurer. The first plan, in the summer of 1973, was to introduce mail order sales from the Wisley kiosk. Because the Society's charitable status might be jeopardised by making a commercial profit, it was decided to form a separate trading company, to be named RHS Enterprises Ltd, which could engage in retail activities and plough its profits back into the Society. John Hamer,

recently retired as Secretary, wanted to take over the running of the company, but was forced to abandon his hopes by a debilitating illness (his doctor thought his life expectancy so reduced that he urged him to take his pension entitlement in cash). And so the management of the new company fell to Barry Ambrose, who turned it into a successful venture over the next two decades.

The new company was incorporated in May 1975, and by October a profit of £12,000 had been made; the Society felt that it could end its initial subsidy and cushioning arrangements, and expose RHS Enterprises to the rigours of the commercial world. 'No purpose would be served in diminishing the Society's direct revenue simply in order to increase the trading company's profits as tax on the latter would have to be reclaimed', as Lord Blakenham said. So far, the content of the retail scheme consisted of printed matter and gifts (RHS Enterprises took over all sales of publications from November 1977), but the possibility of selling plants was being whispered. By 1976 the plant sales centre was being actively planned; Russell Coates became its first manager, and it was hoped that it might produce an annual turnover of £100,000. Some argued that it should concentrate on selling rare plants, or sell plants with such detailed cultural instructions that its work could count as educational, rather than commercially competi-

Barry Ambrose, first Director of RHS Enterprises, with the actress Hannah Gordon at the opening of the extended Wisley shop. Ambrose, trained at the Manchester parks, was one of the last of the old Diploma students at Wisley in the early 1970s. He developed the Wisley shop into the country's largest horticultural bookshop, and an immensely successful commercial enterprise.

tive; and within a couple of years the Society had to face accusations of running a garden centre, undercutting costs, and harming local trade, all of which were rebutted by a nurseryman on Council, Martin Slocock. In 1980, the Charity Commission advised that RHS Enterprises should not own its operating buildings, but that the RHS should repossess them and rent them to its subsidiary; this dashed the hopes that all refurbishments could be paid for by RHS Enterprises, and not cost the Society anything.[54]

By the time of the Ridley Review Committee, RHS Enterprises was contributing about 11 per cent of the Society's annual income, and that Committee held its 'entrepreneurial approach' as an example for the rest of the Society, specifically recommending four areas of enterprise: publications, an improved restaurant at Wisley, sponsorship, and a legacies campaign.

The Wisley restaurant was steadily improved over the succeeding years, and restaurants and outposts of the plant centre and bookshop were among the first considerations for the Society's new gardens. The programme of licensing, which had begun

The refurbished restaurant at Wisley in the 1990s.

with flower plates and spoons, moved on in the late 1980s to the exploitation of images from the Society's library; the publication of the book *Hooker's Finest Fruits* in 1989 resulted in a profitable spin-off in the use of Hooker fruit images on an attractive range of cups. By that time a further limited company, Horticultural Halls Ltd, had been set up to cope with the income from letting the Halls for non-horticultural uses. By the end of the century the success of these two businesses was seen as a model for other potential income-generating activities, and RHS Publications Ltd, HHL Events Ltd, and RHS Special Events Ltd followed in their wake.

As recommended by the Ridley Committee, the RHS set out in search of commercial sponsors. Witan Investments agreed to sponsor a London show in 1990; in 2000 the American firm of Merrill Lynch agreed to sponsor the Chelsea Flower Show for a four-year period. Charitable gala evenings at the Chelsea Flower Show were instituted in 1990, and followed at other shows. The proposal to instigate a legacies campaign was also taken seriously, and in 1991 a Marketing Department was set up, followed by Fundraising. Over the

succeeding decade, Marketing initiatives ranged from a long and inconclusive reconsideration of the Society's logo, through the introduction of an RHS credit card (not widely taken up) and the creation of an RHS Wine Club, to the creation of an American Friends of the RHS.

As the administration of the RHS became progressively more attuned to the world of finance, it began to pick up the habits and idioms of the business world. An arcane vocabulary of 'mission statements', 'corporate identity', and ephemeral management slang crept into the discourse of nearly every department ('corporate identity' dragging in its wake endless debate about logos and letterhead designs). That the RHS was becoming too commercial became a regular theme of complaint in the 1990s, and even some Council members were uneasy about the perceived concentration on income, and wanted to reinforce the Society's status as a charity instead.

Computerisation had begun to hit the Society in the 1970s—in both senses, for in September 1974 a £3,000 petty cash fund was set up, to finance subscription refunds following errors made by banks.[55] Accounts and membership were the first departments to become fully computerised, for fairly obvious reasons; the process gradually extended to registration and the cataloguing of plant collections, and then to the Library catalogue—and wherever plants were involved, anything involving orchids was always first to be computerised, for no other category of plants is likely to throw up any problem that can't be met with among the orchids. As information technology became progressively more important, a separate IT Department evolved from its origins in the Membership Department. The volatility of IT in the larger economy was perfectly reflected in its functions within the RHS: no department has seen a faster turnover of managers, who have ranged from the commandeering to the idealistic, or of staff, who have shown a marked tendency to be lured by the higher salaries obtainable in the commercial world.

Sir Simon Hornby, President 1994-2001, shown here accompanying the Queen at the Chelsea Flower Show. Formerly Chairman of the WH Smith Group, booksellers. At various times a council member or trustee of such organisations as the British Museum, the Victoria and Albert Museum, the National Trust.

The turbulent years

The years of Robin Herbert's Presidency formed a lively decade. Donald Hearn, the first Finance Director, was later to reminisce about the perceived change in the Society's ways:

> Arriving at 80 Vincent Square back in April 1986, there was an overwhelming sense of unchanging tradition. But change was in the air, and the sleeping giant was waiting to be galvanized into action. Those next seven years were exciting times. In 1993 alone we launched three new flower shows (Hampton Court, Wembley, Birmingham); Hyde Hall was taken into our care; the Wisley shop was rebuilt; membership growth was explosive. All this was done with tiny levels of staff.

The years from 1984 to 1994 had seen the acquisition of two new gardens, a regional centre, the Japan Branch, the Hampton Court Flower Show and co-operation with other shows around the country; the first gala evenings for charity at the major shows; significant changes in the format and content of *The Garden*, the beginnings of an intensive publication programme; a devastating storm, and a recovery; the debate over the Society's scientific activities, and the question whether it should try to fill the gap caused by the progressive closure of the horticultural research

stations; and the start of electronic cataloguing and information provision.[56]

In 1993 Christopher Brickell retired, and was succeeded as Director-General by Gordon Rae; the following year, Robin Herbert, having completed his term of ten years as President, retired and was succeeded by Sir Simon Hornby.[57] The insistent pace of reform was about to be quickened into public confrontation. The creation of new bodies of public funding—the Millennium Commission and the Heritage Lottery Fund—created an environment propitious for the planning of large-scale projects, and Wisley, which was rapidly outgrowing its Laboratory accommodation and whose major glasshouses were nearing the end of their projected lives, was an obvious candidate. Sir William Whitfield and Hal Moggridge drew up plans for a new centre for science and advisory services, creating a new formal design for the entrance to the garden, and adding a new path layout, lake, and glasshouse complex. This plan entailed moving the main Library from London to Wisley, and the announcement provoked controversy, as it seemed to have been timed to evade the notice of members until the deadline for submitting a resolution at the AGM had passed. Council's bland assumption that the objectors were few and the objections easily dismissed was rudely shattered at the stormiest annual general meeting since 1875, with a petition of members being presented to prevent Council from making a decision without consultation. A proposal had been drawn up for submission to the Millennium Commission for funding; it had to proceed without the Library element.[58]

The Millennium Commission rejected the Society's application in the summer of 1995, and the decision was immediately taken to re-apply.

Robin Herbert, President 1984-94. Chairman of the merchant bankers Leopold Joseph, and a director of the National Westminster Bank and of Marks and Spencer. Godson of Robert Jenkinson of the Knaphill Nursery, who sparked his interest in plants. He has made several plant-collecting expeditions, and raised many of the specimens at his garden at Abergavenny.

Donald Hearn, the Society's first Financial Director 1986-2001, a role he combined with that of Secretary, 1989-2001. A prime mover in the development of the RHS in the 1990s. Latterly Bursar of Clare College, Cambridge, and a Trustee of the Cambridge Botanic Garden.

Gordon Rae, Director-General 1993-1999. Trained at Wye College, and the Imperial College of Tropical Agriculture in Trinidad, he spent most of his career with ICI, serving terms as General Manager of the Agricultural Chemicals Division in Brazil, and of the Garden and Professional Products Division, before joining the RHS.

Sir Richard Carew Pole, President 2001-. A longstanding County Councillor for Cornwall, where his family home at Antony House is owned by the National Trust, he has been a trustee of the Tate Gallery and President of the Garden History Society, and much involved with agricultural colleges and organisations in the West Country.

Andrew Colquhoun, Director-General since 1999. Trained in agricultural botany, he worked for the Foreign Office in the Middle East before serving in the Cabinet Office and then in the Institute of Chartered Accountants, latterly as Secretary and Chief Executive, before returning to the world of plants at the RHS.

Despite protests that there were insufficient funds to revise the application properly, the application, somewhat adjusted, was submitted in January 1996, to be rejected again. The redevelopment of Wisley was postponed, and by the end of the century only the glasshouse development remained as an active proposal. The focus shifted instead to the London headquarters, long since outgrown by the expanding administration, with various departments operating from nearby rented accommodation. A new application for the rehousing of the Library secured a grant from the Heritage Lottery Fund; Rick Mather drew up plans for an internal refitting of the Vincent Square offices; in 1999, the building was vacated, partly gutted, and rebuilt over a two-year period. The opening of the new Library and offices in 2001 was the last act of Sir Simon's Presidency, a period which had also seen the Society's amalgamation with the Northern Horticultural Society, and its decision to sponsor Britain in Bloom. He retired at the AGM after seven years in office, and was succeeded by Sir Richard Carew Pole, the challenging manner succeeded by the conciliatory.[59]

The new administration inherited a now well-evolved structure of Directorates, an established

impetus toward expansion, and a network of financial and administrative problems, as the Society's evolution from a committee-based to a bureaucratic structure took further steps. Gordon Rae's great innovation in administrative functioning within the Society was his emphasis on strategic planning, and the creation of a planning structure: on the one hand, a set of objectives deduced from the Society's purposes, and on the other, a framework of five-year and three-year plans, continually reviewed, so that the RHS would always have a clearly defined set of goals and a measurable rate of progress. And while Andrew Colquhoun, his successor as Director-General, expressed a cheerful scepticism about the possibilities of accurate prediction—'It was the first Greek strategic planner who is supposed to have said, "If you want to make the gods laugh, tell them your plans for the future"'—he also felt that there was no excuse for not trying, and few significant changes have been made to Rae's Strategic Plan.[60]

Increasingly, the functions formerly assigned to administrative committees had been taken over by departments, and the committees either disbanded (as with the Expeditions and Scholarships Committee) or replaced by purely advisory bodies. When some members of Council expressed their concern that autonomous management decisions should take precedence over the traditional system of deferring to Committees and Panels, Sir Simon Hornby explained that 'it would still be necessary for objectives and strategies to be approved at a high level'. In 2000, a Governance Review was set up under the chairmanship of former RHS Treasurer Lawrence Banks. His report recommended the elimination of most of the remaining administrative committees, and the assignation of their functions to the staff; and, above all, the creation of two boards to deal with administrative matters and policy implementation, reporting to a Council that would henceforth meet less frequently and be concerned solely with strategy. The Business Board and the Horticultural Board were both formally inaugurated in 2002.

4 The Society's Gardens: Chiswick & Kensington

IN 1816, the Society had announced in a letter to an enquirer that it had 'no intention at present, of establishing a public Garden'.[1] But within a couple of years circumstances and intentions had changed. Thousands of fruit tree stocks were arriving for inspection and identification, as part of the programme of nomenclatural reform, and while initially they were sent to nurseries and private gardens, most notably that of the Brompton nurseryman Joseph Kirke, the need for somewhere to grow them was making itself felt; and plants were beginning to arrive as donations from overseas, even before the Society hired its first plant collectors. In January 1818, Council authorised the Secretary, Joseph Sabine, 'to contract for the renting of such small piece of Garden ground as he might deem expedient for the Cultivation of the Fruit trees &c belonging to the Society until the Society shall become possessed of a regular Garden—Mr. Sabine was also authorised to engage a Gardener for the care of the same piece of ground and of such things as may be confided to his care.'[2]

The first Kensington garden

The gardener, one Charles Strachan, was hired even before the site of a garden had been determined. Early in March 1818 Sabine reported that he had located a site in Kensington, comprising a narrow strip of an acre and a half—sufficient for the immediate needs of plant storage. It was located on the south side of the road to Hammersmith, near the southern entrance to Holland Park, and adjacent to Edwardes Square, a major housing development then in progress; Daniel Sutton, the agent with whom Sabine had reached an agreement, was becoming the Square's major promoter.[3] The rent was to be £60 per annum. Thanks to loans from Fellows, all the initial costs were covered by the spring of 1819.

The garden was only intended, it was later said, as 'a repository in which the trees and plants obtained by the Society could be kept as in a nursery until it should become possessed of a capacious garden in which they could be permanently preserved'. Nonetheless, it soon began to develop more permanent features. In the summer of 1818, Sabine presented his collection of hardy bulbs, 'the most complete in the species and varieties of the Liliaceae, not only in England, but in the world ... The collection of Narcissus, Lilium and Crocus, are the best because they have been arranged and described by me as they grew, but the roots of the other genera are equally numerous'. 'Being placed in the Garden of the Society', he went on to say, 'they will be well managed and open to the public eye more than they are at present, as well as exempt from the loss and destruction which is fatal to all private collections of plants on the death of the owner.'[4] A garden frame (cost £5) was one of the first acquisitions; plans for a glasshouse were first broached in June 1818; after two years of making do with a much cheaper glazed pit, a large greenhouse was finally erected.

The initial regulations were simple: the garden was to be open to Council members at all times, and to Fellows between 2 and 6 in the afternoon. The garden staff swelled to include multiple gardeners, porter, and garden clerk. Relations with Mr Sutton did not always run smoothly: he was slow in completing the works he had agreed to undertake (including arranging a water pump); there was argument over who bore the responsibility of paying tithes; in the end there was a dispute over the valuation of the remaining garden stock. Attempts to get a plan of the garden published foundered over financial disputes.[5]

By the middle of 1820 the Kensington garden was becoming cramped, and the search was on for an alternative site. Hugh Ronalds, the Brentford nurseryman and Council member, offered an enclosed ground at Ealing; further offers came in for areas in Wimbledon, Hornsey, Dulwich, St John's Wood, the Harrow Road, and Epping Forest. All were quickly eliminated in favour of the Duke of Devonshire's offer of a large tract of land in Chiswick.[6] Once the lease was arranged, the greenhouse and a number of trees were transferred to the new site, and the old garden was officially closed in October 1822.[7]

The site of the garden began to be built over in the mid-1820s. Today it is occupied by six shopfronts on Kensington High Street (numbers 343-353, once known as Edwardes Terrace), the houses on the east side of St Mary Abbot's Place, and Pembroke Studios at the southern end.

Chiswick: the early years

The new garden was located

> in the parish of Chiswick, between four and five miles from Hyde Park Corner, on the South Side of Turnham Green, and north of the Gardens and demesne of His Grace the Duke of Devonshire, who is the proprietor of the land. The extent is thirty-three acres, and the premises are to be holden by lease from the Duke for a term of 60 years, renewable for that term at the end of every 30 years, upon a fine certain, for ever, at the pleasure of the Society; with a power to the Society of relenquishing [sic] the property at any time, on giving twelve months notice of its intention to do so...

The primary purpose of the garden was fruit culture: introducing new varieties, establishing their correct nomenclature, and testing both varieties and cultivation techniques. Vegetables and ornamental plants also fell within the garden's remit, but those plants 'which cannot be considered as ornamental or useful will be left out of the collection'. The produce of the garden was to be exhibited at the Society's meetings; seeds and cuttings would be distributed to members; and nurseries would be allowed to obtain grafts of approved varieties. There was to be no attempt to compete with nurseries, but rather, by helping to guarantee the quality of their stock, it was hoped that the garden would 'cause an increase of demand on the nurseries'. Fellows could visit and bring guests, while the public would pay for admission (by 1825, there were nearly 4,000 visitors per annum); no gratuities would be allowed for the staff, and no liveried servants would be allowed entrance. In order to finance the works, a separate fund was established for creation, to be kept distinct from the subsequent maintenance budget; the King had promised

£500, not that it was ever paid, and all new Fellows would be charged an extra guinea (an optional payment for those already enrolled). Council hoped 'that in this instance another proof will be given that in Great Britain private funds can create establishments which in Foreign Countries are only founded by national means.'[8] The initial estimate for annual garden costs was £1,200.

The lease was completed in April 1822, and works began with a flurry of infrastructure. Fences and walls had to be built, roads levelled leading to the garden from the nearest highway (with some necessary purchases of land for the purpose), and gates made, including a private door for the Duke of Devonshire (landlord's perquisite). The Chiswick vestry was persuaded to discontinue a footpath cutting across the site. The water table was tested, and wells were dug: 'The Chiswick ground is very porous, and soon parts with its moisture', as the journalist Alexander Dean was later to sum up seventy years of experience.[9] Horses were purchased to help with hauling and carrying. And, in addition to the rent paid to the Duke (£300), there were tithes to pay at £23 p.a., and parish rates at £150 (reduced from over £250, but soon and continuously to rise).

It is worth asking what relation Chiswick bore to the other public gardens, and more especially botanic gardens, of the Kingdom. Kew was not yet the publicly funded home of the Royal Botanic Gardens; it was a royal estate, ruled until recently as a private fief by Sir Joseph Banks, little accessible to the public, and apparently selective in its co-operation with independent botanists. The principal physic and botanic gardens established in previous centuries all seemed to be suffering from stagnation, possibly because of the imposed war economy at the turn of the century: Oxford and Cambridge would have to wait for new administrators in the 1830s to revive them, inaugurate building programmes and, in the case of Cambridge, move to a new site; Edinburgh occupied its new site in the 1820s, but remained underfunded for years, the curator paying for improvements from his private funds. The Royal Caledonian Horticultural Society (founded 1809) acquired a site in 1820; it seemed to function as a mirror-image of its London predecessor, initially booming, sliding towards bankruptcy in the 1850s, and in 1859 handing its garden over to the Ministry of Works and subsequent incorporation into the Edinburgh Botanic Garden. Many private gardens functioned in much the way we now consider botanic gardens to function: most notably Woburn Abbey, where the Duke of Bedford oversaw the publication between 1816 and 1839, by two masterly head gardeners, of a series of five books on his plant collections which functioned both as catalogues and botanical monographs. The royal parks were, as the *Gardeners' Chronicle* was later to describe them, 'large prairies, fairly wooded'; flower gardening was not to reach them until the 1860s. In the 1820s, there was no significant rival to Chiswick, no public garden that could offer the same facilities and programmes. The closest rivals were the small botanic gardens established early in the century at Liverpool and Hull; in the absence of attached chairs of botany, they were really more horticultural than botanical, offering a combination of plant collections and public open space.[10]

neglect of duty, and the annual report commented publicly on the Society's disappointed expectations.[12]

Let us now look at the garden created at Chiswick in the 1820s.[13] Its 33 acres lay between Turnham Green and the northern wall of Chiswick Park, where the Society created a private road that established the line followed today by Ellesmere Road, and between what is now Sutton Court Road on the west and Duke's Avenue on the east (the latter again created as a private road by the Society). Along the south side, nearest Chiswick Park, lay the orchard, planted in its first year with nearly 3,000 standard fruit trees; the private road was flanked by a holly hedge, facing a wall planted with pears, grapes, figs, and peaches. To the west of the orchard, and only about a third of its size, lay the kitchen garden, divided into 36 compartments for different annual vegetables, with borders planted with dwarf plums and cherries. It was flanked by areas for miscellaneous stock and duplicate plants, and northward from it extended areas for glasshouses. The ornamental department, nearly half the entire garden, lay on the north-east, within the L formed by these branches: a pair of rectangular flower gardens, adjacent to an area for further glasshouses, and, separated from these by a holly hedge, the largest single subdivision of the garden, reserved for the arboretum. The Council Room, later described by an assistant as 'an unpretentious Ivy-clad, one-roomed structure ... a dark and cheerless place', was located at the western edge of the arboretum, almost centrally;[14] there were of course entrance lodges, bothies for staff, and miscellaneous sheds, later to be supplemented by exhibition tents, ornamental waiting rooms, and public conveniences. (Glasshouses will be dealt with a little further on.)

A late 19th-century photograph of an ivy-clad building, possibly the Council Room, at the Chiswick garden.

The garden was to be run by salaried head gardeners, but most of the work would be carried out by six under-gardeners and some two dozen labourers under their supervision: two categories of apprentices who would be trained in the course of their work and become qualified for jobs in private gardens, the Society effectively acting as a recruitment agency. The most celebrated example was Joseph Paxton, who arrived as a labourer in 1823, became under-gardener in the arboretum in March 1825, and in April 1826 'left, recommended to a place'—the place being Chatsworth, where he was soon to become the most celebrated gardener in the kingdom.[11] There was a high turnover among the garden staff, even at the highest levels; Strachan, the original gardener at Kensington, was dismissed within a year; William Christie, one of the Kensington staff who moved to Chiswick, resigned in 1824, having been reprimanded for

The fruit collections came in for early and regular praise; the ornamental gardens soon received attention in the newly burgeoning gardening press for their collections of exotics, chrysanthemums, peonies, wisteria, Australian plants.[15] But the feature that attracted the greatest attention was the arboretum, designed by the architect William Atkinson (best known for remodelling Abbotsford for Sir Walter Scott), who was also responsible for the early frames and melon pits.[16]

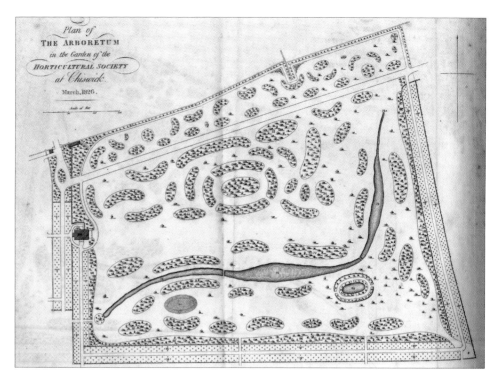

> On the north, it is bounded by a wall, upon which the more tender plants of a trailing or creeping habit are trained. The three other sides, are surrounded by double borders, on each side a walk; those on the east and south are planted with Roses, and those of the west with Azaleas. The area is occupied by clumps irregularly disposed upon turf, in which are planted the various Trees and Shrubs. A few ornamental plants of the same description are occasionally placed upon the grass. Through the centre of the whole has been carried a Canal of Water, supplied by an overflowing well; in this Hardy Aquatics will be grown.
>
> The arrangement of the Arboretum is not systematic, but all the species of each genus are placed as much as possible in the immediate vicinity of each other; thus affording an opportunity of convenient comparative examination.

The arboretum was originally laid as a loose collection of beds, intermixed with some scattered trees; the beds were mostly oval- or lozenge-shaped, though a few were laid out as rings. Some beds, particularly near the entrance, comprised miscellaneous shrubs, but most of them were devoted to one or two groups: hardy heaths, berberis, daphne and aucuba, azaleas, peonies, horse chestnuts, willows, yuccas, roses.[17] So much gravel was extracted in the course of digging the arboretum that it paved all the garden walks.

The design of the arboretum was criticised almost immediately by John Claudius Loudon, who was trying to introduce new ideas of garden design into England, and who could see 'neither beauty nor fitness in any part of the plan of this garden':

> almost all the arboretums in Europe have the trees planted along gravel walks that the botanist may examine them without damping his feet by moist earth or dewy grass; and the genera following each other either alphabetically, or in the order of some botanical system, that he may know where every genus is

to be found ... In the arboretum of the Chiswick garden, the dug clumps are surrounded by grass, which, of course, can only be walked on in fine weather, and the genera are distributed through them at random. As a scientific arboretum therefore, this department of the garden is still more discreditable to the Society, than as a specimen either of natural or artificial landscape-gardening.

It has to be remarked that most of the beds were restricted to one or two genera, so 'random' was not quite an accurate term; also that none of the systems of taxonomy then in use have survived unaltered, so a systematic arrangement would not have been, in the long term, such a benefit. Loudon's alternative proposal was that 'The

The Chiswick arboretum as laid out by William Atkinson: informal planning and rococo revival beds.

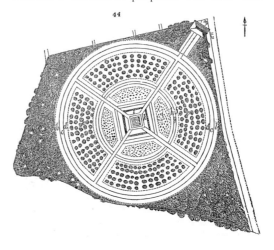

And this is how Loudon would have laid it out: a tight geometric design with all the collections in an intelligible order.

Arboretum should be formed as a belt, combined with hardy herbaceous plants, and arranged in the natural manner'; a few years later he proposed a circular arboretum, geometrically subdivided.[18]

In the 1820s, Loudon's criticisms were extreme and unrepresentative of the general gardening public; within twenty years the taste that he was promoting had triumphed, and there was widespread dismissal of 'the commonplace mode of indiscriminate mixture' seen at Chiswick. The pleasures of formal gardening, of geometric arrangement, symmetry, and patterned beds, of well-defined gravelled walkways and grouping of colours, had become the aesthetic principles of the rising generation of gardeners, and the reputation of Chiswick suffered as a result. The *Gardeners' Chronicle* defended the garden in 1847 by pointing out that 'Tasteful laying out of the grounds in that part was of secondary importance' to horticultural purposes, but acknowledged that the ornamental grounds could nonetheless be improved, noting specifically of the entrance arch that 'from the neglect of its repairs it is kindly intended to become a pure specimen of RUIN, that the visitors may so enlarge their stock of antiquarian knowledge'.[19]

And that remark indicates part of the problem: after 1830, the state of maintenance at Chiswick fluctuated, in line with the Society's finances. As early as 1827 the number of labourers was reduced; in 1830, further staff reductions were accompanied by an injunction to turn parts of the garden over to commercial produce, to bring in some income; and while the 1830s and the beginnings of regular shows brought renewed vigour, expressed in building programmes, the 1840s saw further retrenchments.

Chiswick glass and the great conservatory

The early years of the Chiswick garden saw more than one revolution in the making of glasshouses. Before the 19th century, when wood and masonry were the available structural materials, glasshouses were essentially open-plan buildings with the maximum area of windows consistent with structural stability: they were, by comparison with what came later, dark, hot and dry, for they were heated either directly by braziers or by hot air carried by flues from external boilers. Practical fruit growing frequently relied on pits instead of elevated buildings: a glass roof over a recess in the ground often provided greater light than orangeries did, and a pit filled with dung or tan generated a satisfactory degree of heat. The earliest glasshouses in the Society's gardens were of this sort, most of them designed to test the recommendations of different articles in the *Transactions*.[20] By 1830, there were over 450 feet of glazed pits in the garden, and some 400 feet of hothouses.

In 1815, Sir George Mackenzie read a paper to the Society on the best form of a glasshouse: spherical, so as to be parallel to the dome of the

A view of the Chiswick garden in the late 19th century, with the great conservatory, by then converted into a vinery, in the background.

heavens; that way optimum light would penetrate the building at all times of day. At the time, this was not technically feasible, though some fairly decent domes were already being created, for example only a mile away in the grounds of Chiswick House, in Isaac Ware's camellia house of 1811. But, inspired by Mackenzie's paper, John Claudius Loudon invented a wrought-iron glazing bar that could be made in curved sections; this was patented by the firm of D. and E. Bailey, of Holborn, in 1818. It was now possible, using wrought-iron, to build in conformity to Mackenzie's requirement, and the 1820s saw the initial experiments in curvilinear glasshouse building.[21] (Loudon had already offered to erect a light in the Kensington garden, in 1819.)[22] The end result would be the Great Stove at Chatsworth (1836-40), and the Palm House at Kew (1844-48); but between them came a third major structure, at Chiswick (1840)—a large iron conservatory, erected at a cost of £4,500.

> The range will be nearly 500 feet long, running east and west, with a front both to the north and south; the roof will be constructed entirely of iron, glazed with patent sheet glass, and will have the form of a Gothic arch. The west wing, rather more than 180 feet long and 27 feet high, has been contracted for by Messrs. D. and E. Baileys of Holborn, and will probably be completed by the middle of May. The whole range, when executed, will be one of the most extensive in the world.[23]

Loudon criticised the proposal, on the grounds that a glasshouse should be aligned north to south, rather than east to west, but quoted a letter from George Bentham arguing that cold winds were more likely from the east than from the north. While the glazing bars were of wrought iron, the principal ribs of the arch were of cast iron, a departure from Loudon's early designs; it has been described as the 'first example of a solidly engineered cast-iron barrel vault over a hall'. When the first wing was completed, Loudon praised the good workmanship, but condemned the design as a 'large hand-glass' with a hideous chimney, and also compared it to the hull of a ship inverted. Since the dome and the second wing were never carried out, the incomplete form of the building looked more austere than intended, and late in the century it was dismissed as 'classic'. (An odd comment, since the cross-section was planned to be Gothic; and since in the later years of the century the gardening press showed its awareness of Gothic style as a forerunner of greenhouse style, one can only feel that the Chiswick house was under-appreciated.)[24] Before the end of 1840 it was already housing the Society's collection of camellias and Australian plants.[25]

While the great conservatory remained the largest house at Chiswick, it was continually supplemented by other glass buildings, of varying degrees of permanence. A small span-roofed orchid house of the 1840s was deemed to offer 'much convenience to the amateur of small means'; an older conservatory, built on a wall that divided one portion off as a cactus house, was internally remodelled to make it lighter.[26] In the mid-1840s, James Hartley of Sunderland introduced a process for making sheet glass of uniform quality, free of the bubbles and imperfections that had led earlier greenhouse builders to rely on small panes. In June 1846 Hartley offered to erect a conservatory at Chiswick; it was initially used to house exotic conifers sent back by Theodor Hartweg.[27] In 1852 a rose house was built, on the easily assembled 'orchard house' principles then being propounded by the nurseryman Thomas Rivers; this proved unsuitable for roses, and two years later they were transferred to the Hartley building, where they proved a great success, and

THE ABOVE ENGRAVING REPRESENTS.
THE CONSERVATORY,
ERECTED IN THE
HORTICULTURAL SOCIETY'S GARDEN, CHISWICK,
By HENRY ORMSON, Stanley Bridge, Chelsea,
which was so much admired at the Grand Show in June last, and is now for sale at a very moderate price, the particulars of which may be had on application.

augured a new age of growing tender roses in England.[28] Additional orchard houses were built for fruit. The late 1850s saw new conservatories by Henry Ormson and James Gray, two quondam partners in glasshouse building. And all the while there were experiments with new types of boiler (boilers decayed quickly in the Chiswick soil), steam and hot-water heating (as a result of the popularity of which, the dry atmosphere of early greenhouses was succeeded by humid mid-Victorian), and rainwater collection (Edward Beck, the Isleworth florist and journalist, devised

Advertisement from the Gardeners' Chronicle (1858) for Henry Ormson, formerly partner in the firm of Gray & Ormson, offering his Chiswick glasshouse as a model.

slate rainwater tanks for Chiswick in 1842).[29] For a period in the 1850s, Charles Ewing's glass walls were tried out: freestanding and easily movable, capable of being arranged in different configurations, these were to give support and protection to fruit and other plants without requiring heating apparatus. The results were initially highly promising, but they failed to stand up to stormy weather sufficiently. Despite Lindley's opposition, the Ewing walls were dismantled in 1862 and assembled into a span-roofed house for peaches and vines.[30]

Decline and renewal at Chiswick

By 1849, the example of Chiswick could be held up as a warning to other horticultural societies:

> never let them endeavour to promote horticulture by their example,—never let a local society have a garden; for, if they do, we warn them, from long experience, that it will be worse than a failure. A garden would swallow up their funds ... Subscribers do not care to belong to a society that is ridiculed; and the gardening of a neighbourhood is not improved when a cultivator is able to say, 'Yes, those plants do look bad, but those in the society's garden are worse.'[31]

Much of the early planting at Chiswick had been thick for initial effect, with the intention of removing half or more as things matured. Evidently this did not always happen as intended. By 1850, overgrowth in the arboretum was being commented on publicly: 'the original designers displayed so little taste in laying it out, as to render the Arboretum at the present time little better than a forest scene.'[32] It was to remedy this situation that Robert Glendinning, formerly head gardener at Bicton, latterly nurseryman in Chiswick, journalist, and now Council member, was contracted to remodel the arboretum. Beginning in 1850, he supervised the general thinning of the arboretum, removing the thicket of miscellaneous trees and shrubs, creating new mounds for evergreens and yuccas, masses of rhododendrons, a new 'American' (i.e. peat) garden, and a rockwork bridge whose bases were planted with ferns. New gravel walks, 15 feet wide, lined with flower beds, were dug to give the entrance walk the axis of symmetry which Loudon's aesthetic demanded, and the flanking holly hedge removed. With Robert Thompson, he worked on the orchard, felling half the trees, and replacing them with new stock arranged to demonstrate different systems of pruning. As the works continued, Lindley also took part in the planning: 'In the Arboretum we found Dr. Lindley busily engaged in marking out an

George M'Ewen (c.1820-1858). Head gardener at Arundel Castle. Hired in 1857 as Superintendent of Chiswick, but died a year later. His Culture of the Peach and Nectarine *was published posthumously in 1859.*

alteration in the "Rhododendron clump"', observed the *Chronicle* in 1853.[33]

But these alterations could not long prevail against the deteriorating financial situation, and by 1856 it was once again observed that the garden was suffering. A former gravel path had sunk so much that it was nicknamed 'the Doctor's Ditch'. Plants were being sold, or humiliatingly withdrawn from sale for lack of offers; turnips were being planted extensively to raise short-term income.[34] So, despite the slide towards bankruptcy, the Society head-hunted the celebrated head gardener of Arundel Castle, George M'Ewen, to rescue Chiswick on a minimal budget. M'Ewen's slashing changes were remarked on quite early in 1857: walks widened and made less convex, the iron frame of the exhibition tent turned into a sort of pergola over the main walk, unsightly or problem areas turned over to raspberries, the American garden re-ordered. Most startlingly, after the sale of many of the greenhouse plants, he emptied the great conservatory, and had it replanted as a vinery, thus fulfilling one of Loudon's old demands, that the trial of vine varieties ought to take precedence over exotic ornamentals. The orchid house was similarly turned over to peaches and nectarines.[35] M'Ewen's changes won widespread approval, but his health failed as he entered his second year in his post, and he died in May 1858. (His brother John had helped him in his last days, and stayed on for two months before being dismissed for 'indiscretion'—probably being rude to visitors. George M'Ewen had been similarly censured, but had replied that the visitor had no business picking the flowers.)[36] M'Ewen was succeeded by his assistant Archibald Henderson, who soon left for a more lucrative position at Trentham.

M'Ewen had made Chiswick once again functional; George Eyles, who became the new superintendent in 1859, aimed to keep it that way. But once again Chiswick was to suffer, this time because the Society suddenly found itself with a second garden to maintain.

Kensington in glory

The primary intention behind the garden at Kensington was to secure the Society a venue nearer central London, where its shows could compete more successfully against its rivals at Regent's Park and the Crystal Palace. The anticipated rejuvenation of the Society brought in a sudden rush of new Fellows and benefactors, and while Prince Albert was on hand to keep the newly 'Royal' society and its landlords, the Royal Commissioners, working in co-operation, success

Two proposals for the Kensington garden: above, Sydney Smirke's design for a refreshment pavilion; below, Godfrey Sykes's sketch of arcades with terracotta columns.

seemed certain. The grand opening on 5 June 1861, with its royal panoply and ceremonial, its display of newly introduced Japanese plants, banks of ferns, rhododendrons, heaths, begonias, and flower arrangements, augured a bright new era for the Society, one which the excitements of the 1862 Great Exhibition confirmed.[37]

The garden itself was the culmination of a growing movement in garden design, and an unprecedented experiment in urban horticulture. Because it was a garden close to a city centre, bordered by roads intended to be busy, it was enclosed by arcades on all sides. Nothing unusual in enclosure for an urban garden, but hitherto urban gardens had not earned column inches in the horticultural press, and the only ones that had encroached on the fringes of fashion had been the commercial pleasure-gardens like Vauxhall and Cremorne—good for entertainment, negligible

for horticulture. To focus attention on horticultural achievement in a London setting was, as it turned out, a decided risk. But the immediate shock to the system was the simple fact of enclosure; at a time when the most celebrated gardens offered a prospect—either looking out from a terrace, or over a parterre—a garden that offered walls as the termination of every vista was remarkable. Scarcely less remarkable was the fact that a critic like Dr Lindley, only a few years before outspoken in condemning the idea of an enclosed garden, should now be involved in administering and promoting one.[38]

The arcades themselves were the work of Francis Fowke (later the initial architect of the Albert Hall) and Sydney Smirke (most famous for the Round Reading Room of the British Museum). Three series of arcades summarised the history of Italian architectural style (Italianate

George Eyles (1815-1887). Protégé of Paxton at Chatsworth and the Crystal Palace. At his farewell dinner there, John Spencer praised his 'business habits, kindness of manner, and courtesy to all', as the only means of commanding success in shows. Superintendent of RHS Gardens from 1859 until the 1870s. Landscape gardener.

revival having been, primarily through the work of Sir Charles Barry, the leading secular style of the past quarter-century). On the southern boundary of the garden was the Lateran arcade, modelled in terracotta in imitation of Byzantine work; the Milanese arcades, based on 15th-century Milanese brickwork, ran up the west and east sides; on the northern boundary was the Albani arcade, modelled on the Villa Albani in Rome. Godfrey Sykes devised the ornamentation of the terracotta columns, and the architectural acclaim for his work helped to trigger the immense enthusiasm for terracotta building that swept the 1860s and 1870s. Within the Albani arcade was the conservatory, a curvilinear iron structure designed by Fowke, whose floor was laid by Messrs Minton as a showpiece for the rediscovered art of mosaic, with patterns based on Pompeian, early Italian, and Renaissance originals, including that of the altar slab at Santa Maria Trastevere in Rome.[39]

The landscaping of the garden was the work of William Andrews Nesfield. Nesfield's work as a garden designer was first promoted by Loudon, but did not become well known until his design for the Royal Botanic Gardens, Kew, landed him in the public eye; the gardening press then began to look at his country house commissions, and was originally puzzled by what it saw. Nesfield was most closely associated with the revival of the late 17th-century-style parterre, in which patterns in box were laid out against a backdrop of gravel; such parterres offered no opportunity for gardeners to experiment with colour schemes, and so were initially rejected in the press. But as the 1850s wore on, Nesfield's reputation soared, until on the eve of the Kensington project he basked in the reputation of the greatest landscape designer of the day.[40]

As for a Superintendent, the *Gardeners' Chronicle* indicated the demands that would be placed on him: the new Superintendent 'must be a thoroughly practical

gardener, versed in every department of horticulture ... not a fine gentleman who imagines that fruit growing is the great art and whole duty of man. He must be a skilled ground workman, an experienced manager of men, young enough and active enough to bear the strain ... he must be popular with his brother gardeners, familiar with the management of public exhibitions, and with such an appearance and address as will enable him to receive visitors of all ranks in a manner becoming the magnitude of his charge'. The choice fell on George Eyles, a protégé of Joseph Paxton at Chatsworth and the Crystal Palace: 'eminently qualified both as a Gardener, a man of business, and a person conversant with the management of a great public Garden where Exhibitions are held.' He was hired as Superintendent of Gardens for the Society, with responsibility for both Chiswick and Kensington.[41]

Nesfield drew up plans for the garden, which were revised by the Garden Committee, so that he

Two photographs of the garden in Kensington under construction, taken by an anonymous photographer in 1860.

had to include a system of canals that he had not originally intended. The visitor to the garden encountered, at the southern and lowest end, an ante-garden with two miniature amphitheatres, one containing a holly and hornbeam maze, and one planted with limes, tulip trees and deodars. Beyond lay terraces on rising ground, centred around the canal system: central basins, two rectilinear canals recessed below ground level, and a great cascade fed by an artesian well. The well, a feat of engineering in itself, was 226 feet deep, with a bore plunging a further 175 feet, deeper than the well at Trafalgar Square (because of the higher land?—at any rate, there was much more clay to get through in Kensington).[42] The trees from the original site of Gore House had been swept away before work began; in their place mature trees were transplanted from Chiswick and other sources: Prince Albert donated some, and William Gibbs donated some 25-foot lime trees from Tyntesfield. The maze was composed mostly of holly from Chiswick, and designed so that there were two separate routes to the centre.[43]

Within these broad outlines Nesfield found the space for his latest experiments in parterre planting. As the 1850s had rolled on, he had become progressively interested in the effect of using coloured gravels to create decorative patterns on the ground, patterns which could remain visible all year round and not suffer winter removal as bedding plants did. The *Florist* ensured that the gardening community was primed for developments before the garden was completed:

> We understand that the first landscape gardener of the day is much averse to over-floral decoration, and that, taking advantage of the many suitable forms of evergreens for decorating geometrical gardens, he is employing them more largely on every occasion, as well as more simple figures. We therefore hope to see, at Kensington Gore, good examples in this style of art, by the gentleman we allude to – Mr. Nesfield.

Nesfield's designs took two forms. Alongside the Milanese arcades he created a set of 'friezes' in a Florentine chain pattern based on Italian church floors; these were intended for bedding, but with an admixture of gravels for winter effect. Closer to the centre of the garden, he laid out monogram beds purely of box and gravels (white Derbyshire spar, purple fluorspar, Welsh slate, coloured glass, and crushed brick), in the shape of the four symbolic flowers of the United Kingdom, the rose, thistle, leek, and shamrock. Nesfield and Eyles, who as head gardener supervised the work, issued a joint press statement on the value of gravel parterres for winter decoration; the *Gardeners' Chronicle* depicted the frieze patterns in almost its first colour illustrations (the plan of the Kensington garden was the very first). Donald Beaton, who a decade earlier had criticised

Bird's-eye view of the Kensington garden, from Andrew Murray's Book of the Royal Horticultural Society, 1863: looking north towards Kensington Gardens.

Nesfield for using gravels instead of modern plants, was carried away with enthusiasm—'I never yet saw flower gardening carried on in such high order'—and urged the RHS to set up a 'committee of ladies' to decide on colour schemes for the gravels. (He did chide Nesfield for the error of giving the English rose pattern six petals, but dismissed that as 'a mere matter of detail, which Mr. Eyles could put right for the value of one man's time for two days.')[44]

At the beginning of the 1860s, the new garden in Kensington was the height of fashion. The press tangled itself in intellectual knots trying to find suitable comparisons. Shirley Hibberd summed it up as 'an example of garden architecture which has no match and no parallel for novelty and for unity of design', 'a very complete amalgamation of the French, Italian, and English schools'. The *Athenaeum* elaborated:

> in these magnificent arcades we have something new to our country and our century—something exquisitely Italian ... in these successions of terraces, in these artificial canals, in these highly ornamental water-works we have something of the taste and splendour of Louis Quatorze. It was of such a garden as this that Bacon must have dreamt.

Donald Beaton welcomed the garden as a model for future urban gardens; others urged land-owners to send their gardeners to Kensington to gain fruitful ideas. Not everyone succumbed to the magic, however; take as evidence the sardonic Beresford Hope, writing in the *Quarterly Review*:

> It was comparatively unimportant that the prospects of the horticulturists growing anything in their new allotment were somewhat problematic. They had not given up the useful old nursery at Chiswick, while it was well understood that the object of the new garden was to set up a 'moral Cremorne.' So the brave old trees which skirted the paddock of Gore House were felled, little ramps were raised, and little slopes sliced off, with a fiddling nicety of touch which would have delighted the imperial gardener of the Summer Palace; and the tiny declivities thus manufactured were tortured into curvilinear patterns, where sea-sand, chopped coal, and pounded bricks, atoned for the absence of flower or shrub.

John Robson, the journalist and head gardener at Linton Park in Kent, pointedly queried the limited planting range: 'is it right to call an enclo-sure containing only about fifty species and varieties of plants, the Royal Horticultural Garden?'[45]

The garden brought the Society new sources of financial anxiety, such as an uncertain liability for the repair of adjacent roads, but the first couple of years saw sustained public enthusiasm for the innovations of Kensington. Within a year of its opening, the *Gardeners' Chronicle* could report on its influence:

> The flower gardens of our farmhouses are being laid out *à la Nesfield* ... Vases, statues, Minton pavements, and terra cotta columns are turning out of doors dead walls, dirty gravel walks, box edging, and hideous red flower pots. In effecting this Kensington is taking a great part; old Chiswick standing aghast at innovations which seem to be the very incarnation of horticultural Red Republicanism.[46]

The fine arts at Kensington

Prince Albert's plans for the garden extended beyond horticulture and garden design, and even beyond the encouragement of architectural decoration. A month before the official opening, he set up a Fine Arts Committee under his personal chairmanship, with Sir Charles Dilke, Sir Coutts Lindsay (later the co-founder of the Grosvenor Gallery), the architects Francis Fowke and Sydney Smirke, and the sculptor Richard Westmacott as members. The Committee's remit was largely focused on sculpture, which the Prince thought suffered in England from the lack of facilities for proper exhibition:

> Viewed in a more extended light and with special reference to the influence which the efforts now making by this Society may have in encouraging artists and fostering a taste for art among the people this Garden also possesses singular advantages—Hitherto there has been no place in the Metropolis or even in Britain where the Sculptor or Statuary could expose the creations of his genius in model with such accompani-ments of place and scenery as would give them fair-play—Huddled in confined studios no just conception could be formed of the effect which the larger models would have, when placed in the conditions for which they were intended,—were such a place as these gardens open to artists for the Exhibition of their models, they could be seen under such conditions as would enable their faults to be detected and remedied; their applicability for their intended positions ascer-tained; their beauties to be seen and appreciated; and the encouragement of the Fellows and the public better secured. These advantages would of themselves be sufficient inducement to the Artist not only to end the models which are already lumbering his Studio but also to execute others, and would thus give an impetus to this branch of art, of which the want of such opportunity of Exhibition has hitherto retarded the develop-ment in this country.

Photograph from Murray's *Book of the Royal Horticultural Society, 1863, showing one of the bandstands and the 1862 Great Exhibition building.*

The Committee started with a budget of £500, soon increased to £1,000 per annum, for the purchase of sculptures for the garden, but its first efforts were to arrange loans. The Queen lent two 16th-century statues by Francavilla, and Westmacott sounded out manufacturers of terracotta and artificial stonework for the loan of vases and other ornaments. The first purchase, in 1862, was of four statues of the seasons, by Charles Sharpe (which promptly put the Committee over budget). By that time Prince Albert had died, and was succeeded as Chairman by the Earl of Ducie, whose garden at Torthworth Court boasted one of the nation's finest conifer collections.[47]

In 1863, the Sculptors' Institute collaborated with the Society on an exhibition of work by living sculptors, a follow-up on a smaller but more specific scale to the 1862 Great Exhibition. A hundred and fifty-three works by E.H. Baily, Joseph Durham, Thomas Earle, J.H. Foley, Patrick MacDowell, Matthew Noble, Henry Weekes, and dozens of others were on view in the garden for three months of the summer.[48] Despite encouragement, there was no sequel to this exhibition, though further sculptures were bought for or exhibited in the garden.[49]

Meanwhile, sculpture on a grander scale was also proposed for the garden. For some years discussions had taken place about creating a memorial to the Great Exhibition of 1851; the initial plan, for a statue of Prince Albert, had been vetoed by the intended subject, and something incorporating a figure of Britannia was being discussed instead, when in 1860 George Godwin suggested that it should be located within the new Gardens. A new subscription was undertaken: £6,250 was

eventually collected, some £700 less than the proposed amount; the Society accepted a liability not exceeding £800. Prince Albert became involved in the siting and planning of the Memorial; John Kelk got the tender for erecting it and an accompanying great cascade, for £1,542. Work on this had not proceeded very far, however, by the date scheduled for the grand opening of the garden, or indeed by the time of Albert's death.

The Prince of Wales, in thanking the Society for its letter of condolence, requested that the proposed Memorial to the Great Exhibition be changed to a Memorial to Albert (it would be 'most hurtful to Her feelings were any other statue to surmount this Memorial, but that of the great, good Prince, my dearly beloved Father, to whose honor it is in reality raised'). The Society, and the Commissioners, agreed readily, and the sculptor Joseph Durham was commissioned to make a statue of Albert to surmount the already designed pedestal. The resulting Memorial was unveiled on 10 June 1863, after much discussion, debate, and delay. (This is the statue of Albert that now stands atop the steps leading south from the Royal Albert Hall.)[50]

The Great Exhibition of 1862 resulted in some spillage of artworks into the garden. Early in 1862, the French ironfounder Antoine Durenne got agreement to display two polychrome fountains on the terraces. These were highly admired, and in July the Society advertised a subscription for their purchase, but publicly pointed out that they 'do not in any way press this subscription upon the Fellows'. The press was divided between supporting the purchase, and thinking the garden already over-crowded with ornament. Donald Beaton was enthusiastic, and subscribed his guinea: 'I longed ... from the first day I saw the red-painted fiery horses from France, the horse marines of Neptune ... to get full hold of the biggest of them'. In the event the necessary money was not raised, and the fountains were removed in 1863; one of them was acquired for the garden at Olantigh Towers, and later donated to Victoria Park in Ashford (where it has recently been restored).[51]

Over the following decade and a half, a variety of structures was built in the garden, as temporary displays: greenhouses and garden buildings, iron tents which the gardening press thought would make good conservatories, rustic summerhouses, aviaries and beehives, a rockery by Dick Radclyffe. Frank Buckland, the Inspector of Salmon Fisheries, offered to take charge of pisciculture in the garden, and stocked some of the pools with a selection of salmon and trout; during the 1870s, he organised a large collection of fishery materials in the South Kensington Museum (the eventual nucleus of the Fisheries Exhibition of 1883), and was granted permission to create a salmon rivulet in the garden. Despite remonstrances over leaving the garden entrance unlocked, relations with Buckland were unproblematic.[52] Not so relations with the photographer Louis Birnstingl, who was allowed to erect a photographic studio within the garden, and then carried resistance to eviction to the point of applying for an injunction against the Society.[53] And in the late 1870s came the proposals for a skating rink, defeated by the Commissioners, and subsequently for lawn tennis courts. These proved popular among the Kensington population, alterations in arrangements igniting local protest, and the eventual discontinuation of tennis facilities provoking resignations.[54]

The Society had always provided music at its fêtes and garden events, and the administration of the bands was yet another of the duties that had always fallen to Lindley; not surprisingly, he was entrusted with organising the bands for the grand opening. But, during the brief heyday of Prince Albert's encouragement for public competition in the arts, music became another subject for a Kensington programme. A Music Committee was set up in 1862, under the chairmanship of the Earl of Ducie, with Sir Charles Dilke, Lord Gerald FitzGerald, and Sir John Harrington. Its function was not merely to arrange concerts of military bands (which were intended for almost every weekday between May and September), but to judge them competitively. A form was drawn up for marking the bands according to time, tune, expression, execution, attack, phrasing, ensemble

and solo playing. There were grandiose plans for involving foreign bands in the process. Many of the bands, however, declined to take part in such a system, for £7-£10 per engagement. The dissolution of the Music Committee, however, did not put an end to musical activities in the garden, such as George William Martin's 5,000-voice choir concert in 1869. Provision for the band concerts took the form of two bandstands by Fowke on the upper terrace, whose eventual fate was, on the dismemberment of the garden, to be distributed to London parks (Peckham Rye and Southwark: a copy ended up on Clapham Common).[55]

The sad end of Prince Albert's hopes for a national centre of sculptural exhibitions came in the 1870s. John Henry Foley had exhibited 'A youth at a stream' in the living sculptors' exhibition in 1863, and agreed to make a marble copy for the Gardens for £500. Nothing further was heard until 1871, when he suddenly asked for payment. The Society honoured its commitment to buy the statue, but by then it was felt inappropriate to lavish money on sculptures, and the work was exhibited, to great acclaim, with a view to selling it. All efforts at selling it having fallen through, it was lent to the Commissioners for an exhibition in Sydney, Australia. It then returned, languished, and was eventually given to the Commissioners. (It soon vanished from sight, until it was rediscovered in a cupboard in the Albert Hall in 1985.)[56] There were no more purchases of sculptures: removals, rather. Most intriguing is a statement in Council Minutes for 8 November 1881 that statuary from the Garden, having been spotted in Old Bond Street, was being replaced in the garden; had there been a secret attempt to dispose of it? Those statues left in the garden at the time of its abandonment were moved to Chiswick, and disposed of as soon as possible after.

Chiswick reduced

> The old Horticultural Garden is well nigh forgotten; its glory has departed; and the world's (we mean the gardening world's) eyes are fixed upon South Kensington. The palatial architecture, waterfalls and basins, flower embroidery and tub decoration there have drawn attention from the humble fruit walls and plant houses, green turf, shady walks, fine trees, and country air of Chiswick. Gardening has to make way for music, South Kensington is the High Court of Horticulture, and Chiswick is consigned to the servants' hall.

Under Eyles and his new assistant Archibald Barron, 'Trimness and ornament have been discontinued, but in what concerns the health of

Archibald Barron (1835-1903), foreman at Chiswick from 1859, and later superintendent of the gardens at Chiswick and Kensington. Author of Vines and Vine Culture, *the only English book on the subject to be translated into French.*

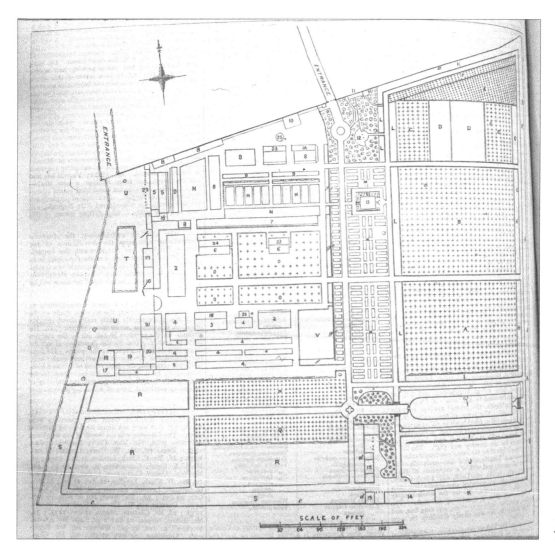

*Plan of the Chiswick
garden after truncation
in the 1870s.*

plants and their successful treatment there is
nothing to desire'.[57] That was in 1862: with the
passage of a few years, the reports on Chiswick
became ever more alarmed. The plants were 'in a
state that would disgrace any nursery garden' in
1865; in 1867, one visitor cried, 'oh, horrible! The
orchard appeared one mass of Sow Thistles,
Groundsel, and Couch Grass. Has the Society let
it to some of the Dudley Street London bird-
catchers? or are the weeds in question left for the
studies of the certificated Chiswick students?' To
which the editors replied: 'It is the old story of
scanty means.' What seemed to be receiving the
greatest attention was the plants being grown for
bedding at Kensington: 'is Chiswick to be for ever
a mere hospital for invalid Kensingtonians?'[58]

In 1870 came the bombshell: the announcement that Chiswick had to be abandoned. The
gardening press struck immediate attitudes, some
opposing, some looking forward to a garden that

would have to be called 'New Chiswick'. When
Council backtracked, the *Gardeners' Chronicle*,
which had publicly gritted its teeth and reconciled
itself to the loss, grumbled, 'So the Council of the
Royal Horticultural Society has had its joke. It
assured us, with tear in eye and hand on heart, that
Chiswick *must* be given up, and assigned sundry
and numerous reasons for the abandonment.'[59] At
any rate, agreement was reached with the Duke of
Devonshire on the abandonment of two-thirds of
the garden, and the retention of the ten acres
nearest Chiswick Park, as more easily managed.
Over the next few years, new streets would be
ploughed through and houses built (but
incorporating some surviving pear trees in back
gardens), so that today the only evidence on the
map that there was once a garden on the site is a
little cul-de-sac called Horticultural Place.

Much of the arboretum, the north-eastern
portion of the garden, was swept away, and the

area retained was sacrificed to the reorganisation of the fruit tree collection, a wet season aiding the work of transplanting. Barron determined to make Chiswick once again the centre for excellence in fruit that it had once been; the vinery at least was consolidating its reputation as the outstanding grape collection in the country; and Barron continued the drive either to build new or convert old glasshouses for further fruit trials. A plan was put forward by the Revd John Fountaine for a glasshouse with a built-in railway, for ease of moving plants indoors and out. A Fountaine house was installed at Chiswick in 1869, and worked well enough to survive for decades.[60]

In the ornamental garden, Chiswick was also responding to changes in fashion. During the 1870s, the herbaceous border was one of the most highly praised features, the curtilage of the Council Room was turned over to a display of smaller perennials, of the sort that got lost in herbaceous borders (daisies, campanulas, primulas), while elsewhere there were trial displays of 167 varieties of double pelargoniums, of achimenes, pansies, and the new tuberous begonias.[61] Most importantly, in 1878, a new rockery was created, and stocked with primulas, saxifrages, campanulas, cyclamens, hepaticas, androsaces, and other alpines donated by George Maw (including iberis he collected in eastern Europe), Isaac Anderson-Henry, and George Fergusson Wilson.[62] Some observers thought that Chiswick would 'brighten and glow into a fuller blaze of floral interest as the clouds of disaster gather over South Kensington'.

But the clouds hung over Chiswick too, and not only because of smog from the encroaching suburbs. Expenditure on Chiswick was cut back in 1876 and again in 1886, this last time by a triumvirate of Council members—Michael Foster, the physician and iris grower, the Duke of Marlborough, and Colonel Beddome, the great authority on Indian ferns. Beddome oversaw a massive sale of orchids in December 1886; Marlborough suggested that Chiswick should develop a nursery, growing plants on a large scale for commerce.[63]

Alterations and decline at Kensington

> When the late lamented Prince Consort conceived the noble plan of uniting Horticulture with Architecture, Sculpture, and Painting as sister arts, the idea was hailed with delight by the foremost and most intelligent of our horticulturists ... The wisest could not foresee that by his untimely death the fundamental idea would not only be rendered abortive but positively reversed—that Horticulture, invited as a sister, would be treated as a slave.[64]

Within a couple of years of the opening of the garden, complaints began to be heard about its lack of shelter, and more particularly about the problems of air pollution. Grumbles about 'sooty shrubs, in mockery called evergreens' and 'miserable-looking, soot-begrimed trees and plants growing (?) there' modulated into denunciations that 'They talked of carrying out a school of Art, when they were not able to keep the gardens in ordinarily proper order.' (By 1869 the araucarias and deodars were dying, and had to be removed.)[65] The Kensington garden Committee called Nesfield back into consultation, to receive from him a rebuke on the way the plans had been handled. 'As mature trees are indispensable adjuncts to scenery, the levels of the architecture should have been adjusted as nearly as possible to the levels of such sites of existing tall trees, as were fit to be retained', he scolded them, whereas the site had been cleared of mature trees and their place supplied by transplanting. The demand for canals had interfered with his plans for massed planting, leaving the entire site too open. His response was to plant more trees and create groves, narrow the open space with hornbeam hedges, and screen the undecorated walls with arbor-vitae up to the height of the copings.[66] By 1864 some of Nesfield's instructions had been carried out: hedges and fences of yew, poplar and laurel had been planted, dividing the ground and narrowing the central walk. Immediately there were complaints about the restrictions of view. The landscape gardener Joseph Newton, at this time a disciple of Nesfield, protested, 'Surely he never can permit his beautiful Italian garden to be converted into a drill ground'. Queen Victoria, however, expressed approval of the alterations.[67]

The improvements had been pushed forward by Sir Henry Cole, now a Council member, as the Society's part of a programme which he demanded the Commissioners take part in as well. The Commissioners proving recalcitrant, a committee was set up including Cole, Sir Joseph Paxton, James Bateman, Samuel Reynolds Hole and other horticultural luminaries, to advise on further changes. Immediate recommendations included planting the grass slopes with variegated ivy, box, and rhododendrons, but budget cuts curtailed any further developments.[68] Additional protected cultivation was also provided: in 1864 an orchard house was erected at the northern entrance, which, after James Bateman had stocked it with orchids at his own expense, slid effortlessly into being an orchid house instead. Some years later, when the Commissioners reclaimed the building, Council determined that Bateman had no rights to the collection, and sold it.[69]

Meanwhile, fashions in gardening were changing, and the box-and-gravel style of Nesfield was rapidly falling from favour; by the 1870s he was being overruled on parterre planting by his own clients. *The Times* took to describing the gravel parterres as 'stony deceptions', and in 1870 the parterres and friezes were grassed over. The maze nearly met the same fate, but was reprieved.[70] The new fashions in bedding, especially carpet-bedding, were essayed at Kensington, and Eyles duly praised for his skill in each new genre. Nonetheless, by the mid-1870s, it was difficult to find articles praising the Kensington garden, although neglect enforced by the Society's increasing financial problems no doubt augmented the purely stylistic rejection. Almost the last significant works to be carried out in the gardens, in the early 1870s, were instigated by the Commissioners: sunken walks across the garden for the benefit of visitors to exhibitions; and work even on these was suspended in 1873. In 1878, however, under the supervision of the Assistant Secretary Samuel Jennings, Karl Siemens carried out an important experiment in electric lighting for a gala event, and illuminations continued to form part of exhibitions during the garden's last decade.[71]

In 1875 a new threat to the gardens emerged as the result of a court case in Brighton. Invoking an 18th-century law, a sabbatarian zealot brought an action against the Brighton Aquarium for opening on Sundays. (In 1862, the Sabbath Alliance had already forced the Edinburgh Botanic Garden's closure on that day.) The consequences of the case for the RHS were mentioned in the press ('There is no distinction between a lion and an octopus and a rhododendron as elements of amusement, and it is evident that the Zoological, the Botanical, and the Horticultural Gardens must, like the Brighton Aquarium, close their gates on Sundays'), and in the court itself. The Lord Chief Baron reluctantly found the Aquarium guilty ('with a degree of repugnance beyond his power to express'), but said in his summing-up that he hoped the case would provoke a reform of the law on Sunday opening: 'Except for the hope he had just expressed, he would feel considerable alarm for the Horticultural gardens.' In the event, a new Act was rushed through Parliament to remit the penalties incurred under the older Act, the Aquarium resumed Sunday opening, and no case involving the RHS came to court.[72]

The arcades were gradually taken back by the Commissioners for use in their exhibitions, beginning with the south arcade, and the entrances to the garden effectively passed out of the Society's control, even before the Commissioners issued their writ of ejectment in 1879. The Royal Albert Hall was built to the north of the garden, and opened in 1871; this was initially a matter of intense interest to the Society, because Council hoped to get exhibition and access privileges. By contrast, the building of the Natural History Museum (opened 1881) to the south of the garden received no comment in Council minutes; the southern arcade effectively no longer belonged to the Society, so there could be little interest in what lay beyond it.[73] The Society did, however, become involved to varying degrees with the smaller International Exhibitions staged in the 1880s. The popularity of these exhibitions was so great that the Metropolitan and District Railway proposed to build a tunnel from South Kensington Station to the entrance of the garden. The tunnel was opened in 1885, and a penny toll charged for its use; the fee was probably too high, and the following year it was closed as unprofitable, and thereafter used for special occasions only; it was finally re-opened, without tolls, in 1908, but by that time the garden it had been intended to reach was a distant memory.[74]

The last years at Chiswick

After 1888, the Society was once again left with Chiswick as its sole garden, which it now concentrated on trying to turn into 'the Kew of horticulture'. The garden's role was defined as focusing on fruit and vegetable cultivation, trials of these and ornamental plants, experiments in culture, and trials of tools.[75] And trials indeed there were, of potatoes, lettuce, rhubarb, of annuals, ivies, asters, carnations, chrysanthemums, pelargoniums, phlox, sweet peas, violas. These, together with the series of conferences beginning in the 1880s, helped to focus the public mind on Chiswick—as, no doubt, did advertising in the local railway stations.

The experiments on boilers and glazing continued; greenhouses underwent continual repair. Skinner Board erected a wire-tension greenhouse, later turned into a peach house. T.C. Bréhaut, the man credited with introducing diagonal espalier training into England, complained in the 1880s of the mixture of different fruits in the same house; as the 1890s progressed, more houses were built specifically for one category (peach house, Gros Colmar house).[76] But all the while came the pressures to bring in some income from commercial produce. In 1889 the garden began to sell cut flowers; in 1894, to supply grapes to the Leadenhall Fruit and Vegetable

Samuel Thomas Wright (1858-1922), last superintendent of Chiswick and first of Wisley. Author of Fruit-culture for Amateurs, etc. The *Journal of Horticulture said of him in 1896, 'He will drop a cultural hint readily enough, but as to extracting his personal opinion on varieties on trial it is clearly no use attempting. He is a good deal like his predecessor in one thing, and that is in the possession of skill in "not knowing".'*

Supply Association. The *Gardeners' Chronicle* condemned efforts to sell Chiswick produce—'to attempt to combine an experimental garden with a commercial establishment is to neglect the one department, and to conduct the other unsatisfactorily'—and recommended that it should be 'a great reference-garden, where authentically-named specimens of the best fruit trees, and the best vegetables, should be grown for reference and comparison', in effect calling for a return to its original purposes of the 1820s.[77] Finally in 1895 came an attack by Peter Barr on the 'starvation allowance' of £1,600 for annual expenditure,[78] followed soon by the forced retirement of Archibald Barron, and one last press attack on the Society's administration for the way he had been treated. Whatever Council's plans were for the rejuvenation of Chiswick under his successor, S.T. Wright, they were not to be accomplished on the traditional site.

For Chiswick no longer enjoyed the environment it once had. The District Railway had reached Turnham Green in 1877, to feed the new garden suburb of Bedford Park, which occupied the site of John Lindley's former garden to the north-east of Chiswick. Domestic coal fires and railway smoke were more than sufficient to bring the gloomy London fog; between the 1860s and the 1890s the local population grew from 6,000 to 40,000. Outdoor plants suffered, the rate of greenhouse repair increased, not to mention the need to wash the grime off the glass regularly; the Scientific Committee examined the question of air pollution; in 1897, James Hudson claimed that the garden he administered at Gunnersbury Park had a more protected climate than Chiswick.[79] Despite the activities of a committee on the improvement of Chiswick, and glasshouse re-building as late as 1898, the conviction was growing that the Society needed a new garden, away from the polluted vicinity of London.

Various locations were scrutinised. A site at Limpsfield, belonging to the Caxton Convalescent Home, seemed the most promising; the negotiations were revealed to the press, a map of the site published, and a special general meeting convened to discuss the matter, before it was abandoned (1899-1900). A site at South Darenth was the next favourite (1901), and got as far as printed notices and a proposed poll of the membership; Swanley was also examined. The press weighed in with recommendations for the new garden, and debate about the relative merits of a garden and an exhibition hall. Meanwhile, a committee on the improvement of Chiswick was meeting, and plants adjudged worthless were being destroyed. In the summer of 1903 came the news that Sir Thomas Hanbury was prepared to acquire the late George Fergusson Wilson's garden at Wisley, to present it to the Society as a replacement for Chiswick, and as soon as the legal negotiations were completed, the plans for Wisley came in a rush. £100 was spent on acquiring a small boundary strip of land for Chiswick, deemed necessary in order to sell the lease. The local council reportedly wanted the garden for public open space, but the Council minutes contain no notice of negotiations. Finally, in August 1904, the sale was agreed of the ten acres through Tyser, the estate agents, for the sum of £12,500, and the deed was sealed that December.[80]

The move to Wisley began in the autumn of 1903, and continued into the spring of 1904. Once the move was completed, all that remained was to dispose of the abandoned garden stock. An auction was held on 10 March, and apart from intense competition for yuccas and carnations, the sales were disappointing. Most of the fruit trees went for small prices, probably because of the difficulty and expense of moving them; 'a choice Fig-tree in a large pot for 2s. was too absurd, but [the auctioneer] could get no more'; the peach trees remained unsold. Sentiment, as the press remarked, was 'notably absent' from the whole proceeding.[81]

> But the scene is changed, and the Chiswick of our sentiment has ended her historical record. With the sale of the plants, shrubs, and trees about a month ago, almost the last event had come to pass, but the finale and exeunt will be performed when the present superintendent closes the small iron gates for the last time on Saturday evening of this week. And he shall say, and we all shall say, 'Chiswick! Farewell!'[82]

5 The Society's Gardens: Wisley

George Fergusson Wilson (1822-1902), industrial chemist and director of Messrs Price, candle makers, whose offices in Wandsworth were demolished while this book was being written. Inventor of Gishurst compound. Council member, and Treasurer 1866-68. Original owner of Wisley.

Right, his design for the 'Wilson raft'.

FACING PAGE
The Wisley Laboratory, with the canal garden boasting a collection of waterlily cultivars.

WHEN G.F. Wilson bought his property at Wisley in 1878, he was already a celebrated horticulturist, whose garden at Heatherbank, near Weybridge, was one of the influential wild gardens of its generation. No plans or even views of Heatherbank were published in the press; the illustrations that appeared were of details—a group of snowdrops or of cyclamens—but that is consistent with the rhetoric of the wild garden at the time, which emphasised the beauty of particular plant combinations rather than large-scale planning.[1] Although it contained greenhouse ranges for orchids and fruit, and a cottage garden ('Gishurst Cottage') for his head gardener, these features were seldom described, and never depicted. Attention focused rather on his naturalised bulbs, his lilies, cistus, and veronicas, the rootery planted with skimmias and andromedas, and the 'Wilson raft', his attempt to create a miniature bog

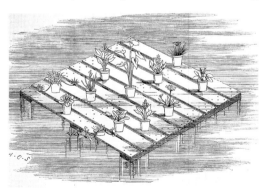

garden—constructed of small logs, with a basal layer of cork to give it buoyancy, but weighted so that it was submerged by a couple of inches, pots being placed at varying heights according to the water requirements of the plants. 'To make a bog without some help from Nature is by no means easy,' wrote Wilson, 'and when made requires attention. Now, any one with an open tank

supplied with water can put into it an inexpensive raft, which will enable water, bog, marsh, and damp soil plants to grow, thrive, and take care of themselves.'[2]

Wilson appears to have offered Heatherbank to the Society in 1870, at a time when the boundaries of the Chiswick garden were being re-negotiated, but nothing came of this.[3] In 1878, he acquired a second property, some five miles from Heatherbank:

> A friend happening to mention a small farm to be sold at Wisley, I went over it, and saw in the old, undisturbed Oak wood such vegetation, showing the richness of the soil, that, on getting home, I said, 'If we get the place, I can make such a garden as has not been made before.'

The resulting garden was named Oakwood, but—possibly because the orchid grower Norman Cookson also had a garden called Oakwood—was often referred to in the press as Wisley. Both Heatherbank and Wisley were described as wild gardens or woodland gardens, but Wilson preferred to use the phrase 'experimental garden' for both: 'It is an enormous advantage to be able in the same garden to try a plant under half a dozen conditions.'

> The greater portion of the Wisley garden occupies the north side of a hill, the ground, sloping gently, terminates in a woody swamp, in some places so quaggy that the soil trembles under the foot as one passes over it. The natural soil in this moist wood is just about the same as that which prevails in some of the German and Belgian forests, and which is so highly prized in those countries for potting purposes.

As with Heatherbank, neither Wilson nor press correspondents commented on principles of design except by remarking on the variety of soil conditions and microclimates. Fairly late in Wilson's career, one writer suggested the influence of Dropmore on its layout, but in view of the

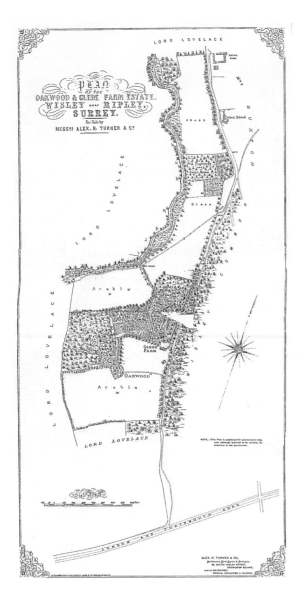

canvas protection in winter; a propagating nursery so subdivided by hurdles (iron, covered with green scrim) that it could be mistaken for a sheepfold. 'The variety of flowers is bewildering': thus summed up the press. Nor was public knowledge of the garden limited to what could be read in the press: visits to Oakwood were well organised, and in the 1890s, when he was in his 70s, Wilson posted a notice: 'Mr G.F. Wilson requests that visitors who have cards of admission will come between three and half past four. Before this time work is interfered with, after it, the "shower-round" is often tired.'

Wilson died in 1902, and Council, then in the throes of looking for a new garden away from the air pollution of the London suburbs, immediately made enquiries about the future of Wisley; but the tension between the advocates of a new exhibition hall and the proponents of a garden paralysed Council when it came to fundraising. At the beginning of August 1903, Sir Thomas Hanbury approached Council with a secret offer: that he buy Wisley and present it to the Society as an experimental garden. One of those privy to the secret was Ellen Willmott, to whom Hanbury revealed that Thiselton-Dyer, the Superintendent of Kew and a former RHS staff member, was opposed to the idea. But Council accepted the proposal, and a Trust was set up to safeguard Hanbury's gift: his cousin Cecil Hanbury, Ellen Willmott, and John T. Bennett-Poë were appointed Trustees. The gift was announced in October. S.T. Wright, the superintendent of Chiswick, was put in charge of planning the move, and over the course of the late autumn and winter of

Plan of Wilson's estate at Wisley, from the 1903 sale prospectus. Below is the first published view of Wisley, from the Gardeners' Chronicle for 1883.

multiplication of different environmental conditions, and Wilson's fondness for features such as rooteries and replications of alpine scenery (in 1888 he created 'a miniature mountain, modelled partly after a very old friend in Perthshire, Schiehallion', and planted it with hardy heaths from Darley Dale and evergreens from Anthony Waterer), James Bateman's Biddulph Grange is an equally likely influence.[4]

At Oakwood, Wilson experimented with a wide range of plants: calochortus, gentians, primulas, ferns, alpines; pitcher plants, waterlilies, poolside plantations of Japanese irises; anemones, trilliums, and hepaticas, not only in the woods but in the open; hedges of *Rosa rugosa*, an avenue of flowering cherries and crabapples; Sikkim rhododendrons with a surrounding framework for

1903-4 various plant collections and the impedimenta of the Chiswick garden were transferred to the new garden. The announcement that Wilson's gardener Tatnall would not be appointed to the Wisley staff caused a minor outcry, but for the most part the news was greeted with enthusiasm.[6]

Getting there

From the beginning, the excitement over the RHS's new garden was tempered with apprehensions over its inaccessibility. Before Hanbury's appearance on the scene, an agreement with an unidentified purchaser had fallen through, because of the travel difficulties. 'If it had been more conveniently situated,' commented the *Gardening World*, 'such a fine garden could hardly fail to excite the envy of many, and the desire to possess it.' Soon after the announcement of its takeover, the fern grower C.T. Druery published a comic 'Dream of Wisley', in which he imagined the problem resolved within the next century by the invention of Röntgen-powered cars which would allow nearly instantaneous transportation. Council indeed devoted much thought to the cost of cab fares to Wisley, and the possibility of organising a bus service; the improvement of a 'disgraceful' road was one of the first priorities on moving in (though a quarter of a century later it was still described as 'shocking'). The nearest railway station, Byfleet (later renamed West Byfleet), was four miles away, and the walk, though pleasant, 'too long for many'. The fact that the Society's first published directions to Wisley contained errors did not help.[7]

The first year for which figures were published was 1905, and the number of visitors was 5,250—already more than Chiswick had received in its last years. By 1908 it had increased to 11,000; during the War it was a popular retreat; by the late 1920s attendance had reached 48,000. When it is considered that at that latter date the number of automobiles in Britain was just passing one million for the first time, these figures bespeak a reasonable enthusiasm on the part of the Fellows (for the garden did not open to the public until 1934). In 1926 Robert Fife proposed a motion, seconded by none other than the Garden's Director, Frederick Chittenden, that the RHS abandon Wisley as unsuitable and look for another more accessible garden; the magazine *Garden Life* responded by urging Fellows 'to acquire the "Wisley habit," then charabanc proprietors will do the rest, for they are not lacking in enterprise'.[8] While one can hear stories of visitors in the post-war years remarking that it was a busy day at Wisley if there were a dozen cars

Sale notice for the Wisley property, 1903.

By Order of the Executors of the Late G. F. Wilson, Esq. F.R.S.,

WISLEY COMMON,

About 3½ miles from Byfleet Station, 4 miles from Horsley Station, 5 miles from Weybridge, and about 1½ miles from Ripley Village.

Particulars, Plan, Views and Conditions of Sale

OF THE

Valuable Freehold Estate

KNOWN AS

"OAKWOOD" & "GLEBE FARM,"

Situate a short distance from the main Portsmouth Road, bounded on one side by the lovely Wisley Common and sloping to the River Wey, with boat-house thereon.

COMPRISING

A GENTLEMAN'S SMALL RESIDENCE,

Farm House and Buildings,

Charming Gardens and Grounds in an Oak Wood,

And far famed

Alpine, Rock, Wood, and Water Gardens,

Probably the finest in this country,

ALSO

WELL TIMBERED GRASS AND ARABLE LAND,

In all about **60** *Acres.*

MESSRS. ALEX. H. TURNER & CO.

Are instructed by the Executors of the late G. F. Wilson, Esq., F.R.S., to sell the foregoing Valuable Freehold Estate by Auction

At the Mart, Tokenhouse Yard, E.C.

On WEDNESDAY, the 6th day of MAY, 1903.

At ONE o'clock, unless previously sold.

Particulars may be obtained of Messrs. WILSON, BRISTOWS & CARPMAEL, Solicitors, 1 Copthall Buildings, E.C., and together with cards to view (without which the property cannot be viewed), of the Auctioneers, 69, South Audley Street, Grosvenor Square, W., and at Weybridge, Woking, Guildford and Reading.

in the carpark, or of staff clustering to a window because there was someone in the Garden, the statistics tell a different story. By 1957 there were 170,000 visitors; in that year a road was being extended through Wisley village. By 1978 the 400,000 mark had been passed, by 1985 the 500,000 mark, and by 1987 the 600,000 mark; by that time two motorways had been carved through Surrey, and Wisley was nestled in the corner of their junction. Public transport was never significantly improved, however, until 1995, when a seasonal minibus service was arranged between Woking and Wisley; the bus shelter on the A25 became a perennial subject for debate with Guildford Council as it repeatedly succumbed to vandalism.

The Wisley Laboratory

The first big building project undertaken at Wisley was the creation of a Laboratory, for the dual purposes of scientific research and training. The Laboratory was opened on Friday, 19 July 1907, by the biologist and social reformer Lord Avebury, who declared:

The erection of this laboratory and research station meets a long-felt want in connection with the Society's work. In the United States and in our Colonies there are several such stations under Government supervision and maintenance, but in the home country the initiation, direction and support is left to private enterprise.

This Laboratory was architecturally unpretentious: a brick building with tiled roofs, looking much like a suburban house, arranged in a T-block with a greenhouse attached to one side, overlooking the glasshouse range.[9]

Within a few years the Laboratory was starting to feel pinched. In 1914, a local firm with the evocative name of Pine-Coffin, Imrie and Angell was hired to expand the building; Imrie was the principal architect. The original Laboratory was encased within wings extending to either side, shifting its orientation by 90 degrees, and its exterior completely rebuilt. The new Laboratory was a building very much in the mode of Lutyens and Webb, modelled on vernacular buildings in Surrey, and adopting the general form of a small manor house.

> Externally the building is treated in a manner probably best described as picturesque. The front towards the road is faced with thin hand-made bricks laid with wide joints; the bricks are rough on the surface and vary in colour, the general tint being a low tone of purple pink. The front facing the Garden has a plinth of similar bricks, with which also the chimney-stacks are faced; above the plinth the walls are treated with oak half-timbering, filled in with rough plastering. The roof is covered with old tiles collected from various parts of the country.
>
> All the window frames are of oak, with metal casements and leaded glazing. The entrance doors are also of oak, studded with wrought-iron nails and hung on armour-bright wrought-iron hinges, with furniture to match ...

The decorative half-timbering is not (or no longer) characteristic of many old Surrey houses, but probably owes more to the example of George Crawley, whose pre-war Surrey houses, like Crowhurst Place, were designed to create the sort of Tudor effect that Norman Shaw had pioneered in other parts of the country. As the laboratory was an extension to an original building, it was designed to create the impression of a building that had been extended over generations, at the expense of an original symmetry. Built on a sloping site, it was given three ground levels, with three corresponding roof levels and three patterns of chimneys.

The entrance lobby on the garden front, protected from the elements by an internal porch

The Laboratory at Wisley, under reconstruction during the First World War.

bounded by a glazed screen, was fitted with an oak dado and oak-panelled ceiling; also in oak were the Jacobean-style staircase and first-floor gallery. The principal windows on the entrance front were decorated with stained glass by Herbert Bryans. From the visitor's point of view, the entrance lobby recalls one of Norman Shaw's great halls, minus fireplace and inglenook. From the staff's point of view, the building suffers from an incapacity for worthwhile expansion: it is a narrow building, all of whose offices open onto a single central corridor, and on no level can one walk the length of the building without ascending or descending stairs—not the most convenient layout for a laboratory. The Library, on the first floor, was also fitted with oak mouldings, but most of the offices were left in more utilitarian style.[10]

The Laboratory, like most neo-Tudor buildings of the early 20th century, was long dismissed by the architectural press, noted by Pevsner only with a sniff, and passed over in silence by county tourists. In the late 20th century, its style gradually returned, if not quite to favour, at least to a degree of sympathetic attention from architectural historians, and it was listed (Grade II) in 1985.

The development of a garden 1

S.T. Wright, the last Superintendent of Chiswick, was also the first Superintendent of Wisley. A practical gardener by training, his role at Chiswick was uncluttered by a school of horticulture or by scientific research, and his role at Wisley carried on seamlessly; until his death in 1922, he was responsible for the maintenance of the garden, the administration of trials, and the distribution of plants. The initial works at Wisley, apart from the erection of greenhouses, involved new planting rather than garden construction; Wilson's wild garden, it was decided, should be kept as far as possible in the manner he had begun it. A collection of ornamental trees was planted in rough pasture to the west of the woodland garden; in 1907, work began on a pinetum, which proved unsuccessful.[11] But one of the last significant features at Chiswick had been a rock garden, and within a few years a new rock garden for Wisley was being planned.

A small rock garden had existed at Wisley, above the waterlily ponds—E.A. Bowles was to describe it as 'poor but honest'. F.W. Meyer, the rockwork designer for the firm of Robert Veitch and Sons, whose writings on rock gardens were to

The rock garden at Wisley, photographed in 1914.

The rock garden at Wisley, from an illuminated vellum album presented to Sir Trevor Lawrence on his retirement, commemorating the achievements of his Presidency.

be published posthumously by *Country Life*, was hired to create a new rock garden, but he had barely received his instructions to secure 500 tons of stone when he died, and the project was suspended. In 1910 it was revived; Ellen Willmott, whose own rock garden had been designed by the firm of Backhouse of York, offered to help with its provision, but the contract had already been put out to tender. Pulham and Son, of Broxbourne, Hertfordshire, won the contract, and made the rock garden under the supervision of the landscape gardener Edward White. A two-acre bank above the ponds was chosen as the site; a 12,000-gallon tank was built at the top with pipes laid eight inches below the surface, and holes bored at intervals for irrigation; hundreds of tons of Sussex sandstone were brought to the site on temporary tramways, and arranged in massive blocks with a waterfall and pools descending the slope. Sir Frank Crisp, whose garden at Friar Park, Henley, boasted one of the most extensive rock gardens in the country, and who had recently gone into partnership with Waterers to provide them with alpines, donated a large quantity of plants. Altogether some 65,000 plants were used initially, and still left enough gaps for critics to grumble about.[12]

The rock garden was a great success, and the first new feature of Wisley to become part of the garden's public image. 'It seems natural for almost everyone who visits Wisley to go first to see the rock-garden', remarked the *Gardeners' Chronicle* in 1920. But the RHS had higher ambitions with the establishment of Wisley than merely a beautiful garden, namely scientific research and a school of horticulture. Frederick Chittenden became Director of the School in 1907, but clearly had his eye on greater things. With the re-organisation of the scientific establishment in 1914, the new post of Director of the Garden was created, and Frederick Keeble was appointed to it over Chittenden's head. Whatever role Keeble might have played in the garden was curtailed by the First World War and his secondment to the Ministry of Agri-

culture; Chittenden finally succeeded him to the Directorship in 1919, and immediately began to institute changes in the garden.

The area now known as Seven Acres had been planted by Wright with a variety of ornamental trees, which did not flourish, because an iron pan militated against satisfactory root growth. This became Chittenden's first big project as Director. It may, of course, be completely coincidental that the first question in the Landscape Gardening section of the NDH final exam in 1916 read:

> The outline plan of the land adjoining the Superintendent's house at Wisley with the position of the house marked is given you. It is proposed to make a garden of the land shown (about 7 acres). Measure it and ascertain the levels (the necessary implements are provided). Draw a plan of the garden you would suggest ...

Whether any of the students' answers had a bearing on the subsequent layout cannot now be determined, as none of the papers has survived. But in 1919 Chittenden organised the digging and replanting of the area, breaking up the pan; a pond was excavated, and the earth thus thrown up formed into mounds on which groups of sorbus, berberis, and other shrubs were planted. The prevalence of heathers on Wisley and Ockham Commons, and the tendency of outcrops of ling to do well in the former pasture, prompted Chittenden to add a heather garden as part of the complex. The resulting composition accorded well with a new taste for glades and open lawns; Francis Hanger was later to exclaim,

> This masterpiece of landscape design will always remain a monument to its designer. Strangers to Wisley emerging from the shady darkness of the Wild Garden, to come suddenly upon the open spaces of Seven Acres, never fail to express appreciation when they view the Heather Garden immediately before them, and away to the east the pond with its Nymphaeas and Weeping Willows.[13]

S.T. Wright died in 1922, to be commemorated by a sundial, and Council decided not to appoint another Superintendent, but instead to create the new role of Assistant Director. (This suggests that there had been a degree of friction between Wright and his effective superior, which Council were determined to eliminate.) The decision proved controversial; Lionel de Rothschild upbraided Council for eliminating the head gardener's role; the garden staff complained about their claims to promotion being passed over (Chittenden's reply was that there were no suitable candidates). A member of the Laboratory staff, the Assistant Demonstrator Arthur

Simmonds, was chosen for the post, even though one prominent Council member, Gerald Loder, thought him 'not the type of man required in the best interests of the Society'. Within a year the press was criticising the management of the garden, complaining of understaffing and poor maintenance, and collectively arguing that 'the function of Wisley is to be beautiful', and that this aim was best accomplished by having a head gardener in position. In 1925 Simmonds was moved to London to become Assistant Secretary for the Society as a whole. Once again the job title was changed, to Keeper (an ambiguous title, because there was already a Keeper of the Laboratory), and Robert Findlay, with experience as head gardener at Logan and at Castle Kennedy, and most recently as Superintendent of Greenwich Park, was hired.[14] By this time there was a hierarchy of posts within the garden, with Floral, Fruit and Vegetable, Rock Garden, and Glasshouse Departments each having a Super-intendent in charge of staff, or frequently students.

Imrie and Angell, in 1925, designed a new gatehouse, which was built by the Wisley staff; memorial gates in honour of William Wilks, incorporating the device of the Shirley poppy, were added at the same time. The other major alterations of the Chittenden years were the creation of a rose garden on Weather Hill, to the south-west of the Laboratory and the floral trial grounds; a partial remodelling of the rock garden; the laying of a broad grass walk from Seven Acres through the pinetum at the northern end of the garden, requiring the bridging of a public footpath; the planting of birches and maples amid the flagging conifers in the pinetum; the replacement of an old orchard by a lilac garden in the area known as Howard's Field, beyond the pinetum; and the creation of the alpine meadow on the east of the rock garden. This meadow, abutting the wild garden and framed on other sides by maples and bamboos, was studded with

boulders supplied by Mark Fenwick of Abbots-wood, so that it would blend gradually into the rock garden, and was planted with naturalised bulbs. Once again, Francis Hanger's infectious enthusiasm shows its reputation at mid-century: 'The Alpine Meadow, so beautifully natural with its plantings of miniature Daffodils, together with Crocus species in their thousands—surely this Alpine Meadow, during March and April, is difficult to rival anywhere in this country!'[15]

Impressive as Seven Acres, the rock garden, and the alpine meadow were, however, the end of the 1920s saw harsh questions being asked about the accomplishments of Wisley.

And for all the money which has been spent on it (about £180,000 in Maintenance and about £50,000 in Capital) how much nearer is Wisley to that envious position the 'foremost horticultural institution of its kind in the world,' which the committee visualised? ... From an arboricultural standpoint the place is of little account; from the horticultural point of view it does not compare too favourably with dozens of private gardens on which far less money is spent ...[16]

A view of the alpine meadow at Wisley.

The old Wisley gatehouse before the development of the modern shop complex.

Another shake-up followed; Chittenden was effectively kicked upstairs, and transferred to London; the Directorship of Wisley was given to R. L. Harrow, who had worked at the Edinburgh Botanic Garden for nearly forty years, and had a great reputation as a cultivator. His years at Wisley, however, were passed under the forbidding scrutiny of a Council and press exercised about the possibility of financial over-reach—not to mention the great depression. Extension of planting schemes rather than new construction was the focus of his term of office: the pinetum was gradually refurbished, Gerald Loder contributed a *Carpinus* collection, and a former dahlia trial ground was remodelled to form an AGM garden, for the display of plants that had received the Award of Garden Merit. The great development was the acquisition of well-wooded new land on the south of the garden, which was immediately seen as a site for rhododendron trials—Battleston Hill; but its development was interrupted by the Second World War.[17]

Wisley glass

Wisley had no glasshouses when the RHS acquired it; Wilson had used frames for propa-gating and winter protection, but his glasshouse ranges were located at his house at Heatherbank. Plans for greenhouses were drawn up in January 1904, and the first range completed the following year, to house the grapevines and figs moved from Chiswick, as well as peaches and melons, with sections for propagation and trials.[18] Before the First World War, orchid and orchard houses were added, and a small alpine house at the top of the rock garden, modelled on that of Eric Hambro at Hayes. The purpose of the alpine house was to provide protection for alpines accustomed to a winter covering of snow, which tended to rot in the wet British winter. This house was replaced in 1926-7 by a large 12-bay span house by Richardson of Darlington, the first glasshouse at Wisley deemed worthy of attention in the press. It received regular attention through the interwar years, but was finally demolished in the mid-1980s, when the deterioration of the wood made it difficult to operate. It was then replaced by two new alpine houses, the larger of which replaced the simple shelves and stages of its predecesor with an interior landscape.[19]

The emphasis on fruit in the early glasshouses was a direct continuation of the work at Chiswick; but after the First World War, the amount of glass

An aerial view of Wisley in the 1950s, looking east: just to right of centre is the Laboratory with the old glasshouse ranges extending to its west.

A view of the Laboratory and the old glasshouse range in 1955.

devoted to fruit was gradually cut back, to create space for increased collections of ornamental plants. By 1927, there was a 'comprehensive collection' of fuchsias under glass; in 1931 the collection of figs was discarded to make more space for greenhouse plant trials, and peaches and nectarines were progressively removed from the first house to accommodate half-hardy plants; one of the central houses was developed as a temperate house.[20] After the Second World War, some £2,700 had to be spent on repairs and renovations, and tentative plans were made for a new glasshouse beyond the model fruit gardens, but nothing happened for two decades. In 1966 a committee was set up to advise on the glass-houses, and George Sheard, the Director of the Glasshouse Crops Research Institute, drew up plans for a new range to be built on the site suggested back in 1949. Construction began in 1968, and the plants from the old range in front of the Laboratory were transferred in the spring of 1969, though it was not until the following year that the new range was fully opened. It consisted of four long rectangular houses, altogether covering over 20,000 square feet, aligned in parallel and connected by a central corridor. At the rear were propagating and service houses, then houses for trials, a vinery, and at the front a larger display house with three sections for different temperatures. Slipped in between the display house and the vinery were two small 'amateur greenhouses' presented by the glass-house manufacturer R.F. Strawson, to demon-

Francis W. Hanger (1900-1961), head gardener at Exbury from 1927, and Curator of Wisley 1946-61. Celebrated for his ability to create magnificent displays at flower shows as well as for his development of Battleston Hill.

strate to visitors the increasing variety of automatic control mechanisms available. The passing of the old glasshouse range, which was demolished to make way for a new water garden, was met with no obvious signs of regret in the press; but one unanticipated effect of the new glasshouse range was that the rates for Wisley suddenly jumped by £1,000.[21]

Within a few years the number of glasshouses had been increased, with a group of three further structures built to the south-east of the large range. The Stanley Smith Trust grant-aided the construction of an orchid house in three sections, which was named in its honour; alongside, a smaller house for epiphytic orchids, and other plants requiring similar conditions, was donated by the Cambridge Glasshouse Company and built of aluminium. The third house, in a line with the latter, was made of cedar wood, devoted to cacti and succulents, and named in honour of Vera Higgins, the Society's former editor, benefactor, and author of several books on the subject. Landscaped internally by Arthur Turner, it incorporated General Oliver Leese's collection of succulents, built up over forty years of collecting, which he donated to the Society.[22] The last addition to the glasshouse collection was a new wing leading from the main display house, constructed in 1991 with funding from Singapore Airlines, for the display of tropical orchids.[23]

The development of a garden 2

R.L. Harrow ran the Garden through the War years, with a new Keeper, J.W. Blakey, who succeeded Findlay in 1938. Blakey was by then an old hand, who had been with the Society since Chiswick, and distinguished himself as a propagator and hybridist. Blakey retired in 1945, and Harrow the following year. For the position of Director, a rising young botanist, John Gilmour, was chosen over the senior figure of John Macqueen Cowan. The title of Keeper was now changed to Curator, and the first man to hold the title was Francis Hanger, Lionel de Rothschild's head gardener at Exbury. Hanger had been a candidate for Blakey's post eight years earlier, and had been seconded to help the Society on food production matters during the War; he was immediately seen as the appropriate successor to Blakey, so much so that when Rothschild asked to be allowed to retain his services to help with post-war refurbishment at Exbury, the Curator-ship was left vacant for six months in anticipation. Hanger was to distinguish himself as an exhibitor, and a designer of exhibition gardens; but his first great project was Battleston Hill.[24]

Initial planting had been carried out on Battleston Hill at the end of the 1930s, fences and hedges installed, and a footpath cleared; but the War had stopped most activity apart from selective tree-felling. But it had immediately been seen as an excellent area for rhododendrons, an acre of ground had already been put to use for trials, and by the war's end there was a sufficient supply of rhododendrons that the Society could send stocks to Eric Savill for the planting of walks at Virginia Water. Over the half-century before its acquisition, a tradition had grown up in England of the creation of woodland gardens, with rhododendrons taking over from conifers as the principal planting, uniting the late Victorian themes of wild gardening and colour massing in the landscape; Bodnant, Sheffield Park, Leonardslee, and Exbury were significant milestones that Hanger would have been familiar

with.[25] He had already been involved with Battleston Hill before the war, when hybrids from Exbury were sent there for trial; now he secured donations of rhododendrons and azaleas from Exbury and Bodnant, from Charles Williams at Caerhays, from Sunningdale Nurseries, and from John Barr Stevenson at Tower Court. The clearance of dead larches from one side of the Hill left an open sunny area, so that azaleas could be distributed according to their tolerance for sun and shade; also planted in the sun was *Rhododendron yakushimanum*, which had caused great excitement at Chelsea in 1947. Through Stevenson's and Williams's contributions, the Hill boasted specimens of all the original 'Wilson 50' species, and a collection of Kurume azaleas, which were at the peak of fashion in the 1940s and 1950s, was added soon after. Hanger made no attempt at

an overt colour scheme, preferring 'one blaze of riotous colour'.[26]

Hanger's other immediate project was the planting of Portsmouth Field, part of the Battleston Hill purchase, consisting of four acres of land adjoining the Portsmouth Road. This had been used during the war for planting potatoes, and now was to be turned into a collection of Japanese cherries; largely through the work of Collingwood Ingram, the number of imported cultivars and new hybrids was steadily increasing both in number and popularity. Two transverse avenues, one of *Prunus yedoensis* and the other of 'Tai-Haku', were planted in 1947-8 to give the area a formal structure, and a large number of cultivars planted in the quadrants thus defined. A strip of woodland on the far side was turned into a camellia walk. Later in the 1950s, an acre and a half of land at the border between Battleston Hill and the cherry garden was devoted to a collection of Wisley-raised hybrid rhododendrons. In 1955, work began on turning one of the steeper slopes of Battleston Hill into a series of peat terraces for further rhododendron planting.

Hanger was to write that he 'had found from experience that Wisley cannot be classified as one of the favourably situated gardens of England', and made sweeping reductions of plants that were not succeeding in Wisley's climate or soil. He carried out major clearances in the Pinetum, replanting with new trees, including *Metasequoia*; removed the old *Rosa* species from Howard's Field and replaced them with a collection of *Malus* cultivars; cleaned out the long ponds and planted a collection of waterlilies donated by Exbury; partially replanted the rock garden, incorporating a collection of sempervivums; planted a collection of ferns from W.B. Cranfield in the wild garden. Two major collections of plants arrived at Wisley during the 1950s: dwarf conifers from A.H. Nisbet—150 plants arrived in the spring of 1956, and were planted in Seven Acres; and a diverse collection of plants from the late E.A. Bowles's garden at Myddelton House. Bowles had kept a portion of his garden as what he called his 'Lunatic Asylum', for atypical forms—variegated plants, contorted forms, unusual colour variants, and the like—and this

A postcard view of Battleston Hill in the 1960s, showing the sort of landscape colour that a later generation reacted against.

Francis Philip Knight (c.1903-1985), managing director of Notcutts' nursery 1944-54, then Director of Wisley 1955-69.

A view in the old potting shed at Wisley, since replaced by the loggia overlooking the canal.

principle governed the selection of planting: the twisted hazel *Corylus avellana* 'Contorta', *Salix babylonica* 'Crispa', *Buxus sempervirens* 'Bowles Blue', a variegated embothrium from Furzey. The area was originally called by Bowles's name of 'The Lunatic Asylum', but soon renamed 'Bowles's Corner'.[27]

The 1950s and 1960s saw a series of changes in the Wisley administration. Gilmour left the Society in 1951 to become Superintendent of the Cambridge Botanic Garden; his successor, Harold Fletcher, lasted three years and then made a similar move to Edinburgh. The Directorship was then back in the hands of a skilled practical gardener, Frank Knight. Hanger died in 1961, and no successor was appointed; Council felt that Knight was more than capable of combining the roles of Director and Curator. Christopher Brickell succeeded Knight in 1968, the first botanist to direct Wisley without a Curator working under him. The 1970s were not a favourable time financially to propose a major staff position, but in 1980, with a return to sounder finances, the position of Curator was re-established, and John Main, the Superintendent of Harlow Carr, was appointed to the position, to be succeeded in 1988 by Jim Gardiner.

Hanger's cherry garden did not long survive him; in 1970 the cherries were cleared from the Portsmouth Field to make way for a new Trials area. The rock garden was extended in 1964, with the addition of some 30 tons of Sussex sandstone and a series of scree beds. Island beds, the post-war alternative to herbaceous borders promoted by Alan Bloom, were laid out on the fringes of Seven Acres opposite the restaurant in the early 1960s.[28] But, apart from the model gardens, to be discussed shortly, the major project of the 1960s and 1970s was the redevelopment of the area in front of the Laboratory. Ever since the First World War, nearly every alteration made within sight of the Laboratory had been justified on the need to bring some more formal structure into that part of the garden, usually with attendant regret that nothing of the sort had been done initially. The terrace at the south end of the Laboratory had been formalised with the Wright memorial sundial in its centre; leading from it to Battleston Hill was the Broad Walk, flanked with herbaceous borders; rose beds had been created near the entrance, and rejuvenated at intervals with other forms of bedding. But the line of glasshouses, while rectilinear enough, necessarily relegated

formal gardening to the fringes of the principal view. With the removal of the old glasshouses, the opportunity was created to create a central formal garden. Geoffrey Jellicoe was hired in 1969 to design a feature, and Lanning Roper, the Assistant Editor, who had by now developed an extensive practice as a garden designer, was commissioned to assist with its planting.

The new water garden was a long rectangular canal, sited asymmetrically with respect to the main door of the Laboratory, but centred on a projecting gabled abutment. Two square stone pools, positioned on either side at the Laboratory end, fed the canal through cascades; a fountain with multiple jets was installed halfway down. On either side a strip of lawn ran parallel to the tank, with walkways on the outer sides. At the opposite end from the Laboratory, the former potting shed was converted into a structure variously described

as a covered pergola, an open-sided pavilion, and a loggia. Roper described the proposed building in the *Journal*:

> At the far end, the potting shed is to be given a new look. It will be adapted to form an open loggia with water balconies, looking east along the canal and to the west over a walled garden, with colourful borders and a formal parterre with bedding schemes to replace those in the small beds along the cross-terrace walk. The brilliant carpet of wallflowers, myosotis, polyanthus and spring bulbs, followed by summer bedding, will make a pleasing contrast to the broad expanse of water in a predominantly green setting.

The loggia was planted with climbing plants, most notably a wisteria—all perhaps a grander echo of the wisteria-covered bridge that dated from Wilson's time, though Roper did not make the comparison. The walled garden was carried out as Roper planned, though some of his more elaborate features, like arches and a pleached lime hedge, either were not carried out or were soon removed.

In design terms, the canal garden quickly became the most frequently photographed view in the garden, and a generally acclaimed success. Behind the scenes, there was less jubilation. The work was completed in 1970; by the summer of 1971 it was discovered to be leaking. Twice during the course of 1972 it was emptied and repaired, and both times the leaks continued. After long disputes with both Jellicoe and the builders, none of whose proposed solutions worked for long, the Society ended by withholding final payments and putting the remaining money from the original contract into its own spot-repairs. But new leaks were reported in 1983, and the canal has since required periodic bouts of urgent maintenance.[29]

Other architectural works were put in hand during the 1960s and 1970s. The most publicised was the Memorial to the Society's President, Sir David Bowes Lyon, who died in 1961. A competition was held, and the design of an architectural student named Derrick Lees was chosen by the assessors as 'a dignified but light and elegant structure'. This was Lees's own explanation of the design:

> The design is contemporary, involving materials, techniques and ideas prevalent in this age. There are some classical elements in the design, which is formal and embodies a geometrical system of order that is carried through in three dimensions. Thus the measurements have their own inevitability ... New materials have made possible new opportunities ...
>
> I envisaged an undulating timber roof apparently floating over the Memorial stone in its site at the top of the rose borders. The two faceted roof lights of perspex are unusual and perhaps the first of their kind while the deeply recessed aluminium mouldings round the pillars, which give strong vertical reflections and shadows, provide some of the qualities of classical pillars. The structure is steel with timber framing and a teak ceiling finish. The paving is formed of reconstructed York stone. In the centre of the floor of the Pavilion is the Memorial stone of black marble, the inscription of which is beautifully carved by Mr. David Kindersley.

Nothing ages like the contemporary, and the Bowes Lyon Pavilion sank in esteem in the later years of the 20th century. Its cost of construction (even when carried out by the Wisley staff rather than outside builders) greatly exceeded the estimate, and perspex and aluminium did not prove the best materials for external use. Nonetheless, now that a renewed appreciation of (some) post-war architecture can be detected, it is possible that its reputation will rise again.[30]

In the mid-1970s, a new information centre was designed by Vernon Gibberd, and the development of RHS Enterprises meant that the gatehouse had to be extended into a new complex of buildings—which eventually swamped the information centre and forced its re-design. The replacement of the alpine house in the 1980s led to the redevelopment of its area: dry stone walls were built on its site, and a paved area created to accommodate stone sinks and troughs; around the smaller of the new alpine houses, raised beds of different kinds of rock were constructed. A new herb garden had already been made not far away, in front of the glasshouses, comprising four beds devoted to dye plants, scented plants, medicinal and culinary herbs. To the south of the Broad Walk, a hedged enclosure was planted in 1973 as a garden of new rose introductions, and in 1980 a demonstration garden of varieties of hedging was installed at the top of Weather Hill.[31]

But the major horticultural works of the 1970s and 1980s were the Jubilee Arboretum and the renovation of the rock garden. The Arboretum, named in honour of the Queen's silver jubilee, and opened by her in 1978, was a 32-acre area of former farmland extending south-west from Weather Hill. Many of the trees were donated by Harold Hillier, who needed to dispose of a large collection of trees from his nursery, supplemented by a grant of money when Council were tempted to reject the gift because of its maintenance costs. The area was landscaped as a series of seasonal walks, emphasising habit, foliage, or bark effect; species and cultivars of particular genera were grouped together, rather as in the Society's original arboretum at Chiswick.[32] The rock garden, meanwhile, had been deteriorating, with much rock gradually slipping downhill, and the narrow paths being eroded by the increased volume of visitor traffic. In 1980, a five-year reconstruction project was begun, starting at the west end nearest the alpine meadow; paths were widened and new foundations made, new stone inserted (Yorkshire stone was found the best match for the original Sussex stone), and the whole area replanted in succession.[33]

In 1984, Christopher Brickell was appointed the first Director-General of the Society, and moved away from the Wisley he had done so much to develop over the previous 16 years. His successors as Director of Wisley were Peter Maudsley, formerly of the Durham Botanic Garden (1985-6), and Philip Macmillan Browse, an experienced horticulturist and author of standard

Christopher Brickell, Director of Wisley 1969–84, and first Director-General of the Society, 1984-94. A traveller and plant collector in many countries; a prolific author and editor, not only of encyclopaedias for the RHS, but of monographs on Daphne *and* Petaloid Monocotyledons.

texts on nursery production (1987-90). By the time Browse left, the Society had acquired a second garden at Rosemoor, and was shortly to add a third; it was decided that a single intelligence ought to be in charge of garden developments at all sites, and the post was changed to Director of Horticulture. Its first incumbent was Bill Simpson, the former Director of Pershore College.

On Friday, 16 October 1987, the worst storm in centuries swept over the south of England, felling millions of trees. At Wisley, the pinetum and wild garden were badly hit; Weather Hill Cottage was narrowly missed by a falling oak; Battleston Hill was the area worst affected, with more than four-fifths of its mature tree cover blown over, and would not reopen to visitors for two years. English Heritage had recently set in motion a programme of grant-aid for historic gardens, which was about to be tested by the flood of applications for assistance with windfall clearance and replanting; Council decided that there were other organisations whose gardens had suffered more, and declined to appeal. Then in January 1990 came a further storm, and this time an appeal was launched, which raised £64,000 by the summer. Massive replanting would change the face of significant portions of Wisley, but none more so than Battleston Hill.[34]

Model gardens

'Wisley, to many people, means the model gardens', recent editions of the guidebook have affirmed, and they have indeed provided the most directly educational aspect of Wisley Garden for the general public.

The original model gardens were an outgrowth of the National Fruit Trials, and were designed by its Director, J.M.S. Potter, in 1946 (and amended in various ways since). The model fruit gardens were laid out near the upper part of the rose borders, between the alpine house and the future site of the Bowes Lyon Pavilion, and comprised three plots intended to show how productive fruit collections could be accommodated in domestic gardens of different sizes; adjacent to these were ranks

The Eros garden, a model garden by Julie Toll which was moved to Wisley after winning a silver medal at the 1995 Chelsea Flower Show.

of cordon fruits. In 1959 they were supplemented (on the other side of the Pavilion site) by a model vegetable garden, laid out on the site of the old pear collection, and for much of its history the responsibility of one staff member, Colin Martin. These gardens were the effective practical counterpart of the Society's publications *The Fruit Garden Displayed* and *The Vegetable Garden Displayed*: educational displays to encourage domestic food production.[35]

In the 1970s, the range of model gardens began to widen. In 1974, Reader's Digest and the Disabled Living Foundation, who had recently collaborated on a book on gardening for the disabled, approached the RHS with a proposal for a model garden to show how a small domestic garden could be adapted for the needs of the blind, infirm or halt. Council fidgeted uneasily: 'It must be anticipated that there would be an association with the Reader's Digest but this would mean improved publicity for the Garden generally and was acceptable.' Reader's Digest made a grant of £2,000 towards the project, and the Foundation advised on its planning. By the time the garden was opened in 1977, a storm had been whipped up in the press over the admission of blind people to Chelsea, so the Garden for Disabled People was valued as tangible evidence of the Society's concern for the disabled. It was extended with a further grant from Reader's Digest in 1980, and redesigned in 1992, with assistance from the Horticultural Society of Messrs Coutts and Co.[36]

The idea of using model gardens as educational tools was now well established. In 1976 the Stanley Smith Horticultural Trust financed a group of additional model gardens, designed by Geoffrey Coombs, the Society's Garden Advisor. The first showed a typical back garden designed for a young couple, with a small greenhouse, borders, and lawn; a family garden showed how to incorporate a children's play area, and fruit and vegetable plots; the third showed what a horti-cultural enthusiast might make of a similar area, with rock and water gardens and an alpine house. In 1984, on the opposite side of the road, a further garden was laid out to serve as the venue for a television series, *Gardeners' Calendar*, made by Granada Television in collaboration with the Society (and also yielding an accompanying book, compiled by the Curator John Main); this garden was designed by Main's Technical Assistant David Mulford, who recorded the difficulties of satis-factorily combining the necessary features for each of the expert presenters' subjects, while 'always in the background was the need for an aesthetic entity'.[37]

Those last words signal a change that came over the rationale for the model gardens in the 1990s. In 1991, Reader's Digest sponsored a further garden, the Garden for all Seasons, opened to accompany the launch of a book of the same title. Showing how a garden could be arranged for year-round effect still loosely fitted the educational remit that had governed the previous gardens, but after that model gardens proliferated, and many seemed to be exercises in garden design rather than horticultural education. At the time of writing, there are ten gardens lining the opposite sides of the road, including two award-winning Chelsea gardens re-erected on site. The choice of the *Daily Telegraph* Reflective garden (1999, by Michael Balston) created some controversy when it was revealed that it had been selected for Wisley before the awards were decided, and as its eye-catching feature was a display of modern tensile fabrics held aloft by steel masts, its choice suggested that the Society was trying hurriedly to compensate for its long-maintained aloofness from the aesthetic questions of garden design.

The development of an estate

Hanbury's original gift of Wisley amounted to some 60 acres; the estate was bordered on one side by the river Wey, on another by Wisley and Ockham Commons, and surrounding it on other sides were parcels of farmland and woods in miscellaneous ownership. Progressively, over the generations, the RHS bought up adjoining land as it came onto the market; even if the financial situation prevented its immediate use, it was better to own the land and let it for farming than to risk unsympathetic use or longer-term alienation. So, in 1914, five acres at the northern end of the garden were purchased from the Lovelace estate; in 1919, a further 160 acres, known as Deers Farm, were acquired from a Mrs Ponsonby. (Much of Deers Farm was let to tenant farmers, and in 1931 a portion sold to Surrey County Council.) Another portion of Lovelace land, including Battleston Hill, was bought in 1936; Bridgefoot Farm in 1948; and further land from the Ockham estate in 1958.[38]

A primary purpose of acquiring more land was to secure accommodation for the staff and students. The original gardener's house, Oakwood, was turned into the Superintendent's house immediately on occupation; the RHS was forthwith summonsed by Guildford Council for allowing the house to be occupied without getting a certificate. This formality having been dealt with, the house, under the new name of Weather Hill Cottage, served successive generations of Keepers and Curators. A new Director's House was built when Keeble was appointed, and a bothy built for the students (later, under the name of 'The Pines', to be converted into flats, and even later into staff offices). But as the staff numbers grew, housing had to be found outside the garden itself. The Lovelace purchase allowed for the building of six cottages, later called 'The Square'; the Ponsonby purchase brought with it part of Wisley village—existing cottages and an old school house (subject to the life interest of a sitting tenant). Six additional cottages were built here in 1924. Deers Farm House was converted into a house for the Fruit Officer, and soon renamed 'The Lilacs'; in the mid-1930s it was converted into a student hostel, and used for the accommodation of Land Army girls during the War.

In 1954, Aberconway House, a new building by Sidney Tatchell sited at the edge of the garden, to the north of the Laboratory, was opened by the Queen Mother as a student hostel. The students taken care of for the moment, work could continue on improving staff accommodation in the village. So desperate for additional housing

Michael Balston's Reflective garden from the 1999 Chelsea Flower Show, re-erected at Wisley as a model garden.

had Council been that it had purchased staff members' houses as far away as Send, some four miles distant. In 1953, the old school house had finally been taken over, renamed Orchard Cottage, and converted into flats; between 1956 and 1961 eight further houses, collectively named Chittenden Cottages, were built in the village; in 1980 the Village Store came into the Society's possession, and was converted into housing. Altogether, there are now 50 staff houses and 38 apartments in the village, and 11 privately owned. But the story was not solely one of progressive expansion. In 1970 the Society planned to demolish a couple of derelict cottages, but was forestalled by the local authority spot-listing them; after an abortive attempt to secure a Consent to Demolish, the cottages were offered on the market, and the freehold sold with protective covenants.[39]

The original gift of Wisley was protected by its investment in a Trust, with three named Trustees. In 1910 William Wilks, the Secretary, had arranged for Council to become the sole Trustee of the Lindley Library Trust; so it must have seemed an easy step to take similar control of the Wisley Trust, and replace the named individuals by Council as Trustee. But Wilks's proposal was defeated by the Charity Commissioners, after press criticism:

The Queen Mother opening the new hostel, Aberconway House, in 1954, accompanied by her brother, the President, Sir David Bowes Lyon.

From that to the suggested creation of an endowment fund, the revenue from which would defray the upkeep of Wisley and so render it independent of the Society's general financial position, was but a step, and a wise one. Endowment funds, however, require trustees, and, characteristically, proposing that the Society itself should become trustees of Wisley, the Secretary, with the Society's interests solely at heart, misjudged the strength of the feeling among the Fellows for the retention of the place under the original Hanbury Trust. So nothing more was heard of the suggested alteration in the Wisley foundation, which would virtually have placed the garden in the hands of the Council.

The Wisley Garden Endowment Trust was created in 1914, to ensure the financial future of the Garden. In 1919, when Deers Farm was acquired, Council wanted the option of being able to sell some of the land if it proved superfluous to requirement; such a provision could not be incorporated into the existing Trust Deed, so the creation of a further Trust was immediately proposed. C.G.A. Nix, the Treasurer, wearily pointed out:

> The affairs of the Society are sufficiently compli-cated at present with (1) Three Charters, (2) a Trust Deed of the main Wisley Garden and (3) a Trust Deed relating to the Wisley Garden Endowment Fund and another Trust Deed of the Ponsonby land would seriously add to the complication.
>
> I fully appreciate the argument that it would be nothing short of a calamity that the research work at Wisley should cease if the Society should get into the hands of creditors, but I fail to see any reason why Wisley should have preferential treatment ... the Society, Vincent Square and Wisley are, to my mind, one indivisible whole which must stand or fall together.

The further Trust did not emerge, but in 1928, with new property in London to add to Wisley expan-sion, a fourth Charter was obtained, to increase the amount of property the Society was entitled to own.[40]

Deers Farm was the largest single purchase of additional land the Society made, and in addition to staff accommodation, it found an additional use for a large portion of land in the 1920s as the site for the National Fruit Trials. Beginning with five acres on the opposite side of the Wisley Village Road from the main Garden, the NFT collection grew until it encompassed 26 acres of trials, plus a five-acre nursery and 19 acres of permanent collections. For nearly forty years, from 1922 until 1960, the Trials occupied this massive area, with the Ministry of Agriculture paying regular contribu-tions for maintenance. The Trials were transferred to Brogdale in 1956, and after 1960 the vacant site was appropriated for staff accommodation purposes, including the creation of a playing field and sports pavilion.

All these developments above ground necessitated a certain amount of infrastructural work below ground, much hampered by distance from surrounding towns. After early and fruitless negotiations with both Guildford and Woking over water supply, the Society dug an artesian well, and set up a pump house on the river Wey to help with irrigation; the pumping system was revised in the 1960s, with new pump houses and a 60,000-gallon storage tank. In 1967, after years of planning and entreaty, Wisley was finally connected to mains sewerage from Woking; for generations, the garden and the village had had to rely on cesspools. The road which ran past the garden to Wisley village also needed upgrading each time the Society added to its property holdings. In the late 1920s, Wilfred Fox of the Roads Beautifying Association supervised ornamental roadside planting along the Wisley road, along with Charles Eley of the Rhododendron Association. In the second half of the 20th century, however, provision for carparking proved a more urgent need than ornamental trees. The enclosure of Wisley Common had been defeated in Parliament in 1870, and a further attempt in 1931 had kept the threat in mind; but with the garden hugging the edge of the Common, carpark expansion (and, in the 1970s, shop expansion) inevitably encroached on common land, and resulted in lengthy negotiations, pleas, and compensatory land exchanges. The carpark was in large part created by re-using the rubble from the demolition of the original glasshouse range in 1969, and eventually developed into a series of partial enclosures so that coaches and private cars could be separately accommodated.[41]

Until the 1960s, the only major road near Wisley was the Portsmouth Road, which ran past the garden on the south on its way to Guildford. In 1966, plans to upgrade the Portsmouth Road into a motorway (the A3) were put into motion, and part of the Society's land was requisitioned for the road's expansion. Work began in 1969, by which time over £5,000 had been spent on screening plantations to reduce the expected noise of the

The centenary of the acquisition of Wisley commemorated in the Wisley carpet bed, 2003.

motorway. The Society's initial fears subsided, as the land requisition was less than anticipated; but the usual long negotiations over compensation had barely ended when further works were required for the closure of the turning from the southbound lane, so that visitors from the north had to drive past the garden for a mile or more to an underpass and return in the northbound lane. Meanwhile, a further land requisition had been made to accommodate the building of the M25 orbital motorway running west to east; the Society's protest was ineffectual, and by the late 1970s Wisley was hemmed in on two sides by busy motorways. A portion of the Society's land remained isolated on the far side of the M25.

During the Second World War, land for an airfield was requisitioned near Wisley—a mere 400 yards away at its nearest point. After the War, Vickers continued to use the airfield for test flying and development; in 1966, they obtained permission to fly over Wisley, despite the Society's objections, and Lord Aberconway jocularly remarked at an AGM that 'these machines already frequently and forcibly interrupt conversation in the Garden, though perhaps this is sometimes a good discipline for gardeners'. Vickers stopped using the airfield in 1972, and the possibility arose that the land could be restored to its previous owners. Various undertakings were given by the government that the site would be restricted to agricultural purposes, and that the runways and buildings would be removed before it was returned; but in the event the land was sold to the former owners with the runways intact, and without restrictions. An application soon followed for the opening of a commercial airfield, and precipitated a public enquiry. The RHS mobilised a letter campaign, and pursued the matter to the House of Lords, where Lord Aberconway, in his maiden speech, spoke against what he described as 'a shoddy, shabby story': 'I am told that 30,000 aircraft movements is the likely height to which the traffic at Wisley Airfield will build up in due course, on seven days a week from 7 a.m. to 11 p.m. That makes, on average, a landing or a take-off every 12 minutes ...' Permission for use as an airfield was refused, and in 1985 Guildford Council purchased the site. But the problem was not over: another application, for use as a helicopter link, was made before the runways were finally bulldozed; and then in 1996 a new and even worse threat emerged. Surrey County Council's draft plan for rubbish disposal envisaged the building of a certain number of incinerators, locations unspecified, but with the airfield site among the possibilities. Another public enquiry, appeals to members and public for support, thousands of pounds spent on legal representation, boxes of archives generated: the airfield site is now secure for the moment from use for in-cineration, but who knows what further threats it will generate?[42]

Wisley in the 1990s: the Millennium initiative

Wisley was 'unrecognisable' after the storm of October 1987, and the replanting pro-gramme was long and arduous. Masses of fallen oaks and Scots pines had to be cleared away from Battle-ston Hill, to be replaced by a mixture of alders and birches; a new rhododen-dron collection was begun on the north side, with an emphasis on new introduc-tions since 1980; deciduous

azaleas were planted on the south side.[43] Elsewhere in the garden, Graham Stuart Thomas was invited to design new borders, as later was Piet Oudolf; John Battye, Superintendent of Garden Technical Services, developed a wildlife conserva-tion area along the river Wey; extensive collections of daffodils, hydrangeas, and escallonias were transferred from Rosewarne Experimental Station when it was closed. During the mid-1990s, work progressed to the area on the south side of the water garden, traditionally nicknamed the 'conifer graveyard': an ambitious programme of embanking and path creation resulted in a raised terrace with a new conifer collection. One aspect of Victorian horticulture that Wilson is not known to have attempted was begun at Wisley in the 1990s: carpet-bedding, in a plot in front of the Laboratory; Ray Waite, who designed all the carpet-beds until his retirement in 1996, was then invited to Japan to create a pair of carpet-beds for the 1997 Hiroshima Garden Festival.[44]

In 1991 the long-standing Wisley Advisory Committee was disbanded, and a new committee structure created so that each of the Society's sites had a Gardens Committee with a comparable remit. The Wisley development suddenly entered a new phase in 1994 under the Presidency of Sir Simon Hornby, who took a great personal interest in the idea of a new centre for science, education, and advisory services, together with proposals for unifying the design, creating a new entrance with a clear and recognisable vista, and a glasshouse complex. The architect Sir William

Battleston Hill after the storm of October 1987.

Whitfield, whose Department of Health building on Whitehall had attracted great acclaim, and the landscape architect Hal Moggridge were selected to produce designs. The scheme was described in *The Garden*, but I will quote here from a more compact version published in the staff magazine *Grassroots*:

> This is the first time such a plan has been developed for Wisley and the garden designs and advanced educational and scientific facilities will be landmarks in the RHS's history ... For the first time Wisley will have an entrance fit for a major national garden and designed to reveal an impressive view beyond. The re-designed path layout will give a more enticing tour around the Garden, encouraging visitors into areas currently little visited, and highlighting fresh vistas, as well as making access for the disabled easier.

Additional features to delight and educate gardening enthusiasts such as model and experimental gardens will demonstrate the diversity of gardens that can be created. The most visible part of the plans will be the construction of a dramatic glasshouse, which promises to become synonymous with Wisley in the future. This will be sited on the edge of an ox-bow lake, overlooked by a hill where an arboretum is currently in its early stages of growth. Visitors to the glasshouse will be able to wind their way, at varying levels, through different climatic zones and planting regimes. A walled garden will be built, adapting a classic feature of our gardening heritage, to illustrate today's walled gardening techniques that are of interest to so many gardeners.

Whitfield's proposed building in neo-vernacular style was deliberately understated:

Sculptures at Wisley: ranging from Henry Moore's 'Large Totem Head', below left, to Donald Foxley's 'Naissance', left, and below, seen from the long mixed border running up to Battleston Hill.

The Queen Mother visits the new Alpine House in 1989 with, from left to right, the Curator, Jim Gardiner, the Glasshouse Superintendent, Ray Waite, the Director of Wisley, Philip Macmillan Browse, and the President, Robin Herbert.

Wisley Garden has its own ethos and is not a setting for a grand building. The existing buildings support rather than justify their setting and the two are seen as an inseparable entity. The old Laboratory building was designed to look like a country house, conveying a domestic rather than an institutional character. To maintain continuity, the new buildings which will house the scientific and educational work of the Society have been designed to blend with the garden and will lie in heavily planted areas.[45]

The Millennium Commission, however, thought that the buildings did not look sufficiently distinctive, and turned down the application—twice. As the fundraising process was diverted to London and the redevelopment of Vincent Square, the Wisley development plan was first postponed, then partially abandoned, with one portion of Moggridge's plan, the redesign of Seven Acres, continuing as the Millennium project. This consisted of a new path system, and a series of round ponds linked with the lake; Sir Simon Hornby introduced some novel birch planting.[46] As the London project was completed and the bicentenary heaved into view as a new focus for fundraising, a more realistic Council found itself having to choose between the Science Centre and the glasshouse complex as the project

to aim for. Much controversy had already attached itself to the glasshouse; Floral C Committee had protested about its location (waterlogged soil, frost pocket) and the likelihood of technical problems; but others advised that modern technology could obviate these difficulties, and the glasshouse was chosen as the bicentenary project for Wisley.[47]

Joyce Stewart, a botanist noted for her work on orchids, had succeeded Bill Simpson as the Director of Horticulture in 1995. The Ridley Review Committee had brought about a reorganisation of staff structure a decade previously, grouping the existing ten departments into larger divisions; together with the Curator, Jim Gardiner, she reinstated the former departmental structure, which had worked more efficiently than its successor. At the time of writing, there were eight departments at Wisley: six devoted to special areas—Trials, Fruit, Rock Garden, Floral, Glass, Woody Ornamental—and two service departments—Estate (dealing with machinery, irrigation, turf management, and landscape work) and Garden Technical (plant records, seeds, information and interpretation).

The garden was continually changing, both visually, horticulturally (in terms of the perpetual renewal and reorganisation of collections), and socially, as it began to accommodate shows and other events. But for the gardening public in general, the continuing image of Wisley remained one of model gardens and ideas for emulation.

> Perhaps the saddest and most chastening moment in a gardener's life is when he returns home from a visit to Wisley and contemplates his own feeble efforts, but no doubt the main purpose of Wisley is the distribution of seeds of discontent whereby we are goaded towards higher things.[48]

To celebrate the Queen Mother's 100th birthday in 2000, all her charities took part in a pageant in London. Shown here are Wisley staff preparing for the parade.

6 The Society's Gardens: Rosemoor, Hyde Hall, Harlow Carr

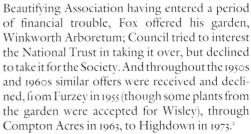

IN 1926, the Society received the offer of another garden. Lord Alfred Milner, the former Governor of the Cape Colony, and later Lloyd George's Minister of War, had an arts-and-crafts garden at Sturry Court, Kent, where he grew a collection of South African plants. He died in 1925, and Lady Milner offered the garden to the Society in April 1926; Council deliberated through its April and May meetings without reaching a decision. To help it to make up its mind, a little press campaign was engineered. On 4 June, *The Times* ran a piece about Sturry which mentioned Lady Milner's offer, and over the next week various local dignitaries published letters hoping that the RHS would accept it. On 15 June, Council finally decided not to take on the garden, and *The Times* carried the news the next day, printing both Lord Lambourne's letter and Lady Milner's reply. What is noteworthy about the episode, apart from the use of the press to put pressure on the Society, is the enthusiasm expressed for the possibility of RHS takeover: despite difficulties of access, the reputation of Wisley and the useful work being carried out there was obviously spreading.[1]

The financial burdens of death duties and rising labour costs were augmented by years of enforced neglect during the Second World War, and even before the War ended, offers of gardens began anew. In 1944 Harold Falkner, the architect who had transformed Farnham in Surrey, offered a rhododendron wood near the town to the Society; after consulting the Rhododendron Association about the possibility of maintenance, Council declined, and immediately after the War turned down a similar offer from Falkner of Byfleet Manor. A.K. Bulley, the nurseryman who had founded Bees' Seeds, died in 1946, and his experimental garden at Ness was offered and re-fused, Lord Aberconway remarking that it 'could never be made into a very beautiful or desirable garden'. The following year, Wilfred Fox's Roads

Lady Anne Palmer (later Berry) in the early 1960s, when she was developing the garden at Rosemoor.

FACING PAGE
The Foliage and Plantsman's Garden at Rosemoor.

Beautifying Association having entered a period of financial trouble, Fox offered his garden, Winkworth Arboretum; Council tried to interest the National Trust in taking it over, but declined to take it for the Society. And throughout the 1950s and 1960s similar offers were received and declined, from Furzey in 1955 (though some plants from the garden were accepted for Wisley), through Compton Acres in 1963, to Highdown in 1973.[2]

In none of these cases was the Society willing to undertake the expense of a further garden, even when, as in the case of Sir Frederick Stern's celebrated chalk garden at Highdown, it offered significant possibilities for horticultural experiment. But in the 1980s Council's attitude changed, as criticism began to be publicly expressed of the Society for being focused on the south-east and irrelevant to the rest of the country. As the idea of increasing activities in the other regions took root, so did a willingness to consider the possibility of having additional gardens. So when, over a five-year period, two gardens with already considerable horticultural reputations were offered to the Society, they were accepted.

Rosemoor before the RHS

The first of these gardens was Rosemoor, near Great Torrington in north Devon, which had been developed over a thirty-year period by Lady Anne Palmer (later Berry).

The small two-storey house at Rosemoor dates from the 1780s, when it had been built as a fishing lodge near the Torridge River. Rosemoor was part of the Rolle estate in the 19th century.[3] Among the chief local industries were iron-founding, timber milling, and limekiln production; much of the woodland surrounding the present Rosemoor estate was planted in the 19th century to provide fuel for the mills. A tumble-down lime kiln still stands near the garden offices and stores; the Devon Historic Buildings Trust has expressed interest in its renovation. Lady Anne's father bought Rosemoor as a part-year fishing lodge in 1923; after his death in 1931, his widow made it her permanent home. The first piece of garden design carried out on the site was the Stone Garden, a flagged terrace below the house on the south, planned by Lady Anne's mother and built by the chauffeur-handyman and woodman. It incorporated a stone lion believed to be an emblem of the Rolle family. After the Second World War, when the house was used to accommodate evacuees from London, Lady Anne and her husband Eric Palmer returned to renovate the estate, ran it as a dairy farm, but eventually let the fields (separated from the house by the main road) for local farmers' grazing.

In 1959, while recovering from measles in Spain, Lady Anne met Collingwood Ingram, who sparked her interest in plants. She made several expeditions with him in Spain and England, was given plants from his garden, and established a collection of the flowering cherries for whose introduction and breeding he was best known. (According to Ingram, the problem with cherry trees was that they were so short-lived: fifty years and they were gone—he himself lived into his 101st year). Ingram was to name in her honour *Cistus* 'Anne Palmer', the plant for which he was awarded the Reginald Cory Memorial Cup in 1960.[4] Lady Anne, having developed a taste for plant introductions, also collected plants in New Zealand along with Harold Hillier.

The garden that Lady Anne made at Rosemoor lay on the east side of the main road, initially in the curtilage of the house. A curving drive divided the garden into two unequal parts: between the drive and the road was an expanse of lawn, flanked with roadside screening and dotted with trees, set with borders of rhododendrons, dogwoods, and hostas, and culminating in a pond set on sloping ground. Nearer the house the garden was divided into sections: the Stone Garden, an alpine scree garden, an old kitchen garden replanted with raised beds of different soil types, a tennis court on which four large beds were constructed for dwarf conifers, a croquet lawn with heavily planted borders, and stretching beyond that an arboretum begun in 1975, devoted to southern hemisphere and other exotic trees, including National Collections of *Cornus* and *Ilex*. The garden designer John Codrington helped with various design improvements, but the work was carried out by Lady Anne's staff and students.

The stone garden at Rosemoor c.1933, soon after its completion.

Rosemoor began to become known in the late 1960s. In 1967 it opened under the National Gardens Scheme for the first time, and five years later it began to open daily between April and October. In 1979, Lady Anne began propagating plants for sale, offering a mail-order service for choice woody plants despatched in litre pots, and issuing a catalogue. In addition to her gardener Peter Locke, who was with her for 25 years, she hired Richard Lee as a propagator to help run the nursery business; the two lived in a pair of cottages at the end of the rented fields across the road. In the later years, Lady Anne also took on students gaining work experience (two of whom were to return as employees after the RHS acquired the estate).[5]

At the beginning of 1987, Lady Anne offered the garden to the RHS.

The development of Rosemoor

The offer of Rosemoor came at a time when Council was actively seeking ways of expanding the Society's activities and services outside the south-east of England. Although some thought that the regionalisation policy ought to be finalised before agreeing, three-quarters of Council voted to accept Lady Anne's offer. Elizabeth Banks Associates were commissioned to report on the garden and its organisation, and produced an initial scheme for its development. It was decided to appoint two senior positions to take charge of the project: one (taken up by Major-General Jeremy Rougier) concerned with general administration and the formation of an RHS centre, the other (taken up by Christopher Bailes) effectively a composite of Curator and Head Gardener. The firm of Ferguson Mann, of Bristol, was chosen to design the RHS centre. Lady Anne was made an Honorary Fellow, and in 1990 married Robert Berry and moved to New Zealand, where she turned her attention to developing the garden at Hackfalls Arboretum.[6]

The donation included not only Lady Anne's eight-acre garden, but also 32 acres of fields, mostly on the west side of the main roadway. Elizabeth Banks Associates were now asked to produce a more detailed plan for the development of the garden, which was submitted in 1987. It proposed that new developments, including the visitor centre, be accommodated on the other side of the road from Lady Anne's garden. The building of the Visitor Centre ran behind schedule, and was opened in June 1990; in 1994, on the occasion of the opening of a new lecture wing, it was renamed the Robin Herbert Visitor Centre, in honour of the retiring President who had overseen the acquisition and early phases of development. The development meant a formidable investment in infrastructure, ranging from the laying of mains and electrical cabling, and the installation of new drainage and sewerage systems, to £260,000 worth of works improving road access, and the construction of an underpass to connect the two gardens without exposing visitors to traffic on the road. Lady Anne had had a small carpark near her nursery, accommodating

a maximum of twenty vehicles if the weather allowed them to get onto the grass: plainly insufficient for the likely attendance at an RHS garden. A first carpark was laid out on the west side of the road, sunk below the field hedge; an overflow carpark to its south was soon added, and eventually, as the visitor figures climbed, a shaded carpark was extended into the adjacent woodland.

Around the garden, especially on the south and east, lay extensive woodlands, which were to prove a major problem, at a time when the Rosemoor project was already exceeding its budget and difficulties were emerging over planting. The woods were in separate ownership, and in 1993 the owners entered into preliminary but abortive negotiations over their future. The owners did not want to sell portions of the woods piecemeal, but they amounted to 133 acres, not all of which were necessary as shelter for the garden. When the woods were offered for sale in 1996, the possibility that a commercial developer might fell them, and thus remove the shelterbelt on which the garden depended, struck fear into the heart of Council, and an appeal was set up to meet the cost of their purchase. The price for the entire woodland was £210,000, but part of the price was met by selling the three blocks most distant from the garden, retaining some 90 acres as shelter. (The sales notice was accidentally sent to some of the people who had just contributed to the appeal, causing some embarrassment, but soon resolved.)

An aerial view of Rosemoor after the formal gardens had been begun: looking south, and showing the extensive woods that form its shelterbelt.

In 1997 Christopher Bailes produced a management plan for the woods. Gradually, over a 40-year period, they were to be returned to the natural woodland type of the area; the crop trees with which large tracts of the woods had been planted—Scots pine, Douglas firs, larches and spruces—would be replaced by oak and ash (beech, although it readily regenerated, was ruled out, as probably not native to the west country). Sorbus, hollies, and other local shrubs would be intermixed, and, in order to reduce the abruptness of the transition to the garden, a certain number of conifers would be retained and other exotic trees planted. Pathways would be made into the woods at various points, and their construction needed careful planning. The existing paths were forestry tracks, and needed to be continued in that status for the time being: the deeply rutted tracks were dug out, filled with crushed stone, rolled flat, and allowed to re-vegetate. Where Sitka spruce dominated among the woods, a new path was created, basically for walking, though wide enough to accommodate a tractor; this was built up rather than excavated, and top-dressed with a carpet of Sitka needles.[7]

On the west, the estate boundary ran along a canal that joined the river Torridge to the north, and had originally been used for bringing lime to be burnt at the Rosemoor kiln. (The towpath is disused but still visible.) The Torridge was a salmon river, and fishing rights along the riverbank had long been granted to a local syndicate, which not only had ten feet of bank granted to its use, but vehicle and parking rights for access. The RHS secured access to the river at one point to enable it to pump river water into a new reservoir (and built a pump house for the purpose in 1990), but it continues to share the riverbank with the fishermen.

The Visitor Centre sits within a pre-existing hedge line, and the boundaries of the major character areas within the garden also conform to existing hedges: a broken hedge line along the stream garden perimeter, another hedge marking the western boundary of the formal garden. These hedge lines demarcated very well the different soil and drainage types within the site; and excavation revealed that the original drainage for the fields consisted of stone drains some five or six feet deep. The challenge for the RHS was to adapt the planting to the soil, and create soil conditions that would allow a wide range of plants to be fostered. The formal gardens area, for example, was largely silt and clay with clay subsoil, so copious amounts of grit needed to be added. Herringbone drains had to be added every five metres or so over much of the site, and within the bog garden area a field drain had to be constructed by sumps. All the principal paths within the field site were laid immediately, and by 1989 work could begin on making the new gardens. In accordance with the Banks master plan of 1987, Banks and Rougier began to develop distinct 'character areas' within the site.

Immediately below the Visitor Centre, work began in 1989 on a formal garden of some 7½ acres to be subdivided by a framework of high hedges of yew, beech, and hornbeam. Each segment of the garden was laid out to a different pattern, ranging from concentric squares through a spiral to asymmetrical and curvilinear paths. The first completed compartments (1990) were devoted to roses: a Shrub Rose Garden, and an adjacent

Work begins on the shrub rose garden at the end of the 1980s.

Modern Rose Garden, with more than 60 recent cultivars. Beyond these, the Square and Spiral Gardens (1991) were planted by colour: hot colours in the Square, and cooler colours in the Spiral. The compartment to the north of these became the Foliage and Plantsman's Garden, and on its east a large compartment housed Potager, Herb and Cottage Gardens, using local vernacular building techniques and raised beds. The last developments in the formal gardens were at the southern end, and consisted of a Winter Garden—plants chosen primarily for beauty of bark and stem—and a set of three model gardens, to demonstrate the layout and planting of shade, terrace, and town gardens for the west country.

plants to create a bog garden. A pipe was laid from the lake to the top of the stream to keep water circulating in dry months, and the bed was diversified into a series of pools and cascades, with water-loving plants forming a ribbon garden for most of its length. At the top of the stream, an underpass was built, a waterfall created to feed the stream, and some 500 tonnes of local stone were embedded in the banks to create a rock gully, planted with bamboos and ferns.

Work on the model gardens near the Visitor Centre, originally scheduled for 1993, was postponed in order to create a fruit and vegetable garden at the north end of the site. The location was chosen, first in order to attract visits to the further reaches of the garden, and to keep it near the nursery for ease of support by the garden staff. A small orchard was planted, the varieties chosen for local conditions, and demonstration vegetable plots, both in traditional manner and using raised

Above, the potager and herb garden, one of the enclosed formal gardens at Rosemoor; right, the stream and bog garden.

At first, all seemed to go well. Despite predictions that roses would not do well in the unpolluted air of the Devonshire countryside, the majority of the planting survived and survived well. But the Torridge valley is closed off like a box where the river turns at Torrington; a frost pocket made itself felt at the bottom of the garden in the early years; the central spine of the formal gardens was a wind tunnel during the spring nor-westers. In the winter of 1993-94, phytophthora infection was discovered among the yews, which succumbed in great num-

bers. The remaining yews were taken up to allow the installation of new pipe drains, and were replanted in imported sandy loam; the dead yews were replaced by holly and box. Some suggested that the RHS should market Rosemoor as the place to go if you wanted to see your major gardening problems overcome.

The major field boundary north of the formal gardens was a ditch that bisected the site and tended to dry up in the summer. Work began on turning this into a stream garden at the same time that the rose gardens were being made. The ditch stream was dammed at the western end in 1990 to provide a reservoir for the garden; its precincts were planted with gunneras and other marginal

beds for ease of cultivation, were laid out within a square enclosure, deliberately not completely walled so as to circumvent frost damage. The original plan was drawn up by Tom Stuart-Smith, and it was intended to display the widest range of fruit and vegetables appropriate to the west country. Advice on selection was provided by the Southwest Committee of the Fruit Group (with George Gilbert and Peter Earl as the main advisers).

The Banks plan proposed that the already established garden be maintained in Lady Anne's style, as a mixed plantsman's garden, upgrading the structure where necessary to cope with increased traffic of visitors. Any new features within this garden were either to increase its diversity, or to take advantage of its microclimate. The Stone Garden, whose paths sloped in a manner inconsistent with modern insistence on health and safety, was refurbished, recycling the existing materials whenever possible. The alpine plants in the 'old kitchen garden' were removed to the alpine garden, and musas and other tender perennials were planted in the shelter of the wall. When replanting was necessary in the Cherry garden, a preference was given to species and near-species associated with Ingram. The pond on the slope, which didn't hold water, was removed in 1991, and Lady Anne said she was 'so glad you did that'—it had only been put in for her husband's ducks. More periphery planting was installed to serve as additional road screening, using Lady Anne's planting mix of trees, rhododendrons and woodland plants. The major change on the east side of the road was the redevelopment of the tennis court and croquet lawn as a 'Mediterranean garden'—i.e. a garden for Mediterranean, South American, and Australasian plants which flourish in dry and poorly retentive soils. The initial planting was savaged by the wet and windy winter of 2000, and much experimental replanting had to be undertaken. Rosemoor House became the Curator's residence, and later also accommodated a trainee.

South of Lady Anne's Garden lies the Arboretum, to be maintained in the manner she had begun, and further still, the South Arboretum (marked on the Banks masterplan as a 'pleasure ground', although it never seems to have served that purpose). This area was comparatively undeveloped, and it is now planned to organise its plantings geographically. At first it was planted with fast-growing trees as a nurse crop, so as to establish a canopy and begin the process of creating a woodland; current plans envisage collections of exotic oaks and other woody genera. In 2000, with the aid of a Heritage Lottery Fund grant, a derelict gazebo from the grounds of Palmer House in Great Torrington was moved into the South Arboretum, and restored with grant aid from the Devon Historic Buildings Trust among others.

The little nursery that Lady Anne had run was removed, and a larger one established at the north end of the redeveloped fields opposite, with a greenhouse and gas-heated polytunnels. The two garages that Lady Anne used as a potting shed have been renovated, but continue to be used for that purpose; an old dairy barn was renovated for machinery and offices for the curatorial team. At first the RHS continued her plant sales service, and issued two catalogues under the same terms,

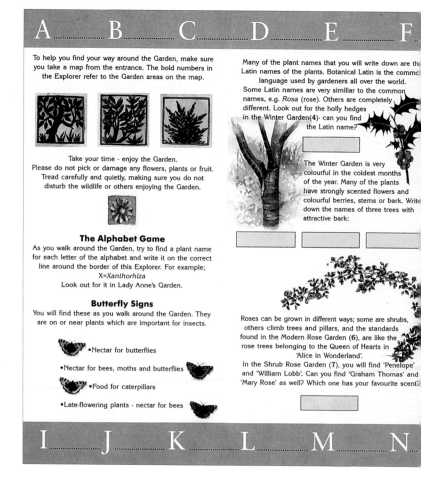

but in the early 1990s made a policy decision that the nursery should be used to provide plants for the garden, rather than for sale; RHS Enterprises, under Jack Gingell, took on the role of establishing a plant centre using commercially supplied plants. At its peak in the late 1990s, the Rosemoor nursery produced 30,000 plants per year, but the scale of production will reduce as the garden matures; Rosemoor is now largely self-sufficient for temporary planting. The cottages where Lady Anne's gardeners lived are still in use, one for staff, the other as temporary accommodation for trainees (at the time of writing, there are four trainees at Rosemoor, working on the Certificate of Practical Horticulture Scheme).

Visitor numbers in 1989 stood at 19,000, and it was hoped to increase attendance to a ceiling of 100,000; that goal had almost been reached two years later. This rapid growth was no doubt due to a careful publicity campaign: the Society's membership was kept abreast of the development of Rosemoor through a series of articles by Bailes and Rougier in *The Garden*.[8] A programme of activities was developed, strongly garden-based in

One of several trail pamphlets produced to help visitors enjoy the Society's gardens at Rosemoor.

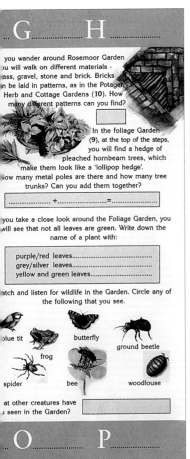

Jeremy Rougier's time, but under his successor Johnny Dean expanding into crafts fairs and educational events for children, promoted by the Education Officer Sarah Chesters. The most recent addition to Rosemoor at the time of writing is its first public greenhouse, an alpine house donated by the manufacturers Hartley Botanic, its construction supervised by Peter Earl and its planting by the gardener Fiona Wilding, opened in 2002. Early responses to the new garden at Rosemoor had included alarm at the prospect of a 'Wisley of the west', pleas for native species only, and worries about overdevelopment; by the time a decade had passed the fears had passed. Rosemoor is still seen as remote and difficult of access, but, as Devon itself changes, the local audience seems likely to increase. In the late 1990s the government claimed that Devon needed more new houses than any county except Essex, and put forward plans for new towns on greenfield sites, provoking local resistance and conflict with developers. Who knows what will result?[9]

Hyde Hall before the RHS

Dick and Helen Robinson bought a 340-acre farm site near Rettendon in Essex in 1955. The house (a typical Essex farmhouse with lath and plaster walls) and barn dated from the late 15th and early 16th centuries; the field boundaries shown on a 1716 tithe map were still largely intact. The Robinsons built up a sizeable mass of deeds, conveyances, land searches, water licences, and other documents dating back to 1713 (all now deposited in the RHS archives), not only for Hyde Hall itself but for adjoining properties that they gradually added to their original purchase, extending the estate to 1,600 acres. The garden was effectively non-existent. There was a ryegrass lawn, with a central rose bed, a clump of pampas grass, a horse-pond, a derelict orchard, and eight trees; on the other hand, there was a 20-foot woodpile, and a slag heap full of domestic rubbish.

Clearing rubbish was the first stage, and much assistance was provided by the Robinsons' pigs—hence the evocative name 'Old Pig Park' for part of the garden. Further help came from F.G. Preston, the former Superintendent of the Cambridge Botanic Garden, who recommended trees and shrubs. During the late 1950s the first parts of the garden were planted, and the pond cleared; gradually, in a piecemeal fashion, areas of ground were cleared and added to the garden.

The house had been built on the summit of a gentle hill, exposed to the north-east winds of East Anglia; it was not until 1963 that the Robinsons planted any windbreaks (screens of Lawson and Leyland cypress). In the same year, the Robinsons first visited the RHS fortnightly flower shows and began to take a serious interest in plants. The immediate result was an enthusiasm for rhododendrons, but to make the Essex clay soil capable of receiving them required a programme of soil

Hyde Hall: a view from the house in 1978 showing how exposed the site was before the development of the shelterbelts.

An aerial view of Hyde Hall in the 1970s; the original design of the rose beds can be seen near the upper right.

acidifying; eventually a woodland garden was created and filled with rhododendrons, magnolias, and camellias. In 1968 the Old Pig Park was taken into the garden and planted with flowering trees, which grew slowly on the still exposed site. Flowering cherries had been the initial focus of planting, but did not flourish on the clay; crab-apples did, however, and a good collection of *Malus* cultivars was assembled.

Immediately in front of the house the Robinsons indulged another enthusiasm: roses. Beyond the pond they planted a pair of long rose beds, and a series of rectangular beds descending the slope like rungs in a ladder; the roses of choice were hybrid teas and floribundas, arranged in groups of thirty or thirty-six. Opposite the end of the beds another pond was made, its margins lined with irises and gunneras. Anthony Huxley, writing in 1974, said that it was 'an attractive and interesting garden now, after less than 20 years; in another 20 it should be one of the most fascinating in Britain'. During the 1980s its collections of *Malus* and *Viburnum* cultivars were given the status of National Collections.[10]

Dick Robinson had meanwhile joined Anthony Huxley in a bid to rescue probably the most celebrated botanical photographic enterprise. Harry Smith had taken over the plant photography business of Ernest Crowson, who had succeeded J.E. Downward, who had in turn succeeded R.A. Malby and his widow, making a line of succession stretching back before the First World War. Dr Robinson began running the Harry Smith Horticultural Photograph Collection in the 1970s, becoming in effect the official photographers at RHS shows.

In 1976 the Robinsons established the Hyde Hall Trust, to finance and maintain the garden, and offer a horticultural service to the vicinity. The Chairman was Eric Maddison, the Principal of Writtle College. The Trust built up a garden library, most of which was dispersed when the Trust was wound up. In 1992 the Trust approached the RHS and offered Hyde Hall to be its third garden.[11]

The development of Hyde Hall

The Gardens Committee for Hyde Hall included John Sales, the former Gardens Advisor to the National Trust, Tim Whiteley, and Carolyn Hardy (the 'godparent' of the garden); Robin Williams and Martin Lane Fox joined later. Savills were chosen to draw up a master plan, including an assessment of the surrounding access roads, and the landscape architect Elisabeth Beasley was appointed as a consultant. It was quickly agreed that Hyde Hall offered the RHS the chance 'to demonstrate gardening practice appropriate for the area of clay soils, low rainfall, minimum input and sustainable gardening as opposed to the high cost and high maintenance of the Society's other gardens—Wisley and Rosemoor'. It was also quickly agreed that the infrastructure needed great improvement: woodlands needed to be planted as soon as possible; the transplanting of mature trees, however desirable for immediate effect, should be resisted, as it was preferable for trees to grow up adapting to the environment; but visitors needed to be distributed around the property rather than concentrated in the gardens around the house, so changes were urgent.

The greatest single problem, since it was to a great extent outside the RHS's control, was access. The roads around Hyde Hall were small, and deemed incapable of taking the sort of traffic that, say, Rosemoor was already getting. (The garden received 42,000 visitors in 1996—a small number by comparison with Rosemoor.) For this reason alone the development of Hyde Hall has been given less publicity in *The Garden* than that of Rosemoor. C.J. Knight, of Savills, negotiated with Chelmsford Borough Council, and reported early in 1995 that 'He had been able to convince the officers that the Society wished to invest in the Garden, itself, rather than in roads. It was his opinion that enforcement action would not be taken against the RHS.' A new road was constructed for access, and new water mains and sewers were laid, but the need to upgrade local roads continues to be problematic at the time of writing. A further problem, but one familiar from other properties, was that portions of the estate were leased to neighbouring farmers; fortunately, the farmers proved co-operative.

Christopher Bailes assumed the duties of Acting Curator while an administrator was sought, and eventually found in the person of Mike Calvert. Calvert oversaw the conversion of the barn into a restaurant, the widening and consolidation of paths to allow disabled access, and the creation of a visitors' centre out of an old cart shed. A small plant centre was established, and a garden library opened; when the Harry Smith Collection moved out, the older photographs were left behind for the RHS, perhaps one day to form the nucleus of a museum of botanical photography. Car-parking has proved more of a problem: at the time of writing, most cars are parked on grass slopes some distance from the house.

Less successful was the attempt to create effective shelterbelts. Elisabeth Beasley had insisted on the importance of woodland planting, and early in 1995 extensive tree planting was carried out to provide windbreaks, but by the summer many of the new trees were suffering from treetop contracture; Christopher Bailes was critical of the way the planting had been handled, and urged that Savills be released from responsi-

Reshaping the lower pond, 1997.

bility for overseeing it, so that the RHS could liaise directly with the contractors.

More recent planting has consisted of alders and poplars, fast-growing exotics for quick effect, and an admixture of wild cherry. From 2001 onwards the planting comprised only native species and in 2002 the Wild Wood Appeal was launched, through which members were able to make donations to help fund the planting and long term care of the woodland.

Around the house, the Robinsons' farmhouse garden and upper pond were augmented with new planting, and an Entrance Garden with a large oak pergola was opened in 1998. They had created an iris garden in one corner, using bearded iris cultivars provided by F.G. Preston, but in the 1970s the irises were overshadowed by their protective hedge, and the area was redeveloped as a Gold Garden in imitation of one seen at Crathes Castle. A collection of almost 600 *Eremurus robustus* specimens occupies a further border, all of them the progeny of half a dozen crowns planted in the late 1960s.

The Robinsons' rose garden had flourished on the heavy clay soil, but by the time the RHS took over the site, signs of disease were appearing, and in 1998 it was agreed that the site had to be excavated and new drainage installed. The surrounding lawns grew on imported topsoil above impacted clay, and became a sort of soup in wet weather; according to the curator Matthew Wilson, 'you could jump and see the ground wobble ten feet away'. Robin Williams designed a new rose garden using rectangular beds edged with yew and box, intended to grow into hedges in due time; pyramidal supports of box section steel, with a dark green painted finish, were installed at regular intervals; 75 cultivars were planted, Sir Simon Hornby having insisted that the number of modern cultivars be augmented. This planting did not fare well, so in 2003 the rose garden was replanted, this time with a selection of 34 of David Austin's English rose cultivars. At the

A view in the rose garden after its first redevelopment.

funding for a Dry Garden project, to be carried out over three years. The first year was devoted to sewer connections, the second to education and publicity, and the third year to making a reservoir and constructing the dry garden. Colvin and Moggridge drew up the plans; a 10-million-gallon reservoir was dug, to be filled by storm water and land drains, and initial tree planting undertaken around its rim. The dry garden, planned by Christopher Carter of Colvin and Moggridge in 1999, with a planting plan by Matthew Wilson, was completed by Wilson and his staff in 2001, digging masses of sandy grit into the soil, making raised bunds (mounds of rubble-filled subsoil topped with gritty topsoil), incorporating gabbro boulders from Scotland to give it the form of a rock garden, and planting over 4500 plants, ranging from agaves to grey- and silver-leaved plants. The dry garden quickly attracted television publicity and a steady stream of photographers.

The *Malus* field, extending from the Old Pig Park downhill and devoted to a collection of crab-apple cultivars and other flowering trees, began to suffer from flooding and from blossom-end wilt. In 1999 the *Malus* collection lost its National Collection status, but a new National Collection had been begun at Brentwood in Essex, and some of Hyde Hall's specimens were transferred there. In the winter of 2000 the lower reaches of the garden were flooded, and a number of mature specimens lost. Plans had already been made for a grand Millennium Avenue running through the Malus field, with a circular pool 50 feet in diameter as a punctuation mark a third of the way along; the trees employed were Hungarian oaks (*Quercus frainetto* 'Hungarian Crown') and ornamental pears (*Pyrus calleryana* 'Chanticleer'), to be interspersed for immediate effect with a quick-growing ash (*Fraxinus excelsior* 'Westhof's Glorie'). But the loss of so many trees from the area forced a reconsideration of the design: the avenue trees were to be planted on mounds, with ditches (locally called 'swales') to collect water running off the avenue and direct it toward the reservoir. At the lowest part of the field, a new riverbed was planned, to be fed from the reservoir and planted with perennials.[12]

bottom of this garden a rose walk, comprising a double row of posts linked with ropes for climbing roses, provides a means of demonstrating techniques of rose pruning and training. Flanking the lawn and running back up toward the house is a long herbaceous border, planted against a yew hedge and subdivided into sections by yew buttresses. This border was created in 1995 by Pamela Schwerdt and Sybille Kreuzberger, the former head gardeners at Sissinghurst, and organised in a sequence of colours from red and orange at the top of the hill to purples at the base.

Despite strong argument, John Sales and Christopher Brickell won the battle in the early 1990s to retain the Robinsons' plantsman's garden, despite its labour-intensive and 'maximum-input' style of cultivation. Outside this plantsman's garden, however, it was agreed that the RHS ought to aim at sustainable horticulture. In 1996 a master plan was drawn up by Chris Carter of Colvin and Moggridge that included a dry garden and the redevelopment of the *Malus* field.

The soil at Hyde Hall was thick clay; during the summer it tended to become rock-hard and allow any rainwater to stand until it evaporated. Only half the national average rainfall descended on this part of Essex. At a time when Essex was widely claimed to be a semi-desert area, and the concept of 'xeriscaping' had arrived from America (to be translated into the concept of the 'Mediterranean garden' in the UK), Hyde Hall provided the perfect opportunity for the RHS to educate the public about water conservation in the garden, and demonstrate what could be achieved with appropriate planting. In 1998, agreement was reached with Essex and Suffolk Water over

The dry garden at Hyde Hall, completed in 2001 as a demonstration of gardening for arid areas.

Harlow Carr and the NHS

Unlike Rosemoor and Hyde Hall, the third of the Society's regional gardens had not been a private estate, but had been planned from the first as a public garden, offering facilities to the membership of a separate horticultural society.

The North of England Horticultural Society had been formed in 1911, and had for years administered the Harrogate Flower Shows. It had tried to extend its activities in other directions; in 1919 it had proposed the creation of a northern branch of the RHS, and a few years later proposed a scheme for trials to be held in the north to complement those at Wisley. The Corporation of Harrogate offered a site on Harlow Moor Drive, the RHS was sympathetic, and for a while the establishment of a northern trial station seemed a distinct possibility. But the site proved unsuitable, the NEHS seemed unable to stir up sufficient local support to run trials without assistance—'Unless therefore the R.H.S. is present on the 29th we may as well close down for the summer and take our holidays free of care!'—and negotiations foundered.[13] After 1927, twenty years and a war were to go by before the idea of a northern trials station resurfaced.

The inaugural meeting of the Northern Horticultural Society (NHS) took place in Manchester in March 1946, and two disparate purposes quickly became apparent: to revive the idea of a northern trials station, and to create an institution for horticultural co-operation throughout the north of England. Colonel Charles Grey, who became the Chairman of the Society the following year, knew nothing of the previous attempts to establish a trials station, but wanted to create a 'counterpart of the Royal Horticultural Society's great station at Wisley, where commercialism plays no part, where trials of newly raised hybrids can be carried out, and where new plants can be tested for hardiness and suitability to inland climatic conditions north of the Trent'. In 1948 Mrs Lane-Fox offered the new Society the use of the grounds of Bramham Park as a garden; after initial enthusiasm the proposal fell through over matters such as maintenance costs; and then W.V. Bishop, the Parks Superintendent for Harrogate, negotiated for the Corporation to lease the NHS a 30-acre site at Harlow Car (later increased to 45 acres), comprising woodlands, a stream, and pastures. The lease was agreed in March 1949; a management committee, including Sir William Milner, Robin Compton of Newby Hall, and Robert James of St Nicholas, was set up; Colonel Grey was responsible for the first phase of the design. The first Superintendent was Robert Hare, from 1950 to 1953, when he was appointed Superintendent of the Royal Parks; he was soon succeeded in 1954 by Geoffrey Smith, who remained for twenty years, overseeing most of the garden's construction.[14]

In 1955, on Colonel Grey's death, Sir William Milner became the Director of Gardens, and the

Management Committee was reconstituted, with separate subcommittees on rock gardens (chaired by Barbara Clough), woodlands and arboretum (A. Sigston Thompson), and ornamental grounds (George Knight). Over the ensuing years, a rock garden was created in a series of stages, beginning with a sandstone rockery north of the stream bed, an adjoining series of limestone outcrops on a flat site above the stream bed, and finally, on the other side of the stream, peat terraces. Geoffrey Smith constructed a rustic stone bridge over the stream. Colonel Grey's original design for the gardens had been rigorously formal, and by the mid-1960s was much criticised for regimented straight lines; so the major developments of the '60s and '70s, including the rock gardens, Tarn Meadows (an area of heathers, conifers and shrubs overlooking the stream), and the woodland areas, were just as rigorously informal.[15] The early reputation of the garden is summed up in this anecdote:

> There was this summer one memory which I will treasure for all time. The Gardens' Superintendent, who as you will know is, very rightly, jealous of the reputation of the Gardens, was one day in June working near to two lady visitors. They stood looking across the stream at the crowds of Blue Poppies in flower there; on each

side there were massed Primulas of many species; the sibirica Iris were coming into flower in many groups nearby; further away in the Gully Bed they could see the red haze of the Harlow Car hybrid Primulas, and beyond it all they could see, like some theatre back-cloth, the flowers of the later rhododendrons and azaleas. Then one visitor turned to the other and said: 'It is, of course, rather between seasons for much colour.' Staff legend relates that Mr. Geoffrey Smith then hastened to the Heath Garden and jumped into the pond there, from which he was retrieved by his staff.[16]

Two views at Harlow Carr at the end of the 20th century. Above, primulas in the streamside garden; below, agapanthus and verbenas in the mixed grasses and perennials border.

A new garden in memory of Barbara Clough was created beside the Gatehouse, and a new rose garden started in the early 1970s. In 1975 Geoffrey Smith was succeeded as Superintendent by John Main, and he in turn five years later by Philip Swindells; the initiatives of their years included the winter garden, the first model gardens, and new trial gardens in the Queen's Meadow. The 1990s saw the creation of a herb garden, scented garden, foliage garden, and perennials border. In 2000, the BBC held its Gardener of the Year Competition at Harlow Carr, and left a new model garden in its wake.

Harlow Carr—the spelling was altered in 1989, partly for etymological reasons, partly to stop people from thinking that the garden was a motor museum—had been the site of a spa in the 19th century, and a hotel and bathhouse were built at the site in the 1840s. The derelict bathhouse was turned into the Charles Grey Memorial Building, opened in 1956, accommodating the library; it was refurbished and altered in 1983 to include an educational department under Jill Oliver, many of whose first activities were dedicated to the study of the local ecology. Harrogate Corporation presented the former gates of the Valley Gardens; the Harrogate Spa Rooms were demolished in 1964, and the Doric columns from its portico re-erected in the woodland as a folly. In 1971 a new entrance lodge was constructed after an appeal to the members, and in 1985 a new office building was grant-aided by the English Tourist Board to the sum of £90,000.

Colonel Grey had originally hoped to build up a membership of 10,000, but growth was slow—by the end of the 1950s, membership had passed the 3,000 mark. In the 1980s it eventually surpassed, but again sank down to, the 10,000 figure. As it grew, the Society increased its range of activities,

on the model of the RHS. It undertook a programme of seed distribution to its members, and by 1963 had distributed some 25,000 packets; it instituted lecture series, educational programmes, an alliance with Harrogate College of Arts and Technology, and a Harlow Carr Medal for northern gardeners, first awarded in 1990. Specialist groups began to be set up in 1961, starting with groups for roses, lilies, and alpines, and eventually extending to delphiniums, edible plants and bonsai. In 1980 Frederic Doerflinger, representing the International Flower-Bulb Centre of Holland, initiated a twice-yearly shipment of bulbs to Harlow Carr, for 'the most important practical research programme into landscaping with bulbs anywhere'.

In 1972 a proposed redevelopment plan for the adjacent *Harrogate Arms Hotel* caused division within the Society. A separate Harlow Car Defence Society was established and at a special general meeting won the right to have seats on Council whenever the plan was discussed; the plan was defeated, and the Defence Society finally wound up in 1974, but at the cost of the first breach in the unity of the NHS.[17] The same years saw the corrosive impact of inflation, as a surplus of £1,500 in 1973 turned effortlessly to a deficit of £2,635 the following year. By the end of the decade, despite financial tinkering, the deficit had grown to £5,000, and the

Harlow Carr's past. Above, the bathhouse and the Harlow Carr Hotel *in the 19th century. Right, the Royal Spa Concert Rooms, from which came the Doric columns re-erected in the garden, far right.*

Society launched its first public appeal in 1979. The first bring-and-buy sale on behalf of the Garden had been held back in 1964; John Main and his wife had established a small garden shop, but it was discontinued when he left for Wisley in 1980. The RHS had by now established its commercial arm, RHS Enterprises, and once again the NHS found a model in what was happening at Wisley. 'The National Trust, many historic houses, and the Royal Horticultural Society, to name but a few, have successful trading ventures of their own, so why not our Society?' Harlow Car Enterprises Ltd was duly formed in February 1981; £12,500 was needed to start it up, and the Society got its first taste of significant fundraising: 'It would no doubt be possible to obtain a bank loan for this purpose but, with current interest rates, the Company would start life with a substantial burden round its neck.' The largest contribution came from the Coulthurst Trust, the then President's charity. The new shop was 'one of the biggest under-takings your Society has ever contemplated', and was formally opened in the summer of 1982; much of the Barbara Clough Garden vanished under its extended sales area. The shop was redesigned in 1990, again on the Wisley model, with a one-way system giving access only from the Garden: 'It has been very difficult to stop dishonest people from slipping into the garden without paying by appearing to use the Plant Centre only.' A few years later, a campaign called Green Shoots for Business! was initiated, to encourage local businesses to make use of the Garden's facilities.[18]

Amalgamation and development

The RHS, remembering the failure of the proposed northern trials station in the 1920s, had greeted the creation of the Northern Horti-cultural Society with an offer of grant aid if it could maintain trial grounds. The first trials to get under way were of delphiniums, in 1954, and the pro-gramme slowly expanded, even if 'due to shortage of staff and pressure of other work [they] have not been regulated with the detailed precision which they entail'; by the late 1950s, chrysanthemums, clematis, dianthus, gladioli, irises, roses, stocks, and tulips were under trial. Over the ensuing years the RHS provided both plants and grants to Harlow Carr. Donald Ineson, lecturing at the RHS in 1964, confirmed, 'The Royal [Horti-cultural] Society have assisted us by gifts of cash, of trees, shrubs, plants, and seeds, and particularly by their sympathetic interest in our affairs.'[19]

As the RHS began to expand its regionalisation programme in the 1980s, Harrogate was an obvious venue for co-operative schemes. In 1987, a reciprocal entry arrangement was worked out between the three societies—RHS, NHS, and NEHS—over entry to shows and gardens. Initially, the shows were the more immediate object of the RHS's attentions; it agreed not to help other flower shows in the area, and provided judges for the Harrogate shows; and it quickly became apparent that more RHS members visited Harlow Carr than NHS visitors did Wisley. Conflicts between the RHS Shows Committee

The wildflower meadow at Harlow Carr.

and the NEHS gradually became apparent, and in 1995 the RHS disengaged itself from the Harrogate shows. Meanwhile, the NHS had exhibited at the Chelsea Flower Show, in 1992.[20]

Andrew Hart, formerly a senior supervisor at Wisley, took over the role of Horticultural Manager at the beginning of 1998, and the Society began working on a five-year plan. But nothing seemed to stop the Society's financial slide, and by 1999 the deficit stood at £80,000. A proposed restaurant and café bar extension, intended to increase income but costing £5,000, proved contentious, opposed by staff who thought the Society could not afford it. The late 1990s saw rapid changes in administration, resignations over policy, and staff restructuring plans which filled the press with news of 'redundancies' and enforced reinstatements. By 2000, in part through appeals, the deficit had been reduced to £18,000; but the tensions within the Society refused to fade. Some disaffected members made overtures to the RHS, and on 18 April 2001, an Extraordinary General Meeting was convened to discuss a proposal that the NHS should merge with the RHS; 95 per cent of the votes (representing about 45 per cent of the membership) were in favour of amalgamation.[21]

The RHS immediately announced its plans for a development programme for Harlow Carr over a five-year period. Paul Griffiths, the former trials officer who had become Administrative Manager in 2000, oversaw the transition. The prospect of the senior society sharing its resources and expertise created great excitement among some of the members; but teething problems inevitably developed, and none more obvious than the discontinuation of *The Northern Gardener* after over fifty years of publication. The RHS's first development was commercial: to stimulate

Harlow Carr's income-generating capacity by upgrading its shop; a team from RHS Enterprises Wisley moved north to create a new shop, working overnight to complete the facilities in time for the official opening. Infrastructural work like carparks quickly loomed as necessary to encourage visitors; a strategic plan was drawn up which included rehousing the library, museum, and educational facilities.

The establishment of a museum of gardening had been one of the most interesting developments at Harlow Carr. Philippa Rakusen, the Director of Gardens in the 1980s and a member of the Garden History Society, had led this initiative, and in 1989 the Museum was officially opened by Kay Sanecki, the author of *Old Garden Tools*. John Tyldesley became the honorary Director of the Museum, and over the ensuing decade, with a very small budget and depending largely on donations, it amassed an increasing collection of old tools. The Museum collection was accommodated in part of the gatehouse complex, and temporary displays arranged. This is the first time that the RHS has been responsible for running a museum, and its future development remains to be seen.[22]

Meanwhile, plans for the gardens were also put in hand. The existing National Collections of *Rheum*, *Dryopteris*, and *Polypodium* were augmented by a further collection of *Fuchsia* section *Quelusia*. Repairs to the rock gardens had been needed for some time. And, as the RHS bicentennial approached, the BBC put forward a plan for a television series entitled 'Gardens through time', in which a series of gardens would be made to represent the different styles that have been favoured at different points in the Society's history; work on the gardens began in 2002, and the result should be the RHS's first practical display of the history of gardening.[23]

7 Shows

THE Horticultural Society's early meetings, once basic organisational matters had been dealt with, were largely devoted to the reading of papers by Fellows. It was not until 1805 that there is any record of an item being exhibited at a meeting: 'A Potatoe was exhibited by Mr. Minier likely to prove a valuable variety, the peculiar property of which is, that its tubers form so late in the season and have so thin a skin that they may be used through the winter, like young Potatoes'.[1] For the best part of a decade, exhibits were sporadic, sometimes only two in a year, but in the aftermath of the Napoleonic Wars, they came to be the rule rather than the exception. Fruit varieties, sometimes single (especially when new cultivars were announced), sometimes comparative displays, formed the major theme until the 1820s, when the proportion of ornamental plants began to increase.

Who exhibited at these meetings? A certain number of exhibits was sent from Fellows or Corresponding Members who lived abroad, but the majority came from private gardeners (estate owners or their head gardeners); fruit varieties dominated, but imported plants newly flowered in Britain, and eventually hybrids or sports (such as the pioneering pansies shown in 1834 by Lady Gambier's gardener), were also shown. Some exhibitors crop up in the lists repeatedly: John Allnut of Clapham,[2] Robert Barclay (who had helped to launch Curtis's *Botanical Magazine* in the 1780s), Sir Abraham Hume of Wormleybury (a leading importer and grower of Chinese plants), the botanist and conifer expert Aylmer Bourke Lambert, William Wells of Redleaf in Kent; also, of course, Council members like John Creswell, James Robert Gowen of Highclere (the raiser of the smooth-leaved hollies, *Ilex ×altaclerensis*), the Comte de Vandes, Roger Wilbraham. Once the Garden at Chiswick had been established, and plants from the Society's collectors were being

grown on there, these introductions formed a major, and sometimes dominant, part of the exhibits. Here is Loudon's account of the meeting of 7 July 1829, as a particularly rich example:

Exhibited. Specimens of Indian corn, from Captain Peter Rainier, F.H.S. Rheum Emodi, from Aylmer Bourke Lambert, Esq. F.H.S. Two Fruit Pieces, sent by permission of His Grace the Duke of Bedford, and drawn from nature expressly for him, by Mr. George Lance, of 15. Clarendon Square. These were noble specimens of the art of painting, and reflected honour upon the artist. They were exhibited in consequence of having been partly executed from fruit supplied from the Society's garden. Dried fruit of Diospyros Kaki, from John Reeves, Esq. F.H.S. These were flat, covered with a grey sugary secretion, sweet, and pleasant. A collection of Pinks from Mr. Hugh Ronalds. Flowers of Larkspurs and Rhododendrons, from Mr. Joseph Kirke, F.H.S. Flowers of Verbena Melindres, from Mr. James Young, F.H.S. A collection of Roses, from Mr. John Lee, F.H.S. Godfrey's Seedling Strawberry, from Mr. George Godfrey of Shirley Gardens, near Southampton. Wilmot's superb Strawberry, from Mr. J. Harman of Uxbridge. Melon, unnamed, from Mr. David Lyon, gardener to Sir Charles Pole, Bart. F.H.S.

Also, from the Garden of the Society. Barnet and Red Antwerp Raspberries, Elton, Black Eagle, Waterloo, May Duke, and Knight's early Black Cherries. Twenty-eight sorts of Strawberries. Flowers of Eccremocarpus scaber, Gesneria bulbosa, Cuphea Melvilla, Combretum purpureum, Quisqualis indiva, Oenothera, Lindleyana quadrivulnera viminea, tenella, pallida, and rose alba; Clarkia pulchella, C. pulchella var. integripetala, Galardia aristata, Eschscholtzia californica, Lupinus ornatus, plumosus, and bicolor; Pentstemon diffusum, venustum, and triphyllum; Sida malvaeflora, Gilia capitata, G. pulchella, Anthemis arabica, Iberis umbellata red and lilac, Malope malacoides, Potentilla atrosanguinea, Collomia grandiflora, Sweetwilliams, Double Poppies, Malva

Munroiana. Geum coccineum, Chelone nemorosa.

The major components of the display from the Garden were new fruits bred by the President, Thomas Andrew Knight, and new plants introduced from America by David Douglas. The exhibitors were mostly amateurs or their gardeners, but included the nurserymen Hugh Ronalds, Joseph Kirke, John Lee, and James Young. The contribution of John Reeves of Canton was Japanese persimmons, a plant introduced 40 years earlier by Sir Joseph Banks, but which had disappeared in the meantime (and which kept having to be reintroduced until the late 19th century).[3]

The first Chiswick fêtes

The Society's anniversary meetings had hitherto taken the form of a dinner held in a tavern, but in 1827 Council decided to make the experiment of a public breakfast, which would give those attending the chance to see the Chiswick Garden. A Breakfast Committee was formed, consisting of eight Council members and 16 others, and a group of aristocratic wives (entitled Ladies Patronesses) was chosen to handle the invitations. Tickets cost one guinea for ladies, and £1 11s. 6d. for gentlemen. In the event, 2,973 tickets were issued, and 2,843 persons admitted. The breakfast, which had been renamed a Fête by the time it took place on 23 June, was a success in most respects; not a single plant was injured.

> Various bands of music were dispersed through the gardens. There were thirty hospital tents, thirty marquees, three state tents, and one horse tent, the latter of which was 200 feet in length. Two of the longest were occupied by tables, extending from one end to the other, and covered with chickens, hams, tongues, lamb-tarts, jellies, pastry, creams, wines, &c., with the names of the ladies patronesses attached to ornamental objects. Some of the marquees were adapted for dancing, in case the weather had been wet. On a platform in the midst of the largest lawn, was a raised stage for collinets, band of 30 performers on numerous instruments, and immediately in front was a roped enclosure for dancing. One of the marquees was set out for, and provided with lemonade, orangeade, ices, teas, &c., whilst in another part was a large marquee, ornamented with festoons of flowers, bays and other shrubs, and containing a rich display of pines [i.e. pineapples], melons, grapes, strawberries, cherries, and other fruits, all of the finest qualities, and in the highest perfection. Each article was ticketed, and some of the grapes were growing on dwarf vines in pots. In another part was an elevated stage or platform over a pond of water, on which the Tyrolese family were occasionally seen, and where they exhibited not only their singular vocal powers and natural airs, but their equally singular costume. Three military bands were stationed in other and distant parts, and consisted on 27 performers of the Grenadier Guards and Miners, and 24 of the Artillery.

The only problem was a shortfall in refreshments, which led to 'a very unpolite and ungallant scramble for the pines fruits, melons, grapes, &c.,' and later to a lawsuit brought by Jarrin, the caterer, for payments the Society had withheld in protest against his work. Jarrin lost his case, and the Society tried to recover costs; Jarrin and his lawyer conducted a campaign in the *Morning Herald* to avert the claim, as the caterer was facing bankruptcy. The Society's response was to threaten the *Morning Herald* with a suit for libel, and the editor backed down and handed over Jarrin's letters. The event earned a profit of some £500, which was used to create a Fruit Room at Chiswick.[4]

Not all viewed this first descent into commerce with equanimity. One anonymous Fellow wrote to the *Gardener's Magazine*: 'I, for one, most exceedingly regret that these objects should have been so far lost sight of, that the Society should be made to pander to the sickly appetite for amusement of the fashionable world. It is beneath the dignity and beside the purpose of the Society'. When Loudon asked 'what can be more harmless than such a fête once a year?' he was asked in return what would be the consequences if it became monthly: 'Are you alarmed for its effects upon the morals of the fashionable visitors to the garden on these occasions? or for the example of the dissipation which it displays to the gardeners?'[5]

The success was largely repeated the next year, despite morning rain. Once again, Ladies Patronesses were given the power of issuing tickets, at two guineas a head except for Fellows and the Ladies Patronesses themselves (John Lindley was given a free ticket). The visitors' carriages 'extended from the entrance of Kensington to Turnham Green, more than two miles'. The arrangements cost over £2,000, but the receipts were over £3,000; the costs of the previous caterer's trial ate into the profits, but the results were handsome enough to warrant an enthusiastic continuation of the custom.[6]

By 1829, *The Times* could say of the Chiswick fête that it 'forms one of the principal attractions of the fashionable season, and is looked forward to with more anxiety than any other fete, either public or private'. This time, however, the weather defeated the best efforts of the organisers:

'The Horticultural Fate', a cartoon by 'Paul Pry' (William Heath), published 30 June 1829, showing the first appearance of what became known as Chiswick weather.

At three o'clock, notwithstanding the very unfavourable appearance of the atmosphere, there were, probably, 3,000 persons of the first respectability assembled in the gardens, all enjoying the delightful promenades which it affords, and not a few waiting with some anxiety for the opening of the refreshment booths, which was announced to take place at half-past three. At that hour a number of persons assembled before the entrance, but in consequence of some disappointment in the arrrangements (we believe arising from the non-arrival of the Duke of Sussex) the refreshments were not attainable until four o'clock, an hour at which the greater portion of the company had been compelled to seek shelter from the heavy rain in the most distant tents through oceans of mud, and under the pelting of one of the heaviest rains of the season ...

The gardens were fitted up with tents and marquees, with the usual elegant and picturesque arrangement; and the Messrs. Gunter did every thing in their power, by the aid of boards and baskets, to obviate those complaints against the impassability of the walks which we heard last year. It was out of their power, however, to contend against the saturating rain which fell in the course of the day, and the walks became, therefore, not so much from their original softness, as from the constant induration of clogs and shoes, a terror to all passengers.

The *Morning Post* was more melodramatic:

But, when the doors were opened, what a rush took place! The standing nearly ancle[*sic*]-deep in water, coming from wet gravel; shrieks were dreadful, and the loss of shoes particularly annoying! Even when parties got possession of standing room at the several tables, what was even then their situation? They were for, it is necessary to observe, that there was no platform, and the tents were erected in a valley, to which all the water from the high grounds found its way ...

We cannot conclude—we shall not name individuals—without again alluding to the conduct of certain persons who were *not gentlemen*; they conducted themselves like centaurs rather than men.

The cartoonist 'Paul Pry' commemorated the event in a cartoon entitled 'The Horticultural Fate'.[7] No fête was held in 1830, though a rather understated one was held in 1831.[8]

These fêtes were not merely parties; each was accompanied by a display of fruits or other produce of the Garden, and one of the attractions of the ill-fated 1829 event was the first flowering of *Clarkia pulchella*, one of the plants brought back from America by David Douglas.

Flower shows at Chiswick and Kensington

In 1831, in the wake of the financial crisis, competitive classes were introduced into the Regent Street meetings for the first time in an attempt to make them more attractive. Banksian Medals were to be awarded for the best displays of rhododendrons and azaleas (May and June meetings), grapes and roses (June and September meetings), melons (July), pineapples (July and February), dahlias (September), and camellias (April). A Large Silver Medal would be awarded for the most ornamental hardy plant exhibited within the year, and a Banksian for the second-best.[9]

This may have been the first time that the Horticultural Society introduced competitive classes into its shows, but competitions for plants already had a history extending back nearly two centuries. 'Florists', meaning by that term not, as today, floral decorators, but amateur growers of flowers, had come to form local societies in the 17th century, whose principal purpose was to allow growers to compete for prizes. Florists' meetings were generally held at public houses, and accompanied by dinners; hence the standard term 'florists' feasts' (and the background to the Society's own anniversary dinners). The prizes tended to be silverware and plate, though, as the 19th century progressed, these were replaced by money prizes. In the 1820s, when the first attempts were made to publish records of florists' competitions on a national basis, the scale of activity was enormous: in 1821, there were 42 auricula and polyanthus shows, 21 tulip shows, five ranunculus shows, and 69 carnation and pink shows held around the country.

Keen attention was given to the production of new varieties for exhibition, even if such varieties were obtained not by cross-breeding, but by selecting sports. In the 17th and 18th centuries, there were eight traditional categories: tulips, carnations, pinks, auriculas, polyanthus, hyacinths, anemones, and ranunculus. In the 19th, as new and highly variable plants were introduced into cultivation, there were attempts to expand this list to include dahlias, calceolarias, and pelargoniums in particular; but the term 'florists' flowers' went on being understood to refer to the older traditional plants.[10]

John Lindley, however, was one of those who used 'florists' flowers' in an expanded sense, to mean any varieties raised and exhibited for the interest of the flowers alone. He disapproved of the old florists' societies and their objects: 'Seedlings of the old races of florists' flowers receive no prizes at Chiswick in future, *because no public object is to be served by conferring them.*' And he expanded this prejudice to include the breeding of new varieties of flowers for exhibition. 'It has invariably happened to all modern races of Florists' Flowers, that they have been the rage for a few years, and then have dropped in estimation as fast as they rose. Dahlias, Pansies, Calceolarias, are so many examples of this change of taste ... The secret is, that the varieties are too similar.' When Edward

Beck, the Isleworth nurseryman who was soon to found the magazine *The Florist*, wrote that, in the absence of a viable national society, florists ought to join the Horticultural Society and swell its income, he received short shrift from Lindley, and was able, a year later, to publish a complaint about Lindley's discourteous behaviour to a group of florists at a show: 'His indifference for florists' flowers we were well acquainted with; but we did not before know that it extended to the exhibitors of them. How is it, that one who can teach so well, cannot learn that the situation he holds entails upon him a respectful attention to exhibitors and their wants?' (Beck himself thought that Lindley was probably showing signs of overwork.)[11] Refusal to give prizes did not mean that the plants themselves were banned from the Society: exhibits of carnations, anemones, pansies, fuchsias, and the like carried on, though preferential attention was given to fruit, and to rarities.

In February 1833, George Bentham, the Secretary, proposed that, as there was pressure from Fellows to have some sort of events in the Garden, while others were disgruntled by the idea of reviving the fêtes, a new idea should be tried: shows to which Fellows and nurserymen would be invited to send displays of plants, as they did to Regent Street, but on a larger scale. Judges would make awards to the exhibits before the gates were opened; to offset the costs, tickets would be sold to the public, each ticket usable at one of the three proposed occasions (May, June, and July). Council accepted the idea, and the first show was held that May.[12]

The Chiswick shows were held thrice yearly from 1833 to 1857, and, especially during the first decade or so, proved productive of horticultural novelties, from the first flowering of *Deutzia scabra* in 1834, to the display of Hartweg's new Mexican conifers in pots in 1843. And let us not forget the occasion when Thomas Appleby exhibited deutzias trained as standards; Donald Beaton later recalled 'the rage the Doctor [Lindley] was in, and the runnings he had hither and thither, looking after Mr Appleby to knock his head off for daring to bring "fly-flappers" to a Chiswick Show!'[13] By 1840 the shows had become a byword for smooth and efficient running (though not for standards of judging), and reports on rival flower shows accused them of being chaotic by comparison.[14] Two sample quotations indicate the general tenor of the gardening press:

> Those who have never had an opportunity of witnessing these Exhibitions, can form but an inadequate idea of the magnificent effect which they produce; far surpassing any other thing of the kind; and, indeed, it would be unreasonable

not to expect such to be the case, when it is considered that they form the central point to which flow all the most beautiful, and interesting horticultural productions, which the wealth of the Fellows, and the talent and perseverance of professional men can command ...

Considerable as has been the number of tickets sold [12,000], we have no doubt that it would be doubled if it were more generally known in the metropolis what a brilliant scene the Horticultural Society's Garden presents on the days of exhibition, and for how little this scene might be enjoyed: that, besides a splendid garden, and an exhibition of the finest fruit and flowers that wealth and skill can produce, enlivened by several bands of music. The principal part of the English aristocracy are present, and mix indiscriminately with the tradesman, the mechanic, and the gardener. This scene may be enjoyed by men, women, and children, for five or six hours, at 3s. 6d. each. There are omnibuses in abundance, by which persons may be conveyed from the metropolis for a shilling, and back again for the same sum ... So much elevating, humanising, and rational enjoyment is not to be obtained for a similar sum, as far as we are aware, in the metropolis, or its neighbourhood.[15]

As that last quotation indicates, Chiswick was once again an integral part of the London season. The Duke of Devonshire, as both President and landlord, opened the grounds of the adjacent Chiswick House during some of the show periods. Royal visits took place in 1842 and 1846. (In 1837, a Show was cancelled so as not to conflict with the funeral of William IV; on two occasions since royal funerals have forced the cancellation of a show, in 1936 for George V, and in 2002 for the Queen Mother.) By 1840, 22,000 tickets were issued during the course of the season. A certain amount of press coverage dwelt on the fashionable society aspects of the shows, and on the non-horticultural parts of the entertainments: 'The road was ... lined with carriages for upwards of a mile and a half ... The number of tickets sold, we are informed, exceeded *fourteen thousand*!'

The bands of the 1st Life Guards, of the Royal Horse Guards (blue), and of the Fusilier Guards were in attendance. The whole of the musical arrangements, which were very excellent, were under the management of Mr. Waddell, of the 1st Life Guards, who acted as general conductor. The march from the opera of *Il Torneo* (Earl of Westmoreland), the overture to *La Syrene* (Auber), the overture to *Fra Diavolo* (Auber), *Oberon* (Weber), *Camp of Silesia* (Meyerbeer), and 'God save the Queen' were played in a masterly style; indeed, a finer musical treat of instrumental music can hardly be imagined.[16]

Show organisation was not without its problems, of course, ranging from tentage and lavatory requirements, through Sabbatarians who demanded that the Shows be moved from Saturdays to midweek, prominent exhibitors who wanted to borrow the tents or have the dates of shows changed for their personal convenience, public declarations of withdrawal from showing by frustrated exhibitors, and rival societies holding shows too close in time (if not on the same day), to outright crime. In 1842 the police seized ticket touts illegally selling tickets, and in 1853, after robberies at the shows, detectives were employed, and seven recognised London thieves stopped at the gates.[17]

The administration of the shows fell largely to Lindley, who became for good or ill the Society's figurehead for relations with exhibitors—good, for his achievement in organising the shows in the first place, ill, for his dictatorial behaviour toward exhibitors, his rigorous enforcement of rules that others found arbitrary, and his inability to preserve an unruffled demeanour when dealing with fractious contestants like George Glenny. Many exhibitors complained about not getting the medals they expected, but Glenny, as the editor of the weekly *Gardeners' Gazette*, was able to publish his complaints, and occasionally Lindley's acerbic replies. In 1837, Glenny refused to accept the Large Silver Medal he was awarded, and got permission to exchange it for money (others made similar requests, and Council eventually had to offer standard exchange prices). In 1838, he got up a subscription among the exhibitors for a piece of plate, to be presented to Lindley in recognition of his work on shows, but Lindley refused to accept anything from such a tainted source. In 1839, Council ruled that Glenny would receive no further awards, because of his libels on the Society; though it is possible that his chairmanship of a rival society, that had recently held shows at another garden in the Chiswick district, was as provoking as his writings.[18]

Indeed, Lindley's behaviour progressively alienated elements of the gardening community besides the florists. By the 1850s, he was being represented in the press not only as a martinet (Glenny accused both Lindley and Bentham of 'indulging in personalities' when dealing with complaints over awards), who instituted pointless rules, was short with exhibitors and closed the door in the face of journalists, but as a snob who managed to be gracious with the Queen while peremptory with the lower orders. (It is possible that an element of political conservatism became more prominent in his character after 1848, when the fear of revolution was such that all the

Society's gardeners were enrolled as special constables to patrol the streets of Chiswick and keep them safe from Chartist insurrection.) His insistence that the queues keep moving without pause ('There was no stopping before the plants ... I laid a pretty deal of it to the Doctor's treading so hard on their toes, and so making 'em keep moving') was specially irritating. Donald Beaton, explaining why many exhibitors in the 1850s preferred to show at the Crystal Palace, was scathing about Lindley:

Depend upon it, the mere free liberty of the subject, which the gardener enjoys here, will go 10,000 times farther in elevating him in the social scale than all the 'laws and regulations' ever invented, or put in force, at Chiswick by Dr Lindley.

    Two years after I left Shrubland Park, I met Mr Davidson, my successor there, at a Chiswick Show, and merely turning round to ask him how Lady Middleton and Sir William were, I was tapped on the shoulder from behind: there was the everlasting Doctor, who told us plainly enough he could not allow such evident signs of revolution under the sanction of the Horticultural Society.

    Here, at the Crystal Palace, gardeners are not only allowed to speak with each other, but actually to shake hands, to ask questions, to give civil answers, to walk about in groups, to look at and watch and hear what the nobility said about the Show.[19]

This quotation also indicates the fatal wound to Chiswick: rivals nearer the centre of London. Chiswick was not accessible by rail until the 1890s; the Royal Botanic Society's garden in the Inner Circle of Regent's Park, and the Crystal Palace Park, were easier to get to. The Royal Botanic Society began holding flower shows in 1842, and they attracted much of the audience that had

formerly made its way to Chiswick. In 1843 the shows cost the Society £2,956 to stage, a sum that slightly exceeded the revenue; by 1845 the exhibition account had fallen to £591, a drop of over £1,000 within a year.[20] By the late 1840s the profits had risen, and the rivalry between the two societies was diagnosed as a sign of healthy competition which resulted in mutual improvement;[21] but they were further hit in the mid-1850s by the inception of the Crystal Palace shows. The Society had courteously cancelled a show so as not to conflict with the opening of Crystal Palace Park, and Paxton was later to offer the Society accommodation there;[22] but in the meantime exhibitors welcomed the free and unrigorous atmosphere of the Crystal Palace shows. Already by 1855 ticket sales had fallen under the thousand mark, the profits had fallen to £300 (from £3,000 a decade earlier), and Lindley warned that the absence of a rail link to Chiswick meant that the shows would have to stop unless they could be significantly revitalised in some way: 'the Society's Garden ... is beaten by distance'. Lindley gave money prizes out of his own pocket in order to save the Society's funds.[23] It must be said that the 1850s were a difficult time for flower shows on a wider scale, possibly through saturation of the market—one commentator in 1856 lamented that 'The Horticultural Society [was] defunct for shows, the South London extinguished altogether, the Cremorne shows reduced to worse than nothing'[24]—but the Royal Botanic and the Crystal Palace gave every sign of triumphing over the downturn in the market.

    As the Society's funds spiralled downward, some exhibitors voluntarily refused their prizes, and the Society took to advertising the shows at railway stations and on omnibuses. In 1855, the shows became sporadic, and in 1857 stopped altogether at Chiswick. St James's Hall, in Piccadilly, was rented when the Regent Street offices were sold, as a replacement venue for the traditional meetings. In 1859 an attempt was made to organise a Fruit Show there; John Spencer, the head gardener at Bowood (and founder of the erstwhile rival organisation, the Pomological Society) was asked to take over its management; he declined, and the offer was extended to the nurseryman Edward Spary instead, until at the last moment it was thought inappropriate that a tradesman should manage one of the Society's functions. The event ended ignominiously with the Society paying St James's Hall compensation

A view of a show at Chiswick, one apparently favoured by good weather, from the Florist for 1848.

for cancelling the show.[25] And with that, the Society's shows disappeared, while Council was swept up in the great effort of creating a new garden in Kensington.

A primary purpose of the Kensington garden was to provide a central London venue for shows, which could then compete more successfully with Regent's Park and the Crystal Palace. After the triumphant opening, shows began in the summer of 1861. The great innovation at Kensington was the Great Spring Show, first held in May 1862, followed by a Great Summer Show in July, which became highlights of the horticultural season for several years. The first Great Show was a somewhat ramshackle affair, as the garden was currently hosting the Second Great Exhibition— 'Beneath two enormous ill-constructed tents there stood a Paradise of flowers'—but as a result the show received some 10,000 paying visitors.[26]

With Kensington as the venue for shows, a change gradually came over the nature of the exhibits. Exhibitors at Chiswick shows had originally been amateurs, but stands of nurserymen had increased in number, especially in the 1850s when they effectively helped to finance the shows. Hosea Waterer, the Bagshot nurseryman, staged a one-man exhibition at Chiswick in 1851, and his brother John followed suit in the 1860s.[27] But many felt that the ordinary exhibitor could not compete on equal terms with the trade, even though the Horticultural Society offered separate prizes for trade and amateur exhibits in the same classes. The *Midland Florist* campaigned against a system whereby the majority of prizes went to the nurserymen who were the official patrons of the shows, and in 1856 the Crystal Palace Company excluded nurserymen from competitions.[28] But at Kensington, nurseries were soon perceived to form the mainstay of the shows. Attempts were made to promote more amateur competitions. In 1864 Paxton chaired a committee on the shows, and made a press statement, praising them in general, but hoping to see 'something like a continuous exhibition, so that a gardener would have no interest in forcing his plants unnaturally into flower' (nobody remarked that only a few years earlier Paxton's shows had been praised precisely for encouraging forcing more than the Horticultural Society's shows did).[29] In 1870, William Marshall proposed 'floral tournaments' in which potential exhibitors were to be encouraged to purchase a quota of plants from shows and enter them for competition two or three years later.[30] Nothing came of either proposal.

Another innovation was the specialist show. The National Rose Society had begun holding a grand annual rose show at the Crystal Palace in the 1850s; in 1862 it amalgamated its show with an RHS summer show, thus beginning an intermittent collaboration. The same year saw shows devoted to camellias and azaleas, and dahlia, pelargonium, hyacinth, potato, and fungus (i.e. mushroom) shows followed, as well as competitions for window gardening (not window boxes, but glass cases). Some specialist societies, including the Carnation and Auricula Societies, were allowed to hold their shows at Kensington (Lindley being dead by then).

The Kensington shows continued into the 1880s, but fluctuating finances meant that the garden was frequently rented out for specialist events (e.g. the British Beekeepers Exhibition), single-firm shows (Carters, various Waterers, Charles Noble), and even a one-man amateur show (Robert Warner exhibiting orchids). In 1875 there was a suggestion of returning to having shows at Chiswick, with a specialist pelargonium show, but this proposal was soon cancelled.[31] In the 1880s, fruit shows were held at Chiswick to accompany conferences, but once the Kensington garden was abandoned in 1888, the normal seasonal shows were held in rented accommodation at the Westminster Drill Hall, rather than risk the low attendances at Chiswick.

By the 1870s, the number of flower shows was rising steadily after its mid-1850s plunge. As early as 1871, D. T. Fish remarked that 'Chiswick in those days had it all to itself. Now every town of note, and almost every village of no note, has its flower show'. In 1881, the nurseryman and pioneering floral decorator John Wills predicted the day 'when a flower show will be held in every village in the United Kingdom'; but in the same year the *Gardeners' Chronicle* complained that flower shows 'have multiplied excessively of late years. The primary object originally in founding these exhibitions was to encourage cultivation ... But in too many cases these laudable aims are overlaid by the desire to get up a great entertainment'. William Robinson added his weight to the attack: 'Shows are now of very doubtful effect on gardening; the real tests of the gardener's skill and taste are in the garden and not at the "Show", and the decadence of the great flower-shows is by no means an unmixed misfortune for horticulture.'[32]

1862 and other Commissioners' exhibitions

A consequence of the shared responsibilities for the Kensington site was the involvement of the RHS in exhibitions created by the Royal Commissioners. Collaboration in the second Great Exhibition had been written into the leasehold conditions, and Lindley was appointed Superintendent of the Colonial Section, a role which wore down his health. The Exhibition was greeted by the public as an overwhelming success—'Until the present assemblage was formed no one could have entertained a correct notion of the enormous wealth of the countries which acknowledge the sovereignty of the QUEEN of ENGLAND; henceforward no political destroyer can dispute it' (*Gardeners' Chronicle*)—though by the Commissioners themselves as a financial failure, which threw into question any idea of a third Great Exhibition.[33]

In 1869, the Commissioners announced their plans for a series of smaller-scale International Exhibitions, which would have implications for the Kensington gardens beyond the provision of access for exhibition visitors. If the Society would re-erect its former palm house within the gardens, the International Exhibition Committee undertook to pay for the heating system; the ante-garden needed rearrangement to provide a 'permanent horticultural exhibition' so long as the International Exhibitions lasted. The first of the Exhibitions, in 1871, had a horticultural division, and £243 worth of prizes was awarded for entries. All these things provided extra work for the Kensington staff during the early 1870s, until the Exhibitions were curtailed.[34] In the 1880s the Commissioners launched a new series of specialist exhibitions, on medicine and health, fisheries, and colonial produce, each of which involved access to the gardens for the visitors, but beyond that, the Society kept a low profile, nursing memories of the debilitating controversies of the 1870s. When Sir Lyon Playfair proposed an exhibition of Horticulture, Floriculture and Forestry in 1883, the Society announced that it was happy to co-operate but not to take responsibility; so naturally nothing came of the idea.[35] For the Colonial and India Exhibition of 1886, the Society undertook to house plants sent from Australia for the purpose, and assisted in the organisation of fruit and vegetable displays from the Colonies. But after that there was only passive involvement in the Commissioners' exhibitions, culminating in 1887 when the Society forced a refund of £80 for the loss of chairs during the Fisheries Exhibition.[36] The following year the Kensington garden was abandoned, and the question no longer arose.

International Horticultural Exhibitions

In 1866, the Great Spring Show was cancelled in order that Britain's first International Horticultural Exhibition could be held in the Kensington garden. This exhibition was organised by a Committee comprising representatives of the RHS, government departments, and botanical gardens. The landscape gardener John Gibson (a former protégé of Paxton's at Chatsworth, who had collected orchids in India for the Duke of Devonshire) laid out the show ground, with the assistance of George Eyles, who was allowed to lend plants from the Society's gardens for the Exhibition on condition that the conservatory was not actually denuded. The Exhibition lasted for four days, the approximate attendance figures being: Monday, 16,000; Tuesday, 30,000; Wednesday, 25,000; Thursday, 11,000. It made a surplus of over £5,000, which the organising Committee was eventually persuaded to allow the RHS to use for the purchase of John Lindley's library.[37]

The *Journal of Horticulture* exhausted itself in the attempt to convey to its readers the wonders of the Exhibition—

> Of what use is it to tell them that there were three acres and a half covered with canvas, making a tent 563 feet long by 293 broad—that the skill of one of the ablest landscape gardeners we have, Mr. Gibson, of Battersea Park, and his accomplished son, had been called into requisition to lay it out—that not only the most celebrated growers of our own land, both amateur and professional, had made the most wonderful efforts to outrival one another, but that the celebrated names of Linden, Verschaffelt, Thibaut and Keteleer, and other foreigners were to be found amongst the exhibitors ... that the Director of the Royal Gardens at Kew forwarded some magnificent specimens—and that the Crystal Palace Company were also competitors with some of their noble tree Ferns? All this to those who were there will afford some notion of what it was; but we fear that to make it all intelligible to those who have not seen it is a difficult task indeed. If any of them have ever seen the Botanic Society's shows [a piquant comparison?], then we may say, Multiply that twentyfold, and you may form some notion of what this great tent was.

—while the *Gardeners' Chronicle* appositely quoted the French horticultural press on the quality of the rose displays: 'The Rose is one of our [French] national glories. Nearly all the varieties at present cultivated in Europe originated in France and bear French names. It is fortunate for us that we have this consolation, for we must confess that our neighbours have in this matter read us a lesson. We have given them the rod for them to beat us with!'[38]

Accompanying the Exhibition was the first International Botanical Congress, an event of great importance in the history of botanical nomenclature. Thomas Moore, the Superintendent of the Chelsea Physic Garden, was the organising secretary for the Exhibition, with a nurseryman and rising horticultural journalist, Richard Dean, as his assistant. Dean made it his life's hobby to remind the public of the event; whenever any of the speakers, judges, or exhibitors died, the obituary in the *Gardeners' Chronicle* would be followed by a little note reminding everyone of his connection with 1866. When three of the jurors died in 1901, he was moved to generalise: 'It is well to recall to mind memories of an exhibition so vast that 110 jurors were required to make the awards! ... Will Old England ever again witness an exhibition the like of that of 1866?'[39]

The monument stand at the Royal International Horticultural Exhibition of 1912, occupied by a characteristic display from Sutton's Seeds.

Dean died in 1905, and so never learned that a sequel would indeed be held. Once again, in 1912, the Great Spring Show was cancelled, so that the Royal International Horticultural Exhibition (RIHE) could be staged in the grounds of the Chelsea Hospital. Once again, this was a collaborative event, in which, officially, the RHS merely had representatives on a committee; the organising secretary this time was T. Geoffrey W. Henslow, later a prolific writer of inter-war books on garden design. Nonetheless, the RHS presence was inescapable. The committee included the RHS Treasurer, Gurney Fowler, as its chairman, Sir Jeremiah Colman of the Orchid Committee as its treasurer, and two Council members as solicitor (W.A. Bilney) and managing director (Edward White) respectively; the Orchid and Floral Committees judged plants as usual. The scale of the event, however, dwarfed not only a

normal RHS show but also the 1866 Exhibition: there were 428 competitive classes, and some 80 special prizes awarded by counties, local authorities, wealthy amateurs, nobility, and nurseries, in addition to the RHS Medals. Reginald Cory, the Welsh coal millionaire and horticultural promoter, undertook the publication of the official chronicle of the exhibition, which appeared in 1914 as *The Horticultural Record*, a massive 500-page volume which lists all the judges and awards, illustrates the exhibits with 187 photographs, 116 in colour, and has an introductory section (comprising reprints of articles from the *Gardeners' Chronicle*) on the contemporary world of gardening by ten contributors, including Reginald Farrer, W.J. Bean, and E.A. Bunyard. The eventual profit from the Exhibition was in the region of £25,000, which was divided between the Gardeners' Royal Benevolent Institution, the Gardeners' Orphan Fund, and the RHS, to help finance the preparation of the *Index Londinensis*.

As in 1866, the Show's international status brought in a heavy influx of continental visitors ('One German was heard to say, in slow, measured tones, "This is the happiest day of my life"'). The press generally agreed that the display of orchids was the finest that had yet been seen in Britain. Nevertheless, criticisms—or perhaps one should say suggestions for improvement—were made, especially by the *Journal of Horticulture*. These included staging, backgrounds for stands, and above all, preparations for the judges: 'much valuable time was lost and much needless tramping about was involved, and several exhibits were not judged for a day or two because of the incompleteness of this part of the organisation.'[40]

The Temple Show

Barely had the dust settled on the abandoned garden in Kensington when the Society announced that it would revive its Great Spring Show, this time to be held in the gardens of the Inner Temple, in late May 1888.

Ten years before, the Society had planned an East End Show, to be held in Victoria Park on a bank holiday weekend, but there had been insufficient time to organise it, and the idea was not resurrected in later years.[40] Now the idea of holding a show in the City was seen as a 'bold venture', a 'new departure ... so remarkable ... that a few superlatives are more than admissible'. With a very short preparation time, the Show was staged in two marquees, one 200 feet by 30, the other 160 by 60; not more than £100 was spent on prizes, the Society having not yet returned to full solvency; and despite torrential rain, the event was greeted with great enthusiasm by the press, as a sign that the RHS had recovered its sense of purpose.[41]

Twenty-four Temple Shows were to be held in succession, progressively growing larger: by 1893 there were four tents, covering nearly 26,000 square feet (though the press thought that 50,000 feet would not be too much); by 1897 there were five tents, and there were stories of exhibitors applying for 1,600 square feet and only getting 250. At first, exhibits consisted purely of groups of plants under the marquees. Gradually, some groups crept into the open air, and by 1904 there were enough of them to be treated as a separate category in the press. The first hints of gardens appeared within the marquees, as small-scale rock gardens were constructed on the tables; in 1893, Henry Selfe-Leonard obtained permission to create a rock garden in the open air; by 1911 the show could be described as 'a huge rock garden', with outdoor rockeries by Carters, Pulhams, the Craven Nursery (Reginald Farrer), the Guildford Hardy Plant Nursery (Selfe-Leonard), Maurice Prichard, Heath & Son, Henri Correvon, and the young Clarence Elliott.[42]

'The Temple Shows differ from all others. There is no schedule of specified classes, but varying amounts of space are allocated to applicants, and they occupy it with the best products at disposal.' By the Edwardian period, the Temple Show was regarded as the 'Derby event' of gardening. Nursery firms continued to form the bulk of exhibits, leading some to complain that 'the shows of the Royal Horticultural Society have grown into trade marts mainly', though comparison with the Ghent Floralies suggested the opposite.[43] The principal problems commented on in the press

were tentage, crowding, and (when it wasn't raining) heat—all of which converged in 1899 to provoke 'letters of complaint too strongly worded for publication' to the *Journal of Horticulture*, and a plea for innovative tent design to improve ventilation.[44] By 1911, there were also traffic difficulties in the area around the Temple. The Templars were not displeased when the 1912 Show was cancelled to make way for the Royal International Horticultural Exhibition; and the following year the Great Spring Show was transferred to the Chelsea Hospital.

Judging and awards

One of the primary purposes of the society that John Wedgwood planned was to give 'premiums' for horticultural achievement; and the first medals given by the Society were very much rewards to individuals for their contributions to the Society. (The Society had pledged itself 'never to give their opinion, as a body, upon any subject, either of Nature or Art, that comes before them', and kept to that pledge until 1858.) The first medal was a Gold Medal, the first recipient Sir Joseph Banks for his work as the most active of the Society's founders; the same design was also issued in Silver and Silver-Gilt, and eventually in Bronze.[45]

In 1820 the Banksian Medal was instituted, 'exclusively confined to rewarding the exhibitors of objects transmitted or brought to the general meetings'. In 1836 a new medal was planned to replace the Banksian, and named the Knightian in honour of the then President, Thomas Andrew Knight; but such was the prestige of the Banksian Medal that it was decided not to withdraw it, and a new hierarchy of medals was drawn up:

> *The Large Medal*, for remarkably handsome ornamental plants of recent introduction, which have never been exhibited previously.
> *The Knightian*, for specimens of eatable fruits, and of ornamental stove or green-house plants.

The Society's original medal, designed by Dr Robert Batty. On the obverse, a greenhouse with a legend meaning 'Summer all year round'; on the reverse, Flora with a herm of the god of gardens. Sir Joseph Banks was the first recipient of the medal, and the greenhouse bears a striking resemblance to Banks's pineapple house at Spring Grove, Isleworth.

The Gold Medal, above, and below the Silver-Gilt, Silver and Bronze Flora Medals: the range of medals normally awarded for flower and ornamental exhibits at the Society's shows.

The Banksian, for specimens of the ornamental hardy plants, and for culinary vegetables.

Council quickly declared that its object 'has not been to excite at these meetings a spirit of rivalry among the exhibitors, by giving medals to the best only of those whose specimens may have been placed before the Society, but, on the contrary, to reward merit wherever it has been sufficient to justify such a measure'.[46]

As financial restrictions began to bite in the 1830s, the expense of the medals came under question. The sheer quantity of medals awarded at the new shows was criticised: 'That so many medals should have been bestowed is extraordinary; and is a proof rather of the liberality of the Society and judges, than affording any information as to the merits of the different exhibitors.'[47] Various economy measures were called for, ranging from a restriction on the sending of medals to provincial societies for them to award at their meetings, to alterations in the medals themselves. A new die was commissioned for the Large Silver Medal, smaller in size than its predecessor; William Wyon's design was ridiculed in the press.[48] Gradually the other original medals were restruck in this smaller format. The (reduced) Large Silver Medal was renamed the Silver Flora Medal in 1864, but the Gold Medal did not take the name of Gold Flora consistently until the 1890s, when a new and much smaller Gold Medal was struck. (In 1927 the Gold Medal was struck once more, at double its former reduced size, but after the Second World War it shrunk once again.)

By the mid-1860s, then, the Society had Gold, Silver-Gilt, Silver, and Bronze Medals to bestow, and while they could still be awarded to individuals who had earned the gratitude of the Society—captains who took their collectors safely across the seas, consuls who looked after them in foreign countries—they were given predominantly to people who had shown meritorious exhibits at shows. In addition, there were the Banksian, Knightian, and Flora Medals. Three more awards were instituted for general use at shows between the 1860s and 1920s:

The Lindley Medal, proposed by Henry Cole and Colonel Scott, and announced as the second most valuable of the Society's medals; it was eagerly sought after by exhibitors, but discontinued after 1878 for financial reasons, then revived in 1903, and since 1930 awarded for exhibits of educational value or special interest

The Hogg Medal, commemorating the Society's former Secretary Robert Hogg and restricted to awards for fruit and vegetable, instituted in 1898

The Grenfell Medal, instituted in 1919 in honour of the former President Lord Grenfell, and originally used for general purposes, but after 1922 restricted to pictures, photographs, or (since 1963) to flower arrangements at Chelsea Show

But during the 1860s and 1870s, perhaps simply because the Kensington garden attracted larger numbers of the fashionable world on a regular basis, an increasing number of people put forward money for extra prizes to be awarded at shows, over and above those that the RHS gave. The most notorious of these was the Davis Medal. In 1870, Alfred Davis left £2,000 to the Society as a permanent fund, and, arriving at a time of acute financial crisis, his bequest was received with temporary hopes that it would help set the Society back on its feet. When it was realised that the fund was specifically for prizes, hopes faded, and a Davis Competition was halfheartedly instituted. It was discontinued in that year of financial crisis 1875; the following year the new administration decided to clear out the Davis Fund, and Davis Medals were issued until the fund ran dry early in 1877.[49] But there was no lack of other prizes offered by nurserymen and wealthy amateurs, right into the beginning of the 20th century, by which time newspapers had become another source of trophies.

The mid-1870s saw the issue of prizes become a political as well as a financial minefield. During Lord Bury's brief administration, the beleaguered Council finally declared that it would withhold payment of awards until its finances had improved. At the stormy AGM of 1875, the treasurer, Bonamy Dobrée, defied gardeners who were suing the Society over the non-payment of prizes, calling them 'rabid prize-men'. A similar fate awaited prizewinners at the less successful provincial shows, where the Society refused to issue awards until the guarantors made good on their promises.[50] Nor did the financial recovery of the late 1880s and 1890s put an end to the problem of the cost of medals. In 1893 the Society stopped the issue of medals, replacing them simply by award cards that were expected to carry the same prestige as a medal; the experiment was stopped in 1899, and new medals, reduced in size, were put into use.[51]

Before looking at the 20th century's additions to the Society's armament of medals and prizes, let us look at the principles by which exhibits were judged.

In the first volume of his new weekly newspaper, the *Gardeners' Chronicle*, Lindley wrote a series of articles on the rules of conduct for flower shows, based on his experience of Chiswick.

If a Committee ever set aside the award of their Judges, if they are so ill-advised as even to question it, they never will have good Judges; for when men feel that they have made an award according to their skill and conscience, to reverse it is to impugn the one or the other. In the one case, a man's vanity is wounded; in the other, his character. The merit of competitors at Horticultural meetings is essentially a matter of opinion; and the Judges have a right to expect that their opinion is placed higher than that of others; else why take them as Judges? The merits of a flower cannot be settled like the termination of a horse-race ... If a Committee are dissatisfied with their Judges, they should change them, but never reverse their decision; if they do, they will be overwhelmed with the complaints of losing exhibitors ...

'The success of the great exhibitions of the Horticultural Society—a success to which there is no parallel, and which has enabled the Society to offer a stimulus to gardeners such as has never been applied elsewhere—has been owing mainly to a steady adherence to these principles.'[52]

And through most of the 19th century, whether from a profession of high ideals or from expediency, the principle of non-interference with judging was adhered to. The provincial shows of the 1870s and 1880s, in particular, threw up nationally publicised complaints about alleged errors of judging, which the Society refused to question: the judges' decision was final. In the early days, when a contestant seemed to have an insuperable case, Council authorised the award of an additional medal, rather than revoking the one originally bestowed, so as not to contradict the judges; in one case the gardener's employer was allowed to purchase a medal to present to him.[53] In the 20th century, however, this position was gradually reversed. Already in 1889 there had been a spat between William Marshall and the new Secretary, William Wilks, over the propriety of placing award cards on exhibits before Council had been consulted; but there had been no suggestion then that Council would alter a proposed award. In 1906 Council overruled the Orchid Committee over an award on the grounds that the orchid in question was too similar to a previously awarded one, and thereafter alterations of Committees' awards became more frequent, until in 1922, responding to a complaint from Vicary Gibbs, Council made it explicit that 'the judges acted as assessors and that the actual award lay with the Council itself'. This did not end the reluctance of committees to surrender their authority, and complaints about alterations have continued to the present day, drawing such responses from Council as (in a 1973 dispute with

Floral A) 'Mrs. Perry might remind the Committee that it was the right and business of Council to vary any award in its entire discretion'. In 1993 the nurseryman John Metcalf asked at the AGM, 'Could Council say what elixir they take that makes them capable of judging all exhibits?', and received the reply that Council had always been the final authority of awards.[54] The modern process of award is for Committees to judge the stands before the show is opened to the public, making their awards by show of hands, and for the Committee Secretaries to present the recommendations to Council for ratification at their meeting. At Westminster shows, ratification takes place at the end of the morning; at Chelsea and other large shows, in the evening, in meetings that frequently stretch well into the night.

It is almost inevitable that accusations of favouritism will surface at some point during a competition's history. In 1836 the complaint was launched that judges at the shows favoured certain exhibitors, prompting George Bentham to reply that the identities of competitors were unknown to the judges at the time of awards. These complaints were instigated largely by George Glenny, who regarded both himself and Louisa Lawrence as discriminated against in the award of medals, and tried to foment rebellion among exhibitors by demanding that they return medals they thought less than they deserved.[55]

Another complaint that has been made at intervals is the accusation that exhibitors have shown plants which they had not grown themselves. In 1834, apparently as a result of accusations at a dahlia competition, Council introduced a form of words which all exhibitors were asked to subscribe to: 'We the undersigned do hereby declare for ourselves or for our employers that every article exhibited by us this day has been brought to its present state by our own cultivation and has been in our possession for four months at least.' How long this guarantee was required is unknown, but it had evidently lapsed by the 1870s, when the *Gardeners' Chronicle* reported grumbles about 'buying plants simply for the purpose of exhibiting'. In 1905 the rules of competition were amended to 'discourage the practice of the introduction into Groups of plants not grown by the Exhibitor and the Judges are directed to take this into account'; again this rule must have fallen into disuse, for in 1919 Sir Jeremiah Colman was proposing as a new rule that exhibitors should use only their own plants. This requirement lasted through the inter-war years—there is a record of an exhibitor's garden being investigated in 1938 to determine whether his exhibited produce was his own—but once again lapsed, and the question was not raised again until the 1990s, when some exhibitors began to complain about the use of bought-in plants on their rivals' stands. A certain degree of buying-in was accepted unproblematically; if, for example, an orchid grower wanted to portray the conditions under which his plants grew naturally, no one would grumble if he acquired the non-orchidaceous part of the display from someone else. But where was the line to be drawn? In 1994, John Metcalf of the Four Seasons Nursery offered himself as a test case and bought in two-thirds of the plants for his exhibit at the February show. When he announced the fact at the AGM, the immediate response from the podium was that judges were concerned with what they saw, not its origins; but the following year all exhibitors were invited to display notices of the extent to which they had grown their own plants. The majority of exhibitors supported the move, the fact that it was a voluntary exercise obviated complaints over compulsion, and the issue has subsided once again.[56]

Cups and prizes, offered for competition, began to multiply from the late 19th century: Nathaniel Norman Sherwood, the Veitch Nurseries, Reginald Farrer, all sponsored challenge cups. Some, like Reginald Cory's, proved hardy perennials at Council discussions, as Cory kept changing his mind about the purpose for which it was to be used. Others gave prizes that were to be won outright, and not repeated after the single award; these were obviously easier to administer. During the First World War, the Society temporarily discontinued all its cups except those for fruit and vegetables, which could be thought of as helping the war effort; when in the wake of the war it returned to its customary practices, Council convened a committee to examine the whole question of cups. Thereafter, Council regularly turned down offers of challenge cups, urging the donors to substitute cups that could be won outright—if not scholarships or something more permanently useful.[57] The new awards that Council accepted tended to be commemorative of Council members, or else accompanied by a significant endowment. A memorial fund for the nurseryman Benjamin S. Williams had been set up in 1896 to fund a medal; in 1907 the RHS undertook its administration.[58] In 1946, when the Rhododendron Association was absorbed into the Society's Rhododendron Committee, it brought with it a battery of six medals and cups, one of which had not even been awarded yet; all were continued as RHS awards.[59] The post-war years saw a purging of older challenge cups, though new ones were added later; some long-standing competition awards have been upgraded

into RHS awards; and the Witan Award, instituted in 1993 by the Witan Corporation for the best exhibit by a newcomer to the shows, was turned into the RHS Award when Witan shifted their sponsorship to the garden advisory service.

In 1988, a Working Party on Awards attempted a simplification of the nomenclature of awards, reducing the range of grades to a standard hierarchy of four: Gold, Silver-Gilt, Silver, and Bronze. (The great publicity effort since then has been to convince exhibitors that Bronze Medals represented a reasonable level of achievement, better than a pass.) The medals that had been historically associated with particular classes of exhibit were retained in a subsidiary position, with a single grade: the Hogg Medal for fruit, the Knightian for vegetables, and the Lindley for educational and scientific exhibits; the Grenfell Medal alone, as the sole award for pictures, was retained with multiple grades. The Banksian Medal, which in 1988 was still retained for ornamental plants, was soon restricted to being the medal issued to affiliated societies for award at their shows.[60]

The rules of judging were only officially codified late in the 19th century, and largely for the benefit of affiliated societies, to ensure that when RHS medals were awarded at their shows, it was for the same standard of exhibit as at the Society's own shows. A committee, comprising nurserymen, head gardeners, the editors of the *Journal of Horticulture* and the *Gardeners' Magazine*, and Archibald Barron, the superintendent of Chiswick, was set up in 1895 to draw up a code, published the following year as *Rules for Judging*. These rules were amended in 1905, when the regulation was added that judges should retire when a plant of theirs came up for discussion, and at intervals thereafter; the ninth edition was published in 1947, and in 1953 it was replaced by a more general *Horticultural Show Handbook*, which has itself been revised at intervals. All exhibits are judged for cultivation and quality, rarity and variety, and general arrangement, with the weighting attached to each of the three criteria varying for plant groups and gardens. Probably the single most consistent and contentious issue over the past century has been the definition of 'amateur' status: could a nurseryman's wife be considered an amateur? could a professional gardener on a country estate have amateur status for plants grown in his private garden? should cottagers who grew plants for their kitchen have a separate status? did an amateur lose that status if he started producing vegetables for the war effort?[61] The rules governing what could be displayed have changed over the years. Onions and leeks were once excluded from the Chelsea Flower Show, but allowed in after the press criticised the rule. While miniature rock gardens on display tables were judged as gardens, smaller groups of alpines in sinks and troughs were long relegated to the category of sundries; Council explained in 1959 that 'experience shows that the majority of miniature gardens exhibited are impracticable and that in many the intrinsic value of the container is greater than that of the plants'. As late as 1976 such miniature gardens were excluded from judging 'unless invited', but this rule had disappeared from the schedule by the time Foxgrove Plants arrived in 1988, and made alpine displays in stone sinks the major theme of their displays.[62]

The judging of gardens developed much later than the judging of plants and exhibits, but during the post-war years assumed a stable form. The day before judging, a team of four assessors looks at each garden—if necessary before the gardens are completed—and assesses them against a set of written criteria, based in part on the exhibitors' statements of intention. The assessors' reports are typed up overnight and given to the judges next day for use in their appraisal. John Sales, the former Gardens Advisor to the National Trust, describing the standards of the judges, explained: 'In such artificial circumstances no one pretends that flower-show exhibits are real gardens, which

change and develop from day to day and year to year. Flower-show gardens are theatrical tableaux contrived for specific purposes—to impress, to shock, to amuse, to educate, to evoke ... and so on.'[63] A certain range of exclusions is specified in the Show Schedules, among them, most notoriously, a ban on coloured sculptures, including garden gnomes; protests over this ban are always good for press attention in an otherwise dull year. Another rule excludes livestock from the gardens; according to legend passed down within the Shows Department, this rule was once invoked by Arthur Simmonds to remove girls in bathing suits from a stand, but no documentation has survived to confirm the story. Some of the rules have reflected the competing claims of horticulture and lifestyle: bathing pools were to be treated as sundries, and if they occupied more than 25 per cent of a site rendered it ineligible for a medal.[64]

The Chelsea Flower Show: administration

Chelsea Hospital had been built in the 1680s by Christopher Wren, as a home for war veterans and invalid soldiers. Originally it had boasted formal gardens by George London and Henry Wise, but these were largely swept away when the Thames Embankment was constructed; John Gibson remodelled the grounds in the 1860s to consist

Judging a rock garden at the Chelsea Show for 1953.

primarily of lawns with a central path on which stood a tall obelisk by Samuel Pepys Cockerell, a memorial to the battle of Chillianwallah. To the east lay the Ranelagh Gardens, a former commercial pleasure garden whose grounds were remodelled by Gibson as part of the same project.

The RHS first became involved with the Chelsea Hospital in 1905. Three years before, it had leased the grounds of Holland House in Kensington to hold what was first advertised as a Coronation Rose Show, but which turned into a more general show (with not many roses) by the time it actually opened in June. Two further two-day summer shows took place at Holland House in 1903 and 1904, but then, to the general satisfaction of exhibitors and press, a three-day Summer Show was staged in the Hospital grounds, a more spacious site than Holland House had allowed, with room for five tents.[65] The Summer Shows reverted to Holland House for the years thereafter, except in 1911, when both it and Chelsea proved unavailable, and the Show was held at the Olympia exhibition hall.

The Royal International Horticultural Exhibition of 1912 demonstrated, at a time when the complaints from the Temple were increasing annually, what an excellent site for a show the grounds of the Chelsea Hospital provided. Accordingly, for 1913, the Great Spring Show was moved there, while the Summer Show reverted to Holland House. The Great Spring Show proved financially the most successful show ever, bringing in a total income of £3,000 (the best the Temple Show ever did was in 1907, when it earned £1,400). Ten acres of the Hospital ground were leased, only half of the applicants got in, and the show lasted for three days (20-22 May). The principal tent was arranged in six spans and spread over two acres of ground; outside the tent there were 17 gardens; there was a total of 244 exhibitors, nearly twice the number accommodated at the Temple.[66] The success meant that there need be no return to the Temple site, and arrangements were made to hold the Great Spring Show at Chelsea the following year.[67]

The Great Spring and Summer shows were held at Chelsea and Holland House until 1916, by which time, despite a shift of focus from ornamental plants to vegetables and a great deal of educational publicity designed to promote home food production, press criticism of the event as a superfluous luxury reached such a pitch that Frederick Keeble, the

Director of Wisley, could refer to 'an agitation to suppress the Society's shows'. In 1916, Entertainment Tax was levied on the Chelsea and Holland House shows, and the Society, although finding the demand 'inequitable', agreed to pay so long as the Westminster Shows were exempted (as having a higher attendance purely of Fellows). Early in 1917 it was decided to cancel both shows for the duration. When the war ended and the shows resumed, their scientific content was deliberately increased in order to justify the claim to exemption from Entertainment Tax. William Wilks wrote Austen Chamberlain, the Chancellor of the Exchequer, a letter demanding 'Justice— plain, simple, straightforward Justice', and after months of argument and the intervention of Lord Balfour of Burleigh, Chamberlain agreed to exempt the Society from the tax, 'so long ... as the Show continues to contain the features now claimed for it and does not include a band or other extraneous attraction'. (In the event, the presence of bands created no problems.)[68] An attempt was made after the War to secure the Show site as a sports ground for troops, but was soon abandoned.[69]

By 1923 it was agreed that the Show was back to its pre-war standard, and the Society began to hear demands for more investment in infrastructure, especially for coping with heavy rains. A new drainage system was laid in the 1920s, the existing plans having proven inaccurate; but flooding still occurred from time to time, most notably in 1971, and even such localised problems as the collapse of the roof of the RHS Enterprises tent in 1995, causing water damage to the stock of books, proved financially onerous.[70] Electrical works for installing telephone boxes; the tarring of the roads to reduce dust; the repair of wartime damage to the main avenue and tennis court in the late 1940s; tree surgery for decaying elms in the 1950s, and

Chelsea weather, the successor to Chiswick weather (for which see page 115). The scene at the Bull Ring gate after heavy rains in 1971.

advice on their replacement; resurfacing of roads in the 1970s; a £100,000 upgrading of the water supply system in the 1980s—all fell to the Society to carry out. In the 1990s, as the number of outdoor stands began to spread into the Ranelagh Gardens, a new Haddonstone stairway was built to improve access from the traditional show-ground area, and named the Sweetingham Steps, after Mavis Sweetingham, who, after a decade in the Shows Department, had become the first Chelsea Show Manager in 1987. Catering (first Lyons, and then Ring & Brymer have been responsible for Chelsea catering for some eighty years between them), the installation of public conveniences, the arrangement of parking facilities (both in Chelsea and across the river in Battersea Park), and local traffic management during the show period, all fall to the Society's responsibility, and the current Shows Director, Stephen Bennett, has greeted successive Directors-General with the announcement that 'the most important things in your job are loos and carparks'.[71]

Leases of the Hospital grounds were taken initially on a five-year, and then on a 15-year, basis. From time to time the Hospital increased the rent, and the Society had no option but to pay up; during the Second World War, the lease agreement meant that the Society continued to pay half the normal rental fee, despite not holding the Show. From the Hospital's point of view, as with the Temple before it, the disruption the

Show caused to normal life frequently came close to outweighing the benefits in income and publicity: a Hospital official suggested in 1950 that the government should grant-aid the Hospital so that it did not need to lease its grounds for the Show.[72] Noise, traffic disruption, and deterioration of the fabric of the grounds have been the traditional grounds for complaint. As the Show increased in size and scale, so the time the RHS needed to occupy the grounds grew. The 1905 show had required five days to put up, and five to take down; by the 1970s the Society's occupation had extended to 40 days. In 1926 B.H.B. Symons-Jeune was so late in clearing his stand that the Society's agreement with the Hospital over evacuation times was violated; thereafter a form was issued to exhibitors binding them individually to clearance times. In the early years Edward White, the representative on Council of the landscaping profession, habitually took the contract for restoring the grounds once the exhibitors had departed; in 1924, to Council's surprise, he declined to compete for the contract, and Edward Cheal took over that responsibility until the Second World War, after which he was succeeded by Thomas Hay, the Superintendent of the Central Royal Parks. In 1950 Frank Knight, the Director of Wisley, took over the role, and it has remained a Wisley function ever since.[73]

Stands for the display of gardening sundries increased steadily from 94 in 1913 to 160 in 1932, by which year it was recognised that 'now the

Stephen Bennett, Shows Director. Having taken a job at Oddbins to help him through college, he rose through the ranks and found himself opening the store's first Liverpool branch during the 1984 International Garden Festival. He speedily stepped sideways into horticulture, and ended up running the Society's shows, including what he described as 'the last of what I call the big bad years – 1986 and 1987'.

The royal visit: King George V and entourage at the Chelsea Show, 1930.

Sundries Avenue is an exceedingly important feature of the Chelsea Show'. (Today the figure is nearly 300; and the 94 sundries stands in 1913 included three artists and one garden designer, categories that by 1932 would have their own separate tents.) The majority of sundries stands were occupied by manufacturers or retailers of garden tools and equipment. Bookshops were present from the beginning, with the publisher Collingridge having a stall in 1913; the *Gardeners' Chronicle* maintained a stand for decades, to be succeeded, as it shrank into a trade magazine, by stands for *Amateur Gardening*, *Popular Gardening*, and later *Garden News* and *Gardens Illustrated*. In the 1920s the charge for sundriesmen's stands was a shilling per square foot; in the post-war years the cost increased at regular intervals, especially after the Society had to lay down new drainage in the Sundries Avenue after the War.[74] But it was only in the sundries avenues that sales could take place: plants have never been sold during the duration of the Show (apart from an incident in 1931 when Symons-Jeune broke the rules), though many stands sold off their exhibited stock once the show ended. In the last third of the 20th century, the sight of crowds of people leaving the Show carrying unwieldy quantities of

A typical scene after 5 pm on the last day of the Chelsea Flower Show, as the streets around the show ground become a moving garden.

plants became the most familiar press image of Chelsea; but the practice had already begun in a small way before the Second World War. Proposals for a sales area at Chelsea, where nurseries could engage in retail sales during the Show, have been aired in the press but have always been defeated at the exhibitors' meetings.[75]

The first Chelsea Show was a three-day event; in 1925 it was experimentally extended to five days (Tuesday to Saturday), but returned to three days the next year. The first day saw judging in the morning, followed by a visit by the royal family, with the Show opening at 3 p.m. to Fellows only. From 1932 the judging and the royal visit took place on the Tuesday, with the Show opening at noon on Wednesday. In 1949 the judging and royal visit were moved to the Monday, with the Tuesday a full-day private view for Fellows. In the 1980s, an age of overcrowding, the Tuesday and Wednesday were reserved for members only. Timed tickets, with a lower fee for evening admission, were already being used in the 1930s.[76] In 1988, the Morgan Guaranty Bank was given

permission to entertain clients at Chelsea, and a small profit was made; the idea was then considered of opening the Show on the Monday or Tuesday evening for charity. Before long, an arrangement was made with Help the Aged to stage a 'Gala' on the Monday the next year, the RHS and Help the Aged to divide the profits between them. The event proved a success, and before long the RHS had a Special Events Department within Shows, running galas at Hampton Court as well as Chelsea.

Entrance rights for the disabled have on occasion posed a special problem. While no objection was made to the use of self-propelled wheelchairs, guide dogs were banned from the Show as a hazard. The issue arose most heatedly in 1975, and Council determined that any blind people desiring admission could be provided with human guides to take them around, but continued the ban on dogs. On 14 January 1976, a letter from Lord Snowdon appeared in *The Times*, protesting against the exclusion of guide dogs, and for over a week each day saw a new letter or two, usually

associating themselves with Snowdon's protest,
though the only letters whose writers showed any
familiarity with the Show suggested that admitting a dog to Chelsea might constitute cruelty to
animals. The rhetoric became more heated with
each passing day, until on 22 January, Lord
Aberconway published a letter saying: 'I do not
care what people think of me: I can however no
longer refrain from saying that my colleagues on
the RHS Council and our officers are not
patronizing or insensitive people: still less are they
imbued with fascist arrogance.' In February
Alfred Morris, the Minister for the Disabled,
issued a statement based on discussions with the
RHS and other parties, agreeing that while guide
dogs would not be allowed into the show ground,
blind persons would be provided with human
guides, and the dogs kennelled for the duration of
the visit. Even though this policy represented no
alteration from what Council had announced
before the controversy arose, it was presented
(even in the Index to *The Times*) as a compromise
on the part of the RHS. Council, meanwhile, had
been involved in the creation of a garden for the
disabled at Wisley, and was urging blind people to
visit the Westminster shows, where there was
more freedom of movement.[77]

Chelsea was interrupted again for the duration
of the Second World War, and in the immediate

*The Queen Mother
sampling a strawberry
at the Chelsea Show in
1969.*

post-war years, the general disruption to the maintenance of gardens, the rationing of fuel, and the
running-down of nursery stock of ornamental
plants, meant that there was no immediate return
to the holding of a great spring show. The RHS
canvassed exhibitors about the possibility of

*Utility gardening,
postwar style: Queen
Mary visits a pre-fab
garden at Chelsea, 1947.*

holding the show in 1947; many thought that even two years after the War's end was too soon, but enough support was found to justify the experiment. The *Gardeners' Chronicle* remarked of the event:

> ... the present Chelsea Show is a great exhibition and one that fully justifies the enterprise of the Royal Horticultural Society. It is a superb display and one that, more than any of its forerunners, tells a brave and beautiful story of difficulties surmounted and a determined effort to keep the fair flag of British horticulture at the masthead and not at half mast. When the Council of the R.H.S. invited Fellows to express their views as to the possibility of holding a Chelsea Show in 1947, a storm of protest arose, chiefly from the traders; nevertheless the Council proceeded with the project, and, as we expected, many of those who most forcefully urged 'let it alone this year also' are among the largest exhibitors.[78]

And the Show went on to increasing popularity throughout the second half of the century—until its popularity became its major problem. Crowding within the tents had been a recurring refrain during the inter-war years, but always mastered by increasing the tentage; photographs show heavy crowds in the open, especially in the vicinity of the rock gardens. In 1950 Lord Aberconway dismissed grumbles about crowding by remarking that 'no one could have the Derby or a Test Match to one's self, and no one could expect to have Chelsea Flower Show to himself'. But the crowds surged on. As the 1970s progressed, the attendance at the Chelsea Show climbed, by as much as 6,000 visitors in a single year (1978). On 22-24 May 1979, crowding became so severe in the mornings that the turnstiles were temporarily closed, and it was clear that some emergency action was needed. It was decided to open the Show at 8 am next year, and close it at 8.30 in the evenings, with a reduced price for entry after 4 pm, to try to draw people away from the morning time-slot; and a one-way system was laid out in the marquee (an expedient that had been rejected as impracticable 20 years earlier). The arrangements worked better than expected in 1980, when a bare majority of Council voted for the imposition of a ceiling on the number of tickets sold. But numbers continued to increase, and in 1987 the turnstiles were closed again. In 1988 a limit of 40,000 visitors per day was imposed—a reduction of 90,000 in total from the previous year—and members were charged for tickets for the first time. An immediate response was a fall in attendance; by April, ticket booking was so slow that national advertisements were taken out to encourage people to come to Chelsea, and the original announcement that tickets would not be available at the gates was rescinded. 1988 was also the first year that ticket touts made their presence felt, and the RHS felt the frustration of seeing its tickets sold at a considerable mark-up without being able to do anything.[79]

An alarmed Council now began to look seriously at the idea of moving the Show to a larger venue. Battersea Park, Osterley Park, and Wisley were suggested; one proposal was that Chelsea should be limited to plant sales, and the sundries rerouted elsewhere; the firm of Land Use Consultants was hired to prepare a feasibility study and, after examining all these options,

concluded that the Show should stay at Chelsea.[80] The real rescue came from the expansion of the shows programme into other venues, and in particular from the takeover of the Hampton Court Palace Flower Show in 1993: the increased options for both members and for exhibitors meant that the intense criticisms and conflict of the 1980s over the future of the Show did not return. (Some argued that the fact of being charged for their tickets made members value the Show more.) The next great alteration at Chelsea was the replacement of the nearly fifty-year-old marquee with a new modular structure. Eddie Farrell, the Commercial Manager of the Shows, was quoted in *The Garden*:

> It will not be made of canvas—which might disappoint traditionalists until the enormous advantages of modern manufactured materials are made

Two views of the new Chelsea pavilions, 2000, within and without.

'We appreciate you're new here but should Her Majesty look in again please don't ask Her if Her ticket is "legit" or did she get it on the market.' Cartoon by Giles commemorating the first appearance of ticket touts at the Chelsea Flower Show, 1988.

clear. For a start, the eaves of the new covered area will be much higher than those of the old marquee, giving a far less-interrupted internal view.

Then there are the tent posts: the old marquee had 278 of them, and you can imagine what restraints that must have imposed on exhibitors, as well as clogging up the aisles. The structural integrity of the new modular construction is in its roof material and it needs only 16 internal uprights. Furthermore, it will transmit light more easily than canvas, and will be more efficiently ventilated.

The new marquee was first erected for the 2000 Show, and was fairly quickly accepted as a suitable replacement. The remains of the old marquee were cut up and reused to make some 7,000 items, including hats, jackets, aprons, and bags, which were sold by a company specially set up for the purpose.[81]

The development of the Shows Department

Piggotts was made responsible for the tentage for the RIHE in 1912 (succeeding John Unite, the previous century's favourite tentage supplier), and remained the contractor for tents and marquees right up to 1999, not without the occasional bit of friction over rising costs. The 1920s saw the arrival at Chelsea of labour troubles, and increasing restrictions by the railway companies on what they would carry. In 1921 Council seriously considered cancelling the Show, and only resumed arrangements after Lord Lambourne negotiated terms with the railways over the transport of exhibits. (In 1926 the Show was postponed for a week because of the General Strike, but not cancelled.)[82] After the Second World War labour troubles augmented, with the rise of militant trade unionism among building and exhibition workers. A closed shop was imposed at Earls Court and Olympia, and

Arranging boulders for rock gardens, 1931.

attempts were made to force Chelsea to follow suit; Arthur Simmonds wrote a peeved memo to Council about his encounters with a militant organiser:

> He then approached the employees of Mr. Bull, a contractor who does much work for the Society in keeping the grounds clean and restoring the levels of the garden sites after the Show. All his men were compelled to join a union and this will doubtless be reflected in higher charges, not only to the Society, but also to exhibitors for whom Mr. Bull moves rocks, debris etc.
>
> ... the Federation Steward also approached those engaged on the preparation of gardens and other exhibits. In 1949 an understanding was reached with the Unions as to what was building trade operatives' work and what was gardening. Having no knowledge of this, and caring less, he successfully intimidated some horticultural workers into joining a Union under threat of a general stoppage, and frightened Mr. Walker from taking an active part in the planting of a tree. I am told that he also commenced to approach lorry drivers although he had no sort of authority to do so ...

Equilibrium was reached within a year or so, but the problem did not go away; in 1962 the Society appointed an industrial liaison officer for Chelsea, and in 1969 there was a potentially damaging 'go slow', which resulted in the withdrawal of at least one exhibitor.[83]

Until the 1980s, not only the tentage but all the build-up of the Chelsea Show was handled by external contractors; the role of the Shows Office was, first, to draw up a plan of the show, then to descend on the show ground with stakes and spray-cans and mark out the site, and finally, once the contractors had built everything, to return and handle negotiations with the exhibitors. All strategic issues relating to the shows were decided by Council; the selection of both exhibitors and contractors was the responsibility of the Shows Committee. This Committee had first been appointed in 1921; since the first Provincial Show in generations had been held the previous year in Cardiff, and there was a current press controversy over vegetable judging, it is easy to see why the idea of a general committee to advise on show matters was felt desirable.

All through the third quarter of the 20th century, the head of the Shows Office was Ronald Sargent, who had been a staff member since before the Second World War, and who retired in 1977, and was commemorated the following year by a water feature in the Royal Parks exhibit (designed by Robert Legge) called 'Sargent's Lock'. He was succeeded by Allan Sawyer, who became a familiar image in the early 1980s overseeing the grounds by bicycle; he in turn by Geoff Harvey, the Assistant Secretary, who added shows to halls administration as one of his duties. By the mid-1980s Harvey had a new assistant

Work in progress at Chelsea: two views of exhibitors arranging stands, in 1962 and 1998.

named Stephen Bennett, and the issue of external contracting began to become an explosive one, as Bennett began to expose overcharging and sharp practice among the contractors, and press for change. (In one notorious incident, when turnstile operators at Chelsea were discovered to have pocketed some of the entrance money, Harvey—who was chairman of the Corinthian Casuals football club—brought in members of the Casuals to man the turnstiles on the next day.) Eventually Harvey, who from 1986 was the first Director of Horticultural Halls Ltd, surrendered the Shows Office to concentrate on the halls, and Bennett began the process of wresting the control of the show build-up from the contractors.

In the mid-1980s the Shows Office comprised four staff under Geoff Harvey's direction; under Stephen Bennett, as the Society became directly responsible for onsite build-up and expanded into a network of shows, the staff total had grown to 25 by the beginning of the 21st century, and is now divided into Commercial Operations, Show Development, and Administration and Special

opened after the First World War, the demand for additional tents made itself felt. Orchid growers lobbied for a separate tent for orchids, and then complained of crowding within it; a tent for roses was added in 1928; from 1920 until 1934 a special tent was erected for the display of pictures; scientific exhibits and displays of garden designs had separate, though connected, tents. In 1930, the two double-spanned marquees were turned into a single four-spanned marquee, gaining extra interior space by covering over a road; in 1937, the rose, orchid, and other tents were replaced by a second four-span marquee. The Monument Road, with the obelisk in its centre, remained as a central open passageway until 1951, when the previous smaller tents were replaced by one large principal marquee, which regularly featured in the *Guinness Book of Records* as the world's largest, covering some three and a half acres. Flower arrangers got a separate tent in 1953, later to swell into two tents, one for amateurs and one for professionals; in 1998, a tent was created for scientific exhibits, called the Lifelong Learning Marquee.[85]

The grand marquee at Chelsea, first erected on this scale in 1951.

Events; in addition, staff are divided according to the locations of the shows. As the number of shows increased, and Stephen Bennett gradually assumed control over their strategic development, the Shows Committee became a purely advisory body.[84]

The Chelsea Flower Show: exhibition

The first Great Spring Show at Chelsea was held in a single tent, which had to enclose the Chillianwallah obelisk. Almost as soon as Chelsea re-

Within the great marquee, there were generally 100 or more exhibits by nurseries and amateurs, with some displays by municipal parks and local authorities, and some by affiliated societies. The number of amateurs fell off sharply in the 1970s, the last of the great amateur exhibitors being Maurice Mason of Fincham Manor, Norfolk, who kept up the tradition of stove and greenhouse plant displays into the 1980s. Of the firms who exhibited in 1913, only five were still there in 2003: Allwoods, the carnation growers; Blackmore and Langdon, the peony and delphinium growers;

Princess Elizabeth negotiating a rock garden at Chelsea in 1949.

assistant Mr Carnell, kept the cottage garden idea, but incorporated a cottage made of plants in it.

A different *Chronicle* reporter found it 'delightful', and over the ensuing years Torbay staged a number of innovative displays, ranging from an automobile to the Pied Piper of Hamelin. Gradually, other local authorities began to recover their lost talents for sculptural bedding; and Robert Sweet of Torbay eventually joined the RHS Shows Department as its Head of Shows Development.[87]

Outside the marquee lay the fertile and controversial world of display gardens. Model gardens had become a feature of the Temple Show in its last decade, and the tradition was transferred to Chelsea. The principal makers of rock gardens were assigned an embankment

McBean's Orchids; Notcutts' tree and shrub nursery; and Suttons' Seeds.[86]

One of the most interesting aspects of marquee display has been the revival of three-dimensional carpet-bedding in the last quarter of the 20th century. In 1977 the Royal Parks exhibited a carpet-bedded crown, and in 1979 a swan; the same year saw a demonstration of well-dressing from Bakewell in Derbyshire, on the theme of the Last Supper; these passed without complaint. But when in 1981 the Royal Parks exhibited a more restrained display of the Prince of Wales's feathers in carpet-bedding, a *Gardeners' Chronicle* reporter condemned 'This relic from a past which should long since have been forgotten', and by so doing probably helped to bring the genre back into prominence. At any rate, the scene was set for a display from Torbay Council in 1983 to become a focus of public attention.

> The original plan was to plant up an 'olde worlde' cottage garden and place a model of Cockington village in it. In real life this is a lovely village in the heart of Torquay, which dates back to the middle ages with thatched cottages and mill ponds.
> The plan was thrown out by the RHS because the model village smacked of 'Gnomedom'. 'I won't be beaten,' said Mr R. Sweet, parks and recreation officer, and along with technical

running along the southern boundary of the Hospital grounds, which became known as the Rock Garden Bank, a name that survived the genre. By 1926 the popularity of these rock gardens was such that they had to be roped off, and the following year they were constructed as one continuous exhibit, without fences separating them. Throughout the inter-war years, the rival firms of J. Wood (whose 1913 rock garden won the first Gold Medal given to a garden at Chelsea—and the only Gold for a garden until after the War), Pulham, Whitelegg, and younger arrivals such as Gavin Jones, Ingwersen, and Symons-Jeune, competed annually. (In 1929 Mark Fenwick proposed discontinuing awards to rock gardens.) But in the post-war years the number of rock gardens gradually declined; in 1955, the *Gardeners' Chronicle* lamented, 'Now, alas, with changing times and smaller gardens, the magnificent rock gardens we were accustomed to see displayed are not in demand and a tide of flowering shrubs advances each year over more of the erstwhile rock bank'. In 1966, with only Gavin Jones applying to make a rock garden the following year, Council faced the possibility 'that there would in future be no large rock gardens at Chelsea and thought should now be given to the possibility of planting up part of the rock garden

Two controversial gardens at Chelsea. Above, His Highness Shaikh Zayed bin Sultan al-Nahyan's desert garden, designed by Christopher Bradley-Hole in 2003; below, Arabella Lennox-Boyd's Daily Telegraph *garden of 1998.*

bank with some of the larger shrubs to provide a screen, to permit the space being used for smaller rock gardens and for exhibits of shrubs in which paths could be included'. In 1968, Wisley stepped in to fill the gap with a massive rock garden made by the students. The unsuitability of geologically modelled rockworks for the small domestic garden was often cited as a reason for the decline, though it was pointed out that where cash prizes accompanied the awards, as at the Southport Show, rock gardens continued to be made. In the 1980s, first Paul Temple and then Douglas Knight revived the rock garden tradition.[88]

The other category of gardens at Chelsea was long known as 'formal gardens', even when they

were decidedly informal in style. Japanese gardens were popular at the first shows, and continued into the 1930s; their principal rivals were gardens in an Arts-and-Crafts style. Some firms, like Ambrose Congreve's Winkfield Manor Nurseries, exhibited both rock and formal gardens in the same years. As early as 1931 the *Daily Express* called for a Chelsea exhibit that would demonstrate a garden suitable for 'ordinary people'—a category rather difficult to define—and in the post-war years the Arts-and-Crafts framework was stripped of much its stone and ornamental paving, and became more of a labour-saving garden. After mid-century the demand for ordinary people's gardens was rivalled by demands for modernist landscaping; Congreve recommended that the Institute of Landscape Architects take over the judging of gardens, and one of that Institute's founders, Brenda Colvin, complained that Chelsea gardens needed 'a more contemporary look with permanent planting of sculptural quality'. But the Society's desire to keep aesthetic questions at arm's length was maintained, and when O.C.A. Slocock proposed a garden competition at Chelsea, the idea was rejected.[89] In the 1990s, however, under the Presidency of Sir Simon Hornby, who had been Chairman of both the Design Council and the Association for Business Sponsorship of the Arts, the fastidiousness about aesthetics was abandoned, and modernism in design positively encouraged. The firm of Wilkinson Sword (having formerly sponsored the Overseas Exhibitors' Trophy) offered an award for the best garden at Chelsea from 1985 to 1993; by the time its sponsorship ended, the selection criteria had come under fire, and it was suggested that there should be two awards, one for 'real' gardens and one for 'theatrical' ones. The high point of this trend was reached in 1999, when Michael Balston's Reflective garden from Chelsea was acquired for re-erection as a model garden at Wisley.[90] The same years, however, saw a counter-trend, perhaps signalled by a humorous article in *Horticulture Week* in 1989, which asked, 'Why don't Chelsea gardens ever have sheds, dustbins or washing lines in them?' The late 1990s saw the arrival of re-creations of what might be called social-history gardens—for example, a wartime garden complete with bomb shelter—so driving home the discrepancy between 'real' and 'theatrical'.[91] The boundaries of real and the theatrical were to be tested in the late 1990s, when the Belgian designer Jacques Wirtz caused a brief controversy by accusing Arabella Lennox-Boyd of plagiarising one of his designs in her *Daily Telegraph* garden, which won Best in Show in 1998.[92]

Since its inception in 1913, Chelsea has almost always had some degree of foreign representation. The exceptions have been the war and post-war recovery years, although in the late 1920s, when the Horticultural Trades Association was campaigning for protective tariffs against foreign imports of plants, the question of banning foreign exhibits from Chelsea was raised repeatedly; the Society's solicitor finally put his foot down and declared that, whatever the status of trade stands, amateurs must not be excluded, since horticulture 'knows nothing of nationality, and must thrive where all comers meet in friendly emulation'.[93] The first foreign firm to be represented at Chelsea was Robichon of Orléans (1913); among others who have exhibited frequently have been the orchid growers Vacherot et Lecoufle; the Dutch nursery Konynenburg & Mark (almost every year from 1951 to 1964); the Zentralverband des Deutsches Gemüse, Obst- und Gartenbaues (1958-65); Kirstenbosch Botanic Garden from South Africa (1987-2000); with the Trinidad and Tobago Horticultural Society in the 1980s, followed by the Barbados Horticultural Society in the 1990s. Not to mention firms such as the Yokohama Nursery Company in the 1920s and Van Tubergen since the 1970s, that started as foreign firms and then opened British branches. The most noteworthy of foreign gardens have been the reconstruction of a classical Spanish garden by the Sociedad Amigos del Paisaje y Jardines in 1952; the *jardin potager* exhibited by the French seed house of Vilmorin-Andrieux in 1958; the Belgian House Plants exhibit in 1981, in which assemblages of plants were grown on suspended trays, prompting accusations of bad taste from parts of the press; the 'Uzbek source garden' of 1992, left radically incomplete by transport problems in eastern Europe, and brought to completion by donations from other exhibitors; and Kay Yamada's 'real Japanese garden' of 2001, sponsored by Barakura English Garden of Nagano. Only once has there been a political controversy at Chelsea, in 1986, during

Julie Toll's seaside garden, awarded Best in Show at the Chelsea Flower Show of 1993.

the height of the controversy over apartheid in South Africa, when Newham Council withdrew its exhibit in protest at the presence of a South African exhibit.[94]

Space is too short to try to describe the significant gardens and exhibits staged at Chelsea over the best part of a century. But the task cannot be left entirely undone, so here is a very brief list:[95]

1929 Mrs Sherman Hoyt's exhibit of American cacti, complete with painted backdrops depicting the Mojave desert, which was acquired for Kew and had its own glasshouse there for over half a century, before being absorbed into the Princess of Wales Conservatory

1930s J. Macdonald's grass gardens—the lone voice declaring the merits of ornamental grasses for his generation

1936 Hilliers' 'Dingley Dell' exhibit

1937 Coronation Year: the Empire Exhibition, with displays of ornamental and economic plants from around the Empire

1953 Another Coronation Year: William Wood of Taplow staged a 'Cutty Sark' garden

1959 *The Times* 'Garden of To-morrow', complete with radio-controlled lawn mower

1960 The great orchid display to accompany the Third World Orchid Conference

1964 *Popular Gardening*'s 'Garden of Today'

1967 The first garden for the disabled at Chelsea

1968 Wisley's exhibit of hostas, which gave a great boost to their popularity

1980 Display of penjing from China

1982 Brenda Hyatt's display of auriculas, which launched these plants back into popularity

1988 John Chambers's honeybee garden

1993 Julie Toll's seaside garden controversially won the last Wilkinson Sword award for best garden, described by David Stevens as 'a sand dune garden that was well planted and beautiful, but visitors said it wasn't a garden'

1994 Isabel and Julian Bannerman's *Daily Telegraph* Old Abbey garden, with a virtuoso display of mature tree transplanting

1996 Dan Pearson's London roof garden for the 1990s

1997 Christopher Bradley-Hole's Latin Garden, the first garden at Chelsea to exhibit the new fashion for sparse planting

2000 The Garden History Society's Le Nôtre Garden, and Piet Oudolf's winning 'Evolution' garden

On one occasion, the Chelsea Show became a subordinate part of a larger exhibition programme. In 1947 the Royal Society of Arts proposed to commemorate the centennial of the Great Exhibition of 1851 with a Festival of Britain, both as a commercial showcase for British design and as a 'tonic for the nation', intended to compensate for years of continued rationing and to stimulate some hope for the future. A garden committee was set up, on which the RHS was represented by John Gilmour and Francis Hanger. On the Battersea Park site where the major part of the Festival was to be held, a series of Festival Gardens was designed by Peter Shepheard, Frank Clark, Peter Youngman, and Maria Shephard-Parpagliolo; the RHS's contribution, it was agreed, would be to expand Chelsea for the occasion and hold a Festival show. Hanger pulled out the stops to create a Wisley exhibit that would surpass all previous efforts:

Wisley was asked to stage an exhibit '... worthy of the Society.' The area allocated to Wisley was 61 × 41 feet, the largest space ever allotted for one exhibit under canvas at any time and the Garden knew that it had a task on its hands. The previous autumn saw Mr Dykes and Mr Boon, ably assisted by students, potting thousands of plants including primulas, lilies, meconopsis, hostas, hardy ferns and other species of woodland plants.

Mr Bolton on Battleston Hill was to supply 'lorry load after lorry load' of rhododendrons, acers and Enkianthus. Notorious Wisley frosts were a worry and so a huge shelter was erected sized 50 x 20 feet and 15 feet high. Larch poles formed the main framework, bamboos threaded through iron fencing were used for the sides whilst wire netting and coconut fibre formed the northern slope of the roof. Sacking was available for further covering if necessary and enabled him (Mr Bolton) '... to sleep at nights as the Show drew near ...' The spring was unkinder than anticipated and two dozen rhododendrons were carted to London and placed in cool air storage at the Docks for five weeks—evergreen plants in complete darkness! Mr Bolton reluctantly handed over his charges to dockers when challenged on union membership.

During Chelsea Week 23 lorry loads of mixed plants were transported to the Show and by 10.30 on Monday night the Himalayan Gorge with a mossy glade was complete. It was acclaimed by all and reckoned to be an exhibit worthy of the Society.

Oh! and the two dozen incarcerated rhododendrons? These emerged from five weeks

Marketing and sponsorship at Chelsea: the Yardley's garden (1997), graced by the 'supermodel' Linda Evangelista.

of total darkness unscathed to 'flower beautifully' on time. They were returned to Battleston Hill after the Show to flourish in future seasons.[96]

In 1980 the Beaminster and District Gardens and Allotment Society staged a garden at Chelsea, the first time a garden had been made by a local society of this sort; it was funded by the BBC, who contributed £20,000 to the construction cost. The *Gardeners' Chronicle* warned that 'This wants watching. If not, before very long, the tail of the media will wag the dog of the Royal Horticultural Society'. As the decades wore on, the amount of money involved in sponsoring a Chelsea garden increased steadily—and so did the accusations that the show was becoming too commercial, 'a horticultural shopping mall'. Some parts of the horticultural press adopted a *faux-naif* attitude toward exhibiting generally; Mirabel Osler, writing about Chelsea in *Hortus*, seemed to have been expecting not so much a flower show as the garden of Eden:

> Hearing a very famous gardening writer greet a very famous gardening photographer by saying, 'This is the best Chelsea ever' I did think, my God, what must the others have been like?
> Impressions fermented. Was there once innocence? Had simplicity and a pure pursuit of displaying the beauty of flowers ever existed? Had gardeners come in the early days with their arms full of flowers and the inculpable motive of showing us what was available in nurseries up and down the country? Were the original Chelsea Flower Shows free of artifice, polystyrene, arty ingenuity, cerebral acrobatics and over-the-top devices of superb bad-taste? Or have there always been rent-a-mobs of ten-inch blooms in psychedelic colours?

To which the only sensible answer is, No, there never was innocence, at any rate not since the florists' societies came into existence in the 17th century.[97]

Some remarks on show layout and display

The exhibits at most early shows were simply collections of plants in pots and tubs. The idea of making an exhibit look like a garden first arose in England with the one-man shows of John Waterer at the Royal Botanic Society, who arranged his rhododendrons in symmetrical groups to suggest possible garden use. During the 1860s, Robert Marnock began using similar principles to create picturesque layouts at the Regent's Park shows, and his disciple Alexander McKenzie followed suit at Alexandra Palace in the 1870s. It can be seen as more than coincidence that the fashion for picturesque display grew up during the decade

which also saw the introduction of flower arranging into shows: D.T. Fish proposed awarding prizes for effective grouping, and said, 'A dozen cultivators can be found to grow a dozen plants well for one who can group them for effect'. From the judges' point of view, however, picturesque layout, by separating the groups of plants to be judged, created extra work, and required extra time before opening for the judges to troop over the site making comparisons, so the fashion, in its extreme form, was short-lived.[98]

Nonetheless, it had a great impact in its time, exemplified in the Society's regional shows of the 1860s and 1870s, where the layout was entrusted to garden designers: usually George Eyles, who was after all Superintendent of the Kensington garden as well as a professional landscaper, but also John Gibson and Joseph Forsyth Johnson. Gibson, whose layout for the 1866 International Exhibition had been highly praised, was hired to lay out the Nottingham Show in 1871. His reputation brought an excitement to the advance press coverage: 'We may ... look for some improvement upon the old-fashioned interminable lines of long, stuffy, narrow tents, with their hideously formal yet shabby tabling, and tier unsymmetrical furnishing in regard to the heights and forms and colours of the different classes of exhibits ...'. The Society's new tent was brought from Kensington, and laid out informally, with winding paths around masses of foliage.

For the layout of the Preston Show in 1878, Joseph Forsyth Johnson, a young Irish garden designer whose show design for Belfast a few years earlier had been highly praised, was put in charge:

> The irregular banks provided for the display of the plants consist of gentle slopes instead of steps, which is a manifest advantage in the setting of the plants, since in most cases it gives them the desired inclination, while the use of ugly supporting blocks and other unsightly contrivances is done away with or reduced to a minimum. A considerable surface of water and a waterfall are introduced, and more or less utilised in setting out the plants for effect, a series of small green banks occupying the bays formed in the margin of the water, and a dozen Tree Ferns being tastefully distributed over the surface of the lake itself, being set just above the water-level ...[99]

The fashion for picturesque landscape under the tent faded after the 1870s, but the demand that Fish had expressed for effective grouping continued as a principle for individual stands. The shows provided two different types of stand organisation: against the outer walls, and on islands within the hall or marquee; perimeter stands have consistently been laid out as banks of shelving or

Continued on p.143

Music at the Chelsea Flower Show

The Royal Horticultural Society is not generally thought of as a musical organisation, but a glance at the past catalogues of the Chelsea Flower Show reveals, in almost every year from 1913 to 1992, a three- or four-day programme of music to be performed by the Grenadier Guards.

This tradition goes further back than Chelsea. While the Society's early fêtes at its garden at Chiswick in the 1820s and 1830s presumably had music, little record of what was played has survived; but with the opening of the Society's new garden in Kensington in 1861, music suddenly became a matter of such importance that a Music Committee was instituted, and competitions between military bands became a regular event in the garden in the 1860s. The reasons for this may be easily guessed. The Crystal Palace, of whose ticket income the Society was highly envious, made concerts part of its life, and had started holding its gigantic Handel Festivals in 1857. And while further problems of income and administration put an end to the Music Committee before long, the association of military bands with the major flower shows continued.

The programme of a military band concert may be varied, but its framework has traditionally been set by the march, with the waltz and other dances appearing at regular intervals in each part of the concert. So it should be no surprise to learn that the most frequently performed composer of all at Chelsea has been Johann Strauss, Jr., with 176 performances.

The British musical stage has been strongly represented from the beginning, with the interesting effect that concert pieces have continued to be performed long after the musicals they were derived from had passed into oblivion. Sir Henry Bishop, the Andrew Lloyd Webber of the mid-19th century, could still be heard at Chelsea in 1928. The history of musical comedy can be traced there, from Sidney Jones and Paul Rubens, through Ivor Novello and Noel Coward, to Lionel Bart and Andrew Lloyd Webber in the present day.

American musicals and American operetta both arrived in the late 1920s. Jerome Kern, as befitting his seniority, appeared first, in 1927, but the first Gershwin piece followed the next day; and then Irving Berlin, Vincent Youmans, Cole

Porter and Richard Rodgers followed in their due course, to be supplemented after the war by Frank Loesser, Jule Styne, and Frederick Loewe. Sondheim has yet to appear.

American operetta made inroads about the same time that American musicals did – interestingly, since apart from Lehar the continental operetta was not well represented; perhaps the English language made a difference. Rudolf Friml was first performed in 1928, and Sigmund Romberg the next year. Film music began to appear in the 1930s, but often with an interesting time lag. 'Dream of Olwen', whose popularity dates from the 1947 film 'While I Live', was not performed at Chelsea until 1974.

One can have much innocent fun with the programmes of music, for over the years they have displayed every solecism possible in dealing with music titles: misspellings, mistranslations of foreign titles, misplaced accents in foreign words, misattributions, substitutions of arranger's name for composer's, imprecision or confusion of genres (is 'Amparito Roca' a march or a paso doble? What sort of march is a patrol?). Most amusing or annoying, depending on temperament, is the continual vacillation between English and foreign languages for titles and terms, as though the excesses of the internationalist in one year were compensated for by the monoglot the year after. 'Suite de ballet' becomes 'ballet music', 'waltz' becomes 'valse', without any clear rationale for the changes.

The earlier programes tried, to a certain extent, to educate the audience; certain pieces would have a little paragraph appended in small print, giving either a potted biography of the composer, or a note about the reception history of the piece. These notes were sometimes subjective, but in most cases genuinely informative. This practice virtually ceased with the Second World War.

A different sort of populism can be seen in the way that titles change in accordance with commercial use. Beginning in 1925, the programmes record performances of excerpts from Schubert's 'Lilac Time'. If you do not recall a work of this title by Schubert, do not be surprised: it is the title of a musical comedy (English version 1922 by Adrian Ross) based on Schubert's life, and therefore using his music for the score. The tendency thus established became more pronounced

after the last war, from reference to Chopin's 'Les Sylphides' (name of a Diaghilev ballet set to pieces by Chopin), to the announcement that Khachaturian had written a piece called 'Theme from The Onedin Line'. A parallel shift (some might call it a decline) took place in the way compilation pieces were referred to in the catalogues; from 'Excerpts' to 'Selection' to 'Melodies' to 'Hit tunes' to 'Showtime'.

The concerts managed to ride out the 1960s without acknowledging the virtual takeover of popular music by rock & roll, but in the 1970s things began to change. In 1971 came the first performance of tunes associated with Herb Alpert and the Tijuana Brass – understandably, because a distinctively new brass sound was of obvious interest to a military band. Over the next few years, anthology pieces devoted to the Seekers and the Carpenters followed; 'Jesus Christ Superstar' appeared in 1974, and in 1978 music by the Beatles was heard for the first time.

In 1993, for the first time in 70 years, the programme of music in the Chelsea catalogue did not list the pieces. A decision had been taken to increase the amount of music performed during the show from two band concerts to a varied range of music all day long. The Band of the Grenadier Guards of course continued their performances, but were supplemented by the Nat West Jazz band, and a harpist. The number of additional bands increased over the next two years, but was reduced again in 1996, with the Grenadier Guards playing on the members-only days, and the Household Division Musicians' Association Band on the public days.

Some pointless miscellanea

First American musical comedy number: Selection from Kern's 'Sunny', 1927; though Gershwin's 'Lady be Good' followed the next day.

First piece of film music: Bliss's theme music for 'Things to Come', 1936.

First television theme: 'Inspector Rose theme' (Hill), 1969.

First rock & roll piece: Andrew Lloyd Webber, music from 'Jesus Christ Superstar', 1974.

Piece least likely to be performed again: 'Parade of the Willies' (A. Spurgin, performed 1960).

vertical displays, but the design of island stands has been subject to great variation. Between the wars, the big seed houses—Sutton, Carter, Webb—were particularly associated with 'mountain-high mounds of annuals', and men like E.R. Janes, of Suttons' Seeds, and Francis Hanger of Wisley, earned great acclaim for their skills in arranging stands and woodland gardens. During the 1960s and 1970s came a tendency for more open exhibits and for accessories associated with flowers—'Some of the latter might disturb the spirit of the late A. Simmonds if, as it may well do, it wanders through the quiet marquee on the night of the Monday preceding the opening'.[100]

At the first Chelsea Flower Show, the orchids were all grouped together on one side of the marquee, and this arrangement continued until they were relocated in a separate tent. The use of tables for certain types of exhibit ensured that alpines, for example, remained together as a category until the Second World War. In the post-war years, the tables were discontinued, and exhibits were increasingly scattered around the marquee without regard to subject. In 1961, Russell Page was to attack this heterogeneity of arrangement:

> What is one to make of the great marquee?—110 separate stands, and no sign of order. Nothing is grouped: cacti, sweet peas, orchids, tulips and vegetables, alpines, roses, ferns, strawberries, perennials and shrubs recur throughout the place in all kinds of combinations. ... this is British horticulture showing and selling its wares to the public. Can it help sales to display goods in a way that even the village general shop has long since abandoned? Any department store arranged on this principle would go bankrupt rapidly.[101]

But the principle of scatter rather than grouping has continued ever since, without any obvious ill consequences, either commercial or aesthetic.

Hampton Court Palace Flower Show

The RHS did not found what became its major show after Chelsea. The Hampton Court Palace Flower Show was the brainchild of the management consultant Adrian Boyd, who saw an opportunity to connect in a joint venture two organisations that were facing times of uncertainty. The Department of the Environment had been dismembered in the 1980s, and one of the cuttings was Historic Royal Palaces, which found itself looking for ways of increasing revenue and attracting a larger audience. Similarly, Network Southeast, one of the temporary aggregations thrown up by the fission of British Rail, was looking for ways of making its rail services more profitable. Boyd's idea was that Network Southeast should sponsor a flower show at Hampton Court, and provide the public transport access. At the time, the RHS Shows Department was working on four new events for 1993, in Birmingham, Harrogate, Wembley, and Glasgow (the exhibition to accompany the World Orchid Conference), and was in no position to compete with any other shows in the London area.

The first Hampton Court Palace Flower Show, in July 1990, was quite successful; special trains were laid on from Waterloo Station, and the porters wore carnations in their hats; even though there was comparatively little trade support for the show, it was impressively marketed and drew in crowds. Network Southeast was pleased: '70 per cent of the estimated 300,000 visitors used rail and that has paid for our sponsorship many times over'. The RHS debated whether to offer to help with the Show, especially when Chelsea reached full capacity; the principal complaint from the RHS's point of view was the quantity of crafts stands which formed the first thing the visitors saw on entering. The organisers, after initial dismissal, indicated that they would welcome an RHS involvement from 1992, and RHS members were granted a reduced admission price at the 1991 show. Adrian Greenoak, the Show's horticultural director, achieved a continuous improvement in the standards; the 1991 Show introduced a British Rose Festival, with the joint involvement of the Royal National Rose Society and the British Rose Growers' Association. But Boyd's firm, Le Teurnier Boyd Management Services, was on unsteady ground: he had come up with the idea, but the legal title to the Show rested with Historic Royal Palaces, and he had to renegotiate the contract every 12 months.

In November 1992 came the announcement that Network Southeast was withdrawing its support for the show. It was paying £750,000 per annum in subsidy, and in the run-up to privatisation was obliged to jettison all its tangential projects. A flurry of negotiations took place: Boyd, having no title to the Show, had to join in competitive tendering by blind bid. Stephen Bennett outlined the benefits of RHS involvement: 'We can reduce the costs hugely ... Apart from saving publicity costs with our extensive media relations network, we have a colossal amount of equipment. We have around £1m worth of tentage and tons and tons of staging equipment. Try to hire that sort of stuff and it costs an arm and a leg. We could do it without any sponsorship ... but that's not to say we should if we have the opportunity to talk to people.' BBC Haymarket was also in the bidding, but Historic

Royal Palaces accepted the RHS bid on condition that it undertook to keep certain staff on the payroll, including Adrian Greenoak. The venture was a risky one, with four new shows already booked for 1993, but, resignedly waving farewell to the expected surplus for the year, Council was prepared to support it.[102]

The first RHS Hampton Court Show took place in 1993, with additional sponsorship from the *Daily Mail*—which did not, in this first year, go smoothly; the March issue of *The Garden* had announced that the show preview would be for RHS members only, but the *Mail* issued 5,000 preview tickets for its readers. The Show was a considerable success, and the following year was declared to be the best outdoor public event of 1994. With a 25-acre show ground, there was room for considerable expansion before the infra-structure would be severely tested, and over the next few years a Heritage Marquee was set up for the NCCPG and its national collections—initially a rather quiet area, but increasing steadily in public interest; crafts pavilions, which under Adrian Boyd were the first sight to greet the visitor, were gradually moved to a less prominent position;

there was room for a couple of dozen display gardens, plus a separate section, on the other side of the Long Water from the major part of the exhibition, for ten water gardens. In 1998 a Hampton Court garden was rebuilt at the Royal Hospital for Neuro-disability. While Chelsea remained the most prestigious of the Society's shows, Hampton Court was the largest, and readily marketed as such; the major problems were the traditional ones of lavatories and parking. Within a couple of years the investment in Hampton Court had been more than recouped, and the half-yearly financial review was now pushed on until after the proceeds of Hampton Court had been counted.[103]

The Scottish and Tatton Park Shows

In the 1860s and 1870s, the RHS had attempted to spread its show coverage throughout the country with a series of Provincial Shows, convened with the assistance of local horticultural societies and the Royal Agricultural Society. After 1873 the programme faltered, was revived by fits and starts,

The Long Water at Hampton Court Palace as it appears during the Flower Show, fringed with stands and seated visitors.

and then extinguished. Throughout the 20th century, the Society sent delegates to take part in judging at regional flower shows, but it was not until the 1980s and the new drive for augmented regional activity that the joint staging of shows with local societies was revived. The story of this is told in more detail in Chapter 19.

By the mid-1990s the Society's confidence in its abilities at staging regional shows had improved, and Council was considering the creation of purely RHS shows in the more far-flung regions. By 1996 negotiations were under way with Tatton Park in Cheshire, and with Strathclyde Council in Scotland. The Island, a 19-acre site between the River Clyde and Strathclyde Loch, in Strathclyde County Park, southeast of Glasgow, was chosen as the site for a show. Stephen Bennett was quoted as saying, 'We have long known that Scotland has enormous potential for a show of international standing, and response to the concept has been overwhelming'. The target was 50,000 visitors in the first year.

Scotland's National Gardening Show was launched in 1997, and billed as the largest flower show in Scotland since the Glasgow Garden Festival of 1988. It was publicised with a special issue of *The Garden* devoted to Scottish themes, and the first year was seen as a great success, with 260 exhibitors and 47,000 visitors. Over 40 per cent of the exhibitors were Scottish, and most of them had never appeared before at an RHS show. Exhibits included a Robert Fortune garden, sponsored by Christian Aid Scotland, devoted to plants that he had introduced; a mining garden; a small wildlife garden from Scottish Natural Heritage; and an exhibit recreating the centre of Inverness, planted with alpines. In its second year exhibitor numbers rose to 300, but attendance fell to 43,000, largely because of adverse weather. The third year, however, was disastrous: while the mounting costs of an expanding show meant that 50,000 visitors were needed for it to break even, the attendance fell to 35,000—a third of the attendance attracted by the Tatton Park Show in the same year. In August 1999, the Society reluctantly announced that it could not afford to stage the show again. The RHS was heavily criticised for thus backing out; it was said in Council that it would be cheaper to buy a train fare to Chelsea for every Scottish member, but the RHS, still slowly and painfully learning the lessons of publicity, did not say this publicly. Scottish horticulturists hurriedly formed a consortium to stage a replacement show, and the Royal Caledonian Horticultural Society became involved in its organisation: 'The RCHS was, at one time, a prestigious society.

A cottage garden in the Daily Mail *marquee at the Hampton Court Palace Flower Show.*

We are trying to get that back', its Secretary was quoted as saying.[104]

The first Tatton Show had been planned for 1998, but in the event it was decided to concentrate on Scotland first, even at the cost of paying compensation for the lost year. Max de Soissons, an experienced organiser of trade exhibitions, who had been hired in 1996 as the RHS manager for the *BBC Gardeners' World* Live show in Birmingham, was appointed the Tatton Show manager. At the first Tatton Show in 1999, there were 12 show gardens, 16 back-to-back gardens (distinct from the small gardens at Birmingham or the courtyard gardens at Chelsea), 77 nurseries in the main marquee, 10 rose growers in the Royal National Rose Show (sponsored by

Manchester Airport), 200 sundries stands, some 20 plant societies in a Specialist Societies Marquee, and about 30 national collections represented in a Heritage Marquee, as well as a crafts pavilion sponsored by *Country Living* magazine and a separate Furniture Pavilion. 70,000 visitors were expected, and 102,000 arrived. Tatton, the RHS staff agreed, had the friendliest atmosphere of any of the Society's shows.[105]

Robert Sweet, the former Torbay Parks Officer, now Head of Shows Development, suggested a competition among parks departments for the best bedding scheme. The plots, each a standard 6 × 4 foot bed so that the local authorities competed on equal terms despite any differences in their size and wealth, were laid out on either side of a principal avenue: there were six competitors in the first year, 12 in the second, rising to 24 in 2003, by which time the competition was having a decided affect on the media coverage of municipal bedding.

In the Show's first year, the proportion of southern exhibitors was deemed to be too high, but as word and experience of the show spread, the number of northern firms exhibiting has steadily increased. Traffic proved a great problem during the first year; the second year saw a great improvement, but northern radio broadcast an unnecessary warning about traffic congestion which may have reduced attendance.

Westminster shows

The Kensington garden had been intended very specifically to give the Society a central London venue, to enable it to compete more effectively against Regent's Park and the Crystal Palace. So when Kensington was abandoned, there was no thought of trying to move the shows back to Chiswick: somewhere more central had to be found, even at the cost of property rental and temporary infrastructure. The Princes Cricket Ground was examined as a possibility, but decided against; and so the London Scottish Royal Volunteers' Drill Hall in James Street was hired, and the Society rented offices sited nearby in Victoria Street. For 16 years all the shows except the Great Spring and Summer Shows were held in the Drill Hall, until in 1904 the Society obtained its own Hall on Vincent Square and was able to hold its shows in its own premises.[106]

Many of the features of Kensington shows were at first carried on in Westminster. For most of the 20th century there was a show in the Hall (later, Halls) each fortnight, except at Christmas and in a slightly extended interval around Chelsea. One-man shows were still possible: Waterers staged one as late as 1914.[107] Specialist shows, such as the Early Market Produce Shows of the 1930s, and the Horticultural Machinery Shows of the late 1940s, were paralleled by shows whose significant features were competitions—daffodils first, from 1911, but soon followed by rhododendrons and camellias, and then by the competitions of specialist plant societies. From 1951 a spring orchid show was staged in the Halls, the first such show being opened by the Queen Mother; in 1985 and 2003, the RHS orchid show was cancelled in favour of, first, the centenary Orchid Conference and Show, and, second, the European Orchid Conference and Show. The Orchid Show of 2001 was the first event in the (yet again) renovated Hall.[108]

Back-to-back gardens at the Tatton Park Flower Show.

In 1921, C.G.A. Nix, the retiring Treasurer, proposed that the Society hold a large autumn show; negotiations over resuming the Great Summer Shows at Holland House were dragging and would shortly be abandoned, and a comparable autumn show seemed a reasonable substitute. First at the Holland Park Skating Rink, then at Olympia and the Crystal Palace, the Great Autumn Show was the Society's largest show after Chelsea. After the Second World War it was not revived as quickly as Chelsea; the fees for Olympia and Earls Court were now so high that Council decided to hold the Great Autumn in their own Halls, but the Horticultural Trades Association cautioned that the two Halls together were

Right, a view at the first show in the Lindley Hall, 1904; below, the Great Autumn Show at the Crystal Palace, 1934.

inadequate for a show of such size. In 1954 the Great Autumn Show was once again held at Olympia, and alternated between Olympia and the Halls for the next decade. In 1966 and 1967 the Great Autumn was held at Alexandra Palace, but as Lord Aberconway said at the next AGM, 'we rattled about in that great hall', and from 1968 the show was held in the Westminster Halls. Attendances dropped in the early 1970s, but by the late 1980s overcrowding rather than sparseness was the complaint. In 1989 the show was reduced from three days to two.[109]

The idea of having a Christmas show was presaged in 1981 when Sir John Wells, of Wells and Winter, staged a Christmas plant bazaar in the Halls, which was confused in the press with an RHS event. In 1992, however, the idea of having a Christmas show was mooted within the RHS itself, and soon agreed on as an occasion with relaxed rules, without serious judging (except for the botanical art competition), at which the exhibitors would be invited to wear fancy dress according to a pre-declared theme. The first Christmas show, in December 1993, was regarded as a most enjoyable occasion, and it continued until 2001, when it was cancelled at fairly short notice. The cancellation provoked expressions of disappointment, most notably from the artists who expected to exhibit.[110]

In 1991, amid anxieties over Chelsea, and the first sightings of the strange new phenomenon of Hampton Court, Martin Slocock suggested that the RHS should launch another major show in London to offer an alternative to Chelsea, for example in a royal park. The Society had not considered a London show outside Westminster since an abortive East End Show in 1878;[111] but suddenly a new venture offered itself. The media corporation News International was proposing to hold a show in Wembley Stadium, and offered to take the financial risks if the RHS would take responsibility for the show organisation. All during the course of 1992 things seemed to be going well, though News International started to get worried as the RHS became progressively involved with *BBC Gardeners' World* Live in Birmingham. The International Spring Gardening Fair took place at Wembley in April 1993, to great disappointment from Council's point of view: the 64,000 visitors were not up to the expected level, benefits for RHS members had been eroded, and the shows staff thought they had been treated in a cavalier manner. Council decided to discontinue relations with News International; when they learned that the next year's show had already been advertised as being held in association with the RHS, they resignedly sighed, 'This illustrated the sort of difficulties experienced in dealing with News International'; eventually the matter was settled out of court, with News International paying the RHS nearly £10,000 for prize money.

The idea of a flower show in a park had been shoved to one side by the RHS, but at a time when the Royal Parks had been the subject of a review committee, when compulsory competitive tendering was running down standards of horticultural maintenance, it was to prove seductive for the Royal Parks Inspectorate. After all, hadn't R.G.B. Evison greatly increased public attendance in the Brighton parks in the 1960s by holding flower shows there?[112] As early as 1993 rumours of a Hyde Park show were transpiring; and in 1999 a flower show was staged in Regent's Park. The RHS was annoyed, because the organisers copied the RHS guidelines for judging without acknowledgement; but the show took place peaceably and seemed to augur a successful future, were it not for traffic and access problems for the exhibitors. The Regent's Park show lasted three years; by the time it disappeared, a House and Garden Show was being held at Alexandra Palace, and the Olympia exhibition centre was staging a similar event.[113]

The problems facing the Westminster Shows increased. During the 1980s and early 1990s the various businesses facing onto Vincent Square gradually disappeared, and their properties were turned into hotels or flats; and as the Square and its adjoining streets became progressively residential, the former latitude allowed to the shows was eroded. A prohibition on noise before 7 a.m. led to the discontinuation of the National Dahlia and Chrysanthemum Societies' shows, as their exhibitors were accustomed to setting up overnight. The introduction of wheel-clamping, especially when it was carried out by contracted officials, posed additional problems for exhibitors; the sight of an exhibitor spending much of the show day in his car, waiting to move it on the appear-

Martin Slocock, Director of Slocock and Knap Hill Nurseries. The third member of his family to receive the Victoria Medal of Honour (Walter C. Slocock, 1916; O.C.A. Slocock, 1964; Martin Slocock, 1973). Treasurer of the RHS, 1992–2002.

A show at Olympia, 1937.

ance of a parking attendant, became common. (At the time of writing, similar anxieties have been felt over the introduction of congestion charging in central London.) The increased power and stringency of fire regulations also helped to catch the Society in a double bind: when one adviser called for greater publicity for the shows to counter falling attendances, another reminded that the Halls had a maximum capacity, and that the inspectors could close the shows if the attendance increased too much.

Throughout the 1990s, the Shows Department pursued several options for invigorating the programme of shows. One strategy was sponsorship: in 1990 Witan, an investment trust, agreed to sponsor the late April show at a rate of £24,500. Accepting sponsorship also involved accepting compromises: in 1994 the March show was limited to the Lindley Hall, so that Witan could hold its shareholders' meeting in the Lawrence Hall, a decision that provoked criticism. Another strategy was publicity in *The Garden*, which began for the first time to feature regular illustrated articles about the shows.[114] In 2001 an April show was held on a weekend, to make it 'easier to get to'; but the major alternative strategies were to reduce the number of Westminster Shows, and to move shows out of London to Wisley.

The idea of holding shows at Wisley had first been mooted in 1974, at a time of slight but uneasy financial upturn, but after a few months of discussion it had been dismissed as impracticable. In 1992 the first Wisley Flower Festival was held in the summer, and deemed a success; by 1994, the show was attracting 20,000 visitors over a three-day period by 1994. It was decided to hold a Wisley show annually, and there was much debate over whether it should overlap with a London show, and more importantly, whether Wisley shows should be additional to, or instead of, London shows?[115] The Wisley shows were initially run by the Shows Department, and the Wisley staff responded with grumbles about wear and tear to the lawns and overflowing carparks. Eventually the Wisley staff took over a greater role in its operation, so that the Shows Department in London was limited to planning dates and select-

The atmosphere of the Christmas shows of the 1990s, here exemplified by Paul Ingwersen, exhibitor and Council member.

ing exhibitors. As Wisley proved a successful venue, and the demands of regionalisation became more pressing, further new locations for shows were canvassed, and a Bournemouth Show was organised for 2003, removing one of the April shows from the London sequence.

Already by the early 1980s the Westminster Shows had ceased to be fortnightly, and plant committees were warning that the reduction in the number of London shows had produced gaps in the award cycle for plants with short seasons. Arguments over the financial implications of the shows became a regular feature of life in the higher echelons of the Society; by the end of the century the cost of the London shows was £400,000 per annum (part of it a rental fee to Horticultural Halls), and each London show lost about £30,000. Arguments were finely balanced between those who looked with dismay on the financial implications of continuing the shows, and those who looked with even greater dismay on the disruption to the competition schedule of reducing them. But as the Society's large shows in the spring and summer multiplied, the arguments in favour of reduction won out. By 2003 a new schedule had settled down, with monthly shows from January to April, plus the Orchid Show in March, then a gap for Chelsea, Hampton Court, Tatton, and Wisley; then the Great Autumn, the October fruit and vegetable show, and a November show—eight London-based shows in all. This is the situation at the time of writing, and it will no doubt continue to spark controversy from one end of the business-horticultural continuum or the other.

ROYAL HORTICULTURAL SOCIETY

OPENING OF THE SOCIETY'S NEW HALL
BY
H·M·THE KING

FRIDAY JULY 22ND
1904

8 *Horticultural Halls*

W HEN the Society abandoned its Kensington garden in 1888, it moved its headquarters into temporary offices at 111 Victoria Street (at the time of writing, the site of a branch of Abbey National). It also found itself without a venue for its flower shows. The experience of the 1850s had taught it that there was no point in trying to stage shows at Chiswick—too far from the centre of London, too many rivals nearer at hand. Accordingly, it rented the London Scottish Royal Volunteers' Drill Hall in Buckingham Gate for its regular shows, while moving the Great Spring Show to the Temple Gardens. For 16 years the Drill Hall saw flower shows at fortnightly intervals throughout the spring and summer seasons.

The building of the Lindley Hall (1904)

Let me now introduce Baron Henry Schröder, a merchant banker and important orchid grower, who served on Council from 1886 to 1893, and again from 1902 to 1905. As early as 1888, at the time of the move from Kensington, he had argued for the importance of a specially constructed hall in London, and his plan certainly caught the ear of the Prince of Wales, who referred to Schröder's plan in opening the 1890 Temple Show: 'The Royal Horticultural Society ... is now devoting its energies to the provision of a great national want— a Central Metropolitan Hall or Home for the Horticulturists of the United Kindom.' In February 1892, however, the New Hall fund was wound up, and the loans returned to those lenders who declined to let their money be transferred to a prize fund. Two years later the matter resurfaced, when Martin R. Smith, the carnation grower, put forward a scheme for providing the Society with a Central Hall of Horticulture; but his timing was not good. Council was already investigating such more modest possibilities as moving into the Imperial Institute's premises.[1]

Official pronouncements dithered. The Annual Report for 1900 stated: 'The Council fully recognise the advantage of the Society's possessing a hall of its own in which plants, flowers and fruits can be seen by the Fellows under more favourable conditions as regards light and space than are possible in the building at present used for the meetings. They do not, however, see their way to its attainment, but will be happy to consider any suggestion concerning it.' But at a special general meeting on 25 April that year, the President said that 'by far the best way of celebrating the centenary of the Society would be the provision of a Hall for its Meetings, and offices for its work, if any arrangement to carry that out could possibly be come to'. In 1902, a Committee under Schröder's chairmanship recommended the acquisition of a site on Vincent Square, the property of the Ecclesiastical Commissioners, on a 999-year lease at £690 p.a. The conflict between the hall and garden parties broke out at the Council meeting of 25 February 1902, with C.E. Shea angrily dissenting from the President; Shea apologised for his behaviour at the next meeting, but along with John T. Bennett-Poë offered his resignation from Council in protest at a Hall being given priority over a Garden.[2]

Schröder, alarmed by the resignations, decided that urgent action was needed to save the Hall proposal. A few weeks after the resignations, at a Special General Meeting, it was reported that the Baron had personally taken out the lease on the Vincent Square site to ensure that the opportunity wouldn't be lost. The estimated costs were £25,000. The lease was transferred to the Society in July, and Baron Schröder's name was cancelled in favour of the Society's on 26 August.[3] Then came the announcement that Wisley had been given to the Society as its experimental garden, so that funds could be devoted to the Hall in good conscience. The estimated costs kept being revised upward until they reached £40,000, and were met by a combination of public appeal and Schröder's own pocket. An appeal brochure was issued, calling for £17,000, and listing the donations already received: Schröder, who signed the appeal, had given £5,000 (about 20 per cent of the original estimated cost), and was to give a further £1,000 to furnish the Library. J. Pierpont Morgan, Lord Rothschild, Nathaniel N. Sherwood, and H.J. Elwes had each given £1,000 (though Elwes only after a tussle over the interpretation of his promise). 'The Society now numbers over 6,000 Fellows, a subscription averaging £1 a year for five years from every Fellow would therefore at once secure the realization of the scheme.' The American orchid grower C.G. Roebling, whose *Zygopetalum* Roeblingianum received a First Class Certificate in 1903, allowed it to be auctioned off as a contribution to the Hall fund (it fetched 50 guineas).[4]

Work began in May 1903, with Edwin Stubbs as the architect. The building illustrated in the appeal brochure consisted of an office block fronting Vincent Square, with the exhibition hall behind, backing onto the triangular yard of the Burdett-Coutts School; the office block had two floors, with a central block at the top of the structure to serve as a caretaker's flat. As illustrated, the entrance steps led up from street level without any covering portico; as built, there was not only a large stone portico over the entrance to the exhibition hall, but the steps were flanked on either side by a large raised terrace. On either side of the main door were additional doorways opening onto entrance lobbies: the left-hand staircase was the public entrance to the Society's offices, the right-hand one eventually restricted to fire-escape use. The combined entrance lobby had a mosaic floor showing the Society's device (altered after the Grant of Arms in 1929) and the heraldic flowers of the United Kingdom. A curving staircase led from the lobby to the basement, where cloakrooms and lavatories were installed. The two upper floors were long and narrow, with offices feeding off a rear corridor which backed against the exhibition hall. The hall itself consisted of a large open space with two raised dais areas on the Vincent Square side, each of which had a service

The fundraising brochure for the new (now Lindley) hall, with interior and exterior views as originally planned.

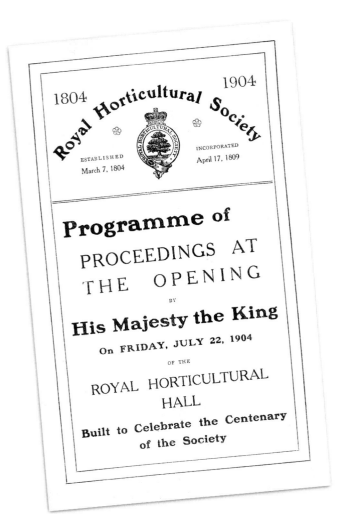

Programme for the opening of the Lindley Hall.

but converted to hot-water heating by Charles Kinnell before the First World War.

By 1911, Council was already investigating possible sites for larger premises; then the war broke out, and threatened what the Society already had. The Hall was quickly requisitioned to accommodate the first rush of soldiers bound for the front. In 1916 it was commandeered on behalf of the Australian army, and not returned to the Society's use until October 1919. The War Office at first tried to refuse compensation, but in 1920 was forced to pay up, and the Society won over £9,000 in reparations.[5]

For its first two decades, the building was known variously as the Horticultural Hall, and as the Society's New Hall. After 1928, when a new New Hall was built, it came to be referred to as the Old Hall, and from 2000 as the Lindley Hall. In what follows I shall refer to it by that name in order to reduce confusion.

The building of the Lawrence Hall (1928)

By the early 1920s, the Hall had come to seem too cramped for the flower shows that regularly filled it. In 1922, a Housing Committee was set up to report on accommodation, under the chairmanship of the Treasurer, C. T. Musgrave. The most active member on the Committee, however, was Henry B. May, the Tottenham nurseryman, now nearing his 80th year, and who had been a member of the Committee for the first Hall.[6] May argued strongly that the Society needed a second hall for its shows; the Committee at first rejected the idea, but before long they were examining sites in Regent's Park, the Embankment, and Greycoat Street, behind the existing hall, as possible locations for a new building.[7]

By November 1924 the Greycoat Street site had been decided upon. Like the Vincent Square site, it was the property of the Ecclesiastical Commissioners, from whom a similar long lease was obtained (the Society acquired the freeholds in 1959). The Ministry of Works owned the adjacent property, and its requirements had to be borne in mind, along with the problems of ancient lights; furthermore, the Society's Charter limited its capacity to own property to an annual value of £5,000. Musgrave lodged an application to obtain a new Charter, which contained a licence in mortmain not limited to any specific sum, and this Charter was granted in 1928.[8]

The Committee called for 'an unencumbered hall 150 ft. by 110 ft.', an area almost twice that of the Vincent Square hall. The architects Easton and Robertson were selected to produce designs, on the strength of a pavilion they had designed at the

entrance; the largest service entrance opened onto Elverton Street, and above it there was a minstrels' gallery. The decoration was loosely based on early Georgian precedents, with round-headed windows. The roof consisted of a large curvilinear span broken at the apex by a raised lantern; a 'travelling gallery', or moving staircase, was installed on the roof in 1910, providing access from the base of the roof to the lantern; this was so lightly poised that I have seen it move in the wind. The Hall was opened by Edward VII on 22 July 1904, and the first show took place four days later. Work on the offices continued after the opening; Baron Schröder undertook the costs of moving the Library and furnishing its new quarters on the second floor. Stubbs was asked to modify the exit so that visitors did not need to have the porter open the door for them; a permanent awning was supplied for the entrance, and bay trees (initially supplied by the Veitch Nurseries, but latterly purchased) were placed to line the approaches to the hall. A kitchen was installed in the basement in 1908. The building was originally steam-heated,

1925 Paris Exposition–John Murray Easton (1889-1975) was the active partner for this project. They put two designs before the Committee:

1. The 'Railway Station Scheme': based on W.H. Barlow's 1860s design of St Pancras Station, with continuous glazing supported on weight-bearing steel trusses carried down to ground level so as to avoid heavy brick piers.

2. The 'Swedish Scheme': based on Arvid Bjerke's design of an exhibition hall built for the Gothenburg Exhibition of 1923, and already used by Easton and Robertson in their Paris pavilion, using high-level glazing in the form of tiers of clerestory windows supported on parabolic arches.

The 'Railway Station Scheme' was consonant with the overall concept of the Vincent Square hall; the 'Swedish Scheme' envisaged a hall divided into a central nave and two side aisles by the piers of the arches, with the nave having roughly the same area as the existing hall, and additional floor space provided by the side aisles. Easton's memorandum set out the advantages of this system of clerestory lighting:

Its advantages are:

a. Natural daylight is admitted through clear glass which can be easily cleaned.

b. Only a fraction of the sun's heat is focused upon the windows since the more vertical the sun the less it strikes upon them.

c. The lights being vertical it is easy to control glare on sunny days by means of an inexpensive system of curtains or blinds which can be readily adjusted.

d. The window can be opened in hot weather thus securing ample and natural ventilation.

e. The vertical glazing and solid roofs are much more weather tight than horizontal glazing.

f. The appearance of the Hall is rendered exceedingly attractive, the railway station effect of ordinary roof glazing being entirely got rid of.

In contrast with this the ordinary type of roof lighting as in the present Hall has the following disadvantages:

1. Its light cannot be controlled and in order to prevent glare from sunshine it must be colour washed thus producing a dull and cheerless effect on sunless days.

2. In strong sunshine the building becomes excessively hot owing to the large area of relatively horizontal glass surfaces.

3. The window cannot be opened.

4. The appearance of the Hall is bound more or less to resemble the railway station type of building.

Easton went on to recommend reinforced concrete as the material for the construction:

The use of modern construction in steel or reinforced concrete eliminates a great deal of the cost of brick work and massive construction which used to constitute the remunerative part of architectural design. In the present instance, for example, walls of 2'3" in thickness would be required under the Building Act whereas by structural design 14" work is all that is necessary.

The Committee's initial response was inconclusive. Dykes, the Society's Secretary, opposed the Swedish Scheme, arguing that the lighting would be unequally distributed in winter, that the dais would be badly lit, and that the loading facilities would be unmanageable. 'I entirely appreciate the Secretary's desire to assist the Council', May replied, 'but his recent contributions do not, I think, materially add to knowledge.' 'The Crystal and Alexandra Palaces are notoriously unsuitable for horticultural purposes', he added; the only factor which should influence the choice of design was the lighting provision of the roof. After much consultation, the Swedish design was approved, and the foundation stone laid by the President, Lord Lambourne, on 19 October 1926.[9] The Hall was known for over seventy years as the New Hall, but in 2000 its name was changed to the Lawrence Hall (after Sir William Lawrence, Treasurer at the time of its building, and not forgetting Sir Trevor Lawrence), on the grounds that, with the internal rebuilding of the former Old Hall, it no longer counted as the newer of the two.

Easton consulted the engineer Dr Oscar Faber of the National Physical Laboratory,[10] who constructed a model for measuring the tensions of the proposed structure. It was soon realised that the arches would suffer from heavy thrust at the level of the aisle roofs, which were accordingly designed as a continuous horizontal girder surrounding the structure and reinforced at their junctions.

At the junction of each arch-rib and the roof there is a horizontal thrust of 45 tons, and the roofs have thus to carry a load of 270 tons from the six arches along each side for a span of 150 ft. Some idea of the reinforcement employed may be obtained from the following figures: There are thirty-three 1¼in. rods in tension and fifteen 1¼in. rods in compression, as well as transverse and shear reinforcement along each side. The ends of these large flat beams are continued round the ends of the building and held together by two tie-beams; that at the front end has also to resist wind pressure on the end wall. It is 3ft. 6in. wide

A photograph of the Lawrence Hall in the course of building, displaying the structure of the parabolic arches.

and 1ft. 6in. deep, and is reinforced by thirty-eight 1¼in. rods.[11]

The Hall was formally opened by H.R.H. Princess Mary, on 26 June 1928, and received an award from the RIBA the following year. The reactions of the different sectors of the press are enlightening. The architectural press greeted the design as revolutionary in a slightly restrained way; according to the *Architect & Building News*, 'Hitherto the walls and roofs of a building have counted as two distinct items ... What we see in the new Horticultural Hall, however, is a break-away from these traditional forms, for in a subtle manner the walls and roof are intermingled with the result that the old distinction between them is in part obliterated'. The writer of that review recognised only aesthetic reasons for the design: the railway station design 'would have been devoid of any architectural distinction'. 'Concrete has been taught to smile', wrote Morton Shand;[12] he praised it in the *Architectural Review* for providing all the benefits of modernism without the extremism:

> All, and more than all, of that unlimited light and air for which St. Corbusier and his fellow Hotgospellers are eternally clamouring in the windy wilderness of rhetoric ... seems to have been joyously captured in that splendidly luminous and intrepid vault.

Elsewhere, he lost control of his metaphors in his enthusiasm; within a few lines the Hall moved from being 'a young building', 'poised on the almost fragile slenderness of its gracefully arching shoulders', to a 'naked monolith' with 'lean, nervous strength and supple muscular anatomy', which 'lives and exults in living'. Charles H. Reilly named it as one of the architectural landmarks of the year. Only the *Architects' Journal* and *Engineering* gave fuel costs and the loss of heat from extensive glazing as motives for the design.[13] And only the *Gardeners' Chronicle*, perhaps not surprisingly, assessed the building for its intended purpose, namely the holding of flower shows. The writer thought the lighting generally superior to that in the Old Hall, but felt that the height of the Hall dwarfed the exhibits, and could have been 25 feet lower with advantage. 'However, the construction of the New Hall was largely by way of experiment; there is no hall like it and, so far as our experience goes, none so well lighted naturally'.[14]

The façade of the Hall was carried out in Ruabon brick on a plinth of Portland stone, with marble friezes above the doors. Lecture and committee rooms were housed in a four-storey block at the west end, an arrangement criticised by some reviewers for an uneasy transition to the main body of the Hall, and by Shand for an unnecessary deviation from symmetry in having a dwarf tower over the side entrance; but the Committee had accepted from the beginning that these rooms could only be accommodated vertically. Some Council members thought that the entrance was excessively understated; indeed, the Society's name was not included as part of the detailing. Compare, however, these varied responses from the architectural press:

> *Architectural Forum*: it 'takes one off guard with its greeting in new, clear phraseology, amid the muffled surrounding Victorian jargon'.

> *Architectural Review*: 'The Quaker discretion of the handsome triple canopy should be an object-lesson in the impossibility of acclimatizing stock models of the florid French type of marquise in London streets.'

> *Architect & Building News*: the 'frontage towards Greycoat Street is a fine example of modern urban design and has the signal merit of taking cognisance of its environment.'

> *Architects' Journal*: the recessed windows, set back some six inches from the wall face, are 'a reflection, intentional I think, of the plaster reveals so often met in the characteristic London style of 1800-1830'.

(Easton and Robertson themselves claimed that the treatment of the façade 'does not arise from the adaptation of "period" style'.)[15]

The main entrance led into a vestibule with a low ceiling, over which lay the dais; the walls were faced with Botticino marble with bands of Ashburton serpentine. Access into the hall was staggered from the line of the main entrance so as to reduce drafts. The vestibule floor was of stone; that of the Hall itself was of pitch pine arranged in a geometrical pattern, with terrazzo laid down at the junction of walls and floor in order to make cleaning easier. The columns and dadoes in the Hall were of dark Manu marble; the east and west ends were covered with acoustical plaster. The basement housed lavatories and a restaurant; Morton Shand thought that the restaurant deserved an article in itself: 'Gourmets will be joining the Royal Horticultural Society in their hundreds if the dishes set before members ... prove anything like as exciting to the palate as those subtle harmonies of grey, green, gold and orange are stimulating to the mind.'

The *Architect & Building News*, ever ready to promote the image of the heroic architect, exulted that 'All the fittings were especially designed by the architects, and this applies to everything in the building, no stock patterns being employed anywhere.' The *Architects' Journal* added that Easton and Roberston 'do not make mistakes'. By 1929, the Society's Council might not have agreed. Instead of using exposed radiators and relying on convection to heat the rooms, the architects employed heating panels, in which the pipes were

The Lawrence Hall as completed in 1928: the façade, which did not yet bear the Society's name on it, and the interior, with chairs laid out for the opening ceremony.

concealed within the floors and walls, providing a barrier against heat loss. (In the Old Hall, with its fully glazed roof, the temperature fell nightly to that of the surroundings, and heating had to start all over again each day.) The *Architectural Forum* called attention to the potential problems of this system: 'The fact that the entire slab must necessarily become thoroughly heated before it can radiate any heat to the air, as well as the sorry predicament in case of a leak, makes it an interesting treatment well worth observing.'

Observation, in fact, was already under way: the first leaks in the roof were reported in August 1928, two months after the opening, and on one night before the end of October no fewer than 41 leaks occurred. The Society's solicitor wrote to Easton and Robertson demanding that they rectify the matter, and after further experiments by Oscar Faber, the matter began to be resolved in the latter part of 1929—but only for the moment, as cracks in the walls were reported during the course of the 1930s. The difficulty of access for repairs continued to bedevil the maintenance staff, however, and eventually the panel system was abandoned for a system of exposed radiators.[16]

Architectural alterations 1930-1983

Edward Harding, the husband of the American garden writer Alice Harding, had offered to fit out a room in the Lawrence Hall as a study centre for American gardening; this idea did not see fruition, nor did it prove practicable to move the Library from its increasingly cramped conditions on the second floor of what now had to be called the Lindley Hall. With the aid of a grant from the Carnegie Trust, a new floor was added to the building in 1930 to house the Library; the architect was William Binnie. As before, a caretaker's flat was built over the central block of the new third floor; an extra fire escape was provided in the form of an external metal staircase leading from the flat to the Library, and rungs in the wall from an opposite landing to the roof gutter (whence one could climb the moving gallery to the lantern, cross to the Greycoat Place side, and yell for help).[17] However, the problem of space for offices had not been solved by the Lawrence Hall, and even before it was opened the Society had begun negotiations to acquire the Express Lift Company's adjacent building for an estimated cost of £10,000. These negotiations flickered off and on until the war, and were resumed immediately afterwards; in 1947, the Society's offer of £45,000 for the site was almost accepted, but the deal fell through; at last in the 1960s the site was sold to another buyer.[18]

During the Second World War, the Halls escaped being requisitioned as they had been during the First; lettings continued until it became apparent that profit-making exhibitions ruined the Society's chances of getting an exemption from wartime rates by virtue of its charitable status. Thereafter, the only lettings allowed for the duration were those with some charitable purpose, and the Lawrence Hall was leased to the Territorial Army for use in anti-aircraft training for the Home Guard. Three times the Halls sustained bomb damage, first in December 1940 when a nearby bomb blew out the glass and doors on the Elverton Street frontage, then in September 1941, undoing all the previous repairs, and finally in June 1944, when both halls were affected. After the war the gable end of the Lindley Hall had to be rebuilt, at a cost of over £4,000.[19]

Once the war was over and its finances restored, the Society determined to rebuild part of the Lindley Hall to increase its office accommodation. Binnie was placed in charge of creating a new wing on the Elverton Street side, by taking out the former minstrels' gallery and creating two floors of offices accessible from the main first-floor level. The Annual General Meeting for 1950 took place during the building work, and Lord Aberconway explained to the assembled members:

> That steel structure which you see in the Old Hall is the beginning ... of a small gallery of new offices for the Staff. We have no room for them on the ground floor; we cannot put them in the basement, and therefore we have to put them up in the air. And if you hear coming from above your heads sweet voices singing as they work, you will know that it is our Staff.

There is no actual report of singing, and as the Elverton Street extension tended to be chilly in winter and overheated in summer, the attitude during the years I knew it was one of resignation.[20]

Life in the second half of the 20th century had a certain recurring rhythm: income from lettings fluctuated; the buildings needed some degree of repair or refurbishment every few years; the Lindley Hall boiler kept being pronounced moribund and yet kept going, spewing out its accumulation of summer soot through the heating grilles every autumn when it was turned on. Each successive repair increased in price in an era of spiralling inflation, as of course did the Corporation Tax, and the early 1970s—when the Society was in financial downturn, in part precipitated by a fall in lettings—was not a good time to learn that the Lawrence Hall needed repairs yet again: the heating system was of a sort the Gas Board would no longer sanction, and needed a further £52,000; the wood-block flooring was wearing out. The need for desperate measures was felt. In 1974, the possibility of selling one of the London Halls was first discussed. As the Lawrence Hall heating repairs stumbled on, to end after two years in an angry flurry of compensation claims, it was the Lindley Hall that was settled on as the building to sell, and researches were conducted into the likelihood of a purchaser being allowed to make alterations to a listed building, let alone demolish it. Inconclusive offers, resistance at the 1977 AGM to the idea of the Library being moved, and more realistic consideration of the costs of the resulting office moves eventually persuaded Council, after three years of machinations, to carry on with the existing building—and, therefore, to renovate it, for it was now the Lindley Hall's turn to show signs of falling apart.

Falling apart, literally: the brick façade on Vincent Square was detaching from the main structure, and in addition the roof needed reglazing, and the heating system updating (this included running heating pipes through the basement, at a height inconsistent with the safety of a staff some of whom were over six feet tall). The total cost of the work, mostly carried out in 1979, was £350,000. But little breathing space was allowed: in February 1981, at the AGM, Lord Aberconway announced that the Lawrence Hall, by then 53 years old and a listed building, was leaking badly again; 'some of its novel structural features', he said laconically, 'have not stood the test of time.' The restoration work began early in 1983, and was completed sufficiently for the Hall to reopen in time for the Great Autumn Show that year; altogether some £900,000 was spent on its repair, financed by a compulsory levy on the members.[21]

Events in the Halls

The Lindley Hall had been opened less than four months when the first concert was held in it; in January 1905 the Bach Choir rented it for a choral concert. Nine months later, musical celebrations were held in the afternoon as part of the centenary of the battle of Trafalgar.[22] For a century now, when the Halls have not been used for the Society's shows, they have been let out for a variety of purposes, ranging from examinations— the Institutes of Chartered Accountants, Surveyors, and Taxation, the Association of Accounting Technicians, the Chartered Insurance Institute, and the University of London have been long-standing and regular customers—to trade and consumer exhibitions, fashion fairs, dances

and private functions, and, in the post-war years, to use by the Post Office for sorting Christmas mail.

Exhibitions of varying degrees of importance were held in the Halls over the decades. The South African Products exhibition of 1907 was not only launched with a royal procession, but earned its organiser a knighthood bestowed on the spot within the Hall. It was at the People and Racing Pigeon Show in January 1940 that Sir Edward Campbell announced that the government would remove its ban on pigeon racing; of probably greater moment was the 'Fight against Rheumatism' launched at the Nursing Exhibition of 1939. The Schoolboys' Exhibition was held in the Halls from 1926 to 1957 (with a few fluctuations of venue), before it moved finally to Earls Court and Olympia; a Schoolgirls' Exhibition was held in August 1949, presided over by Dame Mary Tyrwhitt, the first head of the Women's Royal Army Corps, and offering the astringent message that modern girls should think of pursuing careers, since so many of them would not get the chance to marry.

One of the oldest and longest-lasting of annual exhibitions was the Model Engineering Show, started by Percival Marshall and first held in October 1907. It appeared in the Halls almost consistently until 1960, when it transferred to other, larger venues; more recently it was known as the International Model Show. Marshall also started the Woodworker Show in the Halls, and was associated with the Pioneer Model Racing Car Shows that were also held there. Four important philatelic exhibitions were staged in 1906, 1912, 1923 and 1934; the 1934 Apex International Airpost Exhibition heralded the first winged postmark to be used in the British postal service, sanctioned by the Post Office exclusively for this event. Later on, the annual Stampex exhibition was staged in both Halls from 1969 to 1995, and succeeded by the comparable Philatex exhibition that continues successfully today. Other recent hobby-related events have included Imrex, the International Model Railway Exhibition; Bipex, the Postcard Traders' Association picture postcard show; and the Family History Fair, organised by the Society of Genealogists. The Halls have always been a breeding ground and launch venue for new shows and exhibitions; the Association of Exhibition Organisers has described Horticultural Halls as 'renowned for its role as a launch pad for new shows'. Many still exist today in larger venues around the country, some retaining their original names while others have changed name and emphasis. The *Daily Mail* Ski Show started in 1973, and is now held at Olympia

A display of 'Cinderella stamps', specially issued for events in the Horticultural Halls, ranging from the Bachelor Girls' Exhibition to the Health Exhibition of 1929, and including such stalwart perennials as the Model Engineering Exhibition and the National Cage Birds Exhibition.

(with Snowboard added to its title). The disabilities exhibition Naidex started 1974, and is now held at the National Exhibition Centre, Birmingham); the Christian Resources Exhibition (started by Gospatric Home in 1985) is now held at Sandown Park and other regional venues. The process has also worked the other way: after the destruction of the Crystal Palace, the Halls inherited the National Cage Bird Show.[23]

Political events were avoided as much as possible, and certain political parties were ruled out altogether. In 1926 the Communist Party was refused permission to rent the Hall for 'welcoming certain of their members when they are released after imprisonment for sedition'.[24] However, a Suffragette meeting chaired by Christabel Pankhurst on 23 January 1908 was allowed. (In more recent times, political parties and government departments have been regular users of the Halls and meeting rooms for rallies, conferences, and meetings.) Preferred events included dog, cat, and poultry shows,[25] badminton tournaments, the 1946 World Snooker Championship—and, of course, dances. Throughout the inter-war period, at least one dance was held per week for much of the year; among the regular dancers were the police 'A' Division, Lyons' Shops, the London Union of Training Colleges, the Royal Antediluvian Order of Buffaloes, the National Cyclists' Union, the London Labour Party, and the Widows & Orphans Christmas Hamper Fund. The problem with jollity was complaints about noise from neighbours, and at the beginning of 1921 it was ruled that dances could not continue past midnight. Once the site of the Lawrence Hall had been agreed, in 1926, the RHS applied for a Music Dancing and Cinematograph Licence for the Lawrence Hall, and gave the following particulars to the London County Council as part of the application:

> The premises are primarily required for the Horticultural Shows and Meetings of the Society, but the Lease of the premises will permit public or private meetings concerts, entertainments, exhibitions and other functions. No stage performances are contemplated nor theatrical performances. The premises are, therefore, required for
>
> (a) Exhibitions by the Society and others
>
> (b) Dancing
>
> (c) Banquets
>
> (d) Meetings and Displays
>
> (e) Meetings of any sort confined to Members of the Society
>
> An orchestra would be required for dancing and some entertainments and possibly at Banquets and also professional entertainers might appear but not in stage costumes.

(Cinematograph displays were to be confined to lectures and demonstrations only.) The application was opposed by Miss Murray Smith, a resident in Vincent Square. Cluttons, the Society's surveyors, pointed out in a letter that the Lawrence Hall was only going to be used in the same way as the old one, so they didn't understand why a local resident should object. The RHS brought out the big guns (Sir Henry Curtis Bennett KC, a bigger gun than whom it would have been difficult to find), the opposition was withdrawn, and the licence granted in December 1926.[26]

Along with functions went a necessary infrastructure of catering for the bodily needs of exhibitors and visitors. The Lawrence Hall was equipped with lavatories both indoors and out; Westminster Council demanded the removal of the outdoor lavatories in 1934. The gents' lavatory in the Lindley Hall was generously equipped with a skylight. Both Halls maintained restaurants until 1965, when the Lindley Hall restaurant was closed and its area converted into a storeroom for the Library. The Lawrence Hall restaurant had been praised for its stylish décor on its opening (it was redecorated in 1972, in a colour scheme chosen by Julia Clements); but Morton Shand's fantasy of the food forthcoming from its kitchens was probably doomed to disappointment. Various caterers were given contracts to handle food provision over the years: the Army and Navy Stores, whose offices were only minutes away, operated a successful service, including independent function catering, but were slow to resume proper functioning after the War, and surrendered their contract in 1947. Thereafter reports on the quality of food fluctuated, reaching such a low in 1957-8 that it was deemed to be alienating potential clients. The caterers were expected to provide meals and refreshments for meetings as well as for shows, and here again there were fluctuations; in 1966 Council grumbled about the difficulty of getting a hot meal—similar grumbles back in 1948 had prompted George Monro to donate a hot-plate, to keep Council lunches warm, but it had obviously fallen from use in the interval. From 1947, the caterers were allowed to use the kitchens to service outside functions, at a four per cent commission; but in the 1970s, with the downturn in lettings from the late 1960s, the caterers' profits were so reduced that the Society actually gave them an annual subsidy from 1972 to 1979.[27] Consul Caterers were the longest-lasting firm to run the restaurant, from 1965 until the late 1980s, when they were succeeded first by London Catering Services, then in 1997 by Brookes (a subdivision of Gardner Merchant), which in turn became Sodexho Prestige in 2000.[28]

Despite the immense possibilities, the letting of the Halls provided few occasions for friction. In 1948 complaints were made at a Horticultural and Agricultural Exhibitors' Association meeting, that non-horticultural bodies should not be given preference over kindred societies in the letting process. Three years later, the Society discontinued the use of external agencies for organising lettings, and thereafter the problem of conflict of interest was unlikely to arise, so long as they remained under direct RHS control.[29]

Horticultural Halls Ltd

£900,000 had been spent on the repair of the Lawrence Hall roof; barely had the work finished in 1983 than repairs were yet again required for the Lindley Hall, estimated at a mere £160,000. Before long the Society was discussing the idea of forming a separate organisation to administer Hall lettings; RHS Enterprises was proving a successful venture, ploughing its commercial profits back into the Society, and the profits from lettings demanded similar treatment. And so in 1986 a second commercial arm, Horticultural Halls Ltd (HHL) was formed, and Geoff Harvey, the Society's Assistant Secretary, was its first Managing Director.

Unlike RHS Enterprises, which derived 90 per cent of its profits from the Society's membership, Horticultural Halls operated 'fully in the free market', and in a market niche with approximately a dozen competitors of equal or larger capacity (Alexandra Palace, Olympia, etc.). At the time of its entry into the market in the 1980s, the Halls' image was on the wane and its services had been underpriced. In 1991 Rene Dee was recruited as Sales and Marketing Manager, and introduced a new marketing strategy. A new 'corporate identity' (The Royal Horticultural Halls and Conference Centre) was introduced, marketing improved, and the Hall rental prices steadily increased to improve turnover and profitability. While the recession during this period forced some of HHL's competitors to contract their business, HHL prospered. The commercially unattractive meeting rooms in the Lawrence Hall were developed in 1991-2 and re-launched as a competitive Conference Centre. By the mid-1990s, it was operating in five distinct markets—exhibitions, examinations, conferences, corporate hospitality, and special events (weddings, wine-tastings, fashion shows, product launches, sales auctions and weddings)—and had become a 'price maker', that is, its pricing policies were affecting those of its competitors.[30]

This was the beginning of regular improvements and enhancements both to the facilities and to the resources and staff structure of HHL, under Rene Dee's direction as Sales and Marketing Director; he later became Managing Director after Geoff Harvey's retirement in 1995.[31]

Among the special exhibitions of the 1980s and 1990s were 'The Emperor's Warriors' in 1987-8 (a display of the recently discovered terracotta figures from Qin Dynasty China); 'In the Shadow of the Guillotine', a rather unsatisfactory and gimmicky exhibition about the French Revolution, in 1989; the London Astronomy Show in 1995; 'Fungus 100', the centenary exhibition of the British Mycological Society, in 1996; the International Festival of Chocolate in 1998, complete with the world's largest chocolate bar (9½ feet long, weighing more than a ton); the 'Crisis' Millennium Party for 700 of London's homeless people held on New Year's Eve, 1999. Possibly the most successful of the new shows have been, annually since 1992, the Festival of Mind, Body and Spirit, usually filling the Lawrence Hall while the Chelsea Flower Show is on, and a cutting successfully propagated from it a few years later, the Healing Arts Festival, both of which reliably attract large crowds, and sprinkle the nearby streets with colourful New Age types for a week at a time.[32]

Meanwhile, within the offices, the rapid expansion of the Society's bureaucracy in the 1980s was squeezing departmental space. The former caretaker's flat above the third floor was taken over and converted into further offices; the basement was subdivided into departmental storage areas by a series of wire cages. In 1991, the Shows Department moved out of the Lindley Hall into Assets House, a building on Elverton Street opposite the Lawrence Hall; three years later, when the site was to be developed for flats, it moved again, into Vincent House on the southeast side of the Square. In 1991-2, a further renovation of the Lindley Hall was carried out by Austin Smith Lord architects; solar-controlled blinds were installed in the roof, and a new system of electrical outlets for the use of exhibitors slung through the basement. By 1995, when the proposed move of the Library to Wisley was defeated and the creation of a new home for it became a necessity, it was apparent that the office accommodation also needed a major redevelopment. It was therefore decided to vacate the Lindley Hall altogether, gut and rebuild it internally (saving only the Council Room, as the one room in the building that had retained its original décor), and try to provide space for all the London offices under one roof once again. The works were delayed by the need to raise funds, but at last, in 1999, the various offices were decanted into temporary premises: Secretariat, Publications, Personnel and Marketing into offices in Victoria Street, and Accounts, Shows, Membership, and IT into a building on Vauxhall Bridge Road called Tradewinds (whose lease the RHS had to take over in its entirety when the owners forfeited the head lease in 2000).

Four architects were shortlisted for the project, and Rick Mather, who had carried out important refurbishments at the Maritime Museum in Greenwich and at the Wallace Collection, was

selected; the Society's Project Manager was Martin Harvey. The façade of the building was retained, with alterations affecting only the doorways and the structure of the raised terraces on the Vincent Square frontage, through one of which a ramp for wheelchair access was carved. The Elverton Street entrance became the principal entrance to the Hall, and was considerably augmented; the offices in that wing were expanded outwards into the Hall to provide additional office and corridor space, and a new mezzanine restaurant facility constructed. The accessory staircase was built over to provide an extra office on each floor. (The Library alterations are dealt with in chapter 9.) In the basement, an extensive new kitchen was provided for the caterers, and an ingenious car lift added at one corner, to provide goods access into the Hall (and most especially car access, for Coys' Car Auctions). During the course of works, Westminster Council insisted that a small electricity substation be installed within the building, in order to cope with the computer demand; the glazing subcontractor went into receivership; and so for a variety of reasons the building works overran their original schedule.[33]

Such overrunning is entirely predictable with large-scale building projects, but nonetheless the RHS was caught out. A mixture of terminations of leases and scheduled events meant that when most departments moved back into the building in the spring of 2001, they returned to what was still effectively a building site. Council ruefully acknowledged that the 'staff had shown great tolerance'—not only over the unfinished conditions on their arrival, but over disappointed expectations, for the office plans had altered during the course of works, and some departments did not get all the space or services they had requested. The builders did not vacate the site until February 2002, leaving behind a set of operating manuals for technical services, that, placed side by side, marched all the way around

The Lindley Hall in the course of reconstruction, above left; the great crane seen through the ironwork arches of the roof, above.

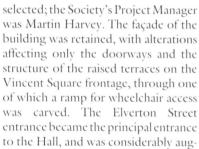

the walls of Rene Dee's office. Five months later the builders returned to continue the process of 'snagging', and remained until the following year.

The distribution of departments within the refurbished Lindley Hall differed in various ways from what had been planned; and it continued to alter and develop after opening. A generous complement of meeting rooms was diminished as some of them were turned into new directorial offices. By late 2002 the first resurvey of accommodation was already being undertaken by Rene Dee, in an effort to rationalise the use of space. Meanwhile, the Halls themselves continued to develop, with the Lawrence Hall basement being examined for possible use as function rooms, an increasing number of television commercials being filmed (most notably, in 2002, the BBC's use of a group of acrobats dangling from the Lawrence Hall ceiling as one of its standard logo inserts), and an increasing number of antique fairs, specialist markets, and fabric and remaindered book sales.[34] At the time of writing, Horticultural Halls has a staff of twenty, including five dealing with business and sales, eight with managing the Halls and Conference Centre, and five with operations and building services. This chapter can conclude with an extract from a description by Rene Dee of a day in the life of Horticultural Halls:

The telephone rings. The walkie-talkie crackles. The mobile interrupts. Dawn breaks on Horticultural Halls. Organic debris and life healing crystals are being cleared from the Halls where Mind Body Spirit has just died. The Conference Centre opens to a babble of intense and high tensile speakers. Delegates jostle. The coffee is late. The flowers are the wrong colour. Another table is required. The speech is in the third cubicle on the right in the Gent's Loos, at the M4 Granada Service Station just past Swindon. The neighbours would like a word. So would the visitor who has collected a Marks & Spencer jacket but claims a Gucci. It's too hot; please open the windows. It's too cold; please turn up the heating. Excuse me but those delegates look like builders. When did you say the Hall had reopened? Can you please move the Great Autumn Show to fit in a 10 day Korean Trade Fair on semi-conductors? The Heavy Metal Convention is coming to the Lindley but don't tell Accounts. The Countryside Alliance rally of 2000 starts outside the Library at 10 am. We need an extra breakout room. Can we use the DG's office? We will need to build through the night and by the way we will be flying trapeze artists from your girders but don't tell Accounts. How many Centurion tanks will fit into the Lawrence? When are you going to build a tunnel between the two Halls?[35]

This photograph was published in The Garden *for January 2000 with the caption: 'Contrary to appearances, this is not the RHS offering for the Turner Prize. It is some of the pipework and cabling that were removed ... at the start of the £4 million renovation to the Society's headquarters ...'*

9 *The Society's Library*

A T the time the Horticultural Society started compiling a library, there was no general resource collection on horticulture, or even botany, available to the general public. There was as yet no public library service; the British Museum Library had not yet begun its statutory collecting policy; the botanic gardens and the Chelsea Physic Garden had libraries, but access was largely restricted to university staff and the members of the Society of Apothecaries respectively. The most important botanical libraries belonged to private individuals: botanists like Aylmer Bourke Lambert, William Roscoe in Liverpool, and above all Sir Joseph Banks, who made their collections available to botanists and scholars on a selective basis (though the contrast between Lambert's generosity and Banks's exclusiveness became a theme for the latter's critics). A five-volume catalogue of Banks's library was published during his lifetime; it was later to become the basis of the Natural History Museum's collection; John Lindley was one of those employed in it before he went to work for the Horticultural Society. These private libraries, in the cases cited, acted effectively as research centres, and in the early 19th century they were assumed as the normal model of library practice. During the 1820s and 1830s, when John Claudius Loudon was campaigning for the establishment of garden libraries as educational tools for gardeners, he meant libraries at country houses, for the use of the estate staff. The creation of a fine library that could be used as a matter of right by fee-paying members was, therefore, a significant step forward in the dissemination of horticultural information.[1]

The first library

The original library was slow to develop. In 1806, John Sims presented five French gardening books to the Society,[2] and the following month the Society purchased a copy of the first edition of Miller's *Gardeners Dictionary*. By 1813 there were enough books for the Society to buy a bookcase. In 1817, the library was moved into the Society's new premises at Church Street, Kensington, much to the relief of the Linnean Society, who had been housing it, and a Library Committee was established, consisting of Roger Pettiward, George Heinrich Noehden, John Creswell, Roger Wilbraham, and the Secretary Joseph Sabine. At their first meeting, they recommended the purchase of Redouté's *Les Roses*, then in the course of publication—one of the Society's more expensive committees.

This first library grew into a fine collection, probably the world's foremost horticultural collection at the time. Its content was limited strictly by Council's interpretation of the Society's purposes: a heavy concentration on fruit, a lesser concentration on ornamental plants, the major floras of the world, a basic reference collection on botany, and no significant attempt to collect works on garden design or aesthetics. Up until 1820 purchasing took place *ad hoc*; in that year a purchasing policy of sorts was finally drawn up. The Committee recommended that it would be 'a fair application of the Capital of the Society, by creating a permanent Collection of Books of Value', and proposed that while modern publications should be purchased out of the Society's normal annual income, a sum equal to five members' compositions per annum (whittled down by Council to four members') should be set aside for 'what, in their future recommendations to the Council they shall denominate *Old Books*'.[3]

On the subject of fruit, at least, the Library seems to have attempted an historically comprehensive collection, acquiring everything it could find that described or depicted fruit cultivars as well as more general works on fruit culture: Batty Langley's *Pomona*, Knoop's *Pomologia*, Mayer's *Pomona Austriaca*, Switzer's *Practical Fruit-gardener*, and others. There seems to have been less effort on extending the antiquarian collection into ornamental gardening, though Thomas Fairchild's *City Gardener* (1726) was there. Garden design was a neglected subject. But when it came to purchases of current and contemporary works, large sums were expended on acquiring works such as the Nouveau Duhamel (*Traité des Arbres Fruitiers*), and as much of *Curtis's Botanical Magazine* as it could find; the *Botanical Register* was subscribed to from its commencement.

All Fellows of the Society could use the Library by prior application, and, occupying the front room of the Regent Street office, it was open without appointment on meeting days. All books could be borrowed for a maximum term of two months, to be replaced by the borrower in the case of loss or damage. (R. A. Salisbury was censured by Council in April 1818 for annotating the copy of the *Annales du Muséum d'Histoire Naturelle* which he had borrowed; he replied that he had annotated it before it was bound, and before the byelaw was created, but did offer to buy a replacement.)[4] Neither attendance books nor loans records survive from this period, but from Council minutes and remarks in the press we know that journalists like John Claudius Loudon and Donald Beaton made extensive use of the Library.

The first financial crisis, of 1830, prompted immediate thoughts of selling books from the Library. An auction of duplicate drawings was proposed first; expensive works in progress, like Blume's *Flora Javae*, were discontinued; George Bentham, the new Secretary, selected a list of works for disposal. At first, this list was intended to consist mostly of duplicates, but it was quickly extended to include works 'entirely unconnected with the objects' of the Society—including many monographs on grasses, foreign floras, and other works which could have been deemed irrelevant only by a criterion of financial desperation. The grand result of the sale was £337 17s. 6d., and apprehensions from an observer like Loudon that the sale of donated books would discourage future donors. (Council minutes at this date never name a librarian, but Loudon ascribed that role to Thomas Goode, officially titled Senior Clerk, who was dismissed as part of the cost-cutting enterprise.)[5] By the late 1830s, calm had been restored, and the Society set about resubscribing and

One of Ferdinand Bauer's title-pages for the Flora Graeca: *volume 8 (1833), the first volume to be edited by John Lindley.*

completing its sets of works it had discontinued a few years before. Most noteworthy of these was Sibthorp's *Flora Graeca*, of which Lindley was by then the editor; £50 was spent on completing it in 1838. (Lindley himself, despite his role in completing the work, was never able to afford a set; his copy consisted solely of the letterpress for the volumes he edited, and is now in the Wisley Laboratory Library.)[6]

With the financial crisis of the 1850s, the Library was once again endangered. In August 1854, Lindley recommended that the post of Librarian be abolished, and amalgamated with that of Assistant Secretary; Council duly agreed and yet, later that autumn, William Beattie Booth was hired as Library Clerk, and not officially made Assistant Secretary until 1859. Soon after his arrival, it was declared that the books in the Regent Street office were never consulted, were covered with dust, and could be sold. Decisions to sell the collection were made, deferred, opposed, and denied in public.[7]

On 7 January 1859 Council demanded that 'every head of expenditure be reduced to the

William Beattie Booth (c.1804-1874), gardener to Sir Charles Lemon at Carclew, Cornwall, between bouts of work for the Horticultural Society. Co-author with Alfred Chandler of Illustrations and Descriptions of ... Camellieae *(1830-31). Librarian and then Assistant Secretary of the Society, 1854-60, though in 1857 he fled the country after the collapse of the Royal British Bank, and was absent from his post for eight months, until the bank's affairs were resolved by Act of Parliament.*

lowest possible point consistent with the existence of the Society', and that included the sale of the Library. Sotheby's agreed to sell the Library so long as Lindley corrected the sale catalogue. The collection of nearly 1,200 drawings was offered for £500, first to the Department of Science and Art, then to the British Museum; these offers failed, and the drawings were included in the auction. In March, the Society's bankers were at last willing to advance them £500—on the surety of the library sale. From that point, even after the financial picture started to improve, there was no reasonable hope that Council would withdraw from the auction. The *Cottage Gardener*, which had been strongly critical of Lindley and the Society in the past, reported the forthcoming sale in tones of outrage: 'Why, the first thing every Society aims at is to obtain a library. Their libraries are the pride of our Mechanics' Institutes ... Will it, then, have to be said, in this age of progress and diffusion of knowledge, that the Horticultural Society sold its library because it could not afford to keep it?' It went on to call for the replacement of the existing Council by a new regime that would keep the Library intact. (The *Gardeners' Chronicle*, which Lindley edited, kept quiet about the matter.)[8]

The sale duly took place over four days, from 2-5 May 1859: 985 lots fetched a total of £1,112 1s. 6d. (Lindley himself bought some books from the sale.) Among the works sold, to list only those the auctioneers found it worth mentioning in their announcement, were Besler's *Hortus Eystettensis*, Sibthorp's *Flora Graeca*, the *Flora Danica*, Tenore's *Flora Napoletana*, Vellozo's *Flora Fluminensis*, Gallesio's *Pomona Italiana*, Bateman's *Orchidaceae of Mexico and Guatemala*, Lindley's *Sertum Orchidaceum*, 'the splendid publications of Jacquin', not to mention the drawings.[9] (Neither the *Flora Napoletana* nor the *Flora Fluminensis* has ever been replaced in the Society's Library, nor has the journal of the Prussian Horticultural Society nor the *Mémoires du Muséum d'Histoire Naturelle*, and only incomplete sets of Humboldt and the *Flora Danica* have been acquired since.) Any trade catalogues that the Society then had were jettisoned as ephemera, or sold as part of job lots; as a result, the current collection of trade catalogues basically begins in 1860, and anything earlier has been either bought or received by donation.

The creation of the Lindley Library

As soon as the initial excitement over the Kensington Garden subsided, the enormity of the Library sale forced its way back into consciousness. 'I for one do hereby protest', wrote Donald Beaton, 'against any more bronzes or brass, except the brass bands, for the new garden, until we have as good a library as the want of brass deprived us of on the fall and folly in Regent Street.' Within a few years, people were coming forward with offers of books, and on his death in 1865 Sir Joseph Paxton bequeathed his books to the Society, most notably his set of *Curtis's Botanical Magazine*, which became the Society's main set.[10]

In November 1865, John Lindley died, and two months later the Society was notified that his personal collection of books was coming up for sale. At the next AGM, in May 1866, it was agreed that the collection should be bought, and Council allocated £600 for this purpose (with, of course, the proviso that it could sell any duplicates already in its possession).[11] In that month also (22-25 May), the first International Horticultural Exhibition and International Botanical Congress were held at the Society's Kensington garden, organised by a joint committee on which the Society was represented; it netted an unforeseen surplus of nearly £3,000, and by September the thought was being voiced, initially by Charles Wentworth Dilke, that the cost of purchasing Lindley's library could be debited to that surplus. George Fergusson Wilson, who had become a Council member the year before, wrote to the *Gardeners' Chronicle*, 'One mode already suggested, viz., the purchase by the Exhibition Committee of the Lindley Library, to be placed in bookcases, where Fellows of the Royal Horticultural Society could easily refer to it, would, I think, be a fair one, deserving the support of those concerned in the disposal of the surplus.'

At the annual general meeting for 1867, the acquisition of Lindley's library came under scrutiny, not only as to the purchase arrangements—could the Society use the Exhibition Committee's profits, and could it afford to buy the collection otherwise?—but as to its long-term welfare. Edgar Bowring, of the Royal Commissioners, argued that 'it would be better that it should not be held as the property of the Society, for fear of what might by any mischance occur, and they would do better to act in the position of trustees'. In due course, after a resolution asserting the Society's right 'morally if not legally' to the Exhibition's surplus, and accusations of bullying levied against Dilke, a compromise was reached between Council and the Exhibition Committee, whereby each party nominated Trustees, and a Trust Deed was drawn up.[12] Among its provisions were the accommodation of the Library by the Society at Kensington, the right of the Trustees to retain the Library intact even if the

Society moved or folded, and the obligation of the Society to pay for a Librarian if one was employed.

At the first meeting of the Lindley Library Trust, on 24 March 1868, the selection of the Trustees was finalised: Thomas Moore (Curator of the Chelsea Physic Garden), Maxwell T. Masters (Lindley's successor as editor of the *Gardeners' Chronicle*), Robert Hogg (editor of the *Journal of Horticulture*, the successor to the *Cottage Gardener*), John Clutton (the Society's Treasurer), Henry Young Darracott Scott (its incoming Secretary), William Wilson Saunders (its outgoing Secretary), and Dilke. The Trust Deed was formally signed on 5 May; the surplus from the Exhibition became the Trust's fund, and the Society was refunded its £600. There was now a new library, held as a trust and inalienable by the Society, partially administered by the Society, and accessible to its fellows.

Public response was immediate and enthusiastic, to judge by the donations that were made in the early years. Lindley's collection amounted to 1,300 volumes, including several journals; by the time the Lindley Library Trust had been established, three years had elapsed since Lindley's death, and the Trust had to advertise for the issues for the intervening years to be donated; in many cases the sets were completed.[13] Donors from Bentham and Hooker, through James Bateman, to Queen Victoria gave books for the new library. It should be emphasised that Lindley's library was in no sense a replacement for the Library that had been sold. Botany predominated over horticulture in Lindley's collection: he seldom purchased for himself books that were accessible to him at the Society's offices. Where there was duplication, it consisted of Lindley's own works, the Society's publications, and gifts from other authors. Lindley's purchases were meant to provide him with the taxonomic works, excluded by the Society's acquisitions policy, that he needed for his work as a botanist.

The botanist Alfred W. Bennett was hired to make an initial catalogue; he did this by the simple expedient of annotating a copy of Pritzel's *Thesaurus Litteraturae Botanicae* (1847-51), but as the late 19th-century librarians followed his example and added new acquisitions to the same volume, it is not a reliable means of identifying the content of Lindley's original collection. Within a few years the Trust was ready to appoint a Librarian. William Thiselton-Dyer was appointed Profes-

sor of Botany in 1871, at a salary of £250; the following year the title of Lindley Librarian was added for an addition of £5 per annum to his salary. He did not last long in his double post: having offered, then withdrawn, his resignation in 1874, he finally left in 1875 to become Assistant Director at Kew.[14] He was succeeded by William Botting Hemsley, who again did not last long, and after 1878 the management of the Library was assumed successively by Samuel Jennings, the Assistant Secretary (1878-80), George Henslow, the Professor of Botany (1880-88), James West, the Royal Microscopical Society's Librarian (1888-90), and finally once again the Assistant Secretary, this time John Weathers (1890-97). Weathers oversaw the publication of the first printed catalogue, and the errors it contained were one of the stated reasons for his dismissal. At no time yet had the post of Lindley Librarian been a full-time one, and the salary usually consisted of a fee of £5 or £10 added to an already existing salary.[15] Finally, in 1897, a young man named John Hutchinson was hired to check through the Society's archives; two years later he was named 'Clerk in charge of the Library' at a salary of 30 shillings per week, then shortly after 'Assistant Cashier and Librarian'; in 1900 he seems to have finally been made the first full-time Librarian since William Beattie Booth.[16] It was Hutchinson who first began keeping a card index of the books, in 1907.

Meanwhile, the Society had been purchasing books out of its revenue budget, quite independently of the Lindley Library Trust. In 1872 Masters suggested that the collections be merged, and this was finally achieved in 1877. At that time

William Turner Thiselton Dyer (later Thiselton-Dyer) (1843-1928) First Lindley Librarian, and Professor of Botany to RHS, 1872-75. Assistant Director, Kew, 1875-85; Director, succeeding Joseph Hooker, 1885-1905. Editor of Flora Capensis *and* Flora of Tropical Africa.

The oldest surviving view of the Library, from the Gardeners' Chronicle, 1897: *during the Victoria Street years, when it doubled as the Council Room and was obviously not expected to attract a large readership.*

the Library was housed in the Society's offices at Kensington; in 1888, when the Society abandoned the Kensington garden and took offices at 117 Victoria Street, the Library was installed in the Council Room, and the Trust assumed the custody of the Society's books as well as its own. Thereafter, Council alternated between consigning its books to the Trust's maintenance, and demanding that the two collections be distinguished or separated; and a combination of staff and Council turnover, poor record-keeping, and corporate amnesia ensured that these positions alternated in a regular cycle.[17] When the Society's Hall on Vincent Square was built in 1904, the Library moved onto the second floor, and Baron Schröder, the principal benefactor of the Hall, paid for the furnishings.

As the original Trustees died, they were replaced by others: E.A. Bowles, John T. Bennett-Poë, William Carruthers of the Natural History Museum, Sir John Bretland Farmer (the editor of *Annals of Botany*), George Maw (author of *The Genus Crocus*), and the nurseryman Harry Veitch, with William Wilks, the Society's Secretary, sitting in *ex officio*. The Trust's last years can be seen as a contest between Masters and Wilks over the control of the Library, with special regard to the question of divided ownership. Masters was the last of the original Trustees to die, and at the very meeting at which his death was announced, in 1907, the possibility was discussed of handing the Trust over to the Society's Council. Bennett-Poë called for a revision of the Trust Deed, so as to emphasise 'the intimate inalienable association of the Library with the Royal Horticultural Society, as long as the Society exists, and wherever it may have its headquarters'—since the old Trust Deed still referred to the Kensington garden as the Library's home. The Trust, indeed, hoped that a revised deed would allow the RHS 'to make an absolute gift to the Trust of all the books at present belonging to the Society and of others purchased in the future'. In 1910 the Charity Commissioners approved a new Deed, which named Council as the sole Trustee. In the Annual Report, Wilks wrote that this move was necessary because there had been nothing to stop the Trust from removing the books from the Society's custody.[18] The revised Deed contained the provision that the Society would appoint a Librarian, paid or unpaid.

Growth of a library

For practical purposes, the Lindley Library Trust was succeeded by a new Library Committee, consisting of the remaining members of the Trust—Bennett-Poë, Bowles, Veitch, and Wilks—along with B. Daydon Jackson of the *Index Kewensis*, C. Harman Payne of the *Florist's Bibliography*, and the orchid grower J. Gurney Fowler as new members. Once the immediate teething problems were over (the Trust's annual budget had been £16, but in the last year it had spent £86), the booksellers William Wesley & Son were brought in to reorganise the collection and revise the card index. So smooth was the transition that no formal statement of library policy was required; as Bowles was to say in 1920, 'every possible book of use to horticulturists should be included'. Subject, of course, to any *ad hoc* restrictions imposed by Council: in 1917 the Revd Joseph Jacob raised a fuss in the press over Council's refusal to purchase Jacques Boyceau's *Traité du Jardinage* (1638), by-passing the Library Committee. (At the time of writing, the Library still has Boyceau only in modern facsimile.)[19] Hutchinson remained the Librarian for another twenty years, though his rate of work seems to have been slow; in 1922 his annual salary increase was kept low because of dissatisfaction with the rate at which pamphlets were being catalogued, and cataloguing was eventually assigned to an assistant. Nonetheless, a printed catalogue—the first reliable one—was published in 1927.[20]

The other great event of this period was the revision yet again of the Trust Deed. Queries had been raised from time to time about the Society's ability to sell the books it had purchased out of its own funds, instead of the Lindley Library Fund. The 1926 Trust Deed asserted that all books owned by the RHS were deemed to be part of the Lindley Library.[21]

By the 1920s the Library was outgrowing its space, and the new Chairman of the Library Committee, G.W.E. Loder (later to become President), objected to proposals to house the overflow in the basement. Plans to add a library to the projected New Hall (which partly involved an offer from Edward Harding to furnish a study centre for American horticulture) came to nothing. A grant of £1,250 was obtained from the Carnegie Trust, on condition that the library be open to the public and take part in the new inter-library loan system, and with its aid the architect William Binnie added a third floor to the Old Hall, dedicated entirely to the Library. The furnishings that Baron Schröder had contributed in 1904 were transferred to the reading room upstairs, and his son Baron Bruno Schröder paid for the extension of the furnishings in the same style: stained oak, with a half-timbered pitched ceiling. There was now a reading room and a stack room of equal size but far greater density of shelving.[22]

In 1930, as part of a general reorganisation at Wisley, Frederick Chittenden, for 23 years the Director, was given the new titles of Technical Adviser and Keeper of the Library, and transferred to Vincent Square; the Council minute discussing the impact on Hutchinson was typed as saying 'at present it would not alter his position', but then coolly amended to 'it would not affect his financial position'.[23] If Hutchinson regarded having to report to a new manager as an indignity, worse was to follow as Council cast about to find a replacement for him. E.A. Bowles found a young man, William T. Stearn, working in Bowes and Bowes's bookshop in Cambridge, who by the age of 21 had already published on plant pathology, and, though lacking university training, was working on a monograph on *Epimedium*. Stearn, in later years, was wont to recall his arrival at Vincent Square in 1932: announcing himself as the new librarian, to the shock of Hutchinson, who hadn't been informed of his replacement, and who hurried off to see Colonel Durham, the Secretary, only to have Stearn's statement curtly endorsed. Stearn was in fact confirmed in the title of Assistant Librarian only in 1934.[24]

On the eve of Stearn's arrival, the *Gardeners' Chronicle* was complaining that 'Economy seems to have been exercised in the purchase of books for the Lindley Library—a point on the wisdom of which there will be difference of opinion.' During Stearn's early years at the Library, it received its largest ever donation: the bequest of Reginald Cory, amounting to over 400 titles and 24 collections of drawings. Some of the works lost in 1859 returned to the Library through Cory's bequest, including the larger portion of the Reeves Chinese drawings. As a by-product of cataloguing the new acquisitions, Stearn wrote several articles for the newly-founded *Journal of the Society for the Bibliography of Natural History*, detailing the publication dates of important botanical works—a matter of considerable importance, since under the international rules of botanical nomenclature it is the first published description that normally determines a plant's name.[25]

In 1939, Chittenden retired from his role as Keeper of the Library, in order to concentrate on completing the *Dictionary of Gardening*. Stearn officially became Librarian, but the role of Keeper was not yet removed. Chittenden was replaced in that capacity by Edward Ashdown Bunyard, who had written on the history of horticultural literature for the *Journal* and built up an excellent private library of antiquarian works on fruit. Bunyard's role lasted for only a year. On 19 October 1939, he left the Library at mid-day, telling Stearn he would be back after lunch to continue work, and went to the Royal Societies Club, where he shot himself. (Stearn, describing the incident, would remark that he must have had the gun in his pocket while talking to him.) His fruit library was bought for the Lindley through funds from the Cory Bequest. Bunyard was succeeded by Daniel Hall, the monographer of the tulip, until 1943, and after that the office of Keeper was deleted.[26]

With the outbreak of war, the more valuable books were sent to safe storage in Aberystwyth, while other parts of the collection were farmed out to Kew and to Wisley (which also safeguarded the rare books from the John Innes Research Institute). After the war the books were returned without incident.[27] Stearn was called up for military service in June 1940; Miss C.M. Lloyd was hired to manage the Library during his absence, but after a year she resigned, and was replaced by Florence Cardew, née Lorimer, a former assistant to Sir Aurel Stein who had catalogued some of his Chinese collections. Mrs Cardew was a dogged worker, even though somewhat inefficient at bibliography; Hutchinson came out of retirement to lend assistance. In 1944 Mrs Cardew was given the task of compiling a supplement to the printed catalogue. Although she remained as Assistant Librarian until the late 1950s, she never completed this task.[28]

Stearn resigned in 1952, and took up a new post as Botany Librarian at the Natural History Museum. His successor was a shadowy figure named Miss L. D. Whiteley, again hired by Bowles—over the protests of the Assistant Secretary Arthur Simmonds, who later blamed her survival of her probation period on Bowles's increasing ill health in his last years. Whiteley lasted nearly five years before Simmonds secured her dismissal; oral tradition attributes this to her tendency to give readers erroneous advice on plant care.[29] She did at least begin the subject catalogue of the Library. She was succeeded in January 1957 by Peter Stageman, recruited from the Cambridge University Library, who saw the Library through its next wave of expansion, modernised many of its facilities, and defended it against financial attrition. One aspect of this attrition was staffing: he used to quip that if a new typist was wanted in the typing pool, the Secretary conducted interviews, but if a new assistant was wanted in the Library, he rang up the Labour Exchange. The present author was hired as his assistant in 1977, and succeeded him as Librarian in 1982.[30]

After the Second World War, the Library gradually expanded into storage areas in the basement of the building; in the early 1960s the Society's consulting architect Sydney Tatchell

William Thomas Stearn (1911-2001), librarian to the Society and pioneering codifier of the nomenclature of cultivated plants. In 1952 he left for the Natural History Museum, but continued to serve as a committee member. Nicknamed the modern Linnaeus for his contributions to taxonomy and nomenclature.

Peter Stageman (1917-2001) worked at the Cambridge University Library, and compiled a pioneering bibliography of the works of the 19th-century naturalist Philip Henry Gosse, before serving the RHS as Librarian, 1957-1982.

Continued on p.173

The treasures of the Lindley Library

The Lindley Library houses the United Kingdom's, and so far as we are aware, the world's, most comprehensive collection of horticultural literature from the 16th century to the present day. While the core collections on entomology, plant pathology, soil science, and other technical and scientific aspects of horticulture are housed at Wisley, the library in London holds the historical (i.e. pre-20th-century) collections on all relevant subjects, and the core collections on garden history, garden design and construction, and floral arts. Horticultural taxonomy and cultivation are shared concerns.

Reginald Cory's was the largest single donation the Library has received, but it has benefited over the decades from many other bequests and library purchases: the notes and drawings of the great mycologist Mordecai Cubitt Cooke, bought in 1911 when he was living in increasing poverty after his retirement from Kew; the libraries of Donald McDonald, the author of *Agricultural Writers* (1908), the cactus grower E. W. Shurly, John Bond, the Ranger of Windsor Great Park, and most recently Graham Stuart Thomas. Extensive donations of books have been received from Sir Frank Crisp, the compiler of *Mediaeval Gardens* (1924); Colonel Beddome, the authority on Indian ferns; Vera Higgins, the cactus expert and former editor of the *Journal*; the lily grower Fred Stoker; Gurney Wilson, the orchid grower and former editor of *Orchid World*; and the alpine collector A.R. Pettitt—and funds for purchasing from the horticultural historian Alice Coats; the architect John Bancroft (in memory of his wife); and the E.H. Wilson Memorial Trust.

While Wisley has a number of antiquarian books, and is increasing its acquisitions, most of the following are concentrated in London. To begin with, there is an excellent collection of 16th- and 17th-century herbals; the major 17th-century florilegia; an outstanding collection of the literature on fruit, from the 16th to the 20th

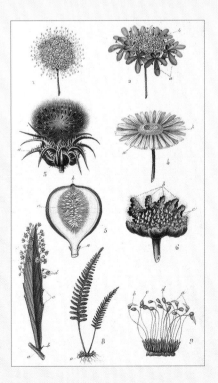

Title-page from the 1586 edition of Pierandrea Mattioli's Kreutter-buch *(second German edition of his* Commentarii in ... Dioscoridis).

Right: The Miyako Rinsen Meisho Zue *[Famous gardens in the capital] by Rito Akizato, an account of the gardens of Kyoto (1799).*

Far right: A plate from the Leçons de Flore *of Turpin and Poiret (1820), a copy printed on vellum and coloured by the artist, formerly belonging to Louis XVIII.*

centuries, in seven languages, mostly accumulated by E.A. Bunyard; the works of John Lindley, in their various editions; a good collection of works on evolution and genetics from the late 19th and early 20th centuries, when the Society was in the forefront of research; possibly the largest publicly accessible collection in Britain of books on flower arranging, from the mid-19th century to the present day; and a fine collection of 18th- and 19th-century Japanese horticultural works.

Any list of special treasures would include: one of two copies of Turpin and Poiret's *Leçons de Flore* (1820), printed on vellum and coloured by the artist (a copy formerly belonging to Louis XVIII, and probably brought to this country by Napoleon III); one of Humphry Repton's Red Books (for Waresley Park, Huntingdonshire); the account book of Capability Brown (on permanent loan); the original edition (1743-50) of Rumphius' *Herbarium Amboinense* and the 1750 Uytwerf reissue; Jean-Jacques Rousseau's signed copy of Albrecht von Haller's *Historia Stirpium Indigenarum Helvetiae* (1768); and both versions of the *Flora Graeca Sibthorpiana* (1806-40), the last volumes of which were edited by Lindley. No more than 50 copies were originally printed; when the work was complete, the bookseller Henry G. Bohn bought up the plates and letterpress, and issued another 40 copies or so. The Society's original copy was sold in 1859; in 1911 a replacement copy was bought from Bernard Quaritch for £200; and in 1936 a copy of the Bohn reprint formed part of the Reginald Cory bequest.

The Library holds some 1,500 periodical titles, from *Curtis's Botanical Magazine* (founded 1787) to the present. This includes all the great gardening newspapers of the 19th century—with the notable exception of Glenny's *Gardener's Gazette*.

In addition to the Society's own archives, it houses those of the Gardeners' Orphan Fund and the International Dendrology Society; the personal papers of E.A. Bowles, the garden designers Lanning Roper and Michael Haworth-Booth, and the flower arranger Constance Spry; portions of the papers of the garden designers Percy Cane and Russell Page; correspondence of William Robinson, Gertrude Jekyll, and George Maw (the tile manufacturer and author of *The Genus Crocus*); the manuscript record books for Gravetye Manor, on which William Robinson based his published account of his garden; Lord Wakehurst's garden books for the garden at Wakehurst Place, Canon Ellacombe's garden book for Bitton Vicarage, and John Wedgwood's of his garden; and Sir Frederick Stern's photographic record of his garden at Highdown.

Divided between London and Wisley, there is an extensive collection of trade catalogues and seed lists of botanic gardens—certainly the largest in the United Kingdom. These date primarily from 1860 to the present, since any catalogues the Society held in 1859 were disposed of, but with various 18th- and early 19th-century titles as well. Some 7,000 firms are represented.

Finally, the drawings collection. Thanks to Reginald Cory and the wealth he ploughed into his antiquarian purchasing, this collection stretches back to the early 17th century, with an album, no doubt intended for publication as a florilegium, by the Dutch artist Pieter van Kouwenhoorn (fl. 1630s). Among the major elements in the drawings collection are: 673 ink drawings by Claude Aubriet (1665-1742), made to illustrate an intended work by Jussieu; drawings by Georg Dionysius Ehret (1708-1770) from the collections of the 3rd Earl of Bute and the 2nd Duchess of Portland; 737 drawings from the Earl of Bute's collection, subsequently acquired by Thomas S. Ralph in the 1840s and rearranged to form a sequence called *Flora Asiatica*; a set of unpublished plates by Pierre-Joseph Redouté; a major collection of the work of Lilian Snelling (1879-1972), probably the most important British botanical artist of the early 20th century; and a number of drawings by the alpine collector Reginald Farrer.

Before and after views from Repton's Red Book *of proposed improvements for Waresley Park, Huntingdonshire (1792).*

Apple 'Minshul Crab': a drawing by Barbara Cotton, made for the Society in 1822.

was commissioned to produce plans for a library extension, which envisaged upper and lower stack rooms, but in the event redundant kitchens in the basement were converted into a library and publications store instead.[31] And still the expansion continued. In the early 1980s, the originally assigned basement area having been filled to repletion, the publications store was moved and the area filled with mobile shelving for further expansion. In the mid-1990s, the Library took over part of the fourth floor (originally the caretaker's flat, but recently converted into offices) to serve as a photographic studio and the office of the Picture Librarian. And the expansion continued.

The staff library at Chiswick and Wisley

Meanwhile, the Society had created a second library, which, unlike its first, was never sold.

A small library for the staff and trainees at Chiswick had been set up, distinct from the Society's main library in London. No clear inception date can be deduced from Council minutes; but when in 1828 it was reported that the garden staff had formed an association for improving themselves, Council allocated £50 to provide extra books for the library. In 1846 a separate reading room for the students was established, and apparently stocked largely by voluntary contributions. Lindley contributed 53 volumes, including some of his own works, and a globe of the world; other contributors to the book stock included Mrs Loudon, William Haseldine Pepys, and Robert Glendinning, who had designed the Chiswick arboretum. The reading room was opened on 23 November with a lecture by Lindley.

In its meetings in December 1846 and January 1847, the Garden Committee passed the following rules: the reading room was to be open every evening except Sunday until 10 p.m., starting at dark in winter, and 6.30 p.m. in summer. The 'frequenters' of the reading room were to take turns acting as its clerks, with the duties of receiving, cataloguing, and shelving new books, and ensuring that they were kept in good condition. Some further rules:

> No one can be permitted to frequent the room unless his hands and face are washed clean.
>
> No conversation is allowed, except on lecture evenings after the lecture is concluded.
>
> The Society furnishes all articles of stationery in moderate quantity, except pens and cedar-pencils.[32]

During the 1850s, as the Society sped through its financial crisis, we may suppose that little was spent on the student library at Chiswick, but at least it remained intact. In 1865, a Committee on the Improved Education of Gardeners reported on the need, among other things, to upgrade that library, and in January 1866 it was duly improved.[33]

In 1899 Council moved that a 'proper library' for the students be set up at Chiswick; this entailed reconstructing the building. Any books at Chiswick not held in the main library at Westminster were to be moved there, and Maxwell T. Masters was to be consulted on the stock.[34] The Society's new Professor of Botany, George Henslow, agreed to give lectures to the students. The refurbished library at Chiswick lasted a mere four years, for in 1903 the Society acquired Wisley as its new experimental garden, and everything was moved there.

The Wisley library was housed on the first floor of the Laboratory, in a wood-panelled room with bays arranged around a central reading desk—and no easy provision for future expansion. Various parts of the library were distributed departmentally, so that the main collections on entomology and plant pathology were to be found in the relevant offices; E. A. Bunyard presented a collection of fruit books for use in the Fruit Room. In 1924 the Wisley Library was officially declared the province of the Wisley Advisory Committee, not the Library Committee, and thereafter its management was kept distinct. Although it had built up an excellent collection of 19th- and early 20th-century gardening books for the general instruction of the student gardeners, its role became more narrowly defined as it effectively became an adjunct to the Laboratory. From 1927 until 1946, it was directed by the Laboratory Keeper, M.A.H. Tincker; he was succeeded in the librarian's role by the Laboratory Steward, Robert Scase.[35] When the latter retired in 1983, he had no direct successor; Audrey Brooks, as chief scientific officer, was instructed to sort the Library out, and arranged for its administration on a part-time basis by a member of the scientific staff. In 1994, Barbara Collecott, formerly Assistant Librarian at Vincent Square, became the first full-time Librarian for over a decade, and the first professional Librarian in Wisley's history.

The Society's drawings collections

By the time the Library was a decade old, it had also begun to acquire drawings. William Hooker (no relation to the Hookers of Kew—his name is commemorated in the colour 'Hooker's green') was appointed the principal artist for the Society's *Transactions*, and from 1815 was also drawing portraits of fruit varieties; he was probably chosen for the task by R.A. Salisbury, whose *Paradisus*

Londinensis (1805-8) he had illustrated. Other artists, like William Clark, Ferdinand Bauer, E.D. Smith, John Curtis, Clara Maria Pope, and Augusta Innes Withers also produced drawings for the Society. Relations between Council and Mrs Withers were occasionally vexed because of the high fees she charged, but Lindley was to use her as the artist for his *Pomological Magazine* in 1827-30, and later in his *Sertum Orchidaceum*.[36] Of comparable importance was a collection of Chinese drawings. In 1817, John Reeves, a tea factor for the East India Company in Canton, proposed sending the Society plants and drawings from China. The drawings, made in a roughly European style, were commissioned from local artists whose names Reeves did not record. They were drawn on by Sabine for his

articles on chrysanthemum cultivars, and Sabine and Lindley abstracted three series of drawings of cultivars—chrysanthemums, camellias, and peonies—for separate study and annotation. So enthusiastic was the response to the drawings that in 1819 Sabine wrote to Nathaniel Wallich, the Superintendent of the Calcutta Botanic Garden, asking him to commission drawings of Indian plants in the Reeves style (duly received in 1821). In 1830, however, as the first financial crisis bit, Council wrote to Reeves asking him to discontinue sending.[37]

One form of plant depiction which the Library originally held was abandoned in the later 19th century and never returned to: wax models. The Society's messenger (i.e. courier), William Tuson, made wax fruit as a hobby, and after the Duke of Saxe-Weimar presented a collection of wax fruits, for which special cabinets were commissioned, the Society woke up to the fact that it had an artist in this genre ready at hand. Tuson began to provide models of fruit in 1819, and continued into the 1820s, receiving three shillings per piece. In 1825 Sir Stamford Raffles had a model of *Rafflesia arnoldii* made for the Society, at a cost of £12; housed in a glass showcase, this served as one of the Society's showpieces for several years, but in 1855, at a time of financial retrenchment, it was decided that the model was in the way, and it was presented to Kew. Wax flowers were exhibited at early meetings, to receive plaudits in the press; but after mid-century the Society declined offers of them, and never commissioned any more itself.[38]

The drawings collection was dispersed in the sale of 1859, and only a few portions of it have since returned: the fruit drawings of Hooker and his successors, and most of the Reeves Chinese drawings. Reginald Cory's bequest yielded a wonderful collection of botanical art from the 17th to the 20th centuries; Stephenson Clarke purchased a collection of late 17th-century German drawings for the Library in the 1920s; Lilian Snelling, for decades the Society's artist for its publications, bequeathed her work in the 1970s.

Late in the 19th century, the Society once again began to commission drawings of plants, with the appointment of Nellie Roberts in 1897 to depict orchids that received awards at the Society's shows. The work of Roberts and her successors had resulted, over a century later, in a collection of 7,000 orchid portraits, held in London for ease of access by the Orchid Committee. In 1922, with grant aid from Reginald Cory, the programme was extended to all award-winning plants. Among the artists employed on this project were Katherine Dykes, the widow of the Society's Secretary W.R. Dykes, and Alfred J. Wise, a Wisley staff member. The project was curtailed in the 1950s, as too heterogeneous in its scope, and the paintings incorporated into the Herbarium; orchids remained as the one category of commissioned work.

In 1913, paintings were allowed to be exhibited at the winter shows for the first time. In 1926 a Committee was asked to examine the exhibited pictures and make awards; two months later, after complaints about the inaccuracy of some of the pictures, a new Paintings Committee was asked to report; it is by no means certain that these two

Drawing of Digitalis *[now* Isoplexis*] sceptrum by Ferdinand Bauer, made for John Lindley's* Digitalium Monographia *(1821).*

Committees were dealing with the same sorts of pictures, for the result of the second Committee's investigation was the hiring of Alfred J. Wise as an artist. It is not until 1935 that a clear distinction can be seen between the Paintings (Record of Awards) Committee and the Paintings (Exhibits) Committee. Artists such as Vera Higgins, Frank Galsworthy, John Nash, Mary Grierson, and most recently Siriol Sherlock have been members of the Committee, as was Wilfred Blunt, the author of *The Art of Botanical Illustration*. In 1985, at Peter Stageman's suggestion, a budget was established for purchasing exhibited pictures; the Picture Committee decided the purchases, until 1990 when Stageman joined it, and more recently the purchases have been decided by a subcommittee consisting of the Librarian, Martin Lane Fox, the Chairman of the Committee, and Dr Shirley Sherwood, the compiler of the country's best private collection of botanical art.[39]

Picture purchasing policy having struck sparks between the Library and Picture Committees, the latter Committee was given a display of the contents of the picture collection, and immediately proposed a series of exhibitions to make the public aware of its contents; the eventual result was a touring exhibition and accompanying book called *Treasures of the Royal Horticultural Society*, and a series of symposia on botanical art, which drew artists from all over the world.[40]

The library controversy of the 1990s

1995 saw the Society's first truly stormy annual general meeting since the Kensington quarrels of the mid-1870s, but the roots of the problem lay twenty years earlier, when the Society found itself facing a deficit, and Council began to emulate its 19th-century predecessors by looking for things to sell. In the autumn of 1974, the idea of selling one of the London Halls began to be discussed secretly—over a year went by before the staff were told—and it was the Lindley Hall (then called the Old Hall) that seemed the obvious candidate. 'The location of the Library was not a major problem in that it could be located at Wisley but this would mean providing accommodation.' That it might mean more than some building works seemed to have dawned on Council by the autumn of 1975: 'No enquiries should be made about re-location of the Library, pending further discussions, in order that complete freedom of action could be preserved.' A year further on, and a minute in the Confidential Minute Book read:

> Members agreed that the Library should be moved to Wisley in view of the saving in the expenditure which would be involved in

construction of a fourth floor. An advantage would be that the Garden library could be sold.

It was agreed that these considerations outweighed the Secretary's [John Cowell's] view that the Library should remain in London, the public transport centre of the country, where it could be used at little personal inconvenience by those who wished to study and to consult reference works. The Secretary had pointed to the increases in Library usage on the occasion of flower shows. He had also expressed doubts both about the number of Fellows who would make casual use of the Library on visits to the Garden and the degree to which those who used it for research would be able to visit it at Wisley.

The proposal to sell the Hall was finally announced at the 1977 AGM, and was vigorously opposed from the floor by W.T. Stearn and W.L. Tjaden. A show of hands was called for, and revealed that some 70 of the audience would find it inconvenient to use the Library at Wisley, while 100 would not. Nonetheless, Council felt a rebuff, and later that spring announced that the plan to sell the Hall and move the Library had been abandoned.[41]

Meanwhile, however, a financial problem was developing. For most of the 20th century, the Lindley Library Fund paid for acquisitions, while the Society paid for the staffing of the Library. All acquisitions were decided upon by the Library Committee, which met every month, on the Tuesday of the flower show; it was only in 1979 that the Librarian was for the first time given a budget to work within. The Fund was topped up from time to time by sales of duplicates; some of the later debates about transferring books to Wisley could have been prevented if the duplicate sales had been less thorough.

In 1985, the Library finances were reorganised by the Treasurer, Lawrence Banks: what was left of the Lindley Library Fund was set aside as a soon exhausted resource for the purchase of important antiquarian books, and the general acquisitions were incorporated into the Society's revenue budget. The last sale of duplicates took place in 1987, to help reimburse the Society for the money advanced to make some major purchases at the sale of the De Belder library at Sotheby's. With the Library's finances at last under proper control, and further basement expansion room secured, a variety of new projects was initiated: the reorganisation of the Library on (modified) Universal Decimal Classification; the beginnings of cataloguing for the trade catalogues, drawings, and archives; the development of an initially small-scale commercial picture library. Meanwhile, both visitor and staff numbers grew: visitors increased from under 2,600 in 1982 to nearly 3,700 in 1990, and staff from two (in 1989) to six (in 1994).

Meanwhile, decisions to move the Library were made, deferred, opposed, and hinted at in public. In 1988-89 a Library Review Committee, chaired by the botanist Ronald Keay, made urgent recommendations about its improvement, drew up an explicit and detailed purchasing policy, and concluded by recommending one of two options: either a new home at Wisley or major construction work at Vincent Square. In 1990 the Prance Committee on the Society's scientific work (Joyce Stewart dissenting) re-affirmed the proposal to move the Library to Wisley, while Anthony Huxley, the chairman of the Library Committee, had turned against the idea. The Annual Report for 1991 contained the promise: 'Council is aware that some members have strong views on the question of the location of the Library, and no decision will be made on thus until members have had an opportunity to express their views on specific proposals', and this promise was renewed at the AGM in 1992.[42]

So matters stood until 1994, when an application was being prepared to the government's recently established Millennium Fund for a major redevelopment at Wisley. Council, over the protests of the Library Committee, voted to move the Library to Wisley to form part of the proposed new science and education centre. No reference to this decision was made in the Annual Report, as it was made after the period that that Report covered; but the announcement was made on the news pages of the January issue of *The Garden*, and at the annual press conference that month.

A spate of articles immediately broke out in the national press. Ursula Buchan in the *Spectator*, followed by Anna Pavord and Mary Keen in *The Independent*, campaigned against the proposed move; *The Times* featured a debate between the President, Sir Simon Hornby, and the journalist Patricia Morrison; Mavis Batey of the Garden History Society, Christopher Lloyd, Sir Roy Strong, Rosemary Verey, and others wrote to various newspapers to protest. 537 letters were received from members, 469 against and 48 in favour of the move; though the President was to describe it as 'disappointingly few', this was the largest number of letters the Society had ever received on a single issue apart from affiliated society privileges. Council hoped that 'once the Society's intention to maintain a reading room at Vincent Square was made known at the AGM, the majority of members would accept the case for the Library to be relocated to Wisley'. A group of opponents of the move prevailed upon the Marchioness of Salisbury, a Vice-President, to speak on the matter at the AGM. The stage was set for the annual general meeting on 21 February 1995 to become probably the longest, and certainly the stormiest, in 120 years.

The discussion turned less on the fate of the Library itself than on the question of consultation, which members had been promised on specific proposals back in 1991, and since there had been no time under the rules to submit a resolution on the subject before the meeting. Meanwhile, at the entrance to the Hall, signatures were being collected on a petition calling for a special general meeting on the question, and Anna Pavord handed this requisition to the President; when the discussion resumed later in the meeting, he concluded: 'Now, because ... [of the] requisition for a Special Meeting, there will be an opportunity for everybody to vote—the whole Membership, which is what I wanted.'[43]

Council was shaken by the AGM, and by the realisation that 'The Central Londoners had been angry and suspicious of Council's plans'. Mary Shirville 'considered that it was not a bad thing to have had this adverse reaction, as it made Council stop and think. It might result in a stronger society in the long term.' In the middle of March, it was reported that 'The issue of the future location of the Library had dominated all else since the AGM, resulting in little other work being undertaken'. Eventually, it was agreed with the

The library in 1994: any spaciousness apparent in the view on p. 164 had long since disappeared under the influx of cabinets and shelves.

Sketch by Rick Mather for the new library, 1998, showing the lower reading room with its skylight on the Vincent Square side.

protesters to replace the proposed Special Meeting with a ballot of the members, to be circulated with *The Garden*. Sir Ralph Gibson, a retired Lord Justice, agreed to supervise the ballot and report on the results. Three options were put forward: A, retention in London (4,903 votes); B, moving to Wisley (2,909 votes); and C, 'one library with two main branches' (8,096 votes). Council had already rescinded the decision to move the Library in June. By now, Nicolas Barker, the former Deputy Keeper of the British Library and author of a study of Besler's *Hortus Eystettensis*, was Chairman of the Library Committee; he agreed to step down temporarily and act as consultant on the development of plans for the new Library that would have to be built.[44]

After a competition, Rick Mather was hired by the RHS to redesign the interior of 80 Vincent Square to accommodate a new library and enlarged offices.[45] The Heritage Lottery Fund made a grant of £1.8 million, and the Society's new Fundraising Department raised an additional £2.2 million from trusts and private individuals. In the summer of 1999, the Library moved out of Vincent Square into temporary accommodation in the basement of the New Hall, while the Old Hall was internally gutted, and its entire basement excavated to its lowest previous level (adding a metre of height over most the area). The interim reading room was a converted pastry store; the Librarian's office and the adjoining work room were converted pantries; the books, and the periodicals deemed necessary for immediate access, were housed in an area normally devoted to the storage of chairs, trestles, and other Shows impedimenta. Some 800 boxes of periodicals and other materials were sent into offsite storage. Under these reduced circumstances, the Library coped for nearly two years.

The opening of the new Library had been scheduled for June 2001, and to meet this deadline the collections and staff moved back into what was still (as with the rest of the offices) effectively a building site. Despite all obstacles, the public areas of the Library were brought to manageable order in line with the schedule, and it opened to readers on 12 June; Sir Simon was able to preside over a press launch for the new Library before he retired as President in July.

The new Library facilities comprise an upper and a lower reading room, the latter designed for

serious study, with separate rooms for rare books and the Picture Library, and access by lift for disabled people. Behind the scenes are a stack room with movable shelving for the bulk of the periodicals collection and trade catalogues, a conservation room and small photographic studio, as well as the Librarian's office, a work room for cataloguing, and other storage areas. Last but assuredly not least, the climatic conditions in the Library are electronically controlled for the first time.[46]

Garden libraries

The Library Review Committee of 1988-9 defined the Wisley library as the scientific library, and the London library the historical library; these two terms not being mutually exclusive, there is a great deal of overlap between the two collections. One of its principal recommendations was the progressive integration of the London and Wisley libraries, in terms of both a clearly defined acquisitions policy and a common budget.

The main step to achieving this aim was the appointment of Barbara Collecott, formerly Assistant Librarian at Vincent Square, as the Wisley Librarian in 1994. She found a library that was cramped for space, starved of funds, in arrears with acquisitions, and heavily used by the scientific staff; spending on acquisitions was quickly brought to equality with London in order to fill the gaps left by nearly a decade of unsystematic policy. (At the time of writing, the Laboratory Library contained some 16,000 volumes, and 400 current periodical titles.) Over the next few years, she developed a Wisley Library Committee comprising representatives of the different scientific departments to advise on purchasing; hired library assistants for the first time in Wisley's history; reorganised the collection on the same classification system as in London, and started to get the Wisley holdings integrated into the computerised catalogue; extended the opening hours for the benefit of the students, and encouraged their increased usage of the collection; began collecting together neglected Wisley archives and photographs, started an oral history project, and created regular displays in the foyer of the Laboratory; and secured some degree of expansion and physical reorganisation for the Library. The most heavily used and most recent parts of the collection were arranged in the reading room, and two annexes across the corridor turned, first, into storage areas for older books and periodicals, and then, as the Library staff increased, into offices.

During the arguments over relocating the main Library in 1994-5, it was urged that an experiment be made of opening the Wisley Library to the public for a specified period, to see what sort of usage it was likely to get. This prospect filled the staff with alarm: not only was the Library on the upper floor of a Laboratory filled with Chemical Hazard notices, to which unsupervised access could not be allowed, but the main room was cramped, with little seating. In 1996, a more satisfactory facility was created: a room—later a pair of adjoining rooms—on the ground floor of the student hostel, Aberconway House, was turned into what was called, first a Reading Room, and then a Garden Library, open to members and the public for a certain number of hours each day. The content, at first, was largely current books and basic reference books; it was hoped that the provision of the Garden Library would help to ease the burden on Advisory services, by allowing people with basic enquiries to answer their own questions, leaving Advisory to cope with the more technical and difficult

matters. The Garden Library soon started to receive a large number of visits, amounting to some 10,000 per annum by the beginning of the 21st century—by which time it housed a stock of 2,000 books and 60 periodical titles, and was staffed by a team of 25 volunteers led by a volunteer professional librarian.

The success of the Garden Library led to plans to provide similar facilities in the Society's other gardens. Hyde Hall was the easiest to equip: office reorganisation freed up a substantial room, which was turned into a library and opened in August 2000. John Bond, the Ranger of Windsor Great Park and a longstanding Council member, died that year, and the Society purchased his personal collection of books to help stock the Hyde Hall Garden Library; at the time of writing it houses 1,000 books and 40 current periodical titles. A similar Garden Library was established at Rosemoor in the winter of 2003-4.

In 2001, the Northern Horticultural Society, based at Harlow Carr, near Harrogate in Yorkshire, was amalgamated with the RHS, and its already existing library was incorporated into the Lindley Library. The NHS library had been opened in 1958, in a building dedicated to the memory of the Society's founder Charles Grey; a

A view in the lower reading room, 2001, with the rare books room visible through the window.

Library Panel had been created to maintain it, and a lending service for Fellows had been started in December 1967. In 2000, on the eve of amalgamation, the Library had an acquisitions budget of £2,000, was run by a team of nearly 40 volunteers, and received over 200 users a month at peak periods. The RHS thus found itself responsible for an existing library of nearly 4,000 volumes and 50 current periodical titles: the third-largest of the Society's collections.[47]

The desire to spread the benefits of the Society's Library around the country had been voiced in preceding generations, most notably by affiliated societies, which had more than once asked the RHS to institute a circulating library for their use.[48] Each of the RHS's sites now has a library collection accessible to its members and the general public, and lending is now being undertaken at more than one site. The Garden Libraries are staffed by a team of a hundred volunteers (across all the sites).

But in the age of information technology, there are other ways of spreading the benefits of library service beside housing new collections in brick and mortar. The last published catalogue of the Library, in 1927, was little more than a list of holdings; under Stearn and Stageman, the London card catalogue had gradually, and intermittently, developed into a more detailed bibliographical account of some of the more important works (the raw material for some of Stearn's articles). In the 1990s, a plan was drawn up for a computerised Library catalogue, that would repair the inconsistencies of the card catalogue, and provide not just a location record, but a bibliographical analysis, of the books; a database on the history of botanical illustration; and a research tool for users for whom physical access to the Library was difficult. Thousands of images from the older books have been digitised to augment the catalogue records; a pioneering project of watermark photography, carried out by Dr Ian Christie-Miller, has added further bibliographic information; and the Library's first full-text digitisation project, of the published works of Humphry Repton, was formally begun in 2003.

TRANSACTIONS,

OF THE

Horticultural Society

OF

LONDON.

Volume 1.

B. Taylor

Sculpebat

LONDON.

Printed by W. Bulmer, & Co. Cleveland Row.
Sold by J. Hatchard, Piccadilly.

MDCCCXII.

10 *Publications*

Ohn Wedgwood's original prospectus for the Horticultural Society contained the provision that 'the Society shall from time to time publish a volume of papers of the same size and form as the Transactions of the Adelphi Society [the Society for the Encouragement of Arts, later renamed the Royal Society of Arts], and that each member shall be entitled to a copy ... That the Committee shall have the power of selecting the papers for publication, and that no paper shall be published before it has been read at a sitting of the Society'.[1]

In the spring of 1807 the Society issued the first part of its *Transactions:* 70 pages on good-quality quarto paper, with two uncoloured engraved plates. Thereafter, at least one part of the *Transactions* appeared every year until 1836, when the momentum started to flag. The initial print-run was 500 copies, but by the fourth volume this had increased to 2,500, with coloured plates outnumbering uncoloured ones. The principal artist for the *Transactions* was William Hooker, but William Clark, Augusta Withers, and Sarah Ann Drake also contributed.

In a spirit of gentlemanly amicableness, the Society made it its policy 'never to give their opinion, as a body, upon any subject, either of Nature or Art, that comes before them', merely to provide a forum for the exchange of information without veto or rancour. By no means all the papers presented at meetings were published in the *Transactions*, but it is not clear how the Publications Committee decided what to publish, and what to reject; the minutes simply indicate approval or refusal. In February 1820, the Reverend George Swayne of Dyrham Rectory near Bath submitted an account of a new hybrid opium poppy; this was referred to the Secretary for experiment, and seeds were distributed at the next meeting. In the end the article was not printed, and one would like to know why.[2] What they did publish was a large number of articles on

Tab. 15.

The Variegated Chasselas.

new fruit varieties, descriptions of new tools and gardening operations, discussions of greenhouse construction and heating, accounts of new plants introduced by the Society's collectors, news from the garden at Chiswick, and theoretical accounts of hybridisation and the life of varieties.

The *Transactions* were a sumptuous and beautiful production, but, like the Society's membership, effectively limited by their high price to a wealthy audience. An alternative approach to periodical publishing was launched in 1826 by John Claudius Loudon, with a small, pocket-sized quarterly called *The Gardener's Magazine*. Note: the gardener, not the country gentleman. One of the correspondents in his *Magazine* complained in 1828 that the *Transactions* were 'a sealed book to country practitioners; quarto paper, large print, and extensive margin little suit our pockets. The publication, to do service to practical men, must be suited to their means.' Loudon aimed to do just that, by reprinting in his *Magazine* extensive chunks of the text of the *Transactions*, making it available to a wider audience, as he pointed out when the Society accused him of plagiarism. 'In the first place,' he responded to these accusations in 1827, 'the quantity of original matter in Part I of the (21s.) volume of our work, completed by the present number is nearly equal to the entire matter of the (£6) quarto volume of the Horticultural Transactions ... Secondly, though our articles are not ornamented by coloured plates, or engravings from copper or steel, yet they are illustrated by a greater number of engravings from wood, sufficiently intelligible for all useful purposes, than is the present or any formed volume of the Horticultural Transactions'.[3]

By its third year, the *Gardener's Magazine* had become a monthly, and was attracting an increasing number of writers, some of whom also wrote for the *Transactions*. Loudon invited controversy, publishing replies to correspondence, and by his fifth volume felt able to criticise the *Transactions* for its tone of gentlemanly good-will and refusal to publish criticisms of its articles: the *Transactions* had 'one advantage in this respect, viz., that, from their high price, they are not likely to be read by practical men; and, therefore, if it were possible that such a thing as an error should creep into them, it would do little harm'.[4]

By the mid-1820s, the duties of editing had fallen to the new Assistant Secretary, John Lindley, who performed that function for the rest of the *Transactions*' history, while also editing the *Botanical Register* and the short-lived *Pomological Magazine*. Meanwhile, the downturn in the Society's fortunes at the end of the 1820s threatened the production of the *Transactions*: when in 1829 the printer presented an invoice for £2,335, the Society, lacking the ready funds, gave him interest-bearing bonds for £2,000. From the late 1830s, the *Transactions* appeared sporadically, and in 1845 Council decided to discontinue the periodical at the end of the third volume of the second series, which appeared in 1848, carrying a cumulative index for the whole work.[5]

The fall of the *Transactions*, despite its origins in the Society's peculiar circumstances, was merely one instance in a general collapse in the market for colour-plate botanical magazines in the 1840s. In 1830, besides the *Transactions*, there were three magazines devoted to plant portraits—Curtis's *Botanical Magazine*, Edwards's *Botanical Register*, and Loddiges's *Botanical Cabinet*—that published hand-coloured plates. Then, in 1833, Joseph Harrison started the *Floricultural Cabinet*, illustrated with colour-printed plates—cheaper to produce, though less attractive; and by 1840 five other magazines had followed suit. Market saturation was the consequence: by 1850, only the *Botanical Magazine* and the *Floricultural Cabinet* were still going.[6]

Proceedings and Journals (to 1970)

In place of the *Transactions*, the Society initiated a *Journal* under Lindley's editorship, smaller in format, and issued in one annual volume. The first two volumes carried some colour-printed engravings, but after that the illustrations were confined to uncoloured engravings and wood-cuts. The first volume, for 1846, made its mark with opposing articles by Lindley and Miles J. Berkeley on the cause of the Irish potato blight. The content of the *Journal* was generally similar to that of the *Transactions*. A potential new direction was opened up with a description of John Dillwyn Llewellyn's orchid-house at Penllergaer—the first time the Society had published a description of a garden, or an ornamental garden feature; but it was not followed up. Nor did Lindley allow articles on design principles or aesthetics to appear—unless he himself was the author; in 1848 he published what was officially an historical talk on Elizabethan gardens, but in reality a polemic against historical revivalism in garden design.[7]

The late 1830s had seen a revolution in the horticultural literature, with the arrival of the first weekly gardening newspaper: George Glenny's *Gardeners' Gazette*, launched in 1837. Of greater importance was its first rival, the *Gardeners' Chronicle*, which Lindley and Joseph Paxton founded in 1841, and which remained the greatest and most influential of gardening magazines until well into the 20th century (from which height it eventually dwindled into a trade magazine, still continuing under the title *Horticulture Week*). Lindley remained its horticultural editor until failing health obliged him to relinquish his duties in 1863. His editorship was dogged by suggestions of conflict of interest, and allegations that he kept his best material for the *Chronicle* instead of the *Journal*. Certainly the *Chronicle* allowed for controversy and reply in a way the Society's publications did not, and Lindley used it as a political force, campaigning for the abolition of

Miles Joseph Berkeley (1803-1889), curate at Margate from 1828 to 1868, and latterly at Sibbertoft. Author of such works as British Fungi *(1833) and* Intro-duction to Cryptogamic Botany *(1857). In 1845 he identified the cause of the Irish potato blight as the fungus, later named* Phytophthora infestans. *First editor of the* RHS Journal, *1866-8.*

the tax on glass, improvements in glass manufacture, improvements in municipal parks, and much of the range of issues for which Loudon had formerly striven. Lindley's successor, Maxwell T. Masters, served as editor until 1905, and during their collective 60-plus years in power, the *Chronicle*, while officially independent and occasionally critical, largely served as an additional outlet for the expression of Society policy—with a more reliable publication schedule than its own output.[8]

Meanwhile, the Society's financial downturn was gathering speed, and the *Journal* was discontinued after nine volumes. A volume of *Proceedings*, giving annual reports and details of awards, had already been published for the years 1838-43, and in 1859, as finances started to pick up, the *Proceedings* were revived under the editorship of the botanist Arthur Henfrey, and continued until 1868, distributed to members but not sold to the public. By that time, a new *Journal* had been begun.

A successor was sought to Lindley, who had died in 1865, and was found in Miles J. Berkeley, his opponent over the potato blight in 1845. The first volume of the *Journal of the Royal Horticultural Society* appeared in 1866. Getting contributors was obviously a problem: Berkeley himself wrote 13 of the 41 articles that first year. He remained as Editor for the first four volumes (1866-73), resigning when his new duties as Rector of Sibbertoft, Northamptonshire, made his London activities difficult. Thereafter, until 1940, the task of editing the *Journal* was a duty passed through the hierarchy of the Society's staff: Secretaries, Assistant Secretaries, a Professor of Botany all undertook it at different times. The longest-running Editor (1908-39) was Frederick Chittenden, who filled just about every function the Society had, whether officially or not. The *Journal* came out irregularly at first, and in some years consisted solely of conference proceedings. From the 1890s to the 1930s it issued two or three parts a year, becoming monthly from 1934.

The *Journal* started the 20th century triumphantly with the English translation of Mendel's paper on heredity. Throughout the early years of the century, it contained a form of current awareness bulletin, by including abstracts of horticultural articles from an international range of periodicals; this was abandoned after the Commonwealth Agricultural Bureaux began publishing *Horticultural Abstracts* in the 1930s. And in the 1890s, the Society's long prejudice against discussing matters of aesthetics was finally breached, when Gertrude Jekyll published a paper on planning herbaceous borders. Accounts of individual gardens did not begin to appear until the later 1920s.

Chittenden was succeeded in 1940 by Sir Daniel Hall; he had two collaborators, first Roy Hay, then Vera Higgins, who succeeded him on his death in 1942, and guided the *Journal* through the war years. She was followed in 1946 by Patrick Synge, whose term as Editor lasted until 1969—the second-longest. From the mid-1950s he had to assist him an able series of Assistant Editors: Lanning Roper (1954-56), Miss G.E. Peterson (1957-9), James Platt (from 1961), and Elspeth Napier (from 1966). Synge introduced colour photographs as illustrations in the late 1940s, lost them to financial pressure in 1952, but was able to claw them back in the mid-1960s, when fortunes seemed to be improving. Articles on gardens were appearing more regularly now, and Lord Morton had started a series on the history of important nurseries in 1958 (he never lived to collect them into his intended book). But Synge and the Society's new Secretary John Hamer were increasingly at loggerheads, with Synge regarding the latter as obstructive on principle and obtuse in manner; eventually, in 1969, Synge resigned.[9]

The formation of a publishing policy

Short-lived publications committees came and went over the years through the Society's history, the first one having been wound up with the first series of the *Transactions*. The longest-lasting Publications Committee dated its origin to 1917 and the initiative of H.J. Elwes.[10] The experience that led to the formation of the Committee was that of publishing pamphlets during the First World War to help with domestic food production, on subjects like autumn vegetables, potatoes, and bottling fruits and vegetables for preserves. The issue of pamphlets languished during the inter-war years, but was stepped up again during the Second World War, in collaboration with the Ministry of Agriculture and the Dig for Victory campaign. Thereafter it remained consistent, culminating in the Wisley Handbooks of the 1970s and 1980s.

In 1956, the President, Sir David Bowes Lyon, distinguished two purposes in the Society's publications: those intended to popularise gardening, whose success could be measured by sales, and which ought not to be ventured upon without some assurances of successful distribution, and 'a certain number of works which were definitely scientific, even though the cost of the latter could not be entirely recovered'.[11] Under the heading of works popularising gardening came the Society's biggest-ever bestseller, *The Vegetable*

Robert Edwin (Roy) Hay (1910-1989), assistant editor of the RHS Journal, 1940. Editor of the Gardeners' Chronicle, 1954-64, and prolific author; wrote Gardening the Modern Way and the Dictionary of Indoor Plants in Colour (1975) for the RHS. Founder of Britain in Bloom.

Vera Cockburn (1892-1968) married the radiologist Frederick William Higgins of the National Physical Laboratory, where she was a scientific officer during the First World War. During the 1920s she began collecting orchids and cacti. Editor of the Cactus and Succulent Society's Journal, the Alpine Garden Society's Bulletin, and the RHS Journal, for a while simultaneously. She wrote ten books, mainly on cacti and succulents, and translated fourteen.

Garden Displayed (first published 1941), and its companion volume *The Fruit Garden Displayed* (first published 1951); cards, calendars, and desk diaries; textbooks intended for use in horticultural colleges, especially the Macmillan series 'Science in horticulture', which began to appear in 1973; books on gardens and garden design—always touched somewhat gingerly; books about the Society itself, its history and art collection.

Books of general advice on plant identification and gardening also fell under the heading of popularising. Among them were 15 gardening handbooks published with Penguin Books between 1958 and 1964; four colour dictionaries (of garden plants, roses, indoor plants, and shrubs) published with Ebury Press; Frances Perry's *Flowers of the World*, published with Hamlyn in 1972; a series of monographs published with Batsford, beginning with Peter Cox's *Dwarf Rhododendrons* in 1972; and the *Encyclopaedia of Practical Gardening*, issued with Mitchell Beazley in 1979-1981 and later revised.

Under Sir David's second category, of scientific works to be published regardless of cost, came checklists and registers, the Colour Chart, conference proceedings, botanical monographs, and plant collectors' notes. The Society published an

First edition of The Vegetable Garden Displayed *(1941).*

Specimens of the range of pamphlets published by the RHS, from the paper issues of the First World War to the Wisley Handbooks of the late 20th century.

edition of David Douglas' journals in 1914, and, in 1929, a volume of George Forrest's field notes from his 1917-19 expedition in western China. A planned collaboration with the Royal Botanic Garden Edinburgh on a *Plantae Forrestianae* was eventually abandoned, and in its place came a memorial volume to Forrest, which appeared in 1952 as *The Journeys and Plant Introductions of George Forrest*. In 1950, the Society gave an honorarium to Joseph Rock, the American plant collector, for a book about his expeditions, but the draft contained more geographical and ethnographical than botanical or horticultural information; the Society declined to publish, and Rock's work never appeared.

The first monographs the Society published were Sir Michael Foster's monograph on *Bulbous Irises* in 1893, the Irish botanist R.L. Praeger's *Account of the Genus Sedum* (1921) and *Account of the Sempervivum Group* in (1932), and H.W. Pugsley's *Monograph of Narcissus, subgenus Ajax* appeared in the *Journal* (1933). The Society's policy for publishing monographs was breaking into a trot, but its next project almost caused it to stumble. In 1929 Council advanced £50 to Camillo Schneider, the great German dendrologist, to assist him in producing a monograph on *Berberis*; by 1935 another £100 had made its way to him. In 1939 Schneider reported that the first part was complete and available for publication; Council decided to wait another year in the hope of having the complete work. What it got instead, of course, was the war; and when in 1945 Schneider, whose collections at Berlin-Dahlem had been destroyed by allied bombing, applied to the Society for extra funds to get his work back on course, Council found it an unpropitious moment for such a request. Eventually, in 1955, a monograph on *Berberis* and *Mahonia* by Leslie Ahrendt was published in the Linnean Society's *Journal*, with a £500 grant from the Society.[12]

In 1935, an ambitious programme for monographs was worked out. The first to appear was *The Genus Tulipa*, by Sir Daniel Hall, in 1940 (Hall had previously published a horticultural mono graph, *The Book of the Tulip*).[13] F.C. Stern's *Study of the Genus Paeonia* had been intended for publication at the same time, but was delivered late; at first, it was thought that it could appear in December 1941, since the paper for it had already been acquired before wartime restrictions came into force, but it was eventually postponed until 1946.[14] George H. Johnstone, whose garden at Trewithen was famous for its magnolia collection, had been asked to write a monograph on *Asiatic Magnolias in Cultivation*. The work dragged on into the 1950s, bedevilled by nomenclatural quarrels; the volume, possibly the finest the Society published, finally appeared in 1955.[15] E.A. Bowles undertook *Galanthus* and *Anemone*; neither was completed by the time of his death in 1954. His *Galanthus* material

was incorporated into F.C. Stern's *Snowdrops and Snowflakes* (1956); portions of his *Anemone* material, written in collaboration with W.T. Stearn, appeared as two articles for the *Journal*.[16] *Old Camellia Varieties*, a very incomplete checklist begun by Chittenden and completed by A.I. Ellis, was published in 1953. J.R. Sealy had proposed a *Revision of the Genus Camellia* in 1948, to be illustrated by his wife, Stella Ross-Craig; it eventually appeared in 1958, but for financial reasons illustrated with line drawings only.[17] Other proposed monographs never appeared. In 1952, anxious about the rising costs of publication in the post-war world, Council insisted that all future recommendations for monographs must be carefully scrutinised, and that mini-monographs to be published in the *Journal* would be given preference.[18]

In 1956, however, the Society felt sufficiently hearty to revive one of H.J. Elwes's projects. Elwes had published *A Monograph of the Genus Lilium*, with chromolithographs by W.H. Fitch, between 1877 and 1880. Arthur Grove and A.D. Cotton published a *Supplement*, using plates by Lilian Snelling, between 1934 and 1940. In 1956, the Society acquired the copyright, and two further supplements, under the editorship of W.B. Turrill, with plates by Margaret Stones, appeared in 1960 and 1962.[19]

Patrick Synge, meanwhile, was planning a complete revision of Elwes's monograph, which he saw as his life's crowning achievement. In 1966 he persuaded various members of the Lily Group to commission lily portraits from Margaret Stones for the purpose, and the following year found a publisher. Synge resigned the Editorship of the *Journal* at the end of 1969, taking the unfinished manuscript with him, and his effort began a relentless slide downhill. Successive publishers expressed interest and backed out, or proposed such changes in the book that the Society refused to be associated with it. Heated correspondence followed between Synge and the Society, with Synge complaining bitterly about Hamer's obstructionism; the drawings that Lily Group members had commissioned were returned to them; two £1,000 donations toward the publication were returned, but then added to the Library funds at the donors' insistence. This left a group of paintings which the Society had commissioned from Margaret Stones, which Synge offered to buy for the £378

Drawing of Paeonia clusii *for Stern's* Study of the Genus Paeonia, *by Lilian Snelling.*

paid for them; but Stones had sold them to the Society at a specially reduced rate, and it was decided that the true price should be over £1,000. As tempers flared over this issue, Hamer took independent action. Collaring the Library keys from Peter Stageman one day in July 1974, he entered the Library that evening with a locksmith in tow, removed the books from one of the stack room cupboards, placed the disputed paintings inside, and had a new lock fitted, to which he had the only key.

The Society had relinquished any claims on the book, leaving Synge to continue his search. Batsford now took an interest in the publication, and with the passage of four years, and the retirement of Hamer, a rapprochement was achieved more calmly. John Cowell, Hamer's successor, willingly acknowledged Synge's claim to the lily paintings, and handed the key to the 'Secretary's cupboard' to the Library staff so that they could be retrieved and passed over to him. The course to publication was still arduous, but *Lilies* was finally published, in association with the Society, in 1980, two years before Synge's death.[20]

Sealy's *Camellia* and the supplements to Elwes were the last monographic works the Society published on its own. From the 1960s on, all such works as appeared were the result of a collaboration between the Society and a commercial publisher. In 1963, the firm of John Murray approached the Society for help with a major revision of W.J. Bean's *Trees and Shrubs Hardy in the British Isles*—an eighth edition in four volumes, under the editorship of Desmond Clarke. The Society agreed to subsidise the work, but £5,000 had been paid by the time the first volume appeared, and 'what had been regarded as an investment had now become a speculation'; the Society's financial contribution was discontinued as of 1974, and the work was not completed until 1980.[21] Similarly, in 1986, the Society gave a £5,000 subsidy toward the preparation of the *European Garden Flora*.

Index Londinensis

In 1909, Council had noted the absence of a good index of botanical illustrations as a deficiency the Society should seek to remedy. The only systematic attempt at indexing published portraits of plants had been Georg August Pritzel's massive *Iconum botanicarum index locupletissimus* (1855-66); but this was long out of print, hard to obtain, incomplete, sometimes difficult to use, and in any case 40 years of further illustration had elapsed since then. Council established a committee to advise on bringing Pritzel up to date. To start with, the

Committee examined two annotated copies of Pritzel's Index, which Kew and Ellen Willmott respectively had tried to update; but as Willmott had entered many cultivars into her copy as well as species, it was decided to use the Kew copy as a basis for further work. Discussions then descended into chaos, as the principles for revision were debated. Council eventually took the extraordinary step of creating two separate committees, each to be chaired by a member of the other one, representing in effect the botanical and the amateur communities: committee (a) to advise 'As to the maximum of information it is desirable to incorporate in the Pritzel'; and committee (b) to advise 'As to the minimum of information they would deem essential'.

With such beginnings, it was obvious that the Pritzel revision was not going to be straightforward. Should hybrids and cultivated varieties be included? 'Rose 'Dorothy Perkins' might, for example, be very interesting from a horticultural point of view, but of no interest to a botanist', said Otto Stapf, to which Sir David Prain replied, 'Yes, quite true; but we must remember that the R.H.S. is paying for the work to be done.' (Cultivars were eventually excluded.) Hopes that the nomenclature could be guaranteed correct were dashed by Stapf, who pointed out that the *Index Kewensis* no longer attempted synonymy. It was agreed that the work would incorporate Pritzel's work, correcting errors, making plate number references less confusing, and adding works that he had omitted, with 1753, the publication date of Linnaeus' *Species Plantarum*, taken as the starting point.—Then came the war, and the project was shelved.[22]

It was revived in 1918, and Stapf appointed editor. The Clarendon Press agreed to publish the work, and their editor, Kenneth Sisam (otherwise best known as a Middle English scholar), became closely involved with the project. The work was completed with some 300,000 entries in 1927, and published in six volumes in 1929-31 under the title *Index Londinensis*. It remains one of the botanist's and plant historian's essential tools: the most complete record of plant portraits ever compiled, chronologically arranged under each plant—an invaluable tool for literature searches as well.[23]

The publication took place, as Sisam later admitted, 'at a rather unfortunate time for libraries'; the great depression was looming, by 1936 only 270 sets had been sold, and the Delegates of the Oxford University Press lost over £4,000 on the production bills alone. Nonetheless, Sisam began to press for the publication of a supplement: 'The Delegates do not complain of making a considerable loss on *Index Londinensis*, because they regard it as a monumental work, and I imagine your Committee will take the same view.' W.C. Worsdell, Stapf's assistant in the later stages of the *Index*, undertook the work of updating it in 1931, adding about 16,000 entries each year. In 1935 new criteria were introduced to curtail the galloping expansion of the work: 'well-known and frequently figured plants' were to be omitted, and works which did not include suitable illustrations were to be eliminated, except where the plant in question was previously unrecorded. The completed supplement was published in two volumes on 31 January 1941, again at a rather unfortunate time for libraries, and Worsdell was awarded a Veitch Medal for his work.[24]

In 1939, A. D. Cotton proposed that the *Index Londinensis* could be continued on cards, with sets deposited at Kew, the RHS, Edinburgh, and the Natural History Museum. The work was undertaken by Kew, but no multiple copies were distributed. In 1971, after discussions about a further supplement had subsided inconclusively, the RHS stopped its subsidy of the work.[25]

The Dictionary of Gardening

The financial repercussions of the *Index Londinensis* left Kenneth Sisam's enthusiasm for collaboration with the Society untouched. Early in 1936 he was proposing, in conversation with Colonel Durham and Sir Arthur Hill, another

revision of a standard classic: Nicholson's *Illustrated Dictionary of Gardening*.

That work had its origin in a proposal from the young William Roberts, later an important horticultural bibliographer, to the publisher L. Upcott Gill, that they publish a gardening dictionary. Roberts worked on the project until 1884, whereupon Gill turned for help to Kew, and was rewarded with George Nicholson, about to become Assistant Curator. Nicholson drew on his colleagues' help, and produced a fine dictionary, published in 1885-88 and frequently reprinted. A Century Supplement in two volumes was issued in 1901, but Nicholson died in 1908, and the work had been out of print since before the First World War.[26]

'I hope you will be thinking about the new Gardening Dictionary', wrote Sisam to Durham in March 1936.

> I am sure it would be a good thing to have a standard book, to which gardeners could turn with the assurance that the information is sound and not distorted by the idea of selling some plant, tool, or manure ... I have it in mind— though I have not consulted the Delegates yet— that we would take some share in the editorial cost, and of course join in the planning because we have a lot of experience in this kind of work; that we should undertake the printing cost; and that there should be a special subscription rate to members of the Society ...[27]

The Society acceded, and formed an advisory committee. The work of compilation fell on that redoubtable beast of burden, Frederick Chittenden, who was relieved of all other duties as of 1939 to devote his full time to the project. His work consisted of overall editing, and the writing of all articles that were not assigned to some other specialist. His major collaborators were William Dallimore (conifers); W.J. Bean (oaks and maples—Nicholson's former specialties—and the rest of trees and shrubs generally); C.E. Hubbard (grasses); and E.W. Cooper (orchids). There were 43 contributors in all, and would have been more but for the war; Chittenden eventually wrote far more of the entries than he had anticipated. Fruit and vegetable cultivation were made the subject of a separate volume, rather than mix the entries with the alphabetically arranged botanical section.

The war slowed production, but completed portions were already being set in type during the late 1940s. In 1950, however, Chittenden died from cancer. The Editor and the Librarian—Synge and W.T. Stearn—were asked to complete the intended four-volume work, two volumes of which had already been printed and lay in sheets at the Oxford University Press—while G.C. Taylor

Title-page of the first volume of the Dictionary of Gardening, *1952.*

THE ROYAL HORTICULTURAL SOCIETY

DICTIONARY OF GARDENING

A PRACTICAL AND SCIENTIFIC
ENCYCLOPAEDIA OF HORTICULTURE

Edited by
FRED J. CHITTENDEN, O.B.E., F.L.S., V.M.H.

Assisted by Specialists

SECOND EDITION
by
PATRICK M. SYNGE, M.A. (Cantab), F.L.S.

VOLUME I : A—CO

OXFORD
AT THE CLARENDON PRESS

was asked to oversee the fifth volume. The consequence for Stearn was, as he jocularly remarked, that he became an expert on plants from So to Z. The work was finally published in 1952.[28]

It became apparent even before publication that there were gaps in the work, the result no doubt of Chittenden's increasing illness, which could not easily be filled because of the premature printing of the first two volumes. A supplement was therefore planned almost immediately; the work mainly of Patrick Synge, it appeared in 1956. A revised supplement was compiled by Elspeth Napier and published in 1969.[29]

Over the ensuing years the question of revision kept raising its head. By the mid-1980s, it loomed too urgently to be brushed aside any longer, and the Society listened to tenders for a complete revision, to be sold at a price of £400 in 1987 terms. In February 1988, a contract was signed, not with Oxford, but with Macmillan, who had produced the more impressive proposal. Macmillan would find a Managing Editor (Margot Levy), the Society an Editor-in-chief (Anthony Huxley, despite initial hopes that the job would go to one of the rising talents on the Wisley staff); Mark Griffiths was hired as Editor under Huxley; 42 people were eventually listed as researchers. Entirely new illustrations were commissioned: over 350 line drawings, almost all comparative treatments of genera rather than portraits of individual species, by 30 artists.

This time, fruit and vegetable cultivation were incorporated into the common alphabetical sequence; but many definitions were taken out, to form separate glossaries of botanical and taxonomic terms at the start of the first volume; and all the entries on pests and diseases were similarly segregated at the end of the fourth. Biographical entries on gardeners, botanists, and designers were added for the first time, as were entries on garden history generally. Contributors not having been asked to contribute bibliographies for their subjects, an emergency bibliography was compiled by the Librarian at the last moment. *The New Royal Horticultural Society Dictionary of Gardening* was published in 1992. Anthony Huxley did not long survive its appearance; increasingly unwell, but determined not to allow anything to interrupt his work, he only sought medical help after he had delivered the typescript.[30]

Work now shifted to finding ways of channelling the material in the *Dictionary* to different markets. Macmillan published a series of *RHS Manuals*, on grasses, climbing plants, bulbs and orchids and an *Index of Garden Plants*. A paperback imprint of the four-volume dictionary appeared in 1999, not long after the one-volume abridgement by Michael Pollock and Mark Griffiths.

Curtis's Botanical Magazine

In 1921, the Society intervened, not for the last time, to save a famous publication from being discontinued. William Curtis had founded *The Botanical Magazine* in 1787, and it had become the world's longest-running illustrated botanical journal; edited first by Curtis's family, then by the various Directors of the Royal Botanic Gardens, Kew, in succession, it had been associated with Kew for three generations without ever being adopted as an official publication. For most of Queen Victoria's reign it had appeared monthly, each volume containing 60 hand-coloured portraits of plants, usually new introductions. Originally engraved, the plant portraits had been lithographed since 1845, its greatest illustrator being Walter Hood Fitch, who made over 2,000 illustrations between 1837 and 1878.[31] But by the First World War the *Magazine* had fallen on hard times; it had shrunk into a quarterly, with a print-run of 400. Lovell Reeve, who had published it since 1844, suspended publication in December 1920. They tried to pass the responsibility for

Patrick Millington Synge (1910-1982) collected plants on expeditions to Sarawak and East Africa in the 1930s, before becoming a director of the publishing house Lindsay Drummond. Editor of RHS publications, 1945-70. Subsequently editor of the International Dendrology Society Yearbook; *continued to collect plants in Nepal and the Mediterranean.*

Anthony John Huxley (1920-1992), son of Julian Huxley and great-grandson of Thomas Henry Huxley; editor of Amateur Gardening 1967-1971. *Co-author with Oleg Polunin of* Flowers of the Mediterranean (1965), *and with William Taylor of* Flowers of Greece and the Aegean (1977), *as well as of a number of books on plants and gardening, and his excellent introduction to botany,* Plant and Planet (1974).

Rhododendron dauricum var. sempervirens. *An illustration by Lilian Snelling for the 'Cory volume' of* Curtis's Botanical Magazine, *published 1938.*

producing the *Magazine* to Kew (that is, the Ministry of Agriculture and Fisheries). H.J. Elwes, who distrusted government control, tried to get the Bentham Trust to take it over, but his overtures were declined. While negotiations were dragging on, the Smithsonian Institution began to make representations about acquiring the copyright.

This was the last straw. At a meeting of the Garden Society on 24 May 1921, the Director of Kew, Sir David Prain, announced that 'there was some danger of the copyright of the Botanical Magazine passing into American hands, since the Government was unable to see its way to carrying on the publication'. It was 'immediately resolved' that Elwes and W.R. Dykes 'should be commissioned to secure the copyright on behalf of the Society for £250'. The Society's offer was accepted, and Lovell Reeve passed over a quarter-million uncoloured plates, 30,000 coloured ones, the patterns for colouring, a stock of letterpress from 1845 to 1920, and a stock of bound volumes.[32]

The Society found a new publisher in H.F. & G. Witherby, who undertook to issue the *Botanical Magazine* in a print-run of 500 copies, on a trial contract to run to the end of 1924. A new artist was found in Lilian Snelling, who had made drawings of Elwes's plant collection in the previous decade, and had then trained at the Edinburgh Botanic Garden. Otto Stapf, who had just retired from Kew and was in the throes of compiling the *Index Londinensis*, was appointed editor. The first part to appear under the Society's auspices came out in October 1922—just in time for Elwes to see a successful conclusion to his negotiations, for he died the following month.[33]

The Society had decided not to try to issue a volume for 1921, but Reginald Cory agreed to finance the publication of the missing volume privately. Stapf agreed to edit the volume, but as time passed, and continued to pass, and his relations with Cory soured over the latter's proprietorial attitude to the text, which he insisted on altering after it had been set in type, he resigned in January 1933. Cory himself died the following year, and John Ramsbottom was appointed editor. The 1921 volume finally appeared in 1938.[34]

Meanwhile, in 1924 the trial contract came to an end, and Messrs Witherby expressed their doubts about the magazine's viability. C.G.A. Nix reported their worries to F.C. Stern: 'there are not enough botanists and scientific institutions to support a Botanical Magazine of this class, and subscribers must be obtained from among those whose interests in plants are purely horticultural. It may be true that the Botanical Magazine is not of use nor interest to gardeners. If so, we may have

to consider considerable alterations in the style and make up of the Magazine.' The proposed options were: continuing as at present; turning it into a popular magazine, which Nix described as 'a "Daily Mail" sort of magazine' ('Personally I should protest against such a magazine being called "The Botanical Magazine". A new name would have to be found.'); or a compromise venture, with Latin replaced by English. Stern angrily replied that 'I do not think that the Magazine has yet had a chance to become a success. It has never been published punctually since it has been issued by the R.H.S., and this alone makes an enormous difference to subscribers.' He objected to any reduction in standards, and insisted that Latin descriptions formed the *Magazine*'s principal chance of appealing to an international market. So it continued as it had been, in the hope that an improving post-war situation would increase its foreign subscription rate, and the Society began subsidising its publication by £500 annually.[35]

In 1934 Sir Arthur Hill succeeded Stapf, continuing the tradition of Directors of Kew acting as editors. The Second World War brought a hiatus to production; volume 164 was spread out over the years 1943-48. Subscriptions stood at 166 at the end of the war. W.B. Turrill succeeded to the editorship in 1947, and aggressive marketing raised the subscription level to 700 by 1954. The illustration process was also changed. From 1935 floral dissections were printed separately in the text, by the cheaper process of wood-engraving. In 1946 the Society finally ended the long tradition of hand-colouring, switching first to a half-tone process, then to photolithography.[36] Lilian Snelling retired in 1952, to be succeeded by Stella Ross-Craig; Margaret Stones became the principal artist by 1960.

After 1951, each volume of the *Magazine* was issued over two years, with two parts appearing each year. The effective reduction of the number of plants illustrated per annum highlights the logistical problems the work was facing. The 19th century had seen a steady rate of new plant introductions, but by the mid-20th century this rate had slowed, even before the Communist takeover in China cut off the most fertile source of new plants. Turrill introduced a new policy of illustrating some first-generation hybrids of importance, and also began filling the gaps in the *Magazine*'s record by including long-established plants that had been missed previously.

In 1966, Oliver Wyatt, the Treasurer, told Council that the annual subsidy, which had now risen to £2,000 per annum, was 'difficult to defend on a work which must be considered as of limited interest'. He was silenced by Lord Aberconway and Sir Edward Salisbury, who maintained that the Society should bear the costs as a contribution to science. With grant aid and a higher price, the situation was stabilised for a few years; but with the financial pressures of 1969-70, Wyatt met with less resistance, and after fairly brief negotiations, the copyright in the *Magazine* was assigned to the Bentham-Moxon Trust from 1 January 1971. At long last it was an official publication of Kew's.[37]

The Society continued to maintain a non-financial interest in the *Magazine*. By 1983, when Kew was discussing its future with all the anxiety that the Society had formerly done, the Society was there on the sidelines, encouraging it to continue. In 1984 its title was changed to *The Kew Magazine*, market research having suggested that Kew was a better recognised name than Curtis; and the commercial publishers Collingridge became associated with its production. So it passed its bicentenary under another name, only to revert in 1995.

Year Books

One of the major features of the Society's publishing programme in the 20th century began as the result of an independent action of one of the floral committees. In 1911, the Narcissus and Tulip Committee set up a Publications Subcommittee to plan a *Daffodil Year Book*, to be edited by Joseph Jacob; and the first issue appeared in 1913, carrying obituaries, show reports, surveys of new cultivars, and Jacob's historical contribution, 'Celebrities of Daffodildom'. Three issues appeared before the war put an end to further publication.[38] Any thoughts of specialist periodicals lay dormant until lily fever gripped the Society at the beginning of the 1930s. The newly formed Lily Committee secured permission to publish a *Lily Year Book* commencing in 1932, with Chittenden as editor, to be issued in a print-run of 500 copies. The first years of the *Lily Year Book* were an immense success. Narcissus and Tulip responded to the enthusiasm, and pressed for the relaunch of the *Daffodil Year Book*, whose fourth issue duly appeared in 1933.[39]

The Second World War threw both publications into disarray. They were revived in 1946, in print-runs of 1,500, and once again the Editor of the *Journal*, now Patrick Synge, took responsibility for editing them. But the number of Year Books was growing. The Rhododendron Association had been incorporated into the Society in 1945, and one of the consequences was a new *Rhododendron Year Book* (to be augmented into a *Rhododendron and Camellia Year Book* from

1954). For this year book alone, Synge had a long-term collaborator from outside his editorial department (Norman Gould, until his death in 1960), a signal perhaps of the residual vigour of the Rhododendron Association. A fourth year book, the *Fruit Year Book*, was added to the roster in 1947; John Bultitude acted as co-editor for the first issue alone. Otherwise, the responsibility for editing all four was Synge's until his retirement, shared, like the *Journal*, with his assistants. The year books, in those halcyon days, attracted prestige to the Society, and were praised as a means of extending the Society's benefits when 'comparatively few of the Fellows are able to enjoy the facilities provided at London and Wisley'.[40] The *Fruit Year Book*, which had been expected to be the most popular of all (initial print-run, 3,000), unfortunately lasted for only ten volumes; the others, with somewhat chastened circulations, were all still in harness in the late 1960s, when the financial storm broke.

Synge had resigned, and the yearbooks were being edited by the team of Elspeth Napier and James Platt, when the Treasurer, Oliver Wyatt, forced the issue of their production costs. In June 1970 Council, over the resistance of Eliot Hodgkin and Sir Giles Loder, took the decision to discontinue the yearbooks, but allowed Hodgkin the option of raising the matter again with the Publications Committee. That Committee's minutes recorded: 'There was a feeling amongst members of the Year Book Committees that they should have been consulted before the decision to discontinue publication was made. In that the decision was taken on financial grounds this was hardly a matter for the Year Book Committees themselves but was one for the Publications Committee and subsequently for Council.' The Year Book Committees formed an unofficial committee with Herbert Barr as chairman, to demand immediate resumption of publication. Meanwhile John Blanchard requested permission for the Narcissus and Tulip Committee to issue an interim publication by its members, which he himself would underwrite; this was agreed by Council so long as the result was not called a Year Book.[41]

The Publications Committee debated the future of the yearbooks in May 1971. Napier said that 'the production of the 3 Year Books last year had taken up too great a proportion of editorial time for six months', and proposed that the former hard-cover volumes be replaced by smaller-format paperbacks (with the attenuated names of *Daffodils*, *Lilies*, and *Rhododendrons*). Lord Blakenham, the new Treasurer, offered to test the proposal in 1972-73, and then see whether to

continue in 1974. Editorship fell, as usual, to Napier, with an honorary assistant editor in each case. By the end of 1973, Blakenham was sufficiently happy with the financial situation for the publications to continue, but the administration remained uneasy over finances.[42] *Lilies* proved the most difficult to keep financially sound, and ceased to appear as an RHS publication after 1979; the Lily Group assumed responsibility for its publication, which was thereafter sporadic, and years could pass without an issue. Susanne Mitchell took over the general editorship from Elspeth Napier as from the 1990 issues. The status of the year books is still unresolved: are they works intended to popularise gardening, whose success must be measured in financial terms, or do they fall into the category of duty publications, which the Society ought to continue regardless of cost?

From New Perspectives to Maxwell

The financial cutbacks of 1970, which saw *Curtis's Botanical Magazine*, the year books, and the subsidy to the *Index Londinensis* continuation all deleted from the Society's accounts, left the *Journal* comparatively unaffected: safe in the hands of Elspeth Napier, who had succeeded Synge. Postage and distribution systems were scrutinised with greater enthusiasm than editorial or printing costs. But within a few years, as membership continued to decline, the future of the *Journal* was thrown into doubt, and a proposal was considered to replace the *Journal* with a quarterly A4 magazine supplemented by a newsletter. The obvious answer was to see what a commercial partner might offer, and New Perspectives, a quasi-autonomous imprint in the publishing house of Mitchell Beazley, seemed to offer the right answers, under the directorship of Hugh Johnson.

After more than a century, the words *Journal of the Royal Horticultural Society* would now become a subtitle; the new title would be *The Garden*. Hugh Johnson, who as a director of New Perspectives now arrived on the Publications Committee, explained the change as a homage to William Robinson's magazine of that name (1871-1927): 'One hundred volumes of the Journal. The centenary of a famous partnership [i.e. 100 years since Gertrude Jekyll first called on Robinson—not exactly a partnership]. Such a concatenation of centuries was irresistible to the committee which is to "conduct" the refurbished Journal. *The Garden* was the only possible name for it.' The new format was introduced with the issue of June 1975.[43]

Some members regretted the changes in the *Journal* as representing a drift from the organ of a learned society to a common-or-garden magazine. In 1978, Hugh Johnson announced that he was investigating the possibility of a new magazine, designed in part to fill the gap in *The Garden*'s content. To be called *The Plantsman*, and edited by Elspeth Napier, who would become a temporary employee of New Perspectives for a certain number of hours a week, it would appear quarterly, with a colour plate in each issue, at an annual subscription of £6 (£4 to Members). The first issue appeared in 1979, with a resounding preface by Johnson:

> For who would have dreamed, a few years ago, that *The Garden, the Journal of the Royal Horticultural Society*, would now have a circulation of 75,000 copies and a readership of perhaps twice that number?

In trying to inform, and be comprehensible to, this wider gardening audience the *Journal* has deliberately widened its scope and done its best to popularize (though not we hope cheapen) both its manner and its matter. Which has meant leaving out, or at any rate abbreviating, the sort of schollarly [*sic*], unhurried, lovingly minute studies of plants which are the true meat of specialist horticultural literature.

You can see that I am describing an editorial quandary. *The Plantsman* is the answer to it. Its intention is to supplement the monthly *Journal* with quarterly studies for the gardener whose passion for plants will never be satisfied—the plantsman of the title.[44]

During the course of the next 15 volumes, *The Plantsman* was to publish horticultural reviews of genera such as *Acer, Achimenes, Arisaema, Betula, Cistus, Deutzia, Euonymus, Hoya, Larix, Peperomia, Pieris, Pulmonaria, Rhodohypoxis, Skimmia, Sorbus, Trillium*, as well as hardiness surveys and, in 1989, an early assessment of genetic engineering.

In 1989 Elspeth Napier retired from the editorship of *The Garden*, to be succeeded by Susanne Mitchell, whose career had hitherto been spent in book publishing, working with Collingridge, Hamlyn and Marshall Cavendish on their gardening lists. At her interview, she specified as her intended improvements to *The Garden* an increase in its size, a better use of illustrations, more articles arranged in series ('stranding' in the trade terminology), and increased attention to neglected subject areas like house plants and conservatories. The move to A4 size had been intermittently proposed and consistently rejected, but in 1991, she finally got the backing of the Publications Committee with a presentation whose conclusions she summarised thus: 'The new style allows more flexibility in design, the use of larger pictures and gives much more editorial scope.' The projected design was displayed at Chelsea, and 60 per cent of the responses were in favour. The first issue in the new format appeared in January 1992, and was badly printed; she recalled the response of the administration as one of absolute silence. But by then working conditions had been screwed to a point of unexpected difficulty.

In 1987, New Perspectives had been bought by Home & Law, a publishing house within the umbrella of Maxwell Consumer Publishing, itself one arm of the enormous conglomerate Maxwell Communication Corporation. The RHS had no apprehensions about the new arrangement; it brought an association with one of the largest and apparently most successful publishing enterprises in the country which could only be gratifying to the new spirit of enthusiasm for business. The

history of Maxwell was either forgotten or overlooked.

Robert Maxwell, an immigré Czech, had made a career out of publishing in post-war Britain. As early as 1954 he was censured by an official receiver for trading while insolvent. He had weathered this, and built up a respected scientific publishing house, Pergamon Press. When he sold the Press to an American firm in 1969, the new owners discovered that the company's accounts were fraudulent, and an investigation by the Department of Trade and Industry resulted in the verdict that Maxwell was 'not in our opinion a person who can be relied upon to exercise proper stewardship of a publicly quoted company'. But this too he weathered, and by 1987 he controlled a vast business empire that included the Mirror Group newspapers, Bishopgate Property, Maxwell Building Enterprises, and the Nuffield Press. Unfortunately, the scale of these enterprises, and the tangled lines of responsibility between them, made it easy for Maxwell to conceal financial crises in one area by transferring funds temporarily from another; and as the potential disasters worsened, the scale of the internal transfers, most famously the plundering of the Mirror Group's pension funds, made the entire structure rickety. And then, on 5 November 1991, Maxwell's body was found floating in the Atlantic, fallen from his yacht. He was buried on the Mount of Olives in Jerusalem before the state of his finances became publicly known.[45]

The problems of Maxwell's finances were reflected in what was happening at Home & Law. Invoices were regularly weeks, if not months, in arrears; by the end of 1991, the RHS was picking up all the printers' bills in order to keep *The Garden* going. Within a week of Maxwell's death, the suppliers of rented office equipment moved in to repossess their stock, and fax machines and water coolers began disappearing from Greater London House (Home & Law's office block in north London). On Christmas eve, Donald Hearn, the Financial Director, sent up a cheque to cover the Christmas pay for all the *Garden* staff (most of whom were officially employed by Maxwell). The RHS decided that *The Garden* had to be pulled away from Home & Law. Specialist publishers began to be circularised secretly in the ten days before Christmas, and in January 1992 the choice fell upon the East Midlands Associated Press. EMAP had started as the *Peterborough Evening Telegraph*, but had gradually built up a chain of magazines, including gardening titles; it had started *Garden News* in 1958, and four years later had bought *Practical Gardening*. It also had an international distribution facility.

By January, the Maxwell edifice was looking increasingly shaky as the revelations multiplied. The fear that the firm might go into liquidation, and that production of *The Garden* might be halted by a lockout, gripped the Society's administration. Early in February Robin Herbert determined to break the contract. Expeditions were launched from Vincent Square to retrieve the editorial files from Greater London House. Home & Law removed the camera-ready copy for the March issue from the printers to use as a bargaining counter; but the printers had prepared a duplicate copy of the editorial content, and the advertisers were circularised to obtain copies of their text.

While this was going on, a management buy-out took place, and the firm's name changed to Headway Home & Law. The contract guaranteed the RHS the option to renegotiate on any change in the firm's name, so the legal motive for breaking the contract now presented itself. The *Garden* staff were all pulled out to Vincent Square, and the offices in the former flat above the Library cleared to accommodate them. By the end of February, the publication unit of *The Garden* was operating out of the top floor of 80 Vincent Square, and all the contractual arrangements lay happily up in Peterborough with EMAP.

The Orchid Review and The New Plantsman

Meanwhile, in 1988 the Society was once again asked to intervene in the fate of a long-standing and prestigious publication. The *Orchid Review* had been founded in 1893 by the Kew orchidologist R.A. Rolfe, who edited it until his death in 1921. Gurney Wilson, who had himself edited a short-lived magazine called *Orchid World*, established a limited company to keep the *Review* going, and edited it until 1932; he was succeeded by Charles H. Curtis, the editor of the *Gardeners' Chronicle*, who ran it for the next quarter-century, continuing to work at it on his deathbed. During all these years, it had established itself as the pre-eminent British orchid magazine, publishing articles on genera, new hybrids, shows, descriptions of orchid collections, and, latterly, notices of registrations of new grexes.

In March 1988 Ray Bilton, the director of McBean's Orchids, approached the RHS on behalf of the *Review*'s Board of Directors, to seek financial assistance in the face of falling subscriptions and increasing costs. The Society's proposal was a 25 per cent shareholding in Orchid Review Ltd, with the following terms: two RHS nominees to sit on the board, a new subtitle identifying the *Review* as 'the orchid journal of the Royal Horticultural Society', with the RHS paying the cost of the registration supplement in exchange for the copyright in that supplement. £500 was agreed as the price of the shareholding, and the Society began to make an annual contribution of £4,000 towards the *Review*'s costs.

Over the next few years, the price rose, subscriptions fell, and the editorship changed hands almost annually. By the end of 1990 the company was technically insolvent, with a £2,000 deficiency of assets. In 1992, the Society agreed to take the responsibility for continuing the publication from the following January; Wilma Rittershausen, a former editor of the *Review*, was re-appointed, a new format instituted, and the subscription rate began to rise once more. At the end of the first year, Rittershausen reported that 'last year many people were extremely worried about the future of the *Orchid Review*. Once it became known that the RHS was to take it over everyone was delighted and enthusiastic again.'[46]

Meanwhile, Home & Law, by acquiring New Perspectives, had also acquired *The Plantsman*—at a cost to the RHS of £10,000 per annum. The directors reported that 2,700 subscriptions were needed to break even, and there were currently only 1,238. The number slowly crept up, but had reached only 1,500 by the time of the collapse of Home & Law. The last issue of the magazine appeared in 1994; Elspeth Napier had continued as editor until the end.

Should there be a successor? and under what terms? During the course of 1993, negotiations took place with Kew over a possible amalgamation of a successor with *Curtis's Botanical Magazine*; instead, the *Magazine*'s editor, Victoria Matthews, who had already once worked for the RHS as Daffodil Registrar, became Editor of the proposed new periodical. The plan was for a quarterly, in larger format than the old *Plantsman*, with six colour plates per issue. *The New Plantsman* appeared in 1994; the first volume was edited by Matthews, who then moved to America, and a new editor was found in Sabina Knees, a former Wisley botanist working at Edinburgh. *The New Plantsman* has published horticultural reviews of such genera as *Coprosma, Incarvillea, Leptospermum, Nomocharis, Rhus, Tillandsia*, as well as articles on nomenclature, historic trees, the biology of variegation, the history of nurseries and of collectors, and a special issue on Chilean plants. Nonetheless, as time passed, the generic reviews diminished, to be outweighed by articles on individual species.[47]

In the mid-1990s, the Society was once again invited to take an endangered publication under

THE NEW PLANTSMAN

THE ROYAL HORTICULTURAL SOCIETY · VOLUME ONE · PART ONE · MARCH 1994

The first issue of The New Plantsman, *1994.*

The widening publishing programme

By the summer of 1992, the Society's book-publishing programme was growing. In 1986, a long-running association with the publishing house of Dorling Kindersley was begun, with a plan for a new plant identification encyclopaedia. Under the general editorship of Christopher Brickell, the RHS *Gardener's Encyclopaedia of Plants and Flowers* (1989) was a major success, selling 20,000 copies to RHS members alone in its first two months. As an exercise in user-friendliness for the amateur gardening public, it organised the photographic portion of the book by habit, colour, and season, leaving only the descriptive appendix in alphabetical order. It was followed by a series of large-scale encyclopaedias and other publications that made Dorling Kindersley the Society's major publishing partner. Meanwhile, the association with Cassell over the Wisley Handbooks was continuing, a new initiative started with Conran Octopus, and the *Dictionary* begun with Macmillan; an extensive programme of foreign publication saw the Society's books issued in the Americas, Australia and New Zealand, Japan, and the continent of Europe, with frequent translations into five languages—though whether the resulting volumes carried the Society's brand varied.[49] Book publication in association with commercial publishers was fast becoming one of the Society's major sources of income. It is probably safe to say that no other organisation has such an international reach with garden-related publications.

But the cumulative impact of this programme, together with *The Garden*, the year books, and the duty publications, was overburdening Mitchell and her small team in a couple of rooms at the top of 80 Vincent Square. In August 1992, she produced a plan for splitting the editorial and publishing components of her job, finding a new editor for *The Garden*, and confining her role to publishing. The new Editor was Ian Hodgson, who had worked for both EMAP and Maxwell, and had been particularly associated with *Garden News*. He took over *The Garden* from the May issue of 1993, but soon found working conditions at Vincent Square cramped and technologically unsuitable. In 1994 he moved *The Garden*'s editorial team out of London to the EMAP offices in Peterborough, where desktop publishing was already tried and familiar, and there was back-up available immediately if any problems occurred with the information technology. There the magazine flourished until the summer of 2002, when Alan Roe, Director of RHS Enterprises, brought the publication of *The Garden* in-house.

its wing. Chris Philip had begun issuing an annual publication called *The Plant Finder* in 1987; frustrated, on taking over a new garden four years earlier, at the absence of a comprehensive directory of plant suppliers, he had set out to remedy the deficiency. The first edition had listed some 20,000 plants, indicating the suppliers by coded references explained in an alphabetical list at the end. Each year's version was larger than its predecessor, in numbers both of plants and of nurseries. In 1993, his health in decline, Philip approached the RHS to see whether it would undertake to keep *The Plant Finder* going. A deal was concluded in October 1994, and a team at Wisley was set to work to make *The Plant Finder* more user-friendly, and to ensure that its nomenclature was accurate. The *RHS Plant Finder* was selling 40,000 copies a year, and had increased its coverage to 70,000 plants and 800 nurseries. Chris Philip was awarded a Veitch Medal in 1998, and his last letters to the Society glowed with pleasure at the honour; but he died before the AGM at which it was to be presented.[48] The *RHS Plant Finder* has had an immense impact on commercial horticulture in the UK, reversing the trend towards the extinction of small specialist nurseries that caused such alarm in the 1980s.

To accomplish this Roe set up a dedicated office in Peterborough and a production company—RHS Publications Ltd—to produce the magazine and support it financially. At the end of 2003, all RHS publishing was integrated to operate as a separate unit as part of RHS Enterprises, and the first managing director was appointed to run it.

In the 1980s the Society had co-operated with commercial publishers in the production of videotapes of the Chelsea Flower Show. In the early 1990s the Society produced its first internally generated video: *Wisley Through the Seasons*, followed by a series of practical videos, and then once again videos of the Chelsea Show. In 2003, technology having moved forward, the first DVDs were produced: once again, *Wisley Through the Seasons* and a Chelsea Show programme, with a special centenary DVD, *100 Years of Wisley*, appearing that autumn. In 1997 the RHS website (www.rhs.org.uk) was inaugurated, initially providing information about subscriptions, events, and facilities for purchasing from the RHS shops. From 1999 the publishing department began to make an impact on the website: the first registers appeared online, along with the RHS *Plant Finder* and the RHS *Garden Finder*. The first web editor was appointed in 2001.

The range of the Society's book publishing at the start of a new century.

Susanne Mitchell and her small staff in London, meanwhile, were responsible for the Proceedings, the year books, Registers, garden guides, and all book publishing, in addition to new ventures in audio-visual and electronic publication. The difference that had once been maintained between books published in collaboration with, and those published in association with, the Society, depending on the amount of staff involvement, had become obsolete; to be published in association, a book now had to be overseen in the planning stages, copy and illustrations approved and thoroughly screened at every proof stage by the Society. A pattern had already been established by the presence of both the RHS *New Dictionary of Gardening*, intended to serve as a standard reference source for botanist and horticulturist, and the Dorling Kindersley Encyclopaedias, geared to the needs of the amateur gardener. By 1998, with the publication of its first book for children, the Society had a range of titles targeting every level of the gardening public, from the beginner to the expert.

II *Plant Introductions*

WHEN in 1825 John Claudius Loudon described the Horticultural Society as 'the most remarkable feature in the modern history of gardening', he specified plant collecting as one of the principal reasons for this eminence: 'This society ... has spared neither cost, nor influence, nor exertions, to accumulate within its bounds all the most rare and valuable productions of the vegetable world.' Over twenty years later, the press concurred: 'We need scarcely say, that to the collectors of the Horticultural Society we are indebted for the introduction of some of the most beautiful plants in existence, and, indeed, for almost nine-tenths of the novelties that have been imported since it was fairly established.'[1]

Even before the Society had a garden, it had received plants from various sources, as part of its programme of rationalising the synonymy of fruits; such plants were generally distributed to commercial nurseries which would grow them on. But in 1817 an important innovation took place. John Reeves, an East India Company tea factor based in Canton, offered to send Chinese plants; the first shipment arrived within a month of the little garden in Kensington being acquired. Thereafter, the range of exotic plants sent to the Society widened: Nathaniel Wallich sent Indian plants from the Calcutta Botanic Garden; Robert Walsh, seeds from Constantinople; Stamford Raffles, tropical fruits from Singapore; George Canning, seeds from Mexico. Reeves himself kept up a continual flow of Chinese plants until 1830, when the Society, hit by financial crisis, asked him to stop. John Livingstone and Thomas Beale, also resident in China, sent additional plants.[2] Some of the gardeners that the Society recommended to positions abroad returned the favour by sending plants back: Robert Heward, the former garden clerk, sent an unsolicited shipment of plants from Jamaica; William McCulloch, who accompanied the Hon. Robert Gordon to the ambassador's residence in Brazil, was allowed to collect plants for the Society as long as this did not conflict with his other duties; similarly, John Brown in Mexico and David Christie in Colombia were sent money by the Society to cover the costs of intermittent plant collecting. Such was the Society's reputation by 1825 that Captain Beechey could ask it for instructions on collecting plants in the south seas, before embarking on his famous expedition in the *Blossom.*[3]

In most cases, these deliveries of plants did not involve exploration as such; they consisted of either the local garden flora, or plants already being grown in botanic gardens. The achievement lay not in the acquisition, but in the transportation. A shipment of plants collected by Stamford Raffles was lost in shipwreck; not a single survivor reached England of 500 variegated azaleas sent by Reeves; even relatively successful shipments frequently arrived in poor condition. John Livingstone, who also sent plants from China, once calculated the survival rate at one plant out of a thousand—so that the average cost of a safe arrival was £300 per plant. Small wonder that many of the Society's medals from the 1820s to the 1840s were awarded to naval captains who had successfully brought shipments to England in good condition. In 1820 nine captains who had brought plants from China received medals at one meeting. The most famous of all these captains were Henry Andrews Drummond of the East Indiaman *Castle Huntley*, who brought back Chinese chrysanthemums and introduced the mangosteen into England, and Richard Rawes of the *Warren Hastings*, who introduced *Primula sinensis*, and is one of the candidates for introducing *Wisteria sinensis*.[4]

Seeds could be transported packed in wet tissue, but living plants posed great logistical problems on board ship. If the plants were kept below deck, they had inadequate light; if above deck, they were exposed to salt spray. The principal means of sending plants by the end of the 18th century was in sealed cases, frequently with a glass panel, or in portable frames called 'plant cabins'. Reeves was particularly noted for sending plants in the equivalent of miniature greenhouses. These solved the lighting problem while increasing the risk of fragility, and in any case the plants still needed regular watering. In 1829 Nathaniel Bagshaw Ward discovered accidentally that plants could flourish in a closely-glazed case as long as they had sufficient soil and water at the start; water could evaporate during the day, but would not leave the case and would re-condense at night. The merits of the 'Wardian case' were demonstrated successfully on an expedition to Australia in 1833, and the Hackney nurseryman George Loddiges, a Vice-President of the Society, who quickly adopted the principle, was soon able to report that 'whereas I used formerly to lose nineteen out of the twenty of the plants I imported during the voyage, nineteen out of the twenty is now the average of those that survive'.[5] The Society's collectors from Theodor Hartweg on travelled equipped with Wardian cases.

Hoya pottsii, *one of John Potts's most important introductions, as drawn by Mrs Withers for the Society's* Transactions, vol. 7 *(1827).*

John Potts

The reputation of the Chinese plants growing in the Society's garden spread quickly. In November 1820, Captain Nairne of the East Indiaman *General Kyd* informed the Society that he was sailing to Bengal and China the following year, and offered to take a plant collector with him. One of the garden staff, John Potts, was engaged for a salary of £100, and paid £25 on account; Nairne was paid £65 to cover expenses, and Potts duly embarked. He made contact with Reeves, who introduced him to the right people, got him safely to Macao when a quarrel between the East India Company and the Chinese authorities made Canton unsafe, and helped him with the despatch of plants. His first shipment arrived in February 1822. Potts himself returned that August, in ill health; Council provided medical attention, and instructed that 'he be kept in the Garden at Kensington and furnished by the Gardener at the Society's expense with every thing necessary to his maintainance and comfort', but despite everything he died at the beginning of October. The Society paid for his funeral and his gravestone in Chiswick churchyard, and then, dissatisfied with the quality of the first stone, paid for a replacement.[6]

What would have been the major achievement of Potts's journey, a collection of 42 chrysanthemum cultivars, was lost on the return voyage. The Society nonetheless felt it had 'every reason to be satisfied with the exertion and attention of Mr

Potts', and praised the 'large stock of Chinese and East Indian plants' he had brought back. *Hoya pottsii* received the most enthusiastic initial attention, but *Hoya angustifolia*, *Paeonia lactiflora* var. *pottsii*, *Diospyros vaccinioides*, *Callicarpa rubella* and some camellias (including *C. euryoides*, used in China as a stock for grafting), soon made their way into greenhouse cultivation. For the outdoor garden, Potts' major contribution was seeds of *Primula sinensis* which he carried back on behalf of Reeves.[7] A later author, E.H.M. Cox, expressed surprise 'at the money wasted by the Society in sending out [Potts and Parks], as at that time it had three exceedingly energetic correspondents, LIVINGSTONE, REEVES and BEALE' already in China; but Potts' expedition at least was a response to external invitation rather than part of a concerted plan.

George Don

The Society's next expedition was similarly the result of an invitation. Edward Sabine, the brother of the Society's Secretary, was preparing a voyage to Africa and the West Indies, and offered to take a collector with him on the same terms as Nairne had taken Potts. George Don (1798-1856), the foreman of the Chelsea Physic Garden, was engaged for the position, and immediately borrowed Swartz's *Flora Indiae Occidentalis* and

Aublet's *Histoire de Plantes de la Guiane Françoise* from the Society's library to prepare himself. The pair departed on the *Iphigenia* under Captain Mendo, in November 1821. Don's instructions make explicit the degree to which collecting policy was determined by its researches on fruit:

> The chief object of your mission is to collect, transport or bring home for the use of the Society, seeds or plants of the different vegetable productions to be obtained in the countries you visit, whether found in a wild or cultivated state, such as are likely to be useful as fruits on account of their first importance and next to take those plants which will be esteemed in our gardens for their beauty or singularity.
>
> The fruits you will find will be all, of course, natives of hot climates, but these the Society are particularly desirous to obtain, you will therefore be particular in your description of them as well as noting and recording every circumstance relating to their habit if in a wild state, and in their cultivation or their treatment when in gardens.

It was also a condition of his contract that both the plants he collected and the notes he made were the Society's property, not to be given to anyone without the Society's permission.

The *Iphigenia* made a circuit of the south Atlantic: in February 1822 it touched at Portuguese Guinea, where Don's party was attacked by natives who feared the ship was a slaver; a fortnight later it reached Sierra Leone, where Don spent two months collecting. The ship then continued along the African coast to Dahomey and São Tomé, before crossing to Brazil and working its way north to the West Indies, where Don had extended sessions collecting in Trinidad, Jamaica, and Cuba. Finally, the ship put in at New York, where Don had a few days to add to his collections before returning to England. Unlike Potts, who had mainly dealt with existing garden flora in China, Don travelled extensively in the wild, exploring African river valleys and climbing the mountains of São Tomé, frequently succumbing to fever, and even, in Sierra Leone, cutting down trees to get the epiphytic orchids growing in their upper reaches. Not all his plants arrived safely: his entire São Tomé collection was killed by frost in New York. But what he did succeed in bringing back roused immense excitement. Joseph Sabine read a paper on his tropical fruits, which included guavas and star apples—altogether 31 types of fruit, 17 of which had not been previously described. Among the plants which went on to flourish in the glasshouses at Chiswick were *Crinum revolutum*, *Mussaenda elegans*, *Zephyranthes rosea*, *Clerodendrum splendens*, *Clematis grandiflora*, and *Nicotiana doniana* (as *N. repanda*, the 'true Havana cigar tobacco').[8]

Don's relations with the Society deteriorated, however, after the initial enthusiasm. His employment was continued while he worked on his paper on the fruits of Sierra Leone; he had already been censured for violating his contract by giving Aylmer Bourke Lambert one of his dried specimens without permission. Don either took no notice, or was goaded by the disciplinary proceeding into testing his contractual limits further. The first of a projected series of articles by him on the flora of Sierra Leone appeared in the *Edinburgh Philosophical Journal*. Sabine wrote to Robert Jameson, the editor, requesting him to discontinue the series. Don was dismissed from the Horticultural Society, which proceeded to take out an injunction against him, prohibiting him from publishing any of his (or rather the Society's) papers in England. The Wernerian Society, who had been preparing to print his further articles, took alarm and told Sabine that they had returned Don's papers to him, though in fact his monograph on *Allium* appeared in their *Journal* between 1826 and 1831, and the Linnean Society published his monograph on *Combretum* in 1826. Don went on to assist Lambert in his *Genus Pinus*, and to produce a well-received modernisation of Philip Miller's *Gardeners' Dictionary* under the title *A General System of Gardening and Botany* (1831-7), which Loudon hailed as 'A book that has long been wanted, will be hailed with joy by numbers, and will create a host of botanists in Britain'.[9]

Crinum revolutum, introduced by John Forbes and depicted for the Botanical Register *in 1822 under the name* Amaryllis revoluta.

John Forbes

The Society's third expedition, once again, was a response to an outside invitation, this time by Captain Owen of the *Leven*, who was to survey the east coast of Africa. John Forbes (1798-1823) was hired on the recommendation of John Shepherd, the Curator of the Liverpool Botanic Garden. The ship touched at Madeira, the Cape Verde Islands, Rio de Janeiro, the Cape of Good Hope, Madagascar, and finally Mozambique, where Forbes spent ten months exploring the areas around the Zambezi River, with a few excursions to the Comoros and other nearby islands. He died on 16 August 1823 while travelling to Senna, about 150 miles upriver from the coast, where he was buried. The news reached England the following April; Council paid for a memorial plaque in Chiswick church, declaring 'their entire approbation of his conduct while in their service', and announced to its members that of the three collectors sent abroad, 'it is melancholy to add, that only one, Mr. George Don, survives'. When Forbes' papers finally arrived in England in January 1825, it was discovered that he had not altered his will, and by virtue of having been overpaid some nine pounds, had no assets to dispose of, leaving only some minor debts that Council paid off for him.

Forbes was commemorated in some of his novel introductions: *Crinum forbesianum*, and the orchids *Oncidium forbesii* and *Cattleya forbesii*. Among his others were *Gloriosa superba* 'Simplex', *Xylobium variegatum*, *Aeranthes grandiflora*, possibly *Gladiolus oppositiflorus*, and 'an unusual number of entirely new plants'.[10]

Captain Owen, meanwhile, had taken matters into his own hands and hired a German collector named Hilsingberg to carry on Forbes' work. Hilsingberg worked in the field for about a year before dying himself, and the Society received nothing, but paid Captain Owen £18 17s. 0d. for his additional expenses.[11]

John Damper Parks

In 1823, for the first time, the Society actively planned an expedition, making arrangements with the East India Company for a follow-up of Potts's Chinese journey. John Damper Parks (c.1792-1866), a Chiswick gardener, travelled to China on the *Lowther Castle* in April 1823, returning in May 1824, and like Potts he was greatly assisted by Reeves and by Beale; unlike Don and Forbes, he did not collect in the wild. However, Beale had had one of his Chinese servants collect plants in outlying hills which were banned to Europeans, and Parks acted as the means of conveying these plants to Europe.

Parks had been specially instructed to look for the yellow form of the Banksian rose, whose existence had been reported by Roxburgh in the previous decade; he duly brought back several specimens, as well as *Rosa indica* var. *ochroleuca*, *Camellia reticulata* and three cultivars of *C. japonica*, 20 different chrysanthemum cultivars (of which 16 were new), *Coelogyne fimbriata*, and the first aspidistra (*A. lurida*) to be seen in England.[12]

David Douglas

Parks's journey to China had initially been conceived as a two-man expedition, with one gardener returning in 1824 and the second staying on for an additional year. But, in what might—or might not—be seen as early evidence of the Society's concern for the health and safety of its staff, Council quickly decided that in view of the 'disasterous [*sic*] state of affairs in China', only one gardener should be sent out at present. That left David Douglas (1799-1834), the second traveller, a young Scotsman who had been recommended by William Jackson Hooker at Glasgow, without a settled destination; and as new fruit varieties had already been sent by Fellows or Corresponding Members in the United States, it was decided to send him to New York in order to bring back fruits and other plants from American nurseries. Although the bulk of his work consisted of visits to gardens and nurseries, he also did a great deal of seed collecting in the wild, and his aptitude for the task might be deduced from his journal comment on Niagara Falls: 'I am like most who have seen them, sensitively impressed with their grandeur, but particularly with a red cedar which grew out of the rocks on the channel of the river.' On his return, the *Transactions* carried a notice that 'This Mission was executed by Mr. Douglas with a success beyond our expectations. He obtained many plants which were much wanted and greatly increased our collection of fruit trees by the acquisition of several sorts only known to us by name'.[13]

In 1825, Loudon's *Gardener's Magazine* could report that 'an enterprizing young man has been dispatched to the north western coast of North America'. Douglas had sailed on the *William and Ann* the previous July, travelling under the auspices of the Hudson's Bay Company, which, in the wake of Lewis and Clark's expedition, was exerting itself to extend the British claim to as much of North America as it could. To this end, in March 1825, the Company established Fort Vancouver on the Columbia River, and it was

Pencil sketch of David Douglas at the age of 30, by his niece Miss Atkinson: as reproduced in the 1914 edition of his Journals.

here that Douglas arrived the following month to make it his base. He spent nearly two years in the area, adjusting himself to the outdoor life ('The luxury of a night's sleep on a bed of pine branches can only be appreciated by those who have experienced it'), suffering from intermittent hunger, an infected knee, and stormy weather, and always under threat of hostility from the natives. In March 1826 his journal recorded an attack by 450 Indians, subsequent peace negotiations, and the discovery of 'a new species of pinus, the most princely of the genus' (*Pinus lambertiana*). In February 1827 he finally set off for England, walking up the Columbia River, crossing the Rocky Mountains and the Canadian prairies on foot, a journey of nearly 2,000 miles in seven months to York Factory on Hudson Bay, where he caught a ship for England.[14]

He arrived to find himself famous. The first instalments of his seeds and plants had arrived over the intervening years, and Captain Hanwell of the *William and Ann* had been given a medal for his assistance. Council were so pleased with his results that they declared he could have the profits of any publications he made. Douglas was speedily elected a Fellow of the Linnean, Zoological, and Geological Societies—for, like most of the Society's collectors, he collected other natural history specimens as well as plants. By 1830, 130 new species were growing at Chiswick, and were being distributed to the Society's members and to botanical gardens.

Simply as a feat of exploration and endurance, Douglas' American journey has few rivals, and he has often been acclaimed as the world's greatest plant hunter. Others have been more sceptical; E.H.M. Cox, noting some of the plants that he would have expected Douglas to find in the areas he surveyed, wrote:

> I have an odd feeling that the peculiar fact about DAVID DOUGLAS is not that he collected and introduced so many well-known plants, but that he did not collect and introduce many that were just as plentiful and are just as beautiful ... [He] must be considered as one of the world's greatest travellers; but I have reluctantly come to the conclusion that he was not one of the world's greatest collectors. He missed too many opportunities in his desire to get on at the greatest possible speed. Today he would probably have been the world's best racing motorist.

But certainly no previous plant hunter had added so many new species to the English garden. Douglas collected in temperate lands, whose flora would prove hardy in the open air in England, while his predecessors' finds had largely entered the glasshouse. Some of the more notable plants

Eschscholzia californica, introduced by David Douglas – although it had previously been introduced, and little noticed, by Archibald Menzies – as illustrated in Mrs Edward Roscoe's Floral Illustrations of the Seasons *(1829).*

he introduced were: *Gaultheria shallon* (the first plant he saw on landing in Oregon), *Ribes sanguineum*, *Camassia esculenta*, *Calochortus luteus* and *C. macrocarpus*, *Arbutus menziesii*, *Lupinus polyphyllus*, *Clematis douglasii*, *Mahonia aquifolium* (not the first introduction), *Mimulus moschatus*, *Garrya elliptica*; the first examples of what came to be known as 'Californian annuals' (with which, as a group, his name continued to be associated for decades)—*Clarkia elegans*, *Nemophila menziesii*, *Gilia capitata*, *Gaillardia aristata*, *Eschscholzia californica*; and above all, American conifers. His name is forever linked to the Douglas fir, *Pseudotsuga menziesii*, but he also introduced *Abies grandis*, *A. amabilis*, *A. procera*, *Picea sitchensis*, *Pinus radiata*, *P. lambertiana*, *P. ponderosa* ... At one point he wrote to Hooker, 'You must think I manufacture pines at my pleasure'.[15]

It was not long before Douglas was being groomed for a further expedition. Edward Sabine, who as the Secretary's brother had his own house at the Chiswick garden, trained him in making magnetic observations, so he could perform yet another useful function en route. In October 1829 he set off once more for the Columbia River, again under the Hudson's Bay Company's auspices. His collecting there was cut short by epidemic and native violence, so he went south to California for 19 months, his best conifer-collecting ground; then, in August 1832, returned to the Columbia via the Sandwich Islands. While in Honolulu he learned that his patron Sabine had resigned as the Society's Secretary, and sent a notice of resignation; thereafter he divided the plants he despatched into two consignments, one for the Society and one for Hooker in Glasgow. Early in 1833, he began to explore the Fraser River, but lost his journals and a large quantity of specimens in a canoeing accident: 'A disastrous day for me, on which I lost, what I may call, my all.' He returned to California, and then at the end of the year he once again sailed to Hawaii, where he climbed the volcanic peak of Mauna Loa, and in July 1834 was found dead in a bull pit, trampled by the trapped bull. He was buried in Honolulu. His death has been variously explained as accident, murder, and suicide, and it seems unlikely that the debate will be resolved.

When the news of Douglas's resignation reached England, Council reacted angrily. Noting that he had ceased his employment as of 9 September 1832, they initially refused to pay any bills drawn on them after that date, but soon calmed down to the point of indemnifying the Hudson's Bay Company for all its expenses. Eventually they ended up paying an additional £90 claim of Douglas's, which the Zoological Society refused to pay, but by that time the news of his death had arrived, and it was once again possible to feel sympathetic towards him.[16] In the 20th century the Society would fund the repair of his gravestone and of his memorial at his birthplace in Scone. His surviving journals were lost for a while, but were rediscovered during an office sort-out around the turn of the century by the then Secretary William Wilks, who in 1914 published them in an edition that met few of the requirements of textual editing; William Botting Hemsley, reviewing it for the *Gardeners' Chronicle*, remarked that neither Wilks nor Hutchinson, the Librarian, who had assisted him, had enough time to do it properly.[17]

The impact of Douglas on the British garden has already been hinted at. At a time when conifers were already rather fashionable, he introduced more new species than any other collector, and thus helped the coniferous landscape to establish a secure grip on Britain for the succeeding half-century. And, uniquely among collectors until the rhododendron specialists of the 20th century, he became identified in the public eye with a significant category of plants, the so-called Californian annuals that played an immense role in the flower garden for a generation, before pride of place in summer bedding was seized by half-hardy perennials from South America and Africa. More narrowly, for the Horticultural Society, his enormous success not only made its fame as a source of new plants more secure, but helped to re-orient the Society from its focus on the glasshouse to a wider view of the hardy ornamental garden.[18]

James MacRae

James MacRae had been a gardener at the Botanical Garden of St Vincent, in the West Indies, and had sent plants from there to the Horticultural Society. His tropical experience probably made him seem a natural candidate for a journey to Mexico; but political unrest made Mexico seem undesirable, and Thomas Coulter had recently been sending worthwhile seeds from Chile, so South America was made the new target.

In the summer of 1824, Kamehameha II, the King of the Sandwich Islands (Hawai'i), and his Queen died in England while on a state visit to George IV. Captain George Byron (who had a few months before succeeded his poetical cousin as Lord Byron), was to carry the bodies back to Honolulu for burial, and would follow the coast of South America for much of the journey; passage was obtained for MacRae, who also had a diplomatic function to serve: he would carry a consignment of fruit trees and other plants for Hawai'i. Lindley had now published detailed instructions for the transportation of plants, based on the previous experience of the Society's collectors. MacRae left behind instructions for £5 of his salary to be paid to his mother every six months.

MacRae's journal (which has never been published despite abortive plans in 1923) has all the excitement one could wish for, from tropical storms and mutiny to volcanoes and a royal Hawai'ian funeral. The *Blonde* stopped at Brazil, Chile, and Hawai'i, where Kamehameha's funeral was duly conducted and MacRae climbed Mauna Loa (as Douglas was to do a few years later), and then returned via the Galapagos Islands, Peru and Chile once again, reaching England in March 1826. Most of the plants MacRae introduced were destined for the greenhouse, as with his predecessors generally: hippeastrums, alstroemerias, *Cleome rosea*, *Solanum elaeagnifolium*, *Oxalis plumieri*. But one introduction is worth attending to, in part for the lesson it teaches about the ambiguity of dates of introduction. *Araucaria araucana*, the monkey puzzle tree, was introduced to Kew by Archibald Menzies in 1795; but no further trees were ever propagated from Menzies' specimens. MacRae sent back a supply of seed, and by October 1826 the first dozen plants had been sent out from Chiswick to Fellows of the Society. There is no record of the recipients, or

The monkey puzzle, Araucaria araucana: *an early specimen at Dropmore, as it was in the 1870s.*

even of the total number propagated. It was not until the early 1840s that commercial nurseries were able to offer monkey puzzles to the public; this is usually credited to William Lobb sending seed to the Veitch Nurseries in Chelsea, but other nurseries had specimens growing on at the same time, and it is quite possible that some portion of the early nursery stock was a second-generation derivation from Chiswick specimens.[19]

MacRae was made a Corresponding Member of the Society, and accepted a post as Superintendent of the new Peradeniya Botanic Garden in Sri Lanka, whither he embarked in August 1826, and where he was to die in 1830.[20]

Carl Theodor Hartweg

The Society commissioned no more collectors after Douglas for a few years, while it recovered from the financial crisis that brought down Sabine's administration. By the time it felt robust enough to organise a new expedition, it had learned from Douglas's accomplishments, and on sending Carl Theodor Hartweg (1812-72) to Mexico, instructed him to concentrate on altitudes at which he would be likely to find hardy or half-hardy plants (making an exception for orchids, whose popularity was increasing, and to which Lindley was turning his attention).[21]

Hartweg arrived in Mexico in December 1836, and was to spend the next six and a half years travelling through Central and South America. The Admiralty had agreed not to charge for transporting his collections, and Hartweg took advantage of the offer to send back large quantities of plants, many of which arrived in good condition, even despite military blockades and shipwrecks. Within a few weeks of arrival, he had sent 65 different orchid species; he was to send such large quantities of conifer seeds that the Society was able to distribute 4,300 packets to Fellows and botanic gardens. (A display of his Mexican conifers was to form one of the most acclaimed of exhibits at the Chiswick shows.)

Hartweg's travels took him to Mexico City, and from there into the Mexican plateau, which he traversed in several directions, sometimes alone and sometimes with other (friendly or rival) collectors. In August 1838, worried by hostilities between Mexico and France, as well as increased danger of mugging at a local level, he wrote to the Society for instructions, and was advised to proceed to Guatemala; but the transmission of letters by sea was slow, and he did not receive these instructions until January 1839, by which time France and Mexico were at war, and equally to the point, Guatemala was on the point of revolution. Hartweg made his way slowly, arriving in Guatemala City at the beginning of 1840. By the summer his situation was once again seen to be alarming, and he was moved on again. Early in 1841 he made his way south to Ecuador, and worked his way gradually back through Peru and Colombia to the Caribbean, finally sailing from Jamaica back to England.[22]

Meanwhile, the Society, once again in financial straits, had invested his accrued salary in 3 per cent annuities to help it through difficult times. Hartweg returned to disputes over his fees, compensation over his mugging in Guatemala, and an offer of promissory notes. Eventually a committee was set up to decide how to handle him, and its decision was to employ him on a further expedition.

> 'Well, Hartweg', said Lindley, 'the Council have resolved to send you to California, and if you find this single plant (Zauschneria) and send home seeds or plants of it in good condition, it will pay the Society for your mission if you send nothing else. Come over to my house ... and see the dried specimen of the plant in my herbarium before you start.'

No lessons learnt from the Douglas case: to send on an expensive expedition a collector who already had some cause to be embittered, was asking for trouble.[23]

And trouble there was. Hartweg arrived in Mexico in November 1845, and after initial collecting proceeded north to California; unfortunately, the United States was in the course of invading Mexico and claiming large chunks of Mexican territory for its own. Hartweg spent months in the vicinity of San Francisco and Monterey before he was able to move about freely. Early in 1847 he was finally able to explore the Sierra Nevada mountains, then forced by illness to return to Monterey. In the autumn he decided to return to England by crossing Mexico, but, persuaded that it was unsafe, continued to Nicaragua and crossed the isthmus there. He reached England in June 1848; the Society had already sent letters recalling him, but he did not receive these. His return was greeted with obloquy, and the *Journal* for 1849 contained a curt note saying that 'the Council had not reason to be satisfied with the manner in which Mr. Hartweg executed the duty intrusted to him, either in keeping the journal of his proceedings or in forming collections of seeds'. 'Animosity was carried to such a pitch against him', wrote William Swale, a Chiswick staff member, 'that a short time after he returned from his last mission for the Society the then Vice-Secretary [Lindley] would

not accept of a set of the dried plants which Hartweg had collected, but returned them by me, and never even opened the parcel nor examined the specimens.' Hartweg's expenses were settled, but when the Vice-Consul in Guatemala applied to the Society for tickets to the Garden as compensation for his efforts on Hartweg's behalf, he was refused. Hartweg returned to Germany, becoming Inspector of Gardens to the Duke of Baden.[24]

Despite the ill feeling and recriminations, Hartweg's list of introductions was impressive. *Zauschneria californica*, which Lindley had requested; *Nemophila maculata*, *Collinsia tinctoria*, *Lupinus affinis*, *L. hartwegii*, various penstemons; several ceanothus, including *C. dentatus*, *C. papillosus*, and *C. rigidus*, *Laurus regalis*, *Ribes menziesii*, diervillas; *Echeveria fulgens*, and various Mexican cacti; *Achimenes grandiflora*, *A. longiflora*, *A. heterophylla*; *Cattleya maxima* and other orchids; *Salvia patens* and *Fuchsia fulgens*, the ancestors of the modern hybrid fuchsias and bedding salvias; and, of greatest immediate excitement, conifers—*Cupressus macrocarpa*, *Sequoia sempervirens*, *Pinus ayacahuite*, *P. montezumae*, *P. patula*, *P. hartwegii*, and *P. engelmannii*. And because he often worked in the field with other explorers, we have anecdotes that reveal aspects of his personality in a way denied us with most of the Society's earlier collectors:

In the center of the valley we found a small isolated fir which caused the greatest surprise to the botanist because this species was entirely unknown to him. In spite of a thorough search we could not find a second tree of this kind in the vicinity. At the end of the valley was a great block of granite, larger than the largest building of Europe. Attracted by this immense mass of rock I called to my companion, 'Tell me, how did this giant stone get here?' Mr. Hartweg, who was already on the block looking for moss and other plants, and holding a beautiful flower in his hand triumphantly replied, 'But, please tell me first how this strange little flower gets here, where the tiniest moss hardly finds nourishment?'

I have often heard him say that Mr. George Ure Skinner [an orchid collector working for James Bateman] and himself discovered the large plant of Lælia superbiens both at the same time when in Mexico, and that they were both determined to have it, but could not get it then, for it was up a very high tree. Hartweg outwitted Mr. Skinner by going early in the morning, taking with him a native and an axe, and chopping the tree down, at the same time conveying away the large Lælia. I recollect helping to unpack it at Chiswick on its arrival, and it just filled one large wooden case, and arrived in excellent health.[25]

Salvia patens, *one of the ancestors of the modern bedding salvias, as illustrated by Miss Drake for the Society's* Transactions, *2nd series vol. 2 (1838).*

Robert Fortune

Robert Fortune (1812-1880), first student to attain distinction in the Society's examinations; superintendent of hothouses at Chiswick. Collected plants for the Society in China, 1843-6. Curator at the Chelsea Physic Garden, 1846-8. Made three further expeditions to China and Japan, 1848-62, for the East India Company and others. Published four books about his travels; served on the organising committee of the 1866 International Botanical Congress.

John Reeves, the Society's benefactor from Canton, was by now living in England, and had served on Council. At the beginning of the 1840s, England was at war with China over its refusal to countenance the trade in opium; by the time China admitted defeat with the Treaty of Nankin in August 1842, the Society was already planning to capitalise on the situation by sending a collector while British arms enforced free access. The collector chosen was Robert Fortune (1812-80), who a few years before had received the highest marks on the Society's new examination for gardeners. Reeves chaired a Chinese Committee that drew up detailed instructions for Fortune, specifying that 'hardy plants are of the first importance and that the value of the plants diminishes as the heat required to cultivate them is increased'—an exception being made, of course, for orchids. Here is an extract listing some of the specific plants he was to search for:

It is needless to particularise at much length the plants for which you must enquire. It is, however, desirable to draw your attention to –

1. The Peaches of Pekin, cultivated in the Emperor's garden and weighing 2 lbs.
2. The plants that yield tea of different qualities.
3. The circumstances under which the Enkianthi grow at Hong Kong, where they are found wild in the mountains.
4. The Double Yellow Roses of which two sorts are said to occur in Chinese gardens exclusive of the Banksian.
5. The Plant which furnishes Rice Paper.
6. The varieties of Nelumbium.
7. Peonies with blue flowers, the existence of which is, however, doubtful.
8. The fingered Citron ... and other curious varieties of the genus Citrus ... [altogether 22 plants].[26]

Fortune arrived at Hong Kong in July 1843, where he established his base, and was helped by the sons of John Reeves and Thomas Beale. After a month he travelled to Amoy, and then, caught by monsoon, to the island of Chusan, where his collecting started in earnest. He visited the nurseries of Shanghai, made an incautious visit to Canton and Macao, the old John Reeves country, where he was nearly stoned to death by a mob, and returned to Shanghai and Chusan, taking care never to stray more than 30 miles from a treaty port. As a result, far more of his plants were derived from the local garden flora than from the wild. He finally returned to England in May 1846; Council had been tempted in his absence to invest his salary, but had managed to refrain.

The results of his expedition exceeded his employers' hopes; as with Douglas in the halcyon days, they were so pleased they allowed Fortune to publish an account of his journey and keep the proceeds for himself. Having accepted the position of Curator of the Chelsea Physic Garden (working under Lindley), he wrote *Three Years' Wanderings in China*, which was published in 1847 and earned a considerable success. He was to make three further expeditions to China (and Japan), but on behalf of the East India Company, and latterly for unspecified sponsors—though both he and John Gould Veitch sent their Japanese conifers to Andrew Murray at the RHS for taxonomic treatment.[27]

Among Fortune's introductions on his first journey were the Japanese anemone *A. hupehensis* var. *japonica* (which, as *A. japonica*, was flowering at Chiswick by 1844), *Dicentra spectabilis, Jasminum nudiflorum, Lonicera fragrantissima, Forsythia viridissima* (the first forsythia to reach English gardens), *Ilex cornuta, Ligustrum sinense, Viburnum plicatum, Weigela florida* (formerly *W. rosea*, formerly *Diervilla florida*), a number of azaleas and camellias, some forty tree peonies, bamboos, and the Chusan palm *Trachycarpus* (formerly *Chamaerops*) *fortunei*.

Jasminum nudiflorum, the winter-flowering jasmine, as illustrated by Samuel Holden in Paxton's Magazine of Botany *for 1849.*

Botteri and Weir

The notice in the Society's *Journal* about its dissatisfaction with Hartweg had ended: 'The Council do not think it prudent to incur the expense of another collector for the present.' Already it had turned down a proposal from William Swainson to provide a collector in Brazil, and, on Fortune's advice, had rejected an offer of seeds from Hugh Cuming.[28] For a while it contented itself with a subsidy to the Oregon Association, which sent John Jeffrey to Canada in 1850; the results of that expedition included *Tsuga mertensiana* and *Calocedrus* [formerly *Libocedrus*] *decurrens*, but most of the plants the Society received were glossed as 'failed' in the acquisitions book.[29] In 1852 the search for a new collector became serious; Lindley negotiated for a while with Joseph von Warscewicz, later to become famous for *Canna warscewiczii*,[30] but after problems sorting out his current employment situation, decided to employ instead an Italian collector named Matteo Botteri. It is noteworthy that the idea of collecting was more important than the actual location, for Madagascar and Argentina were toyed with before finally settling on Mexico, which had proved so productive for Hartweg.

Botteri (1808-77) is today remembered more as an ornithologist than as a plant collector; his name is commemorated in Botteri's sparrow. His journey for the Society was subject to an unusual degree of administrative bungling, with recall notices and confusions over letters on the one hand, and on the other hand, five shipments of plants of which one arrived in bad condition, and two were regarded as of such little interest that Council eventually informed him his services were no longer required—whereupon followed the usual disputes over pay and expenses. He did succeed in sending back 'Chamaecyparis' specimens, which were balloted for by the Fellows.[31] Further Mexican seeds were sent by Benedikt Roezl in exchange for Lindley putting an advertisement for him in the *Gardeners' Chronicle*.[32]

There followed an interregnum in which the Society first courted bankruptcy, and then, as its exchequer had recovered, toyed inconclusively with various collectors[33] before settling on John Weir, an already experienced plant hunter who had worked with Clements Markham. Weir was sent to Brazil in April 1861, where he spent two years, sending back plants that were described in the Society's *Proceedings* as 'of minor interest'; in 1863, already retrenching on expenditure, Council debated recalling him, but eventually, when the Treasurer, Wilson Saunders, put up part of his funding privately (in exchange for plants), agreed to send him to New Granada (Colombia). In the autumn of 1864, Weir was recalled, resigned, and offered his services to James Veitch's nursery instead; but he was then struck down by a fever that left him paralysed from the neck down. The Society undertook his medical expenses and arranged his return to England, organised a public subscription which raised £700 for him, and used it to create a fund for his long-term care; he lived until 1898. Most of his plants were greenhouse exotics, the Bignoniaceae attracting botanical interest at the time; it was his orchids that were received most enthusiastically, but his obituary in the Society's *Journal* said 'the cultivation of Orchids was not so well understood then as now; consequently fewer stand to his credit than might otherwise have been the case'.[34]

Weir was the last collector specifically hired by the RHS. Despite occasional temptation, Council was prepared to subscribe to expeditions, but never again to take the full burden of one. Wilson Saunders sponsored Thomas Cooper (1815-1913) on a journey to South Africa, to which he managed to get Council to contribute; the results included *Asparagus plumosus* and *Aloe cooperi*. Another of Saunders's collectors, David Bowman, a former Chiswick foreman, also sent seeds to the Society, apparently without a formal arrangement. In 1877 H.J. Elwes tried to galvanise the Society into formulating a policy for plant introductions, but nothing substantial came of it.[35]

Plant collection by syndicate

Robert Fortune, on his first voyage, had confined himself to the coastal areas of China; in his later travels for the East India Company he was able to move further inland. But it was not until the turn of the century that British collectors began to penetrate significantly into the interior of China and to approach the Himalayas from the north. Inspired by the published accounts of two Jesuit missionaries, David and Delavay, who discovered a number of new plants and managed to send seeds of some of them to French nurseries,[36] two British firms sent plant hunters to complete the process of introduction. In 1899 the Veitch nursery sent the young E.H. Wilson to find *Davidia involucrata* (Sir Harry Veitch notoriously instructing him that virtually everything else noteworthy in China had already been discovered); in 1904 A.K. Bulley, the proprietor of Bees Seeds, sent George Forrest to collect Chinese alpines. The results of these expeditions triggered a half-century of enthusiastic exploration, most of it financed by syndicates, in which the RHS took part.

George Forrest (1873-1932), who made seven expeditions to Yunnan collecting plants between 1904 and 1932.

Meconopsis
betonicifolia, *as drawn
by Lilian Snelling for
Curtis's Botanical
Magazine (1927).*

*Francis Kingdon-Ward
(1885-1958), who between
1909 and 1956 made
several collecting
expeditions to China,
Tibet, and southeast
Asia, and described his
journeys in a series of
books.*

*Francis Ludlow (1885-
1972) was a teacher in
Tibet when he met
George Sherriff in 1928.
Over the next quarter-
century they made seven
expeditions collecting
plants in the Himalayas.*

*George Sherriff (1898-
1967) was British Vice-
Consul in Kashgar
when he met Ludlow. He
and his wife created a
garden at Ascreavie,
Angus, using the plants
he brought back from
Asia.*

The RHS declined to finance Wilson's further journeys; the first of the Sino-Himalayan expeditions it contributed to was the 1914-15 Tibetan journey of Reginald Farrer and William Purdom, to which it subscribed £200. (When Farrer died in Burma on a later expedition, Council obviously regretted never having given him an award, and debated commemorating him with a medal or a named corner of the Wisley rock garden. The later Farrer Prize was not instituted until 1959.)[37] George Forrest (1873-1932), however, was another matter. His early expeditions having brought back an unexpected number of new rhododendron species, the newly-formed Rhododendron Society set up a syndicate in 1916 to finance his fourth journey; the RHS became his centre of communication, and eventually contributed £575 to his costs. In return, it received a proportion of the plants and seeds he brought back, which included *Rhododendron protistum* var. *giganteum* and *Camellia saluenensis.* Thereafter his plants were regularly described in the *Journal,* and the Society undertook the publication of his field notes. Forrest died in the field in 1932, and the RHS immediately arranged for the editing of his letters, though actual publication was less than immediate. Macqueen Cowan's *Journeys and Plant Introductions of George Forrest* eventually appeared in 1954, as a scaled-down version of the originally intended *Plantae Forrestianae.*[38]

Meanwhile, after Forrest had started working independently, A.K. Bulley had found another plant hunter in the person of Frank Kingdon-Ward (1885-1958); and, like Forrest, he was to leave Bulley and accept financing by syndicate. The RHS did not sponsor his early Chinese expeditions, preferring to concentrate on Forrest, but changed its mind once Kingdon-Ward started to concentrate on Tibet. For its contribution of £150, the Society got seed of *Meconopsis betonicifolia* and *Primula florindae* as well as numerous rhododendrons. Thereafter it helped to finance all of Kingdon-Ward's expeditions, allowing him to use the RHS name in publicity, until the Second World War; this included a further attempt at China, which was detoured to Burma after he was refused entry. After the war, he faced increasing difficulties in getting access to the areas he wanted to explore, and the Society's sponsorship wound down. But a wide range of lilies, primulas and rhododendrons, among other plants, entered British gardens through his journeys.[39]

The last of the celebrated Himalayan plant hunters that the RHS helped to finance were Frank Ludlow and George Sherriff, on their 1933 and 1936 expeditions, which yielded *Primula ludlowii* and *P. sherriffae, Meconopsis sherriffii,* and

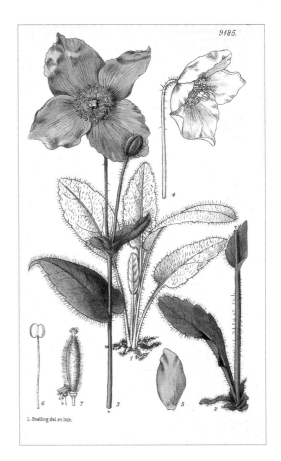

9185.

L. Snelling del.et lith.

Rhododendron sherriffii, and their 1947 expedition, the first to use aeroplanes to transport plants back to England. It offered £1,500 towards an abortive Nepal journey in 1950, but then the pair retired. Despite Sherriff's interest in primulas, it was once again rhododendrons that attracted the sponsorship, and at one point the Society discussed the possibility of a book of their rhododendron introductions, calculating that it would be the size of one of the Year Books. It was never compiled, however, and the literary record of their travels had to wait for Harold Fletcher's *Quest of Flowers* in 1975.[40] The other most prominent plant hunter in China was the American Joseph Rock; although the Society never subsidised him, it did undertake to publish a book of his travels and collections, the manuscript of which was eventually rejected on the grounds that it was too geographical and insufficiently botanical.[41]

The other collector most frequently subsidised by the RHS in the inter-war years was E.K. Balls (1892-1984). Trained at Clarence Elliott's nursery, he was chosen by Dr P. L. Giuseppi as a companion on a plant-hunting journey to Persia and Lebanon in 1932, and the Society contributed to its funding. Interestingly, although the trip had been organised by Giuseppi, it is only Balls's name that appears in Council minutes; Clarence Elliott had introduced him to Frederick Stern, and it was presumably Stern who argued the case for funding. The expedition brought six new species of *Dionysia* into cultivation; heartened by this success, Council invested regularly through the 1930s in Balls's travels to Turkey, Afghanistan, the Atlas Mountains, Mexico and Peru. The sums spent were smaller than those devoted to the Himalayan expeditions—£20 to £50 a time—but the results included *Cyclamen cilicium* var. *intaminatum*, *Fritillaria crassifolia* 'Balls' Form', *Colchicum triphyllum*, *Rubus trilobus*, and the reintroduction of *Salvia haematodes*.[42]

Other expeditions which the RHS helped to sponsor included Francis Younghusband's Everest reconnaissance expedition of 1921;[43] Clarence Elliott and Walter Ingwersen to Patagonia and the Rockies respectively, in search of new alpines; T. Harper Goodspeed and Eugen von Ratibor to the Andes; Hsien-Ling Hu to the interior of China in search of new camellias;[44] and at least eight expeditions by Peter Davis in Turkey and Iran, from the late 1930s to the mid-1960s.[45]

In 1947, the President, Lord Aberconway, proposed to Council that something like the former programme of plant collecting be resumed. The Society was returning to normal after the interruption of the Second World War, and in a short-lived vein of enthusiastic optimism the idea of a return to former glories seemed feasible:

> ... in the early part of last century the Society had sent out its own collectors to unexplored parts of the world. Some, such as Fortune and Douglas, had become famous, and great kudos had accrued to the Society because of the large number of valuable plants which they introduced to cultivation. When, later on, the Society got into financial difficulties, it ceased to send out its own collectors, and the work was taken up by a few of the leading nurserymen, notably Messrs. Veitch, and later by syndicates composed largely of amateur gardeners. ... the Society should again take the initiative in this matter and should, if necessary, be prepared itself to finance collectors who would be able to visit the untrodden parts of the world and collect seeds and plants to be grown and tested at Wisley. ... £1,500 to £2,000 each year would be sufficient to support an expedition of this character ...

Discussions with Sir William Wright Smith suggested Bhutan as a primary place to aim at; Iran and Turkey were similarly emphasised; the Admiralty agreed to co-operate on collecting, and issued an order instructing the Royal Navy's ships to assist with the collection and transportation of seeds.[46] By 1951, the Society had spent nearly £3,000 on expeditions—but as all the expeditions

listed in Council minutes had to seek additional funding from other sources, it could be questioned how far the scheme was really different from the syndicate sponsorship that had characterised the inter-war years. Nonetheless, some degree of funding was provided for the last large-scale British expeditions to the Himalayas under Williams and Sykes; for Oleg Polunin, Adam Stainton, Wilfred Thesiger, Brian Mathew, Paul Furse and T. F. Hewer; and even for the Society's Editor, Patrick Synge, who was given leave for an expedition so long as Lanning Roper edited the *Journal* in his absence.[47] Plants and seeds were distributed between Wisley, the Edinburgh Botanic Garden, and other backers. This programme was run down during the financial tensions of the 1970s, when it became official policy to restrict assistance to expeditions to the writing of letters requesting permission to travel.

The single most exciting introduction of the post-war years, however, did not emerge from an RHS-sponsored expedition. *Metasequoia glyptostroboides*, the dawn redwood, was discovered in China at the end of the war; seed was sent to the Arnold Arboretum in Massachusetts, and Elmer D. Merrill brought a large quantity to the RHS, his pockets so bulging with seed packets that he was at first suspected of purloining plants at the show. It germinated well at Wisley—within a few years Albert Pam was speculating that 'at one time one of the rarest of plants [it] will before long become one of the most common'—and the RHS acted as its first distributor in Britain. Three of the largest British specimens are to be found at Wisley.[48]

Plant distribution

Plants distributed from the Society's gardens were not confined to new introductions—there was a thriving plant exchange between gardens, surplus seeds were distributed every year, and stocks were also bought in to keep supply levels steady for a basic range of plants. New introductions and tested fruit varieties were, however, the most coveted aspect of the plant distribution scheme. Those entitled to take part in the distribution were Fellows, Corresponding Members, and botanic gardens, both British and colonial; collections would occasionally be made for presentation to royal patrons, or foreign nobility who joined. (On the other hand, Bellenden Ker was excluded from the distribution of *Pinus lambertiana* because he did not have a landscape park in which to grow it.) The first woman named as a recipient of plants was Sir Joseph Banks's widow, who was presented with a specimen of the yellow Banksian rose in 1824; a year later Mrs Marryatt, who had a celebrated garden in Wimbledon, was given plants, even though female Fellowship had not yet been introduced. From 1834 the distribution of plants was also extended to provincial horticultural societies who entered into an early version of affiliation. By 1840, the Society had sent out 95,325 plants, 363,594 packets of seeds, and 54,571 parcels of cuttings. During the 1850s, if not earlier, a process of balloting for plants was introduced, and continued until 1874. Thereafter, there were occasional panics and grumbles about the cost and the workload involved in preparing plants for distribution, but the process always continued; on one occasion, when cost savings appeared to dictate an end to the buying-in of stock for distribution, Council members offered to make good the reduction from their own gardens. Increasing rail fares helped to put a brake on plant distribution in the 20th century, and the Second World War made it impossible; since 1942, only seeds have been distributed, but that process continues annually, with over 250,000 packets and over a thousand species and varieties sent out in a typical year. At the time of writing, the Seed Department comprises three full-time and two part-time staff, and 11 volunteers.[49]

Primula sherriffae, as drawn by Stella Ross-Craig (and lithographed by Lilian Snelling) for Curtis's Botanical Magazine *(1937).*

There is too little surviving documentation to permit confident statements about exactly what was distributed when; only rarely, as with MacRae's monkey puzzles, did a plant distribution excite Council sufficiently to be noted in the minutes. Intriguing problems can result. In 1830, the minutes record: 'Read a Letter from Mr. James B. Fraser dated 23d. March transmitting two Cones and a Bag of seed of the Deodara Pine with a small Box of other seeds, and requesting that at any further time he might be supplied with plants that could be spared ...' James Baillie Fraser (1783-1856) had travelled to the Himalayas in 1815; if 15 years later he could supply deodar cones to the Society, the possibility exists that he had brought a deodar back with him and that it had become mature enough to cone in his garden. If so, the date of the deodar's introduction, normally attributed to Leslie Melville in 1831, needs to be adjusted.[50]

And, of course, the fact that a plant has been introduced into Britain tells one nothing about the frequency with which it is grown, or how long

it remains in cultivation. Twice—with Australian and South African plants in the second quarter of the 19th century, and with Sino-Himalayan plants, particularly rhododendrons, in the first half of the 20th—the influx of new species has been so great that many have been lost within a few years of arrival, replaced in people's gardens by the even more interesting novelties that succeeded them. Many of the triumphantly received glories of the Society's early collectors have long since vanished from the UK, as conservatory and stove yielded to border and rock garden; but even introductions as recent as those of Kingdon-Ward and Ludlow and Sherriff have suffered attrition. The finding of *Primula sherriffae* was described as 'one of Sherriff's greatest achievements', but by the time he died, Sir George Taylor warned that it was 'very rare in gardens and could all too easily slip from cultivation'; it last appeared in *The Plant Finder* in the 1994/95 edition.[51]

The ethics of plant collecting

During the 20th century, government restrictions over the movement of plants began to be imposed, initially because of the threat of the introduction of disease. At the end of the First World War the American government announced a blanket restriction on all plant importation, and the Society sprang to the defence of British horticulture, urging the Foreign Office to remonstrate and find ways of licensing nurseries who could satisfy the American inspectors' health standards.[52]

As time went on, a second motive was increasingly added: the desire to protect native flora from extinction. The most notorious offenders against this principle were late 19th-century orchid hunters, who—following the example of Benedikt Roezl, although as we have seen even Hartweg was guilty of this behaviour—would cut down trees wholesale in order to obtain epiphytic species growing near their tops. Concern over the depredation of indigenous floral populations started before the end of that century, but was initially confined to the area where it was most apparent to the complainers: at home; it was in Europe that laws to protect wild flowers from removal were first enacted. The Society actively supported efforts to protect British wildflowers, and when apprised of similar restrictions in other countries, tended to applaud and publicise them.[53] For the time being, the countries most attractive to collectors were too far away for environmental consequences to be appreciated. (Augustine Henry had drawn attention to deforestation in China in 1898, but the result was not an effort at conservation, but a stepping-up of the process of collecting while there was still time.)[54]

By the 1970s, plant hunting was no longer the preserve of a few botanists and specialist collectors. In 1973 the travel agents Thomas Cook organised a plant-collecting tour to Nepal, and RHS members asked the Society to intervene; it turned out that a qualified botanist was leading the tour, but the incident was an augury of things to come. In the same year a controversy arose over the import of cyclamen corms from Turkey, which was to become the focus of a campaign to stop the removal of bulbs from the wild. As China relaxed its restrictions on foreign travel in the 1980s, and the Society considered the possibilities of once again sending collectors there (eventually negotiating an exchange agreement with the Kunming Institute—student places at Wisley in exchange for expeditions), the issue of ecological damage arose: reports of deforestation in the Himalayas, and the progressive loss of the rich flora that Forrest and Kingdon-Ward had found, meant that new restrictions on the activities of collectors had to be imposed. Leave plants where they are, collect only seed, became the new rule; and the maintenance of seed banks took on a new justification as the means of re-introducing vanished plants into their former habitats.[55]

The International Union for the Conservation of Nature was founded in 1948, published several red books listing endangered species of plants and animals, and, beginning in 1963, lobbied for the establishment of an international agreement on the traffic in wildlife. The Convention on the International Trade in Endangered Species of Wild Fauna and Flora (CITES) was agreed in 1973, and entered force in 1975, imposing different grades of restrictions on the sale of red-list species.[56]

In the late 1980s and early 1990s, a couple of high-profile cases showed that public outrage over plant conservation had reached levels beyond the RHS's cautious insistence on the laws. The first was the conviction, in 1989, of Henry Azadehdel for smuggling orchids, a case which attracted considerable, and so far unending, media attention.[57] Then in 1991 John Amand, the proprietor of the bulb nursery Jacques Amand Ltd, was convicted of illegally importing bulbs from Turkey. The Society reacted by banning his firm from exhibiting at shows; then, having taken this high moral line, found that the case was not as iron-clad as it had seemed: his conviction was on a technical point, as the bulbs in question came from gardens (CITES regulations not distinguishing wild and cultivated sources), and further, Amand's actions had been those of a private individual, not connected with his firm. The ban on Jacques Amand Ltd was rescinded, to gestures of fury from those who saw only that a punishment had been escaped.[58] Mike Read of the Fauna and Flora Preservation Society had already published *Grown in Holland?*, in which he exposed the extent to which smuggled plants were entering commerce through the Dutch bulb trade.

In 1993, at a meeting of the Fauna and Flora Preservation Society, Alasdair Morrison, the Chairman of the Orchid Committee, representing the RHS, bluntly said that the Society did not as yet have a fixed conservation policy, and refused to join in blanket condemnation of the collection of plants from the wild. Among the reasons for his caution, as spelled out in a later article, were the disparity between the needs of native peoples and the interests of Euro-American botanists, and the apparent incapacity of CITES to build into its code the difference between the propagation systems of plants and animals.

> The actual achievements of CITES, where plants are concerned, are in my opinion questionable. It was very much designed with animals in mind, and plants are different from animals. The main point is propagation. For instance, if you cut a crocodile into 10 pieces, you get one dead crocodile. If you do the same to many plants, you get 10 live plants—while micropropagation means that plants can be (and are) reproduced by the million. CITES finds it hard to give full recognition to plants' reproductive potential.

In the heat of the moment, however, what appeared in the press was a contrast between the noble intentions of conservationists and the obstinacy of the RHS, as Mike Read and others attacked the Society as reactionary.[59] The incident did at least provoke the Society into greater publicity for the individual conservation policies it had already put into place, and leaflets on CITES and restrictions on the use of endangered timbers were published. Since then *The Garden* has regularly publicised successful conservation projects, drawn British attention to the American experiments in reconstituting prairie habitats, and campaigned for plant protection on a global scale:

> There are nearly seven times as many threatened plants as there are threatened animals listed by WCMC [World Conservation Monitoring Centre], and yet far more money is spent on animal conservation than on plant conservation. In the USA 97 percent of the federal government's conservation expenditure goes to animals and only three percent to plants. The trade in threatened plants continues in many parts of the world, which will inevitably make future volumes of the Red List even thicker. Between the gardening public, the botanic garden community and commercial horticulture we possess the skills, enthusiasm and knowledge to cultivate and conserve these plants. But, just as importantly, we need to have the will.

And at the beginning of the 21st century, the Convention on Biological Diversity introduced the concept of national floral rights, to guarantee some recompense to the country of origin for successful exploitation of plants introduced into foreign environments.[60]

Meanwhile, a new purpose for expeditions had long been implemented by the Society: education. When E.A. Bowles died in 1954, he left money for a memorial fund, and for several years the Bowles Scholarship was made available annually to assist young gardeners to travel; many of them, the young Brian Mathew being one of the first, used their Scholarships to get experience in plant collecting. The administration of the Bowles Scholarship fell to the Expeditions Committee, which thus gradually evolved into a Bursaries Committee as well, before being disbanded in 1991. The RHS continues to administer the Queen Mother Bursary and other bursaries for travel, and to fund expeditions which are increasingly oriented to plant conservation rather than collecting for garden purposes. Other such funds have developed over the years; the Coke Trust, founded in 1985, invited the RHS to take over its management from 1999, and plant study travel is one of the activities it supplies grants for. The Merlin Trust, founded by Valerie Finnis in 1991 to sponsor travel for young gardeners, remains independent of the RHS, but three of the Society's officials are among its Trustees at the time of writing.[61] With all these sources of grant aid, conservation of wild populations is now at least as high a priority as the acquisition of new plants for the garden.

The Bowles Scholarship expedition to Iran and Turkey, 1963, including, left to right, David Pycraft, later a long-serving Wisley staff member, D. Baxter, Stuart Baker, and Brian Mathew.

New plants continue to be introduced into British gardens, even though the quantity has been reduced from the former flood to a sustainable trickle, and new hybrids gather more media attention. The work of—for example—Tony Schilling in the Himalayas, Roy Lancaster and Martyn Rix in China and central Asia, Keith Rushforth in Mexico, and Graham Hutchins in New Zealand, conducted with greater concern than their predecessors showed for the conservation of the wild populations they visit, has enriched our garden flora during the last quarter-century, and is also publicised in *The Garden*.[62]

Victoria R
Patron

12 *Horticultural Taxonomy and Registration*

FACING PAGE
Queen Victoria's royal autograph, on a vellum sheet depicting the Amazonian waterlily that Lindley named in her honour as Victoria regia *(now* V. amazonica*).*

AT the time the Horticultural Society was founded, the Linnaean system was the accepted way of classifying plants. Linnaeus had first propounded his system—in which the flowering plants were grouped according to the numbering and position of the sexual organs, so that plants with a single anther were Monandria, plants with six anthers Hexandria, and so on—in the 1730s, and from the 1750s it had won widespread, if not quite universal, acceptance across Europe. In 1788 Sir James Edward Smith had bought Linnaeus's collections from his widow and brought them to England, where he founded the Linnean Society in 1783; as a result, Linnaeus came to be thought of as virtually an English national treasure. Despite some initial grumbles—for instance, that any washerwoman who could count could pass as a botanist using Linnaeus's system—Linnaean taxonomy had dominated English botany since the 1760s.[1]

On the continent, a concerted opposition to Linnaeus' system arose in the 1780s with the publication of Antoine-Laurent de Jussieu's *Genera Plantarum*, and increasingly European botanists sought to replace Linnaeus' 'artificial' system with a 'natural classification' that would establish the real relationships between plant genera, taking all the parts of the plant, not merely the sexual organs, into consideration. Jussieu divided the flowering plants into Monocotyledons and Dicotyledons, based on the number of the seed-leaves, and subdivided these into 14 classes, based on such factors as the position of the ovary and the perianth. He was succeeded, and improved upon, by Augustin-Pyramus de Candolle at Geneva, who emphasised other aspects of floral morphology, and whose *Prodromus* was the early 19th century's major attempt at a systematic classification of the plant kingdom.

In England, however, Linnaeus reigned supreme for decades after he had been ousted on the continent, and those botanists who wanted to bring England into line with the rest of Europe faced a long uphill struggle. Robert Brown, Jussieu's first important English follower (who improved upon him by distinguishing angiosperms from gymnosperms), persuaded the Chelsea Physic Garden to lay out its taxonomic beds after Jussieu's system in 1821. But the role of principal propagandist for natural classification in England, and most vociferous antagonist to Linnaeus, fell to John Lindley. Through his position as Professor of Botany at University College, and as the author of several works on taxonomy, Lindley repeatedly thundered home the message that the Linnaean system did not work, and that a new system was needed to replace it. Take this passage from his *Ladies' Botany*:

> That the principles of the Linnean system are clear, and simple, and easily remembered is indisputable; that student indeed must be remarkably dull of apprehension, who could not master them in a day. But is its application equally easy? that is the point ... where a genus comprehends species varying in the number of their stamens, as for instance, Polygonum, Salix, Stellaria, and hundreds of others, who is to say which of the species is to determine the classification of the rest? or when this point has been settled, how is the student to know what passed in the mind of the Botanical Systematist? The latter puts a genus into Octandria, because out of ten species, one has constantly, and two occasionally, eight stamens, and he includes in the same class and order, all the other species of the genus, although they have five, six, or ten stamens. Suppose the student meets with one of the last, and wishes to ascertain its name by the Linnean system, he will look for it in Pentandria, or Hexandria, or Decandria, where he will not find it. After wasting his time, and exhausting his patience in a vain pursuit, he must abandon the search in utter hopelessness, for there is no other character that he can make use of as a check upon the first. At last some one will tell him that his

plant is a Polygonum; he turns to his book, wondering how he could have overlooked it; and he finds Polygonum in Octandria. Should he inquire how this is, he will learn that his species belongs to Octandria, not because it is octandrous, *but because it is so very like other Polygonums that it cannot be separated from them, and they belong in most cases to Octandria.* This is the unavoidable answer; and what does it really mean, except that it is not in consequence of its accordance with the system that the student's Polygonum is to be discovered, *but in consequence of its natural relation to other Polygonums;* so that it is necessary to understand the Natural System, to make use of the Artificial System!'[2]

In 1836, Lindley succeeded Sir James Edward Smith as the editor of Sibthorp's *Flora Graeca*; since the work had been begun using Linnaean taxonomy, Lindley continued it that way, but added an appendix in which he listed the plants in the order they should have been dealt with. Lindley was to produce three quite different systems of natural classification during the course of his career—not perhaps a great recommendation for the stability of a system that was offered to replace Linnaeus, and English textbooks did not finally abandon the Linnaean system until the 1860s, the decade of Lindley's death.[3] In the end it was not Lindley but his former superior as Secretary of the Horticultural Society, George Bentham, who produced a lasting system: Bentham and Hooker's *Genera Plantarum* was published from 1867 to 1883, and held sway in England for over half a century.

The International Code of Botanical Nomenclature

While Lindley's work as a taxonomic reformer lay outside his duties for the Horticultural Society, having but little application to practical gardening matters, the question of botanical nomenclature was highly relevant. Linnaeus had a longer-lasting success with his nomenclatural reform: the replacement of the earlier descriptive names by a simple two-word code—generic name, modified by specific epithet—had also won its way throughout Europe by the 1760s, and has never been seriously questioned, though modified in various ways. Lindley once again served as a polemicist for correct and meaningful Latin names, arguing against unpronounceable eponyms, ill agreement of gender and number, and the like, as also for improved Latin grammar and vocabulary in the writing of descriptions. The modern use of Latin in plant descriptions largely follows Lindley's example, and a later official of

the Society, W.T. Stearn, effectively codified this practice in his *Botanical Latin* (1966).[4]

It is worth noting that, in addition to his attempts to reform botanical Latin, Lindley also tried to reform the treatment of English vernacular names. Early in his career he would devise English names for newly introduced plants by translating the Latin names, offering, e.g., swan daisy for *Brachyscome*[5] and fleshlip for *Sarcochilus*; but by 1842 he had become disillusioned—'who employs these names? No one. On the contrary, the universal practice is to adopt the so-called Latin names, and to toss the English ones overboard'. Accordingly, he then took to abbreviating Latin names into English forms, and around mid-century various English publications bristled with Lindleyisms such as gladiole, dendrobe, oncid, odontoglot, and mesembryanth. (He never used chrysanth, to my knowledge, but I am sure he would have approved of it.) Some viewed this innovation with alarm. In 1850 Lindley reported in the *Gardeners' Chronicle* that 'One of our correspondents is alarmed lest his Crocuses should degenerate into Crokes. Crocus is a name not likely to be disturbed; and if it were, the change would not be more disastrous than that of Hyacinthuses into Hyacinths.' Most of Lindley's coinages were being consigned to the dustbin of history by the 1880s, but some are still beneficially in use, like orchids (instead of orchises) and conifers (instead of coniferae).[6]

But to return to the world of Latin names: the success of Linnaean nomenclature did not resolve all problems. Quite apart from the little matter of sub-specific status, where the polynomials rejected for species proliferated for varieties, there was the greater question of competing names for the same plant. During the heroic age of plant exploration, it was not uncommon for a plant to be described and named by different botanists, each unaware of the other's work: and then which name should be followed? An informal tradition had grown up by the end of the 18th century that the first published name should be accepted, but in practice a number of considerations ranging from national rivalries to aesthetic distaste complicated any attempts at agreement; and then there were botanists like Rafinesque, who muddied the waters by arrogantly inventing new names for existing plants.[7]

In 1866, to accompany the International Horticultural Exhibition held in the Society's Kensington garden, the first International Botanical Congress was convened, with Alphonse de Candolle, son of the great pioneer of natural classification, in the chair. Disputes over nomenclature were very much on the agenda. The gardening journalist Shirley Hibberd read a paper in which he called for the creation of a Code of Botanical Nomenclature, which would give clear instruction to growers. De Candolle undertook the drafting of such a Code, and his draft was adopted at the Second Botanical Congress, held in Paris the following year.[8] This first version is now referred to as the Paris Code; amendments have been proposed and debated at each Botanical Congress since then (at roughly five-year intervals).

The 1867 Code made it official that the first published description determined the plant name. The ambiguity in this rule was only realised later, in the 1890s, when the German botanist Otto Kuntze published a massive work, the *Revisio Generum Plantarum*, in which he proposed over 30,000 alterations to recognised names, by adducing pre-Linnaean publications; the Vienna Code of 1905 solved that problem by making 1753, the date of Linnaeus' *Species Plantarum*, the official starting date for modern nomenclature. A further problem eventually surfaced over the demand for a description; so many names already in common use could be traced back to the publication of the name alone, without any attached description, that, in order to avoid wholesale renaming, *nomina nuda* were recognised as valid publications if they preceded the establishment of the rules in the 1860s. The Vienna Code produced a long list of *nomina conservanda* (names that broke the rules but were retained anyway).

The priority rule eventually entailed two great academic research programmes. The first, the *Index Kewensis*, was a list of all published names for flowering plants; the first edition of the *Index* was financed by Sir Joseph Hooker and Charles Darwin, and appeared in two massive volumes in 1895. In that first edition Hooker, as principal editor, attempted to determine synonymies, and had what he considered invalid names printed in italics, followed by the correct name. This attempt led to so many arguments and proposed corrections that, after the first few supplements, subsequent editors abandoned the attempt to determine which were the correct names; the *Index Kewensis* supplements (one every five years for over a century) simply record the names, and let the botanists fight it out over which ones are correct. The second research programme was that of determining the exact dates of publication of the works in which the names appeared. The young W.T. Stearn was to be a major figure in the dating of botanical publications, beginning during his years as the RHS Librarian; and his findings were incorporated with those of many others in Frans Stafleu's *Taxonomic Literature*, a

nine-volume bibliography which gives the dates of nearly 19,000 publications.[9]

The priority rule has, with great impartiality, swept away the favoured names of plants in many different countries, and the general response has been to retain the familiar version as a vernacular name. This has happened in America with *Poinsettia* (= *Euphorbia pulcherrima*), on the continent with *Georgina* (= *Dahlia*), and in England with a large chunk of *Geranium* (= *Pelargonium*—this one is Linnaeus's fault, for *Pelargonium* was a recognised genus before he temporarily abolished it). Lindley's coinages have not been exempt. In 1853 he named a new American tree *Wellingtonia gigantea*, in honour of the Duke of Wellington; but it had already been named *Sequoia gigantea* by Decaisne, and since then has been further separated into a new genus *Sequoiadendron*. Already by the 1880s English botanists were having to face the fact that they were out of step with the rest of the world on this point, but wellingtonia has survived, in England if nowhere else, as a vernacular name.[10] An equally instructive case was Lindley's naming of the giant Amazonian water-lily after the Queen, as *Victoria regia*; alas, it had already been named *Euryale amazonica* by Poeppig, and, since the Vienna Code of 1905, a plant transferred from one genus to another (as from *Euryale* to *Victoria*) must take the first published epithet with it, unless that epithet conflicts with a previously published one in the new genus. So while Lindley's generic coinage is still valid, the epithet has been changed, and the plant is now *Victoria amazonica*.[11]

As this example indicates, the implementation of the Code can be complex. While from time to time the RHS affirms the necessity of scientific nomenclature,[12] the feeling exists even among some botanists that there is more of legalism than of science about the mechanics of some name changes. Two cases in point are the decapitalisation of specific epithets and the periodic attempts to ensure that the people after whom plants are named are recognisable in the resulting names. For the first two centuries of Linnaean nomenclature, epithets based on personal names tended to be capitalised, while those based on place names were more often than not left without capitals. In the 1940s, various botanists instigated a campaign to follow the example of zoologists and remove all capital letters from epithets. Some resisted the change—'The botanists, of course, insist that, like dentistry or spanking, it is all for our own good', said Alice Coats—and decapitalisation has never been made compulsory in the International Code, but the overwhelming majority of botanists adopted it. The RHS, ever in those days cautious, decided not to impose it in the *Dictionary of Gardening*, and did not introduce it into the *Botanical Magazine* until 1956.[13] More recently, there have been efforts to supersede the orthography of first-published names where they rendered eponyms incorrectly, *hookerianus* has been deemed the preferred form over *hookeranus*, and it has even been proposed that names be amended to incorporate the accurate spelling of the personal name.[14]

Taxonomy in the abstract was one thing; putting it into practice was another. In 1913, W. R. Dykes launched an attack on the RHS in *The Times*, complaining of the standards of plant identification among exhibitors at shows:

> The nurseryman seldom finds it worth his while to raise hybrids. He leaves this work to amateurs and is content to buy the showiest results and then to propagate them ... Research on one genus of garden plants [*Iris*] and reference to the original authors of the specific names in use has shown that the usual nomenclature is frequently erroneous, and there is no reason to suppose that the genus in question has suffered more than any other from the vagaries of local botanists. We should expect that the Royal Horticultural Society would be at some pains to see that all plants exhibited under its *aegis* should be correctly named, and that if, as is undoubtedly the case, much confusion existed among the species of such a popular genus as Saxifraga, for example, some attempt would be made in the garden at Wisley to grow specimens of all the species and to see that they were correctly named. It would mean somewhat laborious library work in addition to the trouble of procuring and growing the plants, but surely the comparatively small outlay involved would be well repaid ... Instead of this, however, the society allows the exhibition of plants under any fantastic name that the exhibitor chooses to attach to them, so long as the name is not already in use for another plant.[15]

And even before Dykes became the Society's Secretary, and tried to establish an iris collection at Wisley for taxonomic purposes, the RHS had begun to hold nomenclatural trials. The first notable example was of *Sedum* species, and the result, R. Lloyd Praeger's *Account of the Genus Sedum*, was published in the *Journal* for 1921.[16] The RHS grant-aided the Permanent Committee on Geographical Names set up by the Royal Geographical Society, as an aid to ensuring uniformity of treatment for plant descriptions. In 1928 it established a committee on nomenclature, to stabilise plant names in horticultural use; the scheme was approved by the International Horticultural Conference in 1930, and one of its first fruits was the reference list of conifer names

drawn up by William Dallimore and presented at the Conifer Conference the following year. But stabilisation, despite the precedent of the *nomina conservanda* in the Vienna Code of 1905, was long opposed by the International Commission on Botanical Nomenclature. Proposals for stabilisation were rejected at the 1954 Paris Congress, earning the following diatribe from John Gilmour:

> My own view (and that of the great majority of botanists, pure and applied, including those taxonomists concerned with Nomenclature at Kew and the British Museum) is that the above arguments, though sincerely put forward, are a flagrant case of special pleading by members of an ivory-towered 'priestly caste' who, because the name-changes not only do not affect their work but even give them a sense of progress in it, are blind to the inconvenience they cause to other name-users (who outnumber them by 1000 to 1). They sincerely feel that the Code is for the convenience of taxonomists only—that taxonomists are the only botanists who understand it (which is true)—and that no alteration should be made in it except for the direct benefit of taxonomists.

Gilmour, representing the Society at the IXth International Congress in Montreal in 1959, was defeated in a motion for stabilisation, but a compromise motion put forward by the Utrecht botanist Joseph Lanjouw established the principle that name-changes could be inconvenient, and the way was opened to a tentative programme of name conservation. The RHS grant-aided the International Association for Plant Taxonomy in the compilation of a list of names for conservation, and while in the early days there was much resistance and great pressure to restrict conserved names to plants of 'economic importance', the net was gradually widened to include plants of horticultural significance.[17]

The RHS tended for much of its history to err on the side of conservatism over taxonomic changes; when Stearn proposed that *Viburnum fragrans* should be renamed *Viburnum farreri*, he was censured for proposing to mention this fact in his Masters Memorial Lecture, an improper venue for a name change.[18] Three incidents reveal the gradual change that came over the Society in the second half of the 20th century, as it moved uneasily from a conservative to a progressive role over name-changes.

In 1955 the Society published George H. Johnstone's *Asiatic Magnolias in Cultivation*, possibly the most beautiful of its monographs. The path to publication had proven stormy, however, and nomenclatural corrections proposed by

John Gilmour (1906-1986) had already been Curator of the Herbarium at Cambridge and Assistant Director at Kew when he was appointed Director of Wisley in 1946. From 1951 to 1973 Director of Cambridge Botanic Garden. A major figure in 20th-century taxonomy, and chairman of the Systematics Association.

An illustration by P. Ciccimara for Johnstone's Asiatic Magnolias in Cultivation *(1955):* Magnolia campbellii *subspecies* mollicomata *'Lanarth' (described by Johnstone as convariety* williamsiana*).*

J. E. Dandy, the British Museum botanist, had slowed down the work. Should *Magnolia robusta* (Johnstone's name) be treated as *M. sargentiana* var. *robusta* (Dandy's)? John Gilmour and Sir William Wright Smith, the Society's most authoritative botanists, while favouring Dandy's proposal, thought that 'there should always be room for latitude of opinion in taxonomy' and that the Society should not demand that Johnstone yield. The horticulturists on Council found the debates enervating; Lewis Palmer at one point quipped that 'Botany is not an exact science any more than is theology', while Albert Pam queried 'how botanists who cannot decide on the correct classification and names of British flora could make decisions on a species of magnolia which grows in China'. The greatest crux came over two species, *Magnolia denudata* and *M. liliiflora*, whose names (coined in 1791) Dandy argued should be replaced. Pierre Joseph Buc'hoz, in 1779, had coined the names *Lassonia heptapeta* and *L. quinquepeta* for some plants newly arrived from China; Dandy identified these with the magnolias, and despite the fact that Buc'hoz's

names, based on inaccurate Chinese drawings, miscounted the tepals (*heptapeta* has 9-12 tepals, not seven, and *quinquepeta* six or more instead of five), Dandy felt that a strict application of the rules demanded their adoption. Eventually he changed his mind, and recommended that these epithets be perpetually excluded from use—not that his recantation prevented other botanists since from trying to revive them, but after some controversy in the 1970s, the Buc'hozian names were not adopted in the *New RHS Dictionary of Gardening*.[19]

In contrast to the relatively stable *Magnolia*, the genus *Rhododendron* has been plagued by taxonomic difficulties ever since George Don (formerly one of the Society's plant collectors) announced in the 1830s that the former genus *Azalea* ought to be incorporated into it ('however technically correct ... injudicious in a practical point of view'—Loudon). The flood of Asiatic rhododendrons reaching Europe in the early 20th century led to several attempts at classification, but the one most widely adopted in England was that used in the Rhododendron Society's *Species of Rhododendron* (1930), compiled by John Barr Stevenson—later described as 'not a classification, but a careful avoidance of classification'. This, largely following John Hutton Balfour's 19th-century classification, divided rhododendrons into 42 series of equal rank—handy for the gardener, if not very useful for the taxonomist, and used for nearly half a century. In the 1970s, the botanists Cullen and Chamberlain at Edinburgh proposed a revision of *Rhododendron* which largely followed Sleumer's 1949 classification, and which removed a number of familiar specific and varietal names as synonyms. The proposal was greeted with outrage by many rhododendron growers for whom the discarded names were familiar and the series comfortable: Loudon's remark about Don's earlier revision was echoed by those for whom the new classification ignored taxonomic distinctions that made sense for the plants cultivated in British gardens, however little the plants might observe them in the wild. The RHS decided to make the next edition of the *Rhododendron Handbook* 'a staging post in Rhododendron taxonomy providing ... a bridge between the artificial system used to classify the genus initially and the more natural system resulting from the Edinburgh work'. Alan Leslie, as the Rhododendron Registrar, co-ordinated the two systems on principles laid down by Christopher Brickell in 1978, and the *Handbook* presented both in tabular form, with a mediating 'RHS horticultural revision' that preserved many of the Balfourian taxa as Horticultural Groups which, 'although they have no botanical significance, it is considered horticulturally worthwhile to distinguish'. Some horticulturists and some botanists attacked the *Handbook* for conceding too much to their respective enemies, but many others appreciated the effort to bridge the gap between the two camps.[20]

On the other hand, the proposed reclassification of *Chrysanthemum* in the 1970s brought the Society the reputation of being too precipitate in its acceptance of changes. Linnaeus had used the name for some annual European species; when a number of ornamental Chinese plants of related flower structure were introduced in the early 19th century, they were called chrysanthemums by analogy, even though the Society's Secretary, Joseph Sabine, noted the differences between them and the European plants. Des Moulins, in 1855, proposed renaming the Chinese species *Dendranthema* (using a sectional name proposed by Candolle in his *Prodromus*); this proposal slumbered while chrysanthemum societies were founded all over Europe and the objects of their interest became more familiar than the native species. In the 1970s botanists working on the *Flora Europaea* recommended breaking up the huge and untidy genus *Chrysanthemum* into several different genera, including *Dendranthema*. For a brief period botanic gardens—and Wisley— renamed their plants, and the *New RHS Dictionary of Gardening* adopted the name change. The change provoked outrage among the public—for one thing, existing chrysanthemum societies were not about to change their names. Eventually, Piers Trehane published a proposal for conserving the generic name *Chrysanthemum* for the popular garden varieties; the RHS supported it at the next International Horticultural Conference; and the nomenclatural section agreed by nine votes to three. 'Gardeners will be delighted this year to see', wrote Tony Lord, in 1998, '*Chrysanthemum* has been restored to the florists' chrysanthemum, replacing the despised *Dendranthema*.'[21]

The International Code of Nomenclature for Cultivated Plants

One of the aspects of botanical nomenclature debated at the 1866 Congress was Alefeld's recent attempt to extend Latin names to varieties of vegetables. De Candolle, as Chairman, threw his weight behind a proposal that cultivated varieties should not be given Latin names, but fancy names in the various vernacular languages, so as to be readily distinguished from species that existed in the wild. William Herbert, whose experiments at hybridising gladioli and other ornamental plants had filled the pages of the Society's *Transactions*, had insisted as early as 1818 that 'accidental and cultivated ... varieties' should be given vernacular names. Donald Beaton, one of the pioneer breeders of bedding pelargoniums, abandoned Latin trinomials in favour of easily remembered names like 'Punch' and 'Judy'. But many others continued to use complex Latin names, and were only gradually converted to the new Code's insistence on keeping varietal names linguistically separate from those of species. Fern growers in particular resisted the reform until nearly the end of the 20th century; in the 1980s, the Wisley botanist Peter Barnes and others pushed through a revised nomenclature.[22]

Even once the distinction between wild and cultivated plants had been respected, numerous puzzling questions remained. Was it permissible to enforce changes of varietal name for moral or political reasons—e.g., the plant had a German name (World War I) or was named after a Nazi (World War II)? Should varieties found in the wild be given Latin or fancy names? What if their status was ambiguous? How should as yet unnamed varieties be treated in trials? Could the same plant justifiably trade under different names in different countries? And if a variety was already well known under a Latinised name, should a new fancy name be enforced?[23] The Society's committees found themselves divided on these matters. In 1884, the Daffodil Conference resolved that 'garden varieties of Narcissus, whether known hybrids or natural seedlings, should be named or numbered in the manner adopted by florists, and not in the manner adopted by botanists'; but J.G. Baker, in his classification of daffodils at the same conference, used Latinised names like Leedsii for horticultural groups, as well as retaining some Latin variety names, and was criticised by the conference chairman, Sir Michael Foster, for being 'unphilosophical'—no nomenclatural difference should be made between wild and garden varieties, since the causes of variation were the same, and all should have vernacular names. Orchids displayed the same problem; Maxwell T. Masters, the doyen of the Scientific Committee, attacked the Orchid Committee for using Latin names for natural hybrids.[24]

From 1932, the Society's annual *Book of Arrangements* contained instructions about the naming of plants, including the principles that varietal names should be in Latin only when they expressed some character of the plant, that all other varietal names should be in a vernacular, and not translated into English if originating in a foreign language. As the International Botanical Congress of 1950 approached, the RHS prepared to launch a proposal for a formal Code of Nomenclature for Cultivated Plants. Chittenden, dying of cancer, was unable to go to Stockholm, so the Society was represented by Sir Frederick Stern and W.T. Stearn; the latter was evidently regarded as a potential maverick, for the President 'had impressed upon the Librarian ... that it was important that the deputation from the Society should speak with one voice'. While the delegates toured the city as part of the entertainment package, Stearn hastily drafted the first version of the Code, and distributed photocopies to the botanists as they returned to the hotel. There then followed more than a year of occasionally splenetic correspondence between Stearn and other taxonomists; in 1952 the Society acted as host for the International Horticultural Conference, and the fully fleshed-out Code was adopted.[25] The earlier arguments of Masters and Foster were disregarded, and a distinction between varieties and cultivars decreed:

(1) the term 'variety' should be confined to plants which occur in the wild and which may be given names of Latin form under the regulations of the International Code of Botanical Nomenclature, and

(2) the term 'cultivar' should be applied to plants which originated or are maintained in cultivation and which would not usually be given names of Latin form, e.g. clones, and lines which have been so selected as to be reproducible from seed.

'Originated or are maintained ...'—the term cultivar had been put forward independently in America, by Alfred Rehder, for plants that originated in cultivation, and the two meanings competed with each other for a while; but Stearn's eventually won out, even in America. The term was nonetheless slow to enter general parlance. A memorandum by Arthur Simmonds in 1955 pointed out that:

In the absence of a precise instruction from the Council, it seemed wise to hasten slowly in giving effect to this particular article, and so far little change has been made in the Society's Journal, schedules, or other publications. Thus awards have continued to be made to cultivars 'as *varieties* for garden decoration' or as the case might be, and the show schedules have continued to use the term 'varieties'.[26]

Another of Stearn's terms introduced in this Code was 'grex', for a group of hybrids of common ancestry—examples bred by officials of the RHS being Wilks's Shirley poppies and Lewis Palmer's Headbourne hybrid agapanthus, where these names apply only to the group, not to any individual hybrid within it. Grex eventually

Peter Barr (1826-1909) founded the seed and bulb firm of Barr & Sugden in Covent Garden in 1861 – later to become Barr & Sons, later still to amalgamate with his old rival, Wallace of Colchester, to become Wallace & Barr, and finally in the 1980s to be taken over by De Jager.

proved a controversial term, and during the 1990s it began to be replaced (except for orchids) by 'horticultural group'. An attempt by the Society's Scientific Committee to introduce the term 'strain' was squashed in the early 1990s.

Plant name registrations

The registration of plant names began as one man's obsession before it became an accepted activity of the RHS. Peter Barr (1826-1909), the Covent Garden bulb and seed merchant, became the leading promoter of daffodils of his period; unwilling to believe that the daffodils grown in the 17th century and described in Parkinson's *Paradisus Terrestris* (1629) could have died out, he started a campaign of tracing all the daffodils in cultivation. In 1884, with Barr's assistance, the Society held a Daffodil Conference, under the chairmanship of Michael Foster. At this Conference, a 'Revising Committee' (later 'Nomenclature Committee' and 'Naming Committee') was appointed, with H.J. Elwes as Chairman, to revise the nomenclature of daffodils, and produced what was known as the Conference Catalogue of Narcissi, with a grouping of botanical forms drawn up by J.G. Baker, and a list of garden varieties compiled by Barr. (This Nomenclature Committee modulated by 1886 into the Narcissus Committee, and in 1902 into the Narcissus and Tulip Committee.) Some of the nomenclatural problems facing the Committee have already been discussed.[27] In 1907 the Committee produced its first List of Daffodil Names (compiled by C.H. Curtis); the second list, in 1908, contained the statement that 'The Narcissus Committee are instructed by the Council to refuse in future to register names which are either so nearly like existing names as to be likely to cause confusion, or such as are foolish, or are phrases and not names at all.' In the same year, at the Committee's request, Council appointed a subcommittee on classification, 'to consider the best way of avoiding the confusion, and consequent disputes, likely to arise from the recent multitudinous crossing, recrossing, and intercrossing of the old Divisions of Magni- Medio- and Parvi- Coronati'. A new system of classification was drawn up, and the subcommittee was thereafter reconvened at irregular intervals; C.H. Curtis was appointed Honorary Registrar of Daffodils, and eventually succeeded by Arthur Simmonds, the Society's Assistant Secretary.[28]

Orchids quickly followed daffodils as a recognised source of nomenclatural tangles. A conference on orchid nomenclature had been convened to accompany the Society's provincial show in Liverpool, in 1886, and Heinrich Gustav Reichenbach, who had succeeded Lindley as the period's greatest authority on orchids, attended. The first bigeneric hybrid had been bred in 1883, and given a name combining the names of the parent genera: *Aceras-herminium*. *Laeliocattleya* appeared in 1887, *Brassocattleya* in 1889, and the first trigeneric hybrid, *Brassocatlaelia*, in 1897 (within a decade changed to *Brassolaeliocattleya*, to make its formation consistent with its parents). Deliberations of the Orchid Committee, meetings with

herbarium) tried to bring order into the field by compiling an *Orchid Stud-book*, modelled on the breeding-line anthologies used in horse-racing. The *Stud-book*, by Rolfe and C.C. Hurst, was published in 1909, with financial backing from the Society (which had begun compiling an orchid award list as early as 1899). This was the first attempt to set out the parentage of hybrids, and though in the end the Society refused to adopt its nomenclature—it 'would only make confusion worse confounded'—it recognised its value as a model, and proposed to compile its own register, using improved nomenclature. Rolfe was appointed the Society's Orchid Recorder, but at his death in 1921 he left his work incomplete and virtually unusable.[30] Meanwhile, in 1906, the firm of Frederick Sander at St Albans, probably the world's largest orchid nursery at the time, issued its first list of orchid hybrids, listing not individual cultivars, but only crosses. Sander's list became the orchid grower's indispensable guide, culminating in the production of a cumulative edition in 1947. By that time the nursery was experiencing a reversal of trade; having once had branches in St Albans, Bruges, and the United States, it began to contract until only the American branch was left. In 1949, Sander's approached the RHS to see whether it would take over the responsibility of continuing the register, and Council agreed the compromise of paying the register's production costs; in 1954, the Orchid Committee requested the Society to take over registration altogether.[31]

A Tulip Nomenclature Committee was convened in 1914 and, between the wars, the Society began to issue a checklist of tulip names, again under the editorship of Arthur Simmonds; from 1948 this became a joint project with the Royal Dutch Bulbgrowers' Association, who took it over in its entirety in 1953. Checklists of hybrid lily names were published at intervals in the *Lily Year Book*; a *Tentative Check-list of Delphinium Names* was published in 1947; discussions took place in the inter-war years about registering gladiolus and gentians, and in the 1950s about chrysanthemums. But meanwhile, the idea of registration as a form of name protection was catching on. The J. Horace McFarland Company of Pittsburgh initiated the directory *Modern Roses* in 1930, the American Iris Society began issuing an *Iris Check-list* in 1940.[32]

Brassolaeliocattleya *The Baroness* 'Orchidhurst', a painting by Nellie Roberts of an orchid introduced by Armstrong & Brown (First Class Certificate, 1916).

orchid growers on the naming of hybrids, and even the regulations of the Vienna Code in 1905 left problems unresolved. Finally, in 1909, the Orchid Committee put forward the recommendation that all multigeneric hybrids be given arbitrary names, consisting of the name of some famous orchid grower or botanist with the termination *-ara*. The next trigeneric hybrid to be produced (*Cochlioda* × *Miltonia* × *Odontoglossum*) was accordingly named *Vuylstekeara*, after the Belgian grower Charles Vuylsteke; the proposal was initially controversial, but before long the principle had been accepted worldwide.[29]

As the genealogy of orchids became ever more complicated, Robert A. Rolfe (founder of The *Orchid Review*, and in charge of orchids at the Kew

Camellias also emerged in the late 1940s as a fertile minefield. In 1948, J.R. Sealy offered to produce a revision of the species, which the Society eventually published in 1958; at the same time a checklist of the names of old cultivars, based on the 19th-century literature, was compiled (incompletely) by A.I. Ellis, and published as *Old Camellia Varieties* in 1953, with financial help from the American camellia grower Ralph S. Peer. By the time both works had appeared, the Southern California Camellia Society was already beginning to publish its semi-annual directory *Camellia Nomenclature*.[33] Meanwhile, a new classification of cultivars for exhibition purposes was devised, and published in the *Rhododendron Year Book* for 1957.

In 1947, having absorbed the Rhododendron Association, the RHS issued a *Rhododendron Handbook*, with names of hybrids. In 1952, Hermann J. Grootendorst of Boskoop wrote suggesting that the Society should compile an international register of rhododendrons. 'The Chairman thought it would be a heavy task to compile a complete list, and pointed out that the Society had already published an up-to-date Studlist giving the names and particulars of a great many hybrids'—but there was enthusiasm for the idea nonetheless, and Simmonds suggested that the Society should volunteer for the status of rhododendron registrar at the forthcoming International Horticultural Congress.

As early as 1913 the International Union of Professional Horticulturists had announced the creation of a bureau to register 'new varieties of all kinds of plants'; this project seems to have died with the war, though the Horticultural Trades Association made gestures toward carrying it forward. But in the 1950s, the International Committee on Botanical Nomenclature was actively propounding the idea of International Registration Authorities (later, International Cultivar Registration Authorities) for the different genera of cultivated plants, based on the model of the daffodil and tulip lists that Simmonds had been issuing at intervals. As the RHS had created the prototype, and applied it in so many directions already, it was an easy step to recognising it as the Registrar for a steadily increasing number of categories, beginning in 1955 with daffodils, delphiniums, and rhododendrons. Simmonds became the official Daffodil Registrar, and Harold Fletcher the Rhododendron Registrar. Lilies followed in 1958, with Gillian Peterson as Registrar; at the Third World Orchid Conference in 1960, it was agreed that the RHS should assume responsibility for orchids; dahlias and dianthus followed in 1966. Some plants for

which the Society had already been involved in producing checklists became the responsibility of other organisations: tulips of the Royal Dutch Bulbgrowers' Association; camellias of the International Camellia Society (founded in 1962), which under the editorship of Thomas J. Savige was to produce a three-volume register with 32,000 names. But by the mid-1960s, the RHS was already responsible for the registration of more categories of plants than any other single organisation.[34]

Almost all the early checklists were purely lists of varieties in cultivation, and from time to time it was argued that only cultivars that won awards need be registered; any cultivars that had already disappeared from commerce by the time the checklists began were omitted, so the problem of duplicated names was only partially solved. The *Daffodil Register* was an exception to this rule—the legacy of Peter Barr's hopes of tracking down varieties no longer in cultivation. The great shift took place in the 1970s, in the compilation of the *Dianthus Register*. The first edition, produced by Miss D. Stockwell in 1974, contained upwards of 3,000 names, but was agreed on all sides to be incomplete; many old cultivars of carnations and pinks were known to exist in private collections without entering the commercial market. Audrey Robinson, a carnation enthusiast and horticultural historian, pushed for making the register historically comprehensive, and undertook much of the work of recording all known names of dianthus cultivars over the centuries. The second edition, when it appeared in 1983, contained 27,000 names, and thus became an essential guide for the historian as well as the carnation grower. The 1983 edition of the *Lily Register* was similarly comprehensive, and in Sally Kington's hands, as the result of researches in trade catalogues, the *International Daffodil Checklist* (1989), and the Register, incorporating detailed descriptions as well as names and parentages (1998), swelled to include some 25,000 names. Gradually, the other registers will be made similarly comprehensive.

In 1963 John Gilmour made representations to Council about the urgent need to sort of the nomenclature of 'dwarf and other garden conifers'. Council agreed that the RHS would accept the responsibility of registration, but that it would have to take on board all the conifers, not just the dwarf ones. The International Horticultural Congress in Edinburgh in 1964 agreed to appoint the Society as International Registration Authority. The first Registrar was Humphrey J. Welch, author of a standard work on *Dwarf Conifers* (1966); but differences over nomenclature led him to resign, and publish an alternative

Sally Kington, International Daffodil Registrar (right), at an educational exhibit about daffodils at the spring London Show of 1993.

Conifer Manual in 1991. First John Lewis, and then Piers Trehane, succeeded him as Registrar; an Advisory Committee was set up in 1983; and the Register began to appear in parts, beginning with *Abies* to *Austrotaxus* in 1987 (followed to date by *Belis* to *Pherosphaera*, cypresses, and *Juniperus*).

In 1995 the RHS undertook its ninth category of plants: clematis. Victoria Matthews, who had briefly acted as Daffodil Registrar in the 1980s, undertook the role, and, based in USA, became the first employee of the RHS to work from another country. The *International Clematis Register* was published in 2002, and Matthews then took on the role of revising the *Lily Register*.

The process of registration is purely voluntary; there is no legal penalty for leaving a cultivar unregistered, or indeed for duplicating an existing name. Registration does, of course, involve fees, which in the early days ranged from two shillings and sixpence to register a lily, to a guinea for an orchid. The concept, therefore, has had to be sold to the various plant-breeding communities; some, like orchid growers, rushed to make use of the facility, while it took ten years before the first application to register a conifer name was received. From 1972, all registration was concentrated at Wisley, with one principal registrar supervising; since 1978 that role has been undertaken by Alan Leslie, although several of the individual registrars now work from home (and one from within the Lindley Library). By the late 1980s, with the advent of computerisation, the production of most of the registers was proceeding efficiently and with full co-operation from relevant societies worldwide; registration is in fact the RHS's most important international activity.[35]

At the time of writing, the RHS maintains nine registers.

The Colour Chart

Botanical descriptions can get by with only the roughest of notations for the colour of flowers, but difference of colour is frequently the most important distinguishing factor with cultivars, and a greater degree of precision is needed for their description. As early as the 1860s, the Society's trials of garden plants were frequently organised by their colours, but a list of 42 pelargoniums all described as 'scarlet' can convey to the reader little of the effect of the plants. Unfortunately, no language used by men has a sufficient range of colour terms to make unambiguous identifications of colours. So before the end of the 19th century, the idea of providing collections of colour samples had already been attempted. The problem was not the discrimination of the different colours, but finding a means of printing them that would remain stable.[36]

The first systematic colour identification reference source for gardeners appeared in 1905, from the Société Française des Chrysanthémistes: *Répertoire des Couleurs,* by René Oberthür and Henri Dauthenay, issued in a set of two boxes. The colours in this work were printed on 365 plates, with four tints to the page. This was followed in 1908 by a *Code des Couleurs* by Paul Klincksieck and Th. Valette, incorporating 720 colour samples on painted paper. Alerted to these works by a French deputation to the Temple Show in 1908, Council first thought of producing its own colour chart, but quickly, and more realistically, decided to act as distribution agent for Oberthür's work in England.[37] The problem, however, was that some of the colours in these works deteriorated over time.

From 1929, the Society was a subscriber to the British Colour Council, in order to monitor improvements in colour notation. When in 1934 that Council announced a forthcoming *Dictionary of Colours*, the RHS initiated discussions about its horticultural applications, with the result that the two organisations decided to collaborate on a Horticultural Colour Chart, specifically geared to the colour range of cultivated plants, with Robert F. Wilson of the Colour Council in charge. It took the form of 800 printed samples, printed by a screen process, arranged four to a page as in Oberthür, and issued in 1939-41 in two boxes, with a print-run of 5,000 copies. Wilson was awarded a Gold Veitch Medal in 1941 for his achievement.[38]

In 1958, the Society decided to devise a new chart, as some of the colours could no longer be matched. The colours were now to be arranged on strips instead of sheets, four tints to a strip. The strips were fastened together in four fans (yellow to red; red-purple to blue; blue-green to yellow-green; and greyed colours of all groups), with a total of 792 samples (four tints each of 198 colours). The fans were printed by the McCorquodale Colour Display Company of London, each colour mixed separately, and a subcommittee under the chairmanship of R.H. Stoughton was appointed to supervise the process and authenticate the colours. In order to avoid the problems of the previous Chart, the majority of the colour patches were printed in solid colour, but in order to attain the necessary brightness of some hues, some sheets were printed by a half-tone screen process.

The new Colour Chart was issued in 1966, at a total cost to the Society of £17,000, and references to the former Colour Chart were discontinued in the Society's publications. One major change was the elimination of colour names—canary yellow, Doge purple—in favour of simple numbers—Red 41A, Blue-Green 119C. 'I am desolate that the old names have disappeared and to see that the

The development of colour charts. Top left, the Répertoire des Couleurs *(1905); lower left, Klincksieck's* Code des Couleurs; *top right, the first RHS colour chart (1939-41); lower right and centre: the current RHS colour chart.*

scientists are taking over from the poets', said Fred Whitsey, but otherwise the new Colour Chart was a great success.[39]

The international significance of the Colour Chart led to attempts to harmonise its references with those of colour systems used in other countries. In 1984, the American Rhododendron Society published a pamphlet entitled *A Contribution Toward Standardization of Color Names in Horticulture*, consisting of a table of equivalents between the RHS Colour Chart and the Munsell Universal Colour Language. In 1994, UPOV (the International Union for the Protection of New Varieties of Plants) circulated a list of proposed international colour names based on the RHS references.

In 1986 the Society collaborated with the Flower Council of Holland on reprinting the chart. Lawrence Banks, the Treasurer at the time, met opposition over the cost of the project, but insisted that it be returned to circulation. However, changes in printing technology now caused problems; some of the pigments used in 1966 were no longer commercially available, and some of the red-purple hues in particular did not match the 1966 version. In 1995 a further reprint was issued, this time matched to the 1966 edition. In 2001 a further revised Chart was published, taking 1966 as the standard and adding 76 new colours, the equivalent of 19 sheets, that had previously been difficult to match: dark purples, bright orange, bronze, greys and greens. The pinks and purples formerly printed in four-colour half-tone have been rendered in solid colour instead, putting an end, or so it is hoped, to the problem of reprinting in the future. Since 1986, the fans have also had a hole punched through the middle of each sample so as to isolate the colours under inspection from their surroundings.[40]

The RHS Herbarium

Names and written descriptions are one thing; portraits of award-winning varieties are also a valuable reference source; but there is no substitute for having the plants at hand. Dried specimens mounted on paper have long been the basis of taxonomic collections, and serve as the type specimens for botanical names: if the description leaves identification ambiguous, the original plant that was given the name may survive in some botanical garden's collection, and be available for examination.

The Society sold its original herbarium in 1856, and no record has been found of the purchasers of the specimens; many may lurk unidentified in private collections. John Lindley's private herb-arium (no doubt containing many specimens from the Society's garden) is now housed at the Cambridge Botanic Garden. A herbarium had been built up at Wisley since the early part of the 20th century, greatly augmented by the donation of F.J. Hanbury's collection of some 12,000 sheets in 1936, and containing specimens from the plants collected by the 20th-century plant hunters the Society sponsored. As the Society advanced into its registration project, the decision was taken in 1964 to develop it as a specifically horticultural herbarium, the only one of its kind to focus on cultivars. By the time of the Prance report on the Society's scientific work, the Herbarium contained some 100,000 specimens, seeds, photographs, and illustrations and was recognised as a unique resource.[41]

Pressed specimens are recognised as types for botanical names, but no such process of typification existed for plants raised in cultivation. There is a long tradition of taxonomists dismissing cultivars as irrelevant to the real interests of botany; when Joseph Sabine published his pioneering articles on the cultivars of *Crocus*, *Dahlia*, and *Chrysanthemum* in the Society's *Transactions*, he was mocked by Bellenden Ker for the futility of trying to give a taxonomic status to variable characters ('Was it necessary that a Society should come together for the purpose of printing a volume in quarto on the characters of Sportive Varieties of Chrysanthemums, and figures of fugitive Dahlias?').[42] In the 1980s, Diana Miller, the manager of the Wisley Herbarium, began arguing, in groups like Hortax (the Horticultural Taxonomy Group), for the creation of an analogous system of 'standards', to assist in stabilising cultivar names. The concept was finally ratified in the 1995 revision of the *International Code of Nomenclature for Cultivated Plants*.

> Characters not readily discernible from herbarium specimens such as colour, habit, texture and scent are usually necessary for the identification of cultivars and so detailed descriptions are essential. The value of a Standard is increased further if it is augmented with information such as origin or parentage, references to original publications and any other material which confirms the identity of that plant. It is also useful if the whereabouts of the living plant from which the Standard was prepared, is noted together with dates. Reports of further detailed research and even molecular records, seeds or pollen samples could all be added at a later date.
>
> All this information constitutes the Standard portfolio for the plant. It is not practical for all these items to be stored in herbarium folders but with an efficient database, there is no problem in

recording the data so the whereabouts of these items may be recorded and traced with ease.[43]

An efficient database–welcome to the wonderful world of information technology. Computerisation of plant name registers was quickly followed by attempts to draw up a computerised catalogue of the living plant collections at Wisley, and in 1993, *BG-Base*™, an internationally accepted system, was adopted. The usual catch applied: *BG-Base*™ had been developed by and for botanists, and needed to be adapted for the interests of horticultural taxonomy. Using its software, the *BG-Base*™ administrator, Andrew Sier, and the Wisley botanists built up the RHS Horticultural Database, which was launched on the Internet in 1998.[44] The compilation of this Database is a continuing project, along with the creation of Standard portfolios, the investigation of hybrid status using DNA measurement, and from 1997, the annual revision of the *RHS Plant Finder*, which required a regular name check on some 65,000 cultivated plants, with all proposed amendments reviewed

by an Advisory Panel on Nomenclature and Taxonomy. The beginning of the 21st century added the development of the Plant Selector project, an illustrated plant guide to accompany the Plant Finder on the RHS website, and which entailed the digitisation of both pressed specimens and paintings from the Wisley Herbarium.[45]

National plant collections and the NCCPG

But what about living plants? The idea of a national collection seems to have been first suggested in 1853, when the florist John Edwards proposed that a National Tulip Bed be established at Chiswick. The RHS was assembling collections of plants for nomenclatural trial before the First World War; in 1937 there was a proposal to form a 'standard collection' of montbretias, the exact significance of which is now difficult to discern. But after the Second World War, the proposal to hold collections of the commercially most important flowers was put forward by the Ministry of Agriculture and the Agricultural Research Council: the RHS was to handle dahlias and chrysanthemums, the John Innes Research Institution roses, Kew dianthus, Cambridge Botanic Garden tulips and daffodils. The collections were assembled and planted, but enthusiasm faded, and a decade later the supposed national collections at Wisley consisted of one dahlia and 18 chrysanthemums that no one appeared to be interested in. Was it worth continuing, asked Council rhetorically, and the project seems to have been abandoned. But the idea was not lost; within the next few years proposals were heard for national collections of aquatics, bearded irises, and camellia hybrids to be based at Wisley. When in 1965 a national collection of dwarf conifers was proposed, the RHS having just become International Registration Authority, Council concluded that Wisley was not an appropriate place, and

Diana Miller, Keeper of the Wisley Herbarium, with the range of materials – herbarium specimen, photographs, illustrations, date and description – needed to create a Horticultural Standard.

Westonbirt and Oxford were mooted instead.[46]

In all these discussions, the idea of a 'national collection' appeared to mean a collection of cultivars maintained for purposes of identification, comparison, and perhaps nomenclatural exactitude; the idea of conservation of varieties for its own sake does not seem to have been relevant. But increasingly, public interest was growing in various categories of formerly fashionable plants: old roses began their climb back to popularity between the wars, with the work of E. A. Bunyard and Sacheverell Sitwell; some of the old florists' flowers had their adherents, and Brenda Hyatt single-handedly kickstarted the revival of auriculas with a display at the Chelsea Flower Show in 1982; the efforts of Colin Edwards to assemble a collection of old delphinium cultivars attracted attention in the 1970s.[47] By 1978, when the RHS held a conference on the conservation of plants and gardens, and evidence was presented of the disappearance rate of cultivated plants, both species and cultivars, both genetically and *historically* important, the gardening public was ready for a decisive campaign, and the conference reached the following resolutions:

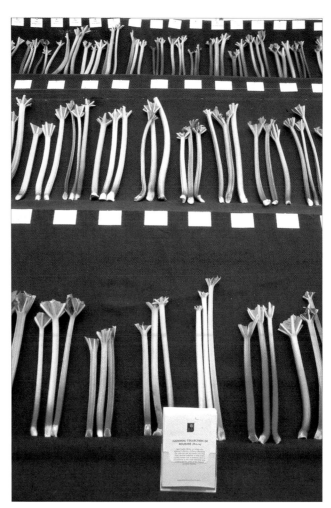

The National Collection of Rhubarb: a demonstration at a Wisley show.

(a) The immediate need for sufficient finance from outside sources to initiate action and to encourage the minimum necessary staff to carry out the primary proposals of the Conference.

(b) The vital importance of documentation and recording of plant collections on a national, local and individual basis.

(c) The essential need to encourage public and political opinion to appreciate the threat to plants and gardens as a major part of the national heritage.

(d) The need to ensure a steady flow of trained gardeners assured of a rewarding career structure and with a wide knowledge of plants and their requirements.

(e) The need to coordinate the activities of nurserymen, botanic gardens, educational and research establishments, specialist societies and other amateurs in the recording, propagation and distribution of rare and threatened plants.

(f) The need to create a national body to be called the Gardens and Plants Council, with functions comparable to those of the Arts Council.

Christopher Brickell, with the help of the Assistant Editor Fay Sharman, compiled a book, *The Vanishing Garden*, to present a survey of endangered cultivars.[48]

The National Council for the Conservation of Plants and Gardens (NCCPG) was duly founded in 1979, and Duncan Donald became its first Director, guiding it through its first five years of life. In 1984 he left to become Curator of the Chelsea Physic Garden, and was succeeded by Tony Lowe. The phrase 'outside sources' in the conference resolution pinpointed the principal problem the new organisation had to cope with: finding money, for it was so structured that it was the local Groups that funded the central office. John Simmons, who became Chairman of the NCCPG on his retirement from the Curatorship at Kew, reported that the Council seemed in retrospect to have 'constantly lived on the verge of collapse'. In 1990, the Department of the Environment reduced its grant-aid; the NCCPG responded by raising its fees and discovering the importance of marketing and fundraising, and by

The National Collection of Heathers at Wisley Garden.

1993 Tony Lowe was able to report a healthy bank balance for the first time.[49]

The new Council's first programme was the survey of vanishing cultivars. Christopher Brickell, Duncan Donald, and Jack Elliott compiled a list of plants believed to have been lost, and a London group volunteer, Sarah Smith, collated it against the *RHS Dictionary*. Through a temporary hiatus in paper supply, the first portions of the list were printed on pink paper, and a tradition was instantly created; a 'pink sheet' plant quickly came to mean an endangered or lost plant that was being sought. The first complete list was published through the Cambridge group in 1991; by the time a new supplement was issued in 1997, nearly 10 per cent of the plants on the list had been recovered from a variety of sources.[50]

The second great project was the establishment of national collections of garden plants, the concept understood this time to mean collections not primarily for commercial or nomenclatural significance, but for the purpose of preserving varieties from extinction. A national collection, whether of a genus or simply of a horticulturally distinct portion of a genus (e.g. cultivars of one

particular species), aims at comprehensiveness; tries to guarantee nomenclatural accuracy, adequacy of cultivation, and a conservation policy (one outbreak of a plant disease could wipe out a collection); and increases the distribution of its plants through group plant sales and the NCCPG plant exchange. Sixty-one national collections had been established by the time the first *NCCPG Newsletter* was published in 1982; twenty years later, the number had climbed to upwards of six hundred. About half are private gardens, a third commercial nurseries, and the remaining sixth public bodies like the National Trust, botanic and university gardens, and the RHS itself. The NCCPG head office, which has since its inception been accommodated at Wisley, has to be ruthless about maintaining its standards, to such an extent that some of the collections at Wisley itself were dropped from the list as being of insufficient quality.[51]

In 1999, the NCCPG launched the Demeter Project, to create a new database for collection holders to use; this received a grant from the Heritage Lottery Fund in 2002, along with funding from the RHS and Edinburgh Botanic Garden.

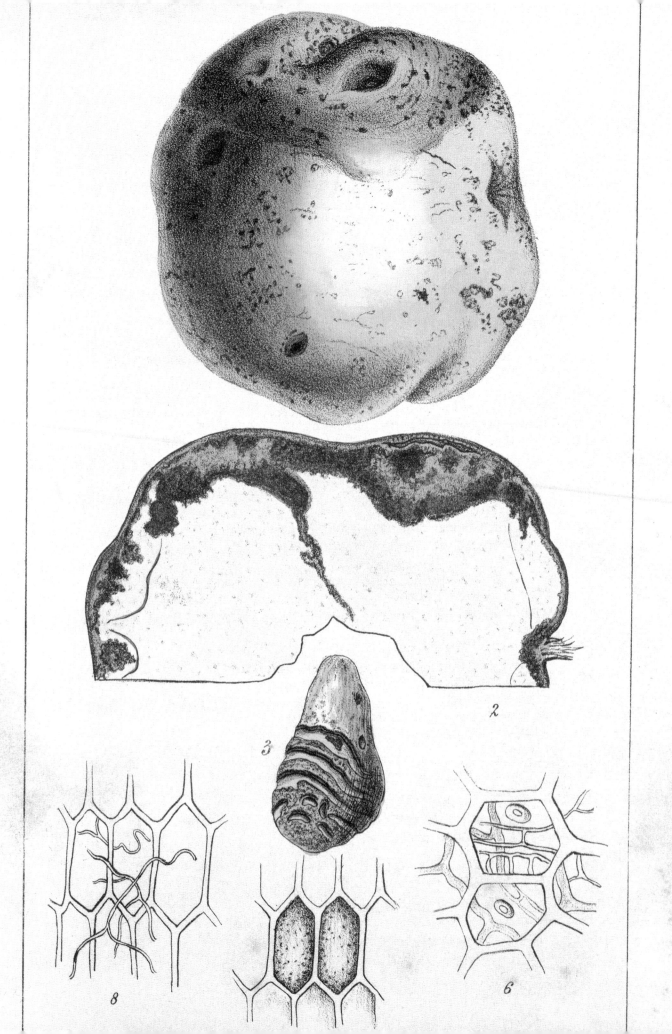

13 *Horticultural Science*

In 1868, the Society announced that, as scientific questions relating to horticultural practice were frequently discussed at its Fruit and Floral Committees, a new Committee would be formed to deal specifically with these matters.

> The Council now consider it advisable to invite the co-operation of physiological botanists and of chemists in the formation of a Committee, whose special functions shall be to promote and encourage the application of physiology and botany to purposes of practical culture, and to originate experiments which may assist in the elucidation of horticultural subjects.

In 1870 the further purpose was added: 'to consider the merits of Plants exhibited at any of the Society's Meetings which may be looked upon rather as Botanical than as Horticultural Specimens'. During the 20th century the purpose was further diversified to include 'diseases, pests, newly imported plants, first hybrids between species, curious plants, inventions, and other objects of horticultural interest and value', in addition to nomenclatural clarification and making recommendations for Botanical Certificates.

The list of the founder members included the luminaries of mid-century botany, chemistry, and entomology: George Bentham and Joseph Hooker, then working on their *Genera Plantarum*; Maxwell T. Masters, Robert Hogg, Thomas Moore of the Chelsea Physic Garden; the plant collectors Robert Fortune and Friedrich Welwitsch; the mycologist Miles J. Berkeley; Sir Edward Frankland, the pioneer of water pollution analysis; the meteorologist James Glaisher; the entomologists Andrew Murray and J.O. Westwood; and the theoretical biologists Charles Darwin, Herbert Spencer, and H.C. Bastian. The Society's President, the Duke of Buccleuch, was the first Chairman, to be succeeded for nearly forty years by Joseph Hooker.[1]

The Society had taken part, two years before, in the organisation of the first International Botanical Conference—which, because it had been accompanied by Britain's first International Horticultural Show, had proved financially as well as intellectually profitable.[2] Thereafter, except occasionally at moments of endangered bank balance, the Society was to be represented regularly at botanical and horticultural congresses, both home and abroad, and was to be the host organisation for the International Horticultural Congress of 1930. On all these occasions, its principal contribution was to lie in the field of horticultural taxonomy, and much of the Scientific Committee's efforts over a century and a quarter was also to be taxonomic and nomenclatural. In this chapter, however, I shall be looking at the other aspects of horticultural science with which the Society has been involved.

Glasshouse technology

Until the 19th century glasshouses were a rarity; the Society played an early role in the innovations that made them widespread and more easily manageable. In 1800, glasshouses were structures of wood or masonry with the maximum provision of windows; they were heated by braziers or by hot air from external boilers. A quick survey of the Society's *Transactions* reveals four articles on the construction of forcing houses and frames in the first volume (1804-12), plus an historical article by Sir Joseph Banks on the forcing houses of the ancient Romans. This total increased in subsequent volumes; altogether, between 1804 and 1841, the *Transactions* published nine papers on glasshouse construction, 20 on glasshouse heating (including pioneering pieces on steam and hot-water heating), two on glazing techniques, four on watering and ventilation systems, and six descriptions of glasshouses that combined any of

Sir Joseph Dalton Hooker (1817-1911), second Director of the Royal Botanic Gardens, Kew, and longstanding chairman of the RHS Scientific Committee. Shown here on his expedition to Sikkim, 1848-51, from which he brought back several species of Himalayan rhododendrons.

FACING PAGE
The potato blight and its symptoms, as depicted in the first volume of the Society's new Journal *in 1846.*

Elevation of the Front.

Fig.1.

Sir George Mackenzie's proposal for a spherically roofed greenhouse, from the Transactions *for 1816.*

these features. In addition, there were three papers on frames and hot-beds.[3]

In 1815, Sir George Mackenzie proposed to the Society that a glasshouse ought to be spherical in shape, so as to parallel the dome of the heavens and admit light at all times of the day. A couple of years later, John Claudius Loudon invented a wrought-iron glazing bar that would make Mackenzie's proposal feasible, and curvilinear glasshouses began to be built in the 1820s.[4]

The Society was to commission a grand curvilinear conservatory for its garden, but thereafter it ceased to be an innovator in glasshouse design, and the great debates on the subject largely passed it by—though Lindley gave them prominence in the *Gardeners' Chronicle*. This neglect is the more surprising in that the next major development was associated with the Society's former gardener Joseph Paxton, but then he had his own magazines in which to air his views. Paxton opposed the curvilinear iron glasshouse as expensive and unnecessary; sufficient light for the plants' purposes could be obtained by a ridge-and-furrow roof angled so as to receive optimum light in the morning and afternoon, and which could be made in more easily maintained wood. The triumph of his approach came with the building he created for

the Great Exhibition of 1851, in Hyde Park: although it had cast-iron supporting columns, and wrought-iron glazing bars for a curved transept required only because he was refused permission to fell a row of elms on the site, most of the structural members and glazing bars were of wood. He was knighted for his achievement; portions of the press were indignant at this breach of class boundaries, as indicated by Beresford Hope's sneer in the Tory journal, the *Quarterly Review*:

> A break down was all but certain, when a gardener dropped in and suggested a big conservatory. Since Cinderella's glass slipper no such success had ever been achieved with that material. The 'Crystal Palace' rose from the turf sparkling and graceful, and the ... elms budded under the transparent roof. Of course toadies and wonder-mongers were not wanting to make the lucky hit of a clever man ridiculous by fulsome praise ...

The lucky hit had been predicted, and promoted, by Lindley, who used the horticultural success of the Crystal Palace to popularise the making of greenhouses on a larger scale; he had already used the leader columns of the *Chronicle* to campaign, successfully, for the abolition of taxes and duties on glass, wood, and brick, thus bringing the costs of greenhouse construction within the reach of the middle classes, and had also promoted Hartley's new sheet glass process, which for the first time made it possible to fit greenhouses with large panes of glass without the imperfections that had made gardeners wary of sheet glass in the past.[5]

The costs of building a greenhouse may have come down by 1850, but the costs of heating one were still high, and heating was always a larger issue in the Society's publications than design. Steam heating had been tried experimentally in the late 18th century, and several articles in the *Transactions* described steam systems; in 1830, a pioneering design for using hot-water pipes was published, the work of the Society's architect William Atkinson. Articles on heating systems and boilers followed at intervals throughout the century, culminating in electric heating at the beginning of the 20th; then interest fell away until inflation in the late 20th century made fuel-saving an issue.[6] During the 1850s, experiments were made at Chiswick in the use of freestanding glass walls for partial protection, Charles Ewing's system proving quite successful until severe storms brought its limitations to notice.[7] But while experiments in glazing were carried out inconclusively at Chiswick in the 1880s, the 20th century's major innovations took place at the John Innes Horticultural Institution—W.J.C. Lawrence's experiments in light intensity and internal climate—and while the Society invited Lawrence to lecture to its Fellows on the matter, it left the research to others, especially the Glasshouse Crops Research Institute, whose Director George Sheard advised it on its own glasshouses.[8]

Weather report

Let us now move away from the greenhouse, as in fact did many plants during the second quarter of the 19th century. One of the great accomplishments of Chiswick in its first thirty years was its experiments in hardiness: the Society had stocks of each plant sufficiently large that it could risk losing some to frost, in order to identify their tolerance levels. As early as 1805 it published an article by Banks on acclimatising plants, followed five years later by a report on exotics which endured the open air in Devonshire. Frost reports formed a regular part of the *Transactions*, and continued to fill the *Journal* well into the 20th century; the first, the result of a survey by Lindley, was published in 1826, and was speedily imitated by J.C. Loudon in his *Gardener's Magazine*. As a result of this collective endeavour, many plants formerly considered delicate glasshouse exotics, like camellias and rhododendrons, moved outdoors and became fixtures in the open air.[9]

In the wake of Lindley's frost survey, in order to make its observations more systematic, the Society installed a battery of meteorological equipment in the Chiswick garden, and daily weather observations became an additional staff duty. William Beattie Booth was the first compiler of the weather records, succeeded by Robert Thompson, and both presented regular instalments of the observations in the Society's publications. The meteorologist James Glaisher, as a founder member of the Scientific Committee, offered his assistance in 1869, and undertook to edit all the existing records: 'These tables', he concluded, 'form one of the most complete records of the kind in existence, only comparable, we believe, with the Greenwich records.' His 'Reduction' of the cumulative record from 1826 to 1869 was issued as a special supplement to volume 2 of the *Journal*.[10]

Glaisher, who effectively began the publication of daily weather reports in newspapers and achieved his greatest notoriety for reaching the maximum height ever achieved in a balloon without breathing apparatus (seven or eight miles, imprecision due to unconsciousness) during the course of his experiments on atmospheric composition, also busied himself in the 1870s with experiments on soil temperature, and read two papers to the RHS on specialised soil thermometers of his own design, manufactured for him by Horne and Thornthwaite, which he offered for sale to RHS members under the Scientific Committee's auspices. (It was not the first time the Society had sponsored meteorological equipment: Lindley had promoted a patent hygrometer in the 1840s.)[11]

In the wake of Glaisher, the Meteorological Office interested itself in the Chiswick observations, and suggested various joint projects, some of which the Society declined as too little related to horticulture. When the Society moved to Wisley, it proudly publicised the establishment of its new weather station.[12] And it has remained in operation to the present day, through storms, frosts, and the tornado that manoeuvred its way through the garden on 21 July 1965, uprooting 174 trees completely, mostly in the fruit field. When the Fruit Officer E.G. Gilbert reported the incident in the *Journal*, his attention was naturally focused on the ways the trees responded to damage—apples being uprooted without breakage while plums were snapped or smashed to pieces—but he also found time to wonder:

> Within 20 feet of the new R.H.S. Meteorological Station numerous apple and peach trees were either uprooted or smashed. Yet on the

The meteorological station at Wisley.

Meteorological Station not a single instrument was found so much as one inch out of place! The devil looks after his own!'[13]

The move to Wisley was the more relevant in that air pollution had been the principal reason for abandoning Chiswick. The Scientific Committee had been granted £100 by the Royal Society for a special study of air pollution, and the results were published in the *Journal* in a two-part article by F.W. Oliver. The Society had already held a Smoke Abatement Exhibition at Kensington in 1882, one result being a sardonic note in Council minutes that the exhibition had damaged plants in the conservatory. The deleterious effects of pollution were seen not only on plants in the open air, but also on greenhouses, in the forms of soot deposit (increased maintenance) and even glass decay.[14]

The excitement generated by the progressive discoveries of hardiness in the second quarter of the 19th century has long since faded, and the aspirations of the period's gardeners came to seem merely amusing. When Donald Beaton, in 1852, looked forward to 'a cottage gardener having a plot of Pine-apples growing at the end of his Rhubarb bed like so many globe Artichokes', he was merely continuing the hopes that Sir Joseph Banks had expressed half a century before, of avocados, mangos, mangosteens and durians becoming commercial crops in England.[15] As these hopes dwindled, one of the immediate responses was attempts to devise external heating systems, comparable with those of glasshouses but acting in secluded parts of the open ground: heated ponds for tropical waterlilies, and even Trevor Clarke's geothermal garden at Welton Place in Northamptonshire, where hot-water pipes were run through the soil to create a (hopefully) suitable environment for tropical plants. A geothermal border was installed at Chiswick in the 1860s, with pineapples among its plants, though the lack of publicity accorded to it suggests that it was not successful for long.[16] Today, it is possible that such hopes and experiments might be revived, to judge from the rhetoric with which the press greets discussions of global warming. Thomas Andrew Knight had conducted an early study of climate change, based on published weather records in England, but had looked to local phenomena like deforestation to explain temperature fluctuations.[17] It was not until the 1970s, a time when the *Journal* was making recommendations about adapting plant choice to the microclimate of the garden,[18] that the problems of climate change forced themselves on public attention.

The hot summer of 1976 saw severe drought in various parts of England, and the beginnings of water rationing and hosepipe bans as a regular fact of life. A Drought Act was passed that brought calls for the RHS to take some action on the matter. The loss of trees, and the fears for various important arboreta, were succeeded by a rash of insurance applications for subsidence related to clay soil shrinkage, with two results: the assembly by scientists at Kew of the first substantial database of tree root extent, and panicky recommendations for the removal of trees near houses that led to fears of 'treeless cities'.[19] The 1980s brought the first of a series of major storms, with further widespread tree damage. By the 1990s, it had become established that the British climate had warmed by 0.5°C (1.3°F) during the preceding century, with the immediate consequence that all the finely tuned details of Arthur Hellyer's once indispensable *Your Garden Week by Week* had been rendered obsolete.

> For each 1°C (1.8°F) increase in temperature in spring, oak trees are breaking into leaf six days earlier. Dry summers are affecting the health of beech trees, causing them to produce fewer buds and shoots and go prematurely into seed production. If dry summers happen repeatedly, dieback will be commonplace. Many pests and insects are sensitive to temperature changes. An increase of only 1°C (1.8°F) in annual average temperatures can trigger certain aphid species to appear 16 days earlier in the season ...

Not to mention premature emergence from winter dormancy, partially abandoned hibernation, and an increasing range of problems that the Advisory Services and *The Garden* have had their attention turned to as the century ended. In 2000, the RHS, the National Trust, and the UK Climate Impacts Programme drew up a joint action plan of research priorities, in which Wisley's scientists are playing a major role. In 2002 the result of this work was published by the UK Climate Impacts Programme in a major report entitled *Gardening in the Global Greenhouse: The Impacts of Climate Change on Gardens in the UK*.[20]

Tools and implements

Garden tools have evolved without any great programmes of research and development speeding them along, and the role of the RHS in developing or promoting any individual items has been small. In 1819, T.A. Knight turned his attention briefly to the reform of pot making, making recommendations for the best design (width at top, width at base, and depth should have the proportions 8:5:6), but there is no evidence that anyone paid attention. A very few articles on particular fumigators, forks, or Alexander Forsyth's combination plumb-line and level appeared in the *Transactions* or *Journal* without attracting overmuch notice.[21]

What the Society could do well was to hold exhibitions and trials of tools and equipment. The first big exhibit of implements formed part of the second Great Exhibition of 1862, and it was followed by a separate exhibition in 1865. Thereafter, tool displays formed a part of the Kensington shows on an *ad hoc* basis, but did not return as a theme in the Westminster shows that succeeded them. During the Second World War, the Ministry of Agriculture drew up plans for research on horticultural machinery; when the Chelsea Show was revived in 1947, and many anticipated exhibitors were as yet unable to put on their

M'Glashan's tree-moving demonstration at Chiswick. Original drawing by Philip Henry Delamotte for an engraving published in the Illustrated London News *of 12 March 1853.*

displays, an exhibit of mechanical appliances was resorted to as a space-filler. It proved so successful that a series of separate Machinery Shows was held in the ensuing years, as well as tractor demonstrations at Wisley. (The Ministry's Horticultural Machinery Development Board was dissolved in 1949, leaving further development in the hands of the National Institute of Agricultural Engineering, with no further input from horticultural representatives.)[22]

The first significant trial of garden equipment held by the Society was of a tree-transplanting machine. The transplanting of mature trees had been an important issue for gardeners and garden designers for generations; many suggestions for improvements in the process were made in the early 19th century, and articles appeared in the Society's publications. In 1853, a machine devised by a Mr M'Glashan was demonstrated at Chiswick; the operation was successful but the patient (a red cedar) died. 'This is not, however, a matter of surprise', said the *Gardeners' Chronicle*, 'for to show the power of the machine, the tree was allowed to dangle in the air on it for two days, thus subjecting its roots to an undue amount of exposure.' In the event, the most successful transplanting system of the century was that of William Barron, which was developed and publicised without the Society's help.[23]

Trials of other sundries took place occasionally at Chiswick: most famously, a trial of path surfaces in 1852 that announced the superiority of the newly-introduced asphalt. In 1912 the Wisley Garden Committee determined to conduct trials of various garden sundries, ranging from tools to pesticides, and issue fixed-term Awards of Merit, which would lapse after ten years (the assumed life-span of a commercial product). Most of the trials were held at Wisley, but in 1925 a trial of lawn mowers was held at Regent's Park, and a trial of garden sprinklers a decade later received respectable press attention. The awards were revived briefly after the Second World War, but in 1950, on the recommendation of Sir Giles Loder, they were discontinued. Over the nearly forty years of the trials, such diverse tools as Green's Silens Messor lawn mower, Pugh's Atco motor mower, Lloyd Lawrence's Pluviette lawn sprinkler ('soundly constructed of cast-iron, and is unlikely to get out of order', 1914), the Planet Jr. double wheeled hoe, and Rolcut secateurs received awards; in 1950, some of the first plastic flower pots (from Moulded Plastics Ltd) were among the last honorands.[24] Thereafter the RHS was involved in consultations with the British Standards Institution over lawn equipment and other tools, but in the 1970s it missed its chance of

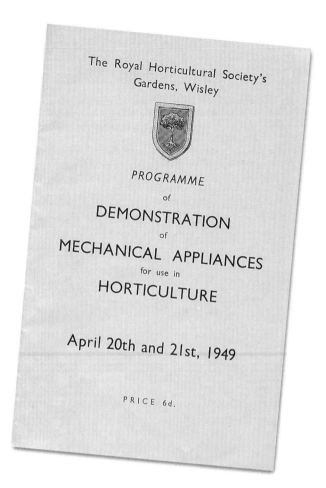

collaborating with the Consumers' Association over the testing of equipment, which resulted in the creation of the magazine *Gardening from Which?*

Programme for an equipment demonstration at Wisley, 1949.

Physiological botany

Thomas Andrew Knight, the Society's second President, was an experimental botanist with interests in plant physiology, including the rising of sap, bud and root formation, leaf motion, and hybridisation. After his death in 1838, Council agreed to publish a collection of his papers in a cheap and convenient form. George Bentham and John Lindley edited *A Selection from the Physiological and Horticultural Papers* (drawn in large part from the Society's *Transactions*), which was published in 1841.[25]

Lindley's own work as a botanist carried him far beyond what was directly relevant to the Society's interests. Nonetheless, as its Editor, Lindley ensured that a certain number of papers on physiological botany appeared in the *Transactions* and *Journal*, many of them his own work. These included articles on double flowers,

Maxwell Tylden Masters (1833-1909), son of the famous Canterbury nurseryman William Masters. Lecturer in botany at St George's Hospital, and from 1865 the editor of the Gardeners' Chronicle; *author of* Vegetable Teratology *(1869) and various monographs, on conifers, Aristolochiaceae, Passifloraceae, etc. Secretary of the International Botanical Congress, 1866.*

diurnal variation in growth rates, evaporation from leaves, geotropism, and Edward Solly's researches on the effects of electrical stimulation on plants; these last were at least commissioned by the Society, as part of his work for the Chemical Committee.[26] Of all these papers, possibly the most immediately important horticulturally was the work on the colours of hydrangeas. The variation between pink and blue had been noted by William Curtis in the 1790s, but he had not made the association with its cultivation conditions. In 1822, Joseph Busch published a note in the *Transactions*, stating that the blue flowers were always associated with the presence of alum in the soil. Twenty years later, in the *Journal*, James Donald published the first systematic experiments to determine what soil conditions induced the change.[27]

After Lindley's time, the purely botanical content of the Society's *Journal* sagged; Maxwell T. Masters on the physiology of root-hairs (1879) was the last important physiological article for the 19th century. When Masters died in 1908, after forty years on the Scientific Committee and even longer as editor of the *Gardeners' Chronicle*, the Society commemorated him by instituting an annual Masters Memorial Lecture whose purpose was to provide Fellows with a summary of current thought and research on some aspect of botany or horticultural science. (The first lecturer was Hugo de Vries, on genetics.) Most of these lectures have been published or abstracted in the *Journal*.[28]

One subject that never featured in the *Transactions* or *Journal* was the physiology of poisonous plants. This issue raised its head in the 1990s, after generations in which the capacity of certain plants to cause skin irritation had been known and accepted as a fact of life by gardeners. In 1991 *Gardening Which?* (as it was now called) ran a feature on the inadequacy of safety labelling on plants; over 80 per cent of poisonous plants on sale in garden centres, it claimed, were not so labelled. The Society set up a working party with the Horticultural Trades Association (HTA), and commissioned a research project in which it collaborated with Kew and the National Poisons Unit at Guy's and St Thomas' Hospitals, reviewing the toxicology of 109 plant groups. Acting on the results of this study, the HTA devised a Code of recommended practice on labelling, and issued a guidance note in 1994. In 1995 *Gardening Which?* was granted an exhibit at the Chelsea Show to publicise the dangers of poisonous plants to the public, which was promptly criticised as unfair to the nursery trade. Legitimate questions remain about variations in allergic response, but the poisonous plant guidelines, in this age of health and safety consciousness, have now become an accepted institution.[29]

Plant nutrition

In May 1841 the Duke of Devonshire, who had succeeded Knight as President, proposed that the Society should 'conduct some experiments in Horticultural Chemistry, more especially for the purpose of investigating the exact nature of the influence produced upon garden plants by soil, and by the substances employed as manures'. The experiments would be funded half by himself, and half by subscription, each contributing £50. A Chemical Committee was forthwith appointed to draw up a research programme; in March of the following year Edward Solly, who had already been a Council member, was hired to carry out the work, and lecture to the Society on chemistry. The Chemical Committee was dissolved in 1846, but Solly was given a new contract of employment as Honorary Professor of Chemistry to the Society.[30]

The question of fertilisers and plant nutrition had hitherto received little attention in the *Transactions*, apart from an essay by Knight on the application of liquid manure.[31] Now Solly's appointment sparked a flurry of activity, and over the course of the 1840s a series of studies appeared, on the chemical composition of plants, soil exhaustion and crop rotation, experimental trials of lawn fertilisers and manures for the kitchen garden, with Robert Thompson supervising the trials, and on growing plants in measured quantities of different media, these experiments carried out by William Haseldine Pepys.[32]

After 1850, the research programme wound down under the impact of financial disaster, and by the time the Society was back on its feet, the centre of fertiliser research had shifted to John Bennet Lawes's estate at Rothamsted. Lawes had worked with Lindley on plant transpiration; in 1843 he had begun systematic experiments on fertilisers, and had already accumulated a valuable body of information by the 1860s. Maxwell T. Masters supervised a trial of fertilisers at Chiswick at the beginning of the 1870s, but there was little impetus to carry out experimental work in depth. The most important piece of chemical research published by the Society in the second half of the 19th century was a translation of Schultz-Schultzenstein's work on the absorption of nutrients by roots, and that was a delayed publication of a piece that Lindley had intended to include in the earlier *Journal*.[33]

Once the Wisley Laboratory had been established, however, Frederick Chittenden began a programme of testing the properties of commercial preparations and of recommended fertiliser mixes, beginning in 1909 with an acclaimed series of experiments on Nitro-Bacterine or bacterial peat, and moving on during the war years to a sludge manure marketed as 'Manchester Corporation Fertiliser'. Between the wars experiments were carried out on the use of potash permanganate (work which Daniel Hall dismissed as of little value), on soil sterilisation, and on the retention of nutrients in plant pots. But during the Second World War, the Society refused to carry out fertiliser trials on behalf of Rothamsted, and thirty years later similarly declined to be a trial centre for soil conditioners. There were other and better-equipped facilities for experimental research on soils and nutrients.[34]

Propagation and seeds

In addition to his work on nutrients, Solly also conducted a series of experiments on steeping seeds in various conditioning fluids, either to speed up germination or improve the vitality of the plants. In 1843, Lindley publicised in the *Gardeners' Chronicle* a claim that ancient Egyptian wheat seeds found in an archaeological investigation had germinated; while the claim was disputed, it focused attention on how much remained to be learned about the properties of seeds, and in particular about dormancy and how to overcome it. One common way of assisting germination was to insert a wheat seed in the base of a cutting (effective because it released growth hormones as it germinated, which helped to stimulate growth in the cutting, though that explanation wasn't available until the 20th century). The idea of dormancy has been challenged in recent years, as an empty rhetoric disguising the fact that we haven't yet understood the optimum conditions for a given plant's germination.[35]

One important by-product of all this was the practical issue of the quality of commercially available seeds. In 1868 Andrew Murray proposed that the Society should conduct trials of seeds from various seedsmen, to assess the degree of adulteration in practice. The adulteration of domestic foods had provoked public controversy two decades earlier, and resulted in government reports on the use of ground chicory in coffee, of alum in bread, and the like; Lindley had collaborated with Sir William Hooker on an investigation of coffee adulteration in the 1850s.[36] So in June 1868 the seed trials began, and the investigative subcommittee published its findings, first in the *Gardeners' Chronicle*, and later in the Society's *Journal*. Four accusations were made: that seed companies tended to keep their seed too

long, so that it had lost its vitality by the time it was sold; that bad seed was mixed with good, and old with new, to bulk out purchase orders; that 'seed whose vitality has been killed' was similarly added; and that (especially with imported seed) artificial colouring and other additives were used to disguise inferior seed. The *Chronicle* expected a flood of denials from the trade, and received instead sniffs and dismissals on the one hand, and corroborative testimony on the other. The Sleaford seedsman Charles Sharpe undertook the role of reformer of his industry and campaigned for legislation to prohibit such abuses; Andrew Murray and Trevor Clarke represented the RHS as expert witnesses before Parliament; and the result was the Adulteration of Seeds Act, 1869.[37]

There was no textbook of propagation until F.W. Burbidge compiled his *Cultivated Plants: their Propagation and Improvement* in 1877, and, apart from the increasingly sophisticated employment of controlled environments through the use of glasshouses, most developments in the 19th and early 20th centuries were a matter of learning the requirements of particular genera of plants. The art of the propagator was to a great extent empirical and dependent on wide knowledge, experience, and intuition. The Society has throughout its history secured the services of great propagators, like Frederick Bause in the 19th century and Frank Knight in the 20th (whose greatest wish, on retiring as Director of Wisley, was to get back to propagating trees); Bause never wrote a treatise on his subject, though as a young man Knight collaborated with G.C. Taylor on a propagation manual.[38] The basic techniques of taking cuttings, on which these men were brought up, have not changed significantly, though research has been carried out at Wisley on improvements in air layering and hardwood cuttings.[39] But the 20th century has seen the development of mist propagation, of hydroponics and nutrient film technique, and of the discovery and use of growth hormones. Although experiments in all these techniques have been made at Wisley, it has always been as a means of testing their viability for domestic horticulture, not as innovations made there.[40]

The use of specialist potting composts was traditionally a matter of empirical testing and mystique—for the complication of some published mixes in the early 19th century suggests deliberate mystification. 'Before peat-based composts', as some recent writers have said, 'there were more recipes for growing media in Britain than in Mrs Beeton's cookbooks.' Despite the introduction of synthetic materials like vermiculite and rockwool, the most influential work on potting composts was carried out at the John Innes Horticultural Institution by W.J.C. Lawrence, and resulted in the specification of a series of 'JI' composts for different categories of plants, all based on proportionate mixtures of loan, sand or grit, and peat (preferred to the traditional manures because of its uniformity, sterility, and slow decomposition rate). These composts were widely adopted in the 1960s by the producers of containerised plants, because they saved labour, and good loam was scarce; so the principal trend in improving potting composts, as in the work that Christopher Bunt carried out at the Glasshouse Crops Research Institute, was that of making them loamless. The RHS helped to publicise all these developments in its *Journal*, and in the 1990s helped to reverse the process by conducting trials of peat-free composts, once the environmental costs of the reliance on peat became known.[41]

Hybridisation and the birth of genetics

Until the end of the 18th century, the production of garden varieties had been a matter of propagation: nature produced the sport, and it was the florist's job to reproduce it vegetatively. The first acknowledged hybrid flower—a cross between a carnation and a sweet william—was produced by Thomas Fairchild in the 1720s, and was nicknamed 'Fairchild's mule'; but it was a long time before the ease of the process or the quality of the results stimulated more than a few to attempt cross-breeding. It was not until the 1790s that the first systematic programme of hybridising plants for the ornamental garden was begun, by the Tooting nurseryman William Rollisson: by 1826 he had bred 285 varieties of Cape heaths. By that time enthusiastic amateurs were joining in the fun, with William Herbert, later Dean of Manchester, trying his hand at amaryllids, gladioli, and other bulbous plants in the 1820s and 1830s.[42]

Practice was one thing, but theory another. Was it possible to predict what the results of a cross between two species, or even two distinct varieties, would be? Apparently not. In 1822, Alexander Seton reported in the Society's *Transactions* the results of crossing two varieties of garden pea, 'Dwarf Imperial' with green peas, and

Hand-coloured engraving of peas, accompanying John Goss's article in the Society's Transactions, *1822.*

a white-fruited variety. The adult plants seemed to be intermediate between the two parents, but Seton had a surprise when he saw the peas that resulted:

> On their ripening it was found that instead of their containing Peas like those of either parent, or of an appearance between the two, almost every one of them had some Peas of the full green colour of the Dwarf Imperial, and others of the whitish colour of that with which it had been impregnated mixed indiscriminately and in undefined numbers; they were all completely either of one colour or the other, none of them having an intermediate tint.

In the same year, John Goss pollinated the 'Blue Prussian' pea (green cotyledon) with pollen from the 'Dwarf Spanish' (yellow cotyledon), and found that the offspring were mostly mixed, but some were distinctly green and some yellow.

> Last spring, I separated all the blue peas from the white and sowed each colour in separate rows; and I now find that the blue produce only blue, while the white seeds yield some pods with all white, and some with both blue and white peas intermixed.

If only they'd recorded the ratios of the offspring; the raw material for Mendel's law was virtually there.[43]

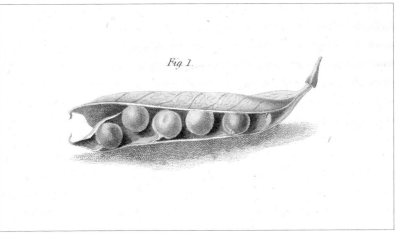

Fig. 1.

The *Transactions*, and after it the *Journal*, were full of articles recording new hybrids, but also of theoretical and reflective articles on the principles involved: how influential was the pollen? what was the relative importance of the male and female ancestors? was there a relation between the qualities of the seed coat and those of the cotyledon? why were some hybrids fertile and others mules? Answers, for reasons now obvious, were not apparent. Behind all these lurked the larger questions of the definition of species and variety, to what extent either category had a real existence or was simply a convenience of human attempts at classification; of truth to type, and the natural range of variation in a population; not to mention whether hybridisation took place in nature, and how natural hybrids could be distinguished from species. Out of this ferment of questions emerged Darwin's *Origin of Species* in 1859, which Lindley arranged to have reviewed in the *Gardeners' Chronicle* by Darwin's friend Joseph Hooker; Darwin's theory found far greater acceptance from botanists than from zoologists initially, in part because it drew extensively on the results of hybridisation experiments published in the *Chronicle*.[44]

By the end of the century, hybridisation seemed to be becoming a fine art; Shirley Hibberd could say in 1883 that 'the hybridist who has thoroughly mastered the art may predetermine, with almost mathematical exactitude, what it is in his power to produce'. This was an exaggeration, as the number of failures attests: Trevor Clarke, one of the period's greatest hybridists, never succeeded in his determination to breed cotton varieties that could be grown in the English climate. Nonetheless, two hybridists at the Veitch nurseries, John Dominy and John Seden, were among the original Victoria Medallists by virtue of their achievements. But, as Lindley's generation would have said critically, it was all empirical: an understanding of the principles involved continued to be elusive.[45]

Darwin's masterpiece had been devoted to the origin of species, but the origin of variation within a species remained mysterious. In the 1880s, August Weismann advanced the hypothesis of the 'continuity of the germplasm'—that what an organism inherited from its parents was essentially what they had inherited from theirs, that characteristics acquired during the course of an organism's lifetime had no influence on heredity. This idea stimulated a new generation of biologists to try to pinpoint the emergence of hereditary characters, in what became known (in Hugo de Vries's phrase) as the mutation theory. Not all accepted the principle; the Society's Professor of Botany, George Henslow, used the *Journal* for twenty years as a forum for his defence of the inheritance of acquired characteristics, and for his attacks on natural selection rather than adaptation as an explanation of evolution—not as an attack on Darwin, but as a defence of the 'real' Darwin whose more fruitful ideas had been submerged in the attention given to his misleading ones.[46]

In 1894 Francis Galton persuaded the Royal Society to appoint a committee to compile statistics on the measurable characters of plants and animals; in 1897 it was renamed the Evolution Committee, and one of its members, William Bateson—who had produced a massive *Materials Toward the Study of Variation*, the major English work on mutation theory—sought the help of the RHS. William Wilks, the Secretary, was excited, a subcommittee was formed, and an appeal sent out to Fellows to help with the survey. One of Wilks's correspondents was a young man named C.C. Hurst, who was working on orchid hybrids and engaging with their theoretical issues. Already in 1896 he was writing to another correspondent:

> With regard to the limits of species, *I* once fondly thought that fertility and non-fertility would be the true test of species, as you seem to do, but my hopes have been sadly dispelled of late, since my experience with orchids. E.g. *Cypripedium barbatum* has been successfully crossed with 24 distinct species out of some 30 species cultivated in gardens ... All are distinct in every way and could not be termed *varieties* merely. If your theory were carried out there would be only *one species* of Cypripedium, and what would be its name? This species would be spread over the whole of the Old World and the present species would be called varieties, which, as you say, would involve the trinomial rather than the binomial method of nomenclature ...[47]

(And that's before the east Asian cypripediums became the new genus *Paphiopedilum*.) Hurst was formulating a theory of evolution by hybridisation, which attracted the sympathetic interest of R.A. Rolfe, Kew's resident orchid expert.

At this point Wilks conceived the idea of an international conference on hybridisation, which Hurst and Bateson helped to organise. (Wilks to Hurst: 'It is so encouraging when one's efforts and plans are cordially seconded. Please do all you can to help me on and get the Conference to go down. Blow the trumpet wherever you can.') The conference was held at Vincent Square on 11-12 July 1899; lectures were given by Bateson ('Hybridization as a method of scientific investigation'), Hurst, De Vries; there was a display of orchid hybrids to draw attention to the problems of character transmission. Bateson emphasised the discontinuity of variation, and the utility of treating variations as complete entities which persisted in crossings; Hurst discussed the phenomenon of characters 'skipping a generation', and used the terms prepotency and latency (where a later generation would say dominance and recession). No consensus was reached; but a great deal of useful networking was done.[48]

Reminiscing about it later, Bateson said: 'The predominant note of our deliberations in 1899 was

Dr E.K. Janaki Ammal trained as a cytologist with C.D. Darlington before joining the RHS. In later years she contributed to the Botanical Survey of India and became President of the Indian Society of Genetics and Plant Breeding; she is commemorated in an award for taxonomy and a medal issued by the Society of Ethnobotanists.

mystery. In 1906 we speak less of mystery than of order.' Three continental botanists, De Vries, Rudolf Tschermak, and Carl Correns, began a thorough literature search for all earlier hybridisation experiments they could find, and in the course of so doing discovered an obscure paper by an Austrian monk named Gregor Mendel, published in the journal of a local natural history society in 1869. De Vries sent a copy of the paper to Bateson, who read it in the train while on his way to give a lecture to the RHS on 'Problems in heredity as a subject for horticultural investigation'. The ratios Mendel had observed for the distribution of characters in offspring were compatible with Bateson's and De Vries's researches; the laws deduced were simple and suggested an immediate answer to the known difficulties; Bateson revised his paper in the train, and the audience of his lecture became the first people in Britain to learn about Mendel. Wilks commissioned Bateson to translate Mendel's paper, and 'Experiments in hybridization' duly appeared as the leading article in the 1901-02 *Journal*—not a bad way of beginning the 20th century.[49]

A second hybridisation conference took place in New York in 1903, with Bateson and Hurst attending as representatives of the RHS, and they found that the gospel according to Mendel was already being well received. Wilks was encouraged:

> I am rather scolded by the Council for spending so much on it but I maintain stoutly that it is almost the only thing we have to show as a *scientific* society and I will not remain Secretary if it is allowed to degenerate into simply the chief Horticultural Soc. on the same lines as other Hort. Socs. only more so.

Hurst was now engaged on a flurry of papers. In the same volume of the *Journal* as Mendel's paper he published the first of two articles showing that Mendel's theory explained the patterns of inheritance he had puzzled over in orchids; and an article on wheat hybrids by the American W.J. Spillman having been brought to his attention, he published a further paper in the *Journal* showing that characters in wheat, too, were inherited on Mendelian lines. Another year, and a report of experiments on peas, replicating Mendel's and rationalising the earlier work of Seton, Goss, and Knight; then his report on the American conference; and then it was time to help Wilks in the organisation of the third hybridisation conference, once again to take place under the Society's auspices. Bateson gave the introductory talk on 31 July 1906, remarking that a new

discipline had come into existence since the first conference, but that it was as yet nameless:

> To meet this difficulty I suggest for the consideration of this Congress the term *Genetics*, which sufficiently indicates that our labours are devoted to the elucidation of the phenomena of heredity and variation: in other words, the physiology of Descent ...[50]

Hurst was to go on to apply Mendel's laws to the history of roses, and to build up a collection of rose species at Wisley for that purpose; Council had decided in 1915 that Wisley was 'the proper place to improve plant varieties'. Experiments on the genetics of important hybrid groups were commissioned between 1906 and the 1920s: Redcliffe Salaman on potatoes, A.J. Bliss on bearded irises, Bertram Buxton on the primrose 'Wisley Blue'.[51] After the Second World War, the work on chromosomes that C.D. Darlington had pioneered offered tempting possibilities for plant taxonomy, and an Indian cytologist, Dr E.K. Janaki Ammal, who had collaborated with Darlington on the *Chromosome Atlas of Cultivated Plants* (1945), was hired in 1946 to work in the Laboratory (the first female scientist in a salaried post at Wisley) on chromosome counts. She represented the RHS at various international conferences on genetics and cytology, and published articles on the implications of chromosome counts for sorting out the taxonomy of philadelphus, nerines, and fruits. She was an early experimenter with the use of colchicine to induce polyploidy, among the first fruits of which were the new magnolia cultivars 'Janaki Ammal' and 'Norman Gould'.[52]

The programme of cytological research at Wisley was wound down in the 1950s, and after Ammal's departure (she became the first Director of the Central Botanical Laboratory of India in 1954), new techniques were developed elsewhere. The immense post-war expansion in vegetable breeding—with the consequence that today, some 40 per cent of carrots, 50 per cent of cabbages and onions, 70 per cent of tomatoes, and nearly 100 per cent of Brussels sprouts are F1 hybrids—was merely noted in passing. The advance from chromosome-counting to DNA sequencing was seized on as an improved taxonomic tool, but the move from chemically induced polyploidy to genetic engineering was observed from a distance, and as the early experiments in making genetically modified plants roused intense controversy, the Society was well placed to air the arguments dispassionately in *The Garden*. As the new century began, the Society's active research lay not in breeding but in studying the genetics of *Lavatera* and *Pelargonium*, and in collaboration with the perfume manufacturers Quest in a study to determine whether the scent of new cultivars could be predicted.[53]

Pest and disease control

When William Forsyth, one of the seven founders of the Society, was appointed to the Royal Gardens at Kensington in 1784, he found many of the fruit trees afflicted with fungal canker. One of his methods of tackling the problem was to experiment with plasters that could be applied to the exposed surfaces after the infected wood had been cut away; he produced what he regarded as a successful formula, which became known as 'Forsyth's plaister' after the Commissioners of Land Revenue asked him to apply it to damaged trees in the royal forests. Forsyth had been keeping the composition of his formula secret, and the Treasury offered him up to £3,000—he eventually received £1,500—for his services on condition that he publish his methods. The result was a pamphlet on tree injuries, published in 1791 and reprinted as an appendix in the various editions of his later *Treatise on Fruit Trees*. The plaister proved to be a mixture of cow dung, urine, wood ash, sand, and powdered lime; it received testimonials, especially from James Anderson and John Coakley Lettsom; it was also bitterly attacked by Thomas Andrew Knight, less for any disproof of its normal practical value than for some of Forsyth's extreme claims about its utility for the rejuvenation of stumps. The controversy that Knight stirred up created embittered feelings all round, and was no doubt the reason why Knight was not invited to the founding meeting of the Society. Forsyth's reputation was much damaged by the controversy, although Knight was wrong on the major issue of the cause of the canker (he regarded it as a by-product of senescence instead of a disease in itself).

Forsyth's methods were not limited to the use of his plaister: in his *Treatise* he also described a treatment for mildew, using a mixture of tobacco, sulphur, elder buds, and unslaked lime boiled together. This was effectively the first recipe for lime-sulphur, the 19th century's primary fungicide.[54]

The subsequent history of plant pathology, and the Society's involve-ment in it, falls into four categories, in chronological but overlapping sequence: physical and environmental methods of pest deterrence; studies of the cause and aetiology of plant diseases; chemical pest control; and biological pest control.

Many suggestions were offered in the *Transactions* and later publications of the Society on methods of deterring or killing slugs, insects, and birds that ate crops. These ranged from the whimsical—the use of cats leashed to overhead wires to keep birds away—to the highly useful, such as Maxwell-Lefroy's Wisley Turnip Fly Trap and Fox Wilson's flea beetle trap.[55] As for how successful they have been, look around you. Fox Wilson, assessing the new pesticides in the 1940s, quoted favourably F.A. Secrett's watchwords—'Neutral soil plus water is the best safeguard against pests', 'Acid soil minus water spells Aphis'—and remarked, 'The importance of overhead watering in arresting pest outbreaks was well illustrated at Wisley in 1945, when a threatened serious attack of Carrot Fly in the Lend-Lease Vegetable Trials was arrested by timely overhead irrigation.' (Well, for pests which thrive in dry conditions at least.)[56] The most

Fox Wilson's flea beetle trap being demonstrated at Wisley.

successful pest treatment ever developed at Wisley was the work of James Kirkham Ramsbottom, a research student who was asked in 1916 to investigate daffodil eelworm, which had recently devastated some major daffodil growers' collections; he discovered that the nematodes could be controlled by a sufficient immersion in hot water. His technique not only saved the daffodil industry from anticipated demise and provided daffodil breeding with a new lease of life, but became a standard precaution in bulb growing generally, always insisted on as a preliminary to planting for trials.[57]

The aetiology of insect infestation is fairly unproblematic in the individual case, although the introduction of new pests requires some entomological research: among the new, or newly significant, pests described in the *Transactions* was the fruit tree tortrix moth, and Sir Joseph Banks devoted an article to tracing the first appearance in Britain of the 'American blight' (*Aphis*, later *Eriosoma*, *lanigera*).[58] Fungal diseases were another matter—Knight, as we have seen, regarded fungi as beneficiaries rather than causes of decline—and the concepts of bacterial and viral infection had to wait until the 1880s and the 1920s respectively. The great test case for fungal disease was the potato blight.

In 1845, reports of a disease laying waste potato fields in Belgium were quickly followed by its appearance in England, and Lindley, as editor of the *Gardeners' Chronicle*, sounded an alarm in August, the week after its first report:

> ... the disease consists in a gradual decay of the leaves and stem, which become a putrid mass, and the tubers are affected by degrees in a similar way. The first obvious sign is the appearance on the edge of the leaf of a black spot which gradually spreads; the gangrene then attacks the haulms, and in a few days the latter are decayed, emitting a peculiar and rather offensive odour. When the attack is severe the tubers also decay ... As to cure for this distemper there is none. One of our correspondents is already angry with us for not telling the public how to stop it; but he ought to consider that Man has no power to arrest the dispensations of Providence. We are visited by a great calamity which we must bear.

The first problem was to determine the cause of the infection. The Revd Miles J. Berkeley, an eminent mycologist, suggested that it was caused by a fungus; Lindley, following the example of Knight, thought the mildew observed by Berkeley was a secondary phenomenon, the fungus taking advantage of the moribund condition of the plant, and that the primary cause was excessive damp. Edward Solly supported Lindley, with additional observations on soil chemistry as a predisposing cause. Lindley published both his and Berkeley's hypotheses in the Society's new *Journal*.

The blight was bad enough in England, but in Ireland, where the potato was virtually a monoculture in large areas of the country, it stood ready to cause mass starvation. The *Gardeners' Chronicle* for 13 September carried Lindley's announcement: 'We stop the Press, with very great regret, to announce that the Potato Murrain has unequivocally declared itself in Ireland. The crops about Dublin are suddenly perishing ... where will *Ireland* be, in the event of a universal potato rot?' The answer, as the ensuing years would reveal, was: in agony, with a million dead of famine, half again that number emigrated, and despite the abolition of the Corn Laws in order to allow food imports, political consequences that continued to fester a century and a half later. Meanwhile, back in the garden, Robert Thompson was making observations on the potato crops at Chiswick, Lindley publishing theories, and both he and Berkeley scouring the literature for relevant information. Lindley gradually became more respectful of Berkeley's fungal hypothesis, although continuing to maintain that the potatoes must have been debilitated by damp in order to succumb; and he began his search for wild forms that could be used in breeding new, resistant varieties.[59]

Berkeley went on to turn his attention to onion smudge, cabbage rust, pear and vine mildew, and other diseases that he identified as caused by fungi, and gradually the weight of evidence inclined the scientific community in his favour. Between 1854 and 1857 he published a series of articles on plant pathology, 173 in all, in the *Gardeners' Chronicle* that were never reprinted in book form, but which constitute the first comprehensive treatise on the subject. In 1865 he succeeded Lindley as the editor of the Society's publications; his last major article for the *Journal* was on the hollyhock mildew that wiped out the older cultivars in the 1870s.[60] But the potato blight continued to figure in the life of the Society. In 1875 the botanical artist Worthington George Smith, having heard Berkeley refer in a lecture to some unidentified spores on infested potatoes, examined the Chiswick crop and found spores which resembled those of the white rust of mustard. He macerated some leaves under water in order to carry out tests, accidentally left some leaves in water for a week, and found that the potato fungus was growing. He announced his discovery of the resting spores of potato blight, for which he was to coin the new name *Phytophthora infestans*. The *Gardeners' Chronicle* 'heartily felicitate[d] the R.H.S. that in this period of deep depression and dire confusion, a member of its Scientific Committee should have cast so much lustre upon it'; the Society gave Smith a Knightian Medal for his achievement. But it was not long before Anton de Bary repeated his experiments, failed to replicate his results, and concluded that Smith's leaves had become independently infected by the potato blight while in the water. The controversy rumbled on for several years before de Bary's conclusion was universally accepted.[61]

Diagnosis was one thing, treatment another. Smoke had been introduced into glasshouses, and chemical agents (urine, soapsuds) sprayed over plants, for generations before the technology began to be improved in the 19th century; and even John Read, who invented the ball-valve for the horticultural syringe, also developed an improved fumigator for spreading tobacco smoke to kill insects. As for the substances used, tobacco remained the most popular insecticide into the 20th century, and in 1866 the RHS lobbied the government to remit the duty on tobacco if imported for horticultural purposes (a matter 'of the greatest importance'). Lime-sulphur and, later, Bordeaux mixture, were the main 19th-century fungicides.[62] The first new pesticides to emerge between the wars were derris dust and tar distillates; tar-oil winter washes were the first insecticides to pass the Ministry of Agriculture's new approval scheme, while the RHS undertook confidential tests of derris for the Ministry before it passed muster. Then, during and after the Second World War, came the introduction of the synthetic chemical pesticides and herbicides, DDT, Aldrin, Dieldrin, Malathion, Methoxone, and an ever-increasing stream of new products promising the gardener further eradi-cations. The RHS pathologist, George Fox Wilson, tested the new chemicals at Wisley and pronounced guardedly on their merits, pointing out that 'The fact that these preparations [specif-ically, DDT] are toxic to beneficial insects ... renders it necessary to time their application with care'.[63]

The RHS helped to publicise the new chemicals, but it equally publi-cised, and became more closely identified with, research into biological control methods. Scientists at Cheshunt Research Station discovered that greenhouse whitefly could be controlled by a parasitic insect, *Encarsia formosa*, which bred on tobacco plants; the RHS spread the news, and became the distribution agent (2s.6d. a small box, 5s. a large box), devoting an entire glasshouse to its production. The parasite was widely used until the Second World War, but was sidelined thereafter in favour of pesticides, though the RHS made a further attempt to popularise it in the 1950s, and was still selling it in the 1970s. (It has since re-emerged, and I have seen a website that markets it with the proclamation 'Finally! Relief from whitefly!')[64] As the synthetic pesticides have come under scrutiny for medical and environmental side-effects, more research has been lavished on biological control and the use of pheromones for trapping insects, with entomologist Andrew Halstead and other Wisley scientists playing their part in the investigations, as well as in finding ways of literally controlling, rather than trying to eradicate, pests. Meanwhile, pure diagnostic work

V.M. Fowler, entomologist at Wisley in the 1950s, with his colleague J. Maynard, collecting rhododendron leafhoppers.

continues, and the Wisley research programmes into armillaria and phytophthora have revealed that in each case more than one species is involved in the infections.[65]

In the 1930s the major problem with pesticides was not their composition, but their availability: when in 1931 the Pharmaceutical Society lobbied for an amendment to the Pharmacy and Poisons Bill, making chemists responsible for the sale of pesticides, the RHS campaigned against it to protect the livelihood of the nursery trade, while supporting the British Mycological Society in its demand that the contents of pesticides ought to be registered with the Ministry and not kept proprietary secrets.[66] But once the new synthetic pesticides became available, fears of their side-effects were not long in appearing. Fox Wilson's cautions about DDT were expressed within two years of its being made available on the domestic market; in 1956 Council asked F.A. Secrett to prepare a memorandum on the damage to crops from the drift of hormone sprays used for weed control, and then launched a campaign with the National Farmers' Union to bring the use of hormone sprays under control.[67] As the evidence accumulated, pressure grew not only for alternatives to pesticides, but for the removal of dangerous pesticides from the market. Beginning in 1991, a European Union initiative towards harmonising the pesticide regulations in its member states led to a review of products, and from 25 July 2003, it was no longer legal to sell unapproved products. Some 500 familiar garden chemicals are being withdrawn from the shelves as this book goes to press. The problem for horticulture is that many of them are being withdrawn not because of evidence of their deleterious effects, but because, in view of the small revenue proportion of their sales, it is inexpedient for the manufacturers to carry out the research needed to determine their safety.

> Few pesticides used on food crops in the small garden would survive because of the cost of obtaining residue data for each crop ... The RHS supports steps that are being taken to ensure that pesticides are thoroughly tested to modern standards, but is concerned that products that have given good service in gardens are being lost on economic rather than safety or environmental grounds.[68]

The Professorship of Botany

In the late 1860s, the Society was reconsidering its educational programme at its garden at Chiswick, and was also seeking to find a way of relieving Miles J. Berkeley from some of his duties on the Scientific Committee and as Editor of the *Journal*, since in 1868 he was made Vicar of Sibbertoft in Northamptonshire and plainly found the double burden of church work and RHS work in two distant places troublesome. Late in 1871, Wilson Saunders, the Secretary, was deputed to find someone who could take over sundry scientific duties, and he reported that he had found a satisfactory person in W.T. Thiselton-Dyer, Professor of Botany at the Royal College of Science in Dublin. Dyer (surname not yet hyphenated) was appointed Professor of Botany to the Society in January 1872; Saunders had spent the previous month drawing up the duties to go with the post:

> 1st. General—to conduct the scientific business of the Society both Horticultural and Botanical. To enter into communication with Horticultural and Botanical establishments at home and abroad and especially with the Societies in union with the Royal Horticultural Society [i.e. affiliated societies]. To visit the chief Horticultural and Botanical establishments near London from time to time and establishments in the country as opportunity may offer for the purpose of examining new and interesting plants and obtaining information respecting them.
>
> 2nd. South Kensington. To attend all meetings and Exhibitions of the Society and there note carefully and report upon all objects of merit for publication by the Society. To aid the Revd. M. J. Berkeley at the Wednesday meetings ... To be at the Offices one afternoon in each week for the purpose of answering any scientific enquiries as may be made by the Fellows. To edit the publications of the Society. To give a series of Lectures on subjects connected with scientific horticulture to the Fellows and others during the season as the Council may direct. To take charge of the Library and look to its increase. To report the names of all plants exhibited at the Exhibitions and Wednesday meetings that may be found with wrong botanical names.
>
> 3rd. Chiswick. To take care that all plants of Botanical interest be properly named. To inspect all scientific experiments made in the garden, to report the results and offer suggestions for further experiments relative to scientific horticulture and the growth of plants. To be present one afternoon each week to give information on such points as may be necessary to Fellows and gardeners of Fellows and to receive from them plants which may require botanical names. To give a series of Lectures each year to the students in the Garden and the Gardeners of Fellows on Scientific horticulture and botany. To report monthly on the meteorological observations made in the garden. To form one of the Horticultural Board of Directors.

Dyer may have helped edit the *Journal*, but documentation is insufficient to establish exactly what if anything he did along these lines; he did administer the Lindley Library. He may have found the range of duties onerous; in 1875, he relinquished the post in order to become Assistant Director of Kew (and of course, eventually, Director).[69]

After a slight hiatus, George Henslow was appointed Professor of Botany in 1880. At the time he held no official post as a botanist; not until 1886 would he become Lecturer in Botany at St Bartholomew's Hospital; but he was the son of the eminent naturalist John Stevens Henslow, and had published on botanical matters. The duties were more or less the same as in Dyer's case, apart from the Library, and the only volume of the *Journal* he edited was that for 1880. His post as Professor of Botany was initially a matter of a renewable one-year contract, and 'termination of Prof. Henslow's duties' crops up regularly for a while in Council minutes, without any formal announcement that they were recommenced in between. One of his eventual duties was to use plants exhibited at the shows for botanical demonstrations. This custom began by accident in 1895, when he was called in at short notice to substitute for Thiselton-Dyer, who could not deliver his scheduled lecture. Henslow delivered a 'conversational discourse' about some of the plants exhibited; the result was so well received that his talks became first an annual, and then a monthly, event. The points to which he repeatedly returned included evolutionary adaptations in plant structure, the doubling of flowers and other abnormalities, the relations between ancestral species and their hybrid descendants, and the procedures involved in hybridisation. Many of these talks, from 1895 to 1901, were published in the *Journal*.

Henslow's duties wound down during the First World War, when the educational programme at Wisley was to a great extent put into abeyance. In 1919 Dr A.B. Rendle, the Keeper of Botany at the Natural History Museum, agreed to succeed Henslow, and give 'horticultural-botanical lectures at every alternate fortnightly meeting when they were resumed at Vincent Square'. When Rendle died, the Professorship was held in turn by Sir William Wright Smith, the Keeper of the Royal Botanic Garden, Edinburgh, and then by two successive Directors of Kew: Sir Edward Salisbury and Sir George Taylor. Sir George Taylor's duties in that capacity were effectively nominal in his last years, the educational programme at Wisley having changed; and in 1994 Professor David Ingram was appointed Professor, not of Botany, but of Horticulture.[70]

From research to advisory services

The first years of the Wisley Laboratory were a great success in terms of public image: the School of Horticulture had started, trials were being organised, Chittenden's experiments with Nitro-Bacterine were acclaimed. Sir Isaac Bayley Balfour made a report on scientific activity that resulted in Frederick Keeble being made Director, and Gerald W. Butcher was able to claim in 1914 that 'The Royal Horticultural Society's gardens at Wisley form a landmark in the progress of horticulture, not alone in this country or in Europe, but of the whole world'. Dissenting voices were heard, most notably an anonymous pamphlet, issued on the announcement of the extension of the Laboratory, arguing that 'the Society is ill-advised to build a costly laboratory for experiments of doubtful value'; but such criticisms had no impact. Work was interrupted by the war; in 1919, while Keeble considered his future, Chittenden was appointed Assistant Director and then succeeded him as Director. Within a couple of years he had an excellent scientific team: Norman Gould as Assistant Botanist, George Fox Wilson as Entomologist (succeeding Maxwell-Lefroy, whose wartime lectures on insect infestations and compost heaps terrified his audiences, and who was soon to found Rentokil), and as mycologist W.J. Dowson, the future author of the *Manual of Bacterial Plant Diseases*. Chittenden, however, found it hard to relinquish his former functions, effectively combining his former role as Director of the Laboratory with his new one of Director of the Garden; it was not until 1927 that the Laboratory had a separate Keeper. By the 1930s the press was asking uncomfortable questions about Wisley's finances, and the list of scientific achievements that had emerged from Wisley, with the hot-water treatment for daffodil eelworm at the top of the list, did not seem to justify either the hype or the expenditure. Two internal committees met during the 1920s to discuss the organisation of the scientific work, and in 1930 a reorganisation of higher staff resulted in Chittenden being moved to London. The immediate response of the press was to see the move as evidence that the 'advisory services have grown at such a pace as to require the whole-time services of an experienced horticulturist'.[71]

Meanwhile, the number of horticultural research stations around the country was increasing. Sir John Bennet Lawes's estate at Rothamsted had been bequeathed to the government as a research centre for soil science; the National Fruit and Cider Institute had been established at Long Ashton in 1905, followed by East Malling;

The primitive beginnings of the advisory stand, at the 1913 Chelsea Flower Show. S.T. Wright, Director of Wisley, is second from the left; H.R. Hutchinson, the Librarian, stands at the rear wearing a bowler.

The advisory stand at the Chelsea Flower Show, ninety years later: the shelves behind the advisers contain advisory leaflets for distribution in particular cases.

Cheshunt had been opened in 1915. In 1932, fresh from the excitement of hosting the International Horticultural Congress, Council had grand visions of the Society's future position:

> The R.H.S. of to-day represents the hub of everything appertaining to horticulture ... the existing research station at Wisley should be appointed to act as the Central Horticultural Research & Distributing Station of the U.K.

It was not to be. Financial depression and criticisms of Wisley, including a detailed dissection of its accounts by the *Gardeners' Chronicle*, all lessened the enthusiasm. Scientific expenditure was cut back in the late 1930s, and the dream of glory replaced by membership in a joint committee with the Agricultural Research Council. Indeed, by 1948 the Society had swung so far in the other direction that it campaigned against J.D. Bernal's proposals for centralised co-ordination of scientific publication.[72]

In the aftermath of the Second World War, a series of discussions, committees, and reports examined the question of scientific work at Wisley. In 1945, M.A.H. Tincker, the Keeper of the Laboratory, proposed that its main efforts should lie in chemicals, mycology, entomology, the general collation of data from Fellows and other enquirers, and meeting special requests from affiliated societies. Already the idea of a centrally directed research programme was being dented by the emphasis on responding to outside requests. In 1949, Sir George Taylor chaired a committee which recommended cutting back on the chemical work, keeping the cytology department together because of the colchicine research, and concentrating on advisory work (a few years later C.D. Darlington was consulted about the cytological work, and said he couldn't see the point of it; it was disbanded). In 1956, a committee consisting of R.H. Stoughton, F.A. Secrett, Eric Savill, and Sir Frederick Stern looked at the scientific staff structure, noted that the mycologist and the entomologist had only a single assistant between them, and suggested that instead of employing specialists, Wisley should employ 'a general practitioner': 'research elsewhere was practically confined to the comparatively few plants which were grown extensively commercially and ... only at Wisley was attention paid to the cultural problems and diseases of the vast majority of ornamental plants commonly grown in gardens'. Enquiries beyond the scope of this staffing arrangement should be re-routed to the research stations, whose number had grown further: the National Vegetable Research Station and the Glasshouse Crops Research Institute had

A view in the pathology laboratory at Wisley, 2003.

both been set up, while the Ministry of Agriculture was developing a network of stations around the country. Firmer links were further being made with research centres abroad, and in 1959 the RHS helped to establish the International Society for Horticultural Science.[73]

When in 1964 it was debated whether there should be a glasshouse reserved for the researches of the entomologist, 'It was emphasised that the function of the scientific staff was advisory and that investigations should stem from problems arising out of this work'. Finally, in 1966, a further committee was appointed to enquire into the scientific staff structure, and reported itself divided over the desirability of research.

> (1) That with the material received and available at Wisley there was scope for important scientific investigations ... (2) That there was no need for a formal scientific establishment at Wisley; that enquiries were on recurrent topics, which could be answered by a series of duplicated leaflets ...

Sir George Taylor dismissively remarked that 'Wisley had acquired a veneer of research', and was opposed by Stoughton. John Gilmour, the former Director, predicted an outcry if the existing services to Fellows changed: 'Without qualified personnel, i.e., if they were replaced by general purpose horticulturists the service would involve snap decisions, mistakes, and delays. Was it not to be accepted that Wisley, by employing young scientists who might move on, was providing a further service to horticulture generally, in offering facilities to obtain valuable practical experience of good stead in their later research studies.' And with that, the matter was

Harold Roy Fletcher (1907-1978) was a botanist at Aberdeen before he joined the RHS, and an authority on primulas and rhododendrons. In 1954 he left the RHS for the Royal Botanic Garden Edinburgh, eventually rising to the position of Keeper.

settled for over twenty years: scientific work at Wisley existed as a support for the advisory services. 'The priorities of the Scientific Staff should be first to answer questions from Fellows, then to instruct the student gardeners.'[74]

The Advisory Services had grown continually since the 1890s, when Augustus Voelcker had first been hired to analyse soil samples for Fellows. An information bureau had been set up to give advice at the Chelsea Flower Show, and as it became better organised it was rejoiced over by the press: 'There was a suggestion of "your troubles are my troubles" at the Bureau, and many worried ones departed bearing the expression of having just acquired a new and sympathetic friend.' Progressively, in the post-war years, as new services like chromosome counts, initially free of charge, were added, Wisley's lines of scientific work had already become integrated into the advisory structure. Service to members became such an article of faith that it came as a rude shock to many staff, later in the century, to find that advisory services are not a charitable object. By that time the work of disseminating advice had to led to an abortive attempt at offering recorded telephone advice through a 'Gardencall' system, and the development of a large number of continuously updated advice sheets sent out by the staff.[75]

During the 1980s, the network of scientific research stations that had grown up around the country began to unravel. The National Fruit Trials were discontinued; East Malling, the National Vegetable Research Station at Wellesbourne, and the Glasshouse Crops Research Institute were amalgamated into a quango called, first, the British Society for Horticultural Research, and later, Horticultural Research International, with the GCRI site closed down; county horticultural stations like Probus and Rosewarne were closed; eventually even Long Ashton was closed, and its functions transferred to Rothamsted. In 2003, funding for East Malling was cut, and the RHS protested to the government. As central funding was progressively discontinued, the RHS began urgently re-examining its scientific programmes: should it try to take on the research that was being abandoned? Committees chaired by Derek Fuller and Ghillean Prance deliberated on the future of research and advisory services; it was agreed that 'filling the research gap left by MAFF' was unrealistic, that the Society should concentrate on development and 'near market' research only, and that while it should revive some of its former abandoned functions—e.g., hiring a soil scientist—it should remember that its greatest strength was in horticultural taxonomy. In 2002, for the first time

in generations, the Society hired a horticultural scientist who was not engaged to be an adviser (and who was stationed at Reading University). After four years of debate, the Society decided in 1995 to try to relieve its over-burdened staff by introducing a charge for advisory services to non-members; ironically, the burden was reduced only temporarily, the rate of enquiries increased, and by the beginning of the 21st century they had reached their former frequency, with more than 45,000 received each year (not counting a third again that number taken at shows).[76]

Conservation of the environment

Harold Fletcher, giving the closing address at the 17th International Horticultural Congress in 1966, offered this vision of the future:

> Who doubts for a moment, for instance, that there will be further additions to the bewildering array of new weed killers, fungicides and insecticides, systemic and otherwise; that there will be additions to our knowledge of plant disease control by antibiotics; that disease-resistant cultivars of fruits, vegetables, and ornamentals, with other desirable qualities, will be bred; additions to our knowledge of the mechanism by which light, for instance, controls such plant responses as the germination of light-sensitive seeds, the growth of seedlings and the regulation of flowering? Who doubts that leaf analysis techniques will add to our knowledge of tree nutrition; that radioactive chemicals will be used more and more to trace the absorption, translocation and utilization of nutrients in plants; that gamma radiation will be used to modify plant growth and effect gene changes; that growth regulators will be increasingly used to hybridize plants which previously have refused to cross; that fertile hybrids will be induced from chemically produced polyploids? Such advances in our knowledge are absolutely inevitable.[77]

Fletcher did not foresee what might be called Nature's response: that pests and disease-causing organisms would prove increasingly resistant to the onslaught of chemical agents; that weed-killers, fungicides and insecticides would be raked off the shelves in the name of public safety; that the English landscape would be altered by epidemic disease, and that at the beginning of the 21st century each succeeding year would bring its moment of panic as yet another epidemic was found waiting offstage; that chastened pathologists would increasingly recommend living peaceably with the enemy rather than trying to extirpate it; that the gene changes he predicted would come to pass with a more precise technology than gamma radiation, but would result in public outcry, rioting, and political dispute.

Fears about the loss of wild plants are hardly new. In 1864, the Society announced a competition for amateur botanical collections, in order 'to encourage and extend the study of British botany throughout the country'; the prize would go to the most complete collection of dried specimens of a given county's flora. Council was not prepared for the outcry. Sir William Hooker organised a petition at Kew, signed by himself and his son, Daniel Oliver, John Smith, Thomas Thomson, and George Bentham, complaining that 'it must result in the wholesale destruction of those rarer plants of the country which all lovers of botany desire to see in their native stations'. Groups of botanists in Manchester and Norwich organised similar testimonials; the largest petition was organised by Professor Charles Babington in Cambridge, and boasted 125 signatures, including those of Charles Darwin, Miles J. Berkeley, and Maxwell T. Masters; John Stuart Mill, who had signed Babington's petition, also sent in an individual remonstrance begging the Society to restrict the terms of the competition to the commoner species of the county. A chastened Council amended the terms to exclude rare plants, and limit the size of the collections to 200 specimens.[78]

The perceived threat was the amateur collector: the loss of ferns, in particular, was well documented by the end of the 19th century, but there was no serious call for protection by legislation until the First World War. In the 1920s, the RHS backed campaigns for wild flower preservation, and appointed Chittenden as its representative on the Wild Plant Observation Board set up by the Council for the Protection of Rural England. Even so, when after the Second World War the government attempted to forbid the sale of certain categories of wild flowers by nurseries, the Horticultural Trades Association tried to get the RHS to organise a protest, as being a more experienced campaigning organisation; and the 1953 Agricultural Land (Removal of Surface Soil) Act was greeted with immediate concern that it might endanger the supply of loam.[79] The most curious campaign to which the RHS lent its voice in the inter-war years was started by the weekly magazine *The Field*, to try to organise the eradication of grey squirrels from Britain, as invasive aliens that were driving the native red squirrel into extinction. (As anyone can see, that campaign didn't work.)[80]

In the immediate wake of the war, the danger to wildlife of DDT was balanced, as a subject of anxiety, by the danger of the indiscriminate flowering of brassicas in disused allotments and waste ground (as a source of uncontrolled pollination for market crops).[81] The extent of environmental deterioration took a long time to sink in. In 1928, a special award was offered at Chelsea for rock gardens using other materials than mountain limestone; but this was purely on aesthetic grounds, to break a growing uniformity, and Council made the proviso, 'while not wishing in any way to discourage the use of mountain limestone'. At its Conservation Conference in 1977, the future of limestone pavements was announced as a subject for concern; even so, it was not until the 1990s that the European Community Habitats Directive listed limestone pavements as a priority habitat. The geologist Eric Robinson published a warning piece in *The Garden*, putting the blame for the current loss rate on unscrupulous suppliers of garden stonework, and recommending a return to the making of artificial-stone rock gardens once associated with the firm of Pulham and Son.[82]

In the 1970s, the Society began increasing its publicity for conservation issues; the Conservation Conference in 1978 led to the creation of the NCCPG, but was about nature conservation as well as the conservation of gardens and garden plants. Pollution was then a greater issue than peat. When legislation to prevent the destruction of sphagnum was first essayed in the 1950s, the Society's response was to complain about confusion in the regulations; peat had by then emerged as the major constituent of the best commercial potting composts (the John Innes range, and the newer loam-free composts), and an increasing industry depended on its harvesting. By 1991, it was estimated that there were 1.6 million hectares of peatland in Great Britain, but possibly no more than 10,000 hectares untouched and active. The Friends of the Earth and other organisations launched intensive campaigns in 1990 demanding that the horticultural use of peat be stopped, and the RHS came under pressure to fall in line. Its response was to conduct trials of peat-free composts, to find out what alternatives could be used with similar success. At Wisley, Ray Waite was already using primarily loam-based composts, so the transition was not difficult: trials of peatless or low-peat composts were carried out with containerised plants in the early 1990s, with promising results, but by 1993 Michael Pollock was forced to report that 'observations and assessments at Wisley of a selection of growing media for containerised plants have not identified products as universally reliable for amateur use as John Innes-type composts or peat-based formulations'. Ironically, despite the highly visible campaigning, the use of peat by domestic gardeners increased by 46 per cent between 1993 and 1999, probably because of ignorance of the contents of the commercially available composts. By the beginning of the 21st century, the National Trust was phasing out the use of peat in all its gardens, and launching its own peat-free compost range; the use of peat at Hyde Hall and Rosemoor had been ended; and the experiments in trying to find effective peat substitutes were continuing. Even what was quaintly becoming known as 'humanure' was tested at Wisley, but 'with unsatisfactory results'.[83]

By the mid-1990s, the RHS was developing an increasing number of conservation policies, and producing leaflets to explain them to the public: by 1995 there were 17 such leaflets, covering such various subjects as the prohibition of products made from endangered hardwoods, through water-saving practices and energy conservation in greenhouses, to the restrictions on the planting of invasive plants. Recycling and the use of domestic compost were heavily promoted by the Society, to reach a minor crisis in 2002 when two different government departments produced conflicting recommendations: on the one hand, that domestic gardeners be encouraged to compost as much household waste as possible, and on the other, that composting be restricted to prevent the spread of contagious diseases. The shock of the foot-and-mouth outbreak the year before, which came close to closing the Chelsea Flower Show,

was still felt. The eventual resolution was that domestic composting was not dangerous and should be encouraged.[84]

By the 1990s, the concept of biodiversity had become a major goal of the conservation movement, amid much ambiguity about what exactly it entailed. (Did nematodes count?) Increasingly, gardens were judged for their wildlife populations, and in 1995, to highlight the trend, an award-winning wildlife garden created at Chelsea by the Royal Society for the Protection of Birds was re-erected as a model garden at Wisley. 'The Society', read a policy statement issued that year, 'actively supports moves to maintain a varied population of fauna, by promoting through its Advisory Service knowledge of the natural role, life-cycle, habitat and other requirements of a wide range of species.' At Wisley, a wildlife enhancement project was carried out along the edge of the river Wey; at Rosemoor and Hyde Hall, experiments in encouraging native plants such as orchids were carried out; in 2002 the RHS convened a Biodiversity Conference with the RSPB and the County Wildlife Trusts to find ways of promoting the use of domestic gardens as protected environments for native species. Green spaces in towns had once been promoted as urban lungs, combatting the spread of air pollution; now they were becoming wildlife havens, with the backing of the government, which was making Biodiversity Action Plans compulsory in every county.[85]

14 *The Orchard and Kitchen Garden*

Thomas Andrew Knight, the Society's second President, had already begun devoting himself to the development of new fruit varieties before the end of the 18th century. When he drew up the initial statement of the Society's objectives for publication in the first instalment of the *Transactions*, he singled out the improvement of fruit as an area of experiment:

> ... almost every ameliorated variety of fruit appears to have been the offspring of accident, or of culture applied to other purposes. We may therefore infer, with little danger of error, that an ample and unexplored field for future discovery and improvement lies before us, in which nature does not appear to have formed any limits to the success of our labours, if properly applied ...[1]

Knight's incentive lay in the fear that existing varieties of fruits had a limited life span, and would soon need to be replaced. Reports of the declining quality of one of the most famous of English apples, the 'Ribston Pippin', and of various other fruits, led Knight to conclude that a variety, like an individual, had a determinate life-span. This was not entirely a new idea—Alexander Hunter had suggested fourteen years as the natural longevity of a variety—but it was Knight who popularised it, and acted on it. In fact, he was reasoning from incorrect premises. Most tree fruits were propagated by grafting, and Knight thought that all grafts were the same age as the parent tree from which the material had first been propagated. The deterioration in cultivars is now deemed more likely to result from using diseased stock than from inherent ageing.[2]

But Knight's hypothesis, while false, was fruitful. His success in the 1790s in breeding annuals gave him the confidence to proceed with experiments on apples and grapes, with the encouragement of Sir Joseph Banks. And during the years of his Presidency of the Society, he introduced an impressive number of new varieties of apples,

peaches, pears, plums, cherries, currants, grapes, and strawberries. In the years 1815-18 he was awarded Large Silver Medals for three cherry cultivars, 'Black Eagle', 'Waterloo', and 'Elton', and was so proud of the last two that he sent a box of them to the Queen; all three were still around in the mid-20th century (seven of his cherry trees still survived at Downton in the 1920s). His apple 'Spring Grove Codlin', named after Banks's garden, is in the Brogdale collection (if true to name). Some of his currants survived into the 20th century, as did his plum 'Ickworth Imperatrice', used for drying. His strawberries 'Elton' and 'Downton' are no longer extant, but were the ancestors of the modern large-fruited forms. But more important than the individual varieties is the incentive he provided, effectively inaugurating the modern age of fruit breeding.[3]

The fruit collection at Chiswick

Articles on fruit outnumber those on any other subject in the early volumes of the *Transactions*, and fruits similarly outnumbered all other categories of plants exhibited at the Society's meetings, especially in the years after the Napoleonic wars. Most of these exhibits were of collections of fruits designed to show quality in cultivation, but new varieties were also brought forward; the most important of these, in the years before the establishment of the Chiswick garden, were Michael Keens' strawberry 'Keens' Seedling', and 'Williams' Bon Chrétien' pear, still familiar in our supermarkets today. Prizes were offered for new fruit and vegetable varieties.[4]

In 1815, the Society started its first important research programme: the resolution of synonymy in fruit varieties. When a variety could be authenticated—new introduction, collected specimen, original tree identified from which grafts were propagated—it had its portrait painted, as a basis for comparison with other claimants to the name, or with other named sorts suspected to be identical. William Hooker, the principal artist for the Society's *Transactions*, was assigned the task of making the portraits; during the course of this work he was also to collaborate with R.A. Salisbury, one of the Society's founders, on a *Pomona Londinensis* (1818). Hooker made a total of 138 fruit portraits, engraving some of them as illustrations for the *Transactions*, and on occasion writing the descriptions of new varieties for publication. In 1820 Hooker had a stroke, and his rate of work fell off; he had already enquired the previous year about another artist for the Society, so perhaps the 1820 stroke was not the first. By 1822 an apprentice named Samuel Galloway was acting for him in his dealings with the Society; in 1823 he was confined, and his effects sold. Although Hooker had agreed that the plates were the Society's property, they were included in this sale; Sabine tried to purchase them but failed. Hooker died in 1827.[5] He had meanwhile been succeeded as fruit artist by Charles John Robertson, Barbara Cotton, and Augusta Innes Withers in succession, but none of them produced the quantity of plates that Hooker had done; the project was winding down, as the Society now had an alternative to portraiture as a means of comparing varieties.

Even before the Society had a garden, it received fruit trees as gifts, a notable example being the 'Seckle' pear sent from America by David Hosack (still available today), and purchased others from foreign nurserymen, especially Dubreuil of Rouen, Van Mons of Louvain, and Noisette of Paris, whose pears and other fruits were highly regarded and frequently found superior to those commonly grown in England. The plants thus received were effectively farmed out to selected recipients for planting and appraisal. In 1818, for example, a shipment of fruit trees from Noisette was distributed as follows: two of each sort for the Society, and the others distributed to Kew, Hampton Court, Cumberland Lodge, Sir Joseph Banks, T.A. Knight, and then to various named nurseries and private estates. By 1820 the authors of papers on new fruits were being pestered by Fellows asking for cuttings, 'to an extent which made it a serious evil', and the Society had to warn its members to make their enquiries through nurseries. (One raiser of a new apple, unwilling to distribute it, returned his award.)[6] It was in large part the problem of

The interior of the great conservatory at Chiswick after it had been turned into a vinery.

accommodating these plants, even in the short term, that determined Council to acquire its first garden in Kensington. But once the Society had a larger garden in Chiswick, Council raised its sights; it now had the space to compile reference collections of fruits, and synonymy could henceforth be checked by comparing the fruits with each other rather than with portraits.

The Chiswick garden had 'one of the most favourable soils in England for fruits', and the Society made the most of this advantage. Between 1823 and 1826 an impressive collection of varieties was planted: 'at no period, nor under any circumstances, has such a collection been before formed'. By 1826, the year of the first published catalogue, 3,825 cultivars had been identified, and there were nearly 1,000 others still in the process of authentication. (Successive editions appeared in 1831 and 1842.) The work of compiling the catalogue devolved on the garden staff, and in particular on Robert Thompson, who was appointed undergardener in the fruit department in 1826. His first duty was the classification of the cherries, apricots, and gooseberries. Fifty-seven cherry cultivars had fruited in time for the catalogue, and Thompson classified them according to leaf shape and fruit characters; some seventy gooseberries he grouped into two broad categories, the Old English and the Lancashire (he also reported that the gooseberries were more often true to name than other fruits, thanks to the activities of the gooseberry shows and societies). Pears, it was discovered, appeared 'not less different in the earliness or lateness of their foliation and inflorescence, than in the leaves and shoots'. By 1830 Thompson's fame was spreading. Loudon reported in that year that 'he has taught himself both the French and German languages, in order to be able to read foreign works on fruits'.

The immediate result of the catalogue was the identification of massive synonymy in the names of fruits available in commerce. Over seventy named apricot cultivars were reduced to 17; 176 nectarines to 19; 182 to 99 grapes. The press resounded with enthusiasm. The catalogue was 'a master-piece of statistical information on the subject of the orchard'. 'For every fruit we have an opinion, and, for the most part, a very sound one, of its quality, its appearance, habit, and general characteristics; and, above all, the many names under which it has been sold to the public. And this information has been obtained by experiment.' Loudon urged everyone to apply to Chiswick for grafts of correctly named fruits, in order 'to effect a fundamental reformation in the nomenclature of European fruits wherever they

A group of apples from Hugh Ronalds's Pyrus Malus Brentfordiensis *(1831):* 'Striped Juneating' *(synonym for* 'Margaret'), 'Summer Oslin' *(not distinct from* 'Oslin'), 'Kerry Pippin', 'Summer Pippin' *(properly* 'Summer Golden Pippin'), 'Tartarian Crab', *and* 'Duchess of Oldenburg'.

are cultivated'. Nurserymen, he predicted, 'will now feel the absolute necessity of beginning *de novo* with their lists of pears, and getting their grafts from the Chiswick garden. In ten years, it will not be the fault of the Horticultural Society, if there is one bad sort of pear sold in the streets of any town in the island.'[7]

Council's first thought had been to publish a pomona, a monograph on fruits, but the scale of the operation meant that nothing larger than the Catalogue appeared under the Society's auspices. Lindley, however, made a stab at an augmented work, and for three years published a *Pomological Magazine*, using Mrs Withers as his artist, and occasionally re-drawn versions of plates from the Society's fruit drawings. (He later re-issued the work under the title of *Pomona Britannica*.) In the same years, a member of Council, Hugh Ronalds, the Brentford nurseryman, compiled a work on apples, the *Pyrus Malus Brentfordiensis*, which was published in 1831, describing and illustrating 180 cultivars. Neither work could have been produced without using the collections at Chiswick, but neither was directly sponsored by the Society.[8]

It is safe to say that it was the *Catalogue of Fruits* that first established the Society's reputation both nationally and internationally, before the work of its major plant collectors bacame known. All through its subsequent reverses of finance and controversies over management, the massive achievement of the fruit collections was held up as both the standard it should be trying to maintain, and the reason why it should not be allowed to succumb. Not that the collection would remain exempt from threat and alarm.

Tropical fruits

The fruit collection at Chiswick was not confined to the hardy fruits growing in the open air. The drawings by Hooker and his successors included melons, pineapples, mangoes, and these and other tender fruits were the first subjects grown in the Society's glasshouses.

As early as 1822, John Lindley was awarded a medal for a paper on the best tropical fruits for the kitchen garden. The same year, Stamford Raffles sent tropical fruits from Singapore, and George Don returned to England with a collection of fruits from Sierra Leone; these latter were greeted with enthu-

1. Striped Juneating
2. Summer Oslin
3. Kerry Pippin
4. Summer Pippin
5. Tartarian Crab
6. Duchess of Oldenburgh

siasm as possible additions for the dessert-table. Lindley and Knight were to turn their attention to Persian melons and their classification, and Knight experimented further with mangoes and cherimoyas.[9] Curiously, despite the long tradition of growing citrus fruits under protected cultivation in England, the Society never accumulated a great collection of oranges or lemons; the only significant publication on the subject to appear in its publications was a late article by Robert Fortune on his celebrated introduction, the kumquat.[10]

Great uncertainty still clouds the introduction of the pineapple into England, but during the 1760s the first two practical manuals on pineapple culture in English appeared. With several varieties being grown in the Caribbean colonies, it is not surprising that English gardeners came to vie in their cultivation at home, and as late as the Edwardian period, long after direct import had superseded glasshouse cropping for the English market, it could still be said that the real standard for judging a gardener was his ability to grow pineapples. For more than a decade, pineapples formed one of the most prestigious features of the Chiswick garden. In 1825 the Garden Committee reported that an 'extensive collection' had been formed in the last year; this included the range of 'new and apparently distinct varieties from Sierra Leone, selected by Mr. George Don, when botanizing in that colony'. In 1831 Donald Munro (normally in charge of ornamental plants) classified the collection in a 34-page report for the *Transactions*, listing over 450 named sorts, which he reduced to 52 distinct cultivars. And then, once the work had been done, the collection was sold at auction, on the rather spurious grounds that it had served its taxonomic purpose. 'No act of the Horticultural Society', wrote Loudon, 'has been viewed by us with more regret than the dispersion of this collection, unequalled in the world.'[11]

During the 1840s and 1850s, while the Society's exchequer crumbled, it continued to publish articles on tropical fruit culture, but they mainly represented the work of private individuals. Robert Schomburgk, the plant collector, wrote a report on West Indian fruits suitable for England, but the Society did not undertake to grow them experimentally. James Bateman emerged as the greatest enthusiast for introducing new varieties, trying starfruit and bananas in his glasshouses at Knypersley Hall in Staffordshire, and as long as he was on Council or otherwise active in the Society's affairs, the interest in tropical fruits was to some extent sustained.[12] But with the sale of exotic plants from Chiswick in 1857, and the conversion of the great conservatory to a vinery, it

was apparent that the Society had largely abandoned its former interest in the subject, beyond the offer of prizes for exhibits.

The Fruit Committee

The 1850s were a hard time in the Chiswick garden, and the fruit collections were not exempt from the general tightening of belts. Robert Thompson, the Superintendent of the Fruit Department, was increasingly compelled to devote his energies to growing fruit for sale rather than for study, and to dig over parts of the orchard for turnips. When most of the existing stock of the *Catalogue of Fruits* was sold off, and instead of a new edition there was merely a supplement in the 1853 Journal, it definitely seemed that the Society had retrenched on its former commitment.

In 1854 came the announcement that a new organisation, the British Pomological Society, had been formed, with the purpose of promoting fruit culture generally, and more specifically of gathering information about local variations in the hardiness and productiveness of fruits, 'and all the contingencies of varied exposures, altitude, and difference of soil, [which] have to be taken into consideration'. The President was the Horticultural Society's former gardener Sir Joseph Paxton; its Secretary, John Spencer, the head gardener at Bowood, who had recently published an account of his vineries in the *Journal*; its frequent Chairman, Robert Hogg, the former nurseryman who would soon publish the first version of his *Fruit Manual*. The gardening press remarked that its creation would have been unnecessary

> if, as was the case in former years, the [Horticultural] Society made a point of procuring both at home and from abroad the new varieties of fruits as they appear, and proving their adaptability, or non-adaptability, to the climate of this country, instead of idly waiting till somebody sends them 'one or two new things' ... [and behaving] as if there were no plants worth cultivating but Orchids, and as if there were no world outside the walls of Chiswick Gardens. A Pomological Society will correct these errors, and supply these deficiencies ...

(The reference to orchids was transparently a dig at Lindley, the father of orchidology.)[13]

The Horticultural Society responded to the challenge. In 1856, it called John Spencer into consultation on the improvement of its garden at Chiswick; one of his recommendations was to reorganise the orchard for fruit trials. Thompson, who only a few months before was being made to count every penny over hiring labourers to prune

Robert Hogg (1818-1897). Nurseryman and editor of the Journal of Horticulture. *Author of* The Fruit Manual *(1860, and later editions to 1884), the greatest guide to fruit varieties in Britain ever published; co-author of the* Herefordshire Pomona *(1876-85). Secretary of the RHS, 1875-84. Died before he could receive the VMH.*

the peaches, was given new powers as an Inspector of Fruits. In July 1857 a 'Pomological Committee' was appointed, consisting of John Spencer, the Hammersmith nurseryman John Lee, and the publisher Henry Bohn, the first two stalwarts of the British Pomological Society. Within a few months this little committee was reprimanded for having failed to meet, and no record survives of what, if anything, it actually did, though Donald Beaton remarked, 'To keep the Pomological Society on its manners, we have instituted a "Pomological Committee", to whose skill and judgment every new fruit will be referred in Regent Street'. One Council member, the Revd Vernon Harcourt, proposed the creation of local committees, wherever two or more could gather in the Society's name, to correspond with the central executive on fruit matters; he amended this to a proposal for a questionnaire on apples, pears, peaches, and nectarines that could be circulated nationwide; the questionnaire that did get circulated was a proposal for the formation of a Fruit Committee. The replies were overwhelmingly in favour, and the move was welcomed in the gardening press.

The Fruit Committee, the Society's first Standing Committee, was officially inaugurated on 5 July 1858. Its purposes were stated in Council Minutes ten days later as: 'examining and reporting upon all fruits or esculents brought under their notice; collecting information concerning the qualities of the Fruits grown in different parts of the United Kingdom, and advising the Council generally as to the best modes of increasing the Society's power of promoting the improvement of Fruits and Esculents cultivated in Great Britain and Ireland.' Its membership comprised landowners, head gardeners, and nurserymen; Vernon Harcourt was its first Chairman, and Robert Thompson the first Secretary. It also, more to the point, included Robert Hogg and John Spencer, who made up the entire administration of the British Pomological Society, thus—once the Committee had demonstrated some efficacy—making that Society redundant; by the summer of 1860 it was in debt, and that autumn its affairs were wound up. It had effectively been merged with the Fruit Committee. In the long term, its major contribution during its independent life was the publicising of the new apple 'Cox's Orange Pippin', introduced into commerce by Charles Turner of the Royal Nurseries, Slough.[14]

In 1859, the committee was renamed the Fruit and Vegetable Committee, and three additional members brought on board because of special

John Spencer (1809-1881). Head gardener at Bowood, Wiltshire, where he designed the arboretum. Founder and secretary of the British Pomological Society. Joint proprietor of The Florist *(1854-62); contributor to* Gardeners' Chronicle.

2. Cox's Orange Pippin.

The apple 'Cox's Orange Pippin', as depicted in the Herefordshire Pomona, *by Robert Hogg and Bull. Introduced into commerce by Charles Turner of the Royal Nurseries, Slough, during the 1850s.*

expertise with vegetables. Over the succeeding years, its membership was to include the Commissioners of Horticulture Sir William Lobjoit and H.V. Taylor, head gardeners such as James Hudson of Gunnersbury and Edwin Beckett of Aldenham, nurserymen such as Clucas, Laxton, and Rivers, and ten of the original Victoria Medallists. It also, more than most committees, brushed the fringes of literature; one of the original members, the Revd Archer Clive, was the husband of the poet and novelist Caroline Clive ('V'), and R.D. Blackmore, the author of *Lorna Doone*, acted as Chairman in 1889.[15]

Fruit shows and conferences

Robert Hogg succeeded Robert Thompson as Secretary of the Fruit and Vegetable Committee in 1860, subject to Council reconsidering the question of preparing new editions of the fruit catalogue—even if, in the event, the new edition was serialised in the *Proceedings* rather than appearing as a separate publication. Hogg left in 1864, and Thomas Moore made a stab at being Secretary of both the Fruit and Floral Committees simultaneously, but within a couple of months the Committee demanded Hogg's return. Hogg was to serve for some years as Secretary of the Society as a whole, but despite periods of absence, he kept returning to the Fruit Committee, as member, Secretary, or Chairman, even during those periods when he and Council vied to see who could be the bigger thorn in the other's side. During these years he revised his *Fruit Manual* into a fifth edition (1884), by which time it had become the largest and most comprehensive survey of British fruits ever compiled (and found time for a plagiarism suit against John Scott of Merriott, who helped himself to some of Hogg's descriptions in his *Orchardist*). In 1906, near the end of his life, Hogg offered the Society the copyright of the *Fruit Manual*, but Council was unwilling to take the responsibility of publishing it. After Hogg's death, E.A. Bunyard proposed that the Society issue a supplement, but this was deemed 'inefficient'. In the end, Bunyard was to compile his own *Handbook of Hardy Fruits*, in two volumes, to made good the Society's deficiency.[16]

Meanwhile, the fruit collections at Chiswick had both suffered and improved. In 1857, George M'Ewen had converted the great conservatory into a vinery, with a collection of 25 different varieties once the synonyms had been reduced, and soon it became famous as the largest reference collection of grape varieties in the country, 'a real temple of Pomona'. The recurrent process of lifting the roots and thinning the vines was always

described in superlatives: a 'Herculean task', 'an almost stupendous work'. At the beginning of the 1870s, the garden was reduced by some two-thirds of its size, and much of the reference collection of fruit trees passed into domestic back gardens or was destroyed altogether. But Archibald Barron, who had now become Superintendent, was determined to return it to its former glory as a centre for the study of fruit; he transferred what was feasible of the old fruit trees and began building up collections of new cultivars. In the 1870s he carried out pioneering work in sorting out the synonymy of apple rootstocks, and in the 1880s, on tomato breeding. But his greatest enthusiasm remained with the grapes, on which he was to write a standard textbook: *Vines and Vine-culture* (1883), which reached five editions and was translated into French.[17]

Besides practical cultivation and the maintenance of reference collections, the best way of restoring Chiswick's reputation for fruit was exhibition. Back in the 1850s, a grand fruit show had been proposed, debated, and eventually held in 1857; a sequel had been held the following year, but the 1859 show had had to be cancelled because of the threatened demise of the Society. The decline of Kensington caused the Society to miss out similarly on the potato exhibitions of the 1870s, which were held instead at Alexandra Palace and the Royal Aquarium in Westminster, although Barron was involved in the judging.[18]

The great conferences got under way in the 1880s, with Barron as the chief organiser and compiler of reports. The National Apple Conference was held at Chiswick in 1883, and Barron was able to put on a display of 328 cultivars from the Society's garden; 236 exhibitors each displayed over two hundred varieties. One of the apples which received a First Class Certificate was 'Bramley's Seedling', not exactly new but not yet familiar; in the wake of the conference it began to be extensively planted. This was followed by the National Pear Conference in 1885, and by a joint Apple and Pear Conference in 1888. At the 1885 Pear Conference, an unnamed cultivar exhibited by Rivers of Sawbridgeworth won high praise, and was subsequently marketed by them as the 'Conference' pear, becoming the most commonly planted British pear of the 20th century. These were followed by a Vegetable Conference in 1889, and over the three following years conferences on small hardy fruits, grapes, and apricots and plums; then from 1894 to 1897 a series of conferences on British-grown fruit, accompanying exhibitions at the Crystal Palace; a joint conference with the National Fruit Growers' Federation in 1905, and one on fruit spraying in 1908.[19] Meanwhile, proposals were made, and continually postponed, for an International Fruit Show, first at Chiswick, then at the Crystal Palace. It was not to be until after Chiswick had been abandoned in favour of Wisley; in 1905 an annual series of Colonial Fruit Shows was instigated, that continued until 1910.[20]

The 20th century saw a slackening of this energy of conference scheduling. A small conference on fruit growing took place in 1919, as Britain emerged from the war, and in 1921 the Society finally managed to convene an International Potato Conference of its own. But it was not until the 1930s that two large-scale conferences were held again: on apples and pears in 1934, and on cherries and soft fruits the next year. Then all fell silent until in 1983 a Centenary Apple and Pear Conference was held. Despite this slowing down, however, it is safe to say that the majority of fruit conferences held in Britain have been the work of the RHS.[21]

Despite the success of the conferences, the fruit collections at Chiswick were beginning to suffer from air pollution by the 1890s; old trees had to be grubbed out; phylloxera was discovered in the vines; the glasshouses deteriorated and were repaired from time to time. In 1895 a committee of enquiry into Chiswick concluded that things were not prospering under Barron's management, and needed to be replanned. Apart from Barron's forced retirement, nothing significant did happen, until Chiswick was abandoned altogether in favour of a new garden remote from the pollution of London.[22]

In the new, cleaner air of Wisley, a new start was made, with a vegetable trial ground established and a reference collection of fruits begun nearby. The staff were well chosen: the Fruit Foreman had bred a melon before becoming a staff member, and was allowed to sell its seeds. Exhibits of Wisley grapes were much praised at Westminster shows in 1908 and 1909—not glasshouse grapes, as at Chiswick, but grapes suitable for an outdoor vineyard. This period saw the beginnings of the movement for English winemaking, with Andrew Pettigrew at Castell Coch the pioneer; he publicised his work in the 1895 *Journal*, and held a wine-tasting that seemed to bode success. H.M. Tod, the donor of many of the Wisley vines, despite being told that wine production was outside Wisley's remit, encouraged the Society to establish a vintage there, but the plans were abandoned on the onset of war. However, half a century later, the Society acted as a communication channel for Ray Barrington Brock, in his survey of grapes in cultivation (which revealed a high degree of synonymy, over a hundred varieties reducing to

about twenty) and his attempts to start an experimental vineyard at Oxted.[23]

From blanched rhubarb to blight-resistant potatoes

The Society's attempt to resolve the synonymy of fruits was paralleled, if not matched, by similar efforts with vegetables. George Gordon, while under-gardener in the kitchen garden at Chiswick, was given the job of classifying the collections of peas and beans, 'to reduce the discordant nomenclature of the seed shops to something like order, to enable the Gardener to know the quality of the sorts he is unaccustomed to cultivate, and above all to prevent his buying the same kind under different names'. The collections contained 43 named varieties of beans, and 130 of peas; by the time Gordon had finished with them, they had been reduced to 11 and 43 varieties respectively.[24] Even before the garden at Chiswick had been acquired, another gardener, William Morgan, had been put to work classifying beets, and his colleague Charles Strachan on onions and radishes; Sabine had worked on tomatoes; William Christie completed Strachan's survey of radishes, went on to carrots, and was working on potatoes when he resigned in 1824, despite an attempt to hold him until he had completed the catalogue. (In later years it would be claimed by critics of the Society that he rebelled against the demand that he compare the taste of all the varieties, but this accusation probably originated as a joke.)[25] A later gardener, Andrew Matthews, was to complete similar surveys of endives, parsnips, and cardoons.[26]

In 1816, a trench was dug at the Chelsea Physic Garden, and some rhubarb buried under the piles of soil. Thomas Hare, the Society's Assistant Secretary, reported the following January on the result: blanched rhubarb, which was found to have had its culinary qualities improved. The publication of Hare's paper was followed by replications of the experiment, and within a few years the blanching of rhubarb had become established as a standard treatment in the kitchen garden.[27] Apart from this, the most important practical contribution to vegetable culture to emerge from the Society's *Transactions* was the description of a mushroom house by Isaac Oldacre, Sir Joseph Banks's gardener at Spring Grove, Isleworth, which was later claimed by William Robinson to be the beginning of successful mushroom growing in England. A mushroom house on Oldacre's model was built at Chiswick, only to be damaged by fire in the 1830s.[28]

Synonymy and classification, rather than improvements in practical culture, were the main results of the Society's work on vegetables. Thompson planned to collaborate with Loudon, providing him with the names of vegetable varieties suitable for suburban gardens, but this project was cut short by Loudon's death.[29] Once the Vegetable component had been added to the Fruit Committee, however, it was immediately proposed that trials of different categories of vegetables be held at Chiswick; reports on trials of peas, lettuce, beets, celery, cucumbers, cabbages, kales, and broccoli were published in the *Proceedings* in 1861-2, and the trials of peas and kales in particular carried on into the 1870s, even after Chiswick was reduced. Many of the vegetables that were then being tried would be unfamiliar today; in large part thanks to the encouragement of awards from the Committee, the range and quality of many sorts has been improved, and the earlier forms have disappeared. The replacement of round-seeded by wrinkle-seeded peas, of the long dark beets of the Victorian period by the modern globe beets; the development of beef and plum tomatoes; the development of white-headed cauliflowers—all these have been signalled by Awards of Merit and First Class Certificates granted at shows before they became standard in the trade.[30]

During the 1830s and 1840s, an increased interest was shown, by Lindley at least, in trying to identify the wild originals of cultivated vegetables, as an aid to future breeding. He published Vilmorin's notes on improving the wild carrot in the *Transactions*, and himself contributed a note on the wild state of maize, before the procedure suddenly became an urgent one with the arrival of the potato blight. He had already arranged for what he then identified as wild potato roots to be planted on the Atlantic islands of Ascension and St Helena, in order to help develop them as victualling stations for passing ships; and both Banks and Sabine had previously looked into the question, and tried to solve the perennial problem of who introduced the potato and when.[31] Once the blight had established itself, Lindley had a new reason for such investigations: to identify forms that might not be susceptible. In the years 1846-7 he assembled as many potatoes as he could that had been collected from identifiable sites in Central and South America, and grew them at Chiswick for observation. One in particular, which he named *Solanum demissum*, and which he found in a sample of 'Mexican potatoes from an elevation of 8000 feet', sent him by a German collector named Uhde, struck him as a good candidate for breeding, since he was convinced that the blight was caused by damp, and it was a dwarf, hard potato that gave hope for good damp-

resistance. Nearly a century was to pass before *Solanum demissum* was to prove the ancestor of some viable blight-resistant cultivars, in the work of Redcliffe N. Salaman and his colleagues at the Potato Virus Research Station. The intervening path had led through sponsored potato-collecting expeditions to South America, Salaman's work on the Mendelian genetics of the potato, and a great deal of international collaboration; but the seed had been sown at Chiswick, when Lindley planted his potato specimens in the 1840s.[32]

Wartime food production

The Society's work on vegetables suddenly assumed national importance with the First World War. As early as February 1915, the Society had issued a press statement on the importance of private gardens growing vegetables, and it began that year to issue pamphlets on fruits and vegetables for the home garden, fruit bottling, and vegetable cookery. Lecture programmes were set up, and demonstrations of bottling and preserve-making held at shows; trials of vegetables and manures were held at Wisley. A government scheme to promote allotments was encouraged, with a national allotment federation and 200,000 new allotments set up by early 1917; the RHS assisted with the creation of model allotments in every major population centre for demonstration purposes. Early in 1917 Sir Arthur Lee, the Director of Food Production, requisitioned the services of Frederick Keeble, the Director of Wisley, whose time was thereafter progressively taken from the Society. A new pamphlet on fruit bottling that year sold 65,000 copies within a couple of months, and news came from America that the botanist David Fairchild was supporting a dried vegetable campaign there, an 'instance of the far-reaching influence of the Society'.[33] One campaign of particular importance, as the Society's most sustained effort to influence the government, was a direct outgrowth of the encouraging of fruit bottling. The RHS lobbied the government to exempt sugar from rationing, so that households could have supplies for jam-making: otherwise, much of the fruit growing that had been so urgently encouraged would be wasted. The initial 1918 campaign was a success, and the government released 10,000 tons of sugar for domestic use; but later that year, despite the Society's opposition, marmalade, syrup, treacle and honey were all rationed, and it was not until 1920 that the rationing came to an end.[34]

War loomed again 20 years later, and this time the Society was better prepared. By the end of

December 1938, E.A. Bunyard had produced a report on the organisation of emergency food growing for wartime. Even before war was declared, the Ministry of Agriculture had arranged for the services of the RHS, and especially of the new garden adviser James Wilson. By mid-September 1939, plans were in place for the creation of horticultural committees in centres of 10,000 or more people to advise on food cultivation and inspect gardens for productive capacity: this was eventually to involve demonstrations by municipal parks staff and the creation of specimen allotments in every district. A joint committee on vegetable growing was established, and the RHS began a programme of lectures and pamphlet publications to teach the public how to contribute to the war effort by increasing domestic production. As shows were progressively suspended because of air-raid threats, they were replaced by displays of photographic panels on vegetable growing, which went on tour around the country. The pamphlet on *Simple Vegetable Cooking* sold 24,000 copies within its first few months; a *Journal* article on 'Vegetables for continuity of supply', in 1943, proved so popular that 10,000 reprints were required.

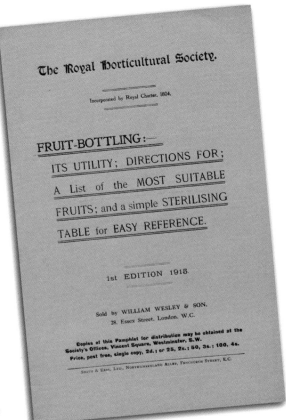

Teaching cookery in two world wars, with specimen recipes.

During the autumn of 1939, an *Evening Standard* editorial coined the suggestive phrase 'Dig for victory', and this was adopted as the name for the Ministry's programme for the promotion of allotment and home garden production. Roy Hay, the new Editor of the Society's *Journal*, who had been exempted from military service to help with the campaign, later described the scene on the morning of 10 September 1940, when the country's Mayors were invited to London to hear an appeal for the creation of a half-million more allotments:

> Everything would have been all right if Hitler had not had the idea of wiping out London's Dockland. We set off that morning for the Mansion House full of doubts whether we would ever get there or, even if we did, whether the Mayoral kitchens would have any gas or electricity to warm up the turtle soup. Buses were running as far as Holborn Viaduct, but Cheapside was a tangle of fire engines and demolition gangs. Great clouds of black smoke swirled round the bank of England, and rivers of filthy water ran in the gutters. By devious routes we reached the Mansion House, tripping over miles of hose pipes and dodging barriers, ignoring the shouts of the City police ... There were as many empty places as guests when we finally sat down at the table. With the turtle soup came an air raid warning. All the speeches were punctuated by the clanging of fire and ambulance bells. Even the Ministry's publicity department could scarcely have staged a more dramatic setting for the Minister's appeal. Mr. Hudson was direct and forceful—as always. He told the Mayors to go home and see to it that the allotments committee was made the most important committee of their Council instead of being the Cinderella of them all. With the warehouses burning all along the river, everybody was impressed.[35]

The RHS was a member of the Allotments Co-ordinating Council, and advised the LCC on its allotments programme. In October 1940 it started work on a larger publication entitled *The Vegetable Garden Displayed*. This was published in 1941, and went through eight impressions during the war, selling for most of that time at a price of one shilling. It became by far the Society's most successful publication. In 1946 it was translated into German, as part of an effort to help with the reconstruction of the Germany domestic economy after the war, the networks of market gardens that accompanied most German towns having been destroyed by the saturation bombing.[36]

A note on the size of vegetables

E.A. Bunyard once remarked, of the growing of giant vegetables, that it was 'as legitimate as any other kind of sport'. Over the years, however, the degree to which fruits and vegetables should be judged by size and other visual, or even tactile qualities, has proved a recurrent subject for controversy. It is one thing for the taste of a variety to be tested before granting it an Award of Merit; but it would be quite another if a display of fruits offered for competition were to be eaten by the judges before granting a prize. So it is not necessarily surprising if suggestions like Sir Harry Veitch's 1896 proposal for a £30 prize for flavour in fruit should not be readily taken up.[37]

Sir Austen Chamberlain, in his role of Chancellor of the Exchequer, exempted the Society from paying Entertainment Tax on the Chelsea Flower Show; and, having got his foot in the door, he proceeded to play a determined role in the Society's activities. On 21 September 1920, a letter from him was read out in Council, 'calling attention to the preposterous size and consequent coarseness of the vegetables usually found on the exhibition tables, particularly at local shows, and

Front cover of the German translation of The Vegetable Garden Displayed, *1946.*

The tradition of vegetable exhibits continues: Medwyn Williams's Gold Medal exhibit at the Chelsea Flower Show, 2000.

asking whether the influence of the Society could not be exerted to eliminate coarseness and to improve the quality'. The Society had already taken an interest in vegetable cookery, mainly because of its wartime work on domestic food production, and had published several articles by Hermann Senn, the chef of the Reform Club, on the cooking of different types of vegetables.[38] Chamberlain was asked to be a judge at the next year's Vegetable Show.

On 12 February 1921, a statement appeared in the *Gardeners' Chronicle* over the names of the President and Secretary: 'The Royal Horticultural Society has resolved to insist that at all its Meetings vegetables shall be judged according to their fitness for table use and not merely by their size and external appearance. With this object in view it has been decided to ask the assistance of eminent chefs as judges in making its awards.' The Fruit and Vegetable Committee complained at not having been consulted first, but the press reaction was more troublesome. The following week, the *Chronicle* objected that to test food value was 'beyond the powers even of a chef, and we must at present admit our ignorance as to whether different varieties of vegetables have different vitamine values'. George Monro, a Council member, argued that cottagers needed the largest size of vegetable consistent with quality, so that size was not a disqualification. Of Fruit and Vegetable Committee members, William Cuthbertson refused to be associated

with a denunciation of big vegetables, and Edwin Beckett, author of *Vegetables for Garden and Exhibition*, asked: 'Why stop at chefs? How would it be to seek the advice of capable cooks and vegetable dealers for the judging of exhibits, and the movement could be extended so that fruiterers and butlers could be asked to judge the chief entries, and parlourmaids to adjudicate on the floral groups? If chefs are to be considered, why not the others? All these are experts from their own points of view.' As a result of this squabble, Chamberlain was asked to form a Committee, along with Lord Lambourne and Herman Senn, to consider the arrangements for the Vegetable Show—possibly the first meeting of the Vegetable Show Schedule Committee. In the event, the show passed off quietly enough.[39]

The issue, however, did not go away, not completely. In 1931, after some debate, Council decided to revise the Award of Garden Merit list, and test vegetables by cooking before including them. In 1934 a symposium was held on 'Quality in early vegetables', at which the question was ventilated again. A quarter of a century later, it blew up once more, when Philip Harben, the BBC's television cook, moved a resolution that fruit and vegetables should be assessed for flavour in judging. F.A. Secrett drew up a memo for Council in response, asserting that culinary value was adequately taken account of in the existing arrangements, and that there was no need for such a change. Finally, in 1990, during a trial of tomatoes at Wisley, 'it was decided to add a tasting trial to the field trials': a panel of 22 tasters was chosen, with six tasters taking part in each of six trials. Tasting trials of melons and potatoes followed in the late 1990s, and in 2003, there were trials of strawberries, rhubarb, beefsteak tomatoes, and salad potatoes (the potatoes were cooked for the Committee and eaten cold on site). The results of a tasting trial are always ambiguous to some degree—much depends not only on the variety but on the conditions of cultivation, maturity, and soil type, not to mention idiosyncrasies of palate among the tasters.[40]

It is worth remarking here that the Society has over the years made some tentative experiments at proposals for vegetable cookery. In 1895, to accompany the Vegetable Show at Chiswick, a vegetarian banquet was offered; the menu included such items as mushroom and potato patty, lentil sausage rolls, tomato salad, fresh and stewed fruits, damson tart; but also cheeses, egg and tomato sandwiches, and blancmange. This pioneering venture was dismissed by the *Gardeners' Chronicle* as 'a novel and interesting, we can scarcely say satisfactory, feature', and it was not to be repeated. During the war years the Society issued a pamphlet on *Simple Vegetable Cooking* (1940), but it was not until the 1980s that any attempt was made to include a cookbook in the range of publications: a small cookery book by Celia Haddon, *Gifts from your Garden* (1985).[41]

The National Fruit Trials

The fruit conferences described so far all took as their primary audience the nurseryman and the professional gardener on the country estate, as the leading market for information. Market gardeners and orchards for mass production were seen as taking their lead from these authorities. But the fruit-growing world was being shaken up in the wake of the agricultural depression that had set in during the 1870s. The *Gardeners' Magazine* had produced a report on *The Wasted Orchards of England*, complaining of a national neglect of fruit cultivation, of failure to compete successfully against continental imports. W.W. Tyler suggested turning railway embankments over to commercial cultivation, remarking (*à propos* lavender) that Britain's cottage industries tended to emigrate to the continent.[42] Commercial pressure was beginning to enforce a cutback in the number of varieties that nurseries offered. Explicit signs came in the response to the final edition of Hogg's *Fruit Manual* (1884), into which he incorporated comments on the quality of fruit varieties from R.D. Blackmore, who maintained an extensive

collection of pears at Teddington. 'Mr. R.D. Blackmore says it never ripens at Teddington ... Mr. R.D. Blackmore says it is no good at all ...' Hogg concluded that his comments were 'quite staggering, and destroy the long-cherished opinion which some of us have held respecting our favourite fruits'. One might have thought that the former chairman of the British Pomological Society would have been more sceptical about remarks based on cultivation in one locality only, but the *Journal of Horticulture* brought the main point into the open:

> Mr. Blackmore was a connoisseur in Pears, and grew an enormous number of varieties. Many of these were quite useless for commercial purposes; and yet because they did not 'pay' he was apt to write letters to the 'Times' against fruit culture generally as a profitable industry. He did not perceive that the most successful growers proceeded on exactly opposite lines to himself, namely, in planting many trees of a few wisely selected varieties, instead of one or two trees of as many varieties as he could obtain or find room for.

This was increasingly the new wisdom: successful, competitive commerce required the effective elimination of most cultivars in favour of the few varieties that paid well.[43]

Shortly before the turn of the century, William Wilks began to be exercised about the state of the fruit industry in Britain. Between 1896 and 1903 he featured in the *Journal* a series of articles from different hands, on the superiority of French market gardening, the failures of English orcharding, the state of the cider and market garden industries, the merits of the Woburn Experimental Fruit Farm, and the importance of setting up fruit instructional stations. Early in 1902 he made a proposal to draw the various fruit-growers' associations together into a single Federation; this proposal was not greeted warmly, but in 1904 he was able to convene a Committee on the state of the fruit industry, including George Monro of Covent Garden and Spencer Pickering of the Woburn Fruit Farm, and published its report in full in the *Journal*, to make sure that Fellows saw it.[44] Among the Committee's recommendations were: the creation of a special sub-department of the Board of Agriculture to oversee fruit growing; legislation to prevent the import of plant diseases; powers to eradicate pests and diseases; reforms to land tenure to ensure that orchards could not be neglected by new owners; government loans to orchard owners, and tax allowances for glasshouses; reform of the railways to ensure speedy delivery of perishable fruit, and the abolition of owner's risk rates; labelling of jam of foreign origin; the experimental establishment of orchards on sewage farms; improved facilities for commerce in the countryside, such as the extension of the telephone into rural districts; and 'That boys in industrial schools be allowed to stay away from such schools for the purpose of fruit picking, subject to suitable regulations'.

Whatever the immediate practical effects of the Committee, the RHS was now established in the government's mind as an organisation of consequence, and after the First World War, when the Ministry of Agriculture became interested in the idea of fruit trials to select varieties of commercial worth, it turned to the Society as a collaborator. A committee was set up, consisting of E.A. Bowles, E.A. Bunyard, Frederick Chittenden, William Cuthbertson, and the Treasurer, C.G.A. Nix, to work out details with the Ministry, and in 1922 the Treasury's sanction was received for a scheme of trials, to be carried out on the Society's land at Wisley. The Deers Farm estate, extending between the original garden and the village, had recently been purchased, and five and a half acres of this new ground were chosen for the initial planting.

Edward Ashdown Bunyard (1878-1939) succeeded his father George as Director of the Royal Nurseries, Maidstone. A gifted writer, author of The Anatomy of Dessert *and* The Epicure's Companion, *he introduced the 'Golden Delicious' apple into England.*

> It was believed then, as indeed it still is, that the future of the fruit-growing industry was dependent upon the ability of the home grower to supply the market with high quality fruit at a price low enough to complete economically with imported fruit, and the primary object of the trials was to help the industry by assessing the commercial merits of new introductions.

Eventually the area devoted to the trials was to expand to 42 acres.[45]

Thus began the noble and doomed experiment of the National Fruit Trials (NFT, until 1943 called the Commercial Fruit Trials, and usually referred to in Council minutes as the joint fruit testing). The RHS provided the land, the buildings, and the staff; the Ministry provided a grant (initially £300 p.a.), which it hoped would lessen as the sale of fruit brought in a profit—but it never did. Only a limited range of fruits was involved; peaches, apricots, nectarines, figs and grapes were rejected, as requiring protected cultivation; cider apples were being dealt with by Long Ashton Research Station; cherries were included initially, but a combination of unsuitable soil and bird damage prompted a reconsideration within a decade, and in 1931 the cherry trials were transferred to the Kent Farm Institute at Sittingbourne. Apples, pears, and plums remained the mainstay of the Trials; it was quickly decided that there was not enough space to experiment with a variety of rootstocks, so few were used. All varieties were sent for trial as

grafts, buds, or cuttings, so they could be propagated at Wisley and all start from a position of equality. The first superintendent of the Trials was A.N. Rawes, Keeble's future collaborator on *Hardy Fruit Growing*; on his resignation in 1935, he was succeeded by J.M.S. Potter. The first Chairman was G.W. Leak, followed by F.A. Secrett. Between them, they struggled on for over thirty years, in the least auspicious of circumstances.

> The trial ground at Wisley, which lies in the valley of the Wey and is only about 60 feet above sea level, has always been subject to late spring frosts. To aggravate matters, the soil is Bagshot sand which warms up rapidly in the spring and so induces early flowering. While it was important to discover which varieties could best withstand spring frosts, low spring temperatures occurred so frequently in the early 'thirties that cropping was seriously interfered with and the value of the records much reduced.

Potter later estimated that 'At least two seasons in every three the crop was largely destroyed by frost'. An experiment using orchard heaters as a defence against frost in 1935 'would undoubtedly have saved the crop in that area but for the fact that there was only enough oil for one night'; in 1950 experiments were made using a rotating helicopter blade and a continuous water spray, but inconclusively. When the available land was full, some trees had to be grubbed out to make room for new varieties, thus 'prematurely terminating some of the trials'. It is a matter for some astonishment that the Trials were kept going as long as they were, although long before they were discontinued various other substations had become involved. Even from the Society's point of view there were further inconveniences: 'after visiting the ornamental gardens, Fellows have not always felt like going a further mile into the village to see the fruit collections'.[46]

In 1945 the Agricultural Research Council set up a review committee for the Trials, and in the resulting reorganisation Potter left the Society's employment and became a civil servant. H.V. Taylor, the Commissioner for Horticulture, succeeded Secrett as Chairman. The limitations of Wisley being established, a search was conducted for a new site, and eventually in 1952 Brogdale Farm, near Faversham in Kent, was purchased to be the new home of the National Fruit Trials. The Trials were kept going at Wisley while Brogdale was made ready; it was planned that the transfer of the collections would be completed by 1956, but that Wisley should continue trials for four years more, just in case.[47]

Brogdale proved to be a much better site than Wisley, and the Trials flourished. A lesson learnt from Wisley was the general inferiority of most of the varieties sent in, so it became customary to hold screening trials before moving the best varieties on into the permanent trials. The RHS lent duplicate fruit books to Brogdale to help with the cataloguing of the collections; and one major work did result, the *National Apple Register* (1969), the most complete reference book on the subject. Only checklists were issued for any of the other categories of fruit, however, before the news came that as part of the government's general cutback on horticultural research, the Fruit Trials at Brogdale were to be closed.

Immediately, of course, the RHS was sounded out to see if it could take the collection back. Council, having been through the process once before, could not offer Wisley as a site unless £60,000 per annum could be fully secured. Some of the collections were transferred to Wye College—the RHS, by now wise to the ways of the government, warning that Wye's funding was dependent on government whim, so that a separate fund would be needed to maintain them. But while encouraging Wye as a site for trials, Council felt that Brogdale was climatically and environmentally by far the best place for the reference collections. In the summer of 1990 an independent Brogdale Horticultural Trust was established, and after some years of struggle, has succeeded in turning Brogdale into a tourist attraction, and the beginnings of a thriving research centre for fruit studies.[48]

Meanwhile, what of the practical effect of the Trials? The fact that from the beginning they were Commercial Fruit Trials gave them a different remit from the sort of trials the Society had conducted previously: they were intended to select cultivars that would ensure high, trouble-free, and continuous yields for British growers—and in consequence the domination of the market by a small number of cultivars. Sir James Mount, reminiscing in 1982 about post-war fruit growing, explained:

> If we go back 50 years to when I started, nurserymen such as Cheals and Bunyards were listing 200 varieties of applies, whereas today you seldom get more than 20. Home Grown Fruits, the marketing organisation, recommends 4 dessert varieties, one cooker and two pears for replanting. What has happened to all the others and why have they disappeared? To complete with the 'Golden Delicious' from France, which is marketed for almost 12 months in the year, the trade wholesalers 'dictate what is acceptable and what is not' ... They only want a red apple, a green apple or 'Cox' and they want as long a season as possible of one variety.

During the Second World War the restriction of varieties in cultivation was advocated as a means of improving national efficiency in food provision. By the 1970s, as the *Grower* magazine commented, 'we reached the position when only plantations on first class sites and soil, capable of regular yields of 750 to 1,200 bushels per acre, could survive.' The Apple and Pear Development Council was established to improve the marketing of British fruit, and began the 1980s with a campaign called 'Polish up your English'—promoting one eating apple (Cox), one cooking apple (Bramley), and one pear (Conference), three cultivars which were apparently to bear the weight of the top fruit industry.[49]

Fruit and vegetables at Wisley

All the while that the National Fruit Trials were taking place down the road, fruit culture was not being neglected in the main garden at Wisley. Changes took place after the First World War; the collections of tender fruit, the figs, peaches, and vines that had originally formed much of the stock of the glasshouse range, were removed to make way for trials of ornamental greenhouse plants. But new interests were emerging as well, among them nuts. The Society's publications had never devoted any significant attention to nuts, but the early 20th century brought a resurgence of interest in the subject. E.A. Bunyard promoted cobnuts and filberts, though it was not until the century's end that the rescue of derelict cobnut orchards in Kent became a matter of public concern, and excitement. In 1918 the Society was offered, and rejected, a £100 bequest to finance walnut distribution; a decade later it was working on a walnut exhibit for the Ministry of Agriculture, publishing articles in its *Journal*, and sponsoring a walnut survey and competition organised by Howard Spence. Nuts were sent in from 314 trees around the country, and few were found to be of satisfactory quality; Spence publicised the failures and promoted an increase in walnut orcharding. The effort that was put into walnut growing was short-lived, however; Spence died young within a few years of his survey; and the production of walnuts in England continued to decline.[50]

Trials of fruits and vegetables proceeded apace. Cooking beets, Brussels sprouts, onions, broccoli, peas, beans, cauliflowers, lettuces, celeriac, strawberries in the first half of the century; rhubarb, tomatoes, carrots, parsley, leeks, celery, onions, pumpkins, cabbages, calabrese in the second half. *The Fruit Garden Displayed*, a companion volume to *The Vegetable Garden Displayed*,

Model fruit gardens at Wisley in the late 1960s.

was published in 1947; both works sold well for decades, but falling sales in the 1990s led to their amalgamation under the title *Fruit and Vegetable Gardening* in 2002. The service of identifying fruits for Fellows led to the creation of the post of Fruit Officer, held at mid-century by E.G. Gilbert. He was followed by Harry Baker, who became the Society's figurehead in dealing with the amateur grower, collaborated with Gilbert on a Wisley Handbook on apricots and tender fruits, and wrote the volume on fruit for the 1979-81 *Encyclopaedia of Practical Gardening*. In the 1990s, a resurgent interest in potato varieties was reflected in large-scale trials and displays at shows, including in 2001 an exhibit of over 500 cultivars.[51]

Once it had been agreed that the National Fruit Trials (NFT) would move from Wisley, some provision had to be made for those Fellows who were interested in fruit. Potter supervised the layout of a group of three model fruit gardens on Weather Hill, adjacent to the NFT collection of cordon pears, intended to show how amateurs could obtain productive fruit cropping on sites of varying size. The soil was sandy, not ideal for fruit, so large quantities of manure were dug in, fertiliser applied, regular mulches of manure and hops added, until the site was productive. Even then all did not go smoothly: the pear 'Doyenné du Comice' was hit by scab, the raspberry 'Norfolk Giant' succumbed to disease; but at least it was less frosty than the old NFT site.[52]

Even if it was no longer conducting commercial trials, the Society wanted to keep some reference collections of fruit in use, especially with a view to the use of the amateur grower. So in 1948 it purchased a further portion of land, continuing the ridgeline of Battleston Hill, as a home for a new fruit collection. This proved much better than the old NFT site: on a hilltop, it had good air drainage, and suffered fewer frosts. The site was sown with mustard as a green manure, and then planted with 150 plum and 500 apple cultivars, the latter on semi-dwarfing rootstocks. In 1988 the fruit field was linked to the model fruit gardens by a new walk and pergola.[53]

Over the course of the 20th century the Society built up an impressive battery of prizes for fruit and vegetables, to be awarded at shows. The Cain Cup, originally awarded for the best amateur exhibit at Chelsea, was changed after the Second

World War into an award for the best display of vegetables by an Armed Forces station; it was discontinued after 1960. The Affiliated Societies' Cup has been awarded since 1908 for the best display of fruit by an Affiliated Society. For competitive exhibits at shows, there are the E.J. White Trophy for apples, the George Monro Memorial Cup for grapes (later changed to vegetables), the Gordon-Lennox Trophy for amateur fruit exhibits, the RHS Vegetable Cup, the Riddell Trophy for Vegetables, and the Stanley Lord Bowl for the year's best exhibit of fruit. And most prestigious of all is the Jones-Bateman Cup, awarded triennially since 1930 for

original research on fruit culture: among its recipients have been Barrington Brock, the promoter of outdoor grape culture; R.R. Williams, for his work on fruit pollination; and Avery Posnette of East Malling for his work on virus diseases.[54]

The National Vegetable Society was founded in 1960, and in 1965 proposed the idea of a Joint Vegetable Committee with the RHS; this was dismissed as having no useful purpose, since the relevant members of the National Vegetable Society were already on the Fruit and Vegetable Committee. Most vegetable research was by that time being conducted, not at Wisley, but at the National Vegetable Research Station in Wellesbourne, though the Society's *Journal* carried updates on its work—most notably, in 1968, revealing that traditional spacings for the planting of vegetables proved unjustified under trial. 'My own conclusion', wrote Elspeth Napier, the Editor, in recounting the results of the trials, 'is that we have been extravagant in the use of the

ground in our vegetable gardens. I suspect that the traditional spacings came to be used because they gave plenty of room to produce the large vegetables that win prizes in competitions.' In the 1980s, however, the Society held joint seminars with the National Vegetable Society at Swansea and Wisley, and set up a joint liaison committee which supervised workshops and lectures on vegetable cultivation.[55]

Vegetable cultivation in the domestic garden has been subject to surges at times of anticipated economic hardship: the wars saw massive programmes of allotment creation, which faded away once peace had come. The self-sufficiency movement of the 1970s, at a time of soaring inflation, sagged as economic stability returned. Neither movement has disappeared, but the boom in garden-making in the 1990s has been primarily a matter of ornamental planting and design theory. The RHS has launched vegetable plot competitions and other efforts to try to stimulate greater interest in food production in the domestic garden, but it remains to be seen how widespread will be the effect. The greatest stimulus to such interest has been, as so often in history, the prospect of loss. The disappearance of hop orchards, cherry orchards, and cobnut plantations; the threat to the future of Brogdale; the campaigns to promote public awareness of the less commercial English apples; the attempts to abridge retail commerce in vegetable seeds on the part of multi-national companies and international legislation; the publicity given to gene banks, and to programmes such as the Henry Doubleday Research Association's vegetable seed bank—all these things have made the recovery of vanishing vegetables, and to a smaller extent fruits, a major horticultural fashion at the turn of the century. *The Garden* reported in 2001 that sales of vegetable seeds had increased dramatically; it remains to be seen where this trend will lead.[56]

The Fruit Group

Representations having been made to the effect that the cultivation of fruit in private gardens might be greatly extended and improved if Fellows and Associates interested in the various

Prince Charles attending a soft fruit demonstration at Wisley, 24 June 1993, RHS President Robin Herbert on the right.

fruits were provided with additional facilities for meeting and exchanging ideas, the Council has decided to establish, within the Society, a Fruit Group which can meet periodically for lectures and discussions and for visits to research stations, private gardens and commercial fruit plantations ... The first Meeting ... will be held at 2.30 p.m. on October 2 in the Lecture Room ... when Dr. T. Wallace will lecture on 'Practical Aspects of the Manuring of Fruit'.

Among the goals which the Committee suggested the Fruit Group should set itself were: 'the desirability of a re-examination of old varieties as, with our present-day knowledge of stocks, nutrition and pest-control, they might get a much higher rating, especially in regard to their suitability for particular purposes, soils and conditions, and as potential parents of new varieties'; 'drawing attention to the merits of little-known varieties'; 'making the results of research more widely known'; and encouraging the 'great desire for knowledge of fruit-growing among the owners of small gardens'. By the appearance of the first *Fruit Year Book* in 1947 the Fruit Group had over 400 members, a figure which has remained steady ever since.

The Fruit Group instigated the publication of *The Fruit Garden Displayed*, and the planting of the three model fruit gardens at Wisley; it assisted in the production of the *Fruit Year Books* from 1947 to 1958, the 21st-anniversary publication *Fruit Present and Future* (1966), its sequel or second volume in 1973, and of the 50th-anniversary volume *Fruit Past and Present*. In addition, it helped to arrange the centenary Fruit Conference in 1983. It has a long tradition of exhibits at the autumn fruit shows at Westminster, and has staged exhibits at Chelsea.

Apple Day at Wisley, 1993: an event which in recent years has become an annual fixture in October, at which the public can see, sample, learn about and buy various cultivars.

In 1957 a proposal was put forward for a Peach Subcommittee, but on H.V. Taylor's advice that it was not wise to create a permanent structure within the Group, a peach panel was assembled instead. That was in the heady days of Justin Brooke's *Peach Orchards in England*; peach growing has not become the industry that was hoped for.[58]

15 *Garden Design*

THE Society's policy of concentrating on practical horticulture, and leaving matters of aesthetics to individual judgment, was reflected emphatically in the content of its *Transactions* and *Journal*. No article on garden design appeared in the *Transactions*: the fringes of the subject were approached with articles on copings for garden walls, tree transplanting, and a report by Sabine on remarkable hedges in Scotland, but all of them treated so as to avoid questions of taste.[1] John Lindley, in his role as editor of the *Gardeners' Chronicle*, regularly published articles on matters of aesthetics, and sometimes weighed in with his own opinions in the leader columns, but for decades he tended to keep the remits of the weekly newspaper and the Society's publications firmly separate.

The absence of articles on the aesthetics of design is the more readily understandable when one considers what was being published on the subject in book form. At the beginning of the 19th century, the dominant, or at least the most publicised, style in garden design was the English landscape garden—a professed imitation of nature whose major features were an open expanse of lawn, fringed with clumps or belts of trees, studded with occasional specimen trees, and excluding from the principal views terraces, flower gardens, kitchen gardens, and other artificial or utilitarian works. While the absence of significant horticulture from the landscape garden has been exaggerated, in this context it is a useful exaggeration to make. Today it can be said that 'Because shrubs and trees are constantly growing and dying, the structure of the garden is shaped by the gardener', but this is not a view expressed in the literature of the 18th century; contrast that with the heyday of the bedding system, when the head gardener could change the visual appearance of the garden annually or even more often, and the difference in horticultural terms is obvious.[2] 'Who loves a garden, loves a greenhouse too', as Cowper said, and it was the kitchen garden and the glasshouse that remained the focus of attention in the Society's *Transactions*.

From the beginning of the 19th century, however, formal design began to return to the garden, and John Claudius Loudon used his *Gardener's Magazine* and the editions of his *Encyclopaedia of Gardening* to promote the cause. The garden at Chiswick, with its lozenge-shaped beds of one plant genus apiece, was often criticised by Loudon and others for design deficiencies, whatever its merits as a reference collection. 'We wish Mr. Bentham and Mr. Lindley were as much attached to landscape-gardening as they are to botany', said Loudon; 'we should then have no fear for the result.' Lindley, by the 1840s, was in many ways a reactionary figure, continuing to invoke the landscape garden as the appropriate standard while his contemporaries were exploring axial layouts, the geometric parterre, and formal bedding. Lindley fought a rearguard action in his weekly leaders, defending Capability Brown when all others had turned against him, attacking the new styles of garden ornament, and in 1847 narrating a laudatory history of the landscape garden.[3] The following year he finally broke the Society's implicit ban on the introduction of aesthetics into its own publications, and made the lead article in the 1848 *Journal* a lecture he had given, allegedly on the history of gardening, but in fact an attack on current trends in design and a plea for the maintenance of the landscape standard.

Lindley's article was a survey of the writings of Sir Francis Bacon, William Lawson, and 'Didymus Mountaine' (Thomas Hill), to show what gardening had been like in the Elizabethan period. But the real focus of the article was the recent efforts by architects and garden designers to promote Elizabethan and Jacobean design as appropriate for the present day, and Lindley's desire to prevent any attempt at reviving the enclosed garden of the period, which seemed to him to reveal 'a most Lilliputian grasp of mind and imagination ... There is no wide expanse of surface; no undulation is spoken of; no changing views created artificially yet natural in effect ...' He argued that instead of making the garden match the style of the house, one should make it harmonise with the surrounding landscape. And when Lindley wrote that 'beyond having pretty flowers in certain seasons, there seems nothing to redeem the offensive ugliness of the whole design', it is difficult not to suspect that his real target was the recent introduction of formal bedding into the principal views from the house.[4]

Within a couple of years the *Gardeners' Chronicle* was to publish a long series of articles about Elvaston Castle, the garden whose division by hedges into a series of garden rooms was to establish a trend that has continued into the 21st century. Ironically, little more than a decade later, Lindley was to appear as a public promoter of the most elaborate enclosed garden of the day: the Society's garden in Kensington. But the most immediate consequence of Lindley's piece was a relaxation in the rules about aesthetic matters in the *Journal*. Over the next few years it was to publish pieces on bedding, edgings for the flower garden, styles of tree planting, and the use of foliage.[5] Then came financial crisis, the cessation of the *Journal*, and the inauguration, after Lindley's death, of a new *Journal* which spent decades primarily as a record of conference proceedings. It was not until 1890, and the resumption of regular service, that the Society had a forum in which aesthetic matters could be discussed; and by that time the old inhibition about dealing with such things was a distant memory.

Bedding and borders

The return of the flower garden from its 18th-century position, secluded from the main views, to the immediate precincts of the house, was accompanied in the 1820s and 1830s by the increasing use, first of North American annuals (primarily the David Douglas introductions), and then of half-hardy perennials from South Africa and South America, to create seasonal displays. In the late 1830s John Caie, the head gardener at Bedford Lodge in Kensington, wrote the first articles on the planning of colour schemes for bedding plants, and by the 1850s the gardening press was producing a flourishing crop of articles debating different colour theories and their application to the flower garden. Virtually nothing of this appeared in the Society's publications. But it could not help but appear in practice, in the Society's gardens, and most notably at Kensington, where George Eyles, the Superintendent, was acclaimed a master at ornamental displays. Each successive fashion from the 1860s to the 1880s was essayed there: the box-and-gravel parterre so associated with the garden's designer, W.A. Nesfield; in four major beds, Nesfield's polychrome beds of coloured gravels; carpet bedding (the use of low-growing foliage plants to create flat patterns) in the 1870s. Eyles, by the end of his career, thought that formal bedding had reached its acme of development, and would be the basis of ornamental gardening for the indefinite future:

> The system has gone on improving ever since, until our flower gardens have become real works of art, and a pleasure to look upon for the whole of the summer and autumn. No doubt the carpet bedding in our parks and public gardens, as well as in many private gardens when the necessary time can be bestowed upon its proper keeping, is as near perfection as can well be. Indeed, I think it very doubtful whether the next generation of horticulturists will witness such a startling revolution, or see such a marked improvement in flower garden decoration as the last has done.[6]

Improvement, perhaps not, but change, certainly. Eyles would have been shocked to see how the status of formal bedding was diminished in the 20th century, but the attack was already under way by the time he was writing.

The attack on bedding was fivefold: on grounds of season, colour, plant selection, moral ideology, and social status. Already by the early 1850s the emphasis on summer bedding was being criticised for leaving the flower garden devoid of interest at other times of year; the response was spring bedding, the use of bulbous plants to extend the bedding system for a further season, an innovation associated primarily with John Fleming at Cliveden, who wrote on the subject in the *Gardeners' Chronicle* in the 1850s and in book form in the 1860s, and with his rival William Ingram of Belvoir Castle. Almost simultaneously came the use of chrysanthemums to extend the system into the autumn, and experiments in winter bedding were occasionally made. But it was not until 1890 that articles on these matters appeared in the Society's *Journal*, with Ingram writing on spring bedding and William Wilks on winter gardening.[7]

Early Victorian gardeners had delighted in using high contrast of colours, with a significant minority—led by Lindley—proposing to adopt the theory of complementary colours associated with the French chemist Chevreul. Lindley began publicising complementary colours in the *Chronicle* even before Chevreul's book was translated:

> Now the complementary colour of red is green; of orange, sky-blue; of yellow, violet; of indigo, orange-yellow; and consequently blue and orange-coloured flowers, yellows and violets, may be placed together, while red and rose-coloured flowers harmonise with their own green leaves ... In all cases, however, where colours do not agree, the placing white between them restores the effect.

Donald Beaton (1802-1863), head gardener at Shrubland Park, Suffolk. Born to a Gaelic-speaking family in Scotland, learned English only as an adult. Influential columnist in The Cottage Gardener *throughout the 1850s. Declined invitation to join the Chiswick Garden Committee, but an early member of the Floral Committee.*

Donald Beaton, writing in the rival weekly *The Cottage Gardener*, rebutted Lindley's arguments on the grounds that in genuine flower beds the colour blocks of the flowers never blotted out the accompanying foliage, and so never approached each other closely enough to create the alleged effects: 'Complementary colours, as they call them, can, therefore, never be obtained from flowers growing on plants, because all flowers are then on one complementary colour, green, of various intensity.' The rival theories came to a public showdown in the years 1856-7, with Chiswick and Hampton Court using complementary colours in their bedding, and Kew and the Crystal Palace adopting more standard contrast under Beaton's supervision. Beaton won: both Chiswick and Hampton Court abandoned their complementary colour schemes, Lindley started criticising Chevreul in the *Chronicle*, and Beaton was able to poke repeated fun at Lindley: 'is it not a cause of rejoicing to see a man like Dr. Lindley turned as completely round from the errors of his flower-garden notions, as if his face were between his shoulder-blades? Verily, the constant dropping of water will not more surely wear down the hardest marble than the force of truth ...'[8]

But by the 1860s, a new generation of gardeners was beginning to turn against high contrast, and it eventually became a mark of praise to describe a gardener as 'no red-hot colourist'. The opening salvo in this battle was fired anonymously by Andrew Murray, the Society's Assistant Secretary. In 1863, in his *Book of the Royal Horticultural Society*, he limited himself to saying that 'There are a good many (some think too many) examples of coloured gravel and ribbon beds in the Garden.' But he had already sent a letter to the *Gardeners' Chronicle*, published under the name 'One of the Old School', in which he denounced brightly coloured flower beds in terms derived from contemporary anthropology:

> Does not the gaudy glitter of these beds address itself to the lower elements of our taste? It is the savage who is caught by the gayest colours, and a liking for them and personal ornament is a remnant of primitive barbarism which is shared by us all, but possessed in smaller and smaller proportions as we ascend the scale of civilisation; we all pay homage to this original weakness, but the highest bred and most cultivated minds feel it least, and when they do yield to it are the first to discard it, and in the present case I am happy to see signs that they are beginning to do so.[9]

The lasting legacy of this letter has been a tendency, continued to the present day, to refer to the colour combinations preferred by the early Victorians as 'primitive'.

In 1871, William Robinson launched his weekly newspaper *The Garden*, in order to promote 'pure horticulture of the natural, or English, school, free from rigid formalities, meretricious ornaments, gypsum, powdered bricks, cockle-shells, and bottle-ends'—the list indicates that Nesfield was the enemy being reacted against, and the RHS garden in Kensington the model for all things bad in gardening. Within a couple of years, Robinson was to open an attack on bedding in general, hoping for the day when science would demonstrate that the laws of aesthetics were immutable, and denying 'that any but the feeblest interest can be excited by it' (he never made clear how two generations of gardeners could have been deceived about their feelings of interest). Initially, at any rate, his objection was more to the colour schemes than to the physical practice of bedding, for he was the first writer to praise carpet-bedding in a book, and even after he had turned against it he continued to have a soft spot for the bedding of succulents. But in his later years he glossed over these inconsistencies, and in the meantime his voice was joined by others who denounced the artificiality of planting for flowering season only, of looking at plants 'as mere masses of colour, instead of as an assemblage of living beings'.[10]

Ultimately, though, these individual arguments faded into the past. To look at 20th-century discussions of Victorian bedding is to find not reasoned arguments but the typical sneers addressed by the advocates of a fashion against the fashions it superseded, coupled with disdain for the masses who still enjoyed the bedding provided by municipal parks. Defences of bedding, usually focused on parks if not actually written by parks staff, seemed always to adopt an apologetic attitude. After the last article on spring bedding in the 1920s, the *RHS Journal* published no further articles on bedding (other than in accounts of municipal park practice) until the 1970s, when a series of articles by Brian Halliwell, who was then responsible for the Palm House parterre at Kew, re-affirmed bedding as a significant aesthetic option for the late 20th century. And gradually, further articles by Richard Fulcher, Christopher Lloyd, and others helped to restore ornamental bedding to a position of respect, while three-dimensional carpet-bedding at Chelsea and the first tentative attempts at restoring Victorian gardens led to a renewed interest in the formerly derided art form.[11]

One reaction to High Victorian bedding, as we have seen, was to attack contrast of colour, and in the 1870s and 1880s there was a widespread repudiation of colour schemes of any sort. Then in 1883, in Robinson's magazine *The Garden*, the first articles on colour planning by Gertrude Jekyll appeared. Instead of high contrast, she proposed such graded colour sequences as the following:

> A progression of colour to be recommended in a mixed border might begin with strong blues, light and dark, grouped with white and pale yellow, passing on to pink. Then rose colour, crimson, and strongest scarlet, leading to orange and bright yellow. A paler yellow followed by white would instantly connect the warm colours with the lilacs and purples, and a colder white would combine them pleasantly with low-growing plants with cool-coloured leaves.

The initial reaction was largely one of scorn: '"G.J." seems only to be attempting in another way, and with greater variety of materials, what the bedding man has been aiming at all along.' But gradually, Jekyll's ideas percolated through the gardening world. In 1891 she contributed to an RHS symposium on hardy flowers; in 1897 she collaborated with H. Selfe-Leonard on a lecture to the RHS about herbaceous border planting, and in the same year became one of the original Victoria Medallists; two years later she published her first book, *Wood and Garden*. During the Edwardian period *Country Life* became a prominent medium for circulating her ideas, and the herbaceous border offered the same focus for colour planning that the formal parterre had done fifty years earlier.[12]

In the wake of Jekyll, the literature on herbaceous borders increased, and several significant articles on the subject appeared in the Society's *Journal*.[13] In the years after the Second World War, the pure herbaceous border began to be modified into the mixed border—with some terminological confusion, for in the 19th century the phrase 'mixed border' had signified a border planted without an overall colour scheme; now it came to mean instead a border in which shrubs were mixed with the herbaceous perennials to provide greater structure and year-round interest.[14]

Rock gardens

Two competing traditions arose during the 19th century, both of which bore the label 'rock garden'. The first, associated with Loudon, Paxton, William Barron, and the Pulham family, saw rock gardening as the creation of a structure of rocks, increasingly, as the century went on, required to be geologically accurate in the placing of its stones, which was then planted in one of a variety of ways. The second, associated with James Backhouse, William Ingram, and later, Reginald Farrer, saw it as the creation of a suitable medium for growing alpine plants, in which the geological accuracy of stone-laying was irrelevant. Many gardeners, such as William Robinson, who wrote the first standard work on the subject, had a foot in both camps, and there was no necessary contradiction between having artificial cliffs and collections of alpines, but the subject was prolific of debate and insult.[15]

What we think of as alpine plants tended to be grown in pots during the early 19th century, as their cultural requirements were poorly understood at first. The Backhouse nursery in York was the first to specialise in alpines, from the 1850s, and in their rock garden, realistic stratification was abandoned in favour of a gravelly growing medium, and the placing of rocks at interesting angles for decorative effect. The RHS garden at Chiswick, constructed in the 1870s, was made in the Backhouse tradition, and from the 1890s through the First World War articles on both alpine cultivation and rock garden construction were featured in the *Journal*. To construct its larger rock garden at Wisley, the Society chose Pulham & Son, under the superintendence of the landscape architect Edward White; although Pulham's reputation rested primarily on rockworks created from artificial stone (a Portland cement mixture poured over masses of brick and clinker, and moulded into shape boulder by boulder), the Wisley rock garden was of natural stone throughout.[16]

The growing popularity of rock gardening was attested to by the number of small-scale examples assembled at the Temple and Chelsea Shows. The second Chelsea Show (1914) was the scene of a protest that revealed the heated feelings which rock garden style could generate. E.A. Bowles's first book, *My Garden in Spring*, had been published, with a preface by Reginald Farrer which took advantage of praise for Bowles's rock garden—in which hardly any rock was visible—to attack an unnamed rock garden, which Sir Frank Crisp thought he recognised as his own.

Gertrude Jekyll (1843-1932), garden designer and prolific writer. She began lecturing to the RHS in the 1890s, and (along with Ellen Willmott) was one of only two women among the original recipients of the Victoria Medal of Honour in 1897.

Ellen Ann Willmott (1858-1934), whose garden at Warley Place, Essex, became celebrated for its varied plant collections. Funded the creation of The Genus Rosa *(1910-14), with text by J.G. Baker and illustrations by Alfred Parsons.*

*Edward Augustus Bowles (1865-1954), whose garden at Myddelton House, Enfield, he described in a series of books (*My Garden in Spring, *1914, and sequels). Author of monographs on* Narcissus, Crocus *and* Colchicum. *For over 40 years Chairman of the Narcissus and Tulip Committee.*

Crowds observing the rock gardens, Chelsea Show, 1930.

... the rich must have their money's worth in show; culture will not give it to them, nor rarity, nor interest of the plants themselves: better a hundred yards of Arabis than half a dozen vernal Gentians ... neither blending nor variety—nothing but a neat unalloyed exhibit like those on 'rockworks' at the Chelsea Show. But what a display is here! You could do no better with coloured gravels. Neat, unbroken blanks of first one colour and then another, until the effect is sumptuous and worthy of the taste that has combined such a garden. But 'garden' why call it? There are no plants; there is nothing but colour, laid on as callously in slabs as if from the paint-box of a child. This is a mosaic, this is a gambol in purple and gold; but it is not a rock garden, though tin chamois peer never so frequent from its cliffs upon the passer by ...

The chamois on the scale-model Matterhorn that formed the centrepiece of Crisp's rock garden at Friar Park, Henley, were cast-iron, but 'tin chamois' was not much of a disguise. Note, however, that the main thrust of the complaint is neither the cliff nor the ornaments, but the colour massing; and this was something that, under the influence of Gertrude Jekyll, William Robinson had come to advocate in the rock garden. Robinson, who had described Crisp's as 'the best natural stone rock garden I have ever seen', associated himself with Crisp, as did Ellen Willmott, whose rock garden at Warley Place, like part of Crisp's, had been designed by Backhouse. Crisp published an article in Robinson's magazine *Gardening Illustrated*, attacking Bowles and not mentioning Farrer by name (Farrer was safely off collecting plants in the Himalayas by this time); Willmott stood at the gates of the Chelsea Show, handing out offprints. The ire of the gardening community flowed the other way, however; Robinson incurred criticism for printing the article, and Crisp's unfair targeting of Bowles earned him a lasting reputation for villainy. A letter from Joseph Jacob, the authority on bulbs, to Bowles sets the tone for most subsequent discussions of Crisp:

> My dear Boy,
> I am sorry I did not see you at Chelsea—Wilks told me of Crisp's scurrilous and 'below the belt'

attack on you, but I did not read it until in the train on the way home. I enclose a copy of the letter I have sent the brute [demanding his resignation as president of the Horticultural Club] by to-nights post. Dont you yourself take the very least notice of it. What a magnificent show it was! The best Chelsea has ever seen –
> Yours ever
> Joseph Jacob

Before dismissing Crisp as a rock gardener, note that his collection of alpines was so large that he went into partnership with Waterer's nursery, which became Waterer Sons & Crisp.[17]

At the first Chelsea Show in 1913, J. Wood of Boston Spa had been awarded a Gold Medal for a rock garden in the form of a series of more or less flat shelves: as far as possible from the mid-Victorian miniature cliff. This shallower model was already increasing in popularity, and spread

through the 1920s; it lent itself to what Farrer called a moraine and the next generation would call a scree: a well-drained gravelly substrate suitable for many alpines, and stylistically descended from the Backhouse rockery with the decoratively angled rocks stripped away. Selfe-Leonard had called in the pages of the *RHS Journal* for a flattening of the rock garden, an end to tilted stones, that legacy of the mid-Victorian obsession with the replication of geological features. By the late 1920s the similarity of designs on the Rock Garden Bank prompted Council to offer a special award for rock gardens made out of some other material than mountain limestone ('while not wishing in any way to discourage the use of mountain limestone'—fears over the stripping of stone from natural sites did not surface until the last quarter of the century); similarly, in the 1930s, their complaint about the universal flatness was answered by William Wood & Sons, who in 1939 exhibited a rock garden in Welsh slate, modelled on a vertical cliff face. The 1930s also saw the emergence, as both an exhibitor and a writer, of B.H.B. Symons-Jeune, whose *Natural Rock Gardening* revived the call for geological accuracy in the placing of stones, though on a flatter scale than that undertaken in the previous century.[18]

Rock gardens at Chelsea reached their peak in the late 1930s; in the post-war years, the number of exhibited gardens began to dwindle, long before the flood of literature on the subject faded into a small trickle. By the mid-1950s shrub gardens were beginning to rival rock gardens on the Rock Garden Bank; by 1967 the number of rock gardens exhibited had been reduced to one, and the great rock gardens of the past had become decidedly a minority pursuit. The post-war years had seen the rise of a new trend in the cultivation of alpines: the use of stone sinks and troughs, and their larger counterpart the raised bed. Lawrence Hills had written the first book on *Alpines Without a Garden* in 1953; the first positive publicity for the idea in the *Journal* came twenty years later, in an article by Valerie Finnis describing the raised rock garden she and Sir David Scott had constructed at The Dower House, Boughton House. By the 1980s the popularity of the alpine trough had grown to such an extent that it could be proclaimed as the democratic form of gardening, as opposed to the rich landowner's rhododendron woodland.[19]

Woodland gardens and landscape colour

William Robinson, who began his career attacking the use of blocks of colour in the flower garden, ended by advocating the use of blocks of colour everywhere else: the rock garden, the herbaceous border, and the wider landscape. The colour massing of trees and shrubs had first been put forward by William Paul, in 1864; James Bateman had lectured to the RHS on coloured-leaved trees in 1865; when Paul returned to the subject in an RHS lecture in 1870, his ideas met with a warm reception from the audience, including D.T. Fish, who described the mixed planting of trees as having been the 'ruin of our landscapes'. By the end of the 19th century, the use of tree colour was attracting widespread attention. Planting for autumn colour, a subject of some interest in the 1840s which had lapsed in the intervening years, returned to attention at the end

of the century, and became a major theme in landscape planting during the first half of the twentieth.[20]

These ideas of colour planning for the wider landscape mingled with the various ideas of the wild garden that were current in the last third of the 19th century—ranging from the naturalising of bulbs in grass to Selfe-Leonard's suggestion for garden seats in the shape of giant fungi—to emerge at the beginning of the 20th as the woodland garden, in which rhododendrons and other flowering shrubs provided the colour masses. Wisley itself was regarded during G.F. Wilson's lifetime as a wild garden, and the addition of Battleston Hill in the 1930s gave it one of the most highly regarded woodland gardens of the period.[21]

To the increasing interest in informal gardening was added, in the last years of the 19th century, a further strand: the Japanese garden. This term covered everything from gardens in the English style planted with Japanese introductions, to gardens laid out by genuine Japanese gardeners specially brought over for the purpose (one of whom, Kenkichi Okubo, wrote for the *RHS Journal*). In practice, only those Japanese precedents were used that could be assimilated to the general style of the wild, rock and water gardens: asymmetrical layout, subdued colour schemes, bamboo groves, the mass planting of waterside irises, Japanese lanterns and stepping stones. James Hudson, the head gardener at Gunnersbury Park, created one of the most famous Japanese gardens of the Edwardian period, which he described in the *Journal*: he did not quote the remark allegedly made by a visiting Japanese ambassador, 'We have nothing like it in Japan'.[22]

The interest in colour grouping in the wider landscape generated a focused movement in the inter-war years: the campaign for the ornamental planting of roadsides. Wilfred Fox, the creator of the Winkworth Arboretum, founded the Roads Beautifying Association in 1928, and promoted the use of flowering trees for road verges. The RHS was represented on the Association's board from the inception, and one of its first projects was roadside planting at Wisley; in the post-war years, when the RBA was wound down, the RHS declined to take over its work, but continued grant-aiding it until the end. Sir David Bowes Lyon chaired a government committee on roadside planting in 1955; by that time the RBA's ornamental ideals (increasingly viewed as suburban) were replaced, as the new motorways were ploughed through the countryside and required planting in their turn, by new ideas from the world of landscape architecture: broad swathes of lawn, coniferous plantation.[23]

Wisley as a wild garden: a scene in George Fergusson Wilson's time, 1899.

Revivalism and modernism in design

Bedding, rock gardens, landscape colour: all these things can readily be regarded as aspects of horticulture. Lindley's 1848 article was the only article in the Society's journals on the architectural side of gardening during the course of the 19th century; despite the importance and influence of the Kensington garden, it was the *Gardeners' Chronicle* in which Nesfield published his press statement on coloured gravels, and which published the major illustrations of the garden. Apart from a couple of early plans, no illustrations of the garden at Chiswick appeared in the Society's own publications either.

This began to change shortly after the turn of the century, when William Wilks published an account of the making of his verandah at his garden in Croydon, and Gertrude Jekyll followed with an account of pergolas. Two years later, Hugh Maule published an article on 'Design in the suburban garden', which introduced to the Society's readers the new ideas of the Arts and Crafts movement, featured the work of designers like John Belcher and Arnold Mitchell, and stressed the importance of vernacular styles, authentic construction, and neatly organised geometric spaces. Pergolas and arches for climbing plants became favoured devices for garden ornament, and were propounded in a trickle of articles, by designers such as Thomas Mawson and Edward White.[24]

Mawson claimed to be the inventor of the phrase 'landscape architect', which was beginning to oust the earlier 'landscape gardener'. By the First World War, an increasing number of designers was adopting the phrase, most notably White, who for years was effectively the representative of the profession on Council. White had married into an impeccable family line: he was the son-in-law of Henry Ernest Milner, author of *The Art and Practice of Landscape Gardening* (1890), himself the son of Paxton's collaborator Edward Milner, the Director in his later years of the Crystal Palace School of Gardening. In addition to his articles on aspects of garden design, White also campaigned, along with Mawson, for the recognition of landscape architecture as a distinct discipline, straddling the boundaries of architecture and horticulture. The moment came when the RHS convened an international conference on garden planning in 1928. The papers were a mixture of historical and national surveys, with Gertrude Jekyll speaking on colour, George Dillistone and Gilbert Jenkins on design, and Christopher Hussey on ornament; the first three were by now members of a passing generation, and only Hussey was to play a role in the forthcoming modern movement. The papers conveyed a general impression that the battle between formal and informal gardening had ended, and that the preferred designs of the day were broadly formal without the hard edges. The young landscape architects assembled for the event determined to create their own professional organisation; the Institute of Landscape Architects was founded the following year, and Mawson was tactfully invited to be its first President (succeeded after a few years by White).[25]

The first generation of the Institute's members—people like Brenda Colvin, Geoffrey Jellicoe, and Sylvia Crowe—had been trained as garden designers, and never lost sight of the private garden as a focus of attention, however much they might later be attracted to larger-scale work in forestry, motorway and power station design, and town planning. A later generation, however, inspired by communitarian ideals, seemed to turn its back on the private garden as inappropriate for the modern age, and to see landscape design as a means of social reform. No doubt this attitude helped the Society to keep the new developments at arm's length; when in the late 1960s it was proposed to include garden design in the NDH Final Exam, Professor Stoughton summed up the deliberations by saying, 'The Society is concerned with horticulture of which landscape design and construction is not a major part'.[26]

Where garden design on the individual scale came closest to the aspirations of these landscape architects was in the emphasis on lawns and ground covers, to create large sweeps of uniform planting, an aesthetic ideal nicely geared to the post-war emphasis on low-maintenance planting. In the early 1960s, the RHS collaborated with Penguin Books on a series of small paperbacks, one of which was to be on labour-saving gardening, by Roy Hay. Penguin wanted the title to be *Gardening the Modern Way*; at first the Publications Committee refused to agree, suggesting *The Modern Garden and Labour Saving* as an alternative, but eventually Council bowed to Penguin's wishes and *Gardening the Modern Way* appeared in 1962. Much of the book was a description of the new machinery for gardening; only one chapter was concerned with design, and that emphasised the importance of simple

Christopher Bradley-Hole's Latin garden at the 1997 Chelsea Flower Show, which sparked controversy for its sparse planting.

outlines, wide walks, easy inclines, ground cover, and a selection of low-maintenance plants. (The late 1950s saw attempts at making the lawn more labour-saving by the use of stoloniferous grasses, such as the briefly fashionable 'Emerald Velvet', which was unsuccessfully tried at Wisley in 1960.)[27]

The heyday of the lawn-and-ground-cover movement lasted roughly from the 1950s to the 1970s, when the tradition of the small formal garden, interrupted or merely temporarily obscured, returned to view. Underlying the formality of the Arts and Crafts garden had been an interest in reviving the garden styles of the Tudor and Stuart periods; the revival of the herb garden as an ornamental feature was one outgrowth of this tendency. By the 1930s, the English landscape garden of the 18th century was returning to critical favour, and in the 1950s the recovered adulation for Capability Brown as the greatest of English gardeners meshed nicely with the emphasis on lawns as the basis of the garden.[28] The rediscovery of Gertrude Jekyll in the 1970s (and restoration of some of her gardens), and the activities of the National Trust, which under the influence of Graham Stuart Thomas and John

Sales was trying to restore the gardens of its country houses as accurate period settings, helped to make garden history an increasingly popular subject, while returning the Arts and Crafts manner to a precarious dominance in the small domestic garden.[29] Already by 1970 the assumption of period accuracy was so engrained that Christopher Brickell felt he had to defend the water garden in front of the Wisley Laboratory by saying:

> Purists may, perhaps, object to the design chosen on the grounds that an Elizabethan manor house should be landscaped in the style of that period, but one must remember that the laboratory building, although Elizabethan in outward appearance, is of relatively modern lineage dating only from 1914-16.[30]

Lindley's argument that the garden need not harmonise with the house had vanished into the past.

The 1990s saw a resurgent campaign for a modernism in the garden, to counteract the perceived dominance of Arts and Crafts design. The garden seen as an outdoor recreation room, promoted by John Brookes since the 1960s; a new interest in gravelled surfaces, fuelled by sources as diverse as the Japanese 'Zen' garden and Derek Jarman's garden on coastal shingle at Dungeness; the fashion for 'high-tech' architecture, promoted as the logical development of a briefly interrupted modernism, and bringing with it a heavy emphasis on glass and metal as construction materials—all these trends dovetailed to create a more or less unified movement, which found expression in newspaper columns and television 'makeover' programmes as well as books and magazines. The model gardens at the Chelsea Flower Show came increasingly to act as public focal points for the new modernism. In 1997 Christopher Bradley-Hole's 'Latin Garden' was voted best in show at Chelsea: a garden characterised by a sparseness of planting that a few years earlier would have been condemned, but which in the age of gravel (and of the sparse planting of a major historical reconstruction, the Privy Garden at Hampton Court) was now becoming fashionable. In 1999, Michael Balston's 'Reflections' garden was similarly fêted for an eyecatching series of sails on metal supports, meeting the material demands of one strand of modernism, and it was recreated at Wisley as a model garden: a sign that the Society had finally abandoned its longstanding reservations about garden design.[31]

A note on some garden ornaments

Garden sculpture is probably the least horticultural aspect of garden design, but it has twice

A view of the exhibition of garden sculpture that Reynolds-Stephens created to accompany the garden design conference in 1928.

metric garden, which the Treasurer, Sir William Lawrence, described as 'an inspired layout'; the *Gardeners' Chronicle* was not so approving, and described it as 'an architect's garden, which differs greatly from ... the landscape gardener's'. The most prestigious sculptors represented in the display were the now senior adherents of the 'New Sculpture' movement, which had emerged in the 1880s: Reynolds-Stephens himself, Goscombe John, Sir William Reid Dick, Gilbert Bayes, and the late Sir Hamo Thornycroft, whose figure of 'The Sower' was acquired for Kew after the exhibition ended. Mixed with these were a number of younger sculptors, the best known being Sergeant Jagger, whose works were harder-edged and more abstract than the Symbolist-influenced pieces of the New Sculptors—Art Deco supplanting an older Art Nouveau. Reynolds-Stephens was given a Veitch Medal for his work on the exhibition, the only sculptor so far to receive it.[32]

The exhibition provided a useful occasion for press campaigning, with Gilbert Bayes and Edward Gleichen (who had chaired one of the conference's sessions) calling in *The Times* for more sculpture and fountains in public gardens, and the organisation Roads for Remembrance for more sculpture on public roads. *Gardening Illustrated* greeted the exhibition as a breath of fresh air: 'After such an exhibition as this ... there can at least not be the excuse of ignorance for the repetition of such Victorian atrocities as one meets with all too frequently today'. That has continued to be the reputation of the exhibition: 'Forty years later', H.R. Fletcher exulted, 'there are not so many "Victorian atrocities".' With the passage of time, what becomes more apparent is the incipient rift between two competing styles of sculpture—both of which were to fall before the arrival of Modernism; by 1960, the works of Henry Moore and Barbara Hepworth represented the critical standard for garden sculpture. At the end of the century, when the newly design-conscious Society decided to provide temporary display space for garden sculptures at Wisley, in an effort to encourage new ideas on the subject, it was sculptures by Moore that were first sought out.[33]

At the other end of the scale of critical approval lay the garden gnome (literally merely a dwarf sculpture, but, to the English imagination, a

'The Sower' by Sir Hamo Thornycroft (1850-1925), exhibited posthumously in Reynolds-Stephens's exhibition, and acquired for the Royal Botanic Gardens, Kew, where it can still be seen.

briefly surfaced as a major theme in the Society's endeavours. The first time was in the early days of the Kensington garden, when Prince Albert hoped that the garden would serve *inter alia* as a forum for the public display of sculpture, and raise the profile of the art; the Society had a short-lived Sculpture Committee, and purchased various works for the decoration of the garden, only to dispose of them later when the fashion and the wealth had passed. The second time was in the 1920s, when the surge of commissions for war memorials was modulating into a more general campaign for the merits of public sculpture.

To accompany its grand conference on Garden Design in 1928, the Society decided to use the occasion for an exhibition of garden sculpture, which would be the first major exhibition in its New Hall (Lawrence Hall) on Greycoat Street. William Reynolds-Stephens, the President of the Royal Society of British Sculptors, was commissioned to assemble and arrange the exhibition, which occupied the central portion of the Hall (displays of garden designs were confined to the periphery). He laid it out in the form of a geo-

A different sort of sculpture for the garden: 'Reclining Figure: Angles', by Henry Moore, exhibited at Wisley in 2000-2001.

sculpture of a dwarf). Promoted in the Edwardian period by the prestigious ceramic firm of Ernst Wahliss, who tried to associate them with the burgeoning (but as yet unnamed) baroque revival, they became widely popular during the inter-war years, but also came to be regarded as the indicator ornaments of the lower middle class, and so despised by the upper strata. The regulations for the Chelsea Flower Show, which showed a clear adherence to the conventions of the new Neo-Georgian taste, prohibited coloured statuary (gnomes specifically mentioned, at a time when the only well-known gnome owner was Sir Frank Crisp) from the show gardens. In the 1980s, the promotion of garden gnomes by garden centres was increasing, and what a Council minute referred to as the 'planned, commercially encouraged, attempt to persuade the Society to allow the inclusion of garden gnomes' reached a peak in 1983 with the staging of a demonstration outside the show ground calling for gnomes to be allowed in. Thereafter the gnome publicity event became an annual fixture. No garden gnomes have been placed at Wisley to encourage new ideas on the subject.[34]

From parks to window-boxes

The polluted atmosphere of cities was a problem that exercised John Evelyn in the 17th century, and plagued the Society in the nineteenth. Within a few years of the Kensington garden's opening, it was being criticised for the sooty and miserable condition of the plants; forty years later it was the increasing air pollution at Chiswick that determined the Society to move to Wisley. Lord Aberdare, the President in the early 1880s, was mocked in the press for his foredoomed attempts to grow conifers in London. Maxwell T. Masters published recommendations for pollution-tolerant city trees in the *Journal* in 1891, work that was later improved on by Angus D. Webster. But the range of plants that would prove long-lived and reliable in the worst urban climate remained sorely limited until the Clean Air Act came into force in 1960.[35]

For park superintendents, whose duty it was to maintain beautiful gardens in town centres, seasonal bedding remained until then the only efficient form of decorative horticulture. The RHS continued into the 1950s to provide advice on bedding in its *Dictionary of Gardening*, at a time when most gardening commentators had turned against it for reasons of aesthetic fashion or social status; two of the 20th century's most important practitioners and theorists of bedding design, Thomas Hay of the Central Royal Parks and J.R.B. Evison of the Brighton Parks, served as Council members and ensured that the tradition was not lost sight of. In 1946, the RHS staged a Municipal Horticulture Exhibition as a means of helping municipal parks services to recover from

Window-box and hanging basket, displayed as part of the competition at the Hampton Court Palace Flower Show in 2001.

their wartime problems; in the 1990s, when cuts in government funding and compulsory competitive tendering for maintenance services inflicted a new blow to parks services already suffering budgetary depletion as a result of local authority reorganisation, Robin Herbert joined Jennifer Jenkins's review committee on the Royal Parks to advise on the maintenance of horticultural standards. (Hal Moggridge, reviewing the Garden History Society's volume on *The Regeneration of Public Parks* in 2001, remarked on compulsory competitive tendering, 'One may observe that RHS gardens are not managed by such stupid methods.') By the mid-1990s, agitation over urban parks had achieved such a high profile that the Heritage Lottery Fund embarked on a scheme of grant-aiding park restoration projects, and David Welch, the Superintendent of the Royal Parks, promoted the scheme in the pages of *The Garden*.[36]

At the other end of the scale from the gigantic parks lay the small domestic garden and the cottage garden, which until the middle of the 20th century were generally seen in terms of food production. In 1904 the RHS instituted a Cottage and Allotment Examination, not for the cottagers but for the county horticultural officers who had to advise them; and although its active involvement in promoting allotments was largely

confined to the World Wars, the Society gave evidence to the Thorpe Committee on allotments in the hope of increasing government grant aid for their provision. As for ornamental horticulture for the town dweller, the Society offered prizes for window-gardening for the working classes in the 1860s, and the 1870s saw the promotion of ferns as window-box plants that could endure the urban smoke. It was not until after the Clean Air Act was proposed that the significant promotion of floral window-boxes and hanging baskets got under way. Window-boxes became admissible at the London shows in 1957, though the Society declined to judge Westminster's window-box competition a few years later. In 1987 the first window-box competition was held at Chelsea, and proved so gratifyingly popular that a hanging basket competition followed it in 1988; both competitions have carried on, growing continuously, ever since.[37]

The garden advisory service

In 1866, the RHS decided to provide advice to its Fellows about their gardens; this duty devolved on George Eyles, as Superintendent of the Kensington garden and also a well-known landscape gardener. In his wake, the successive

Superintendents of Chiswick, Archibald Barron and S.T. Wright, took on the role. By 1912 Council were concerned that Wright's garden-advisory work was taking up too much of his time, and they decided to hire someone to act specifically as a Garden Inspector, who would visit Fellows' gardens and advise them about their planting and layout. The man chosen for the purpose was Ellen Willmott's head gardener at Warley Place, C.R. Fielder, who had already made a name for himself as a garden designer. Willmott consented to his working part-time for the RHS, though once the war broke out there were some tensions about who paid for his coal supply. Fielder continued in this role until he retired in 1924.[38]

The RHS advertised for a successor, at a fee of £300 per annum, and got the services of John E. Vine. Possibly because, as official institutions, their requests came specifically to the attention of Council, it is Vine's work as a landscaper of hospitals that emerges from Council minutes: St David's Home for Disabled Soldiers, at Ealing, 1925; the West Wickham Heart Hospital, 1927. By the mid-1930s, the demand for the work was so great that a second Inspector was hired: W.J. Penton, formerly head gardener at The Node, Welwyn, whose fee was two guineas a day, or one guinea for a half-day. Vine resigned in 1938, and after some months of indecision, Council appointed James Wilson, who had been head gardener to the late Sir Philip Sassoon at Trent Park. Wilson soon found his time taken by wartime duties in charge of the Society's lectures, but after the war was quickly back in harness, advising the National Trust on Montacute, and writing pamphlets on various aspects of gardening for the Society. In 1947, his job was renamed Garden Adviser. Wilson tried to retire in 1956, but was persuaded to stay on for a few years longer, and died in harness in June 1957, to be succeeded by H.R. Tuffin. Tuffin retired in 1970, and as the Society's finances were sliding, it was decided that the next Garden Adviser should recoup part of his salary from his fees.[39]

The next Garden Adviser was Geoffrey Coombs (1971-82), who designed the Stanley Smith model gardens at Wisley in the late 1970s and wrote the Wisley Handbooks on *Plans for Small Gardens*; he was followed by

William Nelmes (1982-93). The service was then discontinued.[40]

Progressively, during the careers of the Garden Advisers, the gardens advised on have shrunk in size, and the definition of 'small garden' has steadily narrowed. There is an unconfirmed rumour that one of the Society's lecturers in the early 20th century advised that 'every garden, no matter how small, should have its two acres of wilderness'. By the late 20th century, Geoffrey Coombs was addressing suburban properties of a much restricted extent, though some were still large enough to require the building of a ha-ha. By the end of the 1990s the RHS had caught up with the majority, and sponsored the publication of Jill Billington's *Really Small Gardens*, a book directed at gardens 'as big as 6m (20ft) square or not much wider than a passage, about 1.5m (5ft) deep'.[41]

The original Enthusiast's Garden, one of the model gardens at Wisley designed by Geoffrey Coombs in the 1970s.

16 *Ornamental Garden Plants*

FOR its first half-century, the Society offered prizes for its competitions, and awarded medals to people for particular achievements, which frequently included the raising of introducing of a new plant; but there were no awards made to plants themselves, no implied system of grading by which the merit of a plant could be assessed. It was only in 1858-9, when the need to re-position itself against its competitors led to the formation of Fruit and Floral Committees, that awards for plants were instituted for the first time.

The Floral Committees

It was consistent with the Society's early priorities that a Fruit Committee should have been established before a Floral Committee; but as the Society has developed, the Fruit Committee has remained with little change, while the Floral Committee has evolved into a network of different committees, many of them forming points of liaison with outside organisations.

The Floral Committee was founded on 24 June 1859, a year after the Fruit Committee, and was given the function of 'examining all plants submitted to it, with a view to decide upon their respective merit and novelty'. This was made more specific in regulations published in the *Gardeners' Chronicle* for 13 August 1859: 'To examine and to report upon the merits of such New Plants and Flowers, whether imported species or seedling florists' flowers, as may be submitted for that purpose.' Two awards were created to be awarded by the Committee: First Class and Second Class Certificates (the latter replaced by the Award of Merit in 1888). These were the Society's first awards to be given to plants instead of to exhibits.[1]

The first Chairman of the Committee was Arthur Henfrey, Professor of Botany at King's College London; his opposite number at University College, John Lindley, was also a member, and effectively the Society's direct representative. The largest number of the founder members of the Committee consisted of nurserymen; there were three clergymen with floral interests, and three head gardeners; and a group of amateur growers, including Dr Allen Maclean of Colchester, who had recently donated a collection of *Tigridia* specimens to the Society. Soon to join the number was Donald Beaton, the pugnacious journalist and one of the pioneers of pelargonium breeding, and he was followed by such men as Maxwell T. Masters, the plant collector George Ure Skinner, William Ingram of Belvoir Castle, H.H. Dombrain, and Shirley Hibberd in the 19th century; W.J. Bean, E.A. Bowles, Amos Perry, and Montagu Allwood in the twentieth.

The longest-serving Chairman was the orchid grower William Marshall, who held that position from 1890 to 1910; he then expressed a desire to stand down and serve as Deputy Chairman, but the Committee couldn't see the distinction between that and the existing role of Vice-Chairman, so from 1911 to 1917 Marshall shared the Chairmanship jointly with the Tottenham nurseryman Henry B. May.

The range of plants to be dealt with by the Floral Committee became a long-standing problem. In 1884 the Floral Committee was divided into two divisions—A, for plants in general, and B, for florists' flowers—with George Fergusson Wilson as the (somewhat reluctant) chairman for both. The following year the two divisions were re-united. Again, in 1907, George Bunyard suggested that the Fruit Committee could take over some of Floral's work-load, but this suggestion was rejected. By this time both orchids and daffodils had been devolved onto separate committees. Attempts to categorise the plants dealt with by the Committee led to problems of definition; in November 1891 the Committee

James Shirley Hibberd (1825-1890), prolific author and pioneer of gardening journalism for the middle classes. Founder-editor of the monthly Floral World *(1858-1880), and in 1884 of the weekly* Amateur Gardening, *which carries on his legacy today.*

FACING PAGE
A trial of delphiniums at Wisley, 1999.

asked Council (unsuccessfully) to legislate on the definition of 'hardy herbaceous plant'.[2] In 1923, the Committee was finally split into sections A and B, with effect from the following year.

The original remit of Floral A was 'to look at florists' flowers, including flowers for the herbaceous border'. In 1964 a Special Committee was appointed to reconsider the division of plants between Floral A and Floral B, and redefined the remit of Floral A as: 'cultivars of horticultural origin which are the result of prolonged breeding and selection, or multiple hybridity, normally grown for garden decoration'. It is now defined in the *Manual for Committee Members and Exhibitors* as 'plants normally grown in the herbaceous border, both species and cultivars (including cultivars of species), cultivars of horticultural origin which are the result of prolonged breeding and selection, or of multiple hybridity, normally grown for garden decoration including bedding. Modern hybrids of roses are included.' Henry B. May, the Edmonton nurseryman who had been the last Chairman of the original Floral Committee, became the first Chairman of Floral A, and has been succeeded in that role by the nurserymen G.W. Leak and Will Ingwersen, the amateur iris grower Geoffrey Pilkington, and Mrs Carolyn Hardy, among others.

Floral B was originally assigned 'plants other than florists' flowers'. In the Arrangements for 1924 this was amended to 'trees, shrubs and botanical species'. The 1964 Special Committee redefined its remit as: 'plants collected in the wild, species and their varieties, cultivars and first generation (F1) hybrids, including all trees and most shrubs, normally grown for garden decoration'. This has been further revised to specify 'hardy trees and shrubs ... including old hybrid roses and species'. It also deals with rhododendrons and camellias when the specialist committee is not meeting. G.W.E. Loder, the Society's future President, was the first Chairman of Floral B, and has been succeeded by several presidents and treasurers—two Lord Aberconways, C.T. Musgrave, Lewis Palmer, Oliver Wyatt, Lord Blakenham—as well as Sir Eric Savill of the Crown Estates.[3]

The 1964 Special Committee further declared that there was 'a need for an additional committee', and recommended the adoption of a plan put forward by Arthur Simmonds, the former Secretary. Accordingly, Section C was established with effect from 1965, to deal with 'flowers and ornamental plants normally grown for decorative effect in heated glasshouses or in dwelling houses'. During the early years of the committee, it was only convened when there were

"It wins it, it wins it not, it......"
Daily Graphic   March 24 '56.

Flower show judging: a cartoon from the Daily Graphic, *24 March 1956.*

enough groups to justify a meeting, cards being sent to members; in more recent years it has met regularly. The nurseryman J.L. Russell was the first Chairman, succeeded by Maurice Mason, one of the last prominent amateur exhibitors of greenhouse plants, and Anthony Huxley, in whose honour a prize was instituted.[4]

Awards have generally been made, or proposed, at shows, and published in the Society's *Proceedings* under each show. Cumulative lists of awards were published between 1893 and the 1930s; all certificated plants had their portraits painted between 1922 and 1951, and certificated orchids have been portrayed consistently since 1897. Photography was discussed as early as 1906, but decided against; and since the Second World War it has become the principal means of recording the plants.[5]

In addition to the two major awards, various preliminary awards, Certificates of Botanical

Interest and Cultural Commendation are also available, and much confusion arose in the early days about the relations between the awards, and which committees are entitled to award them. The Scientific and Orchid Committees fought for a quarter-century over who should award Botanical Certificates for orchids; committees tried to give the awards in the wrong sequence; the most common complaint has been the number of awards, and the excessive similarity of plants awarded. The Certificate of Preliminary Commendation had its origin in a request from the Orchid Committee to provide an award for seedling orchids that seemed likely to prove useful. Council accepted the principle, but left the remit open to any categories of plants.[6] But over the course of more than a century there have been remarkably few instances of flaring tempers, and nomenclatural problems have been far more vexing than the question of the committees' standards.

Joint Committees

The immense number of types of plants dealt with by the Floral Committee led to various proposals for more specialist committees. Successful cuttings were taken before the end of the century in the form of the Orchid and Narcissus Committees, though William Watson's 1894 proposal for a Cactus Committee and an annual exhibition of cacti seems to have died rapidly.

Joint committees with different societies go back to the Edwardian period in an unsystematic way. The first joint committee was apparently with the National Dahlia Society. Further joint committees were formed for irises and sweet peas, and in 1930 a committee was convened to look into the question of joint committees and awards. It recommended the following procedures for the governing of joint committees:

> That every Joint Committee consist of a Chairman, appointed by the Council, and not fewer than ten other Members, half to be appointed by the Council and half by the allied society concerned ... That on a day when a Joint Committee is meeting all plants of the class with which the Joint Committee is concerned (except species and first crosses between species) be referred to it, and that on a day when there is no meeting of the Joint Committee the plants be referred to the appropriate section of the Floral Committee ...

After the International Horticultural Conference of 1930 there was a new rationale for their formation, and the Society applied it systematically. That Conference had recommended that, in any given country, there should be only one body giving awards for any category of plants, in order to avoid confusion. 'Various measures have been sought to this end', reported Chittenden in April 1936, 'and the Joint Committee has proved the most workable. Now for Dahlias, Sweet Peas, Irises, Delphiniums, Carnations, Rhododendrons, only one set of Awards exists in this country.' The elimination of duplication or conflict of awards became the major criterion by which the appropriateness of a joint committee would be judged.[7]

Trials and the Award of Garden Merit

A systematic programme of trials got underway in the 1860s, once the Kensington garden had brought the money flowing back into the Society's depleted coffers. While most of the trials conducted at Chiswick were of fruits and vegetables, the *Proceedings* for 1861 reported on trials of miscellaneous annuals, annual stocks, heliotropes, scarlet and other bedding pelargoniums, variegated begonias, and achimenes. By the turn of the century, in part no doubt because of increasing air pollution at Chiswick, the number of trials was diminishing, but over a forty-year period they had covered a wide range of plants from abutilons and cannas to asters and violas.

Once the Society had moved to Wisley, the trials programme was reinvigorated. Again, fruit and vegetables dominated at first, and renewed their dominance whenever there was a world war,

Floral A Committee judging under wartime conditions (1941), with a sign conveniently pointing to the air raid shelter in case their deliberations were interrupted.

but, especially after the National Fruit Trials became a separate institution, ornamental plants took over the ascendancy. By mid-century a tradition had been established of two different types of trial: permanent and invited. The permanent trials generally correspond to the existence of specialist committees—border carnations and pinks, early-flowering chrysanthemums, daffodils, dahlias, delphiniums, irises, rhododendrons, sweet peas—although in the past there were permanent trials of gladioli, hemerocallis, peonies, phlox, and pyrethrums, that turned out in the event to be merely long-standing. The cultivars are selected by the relevant committee, and grown near a collection of standard cultivars for ease of comparison; if after a set number of years the new cultivars are not recommended for an award, they are removed from the trial. Invited trials are conducted on a more *ad hoc* basis, repeated (if at all) at distinct intervals; cultivars are sent by nurserymen and the public in response to press notification. Over the course of a century, an even wider range of plants has been tried, from cinerarias, coleus, smithianthas, to antirrhinums, oenotheras, heucheras, sidalceas, schizanthus, and pampas grasses. In any given year a couple of thousand cultivars are being tried—since 1970 in the sweeping Portsmouth Field; trial results have been published regularly in the *Proceedings*, and increasingly since the early 1990s articles have appeared in *The Garden* publicising the trials, emphasising their importance, and encouraging visitors to inspect them.[8]

Trials procedures have developed over the generations, and various strategies used at different times to ensure accuracy of results. On occasion the plants have been identified by numbers only, to ensure objectivity. How many specimens of a given cultivar need to be included, to allow for individual variation in performance? Should trials be restricted to plants available in commerce, and what happens if awarded plants disappear from stock? Should the Wisley trials be supplemented by trials elsewhere in the country, since plants that succeed in the south-east do not necessarily do well in the north? (Simultaneous trials have been proposed at various times, and were carried out by the Northern Horticultural Society, with a long-running chrysanthemum trial at Bradford.) In 1968, a new reorganisation reduced the number of trials, in part by excluding from that title the comparative growing of plants for nomenclatural purposes. Complaints have arisen from time to time over the criteria, less often the conduct, of particular trials, but the overall verdict remains the same as even the Society's critics allowed in the early days: there is no other way of ensuring that

the trade and the public can reliably select the best.[9] Within Wisley, of course, there has been another consideration: what proportion of the garden's resources should be devoted to the trials? In the days of Francis Hanger, whose exhibits at Chelsea and Westminster shows excited such admiration, there was a tendency to lavish resources on the growing of plants for exhibition purposes at the expense of the trials. When H.R. Fletcher became Director of Wisley, his inspection revealed that the plants for Chelsea had taken over the room normally allotted to glasshouse trials and other purposes: 'In 1951 the vinery was filled with Lilies, Primulas, Meconopsis, etc. Naturally the vines suffered and after the 1951 Chelsea I remember Mr. Bowes-Lyon looking into the vinery and saying that the grapes grown therein were the worst he had ever seen'.[10]

The advantages of the trials for the nursery trade quickly became apparent, and various schemes have been devised over the years to integrate them more fully into the world of commercial horticulture. In the immediate post-war years the Ministry of Agriculture instituted national reference collections of certain important plants, with the RHS assuming responsibility for dahlias and chrysanthemums; the scheme was inaugurated with great éclat, but was abandoned after a decade. Another experiment was set up by the Seed Trade and Retail Seed Trade Associations, under the chairmanship of T.M. Clucas: the All-Britain seed trials, modelled on the All-American trials, with Wisley as a principal trial ground. 'The object is to enable the public to be informed of the new varieties coming on to the market, and to provide a body which will be able to assess the merits of novelties.' The scheme was formally inaugurated in 1964, with Wisley committed to growing 600 plants in an area of 175 square yards; within a few years, the Society concluded that 'in their present form they were of very little use to the gardening public', though continued membership of the scheme maintained the goodwill of the nursery trade.[11]

A longer-lasting trend was that of securing legal rights for the breeders of new varieties. In the 1930s the Horticultural Trades Association attempted to launch a bill giving legal protection to the raisers of novelties, but it failed, in part no doubt because the RHS declined to support it. But after the war came eager discussions of trademarks, of plant patents, and of Plant Variety Rights; the RHS took part in a committee on the last-named proposal, and after some years of tentative discussions the Plant Breeders' Rights Association was formed in 1962, with L.J. Smith the first Controller. The RHS agreed to undertake trials of dahlias, chrysanthemums, delphiniums, sweet peas and rhododendrons for the Plant Variety Rights Office, and issued regular pronouncements about the system in the *Journal*.[12]

When Lord Lambourne became President after the First World War, he appointed a committee to find ways of enforcing consistency in the making of awards. Various suggestions—such as the 'Congratulations of the Council' for outstanding merit, the use of the Lindley Medal as a supplementary award, and the issue of 'Standard Cups' for exhibits which just missed getting Gold Medals—were tried and discontinued. But one that succeeded was the Award of Garden Merit, given on the advice of the Wisley Garden Committee for plants that had been demonstrated excellent for use in the garden. The first AGM was awarded to *Hamamelis mollis* in January 1922. Chittenden compiled an anthology of the AGM plants, published in 1938 as *Some Good Garden*

The jollity of daffodil judging. On the left, C.H. Curtis, Secretary of the Narcissus Committee, 1903-23, and editor of the Gardeners' Chronicle *and* Orchid Review. *To his right are Guy L. Wilson and George Engleheart, two daffodil breeders who between them named 1,353 cultivars.*

Plants; this went through four editions by 1962, and was supplemented briefly by an annual publication called *New Plants of the Year*. By the 1980s, however, difficulties had developed with the 60-year-old system; AGM plants had disappeared from cultivation, others had been surpassed by new cultivars but were still on the list; some had proved unstable over time, others had fallen prey to newly arrived pests and diseases. In 1988, a working party on awards was convened; the AGM came under particular scrutiny, and in

1992 it was relaunched. All the old AGM designations were rescinded, and a new list of some 3,600 plants was compiled. Provision was also made for a regular review of the AGM list at ten-year intervals, and the first such review, announced in January 2002, dropped over 1,000 plants from the list, replacing them with 889 new ones.[13]

The following review of the Society's work with different categories of ornamental garden plants is organised in roughly chronological order according to the creation—or at least proposal—of the various specialist committees.

Daffodils and tulips

In 1818, Joseph Sabine presented his collections of hardy bulbs to the Society's garden; he specified that the collection of *Narcissus* was one of the best, because he had arranged and described it systematically as it grew. In 1820, the Society commissioned drawings of daffodils from John Curtis, but these were disposed of in 1859, and have not been recovered. After Sabine's time, daffodils remained a matter of but small interest to the Society for half a century. They had fallen from fashion as garden flowers; jonquils played a greater role in the early years of spring bedding than the pseudo-narcissus; but there were nonetheless determined breeders like Edward Leeds who maintained a flow of new cultivars throughout the mid-19th century. The return of the daffodil to favour was in large part the work of the great Covent Garden seedsman Peter Barr, who earned the epithet of the 'Daffodil King' for his efforts, both as a commercial supplier and as a gadfly pushing the RHS into daffodil ventures.[14]

In 1884, largely on Barr's urging, the Society held a Daffodil Conference under the chairmanship of Michael Foster; it appointed a committee to revise the nomenclature of daffodils, and produced what became known as the Conference Catalogue of Narcissi. The nomenclature committee continued to examine new cultivars until in 1888 it was finally made a standing committee of the Society, and daffodils were thenceforth submitted to it rather than the Floral Committee on those occasions when it sat. In 1902 it was retitled the Narcissus and Tulip Committee. In 1912 Peter Barr's heirs presented the Peter Barr Memorial Cup, which has remained in the gift of this Committee; the following year the Engleheart Cup was established for competition. In 1919 Council specifically said that another award for daffodils was undesirable, but further cups and medals have been instituted over the years, and there are now two annual awards and eight prizes given at competition for daffodils.[15]

Most of the important daffodil breeders of the last century (Mrs R.O. Backhouse, G.H. Engleheart, P.D. Williams, Guy L. Wilson, Lionel Richardson, Alex Gray) have been members of the Committee, as have such luminaries of the tulip as W.R. Dykes (*Notes on Tulip Species*), Joseph Jacob (*Tulips*), and Daniel Hall (*The Genus Tulipa*); the Committee also holds the record for longest-lasting chairman (E.A. Bowles, for 43 years). In 1907 the Committee produced its first *List of Daffodil Names*, and the next year appointed a subcommittee on classification; revised lists appeared throughout the century, until the RHS eventually became the International Registration Authority for the genus. Further conferences on daffodils were held in 1899, 1890, and 1927. In 1911 the Committee again successfully sought Council's permission to issue a *Year Book* (first published 1913) and show schedules, and to divide itself into subcommittees for special purposes—so that today there are four additional committees or subcommittees that have originated as cuttings from Narcissus and Tulip. Specialist daffodil shows were held for nearly ten years, until they were discontinued in 1921 because of increasing costs and falling attendances, and requests for further shows under the Committee's auspices were rejected.[16]

Twice in the early 20th century the establishment of a national daffodil society was publicly mooted, in both cases with a background of complaints about the RHS, the limited remit of the Committee, and the conduct of shows. In 1911 a proposal from W.B. Cranfield was defeated, in favour of extending the role of the Narcissus and Tulip Committee. Joseph Jacob, having opposed the idea of a separate society then, proposed his own Narcissus Society in January 1922, but nothing came of this either. On 21 March 1939 a Joint Narcissus Committee was established with the Midland Daffodil Society, E.A. Bowles acting as first chairman; this was discontinued in 1968 because it hadn't met for years. An augmented system of trials was begun in 1932, with major

plantings at Wisley and additional trials convened at Kirton Experimental Station in Lincolnshire. Over the years, other experimental stations built up collections, most notably Rosewarne in Cornwall; Michael Pollock was Director there when the government broke the news of its impending closure, and arranged for the daffodil collection (as also the collections of hydrangeas and escallonias) to be transferred to Wisley in 1989.[17]

Tulips received greater attention than daffodils in the mid-19th century. In 1853 John Edwards proposed that the Society establish a National Tulip Bed at Chiswick—the first proposal for a national plant collection, though not carried out. Thereafter the Society's tulip activities were limited to publishing articles in its *Journal* until the turn of the century, when tulip trials were first carried out at Chiswick.

In order to deal with complaints about multiple names, a Tulip Nomenclature Committee was set up in 1913, trials begun at Wisley, and a conference held, but the First World War threw difficulties in the way of further Dutch involvement for a few years. In 1928 renewed discussions began with the Royal Dutch Bulbgrowers' Association over a checklist, and *A Tentative List of Tulip Names* was published by the Society in 1929; from 1948 the lists were published jointly by the Society and the Bulbgrowers' Association, and from 1960 by the Association alone.[18]

Orchids

The attempt to grow tropical orchids under glass was one of the great research projects of botanical gardens in the early 19th century, mainly because their cultural requirements were not understood. It was long thought that the orchids that could be seen growing on the upper branches of trees must be parasitic; but experiments by Sir Joseph Banks (who seems to have invented the hanging basket as a means of growing them) and others during the 1820s and 1830s established that they were epiphytic, depending on the trees solely for support and not nourishment. From the 1830s, orchids were collected enthusiastically; John Lindley had already turned his attention to their classification, coining such genera as *Cattleya, Coelogyne, Cycnoches, Laelia, Lycaste, Miltonia,* and *Sophronitis.* In the 1840s, John Dillwyn Llewellyn devised the first orchid house that attempted to reproduce a rain-forest setting, and his description of it in the first volume of the Society's new *Journal* (1846) proved influential on others. A decade later, John Dominy, hybridist at the Veitch nurseries in Chelsea, bred the first artificially-produced orchid hybrid, *Calanthe ×*

William Rickatson Dykes (1877-1925), Master of Charterhouse School before he became Secretary of the RHS, where his career was cut short by a fatal car crash. Michael Foster's successor as the leading authority on irises; author of The Genus Iris, *and other books on irises and tulips.*

dominyana; Sir Harry Veitch was later to recall Lindley's reaction on seeing it: 'You will drive the botanists mad!'[19]

The garden at Chiswick became famous for its orchid collection. George Gordon kept his specimens not uniformly warm and moist, but dry and cool during their winter repose, and achieved excellent results, the orchids increasing to the point where they blocked traffic in the glasshouses. Lindley exercised himself in scouring travellers' reports for details on the environmental conditions in which the orchids grew naturally. Theodor Hartweg sent a magnificent *Laelia superbiens* from Mexico, which the *Gardeners' Chronicle* considered 'worth travelling a considerable distance to see'. On the other hand, the attention lavished on orchids at the expense of fruit incurred censure, and helped to prompt the formation of the British Pomological Society as a corrective. In 1852 alone £189 was given in awards to orchids, more than to any other class of plants except general stove plants (despite the major orchid exhibitors grumbling about the medals being reduced in value). The first Lindley Medals were awarded for orchids (to James Veitch and William Bull). By the 1880s orchid hybridising was emerging as the preferred exercise of the wealthy gardener, especially after the first truly ornamental bigeneric hybrid *Laeliocattleya* was produced in 1887, and before long the indexes to the *Gardeners' Chronicle* were listing the descriptions of orchid collections under a separate subheading.[20]

In 1885, the Society staged an Orchid Conference, whose proceedings were published as volume 7 of the *Journal*. The programme had been made the responsibility of a Committee, among whose members were the incoming President Sir Trevor Lawrence, Thiselton-Dyer of Kew, and Michael Foster; Foster at least seems to have tried to keep the Committee alive, because in March 1886 he moved that the Scientific and Orchid Committees—by which latter title he must have meant the Conference Committee—liaise with the Committee for the forthcoming Provincial Show in Liverpool, in order to convene a conference on orchid nomenclature at that Show. This further conference duly took place, with Professor Reichenbach in attendance, but thereafter Foster's committee seems to have lapsed.

On 12 March 1889, James Douglas, the Great Bookham nurseryman, suggested 'the formation of an Orchid Committee to be drawn from the Fruit & Floral Committees', with 'power to recommend certificates &c in the same way as the other Committees'. The first meeting, held on 9 April, was chaired by Sir Trevor Lawrence, and among the first members were John Dominy, Maxwell T. Masters, the horticultural printer and amateur orchid grower Harry M. Pollett, and the leading orchid nurseryman Frederick Sander. Although there have been times when nurserymen dominated the Committee's membership, most major amateur orchid growers of the 20th century have been members, including Sir

A meeting of the Orchid Committee in the early 20th century. Gentlemen on the left, head gardeners on the right. Sir Harry Veitch is seated on the far left.

Jeremiah Colman, De Barri Crawshay, and Eric Young—not to mention K.D. Morgenstern, whose expulsion from the Committee over his truculent behaviour did not prevent him from donating a substantial orchid collection to Wisley. There has even been a foreign member, Prince Tadashige Shimadzu (to use the transliteration of the day), who was made an honorary committee member while in England (1921-31). Two orchid collections have been represented simultaneously by both the owner and the gardener: The Dell, Englefield Green (Baron Schröder and his grower Henry Ballantine), and Westonbirt (Sir George Holford and his grower James O'Brien). O'Brien was to be the Committee's Secretary for many years.[21]

In 1896 the Committee petitioned Council for permission to hire an artist to depict award-winning orchids and provide a permanent record against which to measure progress in future breeding. The artist selected was Nellie Roberts, who had been painting orchids for Sir Trevor Lawrence; she acted as the Society's orchid painter for over 50 years, receiving a Veitch Medal in 1953 for her work. She was succeeded by six other artists in turn; at the time of writing, Cherry-Ann Lavrih has been the orchid painter since 1987. A collection of over 7,000 orchid portraits has been built up over the past century; and in her early days Roberts painted portraits of such of the pre-1897 award winners as could readily be found for her.[22]

The development of the Orchid Register has been described in chapter 12. A further orchid conference was held in 1912, and in 1985 an international conference commemorating the centenary of the original one in 1885. In the meantime, as orchid breeding spread throughout the world, and became particularly popular in eastern Asia, a system of triennial World Orchid Conferences was instigated in the 1950s; the RHS organised the third of these conferences, in 1960, and has played a role in every conference since. Orchid trophies have come and gone in the past, but at the present time there are two awards in the gift of the Orchid Committee: the George Moore Medal (instituted in 1926) and the Westonbirt Orchid Medal (provided from a fund presented in 1960). The Society plays a role in the administration of the Eric Young Orchid Scholarship, which funds a three-year programme for aspiring orchidologists, the first and third years spent training at Wisley, and the middle year in the wild or travelling.[23]

Cacti and succulents

For a while, in the 1830s, it would have been difficult to predict whether orchids or cacti would emerge as the more popular plants; but John Claudius Loudon set his face against the interest in cacti as evidence of a 'vitiated or singular' taste, and orchids won out. Nonetheless, since the late 17th century, there had been a steady interest in South African succulents, and the increasing number of American species that entered England in the 19th century was ensured some degree of welcome. Two important articles on their cultural requirements were published in the *Transactions*, one by Donald Beaton. William Wilson Saunders, the Society's Treasurer and Secretary at different times in the 1860s, was one of the period's major collectors of succulents. So it is not surprising that during his terms of office Queen Victoria should present the Society with a cochineal cactus, or that it should accept a collection of mammillarias. But then interest faded, until the turn of the century witnessed the first episode of a recurring experiment in growing hardy cacti outdoors. E.A. Bowles was scheduled to lecture to the Society on the subject in 1908; by the time his lecture took place, heavy frosts had wiped out his collection:

> I have in consequence a long list of the slain to read to you, and this afternoon's meeting partakes ... of the nature of a memorial service ... Two wheelbarrows full of rotten pieces of Cacti are, then, my qualifications for addressing you.[24]

In 1894, William Watson of Kew proposed the establishment of an annual cactus exhibition, and a Cactus Committee, which would assume the responsibility for judging cacti and awarding certificates like the Orchid and Daffodil Committees. His proposal was rejected, as was H.J. Elwes's later offer of a cup or medal for succulents. At mid-century, the principal promoter of cacti and succulents within the RHS was Vera Higgins, author and translator of several books on the subject, and for a while editor of both the Society's *Journal* and that of the Cactus and Succulent Society; but it was not until the 1970s that a significant trial was held of a succulent (*Schlumbergera*). Nonetheless, cactus nurserymen have always been represented at the shows, and the last regular amateur exhibitors at the Westminster shows, Will and Elsie Tjaden, specialised in schlumbergeras, mesembryanthemums, and conophytums.[25]

Dahlias and chrysanthemums

Dahlias and chrysanthemums were both introduced late in the 18th century, but neither became widespread until the nineteenth. The dahlia began to cause excitement the year the Society was founded, with Humboldt's introductions flowering in France, and the first volume of the *Trans-*

Reginald Cory (1871-1934), coal millionnaire who left his library to the RHS and his money to the Cambridge Botanic Garden. Collected plants in Africa and the West Indies; commissioned Thomas Mawson to develop his garden at The Dyffryn, and to plan a model village called Glen Cory, near Swansea.

actions contained discussions of dahlia species by Salisbury and Wedgwood. Sabine published a review of existing dahlia varieties in 1820, but devoted more energy to chrysanthemums, mainly because John Reeves was sending specimens and drawings of varieties from China; Sabine published accounts of them in the *Transactions*, and approved the Chinese fancy names ('Yellow Tiger's Claw', 'White Waves of Autumn') as alternatives to the dull English ones like 'Semi-double Quilled Pale Orange'.[26] After Sabine's departure, the academic attention devoted to either genus diminished, though the collections at Chiswick continued to attract attention, and dahlias in particular were a subject for competition at the shows. During the 1830s, dahlias changed hands for large sums of money, and were accepted by many as a new florists' flower; and the number of exhibition categories continually increased. Trials of pompon dahlias were held at Chiswick in 1863 and again, along with cactus dahlias, at the turn of the century. The Society's first trials of chrysanthemums took place in the 1880s, and were resumed at Wisley in 1910. After an abortive attempt at a conference and show, a Chrysanthemum Centenary Conference took place in 1890, and a dahlia conference in 1891.[27]

On 24 December 1881, the *Gardeners' Chronicle* announced the formation of a committee 'for the purpose of holding during the next Dahlia season a great exhibition, open to the United Kingdom'. The Crystal Palace Company financed the show, and from its success arose the National Dahlia Society. At what date a Joint Committee was first set up between the two societies for judging dahlias is uncertain: it must have been by 1912, for in that year its existence was referred to in the course of a dispute with the Gladiolus Society. In 1913 a Joint Committee was engaged in judging trials of dahlias set up by Reginald Cory at his garden, The Dyffryn. These were certainly the first trials of dahlias as garden rather than exhibition flowers; Cory, who was later to become President of the National Dahlia Society, arranged and financed the trials himself. The *Gardeners' Chronicle* reported: 'The Dyffryn gardens comprise upwards of 40 acres and the provision of flower beds and borders is so liberal that immense numbers of Dahlias can be cultivated with ease, but this fact notwithstanding, the ground was planted up to the very last foot.' More than 1,000 species and cultivars were inspected by the Committee that first year; Cory was given a Gold Medal for his work, but soon after incurred criticism for the late publishing of the results, which he defended on the grounds that the late-flowering varieties were still being tried in the autumn. In 1914 Cory continued the trial, this time concentrating on seedlings, and offering a silver cup for the best dahlia. When the trials were interrupted by the war, he offered the Cory Cup for Dahlias through the RHS, until in 1923 he tried to widen the scope of the award, and changed its remit to 'the best hardy plant of garden origin shown to the Society in the course of the year'.[28]

The list of Joint Dahlia Committee members was first published by the Dahlia Society in 1927, and by the RHS a year later. Henry B. May was the first Chairman, succeeded by G.W. Leak, Thomas Hay of the Central Royal Parks, and the Covent Garden sundriesman George Monro. This first committee set the pattern for later joint committees: half the membership appointed by the RHS, half by the Dahlia Society, and from 1951 the

A hand-coloured engraving of the new Chinese chrysanthemums, after William Clark, published in the Society's Transactions *for 1825.*

Anemone. Pale. Buff Chrysanthemum.

chairmanship alternated annually between the leading representatives of the two societies.

The National Chrysanthemum Society started life as the Stoke Newington Chrysanthemum Society in 1846; within a few years its shows were being reported in the gardening press, and it was sending chrysanthemums to the shows at Chiswick. (On Henry Cannell's suggestion, it became the National Chrysanthemum Society [NCS] in 1884.)[29] The first discussions about joint arrangements with the RHS took place in 1919, but it was not until 1938 that an official Joint Early-Flowering Chrysanthemum Committee was set up, with G.W. Leak as Chairman, after the RHS had notified the NCS of the new requirement that there be only one award-giving body for any genus in any one country. In 1952 the RHS approached the Chrysanthemum Society with a proposal for a similar committee to judge late-flowering chrysanthemums, arguing that under the existing arrangements there was a danger that chrysanthemums rejected for award by one society might obtain awards on being subsequently submitted to the other. The NCS, while expressing the 'most earnest desire to co-operate with the R.H.S. for the good of the Chrysanthemum', argued that such a joint committee 'would entail the virtual extinction of the N.C.S. Floral Committee', and asked why the RHS didn't recognise it as *the* award body for chrysanthemums. After lengthy debate, a combined meeting was held on 8 July 1953, and it was agreed that a joint committee be established, that neither of the parent societies would make awards to chrysanthemums independently, and (point 12 of the agreement) 'That the advisability of combining the Joint Early-flowering Chrysanthemum Committee and the Joint Late-Flowering Chrysanthemum Committee to form *one* Joint Chrysanthemum Committee from 1954 onwards be considered'. The Late-Flowering Committee, accordingly, had an independent existence of one year before the two Committees were amalgamated.[30] In 1995 the Joint Committee became a Standing Committee.

The late 1960s saw inconclusive discussions about the location of chrysanthemum trials; many on the Joint Committee wanted to stick with Wisley, but there was eagerness in the north of England for trials at a higher latitude. A site at Huddersfield was rejected, but in 1977 an arrangement was made for trials to take place at Bradford. Wisley, meanwhile, went on to build up an impressive collection of Cascade and Charm chrysanthemums. Both the Dahlia and Chrysanthemum Societies held their own annual shows in the RHS Halls in Westminster during the autumn, while their plants rose and fell in fashion. Stuart Ogg, in 1948, offered a rejoinder to those who saw giant exhibition varieties as vulgar: 'The public always amuse me, when they inform me that they do not like the Giant Flowered Types, and my answer to them is always that if I staged an exhibit of smaller varieties alone, half of them would pass my exhibit by, and inform me that they have a far better show in their garden grown from a packet of seed.' By the 1980s the commerce in dahlias had declined, as fashions changed, but then underwent a further revival in the 1990s. In that decade, alas, both shows fell victim to new regulations imposed by Westminster Council, which forbade exhibitors from setting up before 7 a.m., and the two Societies have taken their shows to other locations.[31]

Gladioli and other South African bulbs

The popularity of Cape bulbs had grown steadily in the late 18th century, and *Gladiolus* in particular was a genus on which Dean Herbert expended much effort in his attempts to produce hybrids. The *Transactions* and the first *Journal* are full of articles on gladioli, crinums, nerines, and amaryllids by Herbert, Lindley, J.R. Gowen, John Spencer, and Donald Beaton. In the event, the most successful early hybrids were produced on the continent: the Gandavensis range, followed by new series from Vilmorin, which the RHS distributed in England. It was not until late in the century that James Kelway began to create a lasting series of British hardy gladioli, in particular the Langprim cultivars of the Edwardian period.[32]

In 1912 the Gladiolus Society approached the RHS about a collaboration, so that at two shows the Floral Committee would refrain from making awards to gladioli, and a special joint committee would do so instead. At the first meeting only one gladiolus was presented for award; the problems arose at the second meeting. H.B. May refused to grant a First Class Certificate to a plant previously given an Award of Merit by the Gladiolus Society, and was supported by William Wilks, who wrote that 'it is quite impossible for our Society to recognise the "previous Awards given" by your Society'. The Joint Gladiolus Committee was accordingly dissolved. It was briefly revived in 1931, and dissolved again; in 1948 and 1963 the Gladiolus Society offered to start the Joint Committee again, but Council decided that Floral A was sufficient.[33] Despite the lack of enthusiasm for collaboration, the Society maintains a challenge cup for gladioli: the Foremarke Cup, which has been awarded since 1919.

Sir Michael Foster (1836-1907), Professor of Physiology at Cambridge and author of a ground-breaking textbook on the subject. In his spare time a raiser of irises, and author of the first work on their horticultural classification, Bulbous Irises *(1892). Encouraged W.R. Dykes to carry on his work.*

Irises

The Society's involvement with irises was the work of two successive taxonomists, the Cambridge physiologist Sir Michael Foster, whose monograph on *Bulbous Irises* the Society published in 1893, and his successor W.R. Dykes, who completed Foster's work in his mammoth treatise *The Genus Iris* (1913). Dykes went on to write *A Handbook of Garden Irises*, and numerous articles which were collected after his death by George Dillistone under the title *Dykes on Irises*. He was also a noted iris breeder, but when he became the Secretary of the RHS in 1920, he handed over most of his stock to the Murrells' Orpington Nurseries.

The Iris Society was founded in 1924, with George Yeld as its first President, but Dykes was one of its major promoters, and used the RHS address while editing and writing for the Iris Society's *Bulletin*. His career was cut short by a car crash the year after the new society was founded. Just when the Joint Committee was set up with the Iris Society is ambiguous; it was certainly involved in instituting trials at Wisley in 1924, so Dykes may have been responsible for effecting the linkage.[34] At any rate, Sir William Lawrence chaired the Committee for its first two years, and was then succeeded by F.C. Stern, for over two decades.

The Council note of 27 January 1931 goes on to say that the Christie-Miller Cup, which was in the gift of the Iris Society, should be awarded by the Joint Committee. One of the advantages of this arrangement, as the 1931 *Iris Year Book* informed its readers, was 'that a variety exhibited before or after the Iris Show, if considered worthy, can now receive the recognition it deserves, whereas hitherto its only chance was to secure an award *at the Iris Show* or at Wisley; or, in other words, should its period of flowering not coincide with the Iris Show it might be several years before it was recognised, a state of affairs that did not encourage the exhibition of new Seedlings except at the Iris Show.' It also pointed to numerous anomalies in previous iris awards, and urged that 'the Joint Iris Committee is fully qualified by its intimate knowledge to take the present list of awards as published and confirm such as it thinks are desirable'. A proposal to establish an Iris Group along the lines of the Lily Group was turned down a few years later.

Permanent iris trials have been conducted at Wisley since the 1920s. In 1961 the RHS turned down a collection of pre-1920 cultivars of bearded irises, but four years later determined to establish a collection of 'tall bearded irises of historical interest'. On the other hand, in 1947, Waterers donated a fine collection of *Iris kaempferi*, as they were then known, or *Iris ensata*, as they are called today; this collection has been continuously augmented and renewed, and now provides a great summer attraction between the rock and wild gardens.[35]

Iris trials at Wisley, 1998.

Rhododendrons, camellias, and magnolias

John Reeves sent drawings and specimens not only of chrysanthemums, but also of camellias and tree peonies. One of the Society's gardeners in the 1820s—later to become its Librarian and Assistant Secretary—was William Beattie Booth, who in the 1830s collaborated with the nurseryman Alfred Chandler in producing the first big illustrated English book on *Camellia* species, which he preceded with a substantial article in the *Transactions*. Joseph Sabine had meanwhile written an account of varieties of *Magnolia glauca*. The Society's interest in rhododendrons, on the other hand, developed late; Lindley published an account of Borneo rhododendrons in 1848, but much more important was the note by Standish and Noble, of the Sunningdale nursery, on their first experiments in hardy hybrid rhododendrons two years later. The Society's declining finances meant that it was not in a position to take any significant part in the distribution and development of the new *Rhododendron* species that Joseph Hooker brought back from the Himalayas in the 1850s.[36] By the early 20th century, the number of rhododendron hybrids was increasing rapidly, as new expeditions in China and the Himalayas, some of them funded by the RHS, brought back new species on a regular basis. A chain of societies was set up to administer to the rising fashion.

The Rhododendron Society was founded in 1915 by a small group of enthusiasts, including G.W.E. Loder (later Lord Wakehurst), J.C. and P.D. Williams, Stephenson Clarke, Charles Eley, E.J.P. Magor, J.G. Millais, and Sir Herbert Maxwell. Its membership was never very large, and its most noteworthy achievement was the publication of the three volumes of *Rhododendron Society Notes* (1916-31).

The Rhododendron Association was formed in 1927 in a meeting in the RHS Lecture Theatre, with Lionel de Rothschild presiding. He referred to the 25 members of the Rhododendron Society and suggested that the time had come to try to spread the word about the rhododendron to a wider audience. Loder, Magor, Maxwell, and Millais were among the founding members, despite their role on the rival Society; and after its 1931 AGM, the Rhododendron Society was absorbed into the Association. The Association published a *Year Book* from 1929 to 1939.

In November 1927, Council announced that three members of the Association should act with Floral B to judge rhododendron trials at Exbury, which Lionel de Rothschild was developing as a rhododendron garden: they would concentrate on hardy hybrids introduced since 1918. The

membership of this Joint Committee for Rhododendron Trials was first printed in the *Book of Arrangements* in 1931; the following year, with an expanded membership, it had become the Joint Rhododendron Committee. (The Exbury trials were transferred to Wisley in 1938.) G.W.E.Loder was the first Chairman; among his successors were John Barr Stevenson, Lord Aberconway, Sir Eric Savill, Sir Giles Loder, and John Bond.[37]

On 20 March 1945, Lord Aberconway told Council 'that it might appear to be in the interests of the Rhododendron Association as well as of the Society to suggest that the Rhododendron Association be merged into a Rhododendron Group following the precedent of the Lily Group ... In doing so he pointed out that the Society would have to become responsible for their publications ... The Society would also make itself responsible for the prizes for the annual Rhododendron Show, estimated at about £60. In return the Association would be asked that its Members should become Fellows of the Society, if not already Fellows, and that its existing funds and cups and stock of publications should be handed over to the Society for the purpose of founding the Group.'

The Rhododendron Association agreed, and the transformation was accomplished. The Joint Committee, naturally, ceased to be Joint, and became a Standing Committee instead. A new *Year Book* was initiated for the Group, to succeed, on a larger scale, the Association's old *Year Book*; £250 of the Association's money was put towards rhododendron plates in the *Botanical Magazine*. Five cups and a medal held by the Association were transferred to the RHS; in addition there are two rhododendron awards that began as RHS awards, so that there are, confusingly, both a Loder Cup and a Loder Rhododendron Cup of different provenances.[38]

With a *Year Book*, a Group, such a multiplicity of awards, an increasing collection of rhododendrons planted on Battleston Hill (incorporating gifts from John Barr Stevenson, James Russell of Sunningdale, and successive Rothschilds at Exbury), new rhododendrons being bred by Francis Hanger and his successors (the Francis Hanger Group, followed by the Moonshine Group and other individual cultivars), and two Aberconways as Presidents, the RHS became particularly identified, for good or ill, with rhododendrons in the mid-20th century. But while the comparison between alpines, the democratic plants fit for the smallest garden, and rhododendrons, fit only for the owners of great country estates, was bandied about, it was also possible for the RHS to be attacked for not doing

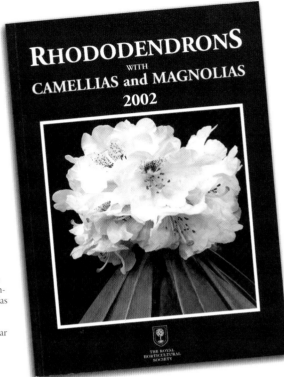

The cover of the 2002 edition of Rhododendrons with Camellias and Magnolias, *the successor to the old* Rhododendron Year Book.

enough to promote the cause of the rhododendron. Dan E. Mayers read a paper in 1977 in which he criticised the RHS for not publishing a membership list of 'this semi-mythical Rhododendron Group', and alleged that 'For 32 years the Royal Horticultural Society systematically discouraged the organization of local Rhododendron clubs and groups by preventing its members from learning the whereabouts of others of like interest.' He tried to enlist the help of *Private Eye*, and only succeeded in provoking an attack on the rhododendron from Germaine Greer, who summarised the institutional history thus: 'The R.H.S. swallowed the Rhododendron Association for the same motive that the whale swallowed Jonah, and is equally incommoded by the fact that it won't stay down.'[39]

In 1957, the Rhododendron Group became the Rhododendron and Camellia Group. The RHS had published two monographs on camellias in the 1950s—Sealy's revision of the species and Ellis's register of old cultivars; the American camellia grower Ralph S. Peer was contributing both finances for these projects and specimens of new American cultivars; and the Society was involved in proposals for camellia as well as rhododendron registration (though eventually an International Camellia Society was formed that took on that responsibility). Peer offered a challenge cup for camellias, but at an inopportune time, so for many years the Leonardslee Bowl was the Society's only

camellia award; the David Trehane Camellia Cup was finally added to the list in 2000.[40] Magnolia was added to its title in 1972—the Society had published George H. Johnstone's magnificent book on Asiatic species, and two valuable magnolias had been bred at Wisley, 'Norman Gould' and 'Janaki Ammal'. As financial crisis stopped the publication of the specialist *Year Books*, it became the Group's responsibility to produce a successor annual out of its own pockets. To quote a later Chairman:

> From 1973 to 1976 the *Year Books* were the only sign that the Rhododendron Group had survived. But in the background another generation of enthusiasts was equally determined that the Group should have a corporate existence. Early in 1976 a small committee of former members met to discuss taking over the administration from the RHS officials. A list of former members was circulated to know if they would be interested; 169 individuals replied in the affirmative and they became the nucleus of the new autonomous Group ... Thus was the Rhododendron Group 'born again' and took charge of its own destiny. Although it never again controlled shows, competitions and trials, those who judged and sat on the relevant committees were inevitably also Group members. In this way close contact and sharing of responsibility with the RHS was maintained and still continues to the mutual advantage of both.[41]

The closing years of the 20th century certainly saw, if not exactly a decline in the public enthusiasm for rhododendrons, at least a reaction against their prominence on the part of an opinion-forming elite, and a programme of their progressive removal from 18th-century landscape gardens such as Stourhead, where they had been extensively planted. *Rhododendron ponticum*, in particular, suffered in esteem. In 1841 the *Gardeners' Chronicle* had published excited correspondence about the fact that it could seed itself in ordinary English soil; within a few years it was being used as planting for game coverts; by the late 20th century it had spread so widely through the countryside that the Forestry Commission declared it a 'noxious alien weed'. But other species, less associated with early 20th-century planting, took rhododendron enthusiasm in new directions. *Rhododendron yakushimanum* was exhibited at Chelsea in 1947, and awarded a First Class Certificate; increasingly toward the end of the century, its hybrids, with their capacity to withstand full sun, attained prominence in garden use. A major ten-year trial of yakushimanum hybrids was started at Wisley in 1996. (Similar hybridisation efforts have focused on the species in the Vireya section; Sir Harry Veitch had turned his hybridists to the vireyas in the 1890s, but these efforts were not followed up in England until a century later, after they had received favourable attention in Australia and America.) Meanwhile, a major trial of *Camellia* × *williamsii* cultivars was held at Wisley in the 1990s, and extensive magnolia plantings were undertaken by the Curator, Jim Gardiner, who emerged in that decade as an important authority on the genus.[42]

Lilies and related plants

In 1818, when Sabine presented his collection of hardy bulbs to the Society's garden, he said, 'they are, I have no doubt, the most complete in the species and varieties of the Liliaceae, not only in England, but in the world'. It included *Lilium japonicum*, specimens of which he presented to Sir Joseph Banks's widow.[43] But after Lindley's time there was little overt activity on the lily front for decades. J.G. Baker published a classification of lilies in the 1877 *Journal*; in 1901 the Society held its first Lily Conference.

In November 1931 it was decided to appoint a standing committee on lilies; F.C. Stern appears to have been the initiator, and became the Secretary. At the Council meeting of 25 October 1932, he presented a memorandum calling for the formation of a Lily Group: 'Many members of the R.H.S. and others have asked me during the past year how to join the Lily Society! The Council will remember that the Lily Committee was created primarily to avoid another new Society being formed, but there is no doubt that there is a want among members and the public to join some body devoted to Lilies and their culture, where they can air their views and hear other views on their especial subject ...' The objects of the Group were to be: 'to encourage the cultivation of Lilies, Fritillaries and Nomocharis by holding meetings for lectures and discussions, by visiting gardens where these plants are well grown, and by holding an annual dinner for those interested in the three genera.' The Lily Committee was to continue in existence, to manage the Lily Group's affairs and to assist Floral B.

The inaugural meeting of the Group took place in the Old Hall on 21 March 1933. The first Group visit was to the gardens of E.A. Bowles and Fred Stoker in July 1933. That same month a Lily Conference was held (11-13 July), the first since 1901, and included Daniel Hall's paper 'A survey of lily soils' (written with M.A.H. Tincker) and Krelage's historical study of the early distribution of lilies in Europe. Ellen Willmott gave the accompanying show a tremendous puff in the *Gardeners'*

Chronicle, quoting the Abbé Souillet: 'He cannot understand how England could ever have been called *perfide Albion*, as he found it the reverse. He was amazed by the magnificent display of lilies in the hall ... Were it not that the Lily week had made such an indelible impression he would have thought it the "dream of a Terrestrial Paradise".' The Abbé was listed in 1933 as one of the Committee's Foreign Correspondents, a number that included the Dutch nurserymen J. Hoog and E.H. Krelage, the Americans A. B. Stout and Carl Purdy, and lily growers and experts from six other countries.[44]

The first *Lily Year Book* appeared in 1932, the second volume being the Conference Number; it was published continuously, apart from a wartime gap, until 1971, when, along with the Society's other Year Books, it was curtailed for financial reasons, and the Lily Group assumed responsibility for producing an intermittent publication, *Lilies and Other Liliaceae*. The reports of the 3rd and 4th International Lily Conferences (1959, 1969) were published in the *Year Books*; in 1989 the Group acted as host to the 5th International Conference, whose Proceedings they have published. In 1939 the Lyttel Lily Cup was presented for the Group to award annually, and it remains the only RHS award for lilies. In the 1970, James Platt, the Group's Secretary, began a seed distribution service. In the hands of his successors, Molly Pottinger and Alan Hooker, this became an important means of encouraging lily growing; recently, for example, the Group has distributed the lily groups raised by Sir Peter Smithers.

Stern was Chairman of the Committee from 1933 to 1967, followed by Oliver Wyatt (1968-73) and Frances Perry (1974-8). In August 1978, she reported that there were two opposing factions within the Group, and that the Vice-Chairman and Secretary both wanted to resign; Council considered that it would be 'more satisfactory if the Committee was given semi-independent status, as had the Rhododendron and Camellia Committee, and if the Committee was empowered to elect a Chairman who should not be a Member or past Member of Council'. In September, it was announced that the Group would henceforth elect its own Committee, and that the Society would no longer issue invitations to serve on it. Gradually it became known as the Lily Group Committee.

In 1949 the Committee helped to organise a trial of lilies at Wisley. In response to an enquiry from Jan de Graaff in Oregon, it was decreed that bulbs for the trial must be propagated vegetatively, not grown from seed; as a result, de Graaff's new trumpet lilies, one of the most important

Sir Frederick Claude Stern (1884-1967), banker and patron of horticulture: helped to finance plant collecting expeditions, and published monographs on peonies and snowdrops. Created the garden at Highdown, Sussex, which he described in his book A Chalk Garden *(1960).*

developments of the time for the future of garden lilies, were excluded. This failure no doubt explains de Graaff's remark in his later book on *Lilies* that 'this is not a field of gardening to be left to the great lily pundits of the Royal Horticultural Society'. Nonetheless, at the Fourth International Lily Conference, the North American Lily Society presented a congratulatory address to the RHS for its work in plant collection, show and conference organising, cultivar testing, awards, registration, and publishing monographs and the *Lily Year Book*.[45]

Delphiniums

In 1891 the RHS held its first conference on hardy perennials, with William Robinson and Gertrude Jekyll speaking. The use of perennial flowers in borders had been promoted by Loudon as early as the 1820s, and had taken on a new lease of life in the 1860s as the process of historical revivalism led to attempts to recapture the planting schemes of the 17th century; Robinson and Jekyll aimed at making them the primary focus of the flower garden without requiring the revivalist justification. Delphiniums were one of the most popular categories of border flowers, with firms like Kelways, from the 1880s, and from 1901 Blackmore and Langdon, breeding new varieties in profusion.[46]

The British Delphinium Society (later simply the Delphinium Society) was founded in September 1928, and within a year had over 200 members. In 1930 the new society wrote to Council about co-operation with the RHS, and on 10 May 1932 Council agreed to the formation of a Joint Committee. In their 1933 *Year Book*, S. Halford Roberts assured the Delphinium Society's members that while 'the *ideal* specialist society is ... one run entirely for the benefit of amateur members', 'to be deprived of our trade members ... would rob the Society of seventy per cent. of its interest'; but 'the personnel of the [Joint] Committee ... is such as to secure for the amateur a maximum of consideration; and the conditions are the easiest which any Joint Committee with the R.H.S. has yet enjoyed'. G.W. Leak was the first Chairman, succeeded by Thomas Hay; later Chairmen have included Stuart Ogg and Miller Gault. The first invited trials of delphiniums at Wisley had already been conducted in 1916, and again in 1923; permanent trials were instituted in the 1930s, and from 1954 these were supplemented by trials at Harlow Carr. By that time cruel fortune had attacked the Delphinium Society, whose financial crisis in 1952 prompted calls for its replacement by a Delphinium Group along the lines of the Lily Group; but the RHS refused, and in due course the Society righted itself again.[47]

The most publicised project in the history of the delphinium must be Robert Legro's attempt to breed red delphiniums. He 'concentrated on the problems of transferring the genes responsible for red and yellow flower colour in *Delphinium nudicaule* and *D. cardinale* to the larger-flowered, border perennials derived from *D. elatum*'; this may well have been the last major breeding programme for ornamental plants before the advent of genetic engineering. He was awarded a Veitch Memorial Medal for his work in 1961; the RHS helped to subsidise it, and undertook to propagate selected clones. The results were displayed at the 1988 Chelsea Show, to muted enthusiasm; by the early 1990s the value of the cultivars seemed likely to deteriorate rapidly; on a tour of the archives, being shown the boxes of documents that had been deposited, Sir Simon Hornby remarked that the documents would quickly outlive the plants.[48]

Sweet peas

In September 1899, George Gordon, a member of the RHS Floral Committee, proposed the creation of a committee to organise an exhibition and conference for July 1900, to celebrate the bicentenary of the introduction of the sweet pea into Britain. (The occasion also prompted a complaint that there was no RHS award for sweet peas.) The exhibition was held at the Crystal Palace, and the conference recommended that a National Sweet Pea Society be formed; its inaugural meeting took place in March 1901. Sweet peas were currently approaching the heights of fashion; comparatively neglected until the 1880s, they had been transformed by the breeding programme of the Shropshire nurseryman Henry Eckford, and by 1911 Walter P. Wright could claim that 'new varieties pour out hotly, like the editions of evening newspapers'. One of the enthusiasts of the cult was Lord Northcliffe, whose *Daily Mail* offered a £1,000 prize for the best sweet pea in 1911.[49]

The RHS first conducted trials of sweet peas in 1911, and again in 1921. In December 1926, the Awards Committee recommended the establishment of a Joint Committee for sweet peas, though it was not until 1932 that it was set up, with G.W. Leak as the first Chairman. The Sweet Pea Society announced the aims of the Committee to its members as the judging both of plants submitted for award and of trials of novelties at Wisley, and of reconsidering the classification list and the list of 'Too-much-alike varieties'. During the Second

A trial of sweet peas at Harlow Carr, 2001.

flowers of a loose truss brought to look you in the face by the flower-stalk being tied to the stem by an almost invisible ligature of fine green silk.' He was indignantly contradicted by other nurserymen, but at the same time it was reported that a plant had been exhibited at a show in Enfield with gum used to prevent its petals falling.[51]

Paul thought that such devices had precipitated the fall from favour of the old florists' societies; but as older societies vanished, newer ones came into existence. The National Carnation and Picotee Society was founded in 1877; the Winter Flowering Carnation Society (later the Perpetual Flowering Carnation Society) was founded in 1906, and changed its name to the British Carnation Society in 1918. Its first annual show was held in Regent's Park, and this fact was held up in the press as a criticism of the RHS:

> It is a matter for disappointment to those Fellows of the Royal Horticultural Society who helped to build the Vincent Square Hall and offices, that more effort is not made by the council to render that Hall the home and place of exhibition of all special horticultural bodies having their shows in London. The newly formed Winter Carnation Society has, because the offers made by a comparatively poor Society (the Royal Botanic) were more liberal, felt compelled to take its first annual exhibition to the Regents Park next December, greatly to the loss of the Royal Horticultural Society's Fellows. Why the Council cannot act as generously to all these respective societies as it does to the Auricula Society seems difficult to understand. The Winter Carnation Growers do much more to help the Royal Horticultural Society to make its ordinary shows than the Auricula Society does.

The next year its show was transferred.[52] In 1949 the two societies amalgamated to form the British National Carnation Society, with George Monro as its first President. (This amalgamation had been advocated by a correspondent in the *Gardeners' Chronicle* while the younger society was still in the planning stages.) Both societies had meanwhile formed joint committees with the RHS.

The Joint Perpetual Flowering Carnation Committee was established in 1934. With the

World War, the Wisley trials were abandoned, and relocated for the interim in various growers' gardens; in 1949 they were resumed at Wisley, and eventually paralleled at Harlow Carr.[50]

Carnations and other florists' flowers

The traditional categories of florists' flowers—auriculas, polyanthus, carnations and pinks—were held in little esteem by Lindley, who got a bad press for slighting their exhibitors at shows, despite the efforts of Edward Beck, the founder-editor of *The Florist*, to apologise for him and gently bring him to see the error of his ways. Lindley refused to allow competitive classes for such plants, partly on the grounds of their lack of botanical interest, but also because of objections to the tricks used by some exhibitors in presenting their flowers:

> The days of porcupine dressing are evidently numbered. It has for some time been a just ground of complaint, that gardeners so disfigure their specimens, by innumerable sticks, that the natural grace of the plants is entirely destroyed; and they are made to bristle with spines ... We cannot but regard this practice as an insidious attempt to bring back the days when ladies cased themselves in hoop petticoats and steel-ribbed stays ...

William Paul, a generation later, continued Lindley's complaint against what he called 'flori-cultural millinery': 'I have seen Hyacinths shown for competition with small pins sticking the flowers close to the stems, and the drooping

National Carnation and Picotee Society, the Hardy Border Carnation Committee (later the Joint Border Carnation and Picotee Committee) was created in the same year, to judge a category of plants that had formerly fallen within the remit of Floral A. In 1980 the responsibilities of the former Joint Dianthus Committee (1946-79), of which the Alpine Garden Society was a third member, were added to this committee, apart from the judging of alpine species, which was added to the duties of Joint Rock. Montagu Allwood, the leading carnation nurseryman of the early 20th century, offered a challenge cup to the Society in the 1920s, but it was not until 1961 that the E H Trophy was instituted as the Society's only dianthus prize (later changed to an award for cut flowers).[53]

The RHS had held a carnation conference in 1890; it never held conferences on auriculas or polyanthus, anemones, or hyacinths, the most popular of the other florists' flowers. In the 1870s it allowed H.H. Dombrain to offer an auricula prize at its shows, and staged a hyacinth show, but it never instituted trials for such plants, until their decline prompted an unsuccessful polyanthus trial in 1957. Auriculas nearly vanished from commerce in the mid-20th century; Brenda Hyatt acquired the stock of James Douglas's nursery at Great Bookham and staged an exhibit at Chelsea in 1982, which galvanised attention and began a revival which now supplies multiple stands every year.[54]

Alpines

The plants that we now think of as alpines were slow to assume their later familiar role in the rock garden, mainly because it took a long time to work out their cultural requirements. Until the middle of the 19th century they were usually grown in pots (for their eventual colonisation of the rock garden, see chapter 15). The RHS held conferences on primulas in 1886, 1895, 1913 and 1928, planned an abortive conference on saxifrages in 1914 and again in 1921, and in the early 1930s became so active with gentians as to consider (but reject) the idea of compiling a gentian stud book. By that time rock gardening had spread through the social scale to become a major British obsession.[55]

The Alpine Garden Society (AGS) was formed in 1929, with Sir William Lawrence, recently retired from the position of Treasurer to the RHS, as its first President. In April 1936, the Alpine Garden Society proposed the creation of a Joint Committee, and despite a warning from the RHS of difficulties 'especially in regard to the time of meeting and to the frequency of meetings proposed', the AGS almost unanimously passed a resolution in favour of a Joint Committee, and the Joint Rock Garden Plant Committee was duly instituted as from 1937. F.C. Stern was the first Chairman; among his successors have been Will Ingwersen, Roy Elliott, and Jack Elliott.

The International Horticultural Conference of 1930 had recommended that there should be only one set of awards per country per plant. 'Not so with rock-garden plants', wrote Chittenden, in response to the AGS proposal. 'Our Society gives its Awards of Merit and the Alpine Garden Society gives its Certificate of Merit. The general public knows no better and is bound to confuse the two different awards for unfortunately they have not been of equal standard ... The present ... seems to give an opportunity of eliminating this source of confusion, and therefore of giving a more certain and indeed a more reliable guide to the gardening public ... The definition of a rock-garden plant can I think be decided only on arbitrary lines ...' The Joint Committee would relieve part of the burden on Floral B by taking away a category of plants it judged. (A proposal for an Alpine Committee had been made back in 1913, but rejected; but the popularity of rock gardening had increased steadily since then.)[56]

In 1954 Council considered a suggestion from the Scottish Rock Garden Club (SRGC, founded 1933) that awards to rock garden plants should be made in Scotland. Sir George Taylor and Sir Frederick Stern formed a special committee to meet the Club, and it was agreed that a Joint Committee composed of two representatives of the RHS, two of the AGS, and four of the Scottish Rock Garden Club would meet twice a year in Scotland for the purpose. The first meeting was in April 1955. Today the Joint Rock Garden Plant Committee is composed of members drawn in equal numbers from the three organisations, each of which appoints a vice-chairman, though the chairman is always an RHS representative. Joint Rock was the first of the floral committees to extend its remit for judging beyond the Society's own shows, and now regularly meets at AGS and SRGC shows as well.[57]

The judging of groups of alpine plants continued to be one of the functions of Floral Committee B until 1964. On 9 April of that year, Lewis Palmer wrote a letter complaining about the inconsistency of standards in judging: 'What I think is worth considering is to have a separate panel to judge alpine groups.' On 26 May, the Awards Committee endorsed his proposal, and Council ratified it on 29 September. The Rock Garden and Alpine Group Committee is not so peripatetic as Joint Rock, but the two committees have worked in tandem for 40 years.

The Society has two medals to offer for alpines, the Farrer Trophy and the Sewell Medal. The latter was intended by its donor to be awarded each year to amateurs and professionals, and long years of controversy ensued over the indifference of the nurseries to compete for it; eventually the terms were changed, and it is now offered to professionals and amateurs in alternate years.[58]

Roses

Roses were also among the plants that Sabine arranged systematically at Chiswick before his ignominious departure, but Chiswick, while it had a collection of rose species, never had an extensive collection of cultivars. Lindley had begun his career as the monographer of the genus *Rosa*; he had been hired by the Society to draw roses; he and Sabine promoted the use of the Burnet or Scotch roses; but Lindley appears to have looked askance at standard roses (introduced in the 1820s), which became the basis of the mid-century rose garden. The typical standard rose consisted of a cultivar grafted onto a rootstock, so that the flower was made the focus of display and brought to a convenient height for individual examination; this meant, for Lindley, turning the rose into a florists' flower, and thus alienating his interest. So during the early decades of hybridisation, and the establishment of Bourbons, Noisettes, Hybrid Perpetuals, and Hybrid Teas as major categories of garden and exhibition roses, these developments were given cursory attention by the Society. (Ironically, Lindley was a friend and correspondent of Giuseppe Manetti, who developed the most widely used of the early rootstocks.) The Society sparked the development of yellow roses by introducing the yellow form of *Rosa banksiae* from China, but had little to do with the subsequent hybridisation programme.[59]

The garden was one thing, but shows were another: roses were one of the first categories of plants for which competitions were established at Chiswick shows in 1831. As the popularity of the new hybrid roses increased, the momentum for a specialist show did likewise, and in 1858 a grand National Rose Show was convened at St James's Hall. The Society was not in a financial position at the time to do more than watch from the sidelines, but in 1861, feeling more robust, it offered to amalgamate the Rose Show with its own summer show, and the combined show became a fixture for a few years. In 1876 the National Rose Society (NRS) was founded, with Samuel Reynolds Hole, one of the original organisers of the Rose Show and more recently an opposition candidate for the RHS Council, as its first President. The NRS held its independent show in the Kensington garden, and held its first provincial show jointly with the RHS provincial show in Preston; but once Kensington was abandoned, it looked to other London venues like the Crystal Palace and the Royal Botanic Society's garden in Regent's Park. In the 20th century, it staged some of its shows in the Westminster Halls, but with continual minor skirmishes over scheduling and entrance fees for non-NRS members.[60]

In 1889 the Society convened its only conference on roses at Chiswick. It has had two challenge cups for roses, both discontinued as such: the Wigan Cup, donated in 1911, and offered for exhibits of roses until 1937 (to be revived after the war with a different remit), and the Clay Cup, which was offered for a new rose from 1914 to 1947. In 1919, rose trials were begun at Wisley, conducted jointly with the NRS, and continued for over a decade; a Joint Rose Committee was set up

A drawing of Rosa banksiae *by an anonymous Chinese artist, commissioned by John Reeves and sent to the Society in the 1820s.*

Rose gardens at Rosemoor, with the Robin Herbert Visitor Centre in the background.

with the NRS in 1959, but was abolished in 1964 because awards for roses were no longer given without an NRS certificate of merit. When they were discontinued in 1931, a border of new cultivars was planted; C.C. Hurst arranged a collection of rose species at Wisley, as part of his work on their genetics. Further rose gardens have been laid out over the years—and, in the 1990s, at Rosemoor and Hyde Hall—generally devoted to the display of new cultivars.[61] E.A. Bunyard helped to foment the revival of old roses in the 20th century, but despite his role on the Society he was unable to stimulate official enthusiasm for the project, and a proposal for an old rose group was rejected in 1947.[62]

Conifers

Conifers were already in fashion by the time the Society opened its garden at Chiswick; Prince Pückler-Muskau, visiting England in 1826, expressed his incomprehension at their popularity, and that was before any of David Douglas's introductions. Throughout the ensuing quarter-century, the Society was the single most important channel for new conifers to arrive in Britain and, through George Gordon's and Andrew Murray's articles in its *Journals*, it helped to establish synonymy and disseminate instructions on propagation.[63] Chiswick boasted an important display collection of the new arrivals, and in the 20th century one of the largest tracts of Wisley was devoted to a pinetum.

But, after the curtailment of the plant collection programme, the most important of the Society's coniferous activities was the holding of conferences: four major international conferences

over the course of slightly over a century. The first conference, held in 1891, was introduced by Maxwell T. Masters, who waxed unusually lyrical over conifers at a time when the reaction was building against their mid-century dominance in landscaping:

> Those who assert, as I have heard them assert, that Conifers are monotonous in point of colour can evidently never have seen the trees either when they put on their spring attire or when they adopt their mature bridal dress.

The conference was accompanied by an exhibit of new conifer hybrids, a subject on which Masters would later write for the *Journal*. A second conference was held in 1931, with William Dallimore presenting a conspectus of the species in cultivation, and Murray Hornibrook of the cultivars of real or alleged dwarf conifers; both this and the third conference in 1970 contained massive statistical surveys. By the time the fourth conference was held in 1999, the Society had become the International Registration Authority for conifers, and was well on the way to completing its initial register of cultivars.[64]

The 20th century saw a fashion for dwarf conifers, many of which proved to be merely juvenile forms of decidedly non-dwarf trees; Hornibrook was the most important early promoter of the trend, and the author of the first book on the subject. His successor in these respects, H.J. Welch, remarked at the 1970 conference that 'innumerable acres of England's green and pleasant land have fallen into the builders' hands and the resulting vast spread of suburbia (regrettable as in some ways it may be) has given just the opening for the use of dwarf conifers which Murray Hornibrook envisaged.' Important donations of dwarf conifers were made to Wisley in the mid-century years, by Lord Ashburton and A.H. Nisbet, whose collection of 260 varieties was transferred to Wisley in 1957. In the 1960s the idea was discussed of establishing a national collection of dwarf conifers at Wisley, but nothing came of it. At the other end of the scale, Arthur Osborn of Kew used the Society's *Journal* in 1941 to popularise a bigeneric hybrid just coming on the market, × *Cupressocyparis leylandii*. It was first significantly used at the Garden House, Buckland Monachorum, to establish windbreaks just after the war; by the late 1990s its capacity to dwarf the houses around which it had been planted as a hedge made it one of the most significant causes of garden-related lawsuits, and led to a press and, eventually, government campaign to restrict it.[65]

Bedding and other ornamental plants

Summer bedding became the decorative mainstay of the garden in the 1820s and 1830s, but its character changed significantly as its popularity increased. J.C. Loudon and others campaigned during those decades for the planting of flowerbeds as masses of single colours; but at the beginning of the period the idea of a solid mass of one colour was an ideal only attainable by comparison with the previously accepted mixed style. Early pelargoniums, for example, tended to be woody-stemmed, with flowers that were small in proportion to the total size of the plant. But once the demand for a solid mass of colour was made, gardeners and nurserymen turned to breeding dwarfer bedding varieties, in which the size of the flower in relation to the stem and foliage was significantly increased. The 1840s saw the introduction of true bedding varieties of pelargoniums, petunias, verbenas, and calceolarias, and these quickly superseded the wide range of miscellaneous species that had hitherto been used. And once the trials programme had begun in the 1860s, pelargoniums became effectively a permanent trial subject, with verbenas and petunias accompanying them in the early years. Specialist pelargonium shows, and an open verbena competition, were held in the 1860s and 1870s.[66]

Coleus (*Solenostemon*) emerged as a plant of foliage interest in the 1860s, and Frederick Bause, the Society's propagator at Chiswick, bred a series of hybrids with royal names like 'Queen Victoria', 'Her Majesty', and 'Princess of Wales'. In 1867 two large sales of Bause's coleus were held by the auctioneer J.C. Stevens, and the plants were eagerly snapped up by nurseries. As the Victorian cult of foliage faded, however, coleus gradually disappeared from view, until a revival began in the late 20th century. In the 1980s, the first trial of seed-raised coleus was held at Wisley, and some new cultivars raised (one of which, 'Wisley', was awarded the AGM).[67]

Pelargonium trials continued in the 20th century; for other bedding plants the trials had faded away, although, under the aegis of Thomas Hay, the Superintendent of the Central Royal Parks, there was a renewed surge of interest in the 1930s. Hay instigated new pelargonium and petunia trials, and also trials of godetias and dimorphothecas, and other plants he wanted to use in his bedding schemes in Hyde Park. In the last decades of the century, the revival of interest

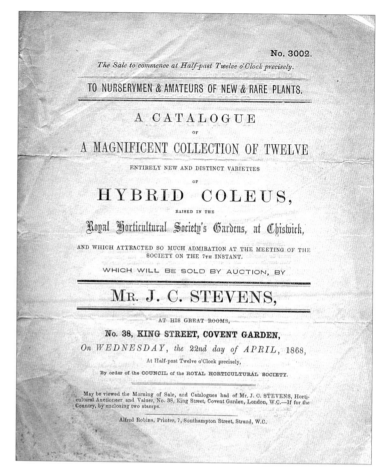

in ornamental bedding led to trials of *Begonia semperflorens*, coleus, nicotiana, and other plants of the sort that Brian Halliwell was promoting in his bedding schemes at Kew. Nonetheless, while Wisley played its part in the bedding revival, interest in bedding plants and their improvement was subdued, and Stuart Ogg, in his last years, used to lament regularly the Society's official indifference to their future.[68]

Tuberous begonias, which emerged onto the market in the 1870s, were a major category of bedding plants in the late 19th century, through the breeding work of John Laing, but were never the subject of a trial. (Variegated begonias—begonias grown as foliage plants for the conservatory—had been put to trial in the 1860s; these fell from favour during the early 20th century, but Maurice Mason promoted a revival from the 1950s.) The Society did at least convene a conference on begonias in 1892. In 1950 a Joint Committee was proposed with the Begonia Society, but fell through over technical difficulties.[69]

Another category of plants which similarly varied between bedding and greenhouse use was the fuchsia, again the subject of trials in the 1860s.

The advertisement for one of two auctions of coleus plants bred at Kensington by Frederick Bause.

Wisley built up a collection of greenhouse fuchsias, already described as 'comprehensive' in the 1920s, and maintained continuously to the present day. When the British Fuchsia Society was formed in 1939, the Society happily took its advice on competitive classes for shows. In 1958 that Society suggested a joint committee meeting annually; Council declined, on the grounds that one meeting a year would not cover all the fuchsias submitted for award, and, as usual, that it was not good that there should be more than one society awarding any class of plants.[70]

Probably the most financially successful of any of the Society's conferences was the Flowering Trees and Shrubs Conference of 1938; certainly its proceedings sold better, and were kept in print longer, than any others. During the post-war years, with the planting of a large number of cultivars in the Portsmouth Field, Wisley became for a couple of decades a major display garden for flowering cherries, and also built up a major peony collection, through the gifts of Sir Frederick Stern and George Churcher. Significant new cultivars imported from abroad, like *Cornus* 'Eddie's White Wonder' (AM, FCC, and Cory Cup), have been promoted through the awards system.[71] *Berberis* has been a recurrent interest of the Society's: Lindley made the first attempt at a classification back in 1850, after Robert Fortune had introduced new Chinese species; in the 20th century, the Society funded two attempts, by Camillo Schneider and Leslie Ahrendt, to revise the classification of the genus. By 1920 Wisley already had the most complete collection of berberis in the country, and during the 1930s J.W. Blakey raised a number of hybrids at Wisley (the × *carminea* and × *wisleyensis* cultivars).[72]

Some of the Society's officials have been associated with breeding programmes of importance. James Robert Gowen, who was first Secretary and then Treasurer between 1845 and 1855, bred the smooth-leaved hollies, *Ilex* × *altaclerensis*. Lewis Palmer, the Treasurer in the 1950s, developed the first successful range of hybrid agapanthus, the Headbourne Hybrids (it was only at the end of the 19th century that it was realised that there was more than one species, so that hybridisation became possible). William Wilks, the Society's longest-serving Secretary, raised the Shirley poppies (named after Shirley, near Croydon,

The gates of Wisley, incorporating the device of the Shirley poppy in honour of William Wilks.

where he was vicar) in the 1880s; he is commemorated by the device of a Shirley poppy worked in the Wisley gate.[73]

But of all the significant plants to be launched at RHS shows, probably the most important were the Russell lupins. The early 20th century had witnessed a long, slow process of augmenting the colour range of lupins; cultivar after cultivar received awards for slight new improvements. Meanwhile, George Russell, a Yorkshire gardener, had been quietly breeding lupins since 1911, and by the mid-1930s had produced a colour range that exceeded anything achieved elsewhere. After showing his lupins at the York Gala, he arranged for the firm of Bakers of Codsall to sell his seedlings, and in June 1937 they staged a display at Vincent Square.

> On a considerable wall space, Messrs. Bakers, Ltd., displayed a magnificent collection of the 'Russell Lupins.' These lovely varieties represent twenty years' work by a little-known gardener, who has produced strains of surpassing excellence, which are characterized by dwarf, sturdy habit and long, erect spikes of many lovely colours ... We understand that seeds of this outstanding type will be available in January of next year.

The war interrupted the spread of the Russells, and it was not until the late 1940s that they became widespread, but when they did they became the fashionable flower of the decade. By 1960 almost all the earlier lupin cultivars had disappeared from commerce.[74]

17 *Floral Arts*

On 25 June 1861, the newly renamed Royal Horticultural Society staged a grand ceremonial opening for its new garden in Kensington, and the most innovative part of the festivities was a competition for table decoration. It was organised by Sir Charles Wentworth Dilke, the Council member who had been the first proponent of the Kensington garden. The announcement circulated with the programme for the opening ceremony read:

> Special prizes for the best three groups of Fruit and Flowers are offered by C. Wentworth Dilke, Esq. V.P.R.H.S. Baskets of any materials, china vases, glass dishes, or epergnes may be used. First Prize, 10 l.; Second, 5 l.; Third, 3 l.; Fourth, 2 l.
>
> The prizes will be awarded by a Jury of Ladies—the Countess of Shelborne, the Countess of Ducie, the Lady Marianne Alford, Lady Middleton and Mrs Holford; Professor Westmacott, R.A. acting as Secretary.

(The Society had used the wives of prominent Fellows as 'Ladies Patronesses' as far back as the first fête of 1827, so this jury was a continuation of an old tradition.)

The competition was described in the *Gardeners' Chronicle* (probably by Lindley) as 'a curious mixture of the hideous and the beautiful, the tawdry and the simple, the grotesque and the refined'. Third prize went to Lady Caroline Kerrison for 'a very elegant arrangement'—bowls of fruit (including pineapples) flanking a central stand in the form of a putto with a further fruit-basket on his head. Second prize went to Lady Rokeby, for 'a rich display in three bowls of various valuable flowers'—a solid mass of foliage with grapes and pineapples. First prize went to Mr Thomas C. March of the Lord Chamberlain's office, though it was understood that he had been helped by his sisters:

> The stands were of glass, apparently a small glass dish on the top of a plain glass rod about 2 feet high, resting on a much larger glass dish; they were decorated with the Maiden-hair Fern, a ring of Forget-me-not, and a centre of Lilies of the Valley, and Lycopodiums creeping up the pedestal; not as much crammed in as the vessels would hold, but each flower and each leaf producing its own effect ... In one of the stands, instead of Forget-me-not, there were Pansies, Rosebuds, and small bunches of Grapes were introduced here and there ...

The *Chronicle* dismissed critics of March's arrangement as 'those who cannot perceive how superior graceful form is to mere heaps of colour', and within a few months had been so won over to the new type of arrangement that it looked back on the second prize-winner as 'lumpish', and on the third as owing its success to its expensive accoutrements.[1]

The month after the competition, epergnes similar to those March had used were being sold at Dobson and Pearce's shop in St James's Street under the name 'March stands'. March capitalised on his success to publish a book the following year on *Flower and Fruit Decoration*, which was quickly greeted by Donald Beaton in the *Journal of Horticulture* as one of the essential books for any gardener to study. Within months of the competition, the *Gardeners' Chronicle* was able to report that 'Mr. Dilke's idea of submitting the grouping of fruit and flowers for the dinner table to competition at our flower shows ... is spreading through the country'.[2]

Dilke's competition was for table decoration, not flower arrangement, and for two reasons. The first was the recent vogue, brought into England in the wake of the Crimean War, for dining *à la russe*: the serving dishes were placed on separate tables, leaving much of the dinner table free, and decoration rushed in to fill the gap. Books with diagrams for table settings formed a sub-genre of floral decoration literature in the 1870s. The second was the popularity of foliage rather than

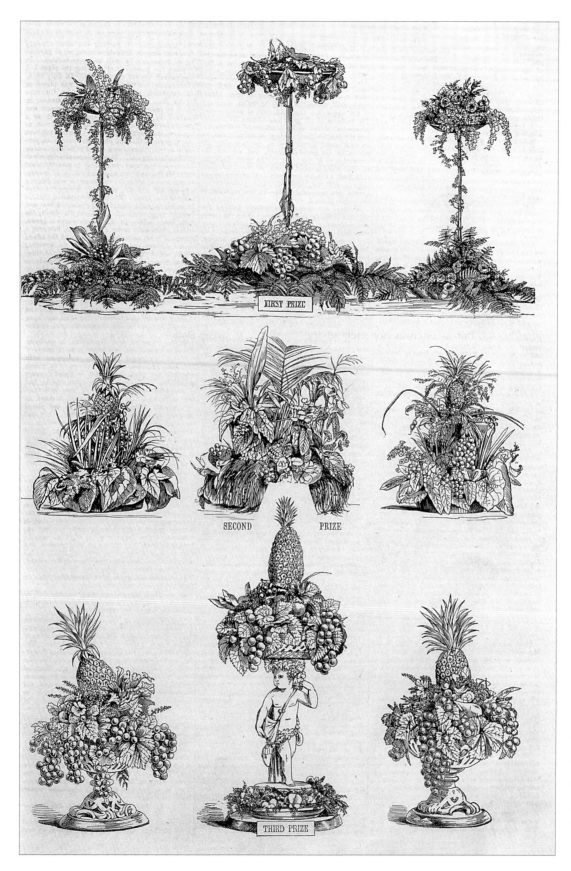

FIRST PRIZE

SECOND PRIZE

THIRD PRIZE

An engraving from the Gardeners' Chronicle, *showing the three winning entries from the 1861 table decoration competition: T.C. March's display of epergnes at the top.*

flowers, which had begun at mid-century with an enthusiasm for ferns and would grow steadily throughout the 1860s, and which was advantageously timed for purposes of interior decoration: in the age of gaslight, foliage plants withstood the indoor environment well, while flowers quickly wilted. Cut flowers continued to be used for table settings, but for longer-term decoration did not return to widespread popularity until the advent of electric light.

This was effectively the first organised competition for flower arrangements, in Britain at least (there had been competitions for bouquets before, but they attracted nothing like the attention that these table arrangements did). It was plainly an idea whose time had come: competing with March's book for the status of first book on flower arranging was Miss E.A. Maling's *Flowers for Ornament and Decoration*. Before 1862, occasional advice on the use of plants for interior decoration can be discovered in more general books, but as often as not such advice related to the use of house plants rather than temporary display (and all through the later 19th century, books on floral decoration regularly elided the boundary between the concepts). After the watershed of the 1860s, the professional floral decorator emerged, with Annie Hassard in the 1870s in a pioneering role (though head gardeners and nurserymen continued to play that role in country houses and for major commissions). But it was the 1861 RHS competition that sparked this process into life.[3]

Table decoration to flower arrangement

The RHS continued its aristocratically judged competitions for a few years (with artists like Henry Redgrave and E.W. Cooke seconded to help), by which time the Royal Botanic Society and the Crystal Palace were staging rival events. Gradually, table decoration became a routine part of the show schedule, not only for the RHS but for societies around the country, attracting press notice only on special occasions like the provincial shows—as at Birmingham in 1872 when a Gaslight Competition was held. In the early 20th century, the popularity of table decoration continued, and the *Journal* for 1904-5 carried an article on the subject; but the competition was dropped from the Temple Shows because of lack of space, and after the First World War table decoration classes were dropped from the specialist shows.[4]

The Society's shows reflected changes in fashion. The 1870s and 1880s saw floral decorations expand from the dinner table to fill the room; the

fashion was led by Sir Edward Scott of Sundridge Park, who in 1871 'gave his house up into his florist's hands for three full days, with carte blanche orders, regardless of expense'. John Wills—of all London nurserymen the most closely identified with floral decoration—carried such display into the RHS shows:

> On July 21, 1873, the first large public entertainment was given in the conservatory of the Royal Horticultural Gardens, in connection with a ball given in honour of H.R.H. the Prince of Wales. Here for the first time ice was largely used for cooling the heated atmosphere of the ball-room, and after this initiative by the Society, as much as forty tons of ice was used on different occasions.

By the end of the century, flowers were once again competing with foliage as material for decoration, and the novel principles of Japanese flower arranging were becoming known. Sir William Lawrence, the Society's Treasurer, later recalled: 'It was left to Queen Alexandra, when Princess of Wales, to sweep all this away. With bated breath Sir Maurice Holzmann told us that the princess had large vases of "common" beech boughs in the drawing-room of Marlborough House.' By the Edwardian period the Society was holding competitions for bouquets in addition to table decoration as formerly understood.[5]

During the inter-war years the Society's support for floral decoration wavered. In 1924 it declined to help the Chamber of Horticulture with a proposed Buttonhole League, although corsages were a recognised exhibition category; it continued to hold flower arrangement competitions for amateurs, but in 1938 published an article on flower arranging in the *Journal* which explicitly denounced existing styles as outmoded, unworthy of appearing in a modern, innovative building like the New (Lawrence) Hall.[6] Meanwhile, however, it had begun a new initiative, as privately run schools of floristry had begun to flourish. In December 1932 George Monro, head of the Covent Garden sundries house, proposed the establishment of a London Diploma of Floral Art; a committee was set up with Monro, E.A. Bowles, Frederick Chittenden, and representatives of the florists' schools, and the British Floral Art Examination Board was established as a Subcommittee of the Examinations Board. In 1935 Sir David Bowes Lyon became its Chairman, and the botanical artist Frank Galsworthy also served as a member. This Board was put into abeyance during the Second World War, and not reconvened after. In January 1952 Julia Clements recommended that the RHS sponsor courses for flower arrangement judges, but Council responded that 'the only rules which could possibly be formulated would be those dealing with schedules and that legislation could not be made to cover matters of taste'—an apparent inconsistency with its own activities twenty years before. In 1953 the Society (along with the Ministry of Education and the schools of floristry) was represented on the Committee for Education in Floristry; in February 1954 it recognised the Society of Floristry as the national examining body in the UK.[7]

Constance Spry had by now emerged as the dominant figure in British flower arranging; her book *Flower Decoration* (1934) had appeared with a preface by the Society's Treasurer, and in 1943 she gave her first official lecture to the Society, on 'Flower decoration in wartime'. As victory in the European war drew nearer, the Society planned to resume its amateur flower arrangement competitions; the result, in September 1945, was deemed a success; and in 1948, at the second post-war Chelsea Flower Show, the south-west corner of the marquee was devoted to a massive flower arrangement competition. (This was in part a means of filling space, since fewer firms than had been hoped were ready to resume their participation in the 1947 Show; but the success of the event determined the Society to continue it even after the exhibitors' level had returned to normal.) In 1956—later referred to by Spry as 'the pinnacle year'—a separate tent was erected to accommodate the flower arrangers; this was augmented in later years with a further tent for professional floristry. And from 1953, it became customary at one fortnightly show each year to give over the whole of the Old (Lindley) Hall to flower arranging.[8]

In the early 1950s, flower arranging was becoming organised as a movement, and the key event took place in the RHS New Hall on 16-17 July 1952: 'The Flower Academy', 'that entrancing exhibition, staged ... by just four clubs and societies in the country'. (The eldest of the four was the

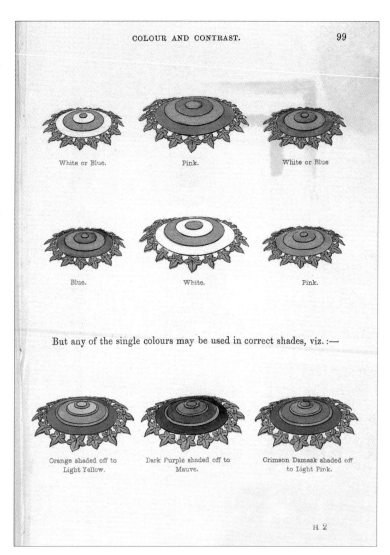

Advice on colour combinations for floral arrangements, from T.C. March's Flower and Fruit Decoration *(1862).*

Dorchester Floral Decoration Society, founded in 1949 by Mary Pope; the other three had all been founded in 1951.) An article by Constance Spry appeared in the same issue of the *Journal* as the announcement of the competition; Mary Pope and her colleagues tried to give the exhibits visual unity by creating a backdrop of corrugated cardboard painted 'as continuous undulating curves'. Eight thousand visitors attended, and no doubt went away with thoughts of new societies in their heads.[9] The Delphinium and Chrysanthemum Societies, in particular, encouraged the new movement—as did some noted gardeners and Council members, such as Stuart Ogg and Maurice Mason; the latter helped to promote the East of England Flower Clubs and staged an exhibit of 'plants interesting for flower arrangers and horticulturists' at a Norwich show. On the other hand, the increasing popularity of flower arrangement also met with opposition from gardeners like Will Ingwersen ('I am driven into frenzies of rage and despair by the raids of demented female flower arrangers, to whom nothing in the garden is sacred') and C.E. Lucas Phillips ('The proper place for flowers is the garden'). The idea that the garden should be planted simply to provide material for the house was greeted with horror by columnists who had no such qualms about the fruit garden; Frank Galsworthy, who had been involved with the Floral Art Diploma, fretted in the pages of *Gardening Illustrated* about the ascendancy of the flower arrangers; and Council members feared 'that it is but the beginnings of strong pressure being brought to bear on the Society to take a more active part in the floral decoration movement'.[10]

In December 1954, a meeting of regional floral decoration societies was held, with the Society's President, Sir David Bowes Lyon, in the Chair, about 'the future of the Floral Decoration Movement'. (The London Floral Decoration Society had changed its name to the National Floral Decoration Society, to some irritation outside London.) The meeting voted unanimously that the RHS should establish a Floral Decoration Committee; Lord Digby became its first Chairman. This Committee was not without its trials; in 1957, 'Lord Digby referred to the unsatisfactory way in which the Members of this Committee, which was unlike any other, took a decision at one meeting and reversed it at the next on instructions from their "constituents".' Mary Pope later remarked that it was the successful formation of this Committee that moved her and her colleagues to start establishing regional branches of the National Society, and eventually, to the creation in 1958 of the National Association of Flower Arrangement Societies of Great Britain (NAFAS), and its inaugural 'Festival of Flower Decoration' in 1959.[11]

There is not much documentation on the judging of flower arrangements at RHS shows for the next 18 years; it seems to have become a matter for Floral Committee A. In November 1977, Council debated whether to ask an expert on flower arrangement to join Floral A, or whether to relieve that Committee of the task of judging flower arrangements and appoint a special panel instead. The latter course being decided upon, Council negotiated with NAFAS, and in April 1978 could report that the 'new panel to recommend awards for exhibits of flower arrangements' had been agreed, with Lady Loder in the Chair, and John Mattock, the prominent rose nurseryman, also representing the RHS. The remaining membership of the panel was chosen by NAFAS, although at Council's request, Julia Clements and Sheila Macqueen were also added. Lady Loder chaired the panel until 1989, when she was succeeded by Mary Newnes (later Shirville), and she in her turn by Colin Ellis. After 1976, affiliation with the RHS was no longer required for flower arrangement clubs to exhibit (by then, NAFAS had over 1,000 such clubs); and in that year, for the first time, NAFAS was invited to stage a major exhibit in the main marquee.[12]

It was understandable in 1861, when the Society had been drawn into Prince Albert's plans for the artistic rejuvenation of England, that it should become involved in matters like table decoration; and that a tradition, once having been started, should continue of its own momentum. But in the 1950s, it was somewhat anomalous that the RHS, which fought shy of making pronouncements on aesthetics, should be promoting an art form unconnected with cultivation. (Some indeed argued that no award cards should be given for flower arrangements, 'because, for one reason, the exhibitors do not necessarily have to grow the flowers'.) Nonetheless, the Society persisted, in the teeth of the most protracted controversy that flower arranging was ever to arouse. In 1954 the new American trend for interpretative flower arranging reached England, and plunged the magazines into 'the uncertain world of art', with accusations of attention-seeking, incomprehensibility, and affectation thrown at the adherents of the new style. The press debate reached a peak in 1958 when Edith Hambly Parker, who had been the organising secretary of the 'Flower Academy' six years earlier, created an interpretative display at a Delphinium Society show that sparked over six months of correspondence.[13] Through it all, the RHS continued to provide a venue, and the exhibits at Chelsea veered back and forth stylistically: in 1999, the NAFAS display in the marquee was rigorously modernistic, while in 2002—conservation of biodiversity having engaged the concern of flower arrangers—it represented the diversity of nature through a series of different climatic zones. And as the century drew to its end, the Society found further ways of promoting flower arrangement: in 1967, Julia Clements began contributing articles to the Society's *Journal*, followed by George Smith and others; while in 1994 Wisley started offering classes in flower arrangement in a joint venture with NAFAS.

The rise of bonsai

The art of ornamentally dwarfing trees originated in China, and it was from China that the first reports reached England, because Japan was

*Bonsai exhibit at
Wisley Show, June
2003.*

closed to foreign visitors. John Livingstone, who
sent plants from China to the Society, contributed
an article on the subject to the *Transactions* in 1820;
Robert Fortune commented on the practice in his
accounts of his travels in China; Lindley remarked
on it with distaste. By the middle of the 19th century the fact was known, but the British showed
no desire to emulate the Chinese in this custom.[14]
The reason for this lack of enthusiasm was not due
to any lack of technical skill—root-pruning was
common enough in the fruit garden—and, indeed,
one instance of ornamental dwarfing was
tolerated and even admired in the mid-century
years: Sir Charles Isham's rock garden at Lamport
Hall, Northamptonshire, where root-pruned
dwarf trees were planted in order to make the rock
garden seem like a scale model of alpine scenery.
But the general attitude was that ornamental
dwarfing represented a depraved taste, or even
that it constituted torture of plants.[15]

From the mid-1860s, however, a fascination for
things Japanese began to grow in England, as the
United States forced the Japanese government to
accept trade and diplomatic relations with the
west, and Japanese artefacts began to reach the
European art market. In 1872, at a banquet held by
the Liverpool Chamber of Commerce in honour
of the Japanese Embassy, the first British display of
bonsai was seen, arranged under the supervision
of George A. Audsley, who was to become
Britain's first authority on Japanese art.[16] By the

turn of the century, Japanese nurseries catering for
the export market were sending bonsai specimens
as well as plants for the flower garden, and private
collections of bonsai were being built up in
England.[17]

At the Temple Show of 1901, there were no
fewer than five exhibits of bonsai: one of them
from an importer, two from private collectors—
Mrs Hart of Fairlawn, Totteridge, whose exhibit
contained 'ships, flamingoes, and Japanese junks
in larch', and John Russell of Richmond, who
exhibited tray landscapes or bonkei (misrendered
'boukei' by the press)—and two from well-
established Covent garden seed houses: Barr and
Sons of Covent Garden, and James Carter and Co.
Barr exhibited a 'miniature Japanese forest' at the
1904 Temple Show, earning the following
comment from the *Gardeners' Magazine*: 'on no
previous occasion have the dwarfed trees so dear
to the Japanese gardener been so extensively
exhibited in this country ... whatever one may
think of them horticulturally, it is impossible not
to admire the patience bestowed upon the plants
by, in many cases, several generations of
gardeners.' Barr's and Carter's specimens were
used as examples by Albert Maumené in the first
major article on bonsai as an art form practised in
Europe, published in the *Journal* for 1908. Barr
went on to exhibit bonsai at the first Chelsea
Shows in 1913-14, while Carters moved in the
direction of model Japanese gardens.[18]

The inter-war years saw an apparent hiatus in the history of bonsai in Britain. There were still private collectors, like Reginald Cory and Hew Dalrymple, but they did not seek, or at least enjoy, publicity. Gwendolyn Anley, the writer on alpine plants, inherited Dalrymple's collection, and gave an account of it to the RHS in a lecture on Japanese gardens read, rather daringly, in 1946, at a time when enthusiasm for things Japanese was at a fairly low point.[19] But during the 1950s the Japanese taste once again became respectable, and with it, on a small scale, the cultivation of bonsai. A bonsai group, the Bonsai Kai (the first bonsai club in Europe), was formed within the Japan Society of London, and in 1961 it staged its first exhibit at the Chelsea Flower Show, winning a Silver-Gilt Banksian Medal. All through the 1960s, the Bonsai Kai was the only society to display bonsai at Chelsea, but the taste was spreading; and by the end of the 1960s specialist nurseries were beginning to appear to cater for the trend. In 1970 the Bonsai Kai was joined at Chelsea by the firms of Bromage and Young, and Tokonoma Bonsai; others followed, including a new bonsai club, the British Bonsai Association, in 1976; Peter Chan exhibited under his own name from 1979 to 1982, and thereafter as Herons Bonsai

Nursery. By 1987 it was estimated that there were 13 stands at Chelsea displaying bonsai, whether as the sole subject of the stand or as part of larger exhibits.[20]

Standards for judging bonsai caused the Society something of the same problem that flower arranging had—but at least cultivation was involved, even if of a sort of which few of the judges had experience in the early days. In 1982, there was discussion about introducing a points system, but this was agreed to be impracticable in the short term. Meanwhile, articles about bonsai had begun to appear in the Society's *Journal* from 1968, with Alan Roger, the chairman of the Bonsai Kai and a member of Floral Committee B, acting as the leading propagandist in the early years; later, Colin Ellis of the Bonsai Kai also wrote on the subject, and in effect represented both the bonsai and the flower arranging fraternities on Council.[21] And in 1989, a decade after the idea had first been proposed, a collection of bonsai was established at Wisley, with a gift of plants, and help in training and maintenance, from Peter and Dawn Chan. By the end of the 1990s there was an annual bonsai weekend at Wisley, and the Society had accepted bonsai as a mature area of horticulture.

ROYAL HORTICULTURAL SOCIETY'S
SCHOOL OF HORTICULTURE.

PROSPECTUS.

The Society admits a limited number of young men to study the Principles and Operations of Horticulture in its Gardens at Wisley, near Ripley in Surrey. The Gardens are 4 miles from Byfleet, 6 from Weybridge, 4 from Effingham, 4½ from Horsley, all on the Southern Ry. Cars can be obtained at the first two stations. Omnibus Route (L.G.O.) No. 115, from the Garage, Kingston Station to North Street, Guildford, passes within 5 minutes of the gardens.

CONDITIONS OF ADMISSION.

The following are the principal conditions of admission :—

1. Applicants for admission as working Students in the Royal Horticultural Society's Gardens at Wisley, are furnished with an application form (p, 11), which, when signed, must be returned to the Secretary, R.H.S., Vincent Square, Westminster, accompanied by a letter in the applicant's own handwriting.

2. Applicants must be between 16 and 22 years of age and qualified from previous general education to profit by the course of instruction provided and must be healthy, free from physical defect, and not so much below average height as to interfere with their prospects as Gardeners. They must also be prepared to perform all kinds of Gardening work, including the humblest.

3. Two testimonials as to character should accompany the application.

4. The applicant will be informed if his name has been entered for admission, and will receive notice of the next vacancy. The terms usually begin on the first Monday in October and the first Monday in April when only can Students be admitted.

5. After any applicant has received notice of his acceptance, an entrance fee of £5 5s. must be forwarded to the Secretary of the Society before the order for admission can be issued. No other fees are charged, but Students provide their own board and lodging, books, stationery, note books, and such like.

6. No wages are given to Students.

18 *Amateur and Professional*

A prospectus for the Wisley School of Horticulture.

OF the seven founding members of the Society, four were gentleman amateurs, and three were professional horticulturists: a nurseryman, and two superintendents of royal gardens. It cannot be said that this even-handedness between the amateur and professional worlds has been smoothly maintained ever since. Conflicts over authority and status have bedevilled both the RHS and the wider society within which it functions.

For its first 80 years, the membership of the Society consisted primarily of nobility and landed gentry. Council minutes in the first half of the 19th century are a record of intermittent genuflection, as dukes and royal families around Europe deigned to become Honorary Fellows, and were presented with specially bound sets of the *Transactions* or collections of trees. The first Royal Patron, or in this case Patroness, was Queen Charlotte, who consented to the role in 1816; the Society's artist, William Hooker, prepared an illustrated vellum sheet for her to autograph—a custom that has continued through the centuries, with every reigning monarch of the United Kingdom asked in turn to be a Patron. (The making of illuminated autographs was also applied to Fellows of royal or sub-royal status, ranging from George III's ducal sons to various continental monarchs, and even Mohammed Said, Viceroy of Egypt in the 1860s.)[1]

Members, or Fellows as they were officially known from 1809, had to be proposed by three or more Fellows, and elected by ballot; the membership fee on admission was five guineas, with annual supplements of two guineas (raised to three in 1818), but a Fellow could compound for the annual payments by a single payment of 20 guineas (raised to thirty in 1818). Such fees could only be afforded by the well-to-do. By contrast, there was an arrangement whereby 'Any person exercising the trade or profession of a Gardener',

having once been awarded a medal or communicated a paper, could be elected for an admission fee and subsequent annual contribution of one guinea. The list of 'Gardeners Admitted to the Privileges of Fellowship' was always small, but boasted some figures of more lasting importance than many of the proper Fellows; as late as 1860 the name of Sir Joseph Paxton appeared under that heading. By that time he was a Vice-President of the Society, so his

Queen Charlotte's royal autograph (1816), drawn by William Hooker, depicting Strelitzia reginae, *which had been named after her (Charlotte Sophia von Mecklenburg-Strelitz) by Sir Joseph Banks.*

appearance in the list might indicate merely that he was getting his subscription at a bargain price. It was of course possible for a Gardener to rise in the ranks to become a Fellow, on payment of the full fee; the Chelsea nurseryman Joseph Knight achieved this in 1817.[2]

This distinction between Gardeners and Fellows effectively continued into the 20th century. In 1888, the invidious 'Gardeners admitted' was replaced by an Associate class created for *bona fide* gardeners (and, eventually, horticultural journalists).[3] Note that after the original reference to 'trade or profession', the phrase 'professional gardener' was never cited in any category of membership; despite the rise of head gardeners to a position of authority, despite the claims of gardeners to be recognised as professionals, they had no professional body to represent them, and were in many circles still regarded as 'trade'. But meanwhile, the Society itself was working in various ways to bring that professionalism about.

Training gardeners at Chiswick

As early as 1820, the Horticultural Society looked forward to the day when it could establish 'a National School for the propagation of Horticultural knowledge'. Looking around, it could certainly see the need for gardeners' education, and its own officials could prove to be objects of complaint. The second President, Thomas Andrew Knight, while an experimental botanist of high repute, was scorned in public for his own benighted staff. In an article in the Society's *Transactions* in 1820, Knight incautiously described his gardener as 'an extremely simple labourer, he does not know a letter or a figure'. John Claudius Loudon, who would soon be campaigning vigorously for improved education in his *Gardener's Magazine*, quipped that this ignorance explained the death of Knight's pineapple crop: 'not knowing "a letter or a figure", of course, he could not take a hint from the thermometer.' When, some years later, Knight's gardener Richard Williams read a paper to the Society, Loudon took note, and remarked:

> We are very happy to learn that Mr. Knight has thought it worth while to keep a gardener who can not only

read, but write. Mr. Knight, by showing the utility of general knowledge to gardeners, and advocating the cause of garden libraries as the means for acquiring this knowledge, might do more for the advancement of horticulture, than by all the practical papers that he has ever written, or ever will write.

The immediate consequence was that the *Gardener's Magazine* was banned from the Society's Library; the longer-term consequence was no doubt a stiffening of resolve on educational matters. But there was general agreement from the rising generation of gardeners that standards of knowledge among their predecessors were low, and that the 18th-century gardening

Joseph Paxton's paragraph of autobiography, from the Handwriting of Gardeners *book. Notice he gives his birthdate as 1801; it is generally agreed that he was born in 1803.*

literature was sorely deficient by comparison with the seventeenth. Donald Beaton was later to claim that 'only four years before the first Reform Bill, some of the best gardeners in the country did not know or understand the principle of potting plants'.[4]

With the acquisition of the Chiswick garden, the possibility of a school of horticulture suddenly came within the Society's grasp. The Council report on the new garden proposed the following staffing arrangement:

> The head Gardeners will be permanent servants of the Society, but the under gardeners and labourers employed will be young men who having acquired some previous knowledge of the first rudiments of the art, will be received into the establishment and having been duly instructed in the various practice of each department will become entitled to recommendation from the Officers of the Society to fill the situations of Gardeners in private or other establishments.[5]

The labourers were to be paid 14 shillings per week—not necessarily a bad wage, when we can find seven shillings a week cited as a working man's common wage before the Napoleonic Wars. Their accommodation was another matter. At the other end of the century, according to C. H. Curtis, who worked for a time as Archibald Barron's assistant, the bothies were 'hovels—no less' right up to the Garden's last days.[6]

A set of 17 rules was established for the conduct of the labourer-students. They had to be recommended by a Fellow of the Society, aged between 18 and 26, unmarried, literate (the test being to write a paragraph of autobiography in a little volume labelled *Handwriting of Gardeners*), with some previous training as a gardener. A month's probation was required, and then the student was on the first step of the employment ladder:

> 9. Each labourer on his first introduction to the garden will be placed in the lowest department, and will be advanced in succession, through the other departments, according to his ability and acquirements, without reference to the time he has been employed in the garden. No person can be admitted for the purpose of study in any *one* department only.

> 12. The *under-gardeners* will be selected from the labourers employed in the garden, solely according to their character, conduct, ability, and acquirements, without any reference whatever to the period of their employment or their age, and they may be removed from the superintendence of one department to that of another, as may be found convenient, without any other consideration.

> 14. The under-gardeners are not permitted to seek for engagement or service for themselves. The nomination to the employment of under-gardener will be presumed to imply that they are considered likely to be recommended in due time to situations of consequence in their profession.[7]

Demeanour and moral conduct were emphasised as much as skill. Some people found these rules pointless and arbitrary; an anonymous correspondent in the *Gardener's Magazine* claimed that they were 'held in derision by all the nurserymen and master gardeners about London who know anything about them, and laughed at by the young men themselves'—though he did not vouchsafe which particular rules were the offending ones. The same correspondent was indignant about the business of recommending gardeners to positions in private gardens: 'so utterly at variance with the dignity of the society, that we are astonished it should be persisted in. An institution with "His sacred Majesty" as a patron, and emperors and kings as members, to keep an office for servants!'[8] No full record has survived of the Society's work as an employment exchange, and the few references in Council minutes can be frustratingly brief. 'April 22 (1826). Joseph Paxton, under-gardener in the Arboretum, left, recommended to a place'—the fact that the place was Chatsworth, the principal seat of the Society's own landlord, was not mentioned. About the same time a new ruling was made that there should be no more than three foreigners at a time among the labourers, suggesting that the scheme had become known internationally; Anton Friedrich Ludwig von Sckell, the son of the famous landscape gardener, was a student at Chiswick in the mid-1820s.[9]

The halcyon days of the early 1820s were soon clouded over by financial hardship. In 1827, hard on the heels of John Turner's embezzlement, the labourers' wages were cut from 14 to 12 shillings, and their number reduced, though not as much as Council had hoped. The garden staff responded by forming a mutual improvement association, one of the first in the country for gardeners, and a grant of £50 was made to buy books for the garden library. This liberality proved pointless, however, for as discomfort modulated into disaster in 1830, Council voted to replace the students with ordinary labourers; student gardeners were allowed to continue without wages.[10]

John Lindley, meanwhile, had taken up his second job as Professor of Botany at University College, and his mind must have turned to the education of his staff. In 1836, the Society announced its return to a new version of its

Sir Joseph Paxton (1803-1865), who rose from under-gardener at Chiswick to become the first gardener to be knighted. Head gardener at Chatsworth, designer of Birkenhead Park, People's Park Halifax, and the Crystal Palace Park, not to mention the Crystal Palace itself. With Lindley a founder of the Gardeners' Chronicle, as well as editor of the Horticultural Register, and Paxton's Magazine of Botany. Author of A Practical Treatise on the Cultivation of the Dahlia (1838).

training programme, this time with examinations. Loudon, who had laboured the question of gardeners' education for years in his *Gardener's Magazine*, could barely contain his enthusiasm:

> A grand step has been taken by the London Horticultural Society for the promotion of gardening, and from which may be dated a new era in the art. It is proposed by the Garden Committee ... to receive no gardeners for permanent employment in the gardens who cannot produce satisfactory evidence that they have received a certain degree of preliminary education; and, after any one has been admitted, he cannot be recommended to any place as a gardener, until he shall have undergone an examination on what may be called horticultural science, and received a certificate, a copy of which will be recorded in a book kept for the purpose [and which does not survive—BE]. We cannot sufficiently express the high opinion which we entertain of the good that will result from this determination of the Society ...
>
> We have said above that this determination of the Horticultural Society will form the commencement of a new era in gardening; but still more effectually will it create a new era among gardeners, by distinguishing and elevating all those that are really worthy of the name; and this will lead to their being more suitably paid, and more respectfully treated by their employers, than many of them are at present ...
>
> We hope all other Horticultural Societies, who have gardens and scientific secretaries, or curators, will institute preliminary regulations of a similar kind; for, though a certificate from a provincial institution can never rank with one from the Metropolitan Society, yet it will be some value, and tend to enhance the worth of that obtained from the Metropolitan Society. We hope, also, that young men, in every part of the country, who are in their apprenticeship, or who are working as journeymen, will prepare themselves for examination by the London Horticultural Society; and will be sufficiently ambitious, not to desire to fill a place till they have proved that, as far as respects the science of their art, they are properly qualified for it.

The examinations were conducted orally and individually, and consisted of accountancy arithmetic, mensuration, plan drawing, geography, botany, and vegetable physiology. The public announcement in Loudon's pages also contained the results of the first three exams, in which an 'extra certificate of the first class' was awarded to the young Robert Fortune. Loudon was in no doubt that the examinations 'originated with Dr. Lindley, who has thus rendered a most important service to the gardening world'.[11]

Lindley was shortly to write a textbook, the *Theory of Horticulture* (1840), which was used at Chiswick though by no means intended solely for the Society's students; within five years it had been translated into Dutch and Russian, and twice into German, and it went into an enlarged second edition in 1855. It was greeted by the young gardeners of the day as marking an epoch in the history of horticulture; Alexander Cramb, the celebrated head gardener of Tortworth Court, later described it as 'raising horticulture almost to an exact science' and 'so demolishing that huge monster—empiricism'.[12] Dedicated to the memory of Thomas Andrew Knight, it was divided into two sections, on vital actions (plant physiology) and the operations of horticulture, including two chapters on the then novel and little-understood problems of plant breeding ('preservation of races by seed' and 'improvement of races'). But, useful as Lindley's work was for the botany requirement, the general thrust of the examinations was better reflected in a posthumous book by Loudon, *Self-instruction for Young Gardeners* (1845), which provided information on arithmetic, book-keeping, geometry, measuring and land-surveying, mapping and architectural drawing, mechanics and hydrostatics. Loudon's book never went beyond a single edition, but deserved to have been much used at Chiswick. Alas! the drawback of books on self-instruction is that, unlike systems of examinations, they do not provide credentials, as D.T. Fish found when he applied for his first job, having trained himself in all the subjects in Loudon, and was offered a place for £30 a year: 'Why couple the knowledge and culture of professional men with the rewards of a livery servant?'[13]

The financial crisis of the 1850s once again curtailed the Society's educational ambitions, but the short-lived recovery of the early 1860s made Council more sanguine. Sir Charles Dilke, who had been instrumental in creating the Kensington garden, now turned his attention to the revitalising of Chiswick, and proposed that a formal School of Horticulture be established, which would aim to be national, if not imperial, in its scope. 'Chiswick, a School of Horticulture!', exulted the *Gardeners' Chronicle*.

> The very idea is refreshing, and the sound of the exclamation musical, after the croakings we have heard of late years to the effect that Chiswick was worn out, Chiswick was obsolete and useless, Chiswick was dead and ought to be dismembered ... We unhesitatingly say it is a necessity; it is one of the wants of the age. The decadence of Chiswick as the fountain of horticultural information, is already telling upon the rising generation of gardeners. We willingly admit that there are bright exceptions, but as a whole, the class is not now what it was when it yielded a PAXTON.

Correspondents looked forward to the day when the Chiswick school would be 'the centre of the horticulture of the empire'.[14] A Committee on the Improved Education of Gardeners was set up, with the Secretary Wilson Saunders as its Chairman, and such members as Dilke, Robert Fortune, Thomas Moore, William Paul, Thomas Rivers, James Veitch, and Paxton. In collaboration with the Royal Society of Arts, which already had a national administrative framework for examinations, it formulated an RHS Certificate comprising subjects necessary for qualification as gardeners (literacy, arithmetic, horticultural operations for the fruit, kitchen, and flower gardens), and subjects necessary for qualification as Associates of the Society ('book-keeping, practical geometry, land-measuring and plan-drawing, theory of horticulture, systematic botany, and the tasteful laying-out of gardens'). The plans incurred some criticism, on the grounds that 'A powerful Society like the Royal Horticultural ought to do its own work', but were generally well received: the first gardener to get full marks on the exams (in 1869) was James Hudson, later the head gardener of Gunnersbury Park (and who was to fund a prize in honour of the 40th anniversary of his passing).[15] Moreover, now that it had some experience with national examinations, the Society proceeded to intervene elsewhere, petitioning the government for improved education in forestry.[16]

More locally, the Chiswick workforce was once again reorganised, with students' weekly wages starting at 13 shillings in the first year, rising to 15 in the third (not much change since the 1820s, but there was not much inflation either). Archibald Barron, as the new Superintendent of Chiswick, was responsible for the training programme, and received an annual £10 bonus because of the high pass rates of his students. The new post of Professor of Botany was created in 1872, with lecturing to the students among its duties; its first incumbent was W.T. Thiselton-Dyer, who left to become Assistant Director of Kew in 1875. Then came the reduction of Chiswick in the 1870s, another winding-down of ambitions, and by the mid-1880s the Society's President could complain publicly that 'this country, which was the greatest gardening country in the world, was the only country which had not got a school of gardening (while Germany had no fewer than thirty-three)'. New proposals to establish a School of Horticulture at Chiswick were dismissed for lack of resources. (A new Professor of Botany, George Henslow, had been appointed after a slight gap in 1880, and filled it intermittently until the First World War.)[17]

James Hudson (1846-1932), head gardener at Gunnersbury Park from 1876, where he became the leading British hybridiser of waterlilies.

National examinations for gardeners

Elementary education had been made compulsory in 1870, and was made free of charge in 1891. Local government reorganisation in the wake of the Third Reform Act resulted in the creation of County Councils in 1888, and the following year the Technical Instruction Act gave them powers to set up courses with a degree of government funding. In 1891 the RHS offered its services to any County Councils which included horticulture in their programmes; the first experiment was quite local—Surrey, for which Maxwell T. Masters and James Douglas, representing the scientific and the practical sides of horticulture, agreed to act as examiners (for a basic fee of five guineas each). The first results, in 1892, were encouraging, and the Society agreed to supervise horticultural examinations anywhere in the country. The old RHS Certificate exams held with the RSA were revised to form a new RHS General Examination that was launched in 1893.[18]

The new exam quickly became established, to such an extent that the London County Council announced that it would be adopted as 'a test for promotion among gardeners'. This proposal was greeted with controversy; William Watson of Kew, who had recently finished revising Thompson's *Gardener's assistant*, reacted by denouncing the whole idea of examinations:

> It is doubtful whether such examinations ... are of much value as a means of training in professional horticulture, or even as a test of knowledge of the principles and practice of the art. Would any practical gardener attach any importance to the success or failure of a young man at an examination in which he is asked to explain or describe the structure and growth of cells, the process of impregnation of the ovule and similar academic question? And even the more practical questions, such as the description and use of implements, manures and their application, are worthless as tests of anything except perhaps memory. This sort of thing has about the same bearing on gardening as questions on the varieties and special uses of saucepans, the origin and chemical constituents of salt, or the effects of heat on vegetable and animal tissue have on cooking. Of course the college students who know little or nothing of gardening do well at the Royal Horticultural Society's examinations, whilst intelligent, experienced young men of proved ability in the garden rarely get into the first class.

The Society's Professor of Botany, George Henslow, agreed in denouncing the LCC's proposal, and defended the examination in a half-hearted way, saying that 'The examinations have great value in securing mental cultivation in the subject of horticulture; but they are unquestionably of little, if indeed it may be of any security, for skill in practical work'. On the other hand, Lewis Castle of the Woburn Fruit Farm and the landscape architect William Goldring defended the examinations as a means of raising the status of gardeners, and the *Gardeners' Chronicle* summed up in a leader, 'The writers from whose letters we quote speak of "college-trained" lads proving unsatisfactory. Is that not an evidence that, however highly certificated the pupils may have been, they have *not* been trained? That, surely, is a defect not to be credited to the examination or to the examiners.'[19]

The RHS General was soon followed by various RHS specifics. In 1904, an examination in Cottage and Allotment Gardening for Teachers was instituted, followed in 1906 by an examination for employees in public parks. Coming immediately in the wake of the Watson controversy, the first year's results were eagerly scrutinised for evidence of relevance. The examiners were William Crump, head gardener at Madresfield Court, C.R. Fielder (later the RHS Gardens Inspector), George Nicholson of Kew, the Royal gardener Owen Thomas, the landscape architect Edward White, and William Wilks, the Society's Secretary. 'Could a better set of examiners have been found?', asked the *Chronicle*, citing their homily to the students as an example of a well-balanced approach: 'The examiners desire to impress on the candidates the absolute necessity of observation as they pursue their daily work, and the application of thought as to the why and the wherefore of what they do and what they notice. A man can never be really fit for high place in any calling in life unless he both thinks and observes.'[20] The injunctions seem to have been necessary. A few years later, the results of the parks exam 'showed but a fragmentary knowledge, uncertain and lacking in conviction, instead of an exhaustive mastership of the subjects of the questions', while an early instance of the teachers' exam revealed a carelessness in filling out forms that 'was not to be expected from school teachers accustomed to examinations... What diversity of opinion was given upon the quantity of seed-peas needful to sow a row thirty feet long! The Examiners were told varying measures, ranging from a quarter of a pint to a quart.'[21]

Students at Wisley over the years. Left, an early view of the lecture theatre in the Laboratory, 1917; right, students in the lecture room, 1907; below right, students gardeners sowing seeds as part of their practical examination in the 1960s.

The first suggestion of a National Diploma as a higher examination in horticulture was made by W.B. Little at a meeting of the recently formed Horticultural Education Association in September 1911. That December the Society formed a new Committee, under the Chairmanship of A.H. Dyke Acland of Killerton, with William Bateson, E.A. Bowles, Frederick Chittenden, James Hudson, and Frederick Keeble among its members (Sir Albert Rollitt was added a fortnight later), to look into the idea. The Committee's report was accepted in August 1913, and negotiations with the University of London began, Rollitt being the chief negotiator. The examination was to be in three stages: a qualifying test, that corresponded in content to the Society's original 1830s exams— literacy, arithmetic, mensurations, geography; a Preliminary Examination covering horticultural operations—

> Choice of site, laying out, levelling, etc., of a garden. Composition of soils ... Cultivation of the soil: trenching, digging, hoeing, raking, rolling; drainage and its effects upon soil and crops; the relation of the plant to the soil. The making of composts ... Nature and uses of manures in the

garden. The part played by root, stem, leaf, flower, fruit, and seed, in the life of the plant. The effect of water, air, light and temperature on the growth of plants ... Seed sowing, transplanting, and permanent planting. Cultivation of kitchen garden plants. Care of lawns, paths, flower-beds, herbaceous borders, and rock gardens. Methods of propagation by seeds and vegetative processes. Cultivation of ornamental plants under glass ... Planting, pruning, and training of fruit-trees and bushes ... Planting, pruning, and training of ornamental trees and shrubs, including Roses. Knowledge of the ordinary names, Latin or English, of garden plants ... Symptoms and treatment of the commonest plant diseases and insect pests. Methods of fumigation and spraying. Use and care of tools and implements ...

—and a Final Examination in a specialist subject of the candidate's choice. The *Gardeners' Chronicle*

hoped that the practical emphasis of the exam would circumvent the old criticisms about academic uselessness, but William Robinson's magazine *The Garden* immediately swung in with precisely that objection: 'It seems to us that the conditions laid down will preclude most of the best gardeners of to-day from obtaining the diploma, even if they desired to do so ... (Arithmetic, mensuration) Knowledge of such subjects is, of course, useful in a way; but we wonder how many of our best gardeners, florists, fruit-growers and seedsmen, or members of the society's own committees, could pass such a qualifying test.'[22]

And after the First World War, the University of London proposed first to discard the practical components of the examination, and then to institute a purely academic examination of its own

which would bypass the National Diploma, all of which caused outrage in the Society.[23] In March 1918, the earlier Diploma Committee had been absorbed into a larger Examinations Board, which added such members as A.B. Rendle, the Keeper of Botany at the Natural History Museum, Sir Arthur Hill of Kew, and C.W. Crook of the National Union of Teachers; this Board was empowered to deal with all the Society's various examinations. It watched the gradual spread of county and other colleges that attempted to run courses in horticulture, and tried to ensure that they adopted the RHS exams. The immediate result was the creation of an honours examination as part of the NDH syllabus, and eventually a new examination, the National Certificate in Elementary Horticultural Practice, in 1937, specifically for students attending full-time courses in horticulture at local colleges.[24]

Probably the most extraordinary episode in the history of horticultural education was the setting of examinations for prisoners of war. The British Red

Cross Society, Prisoners of War Department, had set up an Educational Books Section, which successfully negotiated the despatch of textbooks to interned British soldiers in the German territories, and the RHS ensured that horticultural textbooks were included. Examination papers followed; in July 1942 the first nine candidates in German stalags sat their exams under the invigilation of their sergeants. The system had settled into an efficient rhythm by the time peace broke out in 1945, and Council faced the question: should soldiers, prevented by repatriation from sitting their exams, be allowed an equivalent examination back in Britain free of charge? The answer was: yes, as long as they applied within two years, and some fifty candidates duly took their exams in more conducive circumstances than at first expected.[25]

The history of technical education in Great Britain has demonstrated a consistent trend, whether in engineering, construction, or agriculture. Training by apprenticeship was almost universal in the mid-19th century; it gave way to a network of loosely aligned or competing institutions offering diplomas, which began as supplements to apprenticeship and gradually replaced it as necessary qualifications; finally these in their turn were succeeded by university degrees. (The benefits of this process to the skills involved has been a matter for debate in every case.) The same pattern can be seen in horticulture.[26] In the middle of the 19th century, the best qualification for a gardener was apprenticeship in a garden esteemed as a 'training garden'—which gardens best filled that role depended heavily on the capacities of the head gardener of the time. The RHS, by a mixture of innovation and reaction to competing schemes, pioneered the development of diploma qualifications in horticulture, and by the Second World War had built up a complete educational programme dealing with every level from the beginner to the teacher; the RHS determined the curriculum, conducted the higher examinations at Wisley, approved and supervised the centres for the lower examinations, and rigorously enforced standards (for decades the pass rate on the NDH was approximately 60 per cent). But the same trend toward the downgrading of technical diplomas and their replacement by university degrees began to make an impact on the RHS's educational programme in the post-war years.

Chittenden submitted a memorandum in 1942 in which he observed that few of the successful students went into careers in private gardens, preferring commercial horticulture or the Ministry of Agriculture's ever-expanding network of experimental stations and inspectorships, and recommended that the former purposes of the exam syllabus might be met by introducing more short courses in local colleges and institutes. A ferment of suggestions was made, and some tried, in the post-war years, ranging from the replacement of the NDH Honours exam with a thesis, to abandoning examinations altogether in favour of the Royal Society of Arts. Meanwhile the Society experimentally grant-aided such independent programmes as the YMCA's British Boys for British Horticulture, to encourage more entrants into the profession.[27]

The post-war years saw a protracted debate, analogous to those which took place in every sector of technical education, over the relative importance of academic and practical training. Wye College, and the Universities of Reading and Nottingham, were all offering horticultural degrees before the war, and an increasing number of other universities followed suit after. The Civil Service accepted the NDH as equivalent to a degree (B.Sc. in Horticulture) for purposes of qualification; the great difference between the courses was that the NDH Intermediate Examination required four years of practical training and one year in college, while the Universities effectively reversed the proportion, requiring only one year of practice. But in the 1960s this situation began to change, under demands from two sources: first, from the central government in its attempts to rationalise and centralise the educational system. In 1966 a committee on agricultural education chaired by Sir Harry Pilkington recommended the creation of a Technical Education Council with a common diploma structure throughout all the industries, with the consequent discontinuation of the NDH. Oliver Wyatt, the Society's Treasurer, commented in a memorandum to Council:

> Horticultural training cannot be made to conform to a plan based solely on commercial considerations; an aesthetic element occurs in garden design and public park control, and a purely scientific element occurs in botanic gardens. Therefore a national plan for training or examination in horticulture is not possible on the lines of that proposed for agriculture and poultry rearing where the interest is solely commercial.
>
> No case has been made out for the abolition of the N.D.H. nor for its restriction to matters connected with food production; it would seem that the sole object of the Committee [in] suggesting an alteration of its content is to bring it into line with branches of agriculture ...
>
> The desirability ... of Rationalisation has not been argued, let alone proved. Why should it be 'in the best interests of employers, students and

teaching establishments' to have similarity of standards for various branches of agriculture and horticulture any more than for similarity of standards for e.g. English literature and chinese, or for mathematics and Chartered Accountancy ...

The R.H.S. will not bind itself to take part in the reorganization of the N.D.H. on the lines that the Pilkington Committee seems inclined to propose ...[28]

But the Annual Report for 1966 expressed gloomy resignation:

The Society is in no way concerned to secure a monopoly of examinations in horticulture. The Society accepted responsibility for the establishment, conduct and administration of the National Diploma in Horticulture at the invitation of Government over fifty years ago. If now, over what appears to be less than the whole of the field now covered by the Diploma, it is felt ... that some new structure is necessary, the Society will have no hesitation in discontinuing the facilities it now provides as the need for them disappears.[29]

And so, over the next few years, the RHS educational structure suffered attrition, as first of all the peripheral examinations were discarded. The examination for Parks staff had been run

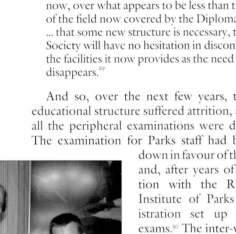

down in favour of the NDH, and, after years of negotiation with the RHS, the Institute of Parks Administration set up its own exams.[30] The inter-war years had been the golden age of the teachers' examination. In 1937 it was taken by 259 teachers; by 1960 this figure had dwindled to 11, and by the early 1970s to an average of four per annum. In 1969 the exam was replaced by a Teachers' Diploma in Horticulture, but within a couple of years it was decided that it served little useful purpose, and was discontinued.[31] The RHS General Exam, on the other hand, reached its pre-war high in 1937, with 343 senior and 117 junior candidates; but in the post-war years it shot up further, to peak at 984 in 1959, 427 of whom passed. The NDH Preliminary Examination was discontinued in 1966; the Annual Report stated that 'there is now no reason why all candidates should not obtain the necessary education qualification either before leaving school or by study afterwards'. The Technical Education Committee continued to press for

Christopher Jones receives his prize from the RHS President Sir Simon Hornby, as winner of the Chittenden Award for 1997 and given on the occasion of his graduation as M.Hort. (RHS).

examinations that were related to the centralised course structure, and in 1969 the administration of the National Certificate was officially handed over to the City and Guilds of London Institute.[32] By 1990, feeling that the RHS General Examination was not meeting the educational requirements of amateurs (no practical examination, and an inhibiting academic exam), the RHS discussed with the City and Guilds the idea of restructuring it as a framework of modular courses. The RHS General is now a Further Education qualification; its popularity has boomed since the 1980s, and it can now be studied at almost a hundred different colleges and other establishments around the country.

The second source of demand for change was the Civil Service unions, who wanted to make university degrees a requirement for employment because of their promotional value. By the time of the Horticultural Education Association's 1980 conference, it was apparent that NDH holders were no longer regarded as equal to degree holders for entry into the Ministry of Agriculture's services. A joint RHS/HEA review panel, chaired by Fred Shepherd, decided to rename and restructure the Diploma, and it emerged in 1985 as the Master of Horticulture (RHS). Over the next few years the new degree unsteadily found its feet, and there were years of negotiations before the National Council for Vocational Qualifications formally recognised it. (The Ridley Review Committee, meanwhile, was urging the RHS to shed its examinations work, but Council refused.)[33] The M.Hort.(RHS) remains an accepted Higher Education qualification, a credential testifying to both theoretical understanding and practical proficiency. As the availability of formal teaching facilities is very limited, registrations have dwindled, and it is currently being argued that it should be reconstituted with a post-qualifying award dimension. In 2001 an Advanced Certificate in Horticulture was introduced as a progressive award, closing the gap in levels between the General and the Diploma (which latter remains the intermediate stage of the M.Hort.(RHS)).

Some attendant matters have still to be discussed: first, prizes. In 1951, the Chittenden Prize was instituted as a money prize for the best student on the General Horticulture section of the NDH, and the Chittenden Award for the student gaining the highest marks on the Intermediate Examination; among the early recipients were Brian Halliwell, Pamela Schwerdt, and David Welch. (Both prizes were transferred in the 1980s to the Master of Horticulture.) For the centenary of the RHS General, Oliver Menhinick established two prizes, the Centenary Prize (a gift of the *New RHS Dictionary of Gardening* for the best student), and the Anne Menhinick Prize (for the candidate under 30 with the highest score). The Hector Harrison Award was instituted in 2002 for the best student on the new Advanced Examination.

One ever-present problem with the examinations was the question of textbooks. The 19th century had had Lindley's *Theory of Horticulture*, but science had moved on, and the last edition of Lindley's book hadn't. After the First World War Chittenden recommended that it be updated, but nothing happened; he pointed out again in 1942 that it was 'hopelessly out of date', but still nothing happened. Gradually, even the newer classics of horticulture, such as Liberty Hyde Bailey's *Pruning Manual* and *Nursery Manual* (first published in 1891 and 1898) became obsolete and were dropped from the syllabus (in 1942). By 1944, wartime shortages of paper had exacerbated matters, and only seven of the 23 course books were available; in 1947, a two-thirds failure rate was blamed in part on the unavailability of textbooks. The post-war years saw the supply remedied, but the absence of a comprehensive scientific textbook continued to bedevil the educational programme, and in 1989 an Ad Hoc Committee on the General Examination recommended the creation of a new book on horticultural botany. The eventual result was *Science and the Garden*, published in 2002.[34]

It is worth briefly comparing this book with its distinguished predecessor. Lindley's *Theory* dealt in its first section, on plant physiology, with germination, root and stem growth, leaf and flower action, the development of fruit, and temperature; in its second part, on horticultural principles, with bottom heat, watering, ventilation, propagation, pruning, training, potting, transplanting, plant breeding, and soils and manures. *Science and the Garden* has chapters on plant anatomy, nomenclature, breeding and genetics, soils, choosing a site, propagation, colour and shape, seasons, greenhouses, pests & diseases, harvest and storage. The principal additions, apart from genetics, are various aspects of physiology (abscission, chlorophyll) that only began to be researched after Lindley's time, and post-harvest physiology, an essentially 20th-century discipline. For Lindley, greenhouse conditions were taken for granted as the basis for most horticultural work, and there was far less attention to the adaptations and requirements of plants in the open air—a reflection of the emphasis in 19th-century gardens on the cultivation of exotics. Most of the operations to which Lindley devoted separate chapters have been abridged into smaller

Pupils of the Bleasdale C of E school, winners of the Greenfingers Challenge project, 1994.

portions of text, sometimes into paragraphs. But Lindley would have recognised the work as a counterpart to his own.

The steady move toward university training in horticulture over the last half-century has provoked fears of a crisis in practical training. Syllabus standardisation has reduced the number of hours required from students from those once needed for the NDH; courses in subjects like garden design have been introduced by various institutions in response to their perceived popularity, without any previous practical requirements; while the reorganisation of the educational system every few years generates an uncertainty about the long-term status of courses and qualifications.[35] Attention has therefore been increasingly focused on the role of the school system in preparing students for future careers in horticulture. School gardening began to be promoted before the end of the 19th century, and after the Second World War modulated into national courses in rural studies; the principal textbooks offered information about RHS and other horticultural examinations.[36] In 1990 Jenny Worsfold became the Society's Assistant Secretary, with responsibility for education; she instituted a Schools Gardening Competition, initially with sponsorship from the *Daily Mirror*, later succeeded by the Greenfingers Challenge (in association with Britain in Bloom). Under Michael

Pollock, Head of Education until 2003, a programme of schools membership followed, and an increasing range of activities in and for schools; travel bursaries for students were augmented, and new forms of educational publishing, notably videotapes, undertaken with the Education Department's involvement. In 2002, the old Examinations Board was replaced with a new Education and Qualifications Policy Board with the wider remit of promoting horticultural education at all levels of the curriculum. 'With our phalanx of committees of knowedgeable people', said Michael Pollock on the verge of his retirement, 'we have a good capacity to preserve standards.'[37]

The Wisley School of Horticulture

Attempts to create a school of horticulture at Chiswick had failed, but then came the new Garden at Wisley. The first Laboratory was opened in 1907, in a grand ceremony with Darwin's protégé Lord Avebury presiding; and the Laboratory was intended from the beginning as a home for the School of Horticulture. The regulations for the students were summarised in eight points, a mere half the number that had been imposed 80 years before, but this time the students received no wages, and were given extra cautions about obedience, regularity and punctuality. The Wisley Diploma would be awarded to those students who

1. Have completed the two years' course of training in the Gardens and have fulfilled the conditions set out in the Prospectus of the School.
2. Pass written and practical examinations in the Principles and Operations of Horticulture upon the syllabus laid down for study.
3. Present an essay upon some approved Horticultural or Scientific subject.
4. Submit a collection of at least 200 properly dried, named, and localized plant specimens collected *outside* the Wisley Gardens.
5. Submit a collection of insects either injurious or helpful in Horticulture.[38]

A fund was raised in memory of George Nicholson, who had been one of the RHS examiners, to provide a Nicholson Prize for the best student in the Wisley examination; James Hudson funded a similar prize. The Society approached the University of London, to see whether Wisley could be made officially a School of the University; the negotiations consistently failed, but yielded the interesting point that Wisley was too far from London to qualify as a School, though if 80 Vincent Square was registered as the address it would be acceptable for the actual training to take place at Wisley.[39]

The students originally lived in lodgings in neighbouring towns and villages, and were encouraged to enter the garden from 6 a.m. to have time for undirected observation before their work began. Eventually two 'makeshift hostels' were built to accommodate them, but what would now be regarded as decent housing had to wait until after the Second World War interrupted proceedings (most of the student gardeners enlisted, and the Women's Land Army and demobbed servicemen became the temporary beneficiaries of Wisley teaching). In 1952, a new hostel was commissioned from Sidney Tatchell to provide accommodation for the new intake of students; built speedily for a cost of £50,000, and named Aberconway House in honour of the recently deceased President, it was opened in August 1954 by the Queen Mother. At the opening ceremony, Sir David Bowes Lyon, the new President, said, 'I hope we may look forward to the steady emergence of a whole string of budding JOSEPH PAXTONS.' Despite a conviction on the part of some Council members that the RHS ought to manage its own hostel, the management was entrusted to the YMCA for several years.[40]

The first director of the Wisley School of Horticulture was Frederick Chittenden; lecturing and supervising the students fell within his duties as Director of the Laboratory. Sir Isaac Bayley Balfour's report on science at Wisley in 1913 envisaged the appointment of an Assistant Director who would be responsible for education among other things, but the war intervened and the post was not created until 1922, when Arthur Simmonds, who had been one of the first Wisley students in 1907, was appointed. It is unclear how much of the educational work Chittenden allowed to pass out of his hands; he had, after all, developed the curriculum for the two-year course, and served a term as Chairman of the Horticultural Education Association in recognition of his achievements. But Council's dissatisfaction was growing. Recommendations for reorganisation made by a committee in 1924 were not immediately acted on, but as student numbers fell in the late 1920s, from nearly 50 to 27, Council finally decided to implement them. In 1930-31 Chittenden was transferred to London, R.L. Harrow (with eventual assistance from Brian Mulligan) replaced him as Director, and the School was reorganised. The existing arrangements were ended as of 1932, and a new class was created of paid journeymen gardeners, who would work in the garden by day and attend lectures by evening.[41]

After the Second World War, the School was re-started, with studentship initially confined to British subjects, but gradually widening again after 1956. The syllabus for the two-year course continued as in pre-war years, until the combination of financial pressure and the Pilkington Report on technical education forced a fee increase, and another rethink. In 1971, Lord Aberconway announced at the AGM:

> ... we have decided to discontinue our student gardener course at Wisley in its present form. For some time past we have been reviewing its usefulness, from the standpoints both of the students and of the Garden. It is not incumbent upon us to duplicate training facilities that exist elsewhere; there are courses, financed by the State or by County Authorities, available to student gardeners such as those whom we train at Wisley. Moreover the great majority of our students go afterwards into municipal service, and while our Fellows derive pleasure from seeing a good standard of gardening in public parks, they would suffer little loss of potential private gardeners if the present Wisley training scheme were ended ... accordingly the two-year course will end in September, 1972. It will of course be sad to see the end of our long sequence of student gardeners, many of whose careers have reached high eminence, in Britain and overseas.

The last of the old Diploma students left in 1974. A 'more flexible' course was substituted, with an annual intake of 12 trainees, who would spend three or four months in each of Wisley's six major departments.[42] Things did not turn out as planned; twice as many staff as expected were needed to take on the functions of the student gardeners; the idea of converting Aberconway House into flats for permanent staff was soon abandoned; the Director was instructed to accept 'sandwich students, foreign students, and school-leavers requiring pre-entry training'. The course was eroded from two years to one year. In the 1990s Michael Pollock was appointed Head of Education and got a two-year course reinstated as the Wisley Diploma in Practical Horticulture. At the time of writing, there are 28 students (14 in each year), aged between 19 and 35, with foreign students amounting to a maximum of one-third; in addition there are 14 one-year Certificate placements annually, divided among the four RHS gardens; there are two training officers in overall supervision.

Women and horticultural education

Women were not invited to play any role in the Society's activities until the 1820s. In 1824, the stewards at the anniversary dinners were issued tickets to allow ladies to attend the annual dinners, and in 1827 a committee of 'Ladies Patronesses' was convened to look after the ticketing arrangements for the first fêtes—the ladies in question being selected from the wives of prominent, and generally noble, Fellows. By this time there was already one female exhibitor, Mrs Marryat, whose garden in Wimbledon was admired by Loudon. In June 1830 ladies were admitted as Fellows for the first time; there had never actually been a clause excluding them from membership, so Council decided that admission would involve no formal change in rule. The first lady Fellow was Lady Radnor, who as the wife of a peer was admitted without a ballot; the Countesses of Guildford and Morton followed a meeting later, Mrs Marryat and three other ladies after a further fortnight.[43] Of all the early female Fellows, the most energetic—or most troublesome—was Louisa Lawrence, whose garden at Drayton Green was also commended by Loudon, and whose son and grandson were later to become President and Treasurer respectively. A skilled gardener and a very competitive exhibitor, she was to succeed in a celebrated race with Kew and Chatsworth to see who could first flower the tropical tree *Amherstia nobilis*; she was also to complain vigorously over prizes for orchid exhibits, and threaten never to exhibit again if she thought herself cheated of her award. In the 1850s her role as gadfly was taken over by Lady Dorothy Nevill.[44]

The role of women in horticulture was promoted in the 1830s and 1840s by Mrs Loudon, whose *Gardening for Ladies* and *Ladies' Companion to the Flower Garden* urged women to go out into the garden, get their feet wet, and start pruning. The women addressed were amateurs: like the future targets of Edith Chamberlain's *Gentlewoman's Book of Gardening*, they were members of a leisure class, not expected to enter horticulture as a profession. No female students were taken at Chiswick—nor at Wisley until after the Second World War, though that was more for reasons of accommodation and propriety than because of a rejection of female participation in horticulture. For the 1890s saw the beginnings of a campaign to secure horticultural training for women, and the creation of specialist educational establishments for women (the first schools of technical education for women having been founded for needlework and cookery in the 1870s).

Swanley College, in Kent, was opened in 1888; before the end of the decade it had started taking female students, and in 1902 it became an all-female college. In 1897 Kew set up an internal school for women gardeners. In 1898 the Countess of Warwick started Warwick Hostel in Reading as a school for women gardeners, later moving it to Studley Castle in Warwickshire, which became Studley College, the longest-lasting of female horticultural institutions; when Edith Bradley, its Secretary, left Studley, she set up her own college at Greenway Court. In 1899, as a result of the International Congress of Women in London, an organisation was set up that was known at first as the Women's Agricultural and Horticultural International Union, and from 1915 as the Women's Farm and Garden Union. Viscountess Wolseley opened her Glynde School for Lady Gardeners in 1902. A scattering of smaller schools for women gardeners grew up around the country, many of them short-lived, while Bedford College, a college of female higher education, instituted courses in botany and horticulture. The Royal Botanic Society, the RHS's long-standing rival in Regent's Park, instituted a three-year training course for women.[45]

What relations did the RHS maintain with these various ventures? At first its policy was one of hands off; in 1907 Council declined affiliation with Glynde, and in 1914 Keeble refused to represent the RHS on the board of Studley College (an 'undesirable precedent'). But the war changed things: Studley was admitted into affiliation, and the Thatcham Fruit and Flower Farm School at Newbury, and Edith Bradley's Greenway Court, were accepted as examination centres. After the war, the Society grant-aided Swanley to help it pay the mortgage on newly acquired land. When the College was damaged by bombing during the Second World War, Council immediately planned to take on the homeless students at Wisley; Lord Aberconway sent a cautionary telegram saying 'we should not be unduly swayed by our deep sympathy for Swanley into taking steps which might hamper for years our Wisley activities', but as soon as accommodation was found in the Ripley area, Swanley's activities were moved to Wisley for the duration of the war.[46]

The eve of the Second World War was probably the peak period for women's horticultural education as a separate venture: most of the early colleges were still going, and they had been joined in 1932 by Waterperry, established by the formidable Beatrix Havergal. The war swept away many of the smaller colleges; the ruined Swanley was amalgamated with Wye College in 1946, and ceased to be a women's institution. This left Studley and Waterperry, and the RHS increasingly supported them both, appointing Patrick Synge to the Studley Board, awarding Havergal a VMH, and providing a scholarship for a female student—the Emmie Clough Scholarship, funded from a bequest received in 1960, though in later years increasingly having to be topped up from other sources—which was used first for Studley, and then from 1965 for Waterperry. But in the 1960s, the Pilkington Committee opposed the idea of single-sex schools, and in 1969 Studley College was closed; Havergal tried to secure a future for Waterperry as a county college, and the RHS hoped it could be reconstituted as a charitable trust, but it too closed in 1971.[47]

Even before the closure of the women's colleges, complaints were heard of falling attendance, and a drift of women away from horticulture in favour of other careers. From the late 1980s, however, there was an apparent resurgence of interest, with an increasing number of women rising to the position of head gardener, and the creation of schemes like WRAGS (Women Returners to Amenity Gardening Scheme).[48] Meanwhile, within the structure of the RHS, women emerged into positions of importance in the second half of the century. The first female salaried staff member at Wisley was the cytologist E.K. Janaki Ammal, in the late 1940s. In 1967 a press controversy erupted when, at the AGM, Lord Aberconway responded to a question from the floor by saying,

> We have never had ladies on the Council. We appoint to the Council people who we believe can best serve the interests of the Society. It so happens that at present there are no ladies who, we think, have as useful experience as the men available ... while we have considered the names of particular ladies in this context, we have always come to choose people who happen to be men.

Enid Bagnold quoted his first sentence in a letter to *The Times*, and although the selective quotation was quickly pointed out, it became received wisdom that the RHS was set against electing women to Council. When Frances Perry was elected the next year, Lord Aberconway made a point of saying that she had not been chosen because she was a woman, but purely because of her horticultural standing. In 1990 Carolyn Hardy became the first women to chair a Council meeting.[49]

RHS staff and personnel management

Throughout the 19th century, and for the first part of the 20th, the Society maintained little more than a skeleton staff. Lindley even cautioned, in 1862, that to have ten salaried posts was only possible at exceptional times. The key offices, of President, Treasurer, and Secretary, were unpaid—until William Wilks's threatened resignation in 1892 moved Council to offer him a salary.

The redoubtable Beatrix Havergal (1901-1980), who founded Waterperry College in 1932 and directed it until its closure in 1971.

Frances Perry (1907-1993), daughter-in-law of the nurseryman Amos Perry, and the mid-20th century's greatest expert on water gardening. Her classic book on the subject first appeared in 1938.

The bulk of the Society's employees were gardeners, at different times students or hired labourers, with a few key permanent staff to supervise them. This situation remained unchanged until the acquisition of Wisley, when the distance of the garden from London meant that show organisation could no longer so easily be devolved onto the garden staff, and a Shows Office had to be set up more formally; and then, first the inception of the Wisley School of Horticulture, and a few years later the inauguration of the scientific research establishment at Wisley, significantly increased the staffing levels. Nonetheless, until the 1980s the Society was effectively run by its Council and Committees, with internal bureaucracy kept to a minimum.

When the Chiswick garden was opened in 1822, principal gardeners received a guinea a week, the garden clerk a pound. Lindley, as Assistant Secretary, received somewhat over twice that amount, at £120 per annum. The labourers earned a wage of 14 shillings per week; but in 1827, with the first financial crisis, this was reduced to 12 shillings. It remained at that level for a generation, despite the criticism of the press, George Glenny remarking that the gardeners were paid less than dustmen. This pattern, of good intentions crippled by financial disaster, was maintained even as general income levels rose over the mid-century period. In 1857, the post of head gardener for Chiswick was advertised at £150 p.a.; the gardening press scorned the idea that a qualified gardener could be found for such a sum, and George M'Ewen eventually secured the position at a salary of £250. The Society's enforced generosity towards a manager was not extended to the staff, however, for M'Ewen had to write a letter to Council complaining that '30/- a week will not secure to me a "good practical Gardener of considerable experience" beyond the time when that man is offered £75. or £80 in a Gentlemans place'. And 30 shillings a week was still the maximum wage for Wisley gardeners in 1919. Managerial salaries, however, rose as the 19th century continued. In 1871 Thiselton-Dyer received a starting salary of £250 p.a. as Professor of Botany, and Archibald Barron's salary was raised to the same figure in an effort to stop him from leaving the Society for the Royal Parks; £250 was also Wilks's initial salary as Secretary.[50]

After the First World War, inflation settled in as a fact of life, and nominal pay began its inexorable rise. In 1922, W.R. Dykes earned £850 as Secretary, soon to rise to £1,000; a few years later, reorganisation in the Cashier's department left the Chief Cashier earning £350, and the Accountants £200-250 p.a.. By the end of the Second World War,

Arthur Simmonds's salary as Deputy Secretary was £1,500, while L.G. Pavey as Chief Cashier got a starting salary of £450, rising to £510. In 1950, when John Gilmour announced his intention of leaving Wisley for Cambridge, Council tried to tempt him back with a salary of £1,700; his successor, Harold Fletcher, received £1,300 initially, but with other emoluments his income was estimated at £1,850.[51] By the early 1970s that was the approximate annual wage of a carpenter working in the Halls. Meanwhile, the Society kept its eye on the regular increases in agricultural wages, as the baseline for remunerating its own labourers. The galloping inflation of the 1970s caught it out, and despite an increase of 18 per cent across the board, a committee in 1980 reported that most staff were barely within their appropriate scales. Thereafter, a decade and a half of adjusting salaries and trying to iron out perceived inconsistencies finally resulted, under Gordon Rae and the first Personnel Officer Martine Postle, in the introduction of the Hay job evaluation system.

Pay, of course, is only part of an employee's financial situation. Most garden staff lived in the Society's own accommodation, and Council made generous allowances in its early days to cover the central London staff, not to mention Lindley, while finding houses; in the 20th century, it was to buy houses for W.R. Dykes and other staff, and thus find itself a proprietor of various cottages scattered around Surrey. After dealing ad hoc with medical bills for staff sent in by independent doctors, Council in 1825 decided to engage a doctor on contract; it also sometimes covered funeral expenses for staff who died in harness. Honoraria and bonus payments were frequently made; Archibald Barron, as has been remarked, regularly received £10 a year because of the pass rate of his students at the garden. John Weathers, as Assistant Secretary in the 1890s, was allowed a 10 per cent commission on the Society's advertising revenues. And while the Society could be peremptory in dismissing staff—when the garden at Kensington was vacated, most of the garden staff were given three weeks' notice—it also provided ad hoc pensions for long-serving staff members, of varying degrees of generosity, before instituting its first pension scheme in 1910. Unemployment insurance followed a decade later.[52] From the 1940s on, the Society increasingly adjusted its standards to government regulations, adopting a five-day week in the London office, introducing mandatory retirement ages, adapting its pension schemes to compulsory employers' contribution levels, introducing contributory medical coverage, eventually paying Poll Tax for staff occupying RHS housing.

*John Woodbridge
(c.1832-1888), head
gardener at Syon Park.
Said his* Gardeners'
Chronicle *obituary,
'he had recently been
selected to represent the
practical gardening
community upon the
Council of the
reorganised Royal
Horticultural Society.
This important post
was accepted by Mr.
Woodbridge ... with a
due sense of the
responsibility he was
undertaking. That this
feeling dominated in
his mind was shown
during the hours of
delirium which
immediately preceded
his death—he alluded
to resolutions he had to
propose at Council
Meetings, and to
weighty matters
impressed on his mind
as necessary to the well-
being of the Society. He
gradually sank to a
semi-unconscious state,
and died about* 10 A.M.
on April 13.'

By that time the Society's staff numbers had begun to increase at an unprecedented rate. In 1862 the Society had had ten salaried staff; in 1975, there were 32 staff in London, and 130 at Wisley; by the end of the century, there were over 500 staff scattered over London, Peterborough (where *The Garden* had its offices), and three gardens. Some of this increase lay within long-existing departments, but much of it was the result of the establishment of a bureaucracy. A separate Shows Department had come into being, and staff were needed to run the Halls; Wisley supported no longer just gardeners, but research scientists and advisers. In the 1980s and 1990s, entire new departments came into existence: Press (the Society had had agency Press Officers, but now brought the process in-house), Marketing, Fundraising, Regional Development, Personnel. And from the 1970s the Society also had commercial companies as part of its structure: RHS Enterprises, Horticultural Halls, and eventually RHS Publications and RHS Special Events.

The Chiswick staff had set up a Mutual Improvement Society back in the 1820s, which continued under different names throughout the garden's history, until, under the name of the Wisley Scientific Society, it was discontinued in 1923. John Gilmour decided to revive the society in 1948; it was proposed to name it the Chittenden Society, but Chittenden recommended that it be named after Lindley instead, and as the Lindley Society it continues to the present day. The Wisley staff also tried their hand at various staff magazines, eventually settling on the *RHS Garden Club Journal*, which began in 1908 and similarly continues. In 1986, a staff newsletter was launched, entitled *Grassroots*, for distribution to staff at all the Society's sites.[53]

Gardening as a profession

During the 1850s, as the Society's shows declined and its rivals' prospered, part of the blame for the situation was attributed to John Lindley and his disaffection from the gardening community. In 1856, the *Cottage Gardener* (probably G.W. Johnson) expressed the

> hope that for many years to come our generation may benefit by the high botanical acquirements of Dr. Lindley: but as fervently do we hope that he may not continue in the Secretariat of the Horticultural Society for as many days. He was brought up in the wrong school to be fitted for this. He never has forgotten the splendour of the Society under Mr. Sabine—that splendour when £3,106 were paid to Mr. Gunter for one repast at Chiswick—and he is equally the faithful disciple

of the same gentleman's doctrine—'look to the patrician order.' This will not do now; nor was it a doctrine which, if acted upon, ever formed a broad, solid, and permanent basis for any Society. No Society in England is evergreen that is not planted and cultivated by the middle classes, and Dr. Lindley neither in temperament nor in habits is calculated to win golden opinions from the men of the spade. We have very abundant evidence of this ...[54]

The 'patrician order' remained a dominant element in the Society until the last decades of the century, and it is worth remembering that Thomas Andrew Knight was the only commoner to hold the title of President for nearly a century. At the controversial AGM of 1873, Dean Hole criticised Council for its largely aristocratic composition: 'The Council of the Royal Horticultural Society did not represent the Fellows of the Society or the gardeners. It was like a municipality composed entirely of mayors.'[55]

The events of the 1850s having shown that it was necessary to keep a livelier contact with the practical gardening community, Council made it a practice from the beginning of the 1860s to have a head gardener among its number. William Coleman of Eastnor Castle, Charles Edmonds of Chiswick House, John Fleming of Cliveden, James Hudson of Gunnersbury, Sir Joseph Paxton, John Spencer of Bowood, and John Woodbridge of Syon House all filled this position at different times from the 1860s into the early years of the 20th century. (It was Woodbridge who proposed the new membership category of 'Associates' in 1888.)[56]

Head gardeners formed a useful management tier on country estates, and the nobility were comfortable about dealing with them; but they represented only one of the two principal categories of the community of practical gardeners. Nurserymen were another matter. Head gardeners talked about being professionals in the mid-19th century; when nurserymen formed an organisation, it was entitled the Horticultural *Trades* Association. A certain suspicion attached itself to nurserymen's motives: they had a vested interest in the promotion of their plants, which could distort the proper pattern of horticulture if they were placed in positions of authority; and so through most of the 19th century nurserymen were banned from election to Council. Exceptions crept in, most notably James Veitch in the 1850s, but after his death the refusal was reinstated.

As early as 1839, the *Gardeners' Gazette* was complaining that the exclusion of nurserymen from Council was causing offence. When the Society was in desperate straits in 1859, it asked the

Birmingham nurseryman Edward Spary to run its shows, but after a spot of deliberation changed its mind about handing them over to a tradesman. In 1875 and 1876 attempts to rescind the ban on nurserymen were defeated. As late as the 1890s it was ruled that nurseries should not present prizes at shows. If anything, the turn of the century saw an intensification of prejudice against nurserymen, with the journalist Alexander Dean leading a campaign to exclude them from RHS committees; and for some years being in the nursery trade excluded one from holding a Committee Secretaryship. The war seems to have wiped this prejudice away, with Sir Harry Veitch the first nurseryman to hold one of the Society's high offices (Treasurer, in 1918).[57]

Head gardeners may have talked about being recognised as professionals, and the gardening press supported them in this aspiration; but did they achieve their goal? Certainly their wealth and power increased during the middle years of the century, in part through the sterling example of Paxton, the first gardener to be knighted; while no one else reached quite the social heights that Paxton did, all could hope to be pulled along a certain distance in his wake. John Spencer of Bowood, for example, who helped found the rival British Pomological Society in the 1850s, continued his head gardenership there even after being director of a bank on the side. By the 1870s famous gardeners were moving from estate to estate rather the way football stars move from club to club today. But whatever their degree of prestige within the gardening community, they were still servants, and a backlash against their perceived breach of class boundaries lay in wait—perhaps triggered by the successful lawsuit (for libel) which James Barnes, recently retired as head gardener at Bicton, brought against his former employer in 1869.[58]

The critical issue proved to be flower-show prizes. In the 1875 lawsuit of Williams vs Leslie, the nurseryman B.S. Williams sued an estate owner for non-payment of bills incurred by his gardener without his knowledge. This case was still in progress when the RHS, in the midst of financial crisis, refused to pay prize money to those who had won awards at recent shows; as a result some of the gardeners took the Society to court. The Treasurer, Bonamy Dobrée, made it clear why some thought the Society biased against the ordinary gardener: 'We owe for prizes, £1400, and, if I were to pay these rabid prize-men, we should come to a dead stand. I will rather cut my hand off than sign a cheque to pay these prizes. By paying them we should give an undue preference to those men who won prizes at their masters'

expense, because those very men who win the prizes win them at the cost of their masters' fuel, hothouses, &c.' The resigning Secretary, W.A. Lindsay, on the other hand, said that he 'sincerely hoped these gardeners would succeed in their actions'.[59] Nor did the issue go away with the election of a new Council and a gradual financial resolution: in 1901 the query, to whom did a prize belong, the gardener or the employer, provoked a lively correspondence in the *Gardeners' Chronicle*, and Alexander Dean, favouring the latter, was able to point out that the RHS's award cards specified the employer. (His brother Richard answered that the employer got the cup, but that the gardener should get the money.)[60]

The backlash did not generally affect the status of gardeners at the great country houses, where they formed a useful layer of the estate hierarchy; but the jobbing gardener, and the gardener at the middle-class villa, who enjoyed no such cushioning management structure, remained vulnerable. The gardening press, having won its battle for the improved status of gardeners on the country estate, shifted its attention to the middle-class villa during the 1870s and 1880s, but was never able to affect the status of the gardener on such lesser estates—let alone on the fruit farm, where much of the employment was seasonal.

At the end of the First World War, when the central government was providing public housing for the first time in the hope of averting Bolshevism among the returning troops, agitation broke out in the gardening world. The British Gardeners' Association was campaigning for standard hours and wages for gardeners, and it was reported that gardeners near Bristol were applying to become a branch of the National Union of General Workers. Fears of unionisation prompted calls for the RHS to form a committee to arbitrate matters, as well as such minor absurdities as H.J. Elwes suggesting that morale could be restored if Kipling's 'Glory of the garden' were posted up in every bothy. And at the fringes of the debate hung the perennial questions of competence, qualifications, and hierarchy. When one correspondent urged that 18-year-olds were entitled to full wages, because they had shown in the army that they could work as well as older men, W.R. Dykes, soon to become Secretary of the RHS, replied, 'in the garden trees cannot profitably be pruned at the word of command nor will the order "As you were" restore a plant that has been killed by transplantation at the wrong season of the year. The mischief that can be done by the inexperienced is untold.'[61] Hard on the heels of this controversy came a government investigation into bribery in various trades, and horticulture was not exempt: the RHS published a list of offenders compiled by the Horticultural Trades Association, while emphasising that the tendency of some gardeners to accept bribes was a consequence of their low pay.[62]

That state of affairs continued; and with the demise of the country house as a significant employment market for gardeners after the Second World War, and the resulting migration of skilled gardeners into the municipal parks and the horticultural advisory services, those gardeners who remained outside the civil service were seen as a pool of semi-skilled workers. What hope of professional status could there be for people whose work could be envisaged in these terms?

> A fully cultivated garden with a little grass, of (say) an acre, needs a full-time gardener. So the owners, if they think of it, are paying about £500 a year for a gardener, perhaps more, if they are providing him with a properly maintained cottage. What taxed income has to be earmarked to provide this sum depends entirely upon which surtax rate applies, but in any case a gardener must cost about a penny a minute. Think of it! Every time a gardener goes up the garden to fetch a hoe, it costs 4d.!

And so, near the end of the 20th century, it remained the case that 'gardeners are still classified as semi-skilled: a low base from which an equally lowly professional hierarchy is constructed, while socially the private house gardener is held in low esteem'.[63]

The Institute of Horticulture

The two vexed questions, of professional status and of educational qualifications, converged at the beginning of the 1980s in the debate over the revision of the National Diploma. In addition to creating a new title and structure for the Diploma, Council proposed the creation of an institute that would have an interest in the new degree, and could become a campaigning body for the status of horticulture as a profession. Lord Aberconway spelled out four requirements: RHS membership should not be required to join it; it should be prepared to represent any aspect of horticulture; some form of achievement must be necessary for membership; and it must be financially viable. In 1983 the proposal for an Institute of Horticulture was formally launched; the Horticultural Education Association approved the plan, and felt that the new body would take over its role. Accordingly, in 1984, the HEA was dissolved, and absorbed into the new Institute.

By August 1984 over 600 applications had been received for membership, and the Institute of Horticulture ('serving the professional interests of all those who gain their living from horticulture') was officially inaugurated the next month. The first President was George Lockie, with Patrick Johns as Secretary; since then such eminent horticulturists as Vic Fowler, J.K.A. Bleasdale, John Simmons, Bill Simpson, David Welch, Peter Thoday, Charles Notcutt, and Jennifer Adams have served as President, while Angela Clarke has been the longest-serving Secretary. At first the Institute was accommodated at 80 Vincent Square, but it cut the umbilical cord within a couple of years, and found a new home in the offices of the Society for Industrial Chemistry on Belgrave Square. By the 1990s it had developed a network of regional groups, sponsored lectures, and instituted prizes, beginning with the Aberconway Prize for young horticulturists; Lord Aberconway became the Institute's first Honorary Fellow. The Institute began publishing a *Newsletter*, and from 1987 a journal entitled *Professional Horticulture* (later changed to *The Horticulturist*).[64]

The Institute has consistently lobbied the government about funding for research and development in horticulture; acted as a source of information for the profession on controversial topics like genetic modification; instituted a National Students Council for horticultural trainees; and established a marketing campaign, ProHort. Above all, it has campaigned for improvements in horticultural education, and been closely involved with the development of the M.Hort. degree; its journal has carried debates on training and its assessment; it has promoted the concept of centres of excellence, and called for increased practical training (as well as for increased attention to training in management). In 2001, the Institute awarded its President's Medal to Michael Pollock in recognition of his work for horticultural education at the RHS.[65]

Awards to people

In 1897, to celebrate the Diamond Jubilee of Queen Victoria, William Wilks proposed that the RHS issue a medal, to be given to 60 eminent horticulturists in honour of the 60 years of the Queen's reign. As Sir Trevor Lawrence later said,

> When the question arose as to what the Royal Horticultural Society was to do to celebrate the Diamond Jubilee, he need scarcely say that the fertile brain of their Secretary had a suggestion to make. He did not mean to say that the Secretary's brain was the only brain that was fertile, but the fertility of his brain produced a more sturdy plant than the fertility of other brains.

Wilks, Lawrence, and J.T. Bennett-Poë formed a subcommittee to consider the design of the medal, which was designed by Margaret Giles, and executed by Messrs Pinches. Another subcommittee, with Sir John Dillwyn Llewellyn, James Douglas, and Harry Veitch replacing Bennett-Poë, was set up to select the recipients. One of the finalists, William Marshall, declined on the grounds that Council members should not be seen to give themselves medals; Sir Trevor accordingly removed the names of all the proposed Council members—most of whom later received the Medal, after retirement.

All seemed in order, but embarrassment lurked around the corner. Early in July, the *Journal of Horticulture* and *The Garden* printed erroneous lists of the recipients; the blame fell on the Assistant Secretary, John Weathers, for having sent out the wrong lists. Weathers was also in trouble for errors in the printed Library catalogue, and in September he was formally asked to resign. Once the air had cleared, the celebratory banquet and official presentation of the Medals took place on 26 October.[66]

Council had resolved that the VMH was not to be used in advertising, and that any recipient who was found abusing it for commercial gain was to be struck off the list. (Arthur W. Sutton was censured as early as 1898 for using the initials in his advertising, but not struck off; the next time a nurseryman was chosen—Henry Cannell of Swanley—he was made to guarantee in advance that he would not use the award for business purposes.) In 1901, on the death of Queen Victoria, Bennett-Poë proposed that the number of holders of the VMH be increased to 63, in commemoration of the total number of years of her reign. Because the number of recipients is strictly limited, no VMHs are appointed until a death causes a vacancy in the ranks. At first, the names of the Medallists were published with no reasons given for their selection, the reasons for eminence presumably being apparent to all; it was only in 1931 that the Annual Report began to specify the achievements for which the medallists were being honoured. To date, there have been 432 recipients of the Victoria Medal, including botanists, gardeners, park superintendents, plant hunters, landscape architects, flower arrangers, and RHS officials. Among those who have refused the VMH over the years have been A.K. Bulley, the founder of Bees' Seeds; William Coleman, the head gardener at Eastnor Castle; William Robinson; and the botanist Marshall Ward.[67]

Meanwhile, another award existed which was increasingly being given to gardeners. The Veitch Memorial Trust had been founded in 1869, to create and administer a fund in memory of James Veitch, the great Chelsea nurseryman. Suggestions for the fund were canvassed in the *Gardeners' Chronicle*: William Thomson, the head gardener of Dalkeith Palace, proposed a Veitch Medal to be awarded 'to the man who during the year shall make the most important additions to our garden productions, whether by importation or hybridisation'; other suggestions included a portrait, sponsorship of an orphan, and (from D.T. Fish) a Veitch circulating library for horticulture—but as the Lindley Library had been established the year before, this suggestion seems to have been felt unnecessary. In the event, a Medal was agreed, and struck in 1873 in gold, silver, and bronze. Most early Veitch Medals were distributed as prizes for exhibits; the first Medals awarded to individuals were made at the 1885 Orchid Conference. Two years later Robert Hogg proposed that, since the Trust account was always in surplus, additional awards could be regularly given to individuals who had distinguished themselves in horticulture—thus, after nearly two decades, carrying out Thomson's original suggestion.

In 1922 Sir Harry Veitch, the Principal Trustee, then in his 80s, arranged that the RHS should take over the Trust (the fund then stood at £1,674) and distribute the Veitch Memorial Medal in future. After a few years the Society began to phase out the awards to exhibits, and with them, the bronze medals. The Veitch Memorial Medal is now solely an award to people who have made distinguished contributions to horticulture; it is the only one of the Society's medals for people which can be given to other than British subjects. To date, over 100 of the nearly 500 Medallists have come from America, continental Europe, Asia and Africa.[68]

In 1929, a new award, the Associateship of Honour, was proposed by a nurseryman on Council, William Cuthbertson, for those who had given distinguished service to horticulture in the course of their employment. The idea can perhaps be seen as the Society's final acknowledgment of the gardener's professional status. (The two vexing questions which have presented themselves over the years have been whether Associates of Honour could continue to enjoy that status when they ceased their employment, and whether salaried directors counted as employed persons.) The first 30 Associates of Honour received their awards at the 1930 Chelsea Show, and the total number at any one time was fixed at 100 Associates. By the time of writing, over 450 nurserymen, market gardeners, head gardeners, park superintendents, horticultural journalists, educationists, and not a few of the Society's own horticultural staff have received the award.[69]

The centenary of the Victoria Medal was celebrated in 1997, not only with a boxed carpet bed set out by Nick Morgan, Glasshouse Superintendent at Wisley, but by a grand ceremonial gathering of the living VMHs, shown assembled here in the Lindley Hall.

The last of the Society's awards for people was the Long Service Medal, instituted in 1958: this was created for gardeners who had spent their working lives in one single establishment, and the minimum requirement was 40 years' service (with bars for each additional decade). The first year alone saw 200 medals given out. The laws enforcing retirement at 65 have gradually reduced the number of bars awarded, but as the government is currently recommending greater flexibility about retirement age, perhaps the bars may return.[70]

Gardeners in the media

The rise of the professional gardener was strongly linked to the rise of the gardening press, and the Society, by the end of the 19th century, had made it a principle that its staff were encouraged to publish, though for many years they had to get permission first. In 1893, when the Assistant Secretary, John Weathers, proposed to publish a series of plant sketches, there were complaints from Fellows, and he was ordered to abandon the project. In 1919 Chittenden wrote a report on Chelsea for the *Daily Graphic*, signed it, and was reprimanded for thus showing favouritism; 12 years later Robert Findlay, the Keeper of Wisley, was censured for writing show reports under his own name for the *Morning Post*. In neither case was the writer told to stop writing reports, merely to do so anonymously.[71]

There was a long association between the RHS and the *Gardeners' Chronicle*, edited for nearly three-quarters of a century by a succession of RHS officials (Lindley, 1841-63; Masters, 1863-1907; John Bretland Farmer, a Scientific Committee member, 1907-10; Frederick Keeble, 1910-17); the *Chronicle* published transcripts of Annual Meetings when the Society did not have a regular periodical in which to do so. With another RHS official, Robert Hogg, editing the rival *Journal of Horticulture* for nearly 25 years (and remaining its proprietor for nearly 20 more), the most important (and rival) organs of the gardening press were effectively in the Society's hands. The non-horticultural press was another matter. The first regular gardening column in a general newspaper appears to have been George Glenny's in the *Edinburgh Weekly Journal*, and the Society may have helped to close that paper down with a threatened libel suit. But by the turn of the century *The Times* had begun running regular gardening articles, and Lord Northcliffe's papers, the *Daily Mail* and the *Daily Mirror*, turned their attention to gardening in the Edwardian period. The *Daily Mail* sponsored a national sweet pea competition, and thus set a model for other newspapers. The *Daily Graphic* sponsored a challenge cup at RHS shows from 1914 to 1926, when it ceased publication; the *Mirror* organised a wartime potato competition, and the *Mail* a post-war fruit show, both of which fell foul of the RHS over judging rules. In the 1970s the RHS finally adjusted to the possibilities that the daily press offered for membership recruitment, encouraging visits to Wisley, and so on. But the disparity can still be seen: 14 independent gardening editors have received awards from the Society (not counting the editors of the *RHS Journal*), and only three journalists for the daily press.

Journal	Editor	Award and date
Gardeners' Chronicle	Charles Curtis, editor	VMH 1930
	Roy Hay, editor	VMM 1957, VMH 1970
Journal of Horticulture	John Wright, editor	VMH 1897
Gardeners' Magazine	George Gordon, editor	VMH 1897
Gardening Illustrated	W.P. Thomson, editor	VMM 1925
Gardening World	John Fraser, editor	VMH 1922, VMM 1928
Amateur Gardening	A. J. Macself, editor	VMH 1950
	J. S. Dakers, assistant editor	AH 1950
	Arthur Hellyer, editor	AH 1953, VMH 1967
	Anthony Huxley, editor	VMM 1958, VMH 1980
Popular Gardening	H. H. Thomas, editor	VMH 1948
	Gordon Forsyth, editor	VMM 1959
	Fred Whitsey, editor	VMM 1979, VMH 1985
Country Life	Tony Venison, gardening editor	VMM 1994
Home Gardening	J. R. Procter, editor	AH 1965
My Garden	Theo Stephens, editor	VMM 1960
Nurseryman and Garden Centre	John Sambrook, editor	AH 1986
Garden News	Jack Wood, editor	AH 1996
Newspaper	**Journalist**	**Award and date**
Daily Mail	P. W. D. Izzard	VMM 1942
Daily Mirror	Xenia Field	VMM 1972
The Sun	Peter Seabrook	AH 1995

VMH = Victoria Medal of Honour

VMM = Veitch Memorial Medal

AH = Associate of Honour

Radio broadcasting in Britain began in 1920, when the Marconi Company began transmitting from Writtle in Essex. Two years later it began regular transmissions, and started a London station known as '2LO'. In order to avoid competition for wavebands, the Post Office (officially in charge of all things to do with telegraphy) invited the leading British wireless manufacturers to form a syndicate, which adopted the title of the British Broadcasting Company (from 1927, Corporation), and began transmitting on 14 November 1922. '2LO' was retained by the BBC as its London station until 1929. In January 1925, the *Gardeners' Chronicle* deemed it a worthy news item that the Earl of Derby had installed a wireless receiver in the reading-room of the gardeners' bothy at Knowsley Hall; by that time about 80 per cent of the British population was within reach of a radio transmitter, and the Post Office had issued one million licences for radio aerials in 1924.[72]

The first person to broadcast gardening bulletins over the radio was Marion Cran (1871-1941), the immensely popular author of *The Garden of Ignorance* (1913) and other accounts of her garden activities: she began broadcasting in 1923, and published the texts of her early '2LO' broadcasts in 1925 under the title *Garden Talks*. In March 1924 (seven months before the first agricultural bulletins), the BBC began broadcasting gardening bulletins supplied by the RHS, organised and in large part written by Chittenden; before the end of the year a separate broadcasting bulletin for the north of England had been arranged as well. In 1931 the BBC decided to end the use of professional announcers for these programmes; the RHS suggested that they use G.C. Taylor and C.H. Middleton to make the broadcasts, and, still under the RHS direction, the talks continued until 1934. By that time Middleton had established himself as a popular speaker, and he was given his own weekly programme, *In Your Garden*, which became something of a national institution. (His wartime broadcasting played an important role in the Dig for Victory campaign.)[73]

The RHS had already experienced tensions with the BBC over its inflexible programme times, refusal to broadcast about Chelsea until the Friday, and the occasional broadcast gaffe, as when in 1933 an announcer suggested stealing plants. As the world of gardening broadcasting discarded the more patrician Taylor and promoted the more plebeian Middleton, and his equally demotic successors Fred Streeter and Arthur Billitt, the RHS seemed to distance itself from the medium. When the Society's former Editor Roy Hay started a programme called *Home*

Grown in the 1950s, Sir David Bowes Lyon at first refused any association with it, as 'undignified', though a year later Council persuaded him to take part. The longest-running gardening series on radio, *Gardeners' Question Time*, began in 1947; it was not until its 1,000th episode, in 1971, that it finally established a link with the RHS. In 1959, Frank Knight, the Director of Wisley, broadcast on *In Your Garden*, the successor programme to *Home Grown*; when in 1970 the BBC announced a plan to discontinue *In Your Garden* and replace it with a repeat of *Gardeners' Question Time*, Arthur Hellyer read a resolution at the Society's AGM calling on Council to intervene with the BBC and save the programme, but the intervention did not succeed.[74]

Research into the possibility of television was conducted throughout the 1920s; the BBC Television Service was opened on 2 November 1936. By 1938 some 5,000 television sets had been bought, but the service was discontinued on the outbreak of war, and not resumed until 1946. Television grew slowly; by 1954 the BBC was transmitting six hours of television every day; but by that time gardening broadcasting had already begun. *Country Calendar* began featuring a gardening slot in 1953; this was transferred to *Out and About*, and then to *Club Night*, a weekly programme of which the 'Gardening club' was a monthly instalment. *Gardening Club* became an independent weekly programme in its own right by the mid-1950s. Some of the prominent radio personalities transferred to the new medium: Percy Thrower, who began broadcasting on radio in 1948, made his first television appearance in 1952, later assisted by Arthur Billitt.

Commercial television in Britain began in 1955, under the supervision of the Independent Television Authority (this became the Independent Broadcasting Authority after independent local radio was established in 1972). After five years of competition, the government set up a Committee under Sir Harry Pilkington to consider the future of British broadcasting; their report, published in 1962, heavily favoured the BBC. The RHS submitted evidence to the Pilkington Report on the television coverage of gardening:

> The B.B.C. were of course first in the field, and although their efforts are open to some criticism, their general policy is on the right lines. They have a long record in gardening broadcasts, and they have in their staff and outside advisers people who know their jobs. ... Generally speaking ... the B.B.C. has the necessary technical knowledge to provide a properly planned gardening service, and their past and present record shows a will to do so. It seems reasonable

Cecil Henry Middleton (1885-1945), whose radio talks on gardening made him a public figure and materially aided the 'Dig for Victory' programme. Many of his talks were collected in print, beginning with Talks about Gardening *(1935).*

Frederick Streeter (1879-1975), head gardener to Albert Pam at Wormleybury, Herts, and then to Lord Leconfield at Petworth, Sussex. Became Middleton's deputy as BBC speaker in the 1940s, and succeeded to his regular broadcasting slot; continued broadcasting into his nineties.

Prince Charles visits the Hampton Court Palace Flower Show, in the company of the TV gardening presenter Alan Titchmarsh and the RHS President Sir Simon Hornby, 1995.

to suppose that, if they were given further facilities, they would use them to improve this important service.

It is to be recorded with regret that independent television has failed to give adequate treatment to gardening. This is probably due to an inherent fault in organization. As the programme time is split up between various independent companies, it is barely likely that a coherent scheme to cover the whole subject could be given the right timing and balance. The impression is that of various people dabbling in the subject in a spasmodic way, and dropping it when it is found that, as might be expected, the individual uncoordinated efforts fail to attract an audience. From press reports of their finances, it can hardly be supposed that the programme companies lack the means to provide a proper service, and presumably therefore they lack the will to do so. Possibly the chief lack is that of imagination.[75]

So the RHS threw its lot in with the BBC. In 1967, the BBC started a new weekly television series called *Gardeners' World*, with Percy Thrower as its presenter; most of the programmes were filmed at his Shropshire garden, The Magnolias, the first in a series of gardens that served as showcases for the programme, to be followed by Arthur Billitt's Clack's Farm, by Geoff Hamilton's Barnsdale and

Alan Titchmarsh's Barleywood. In 1975, two episodes of *Gardeners' World* were filmed at Wisley. The following year, the BBC dismissed Percy Thrower from its service because he had appeared in advertisements for ICI. In 1978, Thrower officially opened the new plant centre at Wisley, and the photographs of the event made it plain that some RHS officials wished they were anywhere rather than in his company. The Society's lack of recognition for media gardeners earned it complaints, especially when the popular Geoff Hamilton died without having been honoured. (Six people primarily associated with broadcasting have received awards from the RHS: Fred Streeter, VMH 1945—more for his work as head gardener at Petworth than for his radio appearances; Percy Thrower, AH 1962 and VMH 1973; Arthur Billitt, VMM 1978; Clay Jones, VMM 1992; Peter Seabrook, AH 1995; Alan Titchmarsh, VMH 2004. Roy Lancaster might qualify as a seventh, but he was awarded the VMH before his television career took off.)[76]

Meanwhile, the ties between the RHS and the BBC had been increased by official arrangements for the television coverage of the Chelsea Flower Show. It was the BBC's proposal for a 75th-anniversary videotape about the Show that led to the Society's first involvement in video publication, in

1988. In 1984, a series called *Gardeners' Calendar* was filmed using a specially-constructed model garden at Wisley. But the relationship became tinctured with rivalry when the BBC started a monthly gardening magazine, *Gardeners' World*, in 1991. And when in the 1990s the air-time devoted to Chelsea was increased, but at the cost of a watering-down of the content, and too great a perceived focus on non-essentials such as fashions and celebrities, the RHS began to reconsider the advantages of the association. In 1998 Gordon Rae, the Director-General, negotiated a new contract with the commercial Channel 4 to present the Chelsea Show; and while in 2002 the BBC regained its contract, the relations between the two organisations were watched with increasing stringency, and it was required by contract to devote a certain proportion of air time to the Society's other large shows, and a certain proportion of *Gardeners' World* to RHS-related matters.[77]

In 1997 the BBC launched a new series called *Ground Force*, in which Alan Titchmarsh and two previously unknown assistants, Tommy Walsh and Charlie Dimmock, secretly transformed someone's garden over the course of a weekend. The garden makeover show quickly became a staple of television. *Home Front in the Garden, Instant Gardens, Real Gardens,* and *Lost Gardens* (this last a Channel 4 production featuring restorations of older gardens rather than new designs, to which the Lindley Library contributed heavily) all appeared within the next two years. Debate has raged, in the pages of *The Garden* among other places, over the value of the makeover shows, and their influence on the gardening attitudes of the public. But the beginning of the 21st century brought with it attempts to improve the coverage of practical horticulture: Alan Titchmarsh offered his series *How to be a Gardener* as a broadcast textbook, and *Gardening with the Experts*, a series filmed at the RHS gardens (with an accompanying book), focusing on different departments in turn, was widely seen as the best publicity the Society had yet received on television. For the RHS bicentenary the BBC planned a series entitled *Gardens Through Time*, surveying the history of garden design during the Society's two centuries, and focusing on a series of period gardens made at Harlow Carr.[78]

平成5年5月20日 第三種郵便物認可 平成15年4月25日発行 (毎月1回 25日発行 No.157)

RHSJ

The Japan Branch of
The Royal Horticultural Society

英国王立園芸協会日本支部

Lilian Snelling

Paeonia Bakerii
May 16. 1931

2003 **5**

IN the Society's first published membership list, in 1818, some 360 Fellows were recorded. Of these, 112 gave London or Middlesex as their sole address, and a further 142 as a second address; 63 lived in Kent and Surrey, including areas now counted as parts of London; the rest were scattered throughout almost all the English counties (Hertfordshire highest, with 19), Wales (eight), Scotland (six), and Ireland (four).

Additional categories were instituted almost from the beginning. Honorary Members (initial maximum of five) and Foreign Members (initial maximum of 20) were instituted under the 1809 Charter. In 1817, the category of Corresponding Members (native or foreign) was established 'In order to increase the Communication of the Society with distant Parts of the Empire', though in the financially stricter days of 1848, this membership category was restricted to those whose papers were actually printed in the *Transactions*.[1] As the Society's membership grew, so did the numbers in these categories. By 1819 there was a total of 576 paying Fellows, 11 Foreign Members, and 110 Corresponding Members, 61 of them foreign. Even in the earliest days, before the Society had either garden or plant collectors, gifts of plants and seeds, not to mention sets of the *Transactions*, were regularly sent to Honorary Members.

These categories of membership remained in force all through the financial ups and downs of the 19th century; Corresponding Membership was discontinued in the 1920s, by which time Foreign Members had simply become Fellows Resident Abroad. By the middle of the 20th century, the Society's membership was climbing towards 50,000, and a Publicity Committee was instituted to plan an event to celebrate the RHS's status as the world's largest learned society; in the event, the 50,000th member was enrolled without fuss and without event. Some 1,500 of those members were affiliated societies.

Affiliated societies

The first hint of a desire for the Society to undertake specific regional activities was whispered in 1818, when it appeared that members in Winchester wanted to hold a local meeting, and asked if Council could provide papers to be read. Council replied that it 'cannot pledge itself to comply regularly with such requests', and left the immediate query to the discretion of the Secretary.[2] The specialist Groups of the 20th century (Lily, Rhododendron, and Fruit)—not to mention the National Council for the Conservation of Plants and Gardens and Institute of Horticulture—organised regional branches; the parent Society did not. When in 1825 an offer was made to start a garden in the Channel Islands under the Society's auspices, it declined; on the other hand, five years earlier Council had made a gift of £20 to the Dumfries Horticultural Society to help them purchase a site for a garden.[3]

Assistance to other societies was the route that Council chose to pursue. In the autumn of 1826 a plan was worked out to give medals to provincial horticultural societies, for them to award at their own meetings on the Society's behalf. (The first societies to receive the medals were in Aberdeen, Cambridge, Dumfries, Edinburgh, Glasgow, Newcastle, and Winchester.) Thereafter large quantities of silver medals were sent regularly to societies 'admitted into correspondence'—at least until the first financial crisis, of 1830, when restrictions were placed on the number of large silver medals distributed. But the flow of medals was not curtailed, even though rules and quantities were occasionally amended.[4]

Falling membership and collapsing finances in the late 1850s prompted the first thoughts of trying to involve other societies more concretely in the Society's affairs. In 1858, Vernon Harcourt proposed that local committees be set up, consisting of two persons in each locality, to correspond with the Society; in successive Council meetings, he whittled away at his proposal until it turned into a mere questionnaire about local fruit-growing. But Sir Charles Dilke had become interested; he sent a circular letter to provincial horticultural societies proposing a 'union' between them and the Horticultural Society. The replies were so few that the matter was dropped, but it was revived in 1865, and a few societies applied; over the next 12 years 52 societies entered into this Union.[5] In 1877, at the proposal of Lord Alfred Churchill, Council agreed that the RHS should 'receive into association Provincial Horticultural and Floral Societies upon an Annual subscription of 5 guineas'. In return, these societies would receive RHS medals for distribution at their local exhibitions (as honorary distinctions, not for their pecuniary value, a point later made in response to queries from the local societies). The existing unions would continue under the new scheme of affiliation.[6]

For the next century, the scheme of affiliation was little changed. Affiliated societies were given a certain number of medals to distribute at their shows, subject to an agreement about the standards of judging; for this purpose a volume of *Rules of Judging*, later developed into the *Horticultural Show Handbook*, was compiled. When the organisers of the Wolverhampton Horticultural Show asked for a medal to award, they were rebuffed: 'the practice of the Council was to assist parochial & Village Flower Shows rather than those on such a large scale.' (While on the other hand medals were also refused to cottage garden societies, who were somewhat below the show-judging horizon.)[7] The Affiliated Societies' Medal was struck in 1901; the Affiliated Societies' Cup was instituted, and the first Affiliated Societies' Conference held, in 1908; proposals for a circulating library for affiliated societies were firmly rejected. In 1907 it was proposed to create a union of Horticultural Mutual Improvement Societies, with a central register kept at Vincent Square; although this did not come to pass, it did yield a lecture programme, expanded in 1916 into an 'RHS panel' of 2,000 speakers 'in order to stimulate the increased production of vegetable food rendered necessary by the War'. This panel passed largely into the hands of the Food Department in 1918, but not before the Society decided to add allotment societies to its range of affiliates, and lobby the government for their promotion. The inter-war years saw the creation and abandonment of a two-tier system of affiliation, and in 1928 Council nervously refunded the expenses of one affiliated society 'due to the distress in the mining districts',

hoping that this action would not be taken as a precedent.[8]

By 1985 there were upwards of 2,000 affiliated societies, and in that year the Ridley Review Committee recommended a review of the Affiliation system. An Affiliated Societies Conference was held in 1987, and called for the creation of a liaison committee. Mrs Carolyn Hardy was appointed Chairman, with the Society's Assistant Secretary Geoff Harvey as committee secretary and conference organiser. A second Conference was held in 1990, together with conferences for specialist societies and county federations; all three categories of organisation were represented on the Committee. In the spring of 1990 an *Affiliated Societies' Newsletter* was started; the distribution of medals was rationalised, with the Banksian Medal henceforth specifically earmarked for affiliated distribution; the window box, hanging basket, and courtyard garden competitions at the major shows have been made the preserve of the affiliated societies, and lists of lecturers and show judges are now published at regular intervals for their use. Perhaps most importantly, in 1988 the RHS introduced a group insurance scheme for affiliated societies, whereby they could get liability cover for running flower shows at less than a third of the market cost, a scheme which has probably saved many local flower shows from having to close down. By 2000, the RHS scheme provided a range of valued benefits to over 2,500 affiliated societies. In that year, the Banks Committee's review of governance recommended that the Affiliated Societies Liaison Committee be disbanded, and the support of local clubs and societies was integrated into the work of the Regional Development department, with guidance from a working group of Federation members.

Regional shows: 1867-1873 and after

As early as 1861, Prince Albert had urged the Society to get involved in organising flower shows in the provinces.[9] In 1866, the Society reached an agreement with the Royal Agricultural Society on a collaborative venture: staging a flower show and an agricultural show together in a provincial town. Bury St Edmunds, as both the centre of a large agricultural district and a town possessing a botanical garden, was chosen as the site for the first experiment. D.T. Fish, the head gardener of the nearby Hardwicke House, became the local negotiator; he secured Vine Fields as the venue, assembled local guarantors who agreed to receive £200 as their share of the profits, and arranged for

Carolyn Hardy, first female vice-chairman of Council, who with her husband Alan Hardy (1926-1999) formed, in the words of The Times, 'one of the most renowned horticultural partnerships of recent years' at their garden at Sandling Park, Kent.

large local gardens to open to the public for the week (Monday to Friday, 15-19 July).

George Eyles planned the layout of the exhibition: a 90-foot circular tent for competitive displays of palms, ferns, and foliage plants, leading through larger tents for flower and fruit arrangements, pelargoniums and fuchsias, to tents devoted to tools and the smaller classes on the schedule, including cottagers' produce. There was a brief flurry of complaints about judging, but the gate receipts totalled £1,416, enough to give the guarantors more than their expected profits. Fish was awarded a 40-guinea Life Fellowship for his efforts as local organiser.[10]

By the time the Bury Show was held, negotiations were already under way with Leicester for the following year's venture. This time, the formalities of organisation becoming more familiar, there was a grand inaugural dinner; the show lasted from Thursday to Wednesday (16-22 July), but was closed on Sunday. Once again, the Show was a great success, with more competitors, and more exhibits, than at Bury. Eyles was once again praised for his arrangement of the show ground, with artificial rockworks, and an avenue of rare conifers leading to the circular tent: the only reported disappointment was with the displays of cut flowers. Once again, a substantial profit, and 40-guinea Life Fellowships to the local organisers.[11]

After East Anglia and the Midlands, it was the turn of the North, but with the Manchester Show of 1869 the run of luck was broken. The Botanical and Horticultural Society of Manchester administered a fine regional Botanic Garden, which made an obvious site for the Show; initially enthusiastic negotiations stumbled over the question of free admission for that Society's members, which the RHS thought would significantly reduce the Show's likely profits. Council offered them £300 as compensation for making their members pay, but on receiving the answer that this would require an amendment to their charter, a special general meeting, and the possibility of refusal, broke off negotiations. Eyles found an alternative site at Old Trafford. Naturally, the accusation that the RHS had refused the help of local horticulturists was aired in the press, along with advance disputes over the offered prizes, all complainants managing to conclude their articles by calls for peace. But worse was to come. The Show reverted to Monday-to-Saturday opening (19-24 July). The Royal Agricultural Society managed to secure the more prominent part of the site, and access to the flower show could only be got by going through the agricultural portion first:

David Taylor Fish (1824-1901), head gardener at Hardwicke House, Suffolk, and author of several works on fruit, bulbs, and chrysanthemums, as well as the portions of Samuel Beeton's Book of Garden Management *(1863) on garden design, and* Cassell's Popular Gardening *(1884-6).*

accomplished by persevering inquiry of ignorant or unwilling officials, and through inches upon inches of dust, and that dust Manchester dust.

The *Gardeners' Chronicle* reported it as a show of only average merit.[12]

A similar disappointment followed in 1870, with a show in Oxford, in the grounds of the Radcliffe Observatory (Tuesday to Friday, 19-22 July). Once again, the Royal Agricultural Society dominated the grounds, 'a repetition of the Manchester muddle'; lack of advertising and signage, unhelpfulness or indifference of local functionaries, all combined to restrict attendance. The gardening press began now to insist that the RHS drop the relationship with the Agricultural Society, and organise its provincial shows on its own—and also call them great flower shows rather than RHS shows, because 'the Society and its objects are not sufficiently well known in the provinces'. For the first time, a Provincial Show made a loss.[13]

In 1871, determined to learn from its mistakes, the Society made significant changes to the show organisation. The Show was planned for Nottingham, and this time the Royal Agricultural Society was not involved. John Gibson, whose layout for the 1866 International Exhibition had been so highly praised, was hired to lay out the Show in Nottingham Park. His reputation brought an excitement to the advance press coverage, and his informal layout of the marquee won praise for its winding paths around masses of foliage. The Nottingham and Midland Counties Horticultural and Agricultural Society, and in particular W.P. Ayres, its Secretary, and the great fern expert E.J. Lowe, undertook the local arrangements. The Show was planned to run from Tuesday to Sunday, but after Sabbatarian complaints it was agreed to close it on the Saturday evening. The major complaint concerned the presence of locally organised 'crafts' stands: 'It is scarcely in keeping with the high purposes for which the Royal Horticultural show is held that the visitor on entering finds himself in the midst of a fancy bazaar.' £2,500-worth of gate receipts were taken. After the two successive fiascos of Manchester and Oxford, the Society was so pleased with the result that it presented three Gold Medals to the Nottingham Society for them to award in successive years at their own shows. E.J. Lowe was given a 40-guinea Life Fellowship.[14]

In 1872, the Society tried even harder. The chosen site was the Lower Grounds at Aston, Birmingham, a commercial public garden run by H.G. Quilter, and E.W. Badger of the Birmingham

Horticultural Society became the local agent; they booked accommodation for visitors, got railway companies to lay on special trains, and arranged for a number of local manufacturers to open their premises to the public while the Show was on. Badger further organised a Birmingham Rose Show, to be held concurrently and adjacent to the main show. Once again, no agricultural component, and this time, no crafts stands: their place was taken by a massive display of implements. Even the flower arrangements met with approval, and the Show was held at the earlier time of 25-29 June (Tuesday to Saturday). Above all, perhaps, there was publicity, on omnibuses, in railways. The *Gardeners' Chronicle* announced the lesson of marketing: 'Do not hide your light under a bushel,

but set it on the hill tops, and take care that every one sees it who ought to do so.' Even though the layout of the long tent was disappointing (lack of any central focus), the show was deemed a great success in every respect except the weather. 'It was a new sensation to eat lobster salad with one hand, hold an umbrella with the other, and watch the streams of water flow from the ribs of the umbrella into the dry (?) champagne.'[15]

Early in the negotiations, Ayres had suggested a competition for glasshouse designs (having recently patented a design of his own). Quilter seized on the idea, and organised special competitions for implements, boilers, and glasshouses. The terms in the schedule were complained of as vague, but it was acknowledged that these competitions were local, and the terms not the RHS's fault, though Ayres complained that the RHS should not delegate its functions. The trial of

greenhouse boilers brought controversy in its train, with disappointed competitors calling for the award to be revoked, organising a petition at a public meeting, and writing letters that the *Gardeners' Chronicle* refused to publish for fear of a libel suit.[16]

Birmingham had brought in a profit of over £2,000, so the following year's show in Bath was looked to hopefully. It was held in probably the most beautiful surroundings yet chosen, the Royal Victoria Park; some of William Edgcumbe Rendle's glazed flower show pavilions were used as an experiment. But by the time the Show took place, the politics of the RHS had erupted into chaos; Council had resigned *en masse*; resources were suddenly straitened, and schedules disrupted. The result was a general lack of finish: 'the obtrusive rafters, the sloppy paths, the unfinished rockery, the wretched central squirt, and, last but not least, the sadly defective arrangements'—judging could not be completed in a single day. At least the Show did not make a loss.[17]

The Society's worsening finances now brought about a hiatus in the schedule of provincial shows. A Brighton Show, planned for 1874, was called off, and other offers refused.[18] The Council that was refusing to pay the prizes at its own shows could hardly afford to lavish funds on further prizes outside London. With the election of Lord Aberdare, a new administration sought to revive the idea of provincial shows. In the summer of 1877 things began to look more hopeful for a show in Preston; T.M. Shuttleworth of Howick Hall, Preston, was enthusiastic about the possibilities. Acting as local secretary, he secured the grounds of the Preston Nursery and Pleasure Gardens Company as a site; the prize money (£1,200) was raised by local subscriptions. The National Rose Society was already planning a rose show at Preston, and agreed to co-operate. After this promising beginning, nothing went smoothly; the Aberdare administration, perhaps lulled by the good auguries, left most of the organising to Shuttleworth and his colleagues. Then on 18 April 1878 a county-wide cotton operatives' strike was called, and by early June panicky communication was taking place by telegraph about the possibility

A photograph of the scene inside the principal tent at the Bath Provincial Show of 1873.

of cancellation. The RHS finally sent Samuel Jennings, its Assistant Secretary, to replace Shuttleworth as site organiser.[19]

For the layout of the exhibition, Joseph Forsyth Johnson, a young Irish landscaper famous for a recent show design in Belfast, produced an informal scheme of rockwork, irregular banks, and waterfalls. The Show was scheduled to run from Wednesday to Sunday; in the event it was extended into Monday to help the finances. In all there were over 24,000 admissions, nearly half of them on the Saturday. It wasn't enough. The Show made a loss of £1,500, at a time when the RHS could ill afford a financial setback. Weather, competing attractions at Blackpool, trade depression, strikes, and a generally unsuitable district were all blamed for the failure. As the loss became more apparent, a further dispute arose between the Society and the Show's guarantors; the Society refused to pay for prizes until the Show proceeds produced the requisite amount—even the Lindley Medal awarded to Shuttleworth for his own display was withheld—while the guarantors brought an action against the Society for liabilities. The printer of the schedules brought his own independent action.[20]

This flurry of lawsuits seems, unsurprisingly, to have discouraged the Society from attempting shows unless there was a guarantee of local public support.[21] But then Lord Aberdare's administration fell in its turn, and the incoming administration under Sir Trevor Lawrence followed its example by reviving the idea. Liverpool was the venue this time; local guarantors were found to promise £1,500 of support. Wavertree Park, adjacent to the Liverpool Botanic Garden, was secured as a site; the *Gardeners' Chronicle* put up special prizes for young gardeners. Everything seemed set for a smooth success. The week after the Show, during a rose show at Kensington, the results from Liverpool came in.

> In spite of the attractions offered by the Rose Show a gloom hung over South Kensington on Tuesday last. The Roses, poor things! did their best in the sweltering heat ... It was the news that the great Provincial Show at Liverpool, from which so much had been hoped, had proved a financial failure. We need not point out in the present state of the affairs of the Society how serious a matter this is ...

'When a great catastrophe has happened', remarked the *Chronicle*, 'the British public looks out for somebody to hang. On this occasion they will have a difficulty in finding anybody to fit the noose.' At least the boiler contest didn't spark controversy this time. The deficit was £2,100, and the guarantors were called on for the whole guaranteed amount; three months later, only £1,000 had been collected, and the Society announced that prize moneys would not be paid until the money became available. Despite all this, the Liverpool Association approached the RHS to see whether it would help to organise their proposed Jubilee Shows the following year; the Society declined.[22]

With the Liverpool debacle, the Society's venture into the provinces was finally halted for a generation. Instead of helping to organise regional shows, the RHS developed a new habit of sending deputations to regional shows, and assisting in the presentation of awards. This first took place at the Chester Flower Show in July 1896, with John Wright as the principal RHS representative; the following year, the Shrewsbury Flower Show received its first RHS delegation.[23]

When the idea of a provincial show was raised again, after the First World War, the Society looked to Cardiff, whose Mayor and Corporation were busy promoting the idea of a Welsh Horticultural Society, and were enthusiastic about the publicity a show might provide. The exhibition was held in the Sophia Gardens, on 6-8 July (Tuesday to Thursday), three days having by then become the customary length of big shows like Chelsea. The event was eagerly anticipated, but once again was bedevilled by the weather:

> Many years have passed since the Royal Horticultural Society held a provincial show, and perchance many other years may pass before the post-war experiment, at Cardiff, is repeated. The weather conditions during the evening and night before the opening of the show were vile and not less so during the morning of July 6. During the greater part of the time our report was being made there was a superfluity of mud and water in the roadway, around the tents and inside the tents ... and in No. 2 tent, orange boxes served as insecure stepping stones across one side of a veritable lagoon, while table tops along the other side were traps to all but those who walked warily over them.
>
> The exhibition was a good one and exhibitors are to be congratulated on their efforts. The canvas of some of the tents was dark, but probably no one would have grumbled much at this, had the weather been brilliant and hot ...

A heavy loss was sustained on the catering, and Council unanimously resolved to stage the next Summer Show in London.[24] And with that, the idea of provincial shows died for another generation.

Kew and the Chelsea Physic Garden

In 1835, Lindley was the Society's Assistant Secretary, and also Professor of Botany at

University College; as if these were not enough to keep him occupied, that November he took up a third position, that of Professor of Botany and Præfectus Horti to the Society of Apothecaries. That Society, which had maintained the Chelsea Physic Garden since 1673, had succeeded 20 years earlier in securing the passage of the Apothecaries Act, which entitled them to examine medical students and license them to practise as apothecaries; this required the establishment of a training programme, and eventually of a professorship. Lindley was already a Professor used to lecturing, and had had experience of training gardeners at Chiswick, so he must have seemed ideally suited for the post—and indeed published a *Flora Medica* within three years of starting work at Chelsea.

Lindley's appointment brought him into speedy and irrevocable conflict with William Anderson, Curator of the Chelsea Physic Garden since 1815. One of his first observations was of the inadequacy of catalogues of the plant collections (which defect Lindley remedied within three months); he criticised the management of the greenhouses, complained that Anderson's attempt to grow a general representation of the plant kingdom distracted attention from the medical purposes the collection was supposed to serve, and condemned incorrect labelling; and not least, Anderson was a staunch supporter of the Linnaean system, which Lindley wanted to replace by natural classification. Before long, Lindley had to complain of Anderson's 'dogged hostility ... to myself', while Anderson complained to Glenny's *Gardeners' Gazette*; but the Garden Committee supported Lindley and brought Anderson to heel.

Anderson died in 1846, and Lindley hired as his replacement Robert Fortune, who had returned from his Chinese expedition a few months earlier. Fortune set to work clearing neglected parts of the garden, and applied to the Apothecaries for £150 for the repair of the greenhouses; they were duly repaired, but at more than twice the specified cost. In 1848, Fortune was hired by the East India Company for a second expedition to China, this time to collect tea plants to help start up a tea industry in India, and Lindley chose Thomas Moore as his successor. A wise choice: Moore was to run the Physic Garden for nearly forty years. Lindley's own career at Chelsea did not last so long. The Physic Garden's future was put into jeopardy by the Thames Embankment proposals, and the Apothecaries' finances plummeted; the Garden's budget was cut by two-thirds, and Lindley's post was abolished in 1853. Moore consoled himself by writing *The Ferns of Great Britain and Ireland*, with Lindley's help as editor; he was eventually to get the Garden's fortunes restored, but by that time Lindley was dead.[25]

A few years after Lindley had begun his work at Chelsea, he was invited to chair a working party on the condition of the royal gardens at Kew. The Treasury, on Queen Victoria's accession to the throne, had appointed Robert Gordon and Edward Ellice to look into the management of the royal gardens; Gordon, who a few years earlier had conducted the investigation of the Horticultural Society's finances, obviously thought that Lindley was the right man for the job. The others on the working party were Joseph Paxton and John Wilson, the gardener to the Earl of Surrey, the Treasurer of the Royal Household, at Worksop Manor. They were given their remit on 8 February 1838; they visited Kew for their survey on 16 and 19 February; Lindley's report was submitted on 28 February, and by 12 March had been handed in to the Treasury with Gordon's and Ellice's approval.

Kew had ceased to be a royal residence, and since the death of Sir Joseph Banks had been under-funded and neglected. Lindley and his colleagues praised the skills of the gardeners and the health of the plants, but condemned the management of the garden: inadequate labelling, cramped conditions, insufficient support from library or herbarium facilities; failure to maintain contact with the colonies, for which Kew was supposed to provide plants on request; administration without a strategic plan. William Townsend Aiton, the Superintendent (and one of the founders of the Horticultural Society), had to endure an uncomfortable grilling from Lindley about his records and finances. The final recommendation of the report was that Kew should cease to be administered by the royal household, and that it should then either be abandoned or, preferably, taken over by the government as a national botanic garden. The Horticultural Society, meanwhile, sent a petition to the government calling for Kew to be saved; and Lindley wrote privately to John Nussey of the Society of Apothecaries to ask whether they would relinquish the Chelsea Physic Garden in return for Kew providing the required service for the medical students.

There followed stagnation. The government delayed; the Commissioners for Woods and Forests waited until the spring of 1839 before agreeing to take Kew over if funding was made available; meanwhile the Earl of Surrey began visiting Kew and measuring up the glasshouses for possible conversion into vineries. On 13 February 1840 Robert Gordon told Council that the government intended to convert Kew into a royal kitchen garden, and offered the plants from the botanic garden to the Society on condition they allowed a degree of public access to them. Lindley had already been told this two days earlier; possibly at his urging, but certainly with his support, Council declined. Lindley had also threatened to bring the matter to the attention of Parliament; and his channel for doing so may have been Donald Beaton, whose article on cactus cultivation he was preparing to publish in the *Transactions*. Beaton later recorded that:

> I was the first of all the gardeners who knew that the Government of the day made an offer of Kew Gardens to the Horticultural Society as if it were dead lumber. Two hours after that offer was made, I had a notice of the fact in the hands of the post-office, for the use and information of Her Majesty's opposition, and 'to morrow night' the Government were 'pulled up' for the rascality.

The matter reached the pages of *The Times* on 21 February, and the outcry stopped Lord Surrey's scheme. Joseph Hume called for the publication of Lindley's report, which finally appeared in print in mid-May. In June the botanical garden at Kew was transferred to the Commissioners of Woods and Forests; Aiton tendered his resignation that autumn. Lindley had probably hoped that he would become the first Director of the new Royal Botanic Gardens, but his old colleague and mentor William Jackson Hooker was appointed instead, and Lindley remained with Chiswick and Chelsea as his responsibilities.[26]

The Society maintained friendly relations with Kew throughout its subsequent history. When in 1872 the Commissioners attempted to divide Kew's administration, so that the Director would be responsible for science only and the Curator for horticulture, Council supported Sir Joseph Hooker in his attempt to retain complete control, and Maxwell T. Masters launched a (successful) petition on his behalf. Similarly, Council defended Kew in imposing an admission fee during the First World War (the fee was one penny, and it was originally expected to be temporary). Hooker was Chairman of the RHS Scientific Committee, his successors from Sir Arthur Hill onward edited the *Botanical Magazine* for the Society, and two later Directors, Sir Edward Salisbury and Sir George Taylor, were also successively Professors of Botany to the RHS. Robin Herbert, on retiring from the Presidency of the RHS, became Chairman of the Kew Trustees.[27]

Since 1840, the Society had suffered the presence of a rival, the Royal Botanic Society (RBS), in Regent's Park. Emerging at the time of the controversy over Kew's continuation, it started by promoting itself as the successor to Kew; but once Kew was re-established and no longer needed a successor, it aimed its rivalry at the Horticultural Society, and for many years excelled it at flower shows. By the turn of the century, it was losing its way; in 1902 it offered its garden as a venue for RHS meetings; by 1909 it faced serious financial problems, with the danger that its site might revert to the Commissioners of Woods and Forests. Council, for reasons insufficiently explained, wrote a letter offering to take their grounds over, but the letter was not read out at the RBS council meeting, and any negotiations were broken off as their fortunes improved. In 1923, when the Society was searching for new London premises, it investigated the RBS site, but this time the majority of Council were unenthusiastic. When in 1931 the Royal Botanical Society was being wound up, it made a last-ditch appeal for help to the RHS, but by then the Lawrence Hall had been built and the quest for premises abandoned. The garden in the inner circle of Regent's Park reverted to the government; and Duncan Campbell designed Queen Mary's Rose Garden on part of the garden site.[28]

Aid for historic gardens

In October 1923, *The Times* published a letter about a threat to the avenue at Stowe, calling for public donations to save it from demolition, and suggesting that the RHS should organise an appeal. By the time a Council meeting took place, a fund had already been set up under the auspices of the Metropolitan Public Gardens Association, and the RHS restricted itself to contributing £25; the sum necessary to purchase the avenue was raised, largely with the help of Eton College. But the fact that the RHS should be publicly proposed as the obvious body to save an historic garden feature says something about its image at the time.[29]

Fifty-five years later, *The Times* reported that a contract had been issued to remove 180 lime trees from the avenue at Hampton Court. A flurry of correspondence followed, with Professor W.T. Stearn, the Society's former Librarian, leading a team which recommended the felling of only 30, the removal of some crowns, and better maintenance, concluding that there was no justification for the removal of the avenue as a whole. The debate continued: should an avenue be of even growth, or did it matter if the trees were of disparate sizes? Did it make a difference that the avenue now pointed, not to open countryside, but into suburbia? (Tree-hugging had yet to emerge as a strategy.) This time the RHS was able to keep out of the press, while writing to the relevant minister in favour of retention (the trees were reprieved).[30] During the half-century that separated these incidents, the image of the RHS had shifted; it no longer came obviously to mind in the context of preserving historic gardens.

Why did the RHS seem to fit that context in the 1920s? Apart from its general reputation as a campaigning body, resulting from its First World War activities, the most obvious reason would be its involvement in the restoration, if that is the right word, of Hampton Court. At the end of the war, a committee was set up to advise on the treatment of the gardens, which in the last quarter of the 19th century had been partially turned into a wild garden, and had also become a popular venue for carpet-bedding. The committee consisted of the architect Sir Aston Webb, the garden historian Ernest Law, Ellen Willmott, William Watson of Kew, the nurseryman and landscape gardener Robert Wallace, and, representing the RHS, F.R.S. Balfour of Dawyck. It soon emerged that the horticultural and architectural factions did not see eye to eye, and the compromise White Paper they produced envisaged the reduction, but not the complete elimination, of flower-beds and herbaceous borders, the clipping of the yews into topiary, and the restoration of the Tudor garden (that last goal not achieved at the time).[31]

Although the National Trust was given its first country house, Barrington Court, in 1907, it was not until the donation of Montacute, in 1931, that it began to consider the possibility of saving other country houses if they came on the market. In 1937 the National Trust Act was passed, giving the Trust powers to acquire houses and hold land and securities for their maintenance: Stourhead was the first house to be acquired under the new arrangements. Before long, the question of the accompanying gardens forced itself on the Trust's attention. In April 1944 Council received a query from the Trust: would the RHS advise on the maintenance of Montacute? Council agreed; E.A. Bowles plunged into the Library to search for visual evidence of period style, while the Trust wondered about creating a Gothic kitchen garden (whatever that would have looked like); James Wilson, the Society's garden adviser, was eventually assigned the task of advising on request.[32]

But a precedent had been set. In June 1947 Harold Nicolson wrote to Council, asking if the RHS would be prepared to take over Hidcote; Lawrence Johnston, who had begun the garden 40 years earlier, was now old and concerned about its fate. Council immediately concluded that the Society could not take it on, but shared Johnston's concern. In November Lord Aberconway approached the National Trust to suggest the formation of a gardens trust under their combined patronage: together they would acquire some of the greatest gardens in England as they came up for sale, and their maintenance would provide standards for the care of the gardens at the Trust's other properties. The Trust's directorate was initially enthusiastic, then began to worry about problems of administration and finance. In January, however, the joint committee was agreed, and the first meeting took place on 23 March 1948: the RHS was represented by Lord Aberconway, Sir Edward Salisbury, and H.V. Taylor, with Lord Rosse, Vita Sackville-West, and Sir David Bowes Lyon representing the Trust—though Bowes Lyon was the RHS Treasurer and had been part of Lord Aberconway's deputation the previous year. Lord Aberconway announced the scheme both to *The Times* and to the annual meeting of the RHS, and at the latter venue his statement of the aims of the Joint Committee went beyond what had been officially agreed: 'Only gardens of great beauty, gardens of outstanding design or historic interest would be considered, and those having collections of plants or trees of value to the nation either botanically, horticulturally or scientifically.'

A fund was set up, and advertised in the Society's *Journal*, but the scheme would have faced exactly the financial problem that the Trust's directors feared, had it not been for a bright idea of Vita Sackville-West's. The Queen's Institute for Nursing was being absorbed into the National Health Service, and the scheme it had operated for over twenty years, of gardens opening to the public to collect donations for the Institute, was about to be wound up. At Sackville-West's insistence, this scheme was reconstituted as the National Gardens Scheme, and in addition to continuing to provide money for nursing institutes, from 1949 to 1955 it advertised on its annual brochures that a fixed percentage of all donations would be paid to the Joint Committee of the RHS and the National Trust.

Hidcote was the first garden to be taken over by the Trust under the Joint Committee's auspices; it was followed by Bodnant, which Lord Aberconway entrusted in 1949, subject to the condition that he and his family continued to live there and develop the gardens in the style to which they had become accustomed. Nymans, Lord Rosse's garden, followed in 1953, and Sheffield Park in 1954, this last requiring the launch of an appeal to provide the necessary funding for its maintenance. All four of these gardens were made freely available to RHS members. As for maintenance, the decisions of the Joint Committee were concerned with horticulture, and not with restoration: Lawrence Johnston's collection of Regency garden furniture at Hidcote was distributed around other Trust properties, his glasshouses demolished, and parts of his planting scheme discarded. It was not until the beginning of the 1960s, when the Trust's Gardens Advisor Graham Stuart Thomas recommended the restoration of the 18th-century landscape garden at Stourhead, that historical accuracy became an operating principle. By that time there had been much friction between Thomas, who had been hired as Adviser in 1954, and the Committee, which he described as a 'dictatorial and opinionated body'; when Sir George Taylor, the Director of Kew, succeeded Sir David Bowes Lyon as the Committee's chairman, Thomas welcomed the appointment as bringing onto the Committee someone whose views were not shaped primarily by his own garden. The Joint Committee was finally dissolved in 1968, and replaced by a properties panel that brought a unified management to the Trust's estates, though the RHS continued to be a nominating body for the Trust, and Christopher Brickell served an active term as the RHS representative on the South-east Region's board.[33]

Bodnant was not the only example of a Council member's garden facing an uncertain future. The Society had long ago assumed an advisory responsibility for The Wilderness, William Wilks's garden in Shirley near Croydon, inspected it regularly, and got involved in objecting to local roadwork plans when they threatened the garden hedges.[34] When in 1948 Tortworth Court, the garden of its former Council member Lord Ducie, was acquired by the government and plans were made for turning it into a prison, the Society protested vigorously against the threat to public access to the great tree collection, but to no avail; but the loss to horticulture was not total, and two generations later Leyhill Open Prison, as it was then called, was to exhibit gardens at the Society's shows.[35] When the Forestry Commission purchased Westonbirt (Sir George Holford's estate), the Society offered to advise on the gardens; when John Barr Stevenson died, and the future of his rhododendron collection at Tower Court was in doubt, Council discussed strategies for saving it, and helped to arrange for Sir Eric Savill to acquire the trees for

Two views of William Wilks's garden at The Wilderness, Shirley, near Croydon: one of them with Wilks himself sitting huddled in a wintry scene. Wilks was Vicar of Shirley, while simultaneously serving as Secretary of the RHS from 1888 to 1920. In the 1880s, at his vicarage, he bred the Shirley poppies.

transplanting in the Valley Garden at Windsor. After the death of Stephenson Clarke, a company was established to maintain his garden at Borde Hill, and Lewis Palmer, the Treasurer, became the RHS's nominee on the company board. In 1958, the Society helped to publicise the National Trust for Scotland's campaign to acquire Brodick

Castle, and a decade later raised funds for its Branklyn campaign. And so on.[36]

In October 1965, the Garden History Society (GHS) was founded in a meeting at the RHS Halls by a group of historians and journalists. Relations between it and the RHS were rather intermittent at first, though a closer association resulted when the present author became the editor of its journal *Garden History* in the 1980s. Already during the 1970s it had established itself as an activist society with its interventions in cases of motorway threats to landscape gardens; in the 1980s it was to lobby the government successfully over the creation of a Register of Historic Parks and Gardens. The GHS, rather than the RHS, came to seem the obvious organisation to call on when an historic garden was endangered. When, a year after the incident of the Hampton Court avenue, the RHS convened its conference on conservation, and formed the National Council for the Conservation of Plants and Gardens, there was some suspicion that it was trying to re-assert itself against the GHS for a priority in the field of endangered gardens; but it did not take long for the NCCPG to settle into its successful mode of protection for cultivars, and the Garden History Society continued to hold the field to itself.[37]

Cemeteries, prisons, and a cathedral or two

During the early years of the First World War, the bodies of soldiers could be, when possible, brought back to England for burial, but by 1916 the scale of the slaughter, and the difficulty of retrieving, let alone identifying, individual bodies was provoking thoughts of creating special war cemeteries at the battlefields. The RHS was invited into discussions in March of that year, but although Edward White, Council's landscaping representative, offered his services, the horticultural aspects of cemetery provision were deferred till the close of the war. In October 1918 a Cemetery Committee was set up, with architectural advice from Reginald Blomfield and Edwin Lutyens, and horticultural from Gertrude Jekyll; the major decision was to institute a series of uniform designs of headstones, and to arrange them uniformly, so to avoid invidious distinctions of rank, while Rudyard Kipling contributed examples of wording ('Their name liveth forevermore') that could be applied with equal uniformity.

The great war cemeteries in France and Belgium were one thing: but their principles of design and management were extended by government dictate to war cemeteries in Great Britain, for soldiers who had died back home. Meanwhile, back in 1920, Colonel Durham, Director of Works for the Imperial War Graves Commission, approached the RHS to ask whether the maintenance of war graves in England could be entrusted to the affiliated societies; Council recommended that the Commission set up a central supervisory committee instead. The Commission proposed an exhibit at Chelsea to explain its activities to the public; Council declined, and it was not until 1967 that the Commission was finally allowed to exhibit in the garden design section. Despite these rebuffs, when Colonel Durham left the Commission, it was to become the Secretary of the RHS, a position he held for nearly twenty years. During his time and after, the Society continued to be represented on the Commission in an advisory role; Sir George Taylor was the longest-serving botanical adviser and, after his death, it became a role that successive Directors of Kew undertook. In the 1950s, when large areas of Brookwood Cemetery were taken over for Second World War graves, the RHS organised a donation of rhododendrons and azaleas for the grounds.[38]

Odour of sanctity would appear to be a good way in general of securing the RHS's involvement: in 1959-60 the only external landscaping projects (other than through the National Trust Joint Committee) on which the RHS advised were the grounds and avenue of the recently completed Guildford Cathedral, and the restoration of the garden at Westminster Abbey, for which Frank Knight served as adviser.[39]

Possibly the most unusual form of garden with which the Society has been involved is the prison garden. Competitions of various sorts—for example, bricklaying, and other technical skills—had been run in prisons for a long time when, in 1983, Lord Windlesham, the Chairman of the Parole Board, approached the RHS with a proposal for a prize to be awarded to the best prison garden. The RHS agreed to administer the competition and, for its first decade, the gardens were judged by Allan Sawyer, an RHS shows official who was also a justice of the peace. (More

A postcard view of Rolincourt in the 1920s: a British war cemetery with a planting plan by Gertrude Jekyll.

The prize-winning garden 'No time to stand and stare' by the inmates of Leyhill Open Prison at the Chelsea Flower Show for 2003.

result of the difficulty of comparing operations at such different categories of prison, a new judging system was introduced, with second- and third-round judging being made on horticultural achievement only, and a handicapping system applied to the marks so that the final mark reflected the difficulties each institution faced. Prison gardening was then about to emerge into the light of day: in 1998 Paula Deitz, the editor of the *Hudson Review*, had published an article in the *New York Times* about Leyhill Open Prison's success in winning a Gold Medal for its garden at Hampton Court, and this was made the basis of the film *Greenfingers*, released in the autumn of 2001.[40]

Regional centres

In 1985, the Society's Review Committee reported that there was widespread dissatisfaction with the perceived south-east bias of the RHS: 'at present there is not much that can be offered to Members who live a long way from London'. Over the ensuing decade, the Society's administration slowly and painfully adjusted itself to the idea of regionalisation. Proposals were discussed enthusiastically, institutions created or extended with difficulty; and always, the institutional reflex arc meant that spending was automatically lavished on Wisley, and then on London. (The internal conflict reached a climax with the 1995 proposal to move the Library to Wisley, when jibes were heard about the desirability of a name change to the Surrey Horticultural Society.)

recently the judge has been a retired Prison Service officer with horticultural experience.) Each year, the area managers for the prison service, the Director of High Security Prisons, and the Operational Manager for Women's Prisons submit their candidates for award. The Windlesham Trophy does not attract much publicity outside its restricted environment, and prison gardening in general tends to take place outside the public view, so here is a rare comment from a newspaper survey of prison conditions in 2001:

> (Best gardens.) A hotly contested category, with a number of institutions furiously trimming their box hedges each spring in a bid to land the coveted Windlesham trophy, awarded each year by the Royal Horticultural Society. The rules have recently been changed to prevent victors winning two years in a row, a move designed to curb the runaway success of Whatton prison in Notts, which won three years in a row in the mid-1990s and is the current trophy holder. Insiders tip Kingston prison in Portsmouth to land the award this year.

But not even the Windlesham Trophy is exempt from controversy, as when in 1997 it was awarded to Kingston Prison just before the announcement of a financial shake-up; the Chief Inspector of Prisons grumbled in his report that 'the Director General had given no hint of what might be to come when he presented the well-earned Windlesham Trophy to the prison'. In 2000, as a

The first detailed proposals for regional development were discussed by Council in November 1987, and it was agreed that a policy should be adopted of extending the Society's work across the country, but that it would be inappropriate to divide the country into geographical regions for the purpose; instead, the Society should set up Regional Centres—on the model of the National Trust, as recommended by the Review Committee—in areas of high population and local enthusiasm from members and affiliated societies. Care should be taken to avoid accusations of 'taking over' existing societies: it would be better to sponsor joint activities. Lectures, demonstrations, and garden visits were the sort of thing envisaged. The Review Committee had suggested Harlow Carr as 'the most obvious place to start', and reciprocal membership benefits were arranged with both Harlow Carr and Ness Gardens, the University of Liverpool's botanic garden; but the first proposed venue for a Regional Centre was Pershore College, which under the direction of Bill Simpson had developed one of the best horticultural training programmes in the country.

A meeting at Pershore having been successful, a steering group was formed, and the RHS Regional Centre was officially opened on 4 September 1988. Michael Jefferson-Brown was the first administrative secretary; RHS members were allowed to use the Pershore library by appointment; affiliated societies had the same arrangements as at Wisley; a newsletter was begun for local members. But it was not long before tensions arose over the relations between the two organisations. The college wanted to set up a Friends of Pershore, and the RHS was puzzled over its status; some thought that the college wanted to run the RHS Centre as it saw fit, excluding the RHS from its administration. The Friends were finally formed in 1996, as a fundraising group. By that time the idea of setting up several regional centres had ground to a halt, and from being the RHS West Midlands Regional Centre, Pershore in 1994 became simply the RHS Regional Centre at Pershore.[41]

Part of the problem with the idea of regional centres, run in conjunction with existing local institutions, was that it was overtaken by the acquisition of gardens: Rosemoor and Hyde Hall were presented to the RHS after the Pershore experiment was begun, their development made heavy demands on funds, and, as freehold properties of the Society, they offered a much less problematic way of establishing a regional presence. In 1991 Council imagined that the Society could finance a new garden every four years or so; this aim proved unrealistic, but it helped the RHS to break free from the idea of regional centres under joint control, in favour of encouraging other horticultural organisations to pursue their own activities. During the 1990s, a wide range of lectures and demonstrations in different parts of the country was set up; by the beginning of the 21st century, the Society had a regional strategy and an energetic policy of expansion outside the south-east. Partnerships had been established with over a hundred gardens of special horticultural interest which, thanks to the generosity of their owners or curators, provided free access to RHS members at set times of the year; horticultural colleges and centres, nurseries and garden centres ran RHS events and local clubs hosted over 50 RHS lectures each year. Co-ordinating all this was the Regional Develop-

ment department, managed in succession by Wendy Crammond and by Rebecca Lewis-Bowen, with the brief of bringing education, information, and inspiration to keen gardeners across the United Kingdom.

Regional shows: the 1980s and after

The idea of regional centres was gradually succeeded by that of regional shows—not an idea that the Review Committee had proposed, but one which developed from practice. The garden festivals of the 1980s, in effect, acted as a training programme.

Familiar since the early post-war years in various parts of the continent, where they were first used as a means of regenerating war-damaged areas, garden festivals had been recommended in the past as promotional events for British tourism, but never seriously attempted. By the 1980s, however, urban dereliction had attained such levels of publicity that the experiment seemed worth trying. Michael Heseltine, the Secretary of State for the Environment, made the establishment of a series of British garden festivals a personal crusade, and in 1981 began negotiations with the RHS and other organisations for an International Garden Festival to be held in Liverpool in 1984, followed by National Garden Festivals at a series of other sites, one every two years. Council was worried about unrealistically short deadlines, but agreed to help; a company was set up to organise the Liverpool Festival, with Lord Aberconway as its Director. The announcement of the forthcoming festival, made so soon after highly publicised riots in Liverpool, was greeted with cynicism by some, including Hugh Johnson in his Tradescant column in *The Garden*:

> What we have been waiting for all this time has apparently been the Liverpool riots of last year and the resulting visit to Merseyside of the Secretary of State for the Environment. Reading between the lines of the Department's circular it seems that what the Liverpudlians were rioting about was the distance between Liverpool and the Chelsea Flower Show. For a Flower Show is what they are going to get. Since Chelsea won't budge they are to have the National Garden Festival ...

Tradescant had not been aware of the years of negotiation and, after Council remonstrated, joined the Festival promotion.[42]

The site of the International Garden Festival was a 250-acre reclaimed industrial site, heavily polluted, haunted by methane, and a prime candidate for regeneration. Once the Festival was finished, part of the site was intended to be used for building, and part would remain as a park—inaccurately hyped as the first urban park of the century—with some of the theme gardens (the prize-winning Japanese garden, and the Chinese pavilion) retained on site. Some ingenious gardens were created for the Festival (Minotaur Designs' Beatles maze); various experiments with large-scale bedding schemes were heavily publicised, and probably helped to boost public perception of the bedding plant industry. John Main, the Curator of Wisley, was responsible for designing and constructing the RHS exhibit, an alpine meadow (an attempt to get away from the traditional banked rock garden), which won a large gold medal. Lord Aberconway organised a panel of experts to give advice on a daily basis; RHS Enterprises maintained a stand in the Gardeners' Bazaar area, and set a high standard, but only just covered its costs. Standards of maintenance after opening were poor, and there were areas of dead trees. There were nearly 3.5 million visitors, and the £30m. development costs were fully covered.[43]

With Liverpool achieving such a success, the outlook for the first National Garden Festival, to take place at Stoke-on-Trent in 1986, seemed good. Once again, Lord Aberconway, now retired as President, became Chairman of the operating company. The RHS created a gold-medal-winning garden, again designed by John Main, with the theme 'The Wide World of Plants'; plants from five continents were displayed in a mixture of beds and solar domes. Late in the day

(June 1985), the RHS was invited to stage a show as part of the Festival, but Council declined as too little time had been allowed. John Ravenscroft, the Director of Bridgemere Garden World, represented the RHS as a judge; his nursery's garden received the highest award; but he was scathing about the quality of the organisation, saying, 'Unfortunately, garden festivals appear to be organised by people who don't understand that visitors like plants'. Haste, lack of involvement by local firms, insufficient publicity, and bad weather all contributed to poor visitor numbers: over 2 million attended, but 4.5 million were needed to meet the development costs. The site was almost entirely turned over to building after the Festival was over, with only a small wooded ridge retained as parkland.[44]

Three more National Garden Festivals had been scheduled: Glasgow in 1988, Gateshead in 1990, Ebbw Vale in 1992. The Society's active involvement diminished further with each one in the series. The RHS was once again asked to stage a show as part of the Glasgow Festival, but only six willing exhibitors were found; the Festival authorities agreed verbally to provide a £750 subsidy for exhibitors, but the RHS feared that the offer might be withdrawn, and eventually declined. Site security was poor; the Festival authorities steadily cut back on their commitments to site preparation and maintenance; but thanks to the efforts of John Battye, the RHS garden was completed in time for opening, and won its usual gold medal. Part of the problem with

The National Garden Festival at Ebbw Vale, 1992.

Glasgow was financial: the site was acquired from the builders Laing Homes, and handed back to them for development after the Festival ended, but the Audit Commission launched an enquiry into the acquisition process; although heralded as creating employment, the Festival also required the demolition of a run-down area, and local businesses complained of their eviction; the Treasury reduced the coffers of the Highlands and Islands Development Agency, one of the major sponsors, on the eve of the opening; and the event ended disastrously, with a fatal fireworks explosion.[45]

In a triumph of hope over experience, the Gateshead organisers asked the RHS to organise a show during the 1990 Festival and, despite considerable tensions, the show went ahead and attracted 53,000 visitors, the greatest number for any event of the Festival. Council agreed to provide a design for a garden (drawn up by the Society's garden adviser William Nelmes), but not to undertake the costs of construction; and when the works on the garden proved to be of an inadequate standard, the RHS withdrew its association. Ironically, the Gateshead Festival was later declared to be the best of all the Festivals from the horticultural industry's point of view.[46] The Ebbw Vale Festival in 1992 attracted the poorest publicity of all; the RHS provided neither show nor garden; John Ravenscroft attacked the sidelining of horticulture, saying, 'There shouldn't be four nurseries at Ebbw Vale, there should be 40'. But in terms of resulting regeneration it achieved more than any Festival since Liverpool, with 40 acres of parkland retained amid the 'urban village' created on the site of a former steelworks.[47]

The garden festival experiment had inconclusive results: much apparent failure could be attributed to haste, excessively tight schedules, externally imposed budget restrictions, and 'festival fatigue' after a new event every two years. Nearly every Festival went through a management crisis and the resignation of a chief executive; an unstable mixture of private and public funding left each Festival uncertain about its finances; commercial pressures hobbled the expected regeneration effect, especially at Stoke and Glasgow, where the landscapes created for the Festivals were quickly lost. Liverpool was the greatest commercial success, in large part because of its novelty value. The RHS was involved from the start in what seemed a hopeful venture, but, as the Festivals continued, they settled into a pattern of excessive demand and financial retrenchment from which Council was eventually pleased to escape.[48]

By that time the Society had become actively involved with a group of annual or twice-yearly flower shows in different parts of the country. The Southport Flower Show, first held in 1924, had become one of the major fixtures in the gardening calendar, but its continuation was threatened as local government spending was squeezed in the 1980s. In 1986 Sefton Council announced that the Show would be cancelled from the following year, but a protest group persuaded the Council to reprieve it if local fundraising could raise a sufficient amount. The RHS publicised the cause, and decided to stage a mobile presentation, including advisory services; Tom Bradshaw, the Secretary of the Southport Show, said, 'We are proud that we have persuaded the Royal Horticultural Society to venture outside London and to hold their Gardeners' Calendar Roadshow at Southport for the first time.' From Southport the roadshow also went to the Shrewsbury, Bristol, East of England, and Malvern Shows.[49]

The Malvern Spring Garden Show was run by the Three Counties Agricultural Society, who proved particularly receptive to the RHS's contribution. The roadshow and advisory services continued in 1988 and 1989; in 1990 the Spring Show became a joint venture of the two societies, with the profits (and risks) divided equally between them after the Three Counties' overhead costs had been settled. By 1991 the Show was such a success that the Society was ready to enter into similar partnerships with other regional organisations. The North of England Horticultural Society (NEHS) had been running the Harrogate Show since before the First World War; from 1990 the RHS helped with judging; in 1992 agreement was reached on joint shows, both spring and autumn, run on the same lines as Malvern. The joint venture was short-lived: from 1993 to 1995, by which time conflicts between the Shows Committee and the NEHS over decision-making and the length of the shows made the RHS resolve to disengage from its involvement in Harrogate. However, 1995 also saw the inception of a jointly run autumn show at Malvern.

Meanwhile, a new show had been announced for Birmingham, to be held in 1990 under the auspices of the BBC, and entitled *Gardeners' World Live*, after the popular television programme. It proved successful, and in 1993 the RHS entered into a contract for its joint administration, holding an RHS flower show within the compass of the larger event. Already by its second year it included over a hundred nurseries, housed in the longest marquee of its type at any RHS flower show. The Malvern and Birmingham Shows became the largest fixtures in the Society's calendar outside

London—until the late 1990s, and the decision to hold a regional show (first in Scotland, then at Tatton Park) that would be entirely an RHS venture.

Britain in Bloom

Probably the greatest single step toward regionalisation, however, was the RHS's involvement with Britain in Bloom.

Roy Hay, the Society's former Editor, had started it, or perhaps rather introduced it into Britain, for the competition was based on the 'Fleurissement de France', begun in 1959 as a means of promoting civic pride and tourism in French towns. A vacation in France having alerted him to the possibilities, Hay persuaded Len Lickorish, the Director-General of the British Travel and Holidays Association (later the British Tourist Authority), to organise a similar competition in Britain. Britain in Bloom was formally launched in 1963, with the RHS in attendance in a godfatherly capacity. A system of judging was soon finalised, with three stages:

an initial competition to select finalists, judging for best in region, and lastly judging for the national winner. (Lewisham was the first regional winner, Bath the first national winner the following year.)

At first, Britain in Bloom had the reputation of being a competition for municipal bedding, and was accordingly dismissed contemptuously by those parts of the gardening community that also sneered at public parks. As the contest gathered strength, more and more local councils began to encourage horticulture as civic decoration in the form of hanging baskets and tubbed floral displays, once again provoking contemptuous rejection. David Welch, while Parks Superintendent for Aberdeen, defended this sort of civic ornament:

> The comments of the judges are the greatest single influence on horticultural fashion. If they applaud the use of hanging baskets then bingo! more appear. If they admire roses, then rose sales rocket. If they like window boxes the windowsills of competing towns become encrusted with them. If they say they prefer shrubs and trees, more are planted. If you doubt it, look around. In the course of the campaign's three decades the number of flower containers has multiplied. Hanging baskets are no longer exclusively suspended from buildings, they are strung from the arms of specially introduced poles lining the sides of streets. The tops of bus shelters are festooned with flowers. Street corners are crowded with tubs. There is nothing wrong with

The Scottish Show held between 1997 and 1999: logo and aerial view of the island site.

this even though it is a troublesome and expensive form of gardening ... Baskets and boxes are justified in a city centre where there is no room for anything else.

But even before Britain in Bloom developed more of an environmental emphasis, and began encouraging projects in urban forestry, greening of waste ground, and ecological planting, it was apparent that it had become a force for urban regeneration. Towns which had the reputation of being 'dumps from Hell' began securing sponsorship for planting schemes and tidying run-down areas. Winning a Britain in Bloom competition guaranteed an increase of tourism, for good or ill:

> A legendary 'bloom' story is that of Chagford, in south Devon, which won the Village Trophy in 1972. The resultant increase in traffic from visitors going to see the flowers led to some residents asking the village to abstain from entering in the future.[50]

Britain in Bloom lasted for two decades of increasing popularity before it suddenly faced its major crisis. In 1983, *Horticulture Week* reported that the British Tourist Authority 'has seen its budget cut by the Government and, before Parliament was dissolved, was told to drop Britain in Bloom from its remit'. Mark Mattock, the rose grower who was then acting as its Secretary, was quoted as saying that while the regional contests would survive, 'there will no longer be a national event unless someone, or something, is willing to spend around £10,000 on it'. That someone or something proved to be Barratts Homes, who agreed to fund the competition, while the Keep Britain Tidy Group, who were already sponsoring a trophy, took over its practical administration. Barratts were succeeded by MacDonalds (the Tidy Britain Group, as it was renamed, itself depended on voluntary funding, and could not sustain the competition unaided). By the end of the century, financial difficulties were returning.

By this time the RHS was in the throes of reaching out to a wider community, and the Marketing Director Sue Coleman was encouraging its presence in garden centres. Robert Sweet, the horticultural manager in the Shows Department, who in his earlier years in the Torbay parks had been both a competitor (twice finalist, once joint winner) and a judge, and from 1991 to 1998 chairman of the regional competition Southwest Bloom, responded by encouraging the RHS to make a stronger link with Britain in Bloom. A certain disparity of enthusiasm was

A municipal display created in Bampton, Devon, six times national winner of Britain in Bloom, village category.

apparent on Council, but the Director-General and Treasurer supported the idea, and negotiations began. In the autumn of 2000, it was formally announced that the RHS was succeeding the Tidy Britain Group as the organisers of Britain in Bloom, with Caroline O'Callaghan from the Group joining the RHS staff.[51]

The first year's competition under RHS auspices proved to be a great success. The BBC devoted an hour's television programme to the event, detailing the different stages of the competition, and for the first time in its media coverage emphasised the variety of environmental improvements it promoted. In many towns the news that the RHS was now in charge was greeted with excitement, and the presence of the RHS logo on Britain in Bloom notices around the country provided valuable publicity.

Foreign members and projects abroad

The Society's international membership was small but impressive from an early date. The membership lists are intermittent, but by the time the Society was 20 years old its foreign members included the botanists De Candolle, Bonpland, Du Petit-Thouars, Brotero, Paula von Schrank, and Tenore; the botanical artists Redouté and Johann Simon Kerner; the garden designers André Thouin and A.F.L. Sckell; the fruit authorities Louis Noisette and Johann Volkmar Sickler; Sir Stamford Raffles and Nathaniel Wallich in the Asian colonies; and De Witt Clinton, the Governor of New York. (The next decade saw botanists like Martius, Reichenbach, and Humboldt added to the list.) The foreign membership was spread across Europe from Portugal to Poland and Russia, China, Singapore, the Azores, Libya, Egypt, Sierra Leone, Canada, the USA, Cuba, Brazil, and St Helena; the members included directors of botanical gardens, head gardeners on royal or private estates (including the Vatican gardens), presidents of foreign horticultural societies, naval doctors in profusion, government attachés, directors of Hudson's Bay Company forts, and the like. Eventually, in the 20th century, even standing committees were to acquire foreign members: Prince Shimadzu of Japan on the Orchid Committee for the duration of his residence in England; Sir Frederick Im Thurn on the Scientific Committee, his address given as the Fiji Islands; and most recently, also on the Scientific Committee, the late Heino Heine from Mannheim, who used to come to England every flower show to attend its meetings. In 1944 the Society acquired its first American Vice-President,

Liberty Hyde Bailey, and has ever since had at least one foreign Vice-President at any given time.

Much of this membership, and much of the Society's related activities, naturally centred on the British colonies. Lindley advised the Admiralty on the planting of Ascension Island, to make it a suitable victualling station for ships; the Society sent wild potato tubers to be planted there, and similarly helped with the potato crop on St Helena.[52] Lindley's work on the Colonial section of the 1862 Great Exhibition brought him into close contact with horticulturists in the colony of Nova Scotia, and he urged the Society to co-operate with the local Horticultural Society, publishing a promotional article on Canada in the last volume of the Society's *Proceedings* he edited.[53] In another direction, the Society maintained links with the Agri-Horticultural Society of India, and with Wallich at the Calcutta Botanic Garden.

The first American members were David Hosack and Andrew Gentle of the Elgin Botanic Garden in New York, both listed in 1818. By 1832, American members included: from New York, Jesse Buel, editor of the *Cultivator*, the seedsman Grant Thorburn, and the nurserymen William Prince and Thomas Hogg; from Baltimore, John S. Skinner, editor of the *American Farmer*; from South Carolina, Stephen Elliot, botanist and co-founder of the *Southern Review*. Later members of note included the nurseryman W. Attlee Burpee, the garden designer Beatrix Farrand, Wilson Popenoe of the United Fruit Company, and C.S. Sargent of the Arnold Arboretum. Although Edward Harding's 1927 proposal to establish a centre for the study of American gardening in the RHS New Hall proved abortive, links with American horticultural societies have been maintained since the 19th century, ranging from seed exchanges to conferences to flower show exhibits. In 1957, the Massachusetts Horticultural Society awarded the RHS the George Robert White Medal of Honour for its contributions to international horticulture.[54]

Foreign membership proved, during the war-torn 20th century, something of a battleground. The anti-German hysteria of the First World War led to calls for the expulsion of enemy aliens from membership—to which the Society replied that enemy aliens had ceased to be members as soon as they were unable to pay their subscriptions; and once economic depression hit Britain in the 1930s, it supported the Horticultural Trades Association in its call for protective tariffs on imported plants. On the other hand, at the end of the Second World War, the Society refused to be involved in the plundering of German nurseries to provide cheap plants for the British market, and provided plants for the International Peace Garden in Salt Lake City.[55] In the half-century since, the foreign garden project with which the Society has been most closely involved has been La Mortola. Originally the Villa Orengo at Ventimiglia, La Mortola was the Italian home and burial place of Sir Thomas Hanbury; and under the direction of his son Sir Cecil, it maintained links with Kew and other British botanical gardens until the Second World War, providing facilities for exchange students, sending fruit to the RHS, and regularly publishing lists of plants in flower on Christmas day. After the war it became increasingly derelict. In 1979 the garden was transferred to the University of Genoa, and a restoration programme begun. The RHS, in honour of Hanbury's gift of Wisley for its garden, became a partner in the restoration, helped to arrange staffing, met the costs of cataloguing the plant collection when the original sponsor withdrew, and has continued to play an advisory role.[56]

As the Society's regionalisation programme expanded in the 1990s, with its roster of partnership gardens admitting RHS members free of charge, Europe also beckoned, and in 1996 the Kalmthout Arboretum in Belgium became the first European partnership garden—since followed by some 20 gardens in France and two in Italy. In 1997 reciprocal rights for members were established with the Singapore Botanic Garden.

Foreign shows

In the 1860s, the Society, perhaps conscious of its new Royal status, began to get involved with flower shows on the Continent, whether by sending representatives to judge (beginning in 1862, when it sent J.J. Blandy to Belgium), by offering medals, or by staging exhibits. The international impact of the Great Exhibition of 1851 made it *de rigeur* for other countries to stage great exhibitions of their own, in a tradition that eventually modulated into the 20th-century tradition of World's Fairs; the RHS, having hosted the 1862 Great Exhibition, helped to organise the British contingent for the 1867 Exposition Internationale in Paris, and subsequently sent exhibits to nearly all its 19th-century successors (Brussels, Cologne, Paris again in 1878—for which it once again organised a combined British display). From 1875 on it regularly sent a representative to the Ghent Floralies. Robert Hogg, Samuel Jennings (the Society's assistant secretary in the 1870s), and the amateur orchid grower Robert Warner were among those sent abroad as RHS representatives. Most tragically from its own point of view, it sent

Sir Charles Wentworth Dilke to an exhibition in St Petersburg, where he died of pneumonia.[57]

This involvement was naturally curtailed during the First World War, but resumed soon afterward, when in 1923 the Society grant-aided the Chamber of Horticulture for its intended British exhibit at the Ghent Floralies. Ten years later it donated £100 directly to the Floralies, and continued regularly to sit on its jury. In 1926 it organised a big display for Valenciennes.[58] In the 1930s the Society offered its first cups to shows in Australia and the United States (Massachusetts Horticultural Society show, 1937), and the President, Gerald Loder, made a tour of American flower shows. In 1951 the RHS sent a challenge cup to a show in Rhodesia, and a decade later grant-aided a major show at Kirstenbosch in South Africa.[59] But European shows remained its main overseas interest, and as the concept of the European Common Market became more tangible during the course of the 1950s, the interest of British commerce in maintaining a horticultural presence abroad became more earnest. In 1957 the Society was invited to take part in the Floralies Internationales de Paris scheduled for 1959. Defeated by the finances of the endeavour, the Society announced in June 1958 that there would be no British representation at the show; but Sir Arthur Morse, Chairman of the British Travel and Holidays Association, agreed to underwrite the costs of the exhibit, and the Dulverton Trust helped with a timely grant. By the time the Floralies had taken place, the Society and the Holidays Association had collaborated in forming the British Committee for Overseas Flower Shows (BCOFS), whose purpose was to organise British exhibits and keep British horticulture in the foreign eye; Sir David Bowes Lyon, the Society's President, was the first chairman. The Board of Trade agreed to put up to £10,000 into foreign exhibits under the right conditions. The first great success for the BCOFS was at the Valenciennes Show for 1962, where the British exhibit was awarded the Prix d'Honneur.[60]

After that, the story is one of steady decline. The expected co-operation fell apart over the Hamburg Show of 1963, where the Federation of British Horticultural Exporters withdrew, and the RHS ended by staging its own independent exhibit, which won a gold medal. The Foreign Office having refused to fund another exhibit at the Paris Floralies, the RHS confined itself to sending Harold Hillier as a judge. Gradually, as the 1960s skidded on, Council found itself rejecting all invitations to exhibit abroad except at the Ghent Floralies; and in 1968 it declined even that, making it its official policy that contributions to

Sir Thomas Hanbury (1832-1907), who had become wealthy as a silk merchant in China in the 1850s and 1860s, acquired the Palazzo Orengo at La Mortola, near Ventimiglia in Italy, and developed it as a garden; in 1892 he founded the Botanical Institute of Genoa. In 1903 he purchased the Wisley estate and donated it to the Society as an experimental garden.

foreign shows were 'rarely possible'.[61] In 1980, on being invited to contribute to the International Garden Fair in Munich, Council noted that an educational exhibit was possible, but 'not an exhibit of the type produced by Mr. Hanger'; in the event, support was found for a joint British exhibit which won several awards. In the late 1980s, in the wake of the British garden festivals, the Society showed a renewed commitment to exhibits at overseas shows, collaborating on gardens for the World's Fair at Osaka in 1990, the Netherlands Floriade in 1992, and the Stuttgart Garden Fair in 1993, where the British garden won five medals. But this impetus did not outlast the decade; there was no British garden at the 2002 Floriade, because of the lack of joint sponsors and government assistance. On the other hand, the Society's mobile information exhibits have formed a regular part of the Courson Flower Shows in France since 1988.[62]

Meanwhile, while the Society had been looking at Europe, a crisis had grown up in the other direction. The RHS had become involved in helping to set up the Cincinnati Flower and Garden Show, first held in 1990 under the sponsorship of the Provident Bank; it remains the only American flower show which the Society directly supports. But in the early flush of enthusiasm over the possibilities of American involvement, the Shows Department gave advice on flower show management to Joni Nelson, an American banker who set up an organisation called the Chelsea America Foundation, and registered its logo as a United States trademark. A Chelsea America show was held in California in February 1993, to advance publicity claiming various degrees of RHS involvement, and to poor reviews. Although the *Wall Street Journal* published an article dissociating the RHS from the exhibition, a report claimed that 'Many horticulturists in California had been under the impression that the RHS was involved with this event, and also considered that the show had damaged the reputation of the horticultural industry in California'.[63]

The RHS Japan Branch

The most curious and unpredictable of the Society's foreign adventures was the establishment of a branch in Japan.

The motor force for the Japan Branch was the Seiyo Corporation, a real estate subsidiary of the immense Seibu Department Store group. In the early 1980s, the Corporation decided to create a park and botanical garden at Mount Akagi, some 80 miles from Tokyo. One of the managers at Seiyo, Hiroyuki Arimasa, suggested that the park should include a rhododendron garden, which would be the first of its kind in Japan, and contacted the RHS for advice. Together with Hideo Suzuki of the Japanese Rhododendron Society, Arimasa visited RHS President Robin Herbert and Director General Christopher Brickell in 1984. The RHS agreed to help with the rhododendron garden, and arranged for James Russell, the great gardener at Castle Howard, to visit the Akagi Park and advise on the Society's behalf.

At the time there were few members of the RHS in Japan, and the visits to the Akagi project were used to publicise the Society's activities and membership benefits—not that these were necessarily apparent in a country with a different language, writing system, and horticultural tradition. As the discussions continued, and came to include participation in the forthcoming Osaka World's Fair, the Seiyo Corporation proposed the establishment, under its sponsorship, of a branch of the RHS within Japan. Foreign branches had been discussed before, and rejected (most notably a Canadian branch in 1950, which got as far as solicitors' advice).[64] But this time Council was excited by the possibilities, and the RHS Japan Branch was formally inaugurated in November 1986, with Minoru Arai, the President of the Seiyo Corporation, as its President and Arimasa as Director-General, and an initial membership of thirty-five. In 1988, the Japan Branch started its own *Journal* under the editorship of Takemi Iida and then Kazuko Yahiro, each issue consisting of an abridged translation of the text of the latest issue of *The Garden*, with additional material for the Japan Branch. Most issues have had a plant illustration from the Lindley Library on their covers.[65]

With the Osaka World's Fair (International Exposition of Flowers and Gardens), the Japan Branch arranged its first annual International Horticultural Forum, as well as an International Camellia Conference; Brickell and Russell, together with John Bond, the Superintendent of Windsor Great Park, attended on behalf of the RHS. The Japan Branch's membership rose to 600, and thus began a steady climb which reached 2,000 members by 1997, and 3,000 by 2002. As its membership grew, the Japan Branch began to diversify its activities. Four regional groups were set up outside the Tokyo area, annual courses of lectures instituted, members' clubs organised for those interested in wild plants and kitchen gardens, and three subsidiary societies were formed: the Japan Hanging Basket Society, Japan Alpine Plants Study Group, and Container

increasing commercial presence in the major department stores and nurseries.[66]

Celebrations

The Society celebrated its centenary by moving into new offices and a new garden; a grand centenary banquet was planned, to be presided over by its Vice-President Joseph Chamberlain, but in the event was cancelled. The Sesquicentenary in 1954 proved to be a glorious event, with celebratory addresses, scrolls, and other testimonials presented to the Society by its coevals and juniors around the world; Fletcher devoted an entire chapter of his history to recounting the celebrations.[67]

The Osaka World's Fair of 1990: below, a view of the British Garden; left, the Emperor's visit.

Garden Society. The last-named was formed in response to new government directives enforcing the provision of roof gardens on apartment buildings, and was run by Kazuko Yahiro, the former editor of the *Japan Branch Journal*. Seed distribution from Wisley and annual tours to England (including the Chelsea Flower Show) provide links with the parent society. For the Japan Branch's tenth anniversary, Gordon Rae and the present author represented the RHS at the celebrations and provided a lecture tour; by that time it was apparent that 'English Gardening' was a popular fashion in Japan, with a thriving literature in books and magazines, and an

How to commemorate the bicentenary of a Society newly committed to extending its activities throughout the regions of the United Kingdom? The first serious effort was made in the 1980s, when Stephen Bennett, the Shows Director, contacted the Post Office to see whether a set of commemorative stamps could be commissioned for the occasion; the Post Office remarked that they seldom received requests so far in advance—and yet it was only at the beginning of 2003 that the commemorative issue was confirmed. Meanwhile a wide variety of activities was set in motion for different parts of

A crystal bowl presented to the RHS by the Royal Society of Arts, in honour of its sesquicentenary in 1954.

the country; in addition, various organisations came forward with largely self-funded proposals that would tie in with the horticultural theme, which the Society agreed to co-operate with.

A programme of events has been organised under the supervision of a Bicentenary Working Party of Council members and staff. RHS activities include activities for horticultural students and children, events at gardens across the UK, exhibits at gardening museums and permanent commemorations at RHS gardens; a lecture series on plant hunting at the Royal Geographical Society, a high-profile radio debate, Lily and Fruit Group conferences, and a 'science exchange' in association with the Natural History Museum. In addition, 2004 has been designated the 'Year of Gardening', and organisations across the country are undertaking their own activities with a gardening theme. With over 80 participants, these include exhibits at gardening museums and the Tate Britain 'Art of the Garden' exhibition. The British Tourist Authority (now renamed 'Visit Britain') is focusing on gardens and gardening as a major promotional initiative for tourism for 2004. A Bicentenary Plant Collection has been launched: a group of new cultivars (including daffodil, tulip, clematis, rose, orchid, malus, hybrid rhododendron), raised so as to be available for sale in 2004.

Not to mention, of course, this book.

Elizabeth R

E. Sartain

20 *On the Eve of a Third Century*

THE first Charter of the Horticultural Society defined its purpose as 'the Improvement of Horticulture in all its branches, ornamental as well as useful'. With slight modifications—'the art, science, and practice of horticulture'—this is still the Society's charitable purpose. Derived from this is the Mission Statement: 'To be the leading organisation demonstrating excellence in horticulture and promoting gardening.' Note the introduction of the word 'gardening' here: there are no agreed definitions that allow an unambiguous dividing line to be drawn between horticulture and gardening, and there is a substantial part of the public which sees 'horticulture' as merely an elitist word for 'gardening'. Those with closer contacts with commercial growing tend to see horticulture as embracing orchards and nurseries as well as gardens; and there is always, of course, the phenomenon of growing for exhibition purposes.

Yesterday all the past

By the end of its second century, the Society had grown from its small beginnings in Mr Hatchard's offices to a massive organisation with a third of a million members, and with staff in six different sites (four gardens; the London offices, with their two exhibition halls; and a publishing department based in Peterborough).

The RHS offers bursaries to students and young gardeners, and is occasionally able to grant-aid other organisations; nonetheless, while it is sometimes seen as a wealthy organisation, the list of projects it would like to undertake is always truncated by limitations on its financial means. The Society depends for the majority of its income on membership subscriptions and on the profits of its major flower shows (Chelsea, Hampton Court Palace, Tatton Park). The shows all require large expenditure on infrastructure, and are precariously dependent on uncontrol-

lable things like the weather; any downturn in the sales of tickets, and belts are tightened after the half-yearly financial review. Since the 1970s, in an effort to free itself from this uncertainty, the Society has plunged into the world of marketing, fundraising, sponsorship and commercial activity, but without yet finding a way of averting intermittent financial troubles—and at the cost of fears that its horticultural work is dominated by its business side.

The Society began with a minimal staff, sufficient only for record-keeping and the convening of meetings. The staffing level increased as soon as it acquired its first garden; to gardeners were eventually added scientists, as the Wisley Laboratory began programmes of research; but the administrative staff remained minimal until well into the 20th century. The Society originally saw itself as a forum for the collective expertise of the general gardening community, and its primary activities—meetings, publications, shows—were all means of bringing parts of that community together. As the Society's activities increased, with the judging and trial of plants, examinations first local and then national, and scientific research, this networking model was adapted to serve each new sector of activity, in the form of committees composed of eminent amateurs and professionals who gave their services voluntarily. As administrative functions became more complex, they too were handled by committees, who advised Council on policy, and instructed the relevant staff.

Increasingly, in the last quarter of the 20th century, the functions formerly assigned to administrative committees were taken over by departments, and the committees either disbanded or replaced by purely advisory bodies. Once, the Library Committee decided on all purchases as well as determining policy; in 1979 the Librarian was first given a purchasing budget to work within, and the Committee's terms of reference began to shift towards policy advice only. Over the next two decades, shows, publications, expeditions and bursaries, and garden administration followed suit, and the committees that had once made the practical decisions ceded those functions to increasingly autonomous departments or directorates within the staff structure.

The Society first acquired a garden in order to accommodate, propagate, and distribute plants that were sent to it. Before long the role of a garden was expanding into scientific research, on the one hand, and the training of gardeners on the other; to these purposes were added trials of plants in cultivation, in the later 19th century; practical demonstrations of gardening techniques, in the 20th; and national collections for conservation purposes, in the late 20th. Aesthetic purposes—the demonstration of ideas in garden design—have generally been accorded a lesser role, though at Kensington in the 1860s, and toward the close of the 20th century, issues of design and decoration have assumed a greater prominence.

Of the original purposes for having a garden, the distribution of plants continues as a regular activity, even though the RHS ceased to employ plant collectors directly before it was a century old. The training of gardeners continues through the Wisley School of Horticulture and the examinations system, subject though the latter has been to fluctuations in official recognition for technical education. In the mid-20th century, the RHS maintained a system of examinations directed at every level of expertise from the beginner to the teacher, though this structure was eroded in the second half of the century. As for scientific research, the Society has throughout its history been better at initiating research programmes than in sustaining them. It helped to pioneer both fertiliser research and genetics, but in each case the initiative passed to other organisations. In the middle of the 20th century, as government-funded research stations proliferated, the Society's scientific role was attenuated in order to concentrate on the provision of advisory services for its members; with the closure of so many research stations since 1980, scientific work has taken on a new significance, but continues to be 'near-market' research, concentrating on the specific gardening problems of the day. Horticultural taxonomy remains the most important of the RHS's research interests. The Society pioneered the taxonomic study of cultivated varieties, in the work of Sabine on bulbs and chrysanthemums in the 1820s, and carried this work through into the 20th century with the Code

of Nomenclature for Cultivated Plants, and the beginnings of cultivar registration.

The Society's career as a publisher began with a learned journal devoted to the printing of papers read at meetings. During the 20th century its journal moved inexorably in the direction of a mass-market publication with a more varied content, despite intermittent fears about the lowering of intellectual standards. To balance this trend, the Society has twice launched rescue operations for more academic journals threatened with closure—*Curtis's Botanical Magazine* in the 1920s, and the *Orchid Review* in the 1980s—as well as maintaining *The Plantsman* as a forum for the sort of monographic articles that once formed the principal content of its journal. Meanwhile, the RHS has built up a publishing programme, mostly in association with commercial publishers, that now targets every level of the gardening market, from the beginner to the professional, as well as making works like cultivar registers and the *Plant Finder* available on the Internet through the RHS website.

Tomorrow, perhaps the future

And what does the future hold? (Apart, of course, from the unexpected.)

The RHS is a scientific organisation. Horticultural taxonomy has been a primary focus of its existence for two centuries, and will undoubtedly continue to be so. It is now the International Registration Authority for more categories of cultivated plants than any other organisation, and will probably take on more in due course. Its scientists continue their research into the identification and control of garden pests and diseases—work that will increase in scope, as climatic change exposes the British garden flora to hitherto unfamiliar predators. The work of monitoring the effects of climate change in the garden, and of adapting our gardens to the increasing demand for the promotion of biodiversity, seems likely to provide a major research agenda for the foreseeable future. Environmentalism became a social and political force of considerable power in the late 20th century, but it is a movement riven with conflicts between competing ideologies. The Society's public image has fluctuated: on the one hand, it helped to pioneer the idea of biological control in the inter-war years, when it acted as the distribution agent for *Encarsia formosa*, but on the other hand it incurred strong criticism in the 1990s for its perceived slowness to discontinue the use of peat. In 2002 the RHS undertook an environmental audit of all its gardens, to ensure that its practices were as environmentally friendly as possible; but the rapid development of environmental issues in the 1980s and 1990s suggests that a stable assessment of ecological value has not yet been achieved, and that controversies will continue.

The RHS is an educational organisation. Progressively, since the 1960s, its programme of examinations has been eroded, as technical education in horticulture has been taken over by the universities. Nonetheless, the meagre emphasis placed on practical training in the existing academic qualifications means that the RHS examinations continue to play an important role, and one that may well be augmented. After the Second World War, the demography of professional gardening changed: the private garden, once the major source of employment for gardeners, dwindled and was replaced by the municipal parks and the government horticultural agencies. But cutbacks in government spending in the 1980s, with the closure of horticultural research stations and the introduction of compulsory competitive tendering in the parks, made deleterious inroads into employment prospects in the public sector. Meanwhile, the private sector was to an extent rejuvenated: there is nothing like a threat of extinction to spark public interest, and the post-war years saw a steadily increasing interest in the country house and its garden; the National Trust and English Heritage sponsored important garden restorations; a resurgent interest in old gardening techniques has been prompted in part by the organic gardening movement and the reaction against synthetic pesticides. (Within the world of the public parks, a similar phenomenon resulted in the revived popularity of 'craftsman horticulture': carpet bedding and municipal flower bedding.) And with the aid of television, head gardeners and park superintendents were receiving greater publicity at the beginning of the 21st century than at any time since the First World War. The relevance of the RHS educational programme, and of the Institute of Horticulture's activities, seems likely to increase, in the near future at least.

And, as a result of administering four gardens, with their infrastructure of restaurants, shops, and activities, the RHS now finds itself as a major participant in the British leisure industry. In 2003, visitor numbers to the four RHS gardens exceeded one million. In addition, its gardens and activities generate media attention, in both the press and television, and its exhibition halls provide an important forum for a wide range of non-horticultural events. On the one hand, its status in the leisure industry puts it in a good position for educational work, for demonstrating horticulture to the public, for disseminating information. On the other hand, it also provides much of the Society's income, and thus compels the Society to keep abreast of trends and fashions. The establishment of model gardens at Wisley, for example, can be seen as prefiguring the garden makeover programmes of the early 21st century, as can the development of competitive gardens at Chelsea and the other major shows.

The RHS began, and is still regarded, as a learned society. When the enrolment of the 50,000th member drew nigh in the 1950s, plans were drawn up for a celebration of the Society's status as the largest learned society in the world; in the event, the celebration was abandoned. In the succeeding years, the increasing size of the membership has been regarded with greater uncertainty: how large can a learned society become and still consider itself learned? Can one appeal to a mass audience without lowering intellectual standards? To this question there is no certain answer, though a formidable amount of inconclusive debate. The Society's policy was expressed by its former Treasurer, Lawrence Banks: the RHS is both elitist *and* populist. Whether it can maintain that delicate balance will be its crucial test as it enters its third century.

Appendices

Appendix 1: Presidents

1804-11	George Legge, 3rd Earl of Dartmouth
1811-38	Thomas Andrew Knight of Downton Castle
1838-58	William George Spencer Cavendish, 6th Duke of Devonshire
1858-61	Albert, the Prince Consort
1862-73	Walter Francis Montagu-Douglas-Scott, 5th Duke of Buccleuch
1873-75	William Coutts Keppel, Lord Bury, later 7th Earl of Albemarle
1875-85	Henry Austin Bruce, 1st Baron Aberdare
1885-1913	Sir Trevor Lawrence
1913-19	Francis Wallace Grenfell, 1st Baron Grenfell
1919-28	Amelius Richard Mark Lockwood, 1st Baron Lambourne
1928-31	George Walter Erskine Loder, later 1st Baron Wakehurst
1931-53	Henry Duncan McLaren, 2nd Baron Aberconway
1953-61	Sir David Bowes-Lyon
1961-84	Charles Melville McLaren, 3rd Baron Aberconway
1984-94	R.A.E. Herbert
1994-2001	Sir Simon Hornby
2001-	Sir Richard Carew Pole

Appendix 2: Secretaries

1804-5	Rev. Alexander Cleeve
1805-16	Richard Anthony Salisbury
1816-30	Joseph Sabine
1830-41	George Bentham
1841-45	Alexander Henderson
1845-50	James Robert Gowen
1850-51	Dr Daniel
1851-58	J. Forbes Royle
1858-62	John Lindley
1863-66	W. Wilson Saunders
1866-73	Henry Young Darracott Scott
1873-75	W.A. Lindsay
1875-84	Robert Hogg
1884-86	Major T. Mason
1886-88	William Lee
1888-1920	Rev. William Wilks
1920-25	W. R. Dykes
1925-46	Col F.R. Durham
1946-56	C.V.L. Lycett
1956-62	Arthur Simmonds
1962-75	John Hamer
1975-88	John Cowell
1989-2001	Donald Hearn

After Donald Hearn the functions he performed were divided into two separate posts.

Appendix 3: Treasurers

1804-06	John Wedgwood
1806-09	Charles Francis Greville
1809-29	John Elliot
1829-30	Robert Henry Jenkinson
1830-55	Alexander Seton
1835-48	Thomas Edgar
1848-50	Robert Hutton
1850-55	James Robert Gowen
1855	A.R. Jackson
1855-62	W. Wilson Saunders
1863-64	John Clutton
1865-66	John Kelk
1866-68	George Fergusson Wilson
1868-73	John Clutton
1874-75	Bonamy Dobrée
1875-81	Henry Webb
1882-88	William Haughton
1888-91	[Sir] Daniel Morris
1891-99	Philip Crowley
1899-1916	J. Gurney Fowler
1916-18	C.G.A. Nix
1918	Sir Harry Veitch
1919-21	C.G.A. Nix
1921-24	C.T. Musgrave
1924-28	Sir William Lawrence
1928-29	C.T. Musgrave
1929-32	R.D. Trotter
1932-33	C.T. Musgrave
1933-38	R.D. Trotter
1938-43	George Monro
1943-48	R.D. Trotter
1948-53	Sir David Bowes Lyon
1953-65	Lewis Palmer
1965-71	Oliver Wyatt
1971-81	Lord Blakenham
1981-92	W.L. Banks
1992-2002	Martin Slocock
2002-	P.N. Buckley

Appendix 4: Directors-General

1985-93	C.D. Brickell
1993-99	Gordon Rae
1999-	Andrew Colquhoun

Appendix 5: Wisley Directors

Note: Title changed to Director of Horticulture in 1990

1914-19	(Sir) Frederick Keeble
1919-31	Frederick J. Chittenden
1931-46	R. L. Harrow
1946-51	John S. L. Gilmour
1951-54	Harold R. Fletcher
1955-69	Frank P. Knight
1969-84	Christopher Brickell
1985-86	Peter A. Maudsley
1987-90	Philip Macmillan Browse
1990-95	W. J. Simpson
1995-2003	Joyce Stewart
2003-	David Gray

Appendix 6: Professors of Botany

1872-75	William Turner Thiselton-Dyer (1843-1928)
1880-1918	George Henslow (1835-1925)
1919-38	Alfred Barton Rendle (1865-1938)
1938-5 6`	Sir William Wright Smith (1871-1956)
1956-72	Sir Edward Salisbury (1886-1978)
1973-93	Sir George Taylor (1904-1993)

PROFESSORS OF HORTICULTURE

1995-2000	David Ingram
2000-	John McLeod

Appendix 7: Editors

1866-72	Miles J. Berkeley
1879	Samuel Jennings [Assistant Secretary]
1880	George Henslow [Professor of Botany]
1889-90	Daniel Morris [Treasurer]
1890-1905	William Wilks [Secretary], assisted by John Weathers [Assistant Secretary], 1891-6
1906-8	George S. Saunders
1908-39	Frederick J. Chittenden
1940-42	Daniel Hall, assisted by Roy Hay, 1940, and Vera Higgins, 1941-2
1943-5	Vera Higgins
1946-69	Patrick M. Synge
1970-89	Elspeth Napier
1989-93	Susanne Mitchell
1993-	Ian Hodgson

Appendix 8: Librarians

1872-75	W. T. Thiselton-Dyer
1875-78	William Botting Hemsley
1878-80	Samuel Jennings (Assistant Secretary)
1880-90	James West
1890-97	John Weathers (Assistant Secretary)
1897-31	H. R. Hutchinson
1931-39	F. J. Chittenden
1939-52	William T. Stearn
1953-56	Miss L. D. Whiteley
1957-82	Peter F. M. Stageman
1982-	Brent Elliott

Appendix 9: Plant Name Registrars

Register	Sequence of registrars	Publication dates	No. of cultivars listed
Conifers	Humphrey J. Welch; John Lewis; Piers Trehane	*International Conifer Register*, 4 parts to date (1987-98)	*c.*7,000
Clematis	Victoria Matthews	*International Clematis Register and Checklist* (2002)	*c.*2,500
Dahlia	David Pycraft; Alan Leslie (Ronald Hodge, Hon. Assistant Registrar)	*Tentative Classified List and International Register of Dahlia Names* (1969); annual supplements to date	*c.*20,000
Delphinium	John Cowell; Sheila Orr; Alan Leslie	*A Tentative Check-list of Delphinium Names* (1949); revisions and addenda (1956-70). Cumulative supplement, 1970-95; annual supplements published in *Delphiniums* (yearbook of the Delphinium Society)	*c.*4000
Dianthus	Mrs D. Stockwell; Alan Leslie	*International Dianthus Register* (1974; 2nd edition, 1983). Annual supplements to date.	*c.*30,000
Lilium	Gillian Peterson; James Platt; Alan Leslie	*International Lily Register* (1960; 2nd edition, 1969; 3rd edition, 1982). Annual supplements to date.	*c.*9,000
Narcissus	Arthur Simmonds; John Cowell; Kate Donald; Victoria Matthews; Sally Kington	*Classified List [& International Register] of Daffodil Names* (1907-69). Supplements to 1969 international register, to date; published in *Daffodil Year Book* until 1987, separately from 1988. *International Daffodil Checklist* (1989). *International Daffodil Register and Checklist* (1999).	*c.*25,500
Orchids	Jack Greatwood; Peter and Doreen Hunt; Julian Shaw and Hannah Griffiths	*Sander's List of Orchid Hybrids* (1947). Supplement 1946-60. Addenda 1961-70; 1971-75; 1976-80; 1981-85; 1986-90; 1991-5; 1996-8; 1999-2001.	*c.*115,000
Rhododendron	Harold Fletcher; R.E. Adams; David Pycraft; Alan Leslie	*International Rhododendron Register* (1958). Supplements to date; published in *Rhododendron Year Book* until 1987, separately from 1988. *Rhododendron Handbook*, 1947. Revised edition, part 1: Rhododendron species (1956, further revised 1963, 1967); part 2: Rhododendron hybrids (1957, further revised 1964, 1969). *Alphabetical Checklist of Rhododendron Species* (1981). *Rhododendron Handbook: Species in Cultivation* (1980). *Rhododendron Handbook* (1998).	*c.*27,000

Appendix 10: Table of Challenge Cups and Medals

Name of award	Date of founding or transfer to RHS	Presenter	Awarded for	Awarded when
A J Waley Medal	1946	Rhododendron Association; instituted by them 1937	To a working gardener who has helped the cultivation of rhododendrons	Annually
Affiliated Societies' Cup	1908	RHS	For a collection of fruit shown by an affiliated society	Competition
Alan Hardy Challenge Salver	2000	Rhododendron, Camellia and Magnolia Group	For exhibitor with highest points in Early Rhododendron Competition	Competition
Anthony Huxley Trophy	1994	RHS, to commemorate Anthony Huxley	For the best group exhibit of plants normally grown for decorative effect in a protected environment (judged by Floral C)	Annual
Blanchard Prize	1969/ 2000	Phyllis Blanchard, to commemorate Douglas Blanchard (1887-1968), daffodil breeder and exhibitor	For the competitor who obtains the most place-points in the Classes for Novices. Until 1999 a cash prize; since 2000 offered as a crystal trophy	Competition
Bowles Cup	1949	Lionel Richardson	For 3 stems of each of 15 daffodil cvs from at least 4 divisions (rules have changed 4 times since founding)	Competition at Daffodil Show
Cain Cup	1920	Sir Charles Nall-Cain (Lord Brocket)	1920-1939: best amateur exhibit at Chelsea; 1950-60: best exhibit of vegetables by an Armed Forces station at autumn Fruit & Vegetable Show. Discontinued 1960	Competition
Clay Challenge Cup	1913	Messrs Clay	For a rose newly introduced into commerce, with true rose scent. Discontinued 1948	Annual
Coronation Cup	1911	RHS, in honour of the coronation of George V	For best exhibit at Great Autumn Show. Not awarded after 1937	Competition
Crosfield Cup	1946	Rhododendron Association; presented to them by J.J. Crosfield	Usually for best exhibit of one truss of each of six rhododendron hybrids raised by exhibitor	Competition
David Trehane Camellia Cup	2000	Jennifer Trehane in memory of her father David C. Trehane (1909-2000)	For a person who has significantly promoted or increased knowledge of *Camellia*.	Annual
Devonshire Trophy	1958	Mary, Duchess of Devonshire	For best exhibit of 12 daffodil cvs. representing at least 3 divisions	Competition
E H Trophy	1961	Provided from a fund bequeathed in 1961 by W.J.M. Hawkey in memory of his grandmother (Mrs Elizabeth Hawkey), mother (Mrs Ellen Hawkey) and wife (Mrs Emma Hawkey)	1961-2001: Best exhibit in which dianthus features, judged by Floral A. 2002- : best display of cut flowers shown during the year	Annual
E J White Trophy	1992?	Dr J. White, in memory of his father, Mr E.J. White	For best dish of apples at autumn Fruit & Vegetable Show	Competition
Engleheart Cup	1913	RHS	For best exhibit of 1 stem of each of 12 daffodil cvs. raised by exhibitor	Competition
Farrer Trophy	1959	RHS	For the year's best exhibit of alpine plants	Annual
Foremarke Cup	1919	Sir Francis Burdett	1920-68: for 20 spikes of gladiolus cvs. in not less than 10 varieties; 1969-: for best exhibit of 1 spike each of 12 gladiolus cvs.	Competition
George Monro Memorial Cup	1921	George Monro & his brother, in memory of their father	1922-38: best exhibit of grapes by an amateur; 1950-70: best exhibit of vegetables by an amateur, or, from 1971, by an affiliated society	Competition

Name of award	Date of founding or transfer to RHS	Presenter	Awarded for	Awarded when
George Moore Medal	1926	George F. Moore	1926-68: to the exhibitor of the best new *Cypripedium / Paphiopedilum*; 1998- : to the exhibit of the best hybrid cv. of *Paphiopedilum*, *Selenipedium*, *Phragmipedium* or intergeneric hybrid between these genera	Annual
Gordon-Lennox Trophy (until 1995, the Gordon-Lennox Cup)	1913	Lady Algernon Gordon-Lennox	For the best exhibit of fruit by an amateur – 1917-49, at the autumn Fruit & Vegetable Show; 1950-71: during the year; 1972- : at a show other than Chelsea	Annual
Guy Wilson Memorial Vase	1982	RHS	For the best exhibit of 6 white daffodil cvs. (Divisions 1-3), three stems of each	Competition
Harlow Carr Medal	2003	Instituted **1990** for the Northern Horticultural Society	For those who have made a significant contribution to horticulture in the North of England	Annual
Holford Medal	1928	Executors of Sir George Holford	For the best amateur exhibit in the Halls	Annual
John Lea Trophy	1999	Daffodil and Tulip Committee, to commemorate John S.B.Lea (1911-1984), daffodil breeder and exhibitor	For 12 daffodil cultivars bred and raised by the exhibitor	Competition
Jones-Bateman Cup	1920	Miss L. Jones-Bateman, of Cae Glas, Abergele	For original research in fruit culture	Triennial
Lawrence Medal	1906	RHS, in honour of Sir Trevor Lawrence's 21 years as President	For exhibits of a generally meritorious character [best overall exhibit of the year]	Annual
Leonardslee Bowl	1965	Sir Giles Loder	Best exhibit of 1 bloom of each of 12 camellias	Competition
Lionel de Rothschild Cup	1946	Rhododendron Association	For the best exhibit of 1 truss of each of 8 rhododendron spp shown at main rhododendron competition	Competition
Loder Cup	1946	Rhododendron Association	For the best exhibit of 1 truss of a rhododendron hybrid shown at main rhododendron competition	Competition
Loder Rhododendron Cup	1921	Gerald Loder (Lord Wakehurst) in memory of his brother Sir Edmund Loder	For important work on rhododendrons	Annual
Lyttel Lily Cup	1939	Professor E. S. Lyttel	To someone who has done good work of some kind in connection with *Lilium*, *Nomocharis* or *Fritillaria*	Annual
McLaren Cup	1946	Rhododendron Association; presented to them by the Hon. Henry McLaren (2nd Lord Aberconway)	For the best exhibit of 1 truss of a rhododendron species shown at the main rhododendron competition	Competition
Mrs F E Rivis Prize	1960	From a fund presented by Miss A.K. Hincks in commemoration of her sister Mrs F.E. Rivis	To the gardener responsible for the cultivation of the Williams Memorial Medal exhibit	Annual
Peter Barr Memorial Cup	1912	Trustees of the Peter Barr Memorial Fund	To someone who has done good work of some kind in connection with *Narcissus*	Annual
Ralph B White Memorial Medal	1991	Ralph Bernard White bequest fund	For best new daffodil cv exhibited during the year	Annual

Name of award	Date of founding or transfer to RHS	Presenter	Awarded for	Awarded when
Reginald Cory Memorial Cup (originally Cory Cup for Dahlias; then Cory Cup 1923-34)	1914	Reginald Cory	1914-20: for dahlia exhibits. 1923-34: for the best hardy plant of garden origin; 1935-96: for a new hardy hybrid of garden origin; 1997- : to a raiser of important hybrids in a particular genus	Annual
RHS Award (formerly Witan Award)	1993	Witan Investment Trust	For year's best award by a new exhibitor	Annual
RHS Vegetable Cup	1910	RHS	For the exhibitor with the highest number of points for vegetable competitions in a year	Annual
Richardson Trophy	1976	RHS, in honour of Lionel Richardson	For the best exhibit of 12 cultivars of daffodils, divisions 1-4	Competition
Riddell Trophy for Vegetables	1931	Fund established by Lord Riddell	For a class in the Fruit & Vegetable show	Competition
Rosse Cup	1980	Anne Countess of Rosse in memory of the 6th Earl of Rosse	To the winner of Class 8 (Conifers shown for their foliage, 3 vases) at the autumn Ornamental Plant Competition	Competition
Rothschild Challenge Cup	1946	Rhododendron Association; presented to them by Lionel de Rothschild	1963-87: for the best exhibit by a trade grower at the Rhododendron Show. 1988- : for the year's best exhibit in which rhododendrons predominate	Annual
Roza Stevenson Cup	1972	Major-general E.G.W. Harrison in memory of his wife	For the best exhibit of one spray of a rhododendron species at the main rhododendron competition	Competition
Sander Medal	1923	Sander & Sons, in memory of H.F.C. Sander	To the exhibitor of the best new greenhouse plant of the year. Discontinued after 1958	Annual
Sewell Medal	1929	A.J. Sewell	For alpine plants (rules vary)	Annual
Sherwood Cup	1920	The Sherwood family, in memory of Nathaniel Norman Sherwood	1920-49: for the best exhibit at Chelsea; 1950-68: for a vegetable exhibit by an Armed Forces station. Discontinued after 1968	Annual
Sherwood Silver Cup	1898	Nathaniel Norman Sherwood	For Council to award as it wished. Discontinued after 1911	Annual
Simmonds Medal	1968	RHS, to commemorate Arthur Simmonds	For daffodil competitions	Competition
Stanley Lord Bowl	1998	Gardeners' Royal Benevolent Society, on loan from Worshipful Company of Gardeners	For the year's best exhibit of fruit	Annual
Stephenson R Clarke Cup	1978	R.N. Stephenson Clarke in memory of his grandfather Stephenson R. Clarke	To an exhibitor in the Tree & Shrub Competition; conditions alternate biennially	Competition
Walter Blom Trophy	1999	Daffodil and Tulip Committee	For the best vase of nine tulips	Competition
Westonbirt Orchid Medal	1960	Fund presented by H.G. Alexander to commemorate the Westonbirt orchid collection	To the exhibitor of the year's best orchid cultivar, most meritorious group of orchids staged in the Halls during the year, most finely grown specimen orchid, or for outstanding personal achievement connected with orchids	Annual
Wigan Cup	1911	A.L. Wigan	1912-37: for an exhibit of roses; 1963 -: for the year's best exhibit by a local authority	Annual
Williams Memorial Medal	1907	Founded by Williams Memorial Fund Committee 1896	For a group of plants showing excellence in cultivation	Annual

Notes

For abbreviations see p.418.

Preface

1. Murray (1863). William Wilks, *A Short Historical Sketch of the Royal Horticultural Society* (privately printed, 1890). Trevor Lawrence, 'The Royal Horticultural Society', *JRHS*, vol. 20 (1896), pp. 77-89. Arthur Simmonds, 'The history of the Royal Horticultural Society', ibid., vol. 79 (1954), pp. 457-88.

2. Council minutes, 7 November 1961; 1-15 September, 27 October 1964; 10-31 October 1967; 16 January 1968 (including Fletcher's letter dated 9 January); 6-20 February, 6 March 1968; 14 April 1970. Minutes of the History of the Society Committee, 1965. Both Fletcher's and Simmonds's typescripts are held in the RHS Archives.

3. Joseph Ewan, 'The Story of the Royal Horticultural Society. By Harold Fletcher', *JRHS*, vol. 94 (1969), pp. 107-15. Ewan's unanswered questions were: what were the five French books that were the first accessions to the Society's library? What lay behind the feud between R.A. Salisbury and Sir James Edward Smith, and behind George Don's break with the Society? Why did Mrs Marryat receive the pot of *Primula sinensis* in 1824? The last question was misconceived: the pot was a donation, not a competitive prize.

4. Glenny: *GardGaz*, 22 March 1848, p. 2 d; 29 March 1848, p. 2 c-d. Council minutes, 13 December 1853.

1 The Formation of a Horticultural Society, pp. 1-12

1. James Laver, *Hatchards of Piccadilly 1797-1947* (1947). In 1932 a memorial tablet was unveiled on the front of Hatchards' premises to commemorate the founding there of the RHS.

2. Minutes of the Horticultural Society, 1804-15. In this book both general meetings and Council meetings are recorded; the first proper Council minute book starts in 1809, with the granting of the Charter, and for some reason was discontinued in 1815 in favour of a new format of minute book that ran continuously until the 1920s and the arrival of typescript. There are trivial differences in wording between the minute book version, quoted here, and the subsequent printed version.

3. For the history of botanical societies up to Wedgwood's time, see A.T. Gage, *A History of the Linnean Society of London* (1938); Douglas McKie, 'Scientific societies to the end of the eighteenth century', in Allan Ferguson, ed., *Natural Philosophy through the 18th Century* (1972), pp. 133-43.

4. For the history of the agricultural societies, see Kenneth Hudson, *Patriotism with Profit: British Agricultural Societies in the Eighteenth and Nineteenth Centuries* (1972); Nicholas Goddard, 'The development and influence of agricultural periodicals and newspapers, 1780-1880', *Agricultural History Review*, vol. 31 (1983), pp. 116-31; Nicholas Goddard, 'Agricultural societies', in G.E. Mingay, ed., *The Victorian Countryside* (1981), vol. 1, pp. 245-59; J.A. Scott Watson, *The History of the Royal Agricultural Society of England 1839-1939* (1940). For the Society of Gardeners, see Henrey (1975), vol. 2, pp. 211-15.

5. Thomas Skip Dyot Bucknall, *The Orchardist* (1797), esp. pp. 64-6.

6. Minutes, 7 March-11 April 1804. Banks made a manuscript list of members suggested on 14 March which differs from those recorded in the minutes: Royal Society, MM 6.48.

7. Wedgwood's letters to Forsyth, 29 June 1801, and 8 March 1802.

8. For Knight's letter to Banks, and more on the background of the feud, see Mylechreest (1984); Simmonds (1941a), esp. pp. 322-3; Simmonds (1941b); Meynell (1979).

9. Minutes, 7 November-5 December 1804; 7 February 1809. Knight (1805). Knight's proposal was first published as a pamphlet in 1805; see the notice in the *British Critic*, vol. 25 (1805), p. 578.

10. Joseph Knight, *On the Cultivation of the Plants belonging to the Natural Order Proteæ* (1809), preface, pp. v-vi. Robert Brown, 'On the Proteaceae of Jussieu', *Trans. Linn. Soc.*, vol. 10 (1810), pp. 15-226. One of the Lindley Library's copies of Knight has been helpfully annotated with Brown's names in the margins. See Simmonds (1944a), esp. pp. 95-7; D.J. Mabberley, 'Generic names published in Salisbury's reviews of Robert Brown's works', *Taxon*, vol. 29 (1980), pp. 597-606; Mabberley (1985), pp. 144-56. According to Mabberley, it was alleged that Salisbury had attempted to further the education of an adolescent protégé of Smith's by fixing him up with an obliging girl, and that Smith's discovery and disapproval of the proposed training scheme was what had broken up the friendship. The controversy with Smith: see *Monthly Magazine*, vol. 23 (1807), p. 619; vol. 25 (1808), p. 91; Smith's reply, pp. 191-2; R.A. Salisbury, *A Letter to the Editor of the Monthly Magazine* (1808), esp. p. 6 for the jibe about Forsyth.

11. For Banks's horticultural accomplishments generally, and his relations with Knight, see Brent Elliott, 'The promotion of horticulture', in Banks (1994), pp. 117-31.

12. Minutes, 25 April 1804-2 January 1805. For Cleeve, see J. Steuart, 'The Rev. Alexander Cleeve, B.A., first Secretary of the Royal Horticultural Society', *JRHS*, vol.58 (1933), pp. 320-3.

13. Minutes, 5 February-8 April 1805; 4 March 1817; 15 December 1818-6 April 1819. Gage, *op. cit.*, pp. 24-26.

14. Council minutes, 4 April-20 June, 7 November 1815; 5 January, 6 February-16 April 1816. On the Cruikshank

cartoon, see Simmonds (1944b), and Fletcher (1969), pp. 107-12, essentially a reprint of Simmonds' discussion, to which nothing has so far been added in the way of new information.

2 From Crisis to Crisis, pp. 13-36

1. Council minutes: report of the committee on the expediency of establishing, means of obtaining and plan of conducting a Garden for the Society, January 1822.
2. Council minutes, 9-20 February 1822.
3. J.C. Loudon, *GM*, vol. 1 (1825), p. 56.
4. Babbage (1830), pp. 43, 48-9. On the Medico-Botanical Society, whose history has not properly been written, see also the *DNB* under John Frost; some of its archives survive in the Natural History Museum. See also *Horticultural Register*, vol. 1 (1831), pp. 171-7, for Joseph Paxton's proposal that the Horticultural, Zoological, and Medico-Botanical Societies should unite to set up one large national garden for their various purposes.
5. Christie: 15 December 1824-19 January 1825. Stolen seeds: 9 December 1828. Expense: 13 October 1824.
6. Jarrin case: *Morning Herald*, 18 November 1828, p. 2 f. Council Minutes, 21 August, 9-30 December 1828. 1829 fête: letter by 'An enemy of humbug', *Sunday Times*, 12 July 1829, p. 2 b.
7. *GM*, vol. 6 (1830), pp. 244-7.
8. *Ibid.*, p. 242.
9. 'Remarks on the constitution and administration of the London Horticultural Society. By a Fellow of the Society', *GM*, vol. 1 (1826), pp. 146-50, esp. p. 147.
10. Babbage (1830), p. 49.
11. Council minutes, 7 October-11 December 1826; 22 February-12 May 1827; 30 April 1828. *GM*, vol. 2 (1827) pp. 105-6.
12. Anon. (1829), esp. p. 4. On p. 3 the author identifies himself as the writer of a previous letter to Sir Humphry Davy on the conduct of the British Museum. I am convinced that the *Letter to Knight*, and the letters cited in the next note, were written by Bellenden Ker. Ker's name appears several times in Council minutes from 1827 on, trying to get access to those minutes, and making 'insinuations very much resembling charges'. He was a botanist of the old Linnaean persuasion, unconvinced of the worth of studying garden varieties; his main claim to the attention of posterity was a thin but lavish book of plates of Chinese plants, *Icones Plantarum sponte China Nascentium* (1821). For appearances of Bellenden Ker in Council minutes, see 18 June 1827; 1 March 1828; 20 June, 14 July, 29 August, 10 November 1829; 22 January 1830.
13. *Times*, 15 January 1830, p. 2 c [letter signed 'B.']. *GM* vol. 6 (1830), p. 114 [letter signed 'B.', and dated 14 January].
14. Council minutes, 22-27 January 1830. The full text of Knight's letter will be found in Fletcher, pp. 120-121.
15. Lindley's letter was published in *GM*, vol. 6 (1830), p. 240, and again in *CottGard*, vol. 15 (29 January 1856), p. 308.
16. *CottGard, ibid.*, pp. 307-9.
17. The proceedings of the committee were published in *GM*, vol. 6 (1830), pp. 235-252. Council minutes, 17 February-24 March 1830.
18. Babbage (1830), p. 43.
19. For Glenny's career, see Tjaden (1983); Tjaden (1986).
20. *GardGaz*, 26 May 1838, p. 328 (the plate); 14 July 1838, p. 440; 19 January 1839, p. 42; 23 March 1839, p. 184-5; 30 March 1839, p. 200; 6 April 1839, pp. 216-17; 20 April 1839, p. 249; 27 April 1839, p. 264; 11 May 1839, pp. 296, 297; 20 July 1839, p. 465 (trees—according to the anonymous letter, Lindley had to return two

trees after Loudon, who had referred to them in his *Arboretum*, objected).
21. The only historical study of the Royal Botanic Society so far is Meynell (1980). What remains of its archives are held by Westminster Libraries, and scattered between the Central (St Martin's Place) and Marylebone branches. Council minutes, 5 August 1845, for the fall in shows revenue.
22. In 1839 there was a peculiar incident in which a complaint was laid against Davis with the police, but later withdrawn; no documentation survives to establish the nature of the complaint, or the identity of the complainant.
23. Council minutes, 15-26 March 1832; 22 December 1845-21 April 1846; 6 July 1847-16 May 1848.
24. *Edinburgh Weekly Journal*, 26 January 1848, p. 2 d; 2 February 1848, p. 2 d; 15 March 1848, p. 2 e-i; 22 March 1848, p. 2 d; 29 March 1848, pp. 2 c-d, and 4a, 4d for the notices of closure. The history of the *Edinburgh Weekly Journal*, founded in 1798, has not been written properly; R.M.W. Cowan's *The Newspaper in Scotland* (1946) offers some material but is cursory about its declining years, and cannot even date its closure more certainly than '1847 or 1848' (p. 136). I have so far failed to find any gossip in the other Edinburgh papers for 1848 about their esteemed contemporary's closure. *GFA*, vol. 3 (1848), pp. 264-5, 315. *GC*, 11 March 1848, p. 174; 6 May 1848, p. 302.
25. The reporting of the special general meeting of 7 March 1839, called to elect a Council member to replace a deceased one, gives some insight into Glenny's journalistic methods. Glenny (*GardGaz*, 15 March 1848, p.2 g) reported ('we happened to have a reporter present') that an unnamed member stood at the meeting and demanded an inquiry, threatening legal action; in another column (2 e), writing under his own name, he used that unnamed member as the authority for his allegations about the prosecution of the embezzling boy. In *GFA*, *op.cit.*, however, the member who stood up and spoke is specifically named as Glenny himself.
26. Proposed Associate status: 12 March, 16 April 1850; 19 December 1854; 13 February, 13 March 1855. Two-guinea Fellows: 1 July 1856.
27. Council minutes, 11 February, 30 October 1851. Annual Reports of the National Floricultural Society, 1851-1858.
28. *CottGard*, vol. 15 (16 October 1856), p. 31.
29. See, e.g., Donald Beaton in *CottGard*, vol. 22 (24 May 1859), pp. 101-4.
30. Council minutes, 1 August, 24 October, 19 December 1854; 17 April, 31 July, 17 August 1855.
31. Council minutes, 17 July 1855.
32. *CottGard*, vol. 15 (16 October 1855), p. 31.
33. Council minutes, 14 March 1856. At that time there were 149 Life Fellows who had paid a combined total of £4,956 more than twenty years before, 106 who had paid a total of £3,960 within the past twenty years, and 250, the big spenders, who had paid a total of £8,916. Assuming that a reduction in refund could be claimed for each year of allowed usage of the garden, calculate the likely total the Society would have had to pay back.
34. Council minutes, 15 April 1856.
35. Tjaden (1987).
36. For the history of the Royal Commissioners and their dealings with the Society, see their *Annual Reports*; Hobhouse (2002), esp. pp. 113-140, 169-175, 178-182.
37. Council minutes, 8 March, 19 June, 24 July, 17 August 1860, 4 January 1861. *GC*, 5 May 1860, pp. 410-11; 16 February 1861, p. 144; 23 March 1861, pp. 264-5.
38. Council minutes, 17 January-7 February 1862.
39. Council minutes, 29 October, 15 November 1861.

40. Council minutes, 19 December 1862. The salaried staff consisted of ten people apart from gatekeepers: Assistant Secretary, three clerks, Garden Superintendent, Accountant, Bookkeeper, Housekeeper and assistant, and Messenger.
41. *JHort*, 23 June 1863, p. 455; response in Council minutes, 24 July 1863.
42. *JHort*, 23 February 1864, pp. 147-8.
43. Council minutes, 20 August 1861; 19 February 1864.
44. Council minutes, 16 February 1870.
45. Council minutes, 3-25 July 1866. Fletcher gives 1871 as the date Eyles left the Society's service, but see Council minutes, 7 January 1875, for his plea to be allowed to continue working without salary on condition that he kept his house—which Council allowed until the next Lady Day.
46. *GC*, 8 February 1873, p. 180. *Times*, 28 March 1873 p. 8 c. The former Director of the Bank of England was John Gellibrand Hubbard.
47. The transcripts of the AGM and its follow-on meetings were published in *GC*, 15 February 1873, pp. 219-21 (AGM, 11 February); 22 February 1873, pp. 258-60 (adjourned AGM, 18 February); 29 March 1873, pp. 437-40 (Special General Meeting, 26 March); and 12 April 1873, pp. 509-12 (Adjourned SGM, 6 April); the exchange quoted is on p. 438.
48. Council minutes, 21 November, 23 December 1873; 8 January, 17 February 1874. *GC*, 22 November 1873, p. 1564 for Cooper's circular (with whose composition it was alleged Wilson had had much to do); 29 November, pp. 1595-6 for W.A. Lindsay's reply; and 13 December, p. 1638 for the remarks of another signatory, John Denny.
49. Wilson (1874). This pamphlet consisted of correspondence reprinted from the *Gardeners' Chronicle* and *The Garden*, as well as some unpublished letters Wilson had received. See also 7 February 1874, p. 183, for a review of Wilson.
50. *GC*, 12 June 1875, p. 762.
51. *GC*, 13 June 1874, pp. 766, 769. Council minutes, 5 November 1867; 5-12 May, 16 June 1874.
52. *GC*, 8 May 1875, p. 596.
53. *GC*, 19 June 1875, p. 788. The transcripts of the AGM and its follow-on meetings were published in 13 February 1875, pp. 211-13 (AGM, 9 February); 13 March 1875, pp. 342-6 (adjourned AGM, 9 March); 29 May 1875, pp. 695-7 (Special General Meeting, 25 May); and 12 June 1875, pp. 761-4 (adjourned SGM, 4 June). See also *GardMag*, 19 June 1875, p. 307: 'Resign, resign. – It used to be considered an axiom that an English gentleman's word was his bond. Is it due to the atmosphere of South Kensington that a sudden deviation from this good old English principle has sprung up? Surely, if there is anything so demoralizing in the locality that even our nobility cannot withstand its influence, would it not be well for us horticulturists to get out of it?'
54. *GC*, 26 June 1875, p. 820.
55. Council minutes, 3 November 1875.
56. For a taste of the fury lavished on, and complications attending, the proxy question, see *GC*, 3 January 1874, p. 24; 10 January, pp. 57-8; 17 January, pp. 84-5, 89-90; 24 January, p. 121; 31 January, p. 154; 21 February, p. 251; 7 March, p. 311; 18 April, pp. 502-3, 509; 25 April, p. 541. Miscellaneous debates over privileges and transferability: Council minutes, 17 June 1864; 19 May-2 June 1874; 27 October 1875; 13 January, 15 March 1876; 18 November 1879.
57. Council minutes, 12 April, 25 May 1876. George Fergusson Wilson first publicly drew attention to the chicanery in a letter in *GC*, 13 December 1873, p. 1674; whether because of lack of solid evidence then, or simply because other issues overwhelmed the

discussion, it did not become a subject for public indignation until the 1877 AGM.
58. Council minutes, 6 December 1876. Tjaden (1974), pp. 3-4.
59. *Daily News,* 26 January 1877, p. 5 d. *GC,* 6 January 1877, pp. 21-22 (Glendinning); 10 February 1877, p. 176 (leader); 17 February 1877, p. 214 (Dyer).
60. Wilson was a prolific contributor to *GC* about this time: see 6 January 1877, p. 21; 10 February, pp. 179-80; 17 March, pp. 343-4; and 3 February, pp. 149-50, for D.T. Fish's response to his suggestion for a new society.
61. *GC*, 17 February 1877, pp. 210, 216-19. See also Mark Doughty, 'A letter to Robert Hogg, Esqr.', *The Garden (JRHS)*, vol. 110 (1985), pp. 488-9.
62. Council minutes, 6 March-8 April, 10 June, 28 October 1879; 27 March, 10 December 1882; 12 February 1883.
63. *GC*, 4 February 1888, pp. 138-9.
64. Ibid., pp. 150-1. As W.H. Divers, the head gardener of Belvoir Castle, said, 'If the Society does not recover from its difficulties it will not be from want of advice'—*ibid.*, 18 February 1888, pp. 213-14.
65. *JHort*, 1 May 1890, pp. 353-4; 29 May 1890, p. 435; 12 June 1890, p. 483; 19 June 1890, pp. 499-500.
66. For the new Charter, see *JRHS*, vol. 28 (1903-04), pp. 181-2.
67. Council minutes, 9 April-26 November 1895, passim. *GC*, 3 August 1895, p. 138; 10 August 1895, pp. 161-2; 24 August 1895, p. 214; 31 August 1895, pp. 244, 246-7; 7 September 1895, p. 270; 14 September 1895, p. 304; 21 September 1895, pp. 335, 337; 28 September 1895, pp. 371-2; 5 October 1895, p. 400; 25 April 1896, p. 524 for the presentation of the testimonial. For Barron's obituary, see *JRHS*, vol. 28 (1903-04), pp. 181-2.
68. *JRHS*, vol. 25 (1900-01), p. viii. *GC*, 3 March 1900, p. 136; 10 March 1900, p. 152.
69. Council minutes, 8 April 1902, 4 August-27 October 1903.

3 The Twentieth Century, pp. 37-58

1. Council minutes, 6 March, 1 May, 12 June, 25 September 1906.
2. Council minutes, 12 June 1906 (Fruit Commissioner); 6 December 1910 (first research grant); 10 September, 5-19 November 1912 (Chamber of Horticulture, proposed Parliamentary Committee).
3. Council minutes, 21 January-1 April 1913. 'The late Sir Trevor Lawrence', *JRHS*, vol. 39 (1913-14), pp. 513-22.
4. Council minutes, 8-22 September 1914 (enlistments and wages contributions); 26 October 1915 (total enlisted); 22 February, 29 August 1916, 14 August 1917 (exemptions); 13 February 1917 (disinclination to register staff for National Service); 2 February, 20 November 1917 (women weeders); 29 April 1919 (war allowances).
5. For Lockwood, see *Punch*, 15 July 1908, p. 49.
6. Council minutes, 6 October, 1 December 1914 (foreign advertisements); 20 October, 3 November 1914 (German spraying equipment, which turned out to be manufactured in Birmingham); 7 January 1919, 27 April 1920 (demands for expulsion of aliens); 5 January 1915 (proposed renaming of plants).
7. Council minutes, 11 January, 22 February, 28 March 1916, Wheldon & Wesley website (Loewe); 2 May 1917, 26 August 1919 (Ingwersen). The biographical notices of Ingwersen do not mention that during his years at Wisley he was officially under internment. It is not documented who arranged for his parole, but Paul Ingwersen informs me that family tradition points to Reginald Malby and Walter Irving; also that he is credited with creating a rock garden in 1915 at the internment camp at Knockaloe on the Isle of Man.

8. Council minutes, 11 August, 3 November 1914; 2-16 February, 2, 30 March 1915, and thereafter *passim* until the end of the War; 20 November 1917, for a notice of 9,000 fruit trees being sent to the Somme; 29 June 1920 for Veitch's decoration; *Times,* 5 April 1920, p. 3b, for the French mayors' thanks. For the fund-raising pony, see *GC*, 22 May 1915, p. 282.

9. Ruhleben: 10 October 1916; 13 March, 3 July, 4 December 1917. See also Elliott (1988).

10. See note 5 to chapter 8 for references. The final compensation figure was £9,694 14s. 4d., with 50 guineas awarded for costs. The turning point over compensation was a suit by De Keyser hotels, which was referred to the House of Lords: see *Times*, 11 May 1920, p. 6 a-d.

11. Council minutes, 31 August, 28 September, 26 October 1915 (Board of Agriculture grant); 1 August, 26 September 1916; 11 September 1917.

12. *GC*, 31 July 1915, p. 66; 7 August 1915, p. 89; 18 September 1915, pp. 185-6. Council minutes, 11-17 August 1915; 30 January 1917. For Lee's letter, see *GC*, 15 December 1917, p. 240; and for the consequences, Council minutes, 20 November, 15 December 1917, 18 January 1918. *Daily Mirror*, 25 February 1918, pp. 1, 2, 6, and thereafter *passim*; Council minutes, 26 February-26 March 1918.

13. Council minutes, 13 February 1917. For the fate of the Chatsworth Stove, see *GC*, 6 March 1920, p. 119, and Francis Thompson, *Chatsworth: a Short History* (1951), pp. 115-16.

14. Exemption for nursery staff: Council minutes, 28 May, 18 June, 13 August 1918. The Japanese bulb affair: 3-31 July 1917.

15. Council minutes, 24 October, 21 November 1916; 6 November 1917 (Albert Rollitt was the one dissenting vote on Council).

16. For the progress of Keeble's resignation, see Council minutes, 28 January, 8 April-13 May, 15 July 1919.

17. Council minutes, 28 June-11 July, 31 October, 28 November, 12 December 1922; 16 January 1923.

18. Council minutes, 12 March, 9 April 1918 (Woburn Fruit Farm). The other proposed garden acquisitions will be discussed in more detail in chapter 14.

19. Council minutes, 7 October 1919 (northern branch); 8 August, 27 November 1923; 29 January 1924 (Royal Botanic Society). The Royal Botanic Society folded in 1930, and its garden was taken over by the Ministry of Works, to be partly turned by Duncan Campbell into Queen Mary's Rose Garden.

20. Council minutes, 7 June 1921: the first typewritten minutes.

21. Council minutes, 1 August, 10 October 1916; 11 April 1917; 4 November 1919; 23 February 1926.

22. For the Utilisation of Vacant Land report, see *Times*, 28 November 1916, p. 8 e, and 30 November, p. 10 d. Council minutes, 5 December 1916; 4 December 1917. *GC*, 15 March 1919, p. 128, for the end of the wartime allotment provision.

23. For Aberconway's letter, see Council minutes, 1 November 1932, and *Times*, 11 November 1932, p. 10 c. Council minutes, 8 January 1935 for a note on the sinking fund.

24. Council minutes, 8 March 1932.

25. Council minutes, 27 September 1938; 4 July-12 September 1939.

26. For staff enlistment and substitutions, see Council minutes, 12-26 September 1939; 16 April, 21 May, 4 June 1940. The Lilacs was made ready for the billeting of children evacuated from London (16 July 1940), but not required.

27. Cropping for Carter *et al.*: Council minutes, 9 December 1942; 4 January 1944. From 15 February 1944 it was decided to restrict retail sales of fruit and vegetables from Wisley to Fellows and customers of long standing. Lend-Lease: 13 April, 18 May, 8 June 1943; 25 July 1944 ('visitors were struck with the first class cultivation of the trials'); 29 May 1945.

28. Women gardeners: Council minutes, 20 May, 17 June 1941; 14 April, 19 May, 16 June 1942; 4 January 1944; 20 February 1945. Swanley: 21 March, 16 May 1944; 29 May 1945.

29. Council minutes, 22 April, 20 May 1941; 6 January, 13 July 1942; 25 July 1944. *JRHS*, vol. 65 (1940), pp. 275-7; vol. 69 (1944), pp. 296-7. Don Lamberth, later Examinations Officer but then a junior office staff member, remembers arriving in the Pacific for military service and finding that he had been seconded to help stage a fundraising flower show in Australia.

30. Council minutes, 12 September 1939; 30 January 1940.

31. Council minutes, 12-26 September 1939; 30 January, 19 March 1940; 25 March 1941. For fuel rationing and the Non-edible Plants (Fuel) Committee, see *ibid.*, 19 May, 16 June, 15 September-9 December 1942; 5 January-16 February 1943, and thereafter *passim* until 1949. Minutes of the Non-edible Plants (Fuel) Committee, passim.

32. Council minutes, 16 March 1943; 4 January 1944.

33. For the arrival of vandalism in municipal parks during the war, and the fears of parks superintendents for the future of ornamental horticulture, see Brent Elliott, 'Bedding schemes', in Woudstra (2000), p. 117, and the articles cited in footnotes 21-23.

34. See Hay (1946), for an expression of these hopes.

35. Council minutes, 14 January 1947; 13 June, 12 September 1950.

36. Council minutes, 13 December 1949; 18 April 1950; 30 October 1956; 27 October 1964; 8-22 March 1966.

37. Simmonds: remark reported by Peter Stageman. *Home Grown*: Council minutes, 1 December 1953; 19 October 1954.

38. Council minutes, 10 January 1956.

39. The Charities Act (1960) imposed a requirement for the official registration of charities; before that, charitable status was rather informally recognised. The Lindley Library was not registered as a charity until 1995.

40. Aberconway's remark re handing over cash: AGM report 1978, p. iii. Examples of misuse of FRHS: Council minutes, 14 March, 24 October 1899; 28 January 1902; 16 April 1912; 24 March-21 April 1914; 23 February-7 April 1926; and many more too long.

41. Council minutes, 26 March 1946 (Northern Horticultural Society); 29 March 1949 (proposed Midland Horticultural Society); 31 January 1950 (proposed national Scottish horticultural society, and 'Scottish Wisley').

42. Fletcher (1969), p. 437.

43. Council minutes, 2 February-4 May 1971 *passim* (Wyatt's cutbacks); 26 September-5 December 1972; 3 April, 7 August 1973; 10 June 1975; 29 March 1977; 16 February, 21 March, 3 May, 8 August 1978; 10 January 1979 (VAT). Lord Aberconway, 'Donations, covenants and legacies', *JRHS*, vol. 97 (1972), pp. 511-12.

44. The first royalty-yielding agreement was with John Pinches, on a set of flower spoons; then came Franklin Mint with flower plates, vases, and first-day covers.

45. Secret planning: the question of selling the Hall was first discussed on 8 October 1974; on 28 October 1975 it was decided that the staff could finally be told about the discussions.

46. For the levy, see annual reports and AGM reports, 1982-3.

47. Geoff Hamilton, 'When will the RHS cater for us all?', *Garden News*, 23 October 1982, p. 24; 'Now it's

down to you!', 13 November 1982, p. 24; 'It's time to branch out', 18 December 1982, p. 20. I have not obeyed the *Garden News* paragraphing style in the quotations. See also *Amateur Gardening*, 27 March 1982, p. 18, for a letter and comment on the compulsory levy, emphasising that 'Members were not given the chance to vote'.

48. *Sunday Telegraph*, 17 February 1980, p. 6 d-e (Mandrake column, under the heading 'Everything in the garden ...') For announcements and reflections on Lord Aberconway's announced retirement, see *GC&HTJ*, 18 February 1983, pp. 3-4; *Garden News*, 19 February 1983, p. 26; 'Atticus', *Sunday Times*, 22 May 1983, p. 35 (referring to Lord Aberconway as an 'old autocrat', a remark which prompted a complaint from Council). *The Garden* (*JRHS*), vol. 108 (1983), AGM report, p. iv; Roderick Cameron, 'Suggestions for future policy', pp. 452-3; 'Council's comments on Mr Cameron's suggestions', pp. 498-9; vol. 109 (1984), AGM report, pp. ii-iii, vii, xi-xiv.

49. *Report of the Review Committee on the Royal Horticultural Society* 1985. The Committee was chaired by Viscount Ridley, of Blagdon Hall in Northumberland. The other members were Bonham Bazeley of Highfield Nurseries (later the author of *Growing Tree Fruits*); Stanley Downs, the former Head of Horticulture at the Hertfordshire College of Agriculture and Horticulture; Richard Eddis, senior partner in the Society's solicitors, Stephenson Harwood; Ronald Keay, the retiring Executive Secretary of the Royal Society, who had spent much of his career as Director of Forestry in Nigeria; Mary Newnes (later Shirville) of the National Association of Flower Arrangement Societies; and Joyce Stewart, the Sainsbury Orchid Fellow at the Royal Botanic Gardens, Kew. AGM 1986 report, pp. iii-v. *HW*, 10 January 1986, pp. 3, 16; 13 June 1986, p. 5.

50. Council minutes, 8 August 1967.

51. The six types of membership: ordinary membership at either a £14 or a £24 rate for single or double tickets; life members (the life membership scheme had been discontinued in 1972, but its existing beneficiaries' privileges were continued); some 100 junior members, at a £5 rate; nearly 7,000 pensioner members at single- or double-ticket rates; 12 honorary memberships conferred by Council; and some 2,000 affiliated societies, at a £24 rate.

52. *JRHS*, vol. 93 (1968), p. 148.

53. For Christopher Brickell, see *The Garden* (*JRHS*), vol. 116 (1991), pp. 457-8.

54. Council minutes, 10 July 1973; 29 January-19 February, 9 July, 19 November 1974; 7-28 January, 11 March, 15 April, 8 July-2 September, 7-28 October 1975; 4 May, 9 December 1976; 12 January—10 February 1977. RHS Enterprises was incorporated on 8 May 1975; the articles of association were signed by Blakenham and Hamer. *The Garden* (*JRHS*), vol. 103 (1978), pp. 249-51; vol. 116 (1991), p. 508. For a look back at 25 years of RHS Enterprises, see *Grassroots*, no. 84 (March/April 2001), p. 3.

55. Council minutes, 24 September 1974.

56. Donald Hearn, 'So much has changed', *Grassroots*, no. 87 (Sept/Oct 2001), p. 1. Lawrence Banks, 'Laying a good foundation', *The Garden* (*JRHS*), vol. 116 (1991), pp. 631-2.

57. For Gordon Rae, see *The Garden* (*JRHS*), vol. 118 (1993), p. 277; *HW*, 7 April 1994, pp. 28-9. For Simon Hornby, see Fred Whitsey, 'Presiding over growth', vol. 126 (2001), pp. 768-771.

58. For the Millennium application, see 'Sir Simon Hornby on new plans for Wisley', *CL*, 1 June 1995, p. 99; *Grassroots*, no. 28 (June 1995), pp. 4-5. See references in chapter 9 for the Library controversy.

59. For Sir Richard Carew Pole, see *Grassroots*, no. 87 (Sept/Oct 2001), p. 1; *English Garden*, August 2001, pp. 76-7; *Gardens Illustrated*, November 2001, p. 44.

60. For the development of the strategic plan, see Gordon Rae, 'Vision of excellence', *The Garden* (*JRHS*), vol. 124 (1999), pp. 82-5; and Andrew Colquhoun, 'Aiming high', vol. 126 (2001), pp. 922-3. The plan underwen t some modifications between the two Directors-General. In Gordon Rae's version, the charitable object was entitled the Mission Statement, and Colquhoun's Mission Statement was Rae's Vision Statement. Rae explained the internal dynamics of these various statements in an interview: 'So we have a Mission Statement, which is timeless and permanent; a Vision Statement, which sets out our objectives for a 10-15-year period; a Five-Year Plan, which sets out our intentions in greater detail; and within that Five-Year Plan, the first year is the budget, and the second and third years are the forecasts.'—'Interview with Director-General about the strategic plan', *Grassroots*, no. 64 (July 1998), p. 1.

4 The Society's Gardens: Chiswick and Kensington, pp. 59-76

1. Council minutes, 16 April 1816.

2. Council minutes, 17 May 1814 (Kirke); 20 January 1818.

3. Council minutes, 17 February-5 March 1818. *Survey of London*, vol. 42: *South Kensington: Kensington Square to Earl's Court* (1986), p. 262.

4. Council minutes, 2 June 1818.

5. Council minutes, 29 April, 15 September 1818; 19 December 1821 (Sutton); 22 September-3 November 1819 (plan).

6. Report of the Committee appointed to report on ... Chiswick, January 1822. Council minutes, 8 March 1820; 28 February-15 June 1821.

7. Council minutes, 20 July, 9 October 1822. A map in the Kensington Public Library of the Edwardes Square area, made (presumably late) in 1822, already fails to show the site as a distinct entity.

8. Report of the Committee appointed to report on ... Chiswick, January 1822.

9. *JHort*, 6 June 1895, pp. 500-1.

10. For Kew, see Desmond (1995), pp. 127-143. Cambridge: S.M. Walters, *The Shaping of Cambridge Botany* (1981), pp. 40-55. Oxford: see R.T. Gunther, *Oxford Gardens* (1912), pp. 22-6, and Mavis Batey, *Oxford Gardens* (1982), pp. 141-7. Edinburgh: see Fletcher (1970), pp. 104-111; and pp. 138-48 for the Royal Caledonian Horticultural Society. Hull: see *GardGaz*, p. 58, for a letter of complaint about Hull Botanic Garden ('or nursery—I scarce know which to call it') 26 January 1839. Woburn Abbey: the works were *Hortus Gramineus Woburnensis* (1816, 1824, 1826 editions), *Hortus Ericaeus Woburnensis* (1825), both by George Sinclair, and *Salictum Woburnense* (1829), *Hortus Woburnensis* (1833), and *Pinetum Woburnense* (1839), all by James Forbes. On the state of the parks, see *GC*, 15 September 1866, pp. 879-80; for the arrival of flower gardening in parks, see Elliott (1986), pp. 134-5. See also Altick (1978), pp. 317-31, on zoos and pleasure gardens generally, with additional material on Vauxhall (pp. 94-6), the Surrey Zoo (486-9), and Ranelagh (p. 96).

11. Handwriting of under gardeners and labourers book. Council minutes, 24 March 1825; 22 April 1826. On Paxton's career, see Chadwick (1961); for his reputation, see *CottGard*, vol. 8(1852), pp. 334-5.

12. Report of the Garden Committee (1825), pp. 5-6; Council minutes, 15 December 1824.

13. There is an extensive magazine literature on Chiswick throughout its career. *GM*, vols. 1 (1825), pp. 87-88, 213-6, 314-5, 344-5; 2 (1827), pp. 105-6, 359-60, 469;

3 (1828), pp. 485-6; 4 (1828), pp. 168-9; 5 (1829), pp. 343-8, 380; 6 (1830), pp. 248-52, 506-7, 730-1; 7 (1831), pp. 251-3, 687; 8 (1832), pp. 471-2; 9 (1833), pp. 234-5, 471-3; 11 (1835), p. 251; 15 (1839), pp. 145-7, 348-52; 16 (1840), pp. 591-2. *BR*, vol. 25 (1839), Miscellaneous notices, pp. 17-18. *FM*, vol. 5 (1840) pp. 155-6; vol. 6 (1842), pp. 197-8. *GC*, 6 February 1841, p. 87; 13 March 1841, p. 167; 17 April 1841, p. 247; 2 October 1841, p. 647; 27 November 1841, pp. 783-4; 9 April 1842, pp. 239-40; 30 July 1842, p. 512; 24 September 1842, p. 640; 25 March 1843, p. 191; 19 August 1843, p. 575; 6 June 1846, p. 371; 22 March 1847, p. 207; 29 May 1847, p. 359; 31 July 1847, pp. 507, 511; 7 August 1847, p. 525; 25 December 1847, p. 852; 1 January 1848, pp. 7-8; 10 June 1848, pp. 383-4; 19 August 1848, pp. 559-60; 14 October 1848, p. 687; 16 December 1848, p. 847; 17 March 1849, p. 167; 9 June 1849, p. 359; 20 October 1849, p. 663; 16 March 1850, p. 167; 18 January 1851, p. 39; 26 April 1851, p. 263; 7 June 1851, p. 359; 21 February 1852, p. 119; 3 April 1852, pp. 214-5; 1 May 1852, pp. 278-9; 5 June 1852, pp. 358-9; 3 July 1852, pp. 422-3; 31 July 1852, pp. 486-7; 4 September 1852, p. 567; 2 October 1852, pp. 630-1; 30 October 1852, p. 695; 4 December 1852, pp. 774-5; 1 January 1853, p. 7; 5 February 1853, p. 87; 5 March 1853, p. 151; 2 April 1853, p. 215; 30 April 1853, p. 279; 4 June 1853, pp. 358-9; 2 July 1853, p. 423; 30 July 1853, p. 487; 3 September 1853, pp. 566-7; 1 October 1853, p. 631; 5 November 1853, pp. 710-11; 3 December 1853, p. 775; 31 December 1853, p. 839; 4 February 1854, p. 71; 4 March 1854, p. 135; 1 April 1854, p. 199; 1 May 1854, p. 287; 3 June 1854, p. 359; 1 July 1854, p. 423; 5 August 1854, pp. 499-500, 503; 9 September 1854, p. 582; 7 October 1854, p. 647; 4 November 1854, p. 711; 2 December 1854, pp. 775-6; 3 February 1855, pp. 71-2; 31 March 1855, p. 207; 5 May 1855, pp. 303-4; 2 June 1855, p. 375; 30 June 1855, p. 439; 4 August 1855, pp. 519-20; 8 September 1855, p. 599; 15 September 1855, pp. 611-12; 19 April 1856, p. 263; 14 June 1856, pp. 403-4; 23 August 1856, pp. 567-8; 21 March 1857, pp. 195-6; 25 April 1857, pp. 291-2; 1 August 1857, p. 535; 22 May 1858, pp. 423-4; 28 August 1858, pp. 655-6; 9 October 1858, p. 758 [advertisement]; 10 September 1859, pp. 743-4; 30 August 1862, pp. 809-10; 20 June 1863, pp. 583-4; 19 March 1864, pp. 267-8; 3 September 1864, p. 845; 8 October 1864, p. 967; 8 July 1865, p. 628; 21 September 1867, p. 976; 15 August 1868, p. 873; 22 August 1868, p. 898; 12 February 1870, p. 209; 19 February 1870, p. 247; 26 February 1870, p. 280; 5 March 1870, p. 313; 2 April 1870, p. 456; 7 May 1870, pp. 628-9; 14 May 1870, p. 663; 6 August 1870, p. 1054; 13 August 1870, pp. 1086-7; 27 August 1870, p. 1155; 3 September 1870, pp. 1182-3; 28 January 1871, p. 102; 2 September 1871, pp. 1129-30; 3 September 1871, p. 1360; 24 August 1872, p. 1130; 29 April 1876, p. 558; 1 July 1876, p. 15; 12 August 1876, p. 202; 30 September 1876, p. 425; 4 August 1877, pp. 133-4; 27 April 1878, p. 529; 22 March 1879, p. 375; 5 July 1879, p. 18; 18 October 1879, pp. 498, 499; 23 December 1882, pp. 816-17; 7 July 1883, p. 16; 6 October 1879, pp. 423-6; 1 May 1886, pp. 561-2; 11 June 1887, p. 770; 18 June 1887, pp. 806-9; 25 June 1887, p. 839; 30 June 1888, pp. 804-5; 10 November 1888, pp. 536-8, 540; 17 November 1888, pp. 574-5; 24 November 1888, pp. 606, 607-8; 19 January 1889, pp. 75-6; 8 June 1889, p. 723; 15 June 1889, p. 752; 19 July 1890, p. 80; 9 August 1890, p. 166; 23 August 1890, pp. 215-6; 18 July 1891, p. 75; 22 August 1891, p. 218; 29 August 1891, pp. 242-3; 5 September 1891, p. 280; 30 January 1892, pp. 151-2; 19 March 1892, p. 369; 10 September 1892, pp. 304-5, 308; 1 July 1893, p. 13; 29 July 1893, p. 128; 5 August 1893, p. 152; 16 September 1893, p. 333; 14 October 1893, pp. 457-8; 4 November 1893, pp. 553-4; 11 November 1893, p. 587; 30 December 1893, p. 802; 7 July 1894, pp. 8-9; 9 February 1895, pp. 175-6; 31 August 1895, pp. 233-4, 246; 2 November 1895, pp. 522-3; 23 November 1895, p.

620; 15 May 1897, p. 321; 9 October 1897, pp. 247-8; 5 November 1898, p. 338; 13 May 1899, pp. 291-2; 8 July 1899, p. 31; 29 July 1899, p. 91; 18 August 1900, p. 132; 13 October 1900, p. 276; 9 February 1901, pp. 93-4; 19 May 1901, p. 318; 14 March 1903, p. 168; 20 February 1904, p. 121; 19 March 1904, p. 185. *Annals of Horticulture*, 1847, pp. 97-8. *GMB*, vol. 1 (1850), pp. 146-50; vol. 2 (1850), pp. 278-9. *Scottish Gardener*, vol. 1 (1852), pp. 219-21, 338-41, 386-8, 425-9 (reprinted articles from *Gardeners' Chronicle*). *JHS*, vol. 6 (1851) pp. 273-4. *CottGard*, vol. 2 (21 June 1849), pp. 139-40; vol. 15 (18 March 1856), pp. 439-40; vol. 18 (21 April 1857), pp. 31-2; 9 June 1857, pp. 156-8. *Florist* 1859, pp. 114-6; 1861, pp. 260-1. *FW*, vol. 3 (1860), pp. 260-1. *JHort*, vol. 3 (12 August 1862), pp. 372-3; 5 July 1864, p. 1; 16 September 1864, pp. 191-2; 28 March 1865, pp. 244-6; 17 March 1870, p. 208; 24 March 1870, p. 224; 9 February 1871, p. 102; 1 June 1871, pp. 386-7; 9 November 1871, pp. 359-61; 1 July 1875, pp. 6-7; 8 February 1877, pp. 98-9; 18 March 1880, p. 217; 15 April 1880, p. 293; 17 March 1881, pp. 207-8; 5 May 1881, pp. 352-3; 30 June 1881, pp. 528-9; 8 December 1881, p. 525; 9 August 1883, pp. 115-6; 18 October 1888, pp. 351-2; 24 January 1889, p. 64; 7 May 1891, p. 357; 21 July 1892, p. 55 (balsams); 6 June 1895, pp. 500-1; 1 August 1895, p. 111; 2 January 1896, pp. 4-6; 16 July 1896, pp. 49-50; 22 July 1897, pp. 65-9; 2 September 1897, p. 218; 25 May 1899, p. 432; 22 February 1900, pp. 151-2; 31 May 1900, p. 463; 16 August 1900, p. 151; 18 July 1901, p. 56; 5 September 1901, p. 224; 6 November 1902, p. 424; 17 March 1904, pp. 231; 21 April 1904, p. 341. *F&P*, vol. 9 (1870), p. 118; 14 (1875), pp. 150-2. *JRHS*, vol. 2 (1870), pp. 44-6. *Gardener* (1870), pp. 145-6, 391-3. *GardMag*, 5 June 1875, p. 275; 27 January 1883, pp. 49-50; vol. 33 (1890), pp. 582; 4 June 1892, p. 302; 27 August 1892, p. 484; 12 March 1898, p. 163 *; 7 May 1898, p. 290; 17 December 1898, pp. 836-8; 13 May 1899, p. 272. *To-day*, 29 June 1899, p. 732. *JRHS*, vol. 65 (1940), pp. 391-8.—Hereafter only quotations and passages of specific relevance will be cited in these notes.

14. Curtis (1940).

15. See for example *GM*, vol. 1 (1825-6), pp. 87-8, 344-5; vol. 6 (1830), p. 248; *Annals of Horticulture*, 1847, p. 98.

16. Brown (1996).

17. Council minutes, 5-17 November 1823. 4th report of the Garden Committee (1826), pp. 5-6, and plan.

18. *GM*, vol. 2 (1827), pp. 344-8, 359-60, 380; Loudon referred the reader to his *Encyclopaedia of Gardening*, 2nd edition (1827), paragraph 7507 for the correct way of laying out an arboretum. For the later proposal, see *GM*, vol. 6 (1830), pp. 248-51.

19. *GM*, vol. 15 (1839), p. 350; *GC*, 31 July 1847, p. 507; 7 August 1847, p. 525.

20. For the early glasshouses, we have no details, merely the record in Council minutes of which proposed models were being tested. See 20 July 1822 (curvilinear, no author); 4 December 1822, 22 January 1823 (Bailey); 1 March 1828 (Bailey's hot-water system); 14 July 1823 (Banks's and Scott's pine pits); 3 September 1823 (Buck's pine pit, Phelps's melon pit); 19 May 1824 (Atkinson's pine pit); 1 March 1828 (Bailey's hot-water system).

21. For the history of the revolution in glasshouses, see Elliott (1986), pp. 28-32, 65-66; John Hix, *The glass house* (1996).

22. Council minutes, 16 March 1819.

23. *BR*, vol. 25 (1839): Miscellaneous notices, pp. 17-18, and see *GM*, vol. 15 (1839), pp. 145-7.

24. *GM*, vol. 15 (1839), p. 352; vol. 16 (1840), pp. 591-2; *GardMag*, 16 October 1880, pp. 517-18; Georg Kohlmaier and Barna von Sartory, *Houses of Glass* (1986), pp. 87, 132.

25. *FM*, vol. 5 (1840), pp. 155-6.

26. *GC*, 24 September 1842, p. 640; 17 March 1849, p. 167.

27. Council minutes, 2 June 1846. *GC*, 6 June 1846, p. 371; 27 March 1847, p. 207; 10 June 1848, pp. 383-4. For Hartley's glass process, see *GC*, 1849 *passim*.

28. *GC*, 21 February 1852, p. 119; 1856, pp. 403-4. *CottGard*, vol. 10 (30 June 1853), p. 239.

29. Beck: *GC*, 24 September 1842, p. 640. Gray and Ormson: *GC*, 22 May 1858, p. 423-4; 12 June 1858, pp. 475-6, and see Ormson's advertisement, 9 October 1858, p. 758. New Bailey boiler, *JHS*, vol. 6 (1851), pp. 273-4.

30. *GC*, 21 February 1852, p. 119; 3 July 1852, pp. 422-3; 31 July 1852, pp. 486-7; 4 September 1852, p. 567; 1 January 1853, p. 7; 4 June 1853, pp. 358-9; 2 July 1853, p. 423. Council minutes, 17 January 1862 (bearing Lindley's annotation, 'I object to this JL', and Andrew Murray's, 'objection not followed out'). *GC*, 1863, pp. 583-4.

31. *CottGard*, vol. 2 (21 June 1849), pp. 139-40.

32. *GMB*, vol. 1 (1850), pp. 146-50, and see vol. 2 (1850), pp. 278-9, for a complaint about failure to cut the grass.

33. *Ibid*. *GC*, 16 March 1850, p. 167; 18 January 1851, p. 39; 26 April 1851, p. 263; 30 July 1853, p. 487.

34. Council minutes, 13 November, 11 December 1855; 3 April, 18-28 August, 23 September 1856. *CottGard*, vol. 18 (21 April 1857), p. 32.

35. Council minutes, 11, 31 March, 10 July 1857. *GC*, 21 March 1857, pp. 195-6; 25 April 1857, pp. 291-2; 1 August 1857, p. 535; 22 May 1858, pp. 423-4; 10 September 1859, pp. 743-4. For the subsequent condition of the orchard houses, see *ibid*., 7 August 1870, p. 1054; 13 August 1870, pp. 1086-7; 3 September 1870, pp. 1182-3.

36. Decline and death of M'Ewen: Council minutes, 7-12 January, 15 April-21 May 1858. John M'Ewen, 28 April, 21 May, 2 July 1858. M'Ewen and the flower-picker, 10 July 1857.

37. For accounts of the opening, see *GC*, 29 September 1860, p. 869; 25 May 1861, p. 479; 29 June 1861, pp. 597-8; *JHort*, vol. 1 (11 June 1861), pp. 192-200; opening programme [bound with vol. 1 of *PRHS* (1861) in the Lindley Library main copy]. *PRHS*, vol. 1 (1861), pp. 43-51, 95-103, 596-608. For the International Exhibition, see *GC*, 7 June 1862, pp. 521-2; Beresford Hope's astringent view in 'The International Exhibition', *QR*, vol. 112 (1862), pp. 179-219, and reply in *GC*, 26 July 1862, p. 695; *Survey of London*, vol. 38: *The Museums area of South Kensington and Westminster* (1975), ch. 9, 'The exhibition building of 1862', pp. 137-147. For the horticultural portions of the exhibition, see *GC*, 17 May 1862, p. 452; 24 May 1862, p. 476 (boilers); 31 May 1862, p. 500 (lawnmowers); 14 June 1862, pp. 547-8 (timber); 21 June 1862, pp. 571, 572 (fruits); 28 June 1862, p. 595 (timber); 28 June 1862, pp. 596-7 (flowers and sundries); 5 July 1862, p. 620 (fruits); 19 July 1862, p. 666 (vases); 26 July 1862, pp. 690-1 (fruits).

38. For Lindley's attack on enclosure, see his 'On the arrangement of gardens and pleasure-grounds in the Elizabethan age', *JHS*, vol. 3 (1848), pp. 1-15. See Elliott (1986), pp. 67-70, for attitudes to enclosure at the time.

39. For descriptions of the Kensington garden, see the following: *FW*, vol. 2 (1859) pp. 171-2, 220, 241-2; vol. 3 (1860) pp. 68, 113-15, 119-20, 236. *Gardeners' Weekly Magazine*, 1860 ii pp. 14, 206. *Florist*, 1860 pp. 144-7; 1861 pp. 258-60. *GC*, 28 January 1860, pp. 71-2; 31 March 1860, p. 288; 12 May 1860, pp. 432-3 & plan [partly a reprint of *Florist* pp. 144-7]; 17 November 1860, pp. 1022-3; 1 June 1861, pp. 502-3; 6 July 1861, pp. 621, 623; 21 September 1860, p. 850; 22 February 1862, pp. 167-8; 26 April 1862, pp. 379-80; 31 May 1862, p. 500 & col pl.; 13 September 1862, pp. 863-4 & col. pl.; 7 February 1863, pp. 127-8; 7 March 1863, pp. 221-2; 11 July 1863, p.

651; 23 January 1864, pp. 75-6; 23 April 1863, pp. 391-2; 30 April 1863, p. 412; 8 October 1863, p. 967; 22 July 1865, p. 676; 10 October 1868, pp. 1069-70; 4 December 1875, pp. 709-10. *JHort*, vol. 1 (14 May 1861), p. 119; 11 June 1861, pp. 192-200; 18 June 1861, pp. 212-14; 13 August 1861, pp. 373-5; vol. 2 (5 November 1861), pp. 113-14; 19 November 1861, p. 148; vol. 3 (29 July 1862), pp. 327-8; 19 August 1862, pp. 387-9; 15 October 1874, pp. 344-6; 1 March 1877, pp. 160-1. *Athenaeum*, 1861, pp. 362-3 [Frederick George Stephens], 727-8 [Lindley], 766 [William Hepworth Dixon], 800 [Stephens]. Murray (1863), pp. 117-79. RHS (1864). *GardMag*, vol. 17 (1874), p. 558; vol. 26 (1884), pp. 492-3. Simmonds (1948). Elliott (1986), pp. 140-3. Elliott (1992). Hereafter references will be cited for specific features only. See also the (incomplete) collection of architectural drawings for the garden held in the RHS archives, including Nesfield's original plan, coloured sketches by Smirke for the arcades, and decorative details by Godfrey Sykes.

40. For Nesfield, see Elliott (1986), pp. 71-4, 138-40; also Christopher Ridgway, ed., *William Andrews Nesfield* (1997).

41. *GC*, 15 October 1859, p. 828; 19 November 1859, p. 925. Council minutes, 18 November 1859.

42. *GC*, 22 February 1862, pp. 167-8. RHS (1864), pp. 27-30. Council minutes, 28 July 1873, for the query whether the well was actually on RHS land.

43. Council minutes, 2 September 1859; 20 January, 18 December 1860. *GC*, 17 November 1860, pp. 1022-3. For the maze, see Nesfield's original drawing in the RHS archives, and RHS (1864), pp. 17-18.

44. *Florist*, 1860, p. 146; 1861, pp. 258-60. *GC*, 26 April 1862, pp. 379-80 (Nesfield/Eyles press statement); 31 May 1862, p. 500 and colour plate; 13 September 1862, pp. 863-4 and colour plate. *CottGard*, vol. 25 (19 February 1861), pp. 299-300. *JHort*, vol. 1 (13 August 1861), pp. 373-5; vol. 3 (20 July 1862), pp. 327-8; 19 August 1862, pp. 387-9.

45. *FW*, vol. 4 (1861), pp. 125-6. *Athenaeum*, 1861, p. 766 [William Hepworth Dixon]. *CottGard*, vol. 25 (19 February 1861), pp. 299-300. *QR*, vol. 112 (1862), p. 182. *JHort*, vol. 2 (5 November 1861), pp. 113-14; vol. 3 (2 September 1862), pp. 426-9. Robson went on to say: 'Most people admire it much at the first visit, and come away almost enchanted with it—their second visit is also pleasing; but repeat this many times, and the Garden is looked at with indifference—there is no change. Nature forms so unimportant part of the picture, that she may be said to be almost set aside.' See also 'What our neighbours think of us and our garden', *PRHS*, vol. 2 (1862), pp. 704-8.

46. *GC*, 30 August 1862, pp. 809-10.

47. Council minutes, 14 June 1861; 3 March 1862. Fine Arts Committee minutes, 1861-63. The quotation is from Prince Albert's opening address to the Committee.

48. Council minutes, 6 February—24 July 1863; *Catalogue of Sculpture by Living Artists. Exhibited in the Royal Horticultural Society's Garden, at South Kensington* (1863). See Benedict Read, *Victorian Sculpture* (1982), for background, but note that it makes no mention of the Sculptors' Institute, which is not proving easy to find information about.

49. Council minutes, 15 April 1864, for Edward Stephens' refusal to let the Institute of Sculpture get involved in a further exhibition. After 1863, the Fine Arts Committee was succeeded by a Sculpture Committee, whose minutes do not survive, but see Council minutes, 22 July, 16 December 1864.

50. Council minutes, 2 January 1862, for the Prince of Wales's letter. *PRHS*, vol. 3 (1863), pp. 265-72. For the history of the Memorial, see Hobhouse, *op. cit.*, pp. 117-18; from the Society's point of view, Council

minutes *passim* from 31 January 1860 (Godwin's approach) to 8 June 1863.

51. Council minutes, 17 February, 23 May, 18 July, 8 October, 5 December 1862; 30 January 1863. *JHort*, vol. 3 (21 October 1862), p. 565; *ibid.*, 28 October 1862, pp. 585-6; 13 January 1863, p. 22. *GC*, 16 August 1862, pp. 764, 766. *PRHS*, vol. 2 (1862), p. 756; vol. 3 (1863), p. 3. Murray (1863), pp. 68-72. Antoine Durenne was the master of a prominent ironworks at Sommevoire, Haute-Marne, and responsible for many public commissions. The restored fountain was opened on 12 November 1998.

52. Council minutes, 4 March 1864; 19 November 1867; 21-28 April, 29 December 1875; 5 January, 6 September 1876; 13 April 1880. *GC*, 23 April 1864, p. 392; RHS (1864), pp. 30-2. For the great tent, see *PRHS*, vol. 4 (1864), pp. 125-6.

53. Council minutes, 4 October, 15-29 November 1861; 7 February—11 April, 18-20 June 1862.

54. Skating rink: Council minutes, 15 January 1867; 30 June, 13 July, 19 October, 11 December 1874; 7 January, 21 April 1875. Tennis: 4 April 1877; 2 July 1878; 16 January 1883; and see 26 April 1881 for a like request from the residents of Chiswick, turned down for lack of space.

55. Council minutes, 27 April 1861; 21 February, 27 June 1862; 18 May 1869; Music Committee minutes. *PRHS*, vol. 4 (1864), pp. 128, 156, 172. Hazel Conway, 'The Royal Horticultural Society bandstand mystery—or, what happened to the first cast-iron bandstands?' *GH*, vol. 29 (2001), pp. 214-16. Band concerts were interrupted during the financial crisis of the mid-1870s, until outstanding prizes were paid, but resumed in 1877.

56. Fine Arts Committee minutes, 17 July 1863. Council minutes, 24 July 1863; 1-9 November 1871; 14 February 1872. *GC*, 29 June 1872, pp. 865-6; 13 March 1875, p. 345 (discussion at AGM). Council minutes, 11 March, 20 May, 10-24 June, 28 October 1879; 8 February, 12 April 1881; 8 May, 11 December 1883; 8, 13, 22 April, 10 June 1884; 13 January 1885.

57. *GC*, 30 August 1862, pp. 809-10. *JHort*, vol. 3 (12 August 1862), pp. 372-3; 5 July 1864, p. 1. See also *Florist*, 1861, pp. 260-1.

58. *GC*, 8 July 1865, p. 628; 21 September 1867, p. 976.

59. Council minutes, 16 February-20 April 1870. *GC*, 12 February 1870, p. 209; 19 February 1870, p. 247; 25 February 1870, p. 280; 5 March 1870, p. 313; 2 April 1870, p. 456; 28 January 1871, p. 102; 24 August 1872, p. 1130 for the plan of the reduced Chiswick. *Gardener* (1870), pp. 145-6. *F&P*, vol. 9 (1870), p. 118.

60. Council minutes, 1 March, 6-20 April, 4 May 1869. *GC*, 21 October 1871, p. 1360.

61. *GC*, 27 August 1870, p. 1155; 29 April 1876, p. 558; 1 July 1876, p. 15; 12 August 1876, p. 202; 30 September 1876, p. 425. *JHort*, 9 August 1883, pp. 115-6. *F&P*, vol. 14 (1875), pp. 150-2.

62. *GC*, 27 April 1878, p. 529; 22 March 1879, p. 375; 5 July 1879, p. 18; 18 October 1879, p. 499. *GardMag*, 27 January 1884, pp. 49-50. D.T. Fish, ed., *Cassell's practical gardening* (1884), frontis. to vol. 2.

63. *GC*, 12 August 1876, p. 202. Council minutes, 24 July, 6 December 1876; 23 March 1886.

64. *JHort*, 1 March 1864, p. 165. See also Sir Trevor Lawrence's statement in *GC*, 18 February 1888, p. 214: 'If it had not been for the death of the Prince Consort, the circumstances of the Society probably would have been totally different. They would have had the enormous advantage to be derived from his prudent and wise advice and great influence; and had he lived, the story of their connection with South Kensington would doubtless have been a far different one.'

65. *GC*, 7 March 1863, pp. 221-2. *JHort*, 1 March 1864, pp. 165-6, 167-71. Council minutes, 19 June 1866 (creepers not growing well); 2 February 1869 (dying trees removed). *GC*, 4 December 1875, pp. 709-10, citing the *Saturday Review*.

66. Kensington garden Committee minutes, 8 December 1862.

67. *GC*, 23 April 1864, pp. 391-2; 30 April 1864, p. 412; 4 June 1864, p. 533. Council minutes, 8 July 1864.

68. Council minutes, 28 December 1863; 15 January, 3 June, 23 December 1864; 3 October 1865.

69. For the orchid house and Bateman's orchids, see Council minutes: 4 March, 15 April 1864; 16 February 1869; 5-19 March 1873; 10 November-18 December 1874; 28 January 1875.

70. *Times*—cited in *GardMag*, 17 October 1874, p. 558 (have yet to track down reference). Council minutes, 5 January 1870. Maze: Council minutes, 4 December 1872, 13 January 1873.

71. Council minutes, 6 December 1871; 6 March 1872; 2-8 April 1873. Praise for Eyles's carpet-bedding: William Robinson, *Alpine Flowers for English Gardens* (1870), pp. 41-2 (figure 35). Brent Elliott, 'Illuminating the garden', *The Garden* (*JRHS*), vol. 111 (1986), pp. 576-7.

72. Council minutes, 16 June 1875. *Morning Post*, 14 June 1875, p. 4 e-f. *Times*, 12 May 1875, p. 12 f.; and see 14 August p. 9 f. for the follow-up Act. For the Sabbath Alliance and Edinburgh, see Fletcher (1970), pp. 164-8.

73. Hobhouse (2002), pp. 142-9 for the Albert Hall, and 154-6 for the Natural History Museum; *Survey of London*, vol. 38: *The Museums Area of South Kensington* (1986), pp. 177-95 for the Albert Hall, and 201-16 for the Natural History Museum; W. T. Stearn, *The Natural History Museum at South Kensington* (1981), pp. 41-5.

74. Hobhouse, *op. cit.*, pp. 185-6.

75. *RHS Arrangements* for 1889. See also *JHort*, 24 January 1889, p. 64. *GC*, 18 June 1887, pp. 806-9; 10 November 1888, pp. 536-8, 540; 17 November 1888, p. 574-5; 24 November 1888, pp. 607-8 (Thiselton-Dyer's proposals for 'a horticultural Kew' and replies); 19 January 1889, pp. 75-6. *JHort*, n.s. vol. 18 (1889), p. 64. Maxwell T. Masters, "What can we do at Chiswick?", *JRHS*, vol. 21 (1897-8), pp. 161-73.

76. J.R. Pearson's boiler: Council minutes, 13 August 1889. Newton's glazing, 12 February, 10 December 1889; 14 January 1890. Pearson's greenhouse, 28 May, 10 November 1891. Skinner Board house, 23 October 1894, and *GardMag*, 12 March 1898, p. 163*. For Bréhaut's criticism, see *GC*, 13 August 1870, pp. 1086-7.

77. Council minutes, 25 June 1889; 23 October 1894. *GC*, 2 November 1895, p. 522.

78. *GC*, 31 August 1895, p. 246.

79. Council minutes, 11 November 1890; 5 November 1892. *JHort*, 2 January 1896, p. 5; 22 July 1897, pp. 65-9 (conference on the future of Chiswick).

80. Council minutes, 21 November 1899 – 13 December 1904 *passim*. For the Chiswick Council's desire for the garden, see *JHort*, 16 August 1900, p. 151. For the opinions of the press on the requirements of the 'new Chiswick', see *GC*, 18 August 1900, p. 132; 13 October 1900, pp. 276, 283; 9 February 1901, p. 95. *GardMag*, 8 April 1899, p. 203 (Alexander Dean on why it was more important than a Hall); 14 April 1900, p. 215; 21 April 1900, p. 230; 19 May 1900, p. 294; 26 May 1900, pp. 308, 317; 2 June 1900, p. 337; 9 June 1900, p. 344; 16 June 1900, p. 360; 23 June 1900, p. 379 (including Dean vs J. L. Wood). *JHort*, 22 March 1900, p. 245 (Dean again); 29 March 1900, pp. 259-60; 12 April 1900, pp. 307-8; 19 April 1900, p. 329; 10 May 1900, p. 395; 17 May 1900, pp. 422-3. For a discussion of Limpsfield with plan, see *GardMag*, 12 May 1900, pp. 287-8.

81. *GC*, 20 February 1904, p. 121; 19 March 1904, p. 185. *JHort*, 17 March 1904, p. 231.

82. *JHort*, 21 April 1904, p. 341.

5 The Society's Gardens: Wisley, pp. 77-96

1. For the aesthetics of the wild garden in the 1870s and 1880s, see Elliott (1986), pp. 194-6.

2. For descriptions of Heatherbank, and Wilson's notes on plants cultivated there, see *GC*, 3 July 1880, pp. 10-11; 4 February 1882, p. 154; 26 January 1884, 110. *GardMag*, 1 December 1883, pp. 674-5; 6 September 1890, p. 536. *Garden*, 18 April 1874, pp. 323-4; 25 April 1874, pp. 345-6; 2 May 1874, p. 372; 9 May 1874, pp. 389-90; 29 May 1875, pp. 449-50; 9 September 1876, p. 254; 16 September 1876, p. 278 (lilies); 23 September 1876, p. 306; 4 November 1876, p. 456; 3 April 1880, pp. 312-13; 24 April 1880, pp. 361-2; 27 May 1880, p. 449; 20 May 1882, pp. 351-2; 7 June 1884, p. 474 (lilies); 28 September 1889, pp. 300-1; 2 November 1889, p. 404; 24 February 1894, p. 145; 12 May 1894, p. 387; 25 August 1894, p. 167; 25 January 1896, p. 70; 30 October 1897, p. 354; 15 January 1898, p. 51; 28 January 1899, p. 65. *GW*, vol. 7 (6 September 1890), pp. 11-12; vol. 10 (21 October 1893), p. 115 (lilies); vol. 11 (8 December 1894), p. 232 (lilies). There is duplication of text among these entries, because Wilson sent the same plant notes to various magazines. For the Wilson raft, see *GC*, 22 July 1876, pp. 100-1; *Garden*, 7 July 1877, p. 15. For Wilson's cat Fat Tommy, and his use as a bird-scarer, see *GC*, 23 November 1872, p. 1556.

3. Council minutes, 16 February 1870. The garden at Weybridge which Wilson was suggesting is not named in the minute.

4. For Biddulph and its influence, see Elliott (1986), pp. 102-6, 121-3. Bateman and Wilson overlapped on Council, were involved together over the Lindley Library negotiations, and would undoubtedly have known of each other's activities.

5. For descriptions of Oakwood/Wisley in Wilson's time, see *Garden*, 11 June 1881, p. 598; 22 November 1884, p. 432; 2 May 1885, p. 388; 23 May 1885, pp. 469-70; 18 February 1888, p. 138; 28 March 1891, pp. 281-2 (gladioli); 11 June 1892, p. 545 (calochorti); 2 July 1892, p. 6; 10 September 1892, p. 229; 31 December 1892, pp. 577-8 (lilies); 1 April 1893, p. 270 (sedum nomenclature); 9 December 1893, p. 529; 25 May 1895, pp. 358-9; 29 June 1895, p. 454; 20 July 1895, pp. 37-8; 17 August 1895, p. 116; 7 December 1895, p. 450; 6 June 1896, p. 419; 24 April 1897, p. 297 (primulas); 5 August 1899, pp. 108-9 (waterlilies); 26 May 1900, p. 373; 25 January 1902, p. 51; 15 February 1902, p. 103; 12 April 1902, p. 238. *GardMag*, 1 December 1883, pp. 674-5; 28 March 1891, p. 180; 1 August 1891, p. 465; 22 August 1891, p. 515; 5 September 1891, pp. 552-3; 24 October 1891, p. 655 (lilies); 3 December 1891, p. 753 (fruit); 17 December 1892, p. 740 (lilies); 9 December 1893, p. 733; 2 May 1903, p. 284 (sale notice); 22 August 1903, p. 556. *GC*, 10 February 1883, pp. 178, 183; 23 June 1883, p. 799; 30 June 1883, p. 823; 26 January 1884, pp. 110-11; 16 April 1887, p. 519; 20 August 1887, pp. 225-6; 24 September 1887, pp. 365-6; 25 February 1888, p. 244; 28 July 1888, pp. 91-2; 16 March 1889, p. 340; 27 April 1889, pp. 522-3; 28 September 1889, p. 362 (lilies); 28 March 1891, p. 396; 24 October 1891, p. 492 (lilies); 5 December 1891, pp. 679-80 (fruit); 25 June 1892, p. 810; 11 March 1893, p. 302; 21 October 1893, pp. 497, 499; 12 May 1894, pp. 600-1; 8 December 1894, p. 701 (lilies); 7 December 1895, pp. 672-3. *GW*, vol. 2 (21 August 1886), pp. 806-7; vol. 4 (18 February 1888), p. 391 (miniature mountain); *ibid.*, 28 July 1888, p. 763; vol. 7 (6 September 1890), pp. 11-12; *ibid.*, 28 March 1891, p. 475; *ibid.*, 29 August 1891, p. 825; vol. 8 (24 October 1891), pp. 117-18; *ibid.*, 5 December 1891, p. 212; vol. 9 (17 December 1892), p.

241 (lilies); vol. 12 (7 December 1895), p. 227 (lilies). *JHort*, 31 May 1888, pp. 448-50; 7 June 1888, pp. 462-3. *CL*, 25 September 1897, pp. 319-21; 9 October 1897, pp. 371-2; 26 August 1899, pp. 230-4; 8 September 1900, pp. 304-10; 27 July 1901, pp. 101-4. *JRHS*, vol. 26 (1901-2), p. 48. Again, there is duplication among these entries, because Wilson sent the same plant notes to various magazines. Wilson's notice: David Mulford, 'The evolution of a garden: 1', *Grassroots*, no. 40 (1996), p. 5.

6. *GC*, 14 June 1902, p. 390 (sale notice for Wisley). Council minutes, 8 April 1902; 4 August-10 November 1903. *JRHS*, vol. 29 (1904-5), pp. 248-52. Le Lievre (1980), p. 100. The Wisley Trust Deed was published in *JRHS*, vol. 28 (1903-04), pp. 538-42.

7. *GW*, vol. 19 (2 May 1903), p. 394. C.T. Druery, 'A dream of Wisley', *GardMag*, 12 December 1903, pp. 826-8—later reprinted in his humorous volume *The Tatur Disees and other Essays* (n.d.). Council minutes, 8-22 March, 9 August, 20 September-4 October 1904. *GC*, 19 March 1904, p. 188 (the way to Wisley). *JRHS*, vol. 31 (1906), p. 76. *GC*, 6 May 1905, pp. 276-7; 24 June 1905, p. 394.

8. *GC*, 28 August 1915, p. 141 ('the number of Fellows visiting the gardens is as great as ever. Nor is this to be wondered at, for where else near London may be found a spot so calculated to beget a little forgetfulness from the worries and anxieties of the war?'); 27 March 1926, p. 224; 14 December 1929, pp. 464-5. *JHort*, 10 February 1910, p. 126. *Garden*, 10 April 1920, p. 180. *Garden Life*, 20 February 1926, p. 201. *GC*, 16 February 1929, p. 113; 17 March 1934, p. 171.

9. Council minutes, 22 January-16 April 1907. *GC*, 13 April 1907, p. 233; 27 July 1907, pp. 70-2. *JRHS*, vol. 33 (1908), pp. 329-46 ('Opening of the Laboratory and Research Station at the Wisley Garden', including the prospectus of the Wisley School of Horticulture). For a brief life of Lord Avebury, see *The Garden* (*JRHS*), vol. 119 (1994), pp. 594-5.

10. Council minutes, 7 April, 5-18 May, 8-22 September 1914; 9 May 1916. *JRHS*, vol. 42 (1916), pp. 115-21 ('The new Laboratories at Wisley'). Arthur Mee, in *The King's England: Surrey* (1955), pp. 326-7, described the Laboratory as having 'the charm of an old country house'. For the stylistic tradition to which the Laboratory belongs, see Roderick Gradidge, *The Surrey Style* (1991). For Crawley and Crowhurst, see Clive Aslet, *The Last Country Houses* (1982), pp. 161-4.

11. For general treatments of the development of the Wisley garden, see S.T. Wright, 'The Society's garden at Wisley', *JRHS*, vol. 31 (1906), pp. 62-76; Chittenden (1933); Gould (1946); RHS (1978); Rix (1989); David Mulford, 'The evolution of a garden', *Grassroots*, from no. 40 (1996) to no. 76 (Oct/Nov 1999). For early accounts of Wisley under the RHS, up to the end of the First World War, see *GC*, 23 January 1904, pp. 52-3; 27 February 1904, p. 138; 30 April 1904, p. 282; 18 June 1904, p. 394; 6 May 1905, pp. 276-7; 30 September 1905, pp. 248-9; 5 May 1906, p. 275; 11 July 1908, p. 21; 9 April 1910, pp. 228-9; 31 January 1914, p. 74; 7 February 1914, p. 95; 21 March 1914, p. 206; 18 April 1914, p. 272; 20 June 1914, p. 432 (the last three are notes on plants in flower); 22 May 1915, pp. 271-2; 29 May 1915, p. 292 (primulas, tulips); 28 August 1915, p. 141; 6 November 1915, p. 297; 9 September 1916, p. 119 (campanulas). *Garden*, 8 July 1905, p. 2; 30 June 1906, p. 339; 24 July 1909, p. 358; 29 June 1912, pp. 329-30; 16 November 1912, p. 574; 27 May 1916, p. 264; 22 March 1919, p. 128; 12 July 1919, pp. 328-9. *GardMag*, 10 August 1907, p. 579; 6 January 1912, p. 2. *JHort*, 23 June 1910, p. 562; 30 June 1910, p. 580; 21 May 1914, pp. 463-8. Eric Parker, *Surrey* (1908), pp. 231-3.

12. Council minutes, 3 April, 1 May, 31 July–14 August

1906; 16 August 1910; 17-31 January, 1 August, 7 November, 5-19 December 1911. James Pulham, 'The Wisley rock garden', *JRHS*, vol. 38 (1912-13), pp. 225-33; vol. 81 (1956), pp. 159-62. *GC*, 4 April 1914, p. 229; 22 July 1911, pp. 45-6; 17 April 1920, pp. 188; 8 May 1920, pp. 231-2. *JHort*, 15 August 1912, p. 165; 22 August 1912, pp. 182-5. *CL*, 16 November 1912, pp. 683-5; 28 June 1919, p. 799. F.W. Meyer, *Rock and Water Gardens* (1910).

13. NDH final examination paper (1916), section 5 question 1. *GC*, 10 December 1921, p. 302; 20 September 1924, p. 197; 21 August 1926, pp. 151-2. Hanger: *JRHS*, vol. 74 (1949), p. 134. For the heathers on Wisley common, see *ibid.*, vol. 29 (1904-5), p. 251, and *GC*, 4 September 1915, p. 157.

14. For Wright's illness and death, and the controversy over the new post, see Council minutes, 14 March, 9 May–11 July, 31 October–12 December 1922; 16 January 1923. *GC*, 2 September 1922, pp. 131; 9 December 1922, p. 334; 23 May 1925, p. 345. *Garden*, 17 March 1923, p. 137 (complaint about neglect in the rock garden); 28 June 1924, pp. 444, 450-1; 19 July 1924, p. 506.

15. For developments at Wisley during the Chittenden years, from the end of the War until 1930, see Chittenden, *op. cit.*; *GC*, 17 April 1920, p. 188 (rock garden); 8 May 1920, pp. 231-2; 9 October 1920, p. 177; 29 October 1921, p. 221; 19 November 1921, p. 261; 10 December 1921, p. 302; 14 January 1922, p. 19; 11 February 1922, p. 70; 11 March 1922, p. 111; 8 April 1922, p. 168; 6 May 1922, p. 224; 27 May 1922, p. 267; 24 June 1922, p. 331; 19 August 1922, p. 109; 30 September 1922, p. 193; 14 October 1922, p. 221; 23 December 1922, p. 366; 13 January 1923, p. 19; 3 March 1923, p. 121; 24 March 1923, pp. 163-4; 21 April 1923, p. 211; 2 June 1923, p. 297; 30 June 1923, p. 363; 11 August 1923, pp. 83-4; 18 September 1923, p. 146; 6 October 1923, p. 202; 20 October 1923, pp. 235-6; 24 November 1923, p. 310; 26 January 1924, p. 49; 8 March 1924, p. 132; 29 March 1924, pp. 172-3; 7 June 1924, p. 334; 28 June 1924, p. 392; 26 July 1924, pp. 60-1; 13 September 1924, p. 183; 20 September 1924, p. 197; 11 October 1924, p. 250; 25 October 1924, p. 283; 8 November 1924, p. 316; 7 February 1925, p. 93; 7 March 1925, p. 162; 4 April 1925, p. 238; 9 May 1925, pp. 316-17; 6 June 1925, p. 395; 4 July 1925, p. 8; 1 August 1925, pp. 91-2; 29 August 1925, p. 168; 3 October 1925, p. 268; 24 October 1925, pp. 331-2 (waterlilies near lab); 2 January 1926, pp. 7-8; 30 January 1926, p. 81; 27 February 1926, p. 153; 27 March 1926, p. 228; 24 April 1926, pp. 303-4; 22 May 1926, p. 370; 26 June 1926, p. 457; 24 July 1926, pp. 71-2; 21 August 1926, pp. 151-2; 4 September 1926, pp. 191-2; 25 September 1926, p. 249; 30 October 1926, p. 351; 27 November 1926, p. 432; 25 December 1926, p. 508; 22 January 1927, p. 64; 5 February 1927, pp. 101-2; 5 March 1927, pp. 163-4; 26 March 1927, pp. 213-14; 7 May 1927, p. 323; 28 May 1927, p. 370; 25 June 1927, pp. 448-9; 23 July 1927, p. 66; 27 August 1927, p. 171; 24 September 1927, p. 250; 15 October 1927, p. 307; 19 November 1927, p. 404; 3 December 1927, p. 444; 10 December 1927, p. 469; 4 February 1928, pp. 82-3; 25 February 1928, p. 136; 31 March 1928, pp. 227-8; 5 May 1928, pp. 316-17; 26 May 1928, pp. 372-3; 7 July 1928, pp. 11-12; 4 August 1928, p. 92; 25 August 1928, pp. 151-2; 22 September 1928, pp. 232-3; 20 October 1928, p. 309; 17 November 1928, p. 386; 9 February 1929, p. 103; 2 March 1929, pp. 163-4; 30 March 1929, p. 246; 27 April 1929, p. 312; 28 September 1929, pp. 244-5; 9 November 1929, p. 364; 14 December 1929, pp. 464-5; 18 January 1930, p. 44; 1 March 1930, pp. 168-9; 29 March 1930, p. 251; 3 May 1930, pp. 346-7; 7 June 1930, p. 456; 5 July 1930, p. 12; 26 July 1930, p. 72; 30 August 1930, pp. 175-6; 27 September 1930, pp. 258-9. (From 1921 to 1933 J.E. Grant White contributed

regular 'Notes from Wisley' to the *Chronicle*, which allow the reader to note changes in planting as well as the more obvious alterations in design.) *Garden*, 10 April 1920, pp. 180-1, 346-7; 15 December 1923, pp. 650-1; 28 June 1924, pp. 450-1. Karl Wagner, 'Wisley, der Garten den englischen Gartenbaugesellschaft', *Gartenschönheit*, vol. 10 (1929), pp. 413-15.

16. *GC*, 16 March 1929, p. 195; 5 April 1930, pp. 259-60; 12 April 1930, pp. 279-80 (passage quoted); 31 January 1931, p. 7; 14 February 1931, p. 121; 21 February 1931, pp. 148-9 (and correction, 28 February, p. 158); 5 March 1932, p. 173; 12 March 1932, pp. 206-7.

17. For developments at Wisley during the Harrow years, from 1931 to 1946, see Gould (1946); Gould *et al.*, *Guide to Wisley Gardens* (1947); John Gilmour and Francis Hanger, 'Recent developments in the gardens at Wisley', *JRHS*, vol. 74 (1949), pp. 133-44, *GC*, 10 January 1931, pp. 33-4; 28 March 1931, p. 242; 18 April 1931, p. 294; 9 May 1931, p. 356; 20 June 1931, p. 474; 25 July 1931, p. 63; 1 August 1931, pp. 92-3; 3 October 1931, pp. 274-6; 31 October 1931, pp. 349-50; 12 December 1931, p. 446; 2 April 1932, pp. 259-60; 23 April 1932, p. 312; 2 July 1932, p. 10; 22 October 1932, p. 305; 8 April 1933, p. 243; 20 May 1933, pp. 350-1; 8 July 1933, p. 30; 5 August 1933, p. 100; 2 September 1933, p. 178; 20 January 1934, p. 48; 10 March 1934, pp. 165-6; 5 May 1934, pp. 296-7; 1 September 1934, p. 158; 3 November 1934, p. 320; 9 March 1935, pp. 158-9; 30 March 1935, pp. 211-12; 21 November 1936, p. 365 & supplementary plate; 12 December 1936, p. 425 (shrubs); 13 March 1937, pp. 173-4 (spring flowers); 26 June 1937, pp. 443-4; 7 August 1937, p. 102; 18 September 1937, p. 216; 1 January 1938, pp. 13-14; 5 February 1938, pp. 95-6; 5 March 1938, p. 166; 23 April 1938, pp. 288-9; 4 June 1938, p. 393; 23 July 1938, p. 67; 17 September 1938, pp. 217-18; 26 November 1938, pp. 391-2; 28 January 1939, p. 58; 25 March 1939, p. 185; 29 April 1939, pp. 267-8; 10 June 1939, p. 372; 8 July 1939, pp. 28-9; 11 October 1941, p. 121; 6 May 1944, p. 185 (spring flowers); 18 January 1947, p. 32; 12 April 1947, p. 128; 24 May 1947, p. 186; 2 August 1947, p. 38; 29 November 1947, p. 185; 29 January 1949, pp. 36-7. *CL*, 18 February 1933, pp. 170-5. For the acquisition and initial treatment of Battleston Hill, see Council minutes, 30 July, 13 August, 15 October, 5 November 1935; 11 February, 23 June, 21 July, 27 October 1936; 5 January-23 February, 8 June 1937; 11 January, 5 April, 13 September 1938; *GC*, 1 January 1938, pp. 13-14; *JRHS*, vol. 81 (1956), pp. 355-6.

18. *JHort*, 4 June 1914, p. 517, for a good early illustration of the original glasshouse range.

19. Council minutes, 26 January, 23 February 1904; 30 April-14 May 1912; 24 August 1926. For the alpine house: *JRHS*, vol. 39 (1913-14), p. v; vol. 78 (1953), pp. 51-4. *GC*, 8 May 1920, pp. 231-2; 21 August 1926, pp. 151-2; 27 November 1926, p. 432; 5 February 1927, pp. 101-2; 26 March 1927, pp. 213-14; 5 April 1930, pp. 272-3; 26 May 1945, p. 225. For its later history and replacement, see *JRHS*, vol. 81 (1956), pp. 115-18; vol. 89 (1964), pp. 96-9; vol. 96 (1971), pp. 105-8; Julian Treyer-Evans, 'Wisley's alpine house', *The Garden (JRHS)*, vol. 101 (1976), pp. 33-4; C.D. Brickell, 'Early spring in the alpine house', *ibid.*, pp. 66-9; John Main, 'Alpine house area', vol. 110 (1985), pp. 244-5; Ralph Haywood, 'The landscaped alpine house', ibid., pp. 581-3; 'Wisley's alpine splendour', vol. 120 (1995), pp. 154-6; and, for a dissenting view ('the new white elephant'), see Christopher Lloyd in *CL*, 4 September 1986, p. 722.

20. Council minutes, 20 October 1931; *GC*, 24 September 1927, p. 250. In later years, the temperate house was to be the best promoted: see *JRHS*, vol. 81 (1956), pp. 81-4; vol. 82 (1957) pp. 454-7; vol. 84 (1959), pp. 440-2.

21. Council minutes, 29 April, 17 June, 2 December 1947; 9 August, 13 December 1949; 5 April, 3 May 1966; 4 April, 2 May, 23 May 1967; 16 January, 6 February, 2-18 April, 4 September-8 October 1968; 15 January, 25 February-1 April, 20 May, 15 July-28 October 1969; 6 January, 17 March 1970; 26 October 1971. *JRHS*, vol. 95 (1970), pp. 144-5, 284-6.

22. Christopher Brickell, 'Notes from Wisley', *JRHS*, vol. 99 (1974), pp. 425-8, and cover of the February 1974 issue for an illustration of the Cambridge Planthouse; Julian Treyer-Evans, 'The new cactus house', vol. 100 (1975), pp. 515-17; Barry Scrase and Jon Surtees, 'Orchids grow free in Wisley's new glasshouse', vol. 101 (1976), pp. 76-9; Randall W. Robinson and Geoff W. Carr, 'Re-organisation of the Orchid House', vol. 108 (1983), pp. 491-3.

23. John Watkins and Lucinda Lachelin, 'The Singapore Airlines Orchid House', *The Garden (JRHS)*, vol. 117 (1992), pp. 133-7.

24. Gilmour vs Cowan: Council minutes, 29 May 1945. Hanger vs Blakey: 29 November-13 December 1938. Hanger's war work: 17 March, 15 September 1942. Appointment as Curator: 15-29 May, 3-24 July 1945.

25. On the developing tradition of the woodland garden, see Elliott (1986), p. 195; Brent Elliott, *The Country House Garden* (1995), pp. 76-87; 'Rhododendrons in British gardens: a short history', in Postan (1996), pp. 156-86, esp. pp. 172-6.

26. Council minutes, 24 July 1945; 30 April 1946; 14 January 1947. Francis Hanger, 'Rhododendrons at Wisley', *Rhododendron Year Book* 1948, pp. 20-34; 'The kurume azalea garden at Wisley', *JRHS*, vol. 81 (1956), pp. 487-8. 'Notes from Wisley', vol. 78 (1953), pp. 122-7; vol. 81 (1956), pp. 224-7, 248-50; vol. 83 (1958), pp. 190-3; vol. 89 (1964), pp. 186-8.

27. For accounts of Wisley in Hanger's time, and of his alterations, see John Gilmour and Francis Hanger, 'Recent developments in the gardens at Wisley', *JRHS*, vol. 74 (1949), pp. 133-44; J.B. Paton, 'The R.H.S. gardens, Wisley', vol. 79 (1954), pp. 495-503; N.K. Gould *et al.*, *Guide to Wisley Gardens* (1958). See also the series of articles in the *Journal* entitled 'Notes from Wisley', begun in 1954, probably because the *Gardeners' Chronicle* had stopped doing its former series. From 1954 until 1957 the author was J.B. Paton; from 1957 until 1960, the majority author was N.K. Gould, followed, from 1961 to 1975, by Christopher Brickell. Up to 1970, they are indexed together in the cumulative index, so the following list is restricted to those articles which specifically discuss new constructions or plantings: vol. 80 (1955), pp. 296-9 (herbaceous borders); vol. 81 (1956), pp. 224-7 (woodland garden), 470-2 (Nisbet's dwarf conifers); vol. 88 (1963), pp. 194-6 (cherry field); vol. 95 (1970), pp. 332-5 (Bowles's Corner). Council minutes, 4 November 1947 (Cranfield ferns); 3 June, 15 July, 12 August 1947, 16 April 1957 (cherry garden); 22 February, 14 June, 29 November 1955, 14 August 1956, 19 February, 19 November-3 December 1957, 24 November, 15 December 1964 (Nisbet conifers); 9 August, 6 September, 15 November 1955; 19 March, 30 July 1957 (Bowles's Corner/lunatic asylum). Eric Parker, *Surrey Gardens* (1954), pp. 108-10. Arthur Simmonds, 'Bowles's Corner: a home for demented plants', *JRHS*, vol. 82 (1957), pp. 512-13.

28. For general works and redevelopments of the Knight and Brickell years, see once again 'Notes from Wisley', *JRHS*, until 1975. (After 1975, the 'Notes' series was retained but turned into a general heading for miscellaneous short notes from the staff.) Again, the list gives only articles on specific projects: vol. 88 (1963), pp. 323-5 (island beds); vol. 89 (1964), pp. 5-7 (rock garden renovation); vol. 95 (1970), pp. 332-5

(Bowles's Corner); vol. 96 (1971), pp. 5-6 (replanning trials area); vol. 97 (1972), pp. 240-41 (redevelopment of old trials squares near mixed borders). See also Christopher Brickell, 'Experts' garden to delight the layman', *CL*, 22 March 1973, pp. 743-6; 'Garden into modern showpiece', 6 September 1979, pp. 646-8; 'Wisley—the changing scene', *The Garden (JRHS)*, vol. 102 (1977), pp. 146-7. See also Geoffrey Smith, 'Visiting Wisley', *ibid.*, pp. 205-9, and the successive editions of the *Guide to Wisley Gardens* (1963, 1972, 1979, 1985).

29. Lanning Roper, 'The new formal garden for Wisley', *JRHS*, vol. 95 (1970), pp. 104-7. For the arduous chronicle of leaks, see Council minutes, 20 April, 22 June, 10 August, 21 September, 16 November, 7 December 1971; 11 January-28 March, 27 June, 5 September-31 October 1972; 13 March-1 May, 22 May-12 June 1973, 7 August-30 October 1973; 21 May, 11 June, 8 October 1974; 29 April 1975.

30. *JRHS*, vol. 88 (1963), pp. 279-80; vol. 89 (1964), pp. 363-4. The assessors were Lord Aberconway, Geoffrey Jellicoe, Sir Peter Shepheard, Sir William Holford, and Peter Youngman. Council minutes, 17 April, 21 May, 31 July-14 August, 25 September-9 October, 6 November 1962; 8 January, 18 April-25 June, 8-22 October, 18 December 1963; 14 January-4 February, 9 June, 15 September 1964. See *Grassroots*, no. 64 (July 1998), p. 5, for David Mulford's comment: 'I would tell [tour parties] that I see the pillars reflecting the fastigiate nature of the area—the two fastigiate beech behind, the catenary flanking the Rose Borders, Ginkgo biloba at the base and the two upright Tulip Trees either side of the pavilion; the roof represents a canopy, like that in a wooded area.'

31. *JRHS*, vol. 100 (1975), pp. 224-5 (information centre); vol. 103 (1978), pp. 249-51 (plant sales centre); *ibid.*, pp. 161-3 (herb garden); vol. 110 (1985), pp. 244-5 (alpine house area). For the rose garden, see vol. 100 (1975), pp. 282-3; vol. 101 (1976), p. 292; vol. 103 (1978), pp. 433-5.

32. John Main, 'The Jubilee Arboretum', *The Garden (JRHS)*, vol. 106 (1981), pp. 459-61. See also, for a survey of Wisley's trees, written before the planting was taken place, Alan Mitchell, 'The conifers at Wisley', vol. 100 (1975), pp. 276-81; 'Deciduous trees at Wisley', vol. 101 (1976), pp. 267-72.

33. Ken Aslet, 'The rock garden and alpines at Wisley', *JRHS*, vol. 95 (1970), pp. 10-16; Osamu Shimidzu, 'A Japanese view of the rock garden', vol. 103 (1978), pp. 117-20; John Main, 'The rock garden', vol. 107 (1982), pp. 408-10.

34. Mark Burleton, 'Trees that grew so fair', *The Garden (JRHS)*, vol. 116 (1991), pp. 68-70; Catherine Collins and Alan Toogood, 'Battleston: battered and unboughed', *ibid.*, vol. 122 (1997), pp. 710-13.

35. Model fruit gardens: Council minutes, 22 October 1946; Bultitude (1947); Gilbert (1953); Harry Baker, 'Remodelling the medium fruit garden', *JRHS*, vol. 97 (1972), pp. 467-71. Model vegetable garden: *ibid.*, vol. 88 (1963), pp. 281-4.

36. Disabled garden: Council minutes, 30 April, 9 January 1974; 12 January, 10 February, 17 May 1977. David Palmer, 'The garden for disabled people', *The Garden (JRHS)*, vol. 102 (1977), pp. 266-7. The book referred to was *The Easy Path to Gardening* (1972).

37. *JRHS*, vol. 100 (1975), pp. 225-7; Alison Goatcher, 'The new small gardens', vol. 104 (1979), pp. 158-60; David Mulford, 'A new model garden', vol. 108 (1983), pp. 358-60.

38. For the Lovelace purchase, see Council minutes, 24 March-21 April, 14 July-8 September, 3 November 1914. For the Ponsonby purchase, see 17 December 1918; 11 February-25 March, 27 May-2 June, 26 August-

23 September, 4 November 1919. For the Battleston Hill purchase, see references in note 17 above. For Bridgefoot Farm, see 30 November 1948. For the further Ockham estate purchase, see 7-28 October 1958; 25 May-23 June 1959, including the amusing discovery that the Ockham estate was trying to sell the RHS some land it had already sold it in 1914.

39. Contretemps with Guildford: Council minutes, 7 November 1905. Cottages at Send: 6 April, 20 April, 8 June 1948.

40. *GC*, 14 February 1914, pp. 117-18; 21 February 1931, pp. 148-9 (quoted). *JRHS*, vol. 40 (1914-15), pp. iv, 493-7. Council minutes, 9 December 1913; 27 January, 24 February 1914; 27 May 1919; 27 January 1920.

41. The complications of well-digging at Wisley: see Council minutes, 22 June 1915 for a full summary up to that time, but the theme is spread uniformly across many years' minutes. Fox and roadside planting: 25 January, 18 October 1927; 13 March 1928. Attempts at enclosure: *Times*, 14 July 1870, p. 5 f; 8 August 1870, p. 12 a; Lord Eversley, *Commons, Forests and Footpaths* (1910), pp. 189-92; Council minutes, 3 November 1931. Use of rubble for the carpark: 1-29 April 1969. In 1999, press attention focused on the the discovery of a body in the woods, but this was outside the garden boundary: see *Evening Standard*, 15 December 1999, p. 16 ('Evil that lurks at the garden gates').

42. *JRHS*, vol. 95 (1970), p. 144; vol. 106 (1981), pp. 113-14; vol. 121 (1996), pp. 65, 529; vol. 122 (1997), pp. 143, 767; vol. 123 (1998), pp. 126-7.

43. *HW*, 23 October 1987, p. 4. Storm appeal: *The Garden (JRHS)*, vol. 115 (1990), p. 159; Jim Gardiner, 'Mediterranean experiment', vol. 117 (1992), pp. 270-2; Catherine Collins and Alan Toogood, 'Battleston: battered and unboughed', vol. 122 (1997), pp. 710-13; vol. 124 (1999), p. 143.

44. *The Garden (JRHS)*, vol. 114 (1989), pp. 23-4; vol. 123 (1998), p. 689. Carpet-bedding: vol. 123 (1998), p. 146.

45. *Grassroots*, no. 28 (June 1995), pp. 4-5. 'Wisley: into the 21st century', *The Garden (JRHS)*, vol. 120 (1995), pp. 316-19. 'Sir Simon Hornby on new plans for Wisley', *CL*, 1 June 1995, p. 99, and ensuing correspondence, 15 June 1995, p. 91; 29 June 1995, p. 88.

46. *The Garden (JRHS)*, vol. 124 (1999), p. 77; vol. 125 (2000), p. 237.

47. Fred Whitsey, 'Great expectations', *The Garden (JRHS)*, vol. 125 (2000), pp. 14-17.

48. D. Lloyd, 'Who will buy our daffodils?', *JRHS*, vol. 96 (1971), p. 227.

6 The Society's Gardens: Rosemoor, Hyde Hall, Harlow Carr, pp. 97-112

1. Council minutes, 20 April, 18 May, 15-22 June 1926. *Times*, 1926: 4 June, p. 17 f; 7 June, p. 10 c; 9 June, p. 12 c; 12 June, p. 10 a; 14 June, p. 18 (photograph); 16 June, p. 16 f. The garden had been illustrated four years earlier in *CL*, vol. 51 (1922), pp. 668-76.

2. Falkner: Council minutes, 25 July, 12 September 1944; 8 October 1946. Ness: 10-24 September 1946. Hascombe: 7 October-4 November 1947; 2 March 1948. Furzey: 12 July 1955. Mrs Kendrick's garden: 17 April 1956. Haughley Park: 30 April 1957. Willoughbridge, Market Drayton: 4 June, 16 July 1957. Brooklands Farm, Sellindge: 2 July 1957. Compton Acres: 11 June 1963. Mrs R. Chope's garden: 1 February 1966.

3. The Rolle estate around Torrington was centred at Stevenstone, where Charles Barry Jr built a grand manor house for Mark Rolle in 1869-74; this has been largely demolished, and never figured significantly in the gardening press. (Loudon had slighted the earlier garden—see *GM*, vol. 19 (1843), pp. 243-4.) See R.J. Blackmore and J. Clemens, 'Last days of the House of Rolle', *Western Morning News*, 29 August 1970, p. 7, for

the only thing I have found of relevance to the garden. The principal Rolle garden was Bicton, near Budleigh Salterton on the south coast, where James Barnes was the most famous gardener.

4. Collingwood Ingram, author of *Ornamental Cherries* (1948), was awarded the VMH in 1952. See Anne Scott-James, '"Cherry" Ingram', *JRHS*, vol. 100 (1975), pp. 518-22; Martyn Rix, 'Cherry's lasting legacy', *The Garden (JRHS)*, vol. 123 (1998), pp. 244-7.

5. Patrick Synge, *The Gardens of Britain*, vol. 1: *Devon and Cornwall* (1977), pp. 71-4. Alvilde Lees-Milne and Rosemary Verey, eds., *The Englishwoman's Garden* (1980), pp. 97-100. Lady Anne Palmer, 'Rosemoor in Devon', *The Garden (JRHS)*, vol. 102 (1977), pp. 210-15. Roy Lancaster, 'A garden shared', *GC&HTJ*, 11 June 1982, pp. 32-33. Arthur Hellyer, 'Rare plants in a composed setting', *CL*, 10 April 1986, pp. 982-4. Richard Lee died in 1993: *The Garden (JRHS)*, vol. 118 (1993), p. 433. Peter Locke died in 2001: vol. 126 (2001), p. 502. Arthur Hellyer, 'Rosemoor Garden Nursery', *The Garden (JRHS)*, vol. 111 (1986), pp. 134-6; Penelope Hobhouse, *Private Gardens of England* (1986), pp. 36-41.

6. Report of Council for 1987, p. 1. Hackfalls Arboretum, near Hawke's Bay, was begun by the Berry family in the 1920s and named after the Aislabie garden in Yorkshire: see *Friars' Guide to New Zealand Gardens* (2001), p. 93.

7. For the Rosemoor Woods, see *HW*, 3 July 1997, p. 15. Status of beech in Devon: see J.M.B. Brown, *Studies on British Beechwoods*, Forestry Commission Bulletin no. 20 (1953), esp. pp. 15, 17-18, for the conclusion that all beechwoods further west than South Wales have been planted.

8. Jeremy Rougier and Christopher Bailes, 'Rosemoor: a national garden in the making', *The Garden (JRHS)*, vol. 114 (1989), pp. 152-6; 'Progress at Rosemoor', vol. 115 (1990), pp. 256-60; 'Rosemoor: a growing delight', vol. 116 (1991), pp. 181-5; 'Rosemoor—muddy, but unbowed', vol. 118 (1993), pp. 162-5; 'Rosemoor, five years on', vol. 119 (1994), pp. 174-7. Bailes, 'West country roses', vol. 120 (1995), pp. 326-31; 'Striking a balance', vol. 121 (1996), pp. 40-3; 'Naturalising narcissi at Rosemoor', ibid., pp. 146-9. Peter Earl and Bailes, 'Fruit and veg by design', ibid., pp. 496-9. John Chesters and John Lanyon, 'Tricyrtis at Rosemoor', ibid., pp. 536-9. Bailes, 'Controlling the heat', ibid., pp. 614-19; 'Progress at our gardens', vol. 122 (1997), pp. 120-1; 'Planting: a pragmatic approach', ibid., pp. 734-6; 'Life on the margins', vol. 123 (1998), pp. 444-7; 'Forget the flowers', ibid., pp. 584-7; Peter Earl and Allan Robinson, 'Raising the floor', vol. 125 (2000), esp. pp. 181-3; Geoff Stebbings, 'Rosemoor: ten years on', ibid., pp. 452-7; Anne Tattersall, 'Cultural harvest', ibid., pp. 608-9. 'Rosemoor: a national garden in the making', special supplement, *North Devon Journal*, 14 June 1990. Karen Wilson *et al.*, *Rosemoor* (RHS guidebook, 2002). Mary Keen, 'Meeting the masterplanner of Rosemoor [Elizabeth Banks]', *Independent on Sunday*, 23 June 1991, magazine section pp. 70-1. Also news announcements in *The Garden (JRHS)*, vol. 123 (1998), p. 127; vol. 124 (1999), pp. 479, 807, 906; vol. 127 (2002), pp. 243, 330, 507.

9. Conflict over development of Rosemoor—see letters in *The Garden (JRHS)*, vol. 116 (1991), pp. 95-6, and reply from Bailes, p. 211. Edward Heathcoat Amory, 'Goodbye to the Devon we love', *CL*, 21 May 1998, pp. 57-9.

10. Anthony Huxley, 'An "open-and-shut" garden', *CL*, 16 May 1974, pp. 1178-80. For a biographical notice of R.H.M. ('Dick') Robinson, see *The Garden (JRHS)*, vol. 122 (1997), p. 388.

11. For the acquisition of Hyde Hall, and initial

negotiations over roads and the Robinsons, see Fred Whitsey, 'A priceless gift', *The Garden (JRHS)*, vol. 118 (1993), pp. 10-14. Nine files of correspondence and reports relating to the acquisition are in the RHS archives, MB1/1.

12. Announcements in *The Garden (JRHS)*, vol. 122 (1997), pp. 121, 127-8, 615; vol. 123 (1998), pp. 127-8, 305-6, 394; vol. 124 (1999), pp. 479-80; vol. 125 (2000), pp. 16-17, 152; vol. 127 (2002), pp. 243, 418. Chris Bailes, 'Eastern promise', *ibid.*, vol. 125 (2000), pp. 266-9. For roses at Hyde Hall, see Lia Leendertz, 'Give it plenty of swagger', vol. 127 (2002), pp. 31-5. Karen Wilson *et al.*, *Hyde Hall* (RHS guidebook, 2002).

13. Council minutes, 7 October 1919; 24 June 1924; 9 June 1925; 9 February, 9 March, 20 April, 19 October 1926; 22 February, 8 March, 26 April, 17 May 1927.

14. Biographical notices of the major figures in the pre-RHS history of Harlow Carr, in *NG*. Barbara Clough: vol. 23 no. 5 (September 1969), pp. 149-51. Jessie Blossom Coulthurst: vol. 39 no. 2 (Spring 1985), p. 41. Fred Dunning: vol. 54 no. 4 (October 2000), p. 117. John Fitton: vol. 47 no. 2 (Spring 1993), p. 18. Colonel Grey: vol. 10 no. 2 (March 1956), pp. 21-4. Robert Hare: vol. 26 no. 5 (September 1972), pp. 160-1. Donald G. Ineson: vol. 21 no. 3 (May 1967), pp. 85-7. George Knight: vol. 27 no. 1 (January 1973), pp. 14-19. Kenneth Lemmon: vol. 40 no. 2 (Spring 1986), p. 7. Sir William Milner: vol. 14 no. 3 (May 1960), pp. 14-15. Geoffrey Smith: vol. 28 no. 6 (November 1974), pp. 161-4.

15. For the development of Harlow Carr, see *NG, passim*, but the following articles are particularly useful as recording milestones and development plans: 'Plans for the future at Harlow', vol. 10 no. 1 (January 1956), pp. 5-9; Donald G. Ineson, 'The rock garden at Harlow', vol. 10 no. 5 (September 1956), pp. 5-9; Geoffrey D. Smith, 'The woodland garden at Harlow', vol. 11 no. 2 (March 1957), pp. 24-7, and see pp. 5-12 for progress and plans; Donald G. Ineson, 'For a change—we look backwards', vol. 11 no. 6 (November 1957), pp. 5-13; Edwin Cherry, 'Memories of Harlow Car', vol. 14 no. 6 (November 1960), pp. 16-23; A. Sigston Thompson: 'Harlow Car: objects and aims explained', vol. 18 no. 2 (March 1964), pp. 5-9; F.C. Barnes, 'A random thought anent Harlow Car', vol. 21 no. 3 (May 1967), pp. 99-100 (against straight lines); 50th-anniversary issue, vol. 44 no. 3 (Summer 1990), esp. pp. 18-25 for reminiscences by A. Sigston Thompson, Nancy Boydell, John Main, and Philip Swindells; Barry Nuttall, 'Light out of darkness', vol. 50 no. 2 (Spring 1996), pp. 16-17; vol. 54 no. 3 (July 2000), the Jubilee number, esp. Andrew Hart and Fred Dunning, 'Whither Harlow Carr? A look into the future', pp. 94-7. For a survey of the soil conditions at Harlow Carr, see vol. 15 no. 6 (November 1961), pp. 5-11. See also Kenneth Lemmon, *The Gardens of Britain*, vol. 5: *Yorkshire and Humberside* (1978), pp. 74-80; Geoffrey Smith, 'It's green not grim up north', *The Garden (JRHS)*, vol. 126 (2001), pp. 562-3. For Colonel Grey as a garden designer, see 'The gardens of Charles Grey', *NG*, vol. 10 no. 2 (March 1956), pp. 21-4.

16. *NG*, vol. 19 no. 6 (November 1965), p. 212.

17. *NG*, vol. 26 no 6. (November 1972), pp. 171-9; vol. 27 no. 1 (January 1973), pp. 3-14; vol. 28 no. 4 (July 1974), p. 102.

18. *NG*, vol. 35 no. 3 (summer 1981), pp. 88-9; vol. 35 no. 4 (autumn 1981), p. 107; vol. 36 no. 1 (Winter 1981-82), p. 8; vol. 36 no. 3 (Summer 1982), pp. 81-2; vol. 44 no. 2 (Spring 1990), p. 9; vol. 49 no. 3 (Summer 1995), p. 8.

19. Council minutes, 5 October 1948; 30 March–13 April 1954; 26 July 1960; 24 September 1963. *NG*, vol. 12 no. 1 (January 1958), p. 9; vol. 19 no. 1 (January 1965), p. 13.

20. *NG*, vol. 41 no. 4 (autumn 1987), p. 7. From 1987, each

issue of *The Northern Gardener* had a section on news of the RHS.

21. *HW*, 20 February 1997, p. 3. *NG*, vol. 51 no. 3 (July 1997), p. 72; vol. 54 no. 3 (July 2000), p. 74; vol. 55 no. 2 (April 2001), p. 42. *The Garden (JRHS)*, vol. 126 (2001), pp. 159, 411; and see the Tradescant column, 'Wisley has another rival', ibid., p. 591.

22. *NG*, vol. 43 no. 3 (summer 1989), p. 9, for the opening of the museum. From 1996 each issue of the *Northern Gardener* carried a piece about an item selected from the museum's collections.

23. Nigel Colborn, 'Northern jewel', *The Garden (JRHS)*, vol. 126 (2001), pp. 534-9. Karen Wilson *et al.*, *Harlow Carr* (RHS guidebook, 2002).

7 Shows, pp. 113-50

1. Council minutes, 8 April 1805.

2. John Allnut was inaccurately described as a nurseryman by Bretschneider (1898), p. 232, and this error has been perpetuated. For accounts of his villa garden at Clapham, see *GM*, vol. 3 (1827), p. 362; *GC*, 19 June 1841, p. 400 [misnumbered '300']; 5 February 1842, p. 96; 6 March 1858, p. 176.

3. As it seems not to have been done before, here is a list of the accounts of exhibits at the Regent Street meetings as published in *GM*: vol. 1 (1826), pp. 87, 211-213, 340-344, 459-61; vol. 2 (1827), pp. 103-5, 241-2, 356-8, 469; vol. 3 (1827-8), pp. 106-7, 229-31, 356-7, 473-4; vol. 4 (1828), pp. 56-7, 166-8, 284-5, 408-9, 514-15; vol. 5 (1829), pp. 85-6, 216-18, 342-3, 466-7, 611-12, 735-6; vol. 6 (1830), pp. 112-14, 234-6 *passim*, 369, 504-6, 618-20, 728-9; vol. 7 (1831), pp. 126, 250-1, 380-1, 509-10, 622-3, 733-36; vol. 8 (1832), pp. 125-7, 252-4, 378-80, 505-7, 614-15, 742-3; vol. 9 (1833), pp. 127-8, 247-8, 382-4, 507-9, 632-4, 725-8; vol. 10 (1834), pp. 188-90, 244, 298-9, 355-6, 410, 468, 523, 579-80; vol. 11 (1835), pp. 110, 214-16, 325-7, 381-2, 439, 494-5, 607-8; vol. 12 (1836), pp. 51-2, 106-7, 163-4, 220, 273, 330-2, 379-80, 499-500, 556, 721-3; vol. 13 (1837), pp. 48, 96, 191-2, 240, 333-5, 382-3, 478-9, 526-8; vol. 14 (1838), pp. 62-3, 158-9, 207-8, 352, 395-7; vol. 15 (1839), pp. 42-7, 202-7, 480, 531-6, 574-85. In the later years the accounts of papers read, previously kept separate, were included in the accounts of the meetings; hence the increased page counts. Donald Beaton began reviewing the Society's meetings for *CottGard* in 1852: see vol. 9 (4 November 1852), pp. 8-9; 18 November 1852, pp. 122-4; 23 December 1852, pp. 220-1; 3 February 1853, pp. 341-2; 3 March 1853, pp. 420-1; 17 March 1853, pp. 457-9; 31 March 1853, pp. 498-500; vol. 10 (21 April 1853), pp. 37-40; 5 May 1853, pp. 78-9; 18 August 1853, pp. 377-9; vol. 11 (3 November 1853), pp. 76-8; 22 December 1853, pp. 215-17; 2 February 1854, pp. 336-9; 9 March 1854, pp. 437-40; 23 March 1854, pp. 478-80; vol. 12 (6 April 1854), pp. 4-6; 20 April 1854, pp. 34-6; 4 May 1854, pp. 72-4; vol. 13 (14 November 1854), pp. 116-18; 21 November 1854, pp. 136-8; 12 December 1854, pp. 197-8; 19 December 1854, pp. 217-19; 13 February 1855, pp. 370-2; 20 February 1855, pp. 390-3; 13 March 1855, pp. 448-51; 20 March 1855, pp. 469-71; vol. 14 (10 April 1855), pp. 20-3; 17 April 1855, pp. 34-6; 15 May 1855, pp. 104-7; 3 July 1855, pp. 231-4; 10 July 1855, pp. 248-50; vol. 15 (27 November 1855), pp. 140-2; 4 December 1855, p. 160; vol. 16 (29 April 1856), pp. 76-8; vol. 17 (2 December 1856), pp. 141-3; 3 February 1857, pp. 319-21; 10 March 1857, pp. 391-3; vol. 18 (14 April 1857), pp. 16-18; 5 May 1857, pp. 81-3; 7 July 1857, pp. 229-31; vol. 19 (2 February 1858), pp. 289-91; 9 March 1858, pp. 347-9.

4. Council minutes, 9 April–29 June 1827 *passim*. *Times*, 25 June 1827, p. 7 b (quoted). Jarrin case: *Morning Herald*, 18 November 1828. p. 2 f. Council Minutes for 21 August, 9-30 December 1828.

5. *GM*, vol. 3 (1827), pp. 108-9, 231-3, 357-9.

6. Council minutes, 5 May–19 June 1828; and 21 August

for the financial results. *Times*, 23 June 1828, p. 7 a; 25 June 1828, p. 3 c (on police control).

7. Council minutes, 20 June–3 July 1829. *GM*, vol. 5 (1829), pp. 467-9. *Times*, 29 June 1829, p. 2 e. *Morning Post*, 29 June 1829, p. 3 c. For Paul Pry, see Simmonds (1946).

8. Council minutes, 24 March 1830; 25 March 1831. *GM*, vol. 7 (1831), pp. 126, 510, 716. This last entry contains a tantalising line from Loudon about a pseudonymous contributor's criticism of the fête: 'as it is rather severe, we cannot publish it unless he will give his real name'.

9. *Transactions*, unpaginated appendix to Second Series vol. 1 (1831-35). Fletcher (1969), pp. 128-9, implies that the competitions started in February 1831, with pineapples; but the year's cycle of competitions was set to run from May to April, so the pineapple competition would not have been held until February 1832, and camellias not until April 1832.

10. For florists' societies, see the works of Ruth Duthie: 'English florists' societies and feasts in the seventeenth and first half of the eighteenth centuries', *GH*, vol. 10 (1982), pp. 17-35, and 'Florists' societies and feasts after 1750', *ibid.*, vol. 12 (1988), pp. 8-38; *Florists' Flowers and Societies* (1988). For the records of florists' shows, see *An Account of the Different Flower Shews, held in Lancashire, Cheshire, Yorkshire, &c., for the Year 1821; An Account of the Different Auricula and Tulip Shews ... in the Year 1823; The Florist's Gazette ... for the Year 1824* (all published in Manchester by R. and W. Dean); succeeded by *An Account of the Different Flower Shews ... in the Year 1826* (published in Ashton-under-Lyne).

11. *GC*, 26 June 1847, pp. 419, 420; 2 October 1847, p. 654; 9 October 1847, p. 667. *Florist*, vol. 1 (1848), pp. 177-8. A more sympathetic portrayal of Lindley appears in 'Gregory' (1841), p. 114.

12. Council minutes, 23 February 1833. *The Times*, 28 May 1833, p. 4 f, for an account of the first show.

13. Here is a list of the accounts of Chiswick shows, from *GM*: vol. 9 (1833), pp. 383, 509-11; vol. 10 (1834), pp. 299-300, 356, 410-12, 523-4; vol. 11 (1835), pp. 325-7, 382-3, 438-9; vol. 12 (1836), pp. 273, 332, 380-2, 443-4; vol. 13 (1837), pp. 379-82; vol. 14 (1838), pp. 397-400; vol. 16 (1840), pp. 310-11, 360; vol. 17 (1841), p. 331; vol. 18 (1842), p. 381; vol. 19 (1843), p. 453. In vol. 18 Loudon announced his intention of henceforth paying no attention to ephemeral things such as shows, but did not stick rigorously to it. See also *FM*, vol. 5 (1840), pp. 60-2; vol. 6 (1841), pp. 21, 29-31, 56-59. *Florist*, vol. 1 (1848), pp. 179-84. *GMB*, vol. 3 (1851), pp. 140-41. *CottGard*, vol. 10 (26 May 1853), pp. 139-42; 23 June 1853, pp. 218-20; 30 June 1853, pp. 238-40; 21 July 1853, pp. 300-1; 28 July 1853, pp. 314-16; vol. 12 (25 May 1854), pp. 133-5; 1 June 1854, pp. 154-6; 15 June 1854, pp. 192-4; 22 June 1854, pp. 214-16; 6 July 1854, pp. 252-4; 20 July 1854, pp. 294-6; 27 July 1854, pp. 314-17; vol. 14 (24 July 1855), pp. 287-91; 4 September 1855, pp. 406-8; vol. 18 (9 June 1857), pp. 157-8; 16 June 1857, pp. 166-7; vol. 20 (15 June 1858), pp. 155-8. A semi-fictionalised account of a Chiswick show appears in 'Gregory' (1864), pp. 113-17. The deutzia standard incident was recalled by Beaton in *CottGard*, vol. 22 (17 May 1859), p. 90. See also 'Chiswick shows in old days', *GardMag*, 17 December 1898, p. 838.

14. For examples of such comparisons, see *FM*, vol. 5 (1840), pp. 126-8; vol. 6 (1841), pp. 104-6. *GMB*, vol. 1 (1850), pp. 196-8.

15. *FM*, vol. 6 (1841), p. 21. *GM*, vol. 12 (1836), pp. 380-1.

16. *FM*, vol. 1 (1836), p. 72. *GFA*, 3 June 1848, p. 118. For the subsequent history of music at the Society's shows, see the chapter on Chiswick and Kensington, subsection 'The fine arts at Kensington', and on

17. Sabbatarian demand: *GM*, vol. 19 (1843), pp. 222-4. Ladies' cloakroom: Council minutes, 25 April 1838. Mrs Marryat borrowing tent, 12 July 1838. Louisa Lawrence's complaints about medals, ill-treatment at the gate, and finally her decision to sell her orchids, 25 January, 19 July 1853, 14 March 1854. Cremorne holding a show on the same day as Chiswick: *Midland Florist*, vol. 10 (1841), pp. 334-6. Crime: Council minutes, 4 July 1842, 21 June 1853.

18. Council minutes, 7 June, 11 August 1837; 9 March 1839. *GardGaz*, 18 February 1837, p. 104; 25 March 1837, p. 185; 8 April 1837, p. 216; 20 May 1837, p. 318; 27 May 1837, pp. 334, 335; 3 June 1837, p. 351; 17 June 1837, pp. 382-3; 6 January 1838, p. 8; 17 March 1838, pp. 170-1; 14 April 1838, p. 233; 26 May 1838, p. 328 (the plate incident); 9 June 1838, p. 360; 19 January 1839, p. 40; 16 March 1839, pp. 168-9 (refusal of further awards to Glenny); 23 March 1839, pp. 184-5; 30 March 1839, p. 200; 6 April 1839, pp. 216-17; 20 April 1839, p. 249; 27 April 1839, p. 264 (five open letters to the Society); 11 May 1839, p. 297; 15 June 1839, p. 377; 16 November 1839, p. 736. For Glenny more generally, see Tjaden (1986); Tjaden (1983).

19. *GardGaz*, vol. 2 (1838), p. 392. 'Gregory' (1841), p. 117. *CottGard*, vol. 22 (24 May 1859), pp. 101-2. Special constables: Council minutes, 11 April 1848.

20. Council minutes, 1 August 1843; 5 August 1845; 13 May 1846; 24 July 1849. See Altick (1978), pp. 420-1, for the economics of early 19th-century shows generally.

21. *GMB*, vol. 1 (1850), pp. 196-8: 'To the Horticultural Society belongs the merit of raising horticulture, when it had to work single handed; but the Royal Botanic Society deserves considerable praise for having aroused the older Society from a kind of lethargy into which it had fallen, and which in a few years must have done it considerable injury. But now, thanks to competition, each is trying to eclipse the other; and hence we have two active institutions espousing the cause of horticultural progress, instead of one ancient "inutility".'

22. Council minutes, 16 May 1854; 29 April 1856.

23. Council minutes, 17 July 1855; 4 November 1856; 26 May 1857. *GC*, 27 October 1855, p. 709. Lindley's £5 prize was noted in *CottGard*, vol. 17 (2 December 1856), p. 142.

24. *Midland Florist*, vol. 10 (1856), p. 343.

25. Council minutes, 25 March, 1 April, 15 April, 24 June 1859. For reports of the actually achieved St James's shows, see Donald Beaton's accounts in *CottGard*, vol. 19 (3 November 1857), pp. 61-4; vol. 20 (27 April 1858), pp. 51-4; 11 May 1858, pp. 79-81; 23 November 1858, pp. 111-14; vol. 22 (17 May 1859), pp. 90-91; also *PRHS*, vol. 1 (1861), pp. 38-41.

26. *GC*, 24 May 1862, pp. 475, 477-8.

27. Council minutes, 11 February, 11 March 1851. *GC*, 7 June 1856, p. 359. See *GMB*, vol. 2 (1850), p. 1, for a view of a John Waterer show at Regent's Park.

28. *Midland Florist*, vol. 10 (1856), pp. 334-6, 339-43.

29. Council minutes, 3 June 1864. *JHort*, 16 August 1864, pp. 126-7; 30 August 1864, pp. 169-70. For forced flowers at the Crystal Palace, see *CottGard*, vol. 19 (1858), pp. 333-5, and pp. 289-91 for grumbles about the lack of forced winter flowers at the Horticultural.

30. *GC*, 15 January 1870, p. 70; Council minutes, 16 March 1870.

31. Council minutes, 17 March, 7 April 1875.

32. Fish: *GC*, 29 April 1871, p. 551 (and see 7 January p. 9, 28 January p. 109, 25 February p. 239, 11 March pp. 310-11, and 25 March p. 382 for an entertaining quarrel about flower shows between Thomas Baines and W.P. Ayres). Wills: *JHort*, 27 January 1881, p. 63. *GC*, 27 November 1875, p. 684. Robinson: *THE GARDEN*,

vol. 9 (1876), p. 854. For various aspects of the history of 19th-century shows, see Elliott (2001).

33. Council minutes, 27 March, 9 October 1860; 4 January 1861; 28 March, 4 April, 18 July, 1 August 1862. *GC*, 7 June 1862, pp. 521-2.

34. Council minutes, 30 July, 10 August 1869; 16 March, 6 April, 13 May, 29 June 1870. *GC*, 29 April 1871, pp. 545-6; 13 May 1871, p. 610.

35. Council minutes, 2 August 1883. The Health Exhibition of 1884 included a model tea garden, as a way of stimulating the public's interest in tea, but the RHS seems not to have been involved in its creation.

36. Council minutes, 14 April, 14 July 1885; 12 January 1886; 22 March, 12 April 1887. See Peter H. Hoffenberg, *An Empire on Display: English, Indian, and Australian Exhibitions from the Crystal Palace to the Great War* (2001), for more on the Colonial and Indian Exhibition.

37. Council minutes, 25 July, 31 October 1865; 23 January, 15-24 May 1866. *GC*, 13 January 1866, p. 30; 24 February 1866, pp. 170, 173; 31 March 1866, pp. 289-90; 7 April 1866, p. 314; 14 April 1866, pp. 337-8, 340; 28 April 1866, pp. 386-7 [plan]; 12 May 1866, p. 434; 26 May 1866, pp. 481-8; 2 June 1866, pp. 512-13; 14 July 1866, pp. 656-7; 29 September 1866, pp. 924-5; 17 November 1866, p. 1093. *JHort*, 29 May 1866, pp. 390-7, 401-3 [£5,212]; 5 June 1866, p. 419; 14 August 1866, pp. 121-2.

38. *Ibid.*, p. 121. For the roses, see *GC*, 14 July 1866, p. 656—the original passage was in *Revue Horticole*, 1866, p. 234, and see pp. 233-6, 257-60, 273-7 for Edouard André's coverage of the exhibition as a whole.

39. *GC*, 26 January 1901, pp. 62-3. The departed jurors were Charles Pilcher, George Thomson and William Dodds. For Dean's career, see *ibid.*, 26 August 1905, pp. 168-9.

40. *GC*, 4 May 1912, pp. 302-3 (including photograph of tent being erected); 18 May 1912, pp. 330-1, 336; 25 May 1912, pp. 352, 357-8; 22 June 1912, p. 413; 29 June 1912, p. 431; supplements to issues of 25 May, 1 June, 8 June (pp. i-xlviii); 7 December 1912, p. 431. *JHort*, 30 May 1912, pp. 485-6, 487-503. Reginald Cory, *The Horticultural Record* (1914). The Minutes of the Directors and the Finance Committee, Edward White's correspondence file, and an album of views of the Exhibition are held in the RHS Archives.

40. Council minutes, 18 June, 2 July, 23 July 1878.

41. Council minutes, 27 March, 21 April, 1 May 1888. *GC*, 19 May 1888, p. 624, and report, pp. 629-30. *JHort*, 17 May 1888, pp. 397-8; 24 May 1888, pp. 417-18, 421-4.

42. *JHort*, 25 May 1911, p. 472. Selfe-Leonard: Council minutes, 13 February 1893.

43. *JHort*, 26 May 1898, pp. 437-8; 1 June 1893, p. 429.

44. *JHort*, 8 June 1899, pp. 474-5. As early as 1893 there was an account of tents 'wedged with people panting in the heat and longing to "get out of it"'—*JHort*, 1 June 1893, p. 429.

45. The history of the Society's Medals has been written in Tjaden (1994). For the rest of the discussion of medals, only specific quotations and additional information will be footnoted; see Tjaden for everything else.

46. Council minutes, 16 April 1836. *GM*, vol. 12 (1836), pp. 329-30. A scale of values was assigned to the Medals, so that those who accumulated enough could exchange them for other medals, for sets of the *Transactions*, etc. 'A silver Banksian medal is valued at 25, a silver Knightian at 50, a large silver at 100, a gold Banksian at 200, a gold Knightian at 300, a large gold at 500. Thus two awards of silver Banksian medals will entitle an exhibitor to a silver Knightian ... [&c &c]'.

47. *GM*, vol. 9 (1833), pp. 509-11.

48. *GardGaz*, vol. 2 (1838), pp. 154-5: Wyon described as 'a wag of the first water' for a design showing a lady upside-down.

49. Council minutes, 20 July, 3 August 1870; 1 March, 4 October, 8 November 1876.

50. *GC*, 29 May 1875, p. 697. Council minutes, 7-12, 25 May, 9 June 1875.

51. Council minutes, 10 October, 14 November 1893. *GC*, 18 February 1899, p. 109.

52. *GC*, 22 May 1841, p. 323; 29 May 1841, p. 339; 5 June 1841, p. 363.

53. Examples of complaints resolved by the award of additional medals: 2 June 1838 (Antrobus versus Louisa Lawrence); 22 September 1838 (Channing's roses); 21 May, 18 June 1850 (Green's azaleas found equal to the awarded competitor's). In 1847 the Duke of Northumberland was given permission to give his gardener a medal at his own cost, in circumstances which suggest that it was to remedy a perceived discrepancy: Council minutes, 8 December 1847.

54. Council minutes, 23 July 1889; 20 November 1906; 23 November-7 December 1915; 7 June 1922; 4 September 1923; 9 October 1973. 1993 AGM report, p. iv.

55. *GM*, vol. 12 (1836), pp. 380-1. *GardGaz*, vol. 1 (1837), pp. 104, 185, 318, 334-5, 351, 382-3; vol. 2 (1838), pp. 8, 170-1, 233, 360; vol. 3 (1839), pp. 40, 168-9.

56. Council minutes, 23 August 1834; 5 December 1905; 28 January 1919; 11 October 1938. *GardGaz*, vol. 1 (1837), pp. 202-3, 216, 488. *GC*, 27 November 1875, p. 684. For the 1990s fuss, see the 1994 AGM minutes, pp. vii-viii, and *HW*, 26 May 1994, p. 6.

57. Council minutes, 17 October 1922; 26 June 1923; 11-25 June 1929 (proposed Corsar Cup); 17 April 1934; 5 April 1938 (proposed Hanbury Cup); 14 June 1949.

58. Council minutes, 5-19 March 1907; 31 January 1911; 21 January 1913.

59. These were the A.J. Waley Medal (instituted in 1937, but not awarded until after its takeover by the RHS), the Crosfield Cup, the Lionel de Rothschild Cup, the Loder Cup, the McLaren Cup, and the Rothschild Challenge Cup. As the Society already had a Loder Rhododendron Cup, there was some nice scope for confusion, which has somehow been avoided.

60. Council minutes, 9 May 1911.

61. Thomas Moore, 'On judging new plants', *JRHS*, vol. 1 (1865), pp. 99-107; James Douglas, 'Principles of judging at flower-shows', vol. 17 (1895), pp. 134-40; John Wright, 'Horticultural exhibitions and schedules, with the principles and practice of judging', vol. 21 (1897-8), pp. 499-537; William Wilks, 'Some difficulties in flower show schedules', vol. 37 (1911-12), pp. 497-504, and vol. 39 (1913-14), pp. 535-40; A. J. Cobb, 'Suggestions to amateur exhibitors', vol. 53 (1928), pp. 8-24. *GC*, 8 March 1924, p. 127. On the amateur question, see also Council minutes, 21 October, 18 November 1913; 14 November 1922; 6 February 1951; 22 July 1952; 17 February 1953. Vicary Gibbs and Lionel de Rothschild both incurred criticism for exhibiting as amateurs, and the latter offered to withdraw from competition: see 7 October 1924; 30 June 1931.

62. Onions: *GC*, 8 March 1924, p. 127; Council minutes, 5 June 1928. Miniature gardens: 16 December 1924; 12 February-12 March 1929; 17 February 1953; 18 February 1958; 23 June 1959.

63. John Sales, 'Marks of success', *The Garden* (*JRHS*), vol. 124 (1999), pp. 346-7.

64. For gnomes, see chapter 15. Whiten (1982), p. 49, repeated in good faith a story that must have been passed down from Ron Sargent, that it had been a garden by Winkfield Manor Nurseries that had been cleared of bathing beauties by invoking the livestock rule. Ambrose Congreve, the former director of Winkfield, indignantly denied the story, and while society beauties like the young Katie Boyle can be

found amid his display gardens in press photographs, nothing has come to light to support the livestock story. Bathing pools: Council minutes, 22 January, 18 June 1935.

65. Council minutes, 24 January, 1 August, 26 September 1905. *GC*, 28 June 1902, pp. 425-8; 15 July 1905, pp. 53-7.

66. *GC*, 17 May 1913, p. 329; 24 May 1913, p. 346, and report, pp. 349-59; 31 May 1913, pp. 369-70, and report, pp. 372-3. *JHort*, 22 May 1913, pp. 488-92, 497-99; 29 May 1913, pp. 521-2.

67. There have been three published histories of the Chelsea Show: Marsden-Smedley (1975); Whiten (1982); Geddes-Brown (2000). All have been drawn on in this text.

68. For the defence of the 1916 Chelsea, see *Times*, 23 May 1916, p. 11 c; for Keeble's remark, Council minutes, 6 June 1916. Entertainment Tax: *ibid.*, 2-16 May, 29 August, 24 October-19 December 1916; 17 December 1918; 7 January, 11 March-8 April 1919. See also Brent Elliott, 'A political family', *The Garden (JRHS)*, vol. 117 (1992), pp. 37-9.

69. Council minutes, 28 January, 17 June 1919.

70. Council minutes, 17 May 1921 (first report of bad weather insurance); 5 June 1928 (letter from the King referring to the wintry weather!). *GC*, 9 June 1923, p. 313.

71. A very selective list: Council minutes, 24 February 1914 (earliest report on infrastructure costs); 9 May 1922, 10 February 1931 (drainage); 3 December 1946, 4 February, 17 June 1947 (avenue); 8 June 1948 (drainage, tennis courts); 3 April 1951, 8 July-4 November 1952 *passim* (elms); 20 January 1953 (parking). For an account of what Chelsea is like from the organiser's point of view, see Stephen Bennett, 'Countdown to Chelsea', *The Garden (JRHS)*, vol. 119 (1994), pp. 202-5.

72. G.C.T. Dean, *The Royal Hospital, Chelsea* (1950), p. 287.

73. Symons-Jeune: Council minutes, 15 June 1926; 22 February 1927. Grounds restoration: 11 June 1924; 14 June 1949; 18 April 1950.

74. Council minutes, 31 January 1928; 3 December 1946; 20 March 1951. *GC*, 14 June 1932, p. 431.

75. For pre-war plant sales, see Marsden-Smedley, *op. cit.*, p. 15. Debates over sales: Council minutes, 28 July 1931; 10 January 1950; 8 March 1960; 8 June, 13 July, 16 November 1971. *GC*, 18 May 1973, p. 7; 1 June 1973, p. 5.

76. For debates and amendments to opening times, see Council minutes, 21 June 1927; 11 June 1929; 14 July, 11-25 August, 23 September, 3 November 1931; 5 July 1932; 5 February 1935; 11 January 1949.

77. *Times*, 14 January 1976, p. 15 a-b; 15 January 1976, p. 15 e-f; 16 January 1976, p. 15 e-f; 17 January 1976, p. 13e-f; 19 January 1976, p. 13 e-f; 20 January 1976, pp. 4 a, 13 e-f; 21 January 1976, p. 17 e-f; 22 January 1976, p. 15 f-g; 23 January 1976, p. 2 h; 14 February 1976, p. 15 e-f. 1976 AGM report, p. vi. *GC&HTJ*, 20 February 1981, p. 4. Note that at this time guide dogs were also excluded from the lobby of the House of Commons. The letters and extracts from Council minutes are held in a file in the Library.

78. Council minutes, 13 August 1946. *GC*, 24 May 1947, p. 191.

79. *HW*, 27 May 1988, p. 3; 3 June 1988, p. 3.

80. *GC*, 3 June 1950, p. 213. Council minutes, 28 June 1960; 10-24 January, 29 August—7 November 1961; 5 June 1962; 14 June 1966. *GC&HTJ*, 16 May 1980, pp. 18-19. *HW*, 10 January 1986, p. 3; 7 March 1986, p. 3.

81. Nigel Colborn, 'Material improvements', *The Garden (JRHS)*, vol. 124 (1999), pp. 414-17, and 'Seeing Chelsea in a new light', vol. 125 (2000), pp. 104-5. For the recycling of the marquee, see *Grassroots*, no. 79 (June/July 2000), p. 6. The Old Chelsea Marquee Company was not an RHS trading arm, but an independent company that paid the RHS a royalty.

82. Council minutes, 11 March 1919; 10-17 May 1921; 4-18 May 1926.

83. Council minutes, 26 July 1949; 31 January 1950; 10 June 1952; 20 March 1962; 15-29 April, 9 September 1969.

84. *Grassroots*, no. 24 (February 1995), pp. 4-5.

85. Council minutes, 11 May 1920; 27 January 1925; 11 September 1928; 4 April 1934; 19 February 1935; 18 July 1939; 6 September, 1 November, 13 December 1949; 11 July 1950; 3 March 1953. Orchid tent: *GC*, 19 June 1920, p. 305; 14 June 1924, p. 354. Discontinuation of art tent: *ibid.*, 1 June 1935, p. 368. For an account of the process of erecting the marquee, see Whiten, *op. cit.*, pp. 70-2.

86. A.E. Usher, 'Thirty years an exhibitor', *JRHS*, vol. 63 (1938), pp. 553-60; Louis Russell, 'Fifty years of showing at Chelsea', *The Garden (JRHS)*, vol. 105 (1980), pp. 471-7. For Maurice Mason, see *ibid.*, vol. 119 (1994), pp. 102-3, and *GI*, 1954, p. 161.

87. Woodsman (i.e. John Street), *GC&HTJ*, 22 May 1981, p. 20. For the crown, see *ibid.*, 20 May 1977, pp. 5, 7; for the swan, *CL*, 31 May 1979, pp. 1716-17. For Bob Sweet's cottage, *GC&HTJ*, 3 June 1983, p. 9.

88. Council minutes, 20 April 1926; 26 April 1927; 12 February, 25 June 1929; 6 October 1953; 8 November 1966. *GC*, 28 May 1955, p. 211; 8 June 1973, p. 41. See 'Senex', ' "Chelsea" Show in 1950', *GI*, 8 June 1929, p. 398, for a humorous prediction of the development of show rock gardens.

89. *Daily Express*: Council minutes, 16 June, 20 October 1931. Slocock: 30 September 1958. Edward White on excessively architectural gardens: *GC*, 13 June 1931, p. 456; 27 June 1931, p. 493. Congreve: *GI*, 1952, p. 14. Colvin: *GC*, 5 June 1970, pp. 8-9.

90. *HW*, 2 June 1994, pp. 18-19. For the 'Reflections' garden going to Wisley: *The Garden (JRHS)*, vol. 124 (1999), p. 489. A selection of Chelsea gardens from the 1990s is described and illustrated in John Moreland, *Chelsea Gold* (2000). For accounts of what goes into designing a garden at Chelsea, see Ian G. Walker, 'Making a Chelsea garden', *GI*, 1952, p. 131; Elizabeth Banks, 'Chelsea challenge', *The Garden (JRHS)*, vol. 116 (1991), pp. 266-8; Robert Burton, 'Creating a nectar haven', vol. 123 (1998), pp. 330-3; Gillian Temple, 'It's that Show again', *ProfHort*, vol. 5 (1991), pp. 142-4. And, for an American viewpoint, see Christopher Reed, 'The greatest show on earth', *Horticulture*, March 1984, pp. 32-52.

91. 'A Chelsea visitor's diary', *HW*, 2 June 1989, p. 29.

92. 'Top garden designer denies copying rival's classic plot', *Sunday Telegraph*, 1 November 1998, p. 3; 'Duchess plans garden to rival Versailles', *Guardian*, 5 February 1999, p. 11. The Alnwick designs were the work of Peter Wirtz and Paul Robbrecht; see *The Garden (JRHS)*, vol. 124 (1999), pp. 852-7; vol. 125 (2000), p. 824, and much else in the press. To date, the question of copyright in garden designs has yet to be the subject of a court case, so it is unclear what degree of rigour attaches to the subject, but 'the types of gardens', as quoted in the press, is almost certainly not an actionable concept. For Arabella Lennox-Boyd, see Stephen Anderton, 'The designer designs for herself', *CL*, 21 June 2001, pp. 166-71.

93. Foreign firms at Chelsea: Council minutes, 8 February 1927; 3 July 1928; 10 February, 10 March, 8 April 1931. For the HTA's Buy British campaign, see 29 June 1926; for debate over the marking of foreign rose trees, and tariffs on roses and shrubs, see 10 January, 13 March, 5 June, 11 September 1928; 24 November 1931; 10 May 1932.

94. *GC&HTJ*, 14 February 1986, pp. 13-14.

95. Hoyt cacti: *GC*, 11 March 1929, p. 340; 25 May 1929, pp. 372, 383; 1 June 1929, p. 395. *Times* Garden of To-

morrow: *GC*, 23 May 1959, pp. 323-43. Bradley-Hole: *The Garden* (*JRHS*), vol. 122 (1997), p. 467.

96. Council minutes, 14 January 1947; 2 November 1948; 1 March 1949; 31 January, 13 June, 1 August, 12-26 September 1950. David Mulford, *Grassroots*, no. 58 (January 1998), p. 4. See also Peter Shepheard, 'The Festival of Britain', *Landscape Design*, no. 160 (April 1986), pp. 11-13.

97. Beaminster: *GC&HTJ*, 23 May 1980, pp. 4-5. Shopping mall: *CL*, 7 June 2001, p. 195. Mirabel Osler, 'Was there once innocence?', *Hortus*, no. 11 (autumn 1989), pp. 82-7, esp. p. 83.

98. Fish: *GC*, 24 June 1876, pp. 817-8. For the history of the picturesque display movement, see Elliott (2001), pp. 175-80.

99. Nottingham: *GC*, 29 April 1871, p. 546. Preston: *GC*, 13 July 1878, pp. 54-8; 20 July 1878, p. 86.

100. *GC*, 29 May 1965, p. 526; 23 May 1969, p. 8; 22 May 1970, pp. 20-1; 8 June 1973, p. 40.

101. *GC*, 24 June 1961, p. 548.

102. *HW*, 20 July 1990, p. 4; 19 July 1991, pp. 12-13; 4 December 1992, p. 3.

103. *The Garden* (*JRHS*), vol. 120 (1995), pp. 400-1, 482-5; vol. 123 (1998), pp. 309, 476. Each year *The Garden* runs pages of photographs of both Chelsea and Hampton Court shows.

104. Jon Ardle, 'Countdown to Scotland's new flower show', *The Garden* (*JRHS*), vol. 122 (1997), pp. 332-5, and also pp. 301, 541; vol. 123 (1998), p. 544. *HW*, 30 April 1998, p. 5; 4 June 1998, pp. 3, 6-7; 19 August 1999, p. 3; 26 August 1999, p. 13; 30 September 1999, p. 5; 21 October 1999, p. 17.

105. *The Garden* (*JRHS*), vol. 124 (1999), pp. 432-3, 645, 726; vol. 125 (2000), pp. 499, 694-7; vol. 127 (2002), pp. 374-5, 698-701.

106. Council minutes, 14 February 1888. For the campaign to secure a Hall, see chapter 8.

107. *GC*, 30 May 1914, p. 382.

108. *The Garden* (*JRHS*), vol. 122 (1997), p. 303; vol. 123 (1998), p. 307; vol. 125 (2000), pp. 204-5; vol. 126 (2001), p. 320. See also vol. 115 (1990), p. 108, for a profile of Pippa Sergeant (later Hichens), then the administrator of the London shows.

109. Council minutes, 9 August-20 September 1921; 2 October 1929; 9 September, 18 November 1952; 7 July-25 August 1953. On Alexandra Palace, see *JRHS*, vol. 92 (1967), p. 143; vol. 93 (1968), p. 150; vol. 94 (1969), p. 146.

110. *The Garden* (*JRHS*), vol. 126 (2001), pp. 81, 808; vol. 127 (2002), p. 15.

111. Council minutes, 18 June, 2 July, 23 July, 7 November 1878.

112. J.R.B. Evison, 'Brighton florealis?', *Parks and Recreation*, vol. 36 no. 12 (December 1971), pp. 12-13.

113. Alexandra Palace had already hosted a London Garden Show for two years, in 1989-90. See *HW*, 25 May 1990, p. 5.

114. Alan Toogood, 'Winter highlights at Westminster', *The Garden* (*JRHS*), vol. 117 (1992), pp. 207-9; 'Exotic refugees put their case at Westminster', pp. 479-81; 'Autumn in all its fiery glory at Westminster', pp. 570-3. In later years these substantial articles tended to be replaced by briefer news items.

115. *The Garden* (*JRHS*), vol. 123 (1998), p. 615; vol. 125 (2000), p. 654.

8 Horticultural Halls, pp. 151-64

1. Council minutes, 9 February, 7 June 1892; 13 March 1894; 12 January 1897. *GardMag*, vol. 33 (1890), p. 535.

2. Council minutes, 5 June, 9 October 1900; 4 June 1901; 25 February-11 March 1902. *Garden*, vol. 61 (1902), pp. 215-16.

3. Council minutes, 18 March, 8-22 July 1902. Docu-

ments relating to the site acquisition, architect, etc., are in the RHS archives.

4. Council minutes, 23 September 1902; 10-24 March, 7-21 July, 15 September, 27 October 1903; 9 February 1904; 3 January 1905. *JRHS*, vol. 29 (1904-5), pp. 284-294 for the full list of donors.

5. Council minutes, 26 November 1907; 25 August, 22 September, 6-20 October, 15 December 1914, 5 January 1915, for the first wave of interest; then 7 December 1915, 1 August-7 November 1916 for the commandeering. Recovery of the Hall: 27 May, 1 July, 9-23 September, 7 October 1919; for negotiations over dilapidations, 10-24 February, 11 May, 15 June, 13 July 1920; 28 February 1922. The final compensation figure was £9694 14s. 4d, with 50 guineas awarded for costs. The turning point over compensation was a suit by De Keyser hotels, which was referred to the House of Lords: see *Times*, 11 May 1920 p. 6 a-d. Files Q2/1-Q2/2 in RHS archives.

6. Henry Benjamin May (c1845-1936), nurseryman in Tottenham from 1870, and author of *Seventy Years in Horticulture* (1928).

7. This discussion of the building of the Hall is taken with but few changes from my article 'The Royal Horticultural Society's New Hall', *Thirties Society Journal*, no. 7 (1991), pp. 15-19.

8. Council minutes, 11 July 1922; 27 March, 12 June, 10 July, 8 August, 27 November 1923; 15 January-11 March, 24 June, 21 October-2 December 1924; 13 January, 5 May, 25 August, 6-20 October, 1-15 December 1925; 22 November 1927; 21 February 1928.

9. Council minutes, 28 July, 11 August, 8 September, 1 December 1925; 4 May, 19 October 1926. Peter Stageman, 'Golden jubilee of the RHS New Hall', *The Garden* (*JRHS*), vol. 103 (1978), pp. 444-5.

10. Oscar Faber (1886-1956), later the President of the Institution of Heating and Ventilating Engineers, and founder of an engineering company that still bears his name.

11. *Architects' Journal*, 24 October 1928, pp. 572-3.

12. Philip Morton Shand (1888-1960), author of *A Book of French wines* (1928).

13. Quotations from the architectural press are taken from the following articles, and will not be further footnoted: *Architect & Building News*, vols. 119 (29 June 1928), pp. 925-34, and 120 (19 October 1928), pp. 312-15; *Architectural Forum*, May 1931, pp. 566-78 (author, Gerald K. Geerlings); *Architectural Review*, vol. 65 (January 1929), pp. 17-31 (author, Morton Shand); *Architects' Journal*, vols. 68 (24 October 1928), pp. 566-573 (author, Vernon O. Rees), and 69 (1929), pp. 47-8 (author, Charles H. Reilly); *Engineering*, 21 December 1928, pp. 763-4; *Wasmuths Monatshefte für Baukunst*, vol. 1 (1929), pp. 32-5.

14. *GC*, 6 October 1928, p. 261.

15. *JRHS*, vol. 54 (1929), pp. 113-14.

16. Council minutes, 9-30 October 1928; 7 May 1929; 26 April 1932; 27 September-11 October 1938.

17. Council minutes, 3 August, 27 September-15 November 1927; 3-17 July, 11 September 1928; 1 January, 12-26 March, 10 December 1929.

18. Council minutes, 1928-1939 *passim*; 20 May, 29 July-12 August 1947; 27 July-10 August 1965

19. Council minutes: 25 March, 4 November 1941; 14 July, 15 September 1942 (lettings and lease); 10 December 1940; 16 December 1941; 20 May, 16 September, 20 June-25 July, 7 November 1944; 14 January-4 February, 1 April 1947 (bomb damage and repairs). The repairs to the Old Hall were carried out by Foster and Dicksee, those to the New Hall by Brian Colquhoun. File in RHS archives for the Home Guard's occupation.

20. Council minutes, 6 July, 7-21 September 1948;

9 August 1949; 7 March 1950. *JRHS*, vol. 75 (1950), Proceedings, pp. xlv-xlvi; also vol. 76 (1951), p. xlvii.

21. AGM report for 1981, p. ii; AGM report for 1982, pp. iii-iv, vi.

22. Council minutes, 29 November 1904. The Bach Choir concert did not appear in Council minutes, and there are no surviving files of records of lettings until the 1920s: thanks to Basil Keen for the information.

23. South African Products: see *Times*, 25 February 1907, p. 4 a-d, and *Daily Mirror*, 25 February 1907, p. 1 for the knighting of Sir Pieter Bam in the Hall. For the Racing Pigeon Show, see *The Times*, 27 January 1940, p. 3 c. Nursing Exhibition: 10 February 1939, p. 9 f; and see *Nursing Mirror*, 11 February 1939, pp. 663-6, and 18 February 1939, pp. 706-7. Schoolboys: 4 January 1926, p. 10 d; 9 January 1926, p. 8 a. Schoolgirls: 6 August 1949, p. 3 b. Few exhibitions' websites give any past history, especially of previous venues. A rare exception is the Christian Resources Exhibition, at www.resourcex.co.uk. The National Cage Birds Show was held in 1937-38 at Dorland Hall, and moved to the Halls in 1939: see *Times*, 5 January 1939, p. 9 g, and 20 January 1939, p. 9 c. Quotation from the Association of Exhibition Organisers' website, aeo.org.uk.

24. Council minutes, 23 March 1926. The Communists were refused again after the War: 29 November 1949.

25. After the Second World War in particular, dog shows featured largely among lettings. Surviving lettings files record the Afghan Hound Association, the British Alsatian Association, the Chow Club, the Dachshund Association, the English Shetland Sheepdog Club, the Gordon Setter Association, the London Cocker Spaniel Society, the Scottish Terrier Club, the Southern Cairn Terrier Club, and the Wimbledon District Canine Society. Not to mention the National Small Livestock Exhibition, and the Kensington Neutered Cats Club.

26. Council minutes, 19 October 1920; 11 January 1921; 3-17 January 1928. Miss Murray Smith had complained about the noise of dog shows nearly twenty years before (11 June 1907), and complaints about night noises had compelled Council to get a legal opinion a few years after that (17 December 1912; 7 January 1913).

27. 20 February, 8 May 1934 (outside lavatories); 22 January, 16-30 April 1946; 9 September 1947; 2 October 1956; 16 April, 8 October 1957; 5 May 1964 (some significant landmarks in catering).

28. Some notices of the caterers' products can be seen in successive HHL advertisement brochures. For Brookes, see *The Garden* (*JRHS*), vol. 123 (1998), p. 222.

29. Council minutes, 17 February 1948.

30. Relaunch of halls and conference centre, *The Garden* (*JRHS*), vol. 116 (1991), p. 625. Rene Dee, 'Paying our way', vol. 119 (1994), p. 7.

31. One of Rene Dee's most important actions, taken in July 1997, was to protect the RHS from actions that might have been brought, in the increasingly litigious atmosphere of the late 20th century, for unlawful use of their buildings as a multi-purpose venue. This involved the application for Certificates of Lawful Use relating to both Halls from the City of Westminster Environment and Planning Department. These confirm the lawfulness of their use under the Town and Country Planning Act 1990, sections 191-192 (as amended by section 10 of the Planning and Compensation Act 1991), and the Town and Country Planning (General Development Procedure) Order 1995, article 24.

32. See *Grassroots*, no. 62 (May 1998), p. 6, for a squib on the Festival of Mind Body and Spirit by the present author.

33. See *The Garden* (*JRHS*), vol. 125 (2000), p. 4 for a photograph of the cabling removed from the Lindley Hall, and the joke about the Turner Prize. For Rick Mather's work, see Hugh Pearman, *Rick Mather: Urban Approaches* (1992).

34. *The Garden* (*JRHS*), vol. 127 (2002), p. 420.

35. Rene Dee, 'A day in the life of HHL', *Grassroots*, no 89 (January/February 2002), pp. 4-5. And just in case you're wondering what the impact of all this is on horticulture, attend to this further quotation from Rene Dee's article: 'Ultimately, we have to give all that lovely money we make each year to the Society so that Brent can buy more books.'

9 The Society's Library, pp. 165-80

1. For the history of the Library generally, see Peter Stageman's account in Fletcher (1969); Peter Stageman, 'Lindley Library centenary', *JRHS*, vol. 93 (1968), pp. 509-15; Tjaden (1987); Tjaden (1993); and Brent Elliott, 'The Lindley Library and John Lindley's library', in Stearn (1999), pp. 175-98. For the significance of botanical libraries in the Society's early years, see Henrey (1975), vol. 2, pp. 33-6; and Hortense S. Miller, 'The herbarium of Aylmer Bourke Lambert', *Taxon*, vol. 19 (1970), pp. 489-553, esp. pp. 496-7.

2. First minute book, 4 November 1806. The five books were Jacques Boyceau's *Traité du Jardinage*; *Le Jardinier d'Artois*; a 1535 Basel edition of *Libri de Rei Rusticae*; La Quintinye's *Instructions pour les Jardins* (1715); and Liger's *Nouvelle Maison Rustique* (1768).

3. Council minutes, 15 February 1820.

4. *Charter and Bye-laws of the Horticultural Society of London* (1816), p. 44. Council minutes, 29 April, 5 May 1818.

5. Council minutes, 24 March, 30 April, 7-15 May, 21 July 1830. See *GM*, vol. 6 (1830), p. 505: 'We cannot but lament that such a collection should have been sold, because we think this circumstance enough to discourage any one from making similar presents to the Society in future.' See *ibid.*, pp. 729-30, for Goode, and see also vol. 5 (1829), p. 279, for Goode's invention of a wasp trap.

6. Council minutes, 25 April, 20 June 1838. For the *Flora Graeca* and its story, see W.T. Stearn, 'Sibthorp, Smith, the "Flora Graeca" and the "Florae Graecae Prodromus"', *Taxon*, vol. 16 (1967), pp. 168-78; Stearn, 'From Theophrastus and Dioscorides to Sibthorp and Smith: the background and origin of the Flora Graeca', *Biological Journal of the Linnean Society*, vol. 8 (1976), pp. 285-98; H.W. Lack and D.J. Mabberley, *The Flora Graeca Story* (1999). The Lindley Library is one of the very few places where both the original edition and the Bohn reprint of the *Flora Graeca* can be put side by side for comparison. Twice within living memory the proposal was made to sell the Bohn reprint as a 'duplicate', but was successfully opposed each time, in 1961 by Sir George Taylor, and in 1990 by the present author.

7. Lindley's memo on reductions: Council minutes, 1 August 1854. Booth's arrival: 24 October, 21 November 1854. Book sale proposals and debates: 19 December 1854; 23 October, 13 November 1855; 23 September 1856 (Dr Henderson opposing the sale of unique copies). For a public denial, issued through the mouth of Donald Beaton, see *CottGard*, vol. 16 (9 September 1856), p. 419. Booth's levanting, and unsatisfactory replacement by Joseph Tauton: 6-15 January, 3 July, 24 September 1857; the only obituary which mentioned his involvement with the bank was that in *JHort*, 25 June 1871, p. 511.

8. Council minutes, 7, 25 January, 11 February, 4 March 1859—and there it ends; no announcement of the

proceeds of the sale was recorded in the minutes. *CottGard*, vol. 21 (18 January 1859), p. 241.

9. *Catalogue of the Valuable Library of the Horticultural Society* (2-5 May, 1859). A photocopy of the Sotheby's copy, annotated to show sale prices but not purchasers, is held in the Lindley Library.

10. *JHort*, 13 January 1862, pp. 22-3. Council minutes, 30 May, 13-27 June 1865.

11. Council minutes, 23 January, 13-20 February, 30 April 1866.

12. *GC*, 29 September 1866, p. 924; 16 February 1867, p. 154. Council minutes, 12-19 February, 16 April 1867; 3 March 1868. See also Tjaden (1993), pp. 100-05, for the complications and timings of the various proposals and negotiations.

13. *GC*, 5 December 1868, pp. 1258-9.

14. Thiselton Dyer: Council minutes, 19 July, 6 December 1871; 17 January, 3 April 1872; 2-16 June 1874; 23 June 1875.

15. Hemsley: Council minutes, 10 November 1875; 1 March 1876. Henslow: 11 May 1880; 22 March 1881. West: 6 March, 10 July 1888. Weathers: 11 March 1890; 13 March 1894; 10 August, 21 September 1897.

16. Hutchinson: 8 February 1898; 14-28 February 1899; 9 January, 27 February 1900.

17. Council minutes: 14 February 1872; 15 May 1877; 28 February, 24 July 1888; 12 March 1889; 20 March 1906; 29 September 1908; 23 March 1909; 6 October 1925. Lindley Library Trust minutes, 7-28 February 1888.

18. Lindley Library Trust minutes, 20 April, 26 October 1909. Council minutes, 21 December 1909; 22 November 1910.

19. Council minutes, 2 February 1917. *GC*, 24 March 1917, p. 127; 31 March 1917, p. 137. Bowles's comment was made in Council minutes, 9 March 1920.

20. Council minutes, 28 February 1922; 13-27 March 1923; 11 June 1924; 24 August 1926; 22 March, 3 August 1927.

21. Council minutes, 6 October, 3 November-15 December 1925; 13 July 1926. One would have thought that the Trust Deed revision would have settled matters; but as late as late as 5 August 1975, during the secret plans to sell one of the London Halls, the Council minutes recorded, as a matter to be reported on, the question: could the books not belonging to the Lindley Library be sold? Someone must have reported to Council that there were no such books, but this disillusionment was not recorded in the Minutes.

22. Council minutes, 22 February, 4 October, 15 November 1921; 10 August 1926; 3 August, 27 September, 1-15 November 1927; 7 February, 27 March, 11 April 1928; 26 March 1929.

23. Council minutes, 30 December 1930.

24. Council minutes, 9 August, 22 November 1932; 9 January 1934. See Brent Elliott, 'W.T. Stearn: the Royal Horticultural Society years', *The Linnean*, vol. 18:4 (2002), pp. 34-6.

25. *GC*, 21 February 1931, pp. 148-9. For a capsule biography of Cory, see Brent Elliott, 'A priceless legacy', *The Garden* (*JRHS*), vol. 123 (1998), pp. 716-9. The list of Cory bequest acquisitions was published in instalments in the *Proceedings*, from 1937 to 1939. Library Committee minutes, 4 March 1952, for Stearn's survey of his accomplishment while Librarian.

26. Bunyard: Council minutes, 4 July, 24 October 1939. Brent Elliott, 'The gastronomic works of Edward Ashdown Bunyard', *The Garden* (*JRHS*), vol. 116 (1991), pp. 320-1. For the acquisition of the Bunyard library, see Council minutes, 20 February–30 April 1940. Bunyard's articles include 'Some early Italian gardening books', *JRHS*, vol. 48 (1923), pp. 177-87, and

lists of illustrations of apples and pears, not to mention others in the *Gardeners' Chronicle*.

27. Council minutes, 27 September, 25 October, 8 November 1938; 29 August 1939; 17 September 1940; 25 February, 25 March, 20 May, 17 June 1941; 13 November 1945; 16 April 1946.

28. Council minutes, 30 April, 4 June 1940; 16 September 1941; 5 December 1944; 26 March 1946. For Hutchinson's death, see 28 June 1949. Helen Wang, 'Stein's recording angel—Miss F.M.G. Lorimer', *Journal of the Royal Asiatic Society*, 3rd series, vol. 8 (1998), pp. 207-28. Mrs Cardew did publish some extremely important contributions to horticultural bibliography, most notably two articles on Thornton's *Temple of Flora*, in *JRHS*, vol. 72 (1947), pp. 281-5, 450-3, and 'L.S.A.I.D.A.: a riddle of horticultural authorship', on the identification of Dezallier d'Argenville as the author of the *Théorie et Pratique du Jardinage*, *ibid.*, vol. 74 (1949), pp. 256-61.

29. Library Committee minutes, 22 March 1955; Council minutes, 14 February 1956, for Simmonds's memo of complaint.

30. For Peter Stageman, see Anne Scott-James, 'The Lindley Librarian', *The Garden* (*JRHS*), vol. 107 (1982), pp. 18-19; Glenn Barker, 'Capturing the spirit of adventure', *Garden News*, 16 January 1982, pp. 2-3. For myself, see *Gardens Illustrated*, July/August 2001, p. 58.

31. Council minutes, 29 August 1961; 3 April, 5 June, 3 July, 11 September 1962; 20 May, 8 October 1963; 4-25 February, 11 August, 1 September 1964. This may also be the place to notice that the 1979 Hall repairs resulted in heating pipes being driven through the basement storage room at such a height that I could not walk upright down the main corridor; Peter Stageman, who had often referred to the basement store as his pride and joy, went there as seldom as possible during his last three years as Librarian. Oh, and there was a flood one day when the workmen went to lunch without covering the roof aperture they were working on, and it rained, and the water found its way into the basement, where it just happened that, in order to keep books safe from sparks during the drilling of the wall for the heating pipes, the best part of a corridor had had its shelves emptied onto the floor of the adjoining corridor …

32. Council minutes, 21 August 1828. *JHS*, vol. 2 (1847), pp. 171-6.

33. Council minutes, 20 February 1866; 17 March 1868.

34. Council minutes, 31 January—28 February 1899.

35. Council minutes, 24 June, 21 October 1924; 15 November 1927; 27 March 1928.

36. Withers: see Council minutes, 2 December 1825; 8 May 1829; 24 December 1830; 28 February 1837. For an account of her life, see Audrey Le Lievre, 'Flower painter extraordinary', *CL*, 2 February 1989, pp. 66-9. For Bauer's passionflowers, see Council minutes, 17 November 1820; 20 February 1822; 9 January 1829. Hans Walter Lack, 'The Berlin flowers—Ferdinand Bauer's swan-song', *Curtis's Botanical Magazine*, vol. 16 (1999), pp. 286-96.

37. Council minutes: 18 February 1817; 26 August 1819; 2 July 1830. For Wallich, 23 July 1819; 22 March 1821. Some duplicate Chinese drawings were sold off as early as 1822: 18 January 1822. For modern considerations of the Reeves drawings, see Brent Elliott, 'Treasures from the east', *CL*, 5 September 2002, pp. 128-31, and John Tooby, 'The Reeves paintings', *International Camellia Journal*, vol. 16 (1984), pp. 20-1.

38. Saxe-Weimar: Council minutes, 5 May 1818; 24 May 1819. Tuson: 1 December 1819; 7 July, 17 November, 4 December 1820; 21 May 1830. Raffles: 22 June, 8 July

1825; 13 February 1855, and see Sir George Taylor's letter of 29 January 1963 to Arthur Simmonds, in Council minutes for 1963. Models by Acerbi: 21 August 1822. Housing of models: 7 July 1826; 15 May 1830. Rejection of James Yates's proposal for a model of an encephelartos: 7 March 1848. *GM*, vol. 1 (1826), p. 341, for an exhibit of wax flowers by Montaban. Council minutes, 11 March 1930 for a formal refusal of model flowers at Chelsea, or anywhere else.

39. Council minutes, 29 July, 12 August 1913; 23 March, 20 April, 4 May 1926; 8 June 1937. A.J. Wise: 13 July 1926; 6 March 1951. See also Brent Elliott, 'Post-war popularity', *The Garden (JRHS)*, vol. 121 (1996), pp. 762-7, for the Picture Committee's recommendations on standards in botanical art. For Shirley Sherwood, see her *Contemporary Botanical Artists* (1997).

40. Brent Elliott, 'Pictures at an exhibition', *The Garden (JRHS)*, vol. 118 (1993), pp. 108-12; *Treasures of the Royal Horticultural Society* (1994). The proceedings of the first symposium were circulated in ring-bound form, and those of the third as part of a Linnean Society publication, *Biological Collections and Biodiversity* (2001).

41. Council minutes, 8 October 1974; 5 August, 23 September 1975; 12 October 1976; 1977 *passim*; Confidential minute book, 13 January-17 February, 28 September 1976. *The Garden (JRHS)*, vol. 102 (1977), AGM report, pp. vi-vii.

42. Report of the Library Review Committee (1989). *The Garden (JRHS)*, vol. 115 (1990), p. 215; vol. 116 (1991), Annual Report p. ii, AGM report p. iii; vol. 117 (1992), AGM report p. iii. Membership of the review committee: Ronald Keay (chairman), Rex Banks of the Natural History Museum, Elisabeth Hall of the Garden History Society, Anthony Huxley (chairman of the Library Committee), Beryl Leigh of the British Library, and Alasdair Morrison (Council). Mrs Hall was the principal opponent of moving the Library; she secured the services of Donald Buttress, the consulting architect for Westminster Abbey, to report on the possibilities of building an extension at Vincent Square, but the proposal seemed likely to be twice the cost of a new building at Wisley.

43. *The Garden (JRHS)*, vol. 120 (1995), p. 3; AGM report, pp. i-xvi *passim*. Ursula Buchan, 'A row is growing', *Spectator*, 7 January 1995; Anna Pavord, 'Don't bury the books in the garden', *Independent*, 11 January 1995; Sir Simon Hornby vs Patricia Morrison, 'Grafting on new life or an unkind cut?', *Times*, 28 January 1995; Mary Keen, 'The great horticultural library row', *Independent on Sunday*, 29 January 1995; Anna Pavord, 'Look no bugs, and no weather', *ibid.*, 19 February 1995; correspondence in *Times*, 14 , 20, 25 January 1995, and in *Independent*, 13, 20, 23 January 1995. After the AGM, a little selection in chronological order: 'Grass roots' column, *Times*, 27 February; Roy Strong, 'Battle of the Lindley Library', *CL*, 2 March 1995, p. 31, and correspondence, 16 March p. 70, 23 March p. 102, 30 March pp. 82-4; 'Diary' column, *Times*, 9 March 1995, for the rumour that the protesters had been nicknamed 'Brent-a-mob' after the present author; Maurice Weaver, 'Grandees of the garden look for common ground in library row', *Daily Telegraph*, 23 March 1995; Richard Boston, 'The garden war', *Guardian Weekend Magazine*, 15 April 1995, including a comparison of the time and cost of getting to London and to Wisley; Graham Rose, 'Seeds of discord', *Times Style Magazine*, 23 April 1995; James Fenton, 'Rare collection that inspires passion', *Independent*, 24 April 1995; Marianne Macdonald, 'Gardening world takes to polls in great library row', *Independent*, 28 July 1995; Maurice Weaver, 'RHS wants its library to have two branches', *Daily*

Telegraph, 28 July 1995; Dominic Kennedy, 'RHS gives ground to library rebels', *Times*, 28 July 1995; Anna Pavord, 'A little matter of 198,000 votes', *Independent*, 12 August 1995; Ursula Buchan, 'Seeds of discontent', *Spectator*, 11 November 1995.

44. *The Garden (JRHS)*, vol. 120 (1995), pp. 231, 463, 456-60, 594, 663, 733.

45. Rick Mather was first brought into the situation by Anna Pavord, who had commissioned him to draw up an outline development plan for the conversion of the nearby Rochester Row Police Station, then in the process of closing, into a library. Her costs were met by Deenagh Goold-Adams. The Police Station proposal fell through, however; the property developer who owned the rest of the block agreed a larger-scale redevelopment scheme with the Police, which had to be abandoned after part of the station was listed; both station and adjoining shops are, at the time of writing, derelict.

46. For preliminary articles on Mather's design, see Mary Keen, 'A library of cultivation', *Perspectives on Architecture*, May 1995, pp. 44-45, and Jonathan Glancey, 'Sweet campaign blossoms', *Independent*, 19 June 1995. For progress and completion reports on the new Library, see *The Garden (JRHS)*, vol. 122 (1997), p. 842; vol. 123 (1998), pp. 124-5, 713-15; vol. 126 (2001), pp. 706-11; *Times*, 28 October 2002, p. 11 c-f; Ursula Buchan, 'Treasure store', *Spectator*, 18 September 1999, pp. 72-3.

47. For the Harlow Carr Library, see *NG*, vol. 11 no. 3 (May 1957), p. 3, for the donation of a copy of Sitwell and Blunt's *Great Flower Books* 'For the Library which I hope one day will be established at Harlow Car from a Fellow who wishes to remain anonymous'; *ibid.*, no. 4 (July 1957), p. 5; no. 5 (September 1957), pp. 5-9; vol. 12 no. 2 (March 1958), p. 7, for the opening of the Grey Memorial Building; vol. 21 no. 6 (November 1967), pp. 187-9, and vol. 22 no. 2 (March 1968), p. 43, for the inception of lending; vol. 34 no. 1 (Winter 1979-80), p. 17, on budgetary restrictions; Philip Swindells, 'Harlow Car Library', *ibid.*, vol. 41 no. 2 (Spring 1987), p. 10, for a later survey. For a view of the library on the eve of amalgamation, see Allan Smith, 'The Library—past and future', *ibid.*, vol. 54 no. 3 (July 2000), p. 81. From 1997 to 2001 each issue of *The Northern Gardener* carried a note of new acquisitions.

48. Council minutes, 24 October 1911; 27 August 1935.

10 Publications, pp. 181-96

1. Wedgwood's prospectus, as circulated to the founding members, 1804.

2. Advertisement, *Transactions*, vol. 1 (1805). Minutes of the Publications Committee, 1820-9; for Swayne, see minutes for 23 February 1820.

3. *GM*, vol. 2 (1827), pp. 438-9; vol. 3 (1828), p. 32. For Loudon's journalism generally, see Ray Desmond, 'Loudon and nineteenth-century horticultural journalism', in Elisabeth B. Macdougall, ed., *John Claudius Loudon and the Early Nineteenth Century in Great Britain* (Dumbarton Oaks Colloquium on the History of Landscape Architecture no. 6) (1980), pp. 77-97.

4. *GM*, vol 5 (1829), p. 105.

5. Dealings with Nicol, the printer: Council minutes, 29 August, 10 November 1829; 20 October 1831. Termination of first series of *Transactions*: 5 February 1830. Final termination: 20 May, 13 June, 5 August 1845.

6. For Victorian horticultural journalism generally, see Ray Desmond, 'Victorian gardening magazines', *Garden History*, vol. 5 no. 3 (winter 1977), pp. 47-66; Brent Elliott, 'Gardening times', *The Garden (JRHS)*, vol. 118 (1993), pp. 411-13.

7. Penllergare: J.D. Llewelyn, 'Some account of an

orchideous house, constructed at Penllergare, South Wales', *JHS*, vol. I (1846), pp.I-8. The influence of the accompanying engraving may be gauged from the fact that a copy, with right-to-left reversal, was used as the frontispiece of F.W. Burbidge's *Cool Orchids, and how to Grow them* (1874). Berkeley and the potato blight are discussed in chapter 13, and Lindley and garden aesthetics in chapter 15.

8. Tjaden (1983); Tjaden (1986). *GC,* 4 January 1941, p. 1.
9. Lord Morton's proposed book: Publications Committee minutes, 25 March 1958. Synge's retirement: Peter Stageman, the Librarian, knowing their antipathy, mischievously suggested to Hamer that an issue of the *Journal* be set aside as a festschrift for Synge; he reported Hamer's response as: 'If you make any more such bloody silly suggestions, I'll have your guts for garters, and the rest of you skinned, dried, and pinned up on my wall.'
10. Council minutes, 4, 18 December 1917.
11. Council minutes, 1 May 1956.
12. Schneider: Council minutes, 13 November 1923; 11 June 1929; 25 February, 8 April, 6 May 1930; 2 June 1931; 9, 23 February 1932; 7 March, 12 September, 7 November 1933; 4 March 1947. A file of correspondence and extracts from Council minutes is held in the archives. Ahrendt: Publications Committee minutes, 17 June 1941; Council minutes, 18 February 1958; 10 January 1961.
13. Council minutes, 25 October 1938; 30 January, 16 July 1940. Publications Committee minutes, 19 December 1939; 19 March 1940.
14. Council minutes, 8 October 1935; 30 January 1940; 25 February 1941; 21 September 1943; 22 January, 19 February, 26 March, 18 June, 5 November 1946; 14 January 1947; 31 January 1950. Publications Committee minutes, 19 December 1939-15 September 1942; 3 October 1944; 22 January, 24 September-5 November 1946.
15. Publications Committee minutes, 29 March 1938; 3 October 1944; 26 March 1946; 7 October 1947; 20 March 1951-5 October 1954. Council minutes, 22 January-16 April 1946; 1 April, 4 November, 2 December 1947; 4-18 April, 13 June, 1 August 1950; 22 April, 22 July 1952; 22 September, 1 December 1953; 2 February-2 March, 5 October 1954.
16. *Galanthus* monograph: Council minutes, 22 January 1946; 14 August 1956. Publications Committee minutes, 9 October 1951; 8 October 1952-10 January 1956 *passim. Anemone* monograph: Publications Committee minutes, 3 December 1935; 19 December 1939; 23 June, 16 December 1941; 22 January 1946. Council minutes, 18 June 1946. E.A. Bowles and W.T. Stearn, 'The history of *Anemone japonica*', *JRHS*, vol. 72 (1947), pp. 261-8, 297-308; '*Anemone hortensis* and *Anemone pavonina*: a history of confusion', vol. 73 (1948), pp. 57-70.
17. *Old Camellia Varieties*: Council minutes, 2 May, 13 June, 11 July, 29 August, 12 September, 5 December 1950; 3-17 April 1951; 23 June 1953; 3 May 1955. Sealy's monograph: Council minutes, 2, 30 November 1948; 11 January 1949; 6-20 January, 22 September, 6 October 1953; 1 May, 13 November 1956; 1, 29 July 1958. Publications Committee minutes: 12 February 1952; 8 October 1952-16 September 1953; 1 May 1956-9 October 1957 *passim*.
18. Other planned monographs included a projected work on dwarf conifers by Murray Hornibrook (Publications Committee minutes, 13 March 1934), and one on *Cyclamen* by Schwarz (Publications Committee minutes, 6 April 1948; Council minutes, 2 November 1948). A monograph on *Sorbus* was sought, first from John Hutchinson and then from Wilfred Fox, before the latter's manuscript was

rejected (Publications Committee minutes, 18 June-24 September 1946; 16 September 1953; 31 October 1956; 13 February 1957; 8 October 1958; Council minutes, 16 February, 1 December 1943; 2-16 September, 14 October 1958; 13 January, 10 February, 10 March 1959). Sir William Wright Smith's projected monograph on *Primula* was published as a series of papers in the *Transactions of the Botanical Society of Edinburgh* and *Transactions of the Royal Society of Edinburgh*; they were not collected into book form until 1977, when Messrs Cramer issued the facsimile reprints in one volume. Council minutes, 17 March 1942; 24 July 1945; 26 March, 16 April 1946; 22 June 1948; 5 December 1950; 17 April, 12 June 1951; Publications Committee minutes, 9 October 1951; 12 February, 8 October 1952.
19. Council minutes, 13 November 1956; 5-19 February, 2 July 1957; 9 January 1958; 10 February 1959; 22 November 1966. Publications Committee minutes, 1 May, 31 October 1956; 11 March 1959-21 April 1960; 15 March, 7 November 1951; 6 June 1962; 11 April 1967.
20. Publications Committee minutes, 11 April 1967-8 November 1968; 5 July 1972; 21 November 1973. Council minutes, 11 July 1972.
21. Council minutes, 19 March, 3 September 1963; 16 January, 10 March 1964; 11 August 1970; 5 January 1971. Publications Committee minutes, 17 June 1963; 21 January 1964; 21 November 1972. *JRHS*, vol. 96 (1971), p. 54.
22. Council minutes, 23 February 1909; 19 July 1910; 11 April-9 May 1911; 21 January, 18 March, 12 August 1913 (Pritzel Fund); 8 June 1915 (postponement until postwar). Minutes of the Pritzel Index Committee. See B. Daydon Jackson, 'Pritzel's Index', *JRHS*, vol. 45 (1919-20), pp. 14-23.
23. Council minutes, 13 March 1928; 11-25 June, 19 September 1929; 25 February, 6 May, 1-15 July, 26 August, 14 October 1930; 10 August 1933 (destruction of manuscript).
24. Council minutes, 2 July 1935; 23 June 1936; 30 August, 8 November 1938; 3, 24 January 1939; 30 January 1940. Publications Committee minutes: 4 December 1934-16 December 1941 *passim*.
25. Council minutes, 3 March 1965.
26. *The Illustrated Dictionary of Gardening* (1884-87); Century Supplement (1900-1901). William Roberts, 'Nicholson's Dictionary of Gardening: some reminiscences', unpublished (*c*.193-), in RHS archives.
27. Letter from Sisam to Durham, 14 April 1936, fastened in Publications Committee minutes for 16 June 1936.
28. Publications Committee minutes, 7 December 1937; 17 June 1947; 20 March 1951; and for the supplement, 12 February, 8 October 1952. *GC*, 15 December 1951, p. 223.
29. Publications Committee minutes, 16 September 1953; 30 March, 2 June 1954; 29 June 1955; 10 January 1956; 13 December 1962; 3 March 1965-8 November 1968 *passim*.
30. Report of Council for 1992, p. ii. *The Garden (JRHS)*, vol. 117 (1992), p. 155.
31. See Ray Desmond, *A Celebration of Flowers* (1987), and Brent Elliott, 'The artwork of *Curtis's Botanical Magazine*', *Curtis's Botanical Magazine*, n.s. vol. 17 (2000), pp. 35-41.
32. Council minutes, 29 November 1921. Memorandum by W.R. Dykes re Garden Society dinner, dated 13 July 1921, and subsequent correspondence and memoranda, held in file in RHS archives.
33. Documents in file in RHS archives.
34. Council minutes, 13, 20 December 1921; 31 January, 28 February 1922; 10 March 1925; 30 June 1931; 10 January, 7 February, 25 April 1933; 26 June 1934; 5 March 1935. Publications Committee minutes,

12 March 1935; 7 December 1937.

35. Letter from Messrs Witherby, 13 March 1924; Nix, Memorandum to Botanical Magazine Committee, 21 March 1924; letter from Stern to Nix, 25 March 1924—all in file in RHS archives.

36. Council minutes, 4 February, 1 April 1947. Publications Committee minutes, 3 July 1945. Desmond, *Celebration of Flowers, op. cit.*, pp. 188-91.

37. Wyatt's attempted termination; Publications Committee minutes, 6 April 1966. Bentham-Moxon Trust transfer: Council minutes, 5 January-16 March, 20 April, 13 July 1971. Publications Committee minutes, 18 February 1971. *JRHS*, vol. 96 (1971), pp. 148, 151.

38. Council minutes, 14 March 1911; 16 February, 16 March 1915; 16 May, 18 July 1916; 3 July 1917.

39. Council minutes, 2 February, 22 March 1932 indicate the holding of a special meeting of the Publications Committee to discuss the *Lily Year Book*; but those minutes themselves no longer survive. Reprinting of *Lily Year Book*, 13 December 1932. Revival of the *Daffodil Year Book*, 5 July 1932.

40. *GC*, 28 February 1953, p. 75.

41. Council minutes, 9 June, 14 July, 8 December 1970; 20 April 1971. Publications Committee minutes, 5 June, 29 October 1970. *JRHS*, vol. 96 (1971), pp. 55, 148, 151-2, 154, 156.

42. Council minutes, 4 May, 8 June, 13 July, 7-21 September, 5 October 1971; 22 February-28 March 1972; 3 April 1973. Publications Committee minutes, 5 May, 23 June, 22 September 1971; 2 May, 5 July 1972; 14 March, 21 November 1973.

43. *The Garden (JRHS)*, vol. 100 (1975), p. 22; vol. 115 (1990), p. 345. Report of Council for 1975, pp. vi-vii.

44. *The Garden (JRHS)*, vol. 104 (1979), pp. 44, 130, 180. *Plantsman*, vol. 1 (1979), pp. 1, 3-4.

45. A crop of books appeared after Maxwell's death, which was attributed to everything from suicide to Israeli assassination. Reasonably standard works are Roy Greenslade, *Maxwell's Fall* (1992) and Tom Bower, *Maxwell: the Final Verdict* (1996).

46. *OR*, vol. 96 (1988), p. 341; vol. 97 (1989), p. 3; vol. 101 (1993), pp. 2-3. Report of Council for 1993, p. ii.

47. Report of Council for 1993, p. ii; for 1994, pp. ii-iii. *The Garden (JRHS)*, vol. 118 (1993), p. 333; vol. 119 (1994), p. 97. *New Plantsman*, vol. 1 (1994), p. 4.

48. *The Garden (JRHS)*, vol. 116 (1991), p. 463; vol. 117 (1992), p. 7. Tony Lord, 'Developing *The Plant Finder*', vol. 120 (1995), pp. 202-3; '*The RHS Plant Finder*', vol. 122 (1997), pp. 424-7; letter on the origins of *The Plant Finder*, vol. 123 (1998), p. 674; 'Trends and temptations', vol. 126 (2001), pp. 474-7. Obituary for Chris Philip: vol. 123 (1998), p. 150.

49. The Dorling Kindersley encyclopaedias, for example, were published in America, with the name of the American Horticultural Society replacing that of the RHS. One implication of this international publishing scale is that books must now be adapted in advance to foreign climatic conditions; text can be altered readily, but the cost of altering colour-printed pages is enormous, so every effort is made to ensure that they can be incorporated into a foreign edition without change.

11 Plant Introductions, pp. 197-212

1. *GM*, vol. 1 (1825), p. 56; *Annals of Horticulture*, 1847, p. 98. For general contemporary reports on plants introduced by the Society's collectors or otherwise through its auspices, see Lindley's reports on new plants flowered at Chiswick, *Transactions*, vol. 6 (1826), pp. 62-100, 261-99; vol. 7 (1830), pp. 46-75, 224-53; and the notes on 'New plants' published regularly in *JHS*: vol. 1 (1846), pp. 61-77, 146-59, 226-40, 298-308;

vol. 2 (1847), pp. 77-80, 157-60, 243-8, 306-16; vol. 3 (1848), pp. 73-80, 165-7, 236-48, 311-20; vol. 4 (1849), pp. 77-84, 111-16, 221-6; vol. 5 (1850), pp. 79-88, 137-44, 192-8; vol. 6 (1851), pp. 52-60; vol. 7 (1852), pp. 266-86; vol. 8 (1853), pp. 125-36, 318-22; vol. 9 (1854), pp. 52-6. Lindley also published articles listing new introductions through other sources than the Society, for which generous gesture see *JHS*, vol. 5 (1850), pp. 32-7; vol. 6 (1851), pp. 258-72.

2. For Reeves, see Council minutes, 18 February, 1 April 1817; 2 July 1830. For Wallich, 15 July 1819; Raffles, 20 July 1822, 15 December 1824; Canning, Garden Committee Report 1825, p. 5 (where did he get his Mexican seeds?—he never went to Mexico). For Walsh, see *Transactions*, vol. 6 (1826), pp. 32-58. For Livingstone and Beale, see Bretschneider (1898), pp. 266-8, 306-7, and Livingstone's articles in *Transactions*, 'Account of a method of ripening seeds in a wet season; with some notices of the cultivation of certain vegetables and plants in China', vol. 3 (1820), 183-6, and 'On the state of Chinese horticulture and agriculture', vol. 5 (1824), pp. 49-57.

3. For Heward, see Council minutes, 21 August 1823; McCulloch, 4 August 1826 (and for a note on his life, *GC*, 3 November 1877, p. 571); Brown and Christie, 8 August 1825. For Beechey's request for instruction, see 24 March 1825, and for the results of his voyage, see W.J. Hooker and G.A.W. Arnott, *The Botany of Captain Beechey's Voyage* (1830-41).

4. For the losses cited, see Council minutes, 15 December 1824. For medals to captains, see 18 December 1820, 30 April 1821, 11 March 1841; and see 20 July 1822 for a list of importations arranged by captain. Drummond: 18 June 1827. Rawes: 22 March 1821, 29 March 1826. For *Wisteria sinensis*, see Joseph Sabine, 'On *Glycine sinensis*', *Transactions*, vol. 6 (1826), pp. 460-4, and Peter Valder, *Wisterias* (1995), p. 42.

5. The handiest summary of plant transportation techniques is Ray Desmond, 'The problems of transporting plants', in John Harris, ed., *The Garden: a Celebration of One Thousand Years of British Gardening* (1979), pp. 99-104. See also John Livingstone, 'On the difficulties which have existed in the transportation of plants from China to England', *Transactions*, vol. 2 (1819), pp. 421-9, and John Lindley, 'Instructions for packing living plants in foreign countries', *ibid.*, vol. 5 (1822), pp. 192-200; John Damper Parks, 'Upon the proper management of plants during their voyage from China to England', vol. 7 (1830), pp. 396-9; Nathaniel Wallich, 'Upon the preparation and management of plants during a voyage from India', 2nd series vol. 1 (1831-35), pp. 140-3; Robert Fortune, 'Experience in the transmission of living plants to and from distant countries by sea', *JHS*, vol. 2 (1847), pp. 115-21; 'Observations upon the best methods of packing seeds for a voyage to India or China', vol. 3 (1848), pp. 41-4. For the development of the Wardian case, see David Elliston Allen, *The Victorian Fern Craze* (1969), pp. 8-16. The introduction of the Wardian case has been misdated in both directions: before Allen, Robert Fortune was often cited as the first collector to use the cases, because Ward was so late in publishing an essay on his invention; on the other hand, Cox (1955), p. 270, confuses Wardian cases with the miniature greenhouses Reeves and Parks used in the 1820s.

6. Potts's journal, in two MS volumes, is held in the Lindley Library. *Transactions*, vol. 5 (1824), pp. iii, 427, and vol. 7 (1830), p. 25. Bretschneider (1898), pp. 269-71. Cox (1945), p. 58. Cox (1955), pp. 269-70. Council minutes, 17 November, 4 December 1820; 5 January 1821; 9 February, 1 June, 20 July, 6 September, 9 October 1822; 26 May, 21 August 1823.

7. For *Hoya pottsii*, see *BM*, tab. 3425 (1835). Notices of significant plants introduced by Potts, Don, Forbes, Parks, and MacRae will be found scattered through volume 6 of the *Transactions*.

8. Don's journal, in eight MS volumes, is held in the Lindley Library. Joseph Sabine, 'Some account of the edible fruits of Sierra Leone', *Transactions*, vol. 5 (1823), pp. 430-66. *CottGard*, vol. 16 (1856), pp. 152-3. Cox (1955), p. 271. Lemmon (1968), pp. 121-49. Council minutes, 15 June, 5 September, 23 November 1821; 20 July, 21 August 1822; 19 February 1823. See *BM*, tab. 2484, for *Nicotiana repanda*.

9. Council minutes, 26 May, 3 September 1823; 13 October, 15 December 1824; 19 January, 24 March 1825; 29 November 1832. See also *GM*, vol. 8 (1832), pp. 203-4, for Loudon's review of Don's *General System*. Don's articles referred to in the text are 'A review of the genus *Combretum*', *Transactions of the Linnean Society*, vol. 15 (1827), pp. 412-41, and 'A monograph of the genus *Allium*', *Memoirs of the Wernerian Society*, vol. 6 (1832), pp. 1-102 (actually published 1827—see W.T. Stearn, 'Don's "Monograph of the genus *Allium*"', *Journal of Botany*, vol, 74 (1936), pp. 322-3.

10. Forbes's correspondence is held in the Lindley Library. *Transactions*, vol. 4 (1822), p iii, and vol. 5 (1824), p. iii. Cox (1955), pp. 271-2. A.W. Exell and G.A. Hayes, 'Henry Salt and John Forbes', *Kirkia*, vol. (1961), esp. pp. 133-7; Mary Gunn and L.E. Codd, *Botanical Exploration of South Africa* (1981), pp. 156-7. Council minutes, 5 September, 18 October, 23 November 1821; 20 February, 21 August 1822; 3 April 1824; 19 January 1825. For *Gladiolus oppositiflorus*, see William Herbert, *Amaryllidaceae* (1837), p. 366—he does not name Forbes, but the time and place point to him.

11. Council minutes, 13 October 1824; 24 March 1825; 29 June 1827.

12. Parks's journal is held in the Lindley Library. *Transactions*, vol. 5 (1824), pp. v, 427-8. *GM*, vol. 5 (1829), pp. 572-3. Bretschneider, (1898), pp. 271-4. Cox (1945), pp. 58-9; Cox (1955), p. 270. Council minutes, 19 February, 24 March, 18 April 1823. For the camellias, see *Transactions*, vol. 7 (1829), pp. 555-7; for *Rosa banksiae lutea*, see *Botanical Register* tab. 1105.

13. The rough and fair journals for Douglas's first expedition are held in the Lindley Library. Council minutes, 19 February, 24 March, 18 April, 24 June 1823; 3 March 1824. *Transactions*, vol. 5 (1824), pp. iv-v.

14. *GM*, vol. 1 (1825), p. 56. The rough and fair journals for Douglas's second expedition are held in the Lindley Library. Council minutes, 2-27 July 1824; 4 May, 11 November 1826; 1 March, 2-25 April 1828; 10 April 1829. *Transactions*, vol. 5 (1824), p. vi; vol. 6 (1826) pp. iv-v; vol. 7 (1830), pp. ii-iii. Fort Vancouver was eventually ceded to the United States, and is now Vancouver, Washington—not to be confused with the Canadian Vancouver to the north.

15. Cox (1955), p. 274. Jane Loudon, *The Ladies' Companion to the Flower Garden*, 2nd edition (1842), p. 47: the entry on 'Californian annuals', 'mostly sent home by Douglas'—a passage unchanged in later editions into the 1860s. For notices of Douglas's plants, see *Transactions*, 2nd series vol. 1 (1835), pp. 403-14, 476-81; an important series of articles by John Thomas Howell, on Douglas plants in the St Petersburg herbarium, in *Leaflets of Western Botany*, vol. 2 (1937-40), pp. 59-62, 74-7, 94-8, 116-19; Susan Delano McKelvey, *Botanical Exploration of the Trans-Mississippi West* (1955), pp. 299-341, 393-427.

16. Council minutes, 21 August, 9 December 1828; 20 June, 3 July, 10 November 1829; 22 January, 12 February 1830; 21, 30 April, 4 November 1831; 12 February, 16 March, 14 May, 18 October, 8 November 1834; 22 January, 28 March, 12 June 1835; 4-18 June, 1 Octo-ber 1836. Because Douglas's journal for this expedition was lost on the Fraser, its narrative was pieced together from his correspondence to Hooker and eyewitness sources; see *Companion to the Botanical Magazine*, vol. 2 (1836), pp. 79-182, and A.G. Harvey, 'David Douglas in British Columbia', *British Columbia Historical Quarterly*, vol. 4 (1940), pp 221-43.

17. Council minutes, 19 March, 2 April 1912; 8 September 1914; 5 January 1915. Hemsley's review: *GC*, 13 February 1915, p. 75.

18. The literature on Douglas is immense. A biographical notice, including extracts from the journals, was published in *Companion to the Botanical Magazine*, *op. cit.* There have been five full-length biographies: A.G. Harvey, *Douglas of the Fir* (1947); William Morwood, *Traveller in a Vanished Landscape* (1973); John Davies, *Douglas of the Forests* (1980); Rémy Claire, *David Douglas* (1998); and Ann L. Mitchell, *David Douglas* (1999). See also Lemmon (1968), pp. 150-81; and Coats (1969), pp. 304-14; and, for the mystery of what happened to the fund invested for the repair of his tombstone, see Peter Hunt, 'The strange case of the missing ten pounds', *GC*, 12 June 1965, p. 576. For the coniferous landscape, see Elliott (1986), pp. 115-18. Andrew Murray, a later Assistant Secretary of the RHS, attributed to Douglas's and Hartweg's American travels the impulse behind the mid-century bedding system: 'It was the Nemophilas, the Coreopsides, the Eschscholtzias of these plains that first formed the glowing beds'–*GC*, 27 December 1862, p. 1218.

19. In 1841, the *Gardeners' Chronicle* reported that Pontey's nursery in Plymouth was raising a fine crop of araucarias from seed (1 January, p. 7; 20 February, p. 123); in 1842, that Philip Frost was propagating them at Dropmore (24 September, p. 641); and in 1843, that Youell's Great Yarmouth nursery was offering four-year-old specimens (25 November, advertisement, p. 817). Council minutes, 4 October 1826, for the distribution of the first dozen specimens from Chiswick.

20. MacRae's journal is held in the Lindley Library. *Transactions*, vol. 5 (1824), pp. v-vi, and vol. 6 (1826), pp. iii-iv. Cox (1955), p. 275. Council minutes, 21 August 1823; 3 April, 27 August, 15 December 1824; 24 March 1825; 7 April, 4 August, 4 October 1826. Notes on some of MacRae's plants were published in the *Transactions*, vols. 6-7. Peradeniya: the earliest surviving plan of the botanic garden (actually little more than an outline of the ground) is in an album formerly belonging to Lindley (probably sent him by MacRae) and now in the Lindley Library.

21. Hartweg's journals and miscellaneous correspondence, in three volumes, are held in the Lindley Library; portions were published in the *JHS*, vol. 1 (1846), pp. 180-5; vol. 2 (1847), pp. 121-5, 187-91; vol. 3 (1848), pp. 217-28 (Californian travels), and in *Transactions*, 2nd series vol. 2 (1848), pp. 378-409; vol. 3 (1848), pp. 115-62 (Mexico, Guatemala and Equatorial America). For biographical notices, see *GC*, 11 March 1871, p. 313; *JHort*, 16 March 1871, pp. 199-200; 21 September 1871, pp. 214-15 (memoir by William Swale); *Leaflets of Western Botany*, vol. 1 (1935), pp. 180-1; Coats (1969), pp. 317-19, 344-6, 374. For details of his plants, see George Bentham, *Plantae Hartwegianae* (1839-57), and George Gordon, 'Notes upon some newly-introduced conifers collected by Mr. Hartweg in Upper California', *JHS*, vol. 4 (1849), pp. 211-20.

22. Council minutes, 26 February, 14 July, 1 October, 14 November 1836; 28 February 1837; 7 March, 2-20 June, 12 July, 13 November, 8 December 1838; 25 January 1839; 9 July 1840; 5 February 1841; 4 July 1842; 9 February, 23 May, 1 August, 5 September 1843.

23. Council minutes, 5 February, 24 November 1841; 20 April 1842; 25 April, 5 September 1843; 16 January, 20 February, 16 April, 16 July, 18 December 1844; 16 January, 4-26 February, 20 May 1845. The quotation is from William Swale's memorial notice, in *JHort, op. cit.*

24. Council minutes, 5 August 1845; 13 February, 1 September 1846; 9 February, 20 June, 14 July, 12 September, 21 October 1848. *JHS*, vol. 2 (1847), pp. 165-8; vol. 4 (1849), pp. 184-6. Swale, *op. cit.*

25. Theodor Cordua, quoted in *Leaflets of Western Botany*, vol. 1 (1935), pp. 180-1; Swale, *op. cit.*

26. Fortune's correspondence, and instructions from the Chinese Committee, are held in the Lindley Library. He described his journey for the Society in 'Sketch of a visit to China, in search of new plants', *JHS*, vol. 1 (1846), pp. 208-24, as well as several articles on individual plants he collected, and in *Three Years' Wanderings in China* (1847). The literature on Fortune is second only to that on Douglas in quantity, as far as the Society's collectors go, so here are a few items of importance only: *GC*, 17 April 1880, pp. 487-9; Bretschneider (1898), pp. 403-518; E.H.M. Cox, in *New Flora and Silva*, vol. 8 (1936), pp. 172-9, in *JRHS* (1943), pp. 161-71; Cox (1945), pp. 76-92; E. Nelmes in *Proceedings of the Linnean Society*, session 156 (1943-4), pp. 8-16; Coats (1969), pp. 71-5, 101-10; Dawn Macleod, 'A mystery solved', *The Garden (JRHS)*, vol. 117 (1992), pp. 214-17.

27. Council minutes, 19 May, 21 July, 25 November-9 December 1842; 7 November 1843; 19 July 1844; 26 February, 15 April, 5 August, 2 September 1845; 13 May, 3 November 1846; 15 April, 6 July 1847. For his later travels, see his books *Journey to the Tea Countries of China* (1852); *Residence among the Chinese* (1857); *Yedo and Peking* (1863). See also Andrew Murray, *Pines and Firs of Japan* (1863); that collection of specimens came to an inglorious end at Kensington—see Council minutes, 6 November 1872, for the statement that Murray's pine cone collection 'at present stowed away in the Societys [*sic*] Cellars might be given to the Royal Gardens, Kew'.

28. *JHS*, vol. 4 (1849), p. 186. Council minutes, 10 April, 24 November 1841.

29. Council minutes, 19 February 1850; 7 January 1851; 12 October 1852; 13 March 1855. For Jeffrey's collections, see James M'Nab, 'Coniferous plants from British Columbia', *GC*, 6 April 1872, pp. 464-5; 27 April 1872, pp. 573-4; 11 May 1872, pp. 636-7. The Oregon Association's Secretary was Andrew Murray, later Assistant Secretary of the RHS. See also James Todd Johnstone, 'John Jeffrey and the Oregon expedition', *Notes from the Royal Botanic Garden Edinburgh*, vol. 20 (1939), pp. 1-53. Chiswick acquisitions book, 1852-56.

30. Council minutes, 9 March-21 April, 15 June, 9 November 1852. Warscewicz (1812-66) later became a specialist in collecting orchids.

31. Botteri kept no journal—hence the lack of information on his plants. Council minutes, 15 June, 9 November 1852; 25 January-22 March, 10 May-21 June 1853; 14 February-11 April, 24 October-19 December 1854; 13 March-17 April, 22 May, 23 October 1855; 22 January, 14 March, 23 September 1856; 26 February 1857. For the 'Chamaecyparis' ballot, see *CottGard*, vol. 18 (14 July 1857), p. 229, and *GC*, 22 November 1856, p. 772. The identity of this plant is nicely uncertain. R.A. Dümmer examined Lindley's herbarium specimen at Cambridge, and determined it to be *Thuja orientalis* var. *mexicana*—a mutant form of an Asiatic garden escape!—see his 'Three conifers', *Journal of Botany*, vol. 52 (1914), pp. 236-8. As the plant has long since disappeared from cultivation, and

does not appear to have been identified again in the wild, I think the evidence can only be described as inconclusive.

32. Council minutes, 3 July 1857; 12 January 1858. The notice appeared in *GC*, 25 July 1857, pp. 516-17.

33. Council minutes, 31 January, 3 July, 4 September, 26 October 1860; 26 February 1861. The collectors briefly entertained during this period were George Badcock, — Maytner, Gustav Nagel, and Marius Porte, about none of whom have I yet unearthed anything.

34. An acquisitions book for Weir's plants is held in the Lindley Library. Council minutes, 5 March, 9 April, 6 August 1861; 30 January, 2 October, 11 December 1863; 15 April, 14 October-16 December 1864; 4 April, 30 May, 21 November 1865; 6 March-17 April 1866; 22 July, 14 October 1884. Extracts from Weir's correspondence and journal were published in *PRHS*, vol. 1 (1861), pp. 627-8, 643-5, 663-4, 683-5, 723-4; vol. 2 (1862), pp. 34-60, 93, 559-72, 579-96, 784-95; vol. 3 (1863), pp. 67-8, 221-2, 233-45, 336-44; vol. 4 (1864), pp. 24, 38, 73-4, 108-9, 138, 179-85. John Miers's reports on his plants were published in *ibid.*, vol. 3 (1863), pp. 179-202 (Bignoniaceae), 294-6, 344-9, and vol. 4 (1864), pp. 160-2, 185-6. See also *PRHS*, vol. 2 (1862), p. 763; vol. 5 (1865), pp. 22, 181-3; vol. 1 n.s. (1866), pp. liii-lv; *GC*, 1866, p. 170; *JRHS*, vol. 22 (1898-99), pp. 115-16. Weir's only article for the Society, on *Myroxylon toluiferum*, appeared in *PRHS*, vol. 4 (1864), pp. 99-101.

35. Cooper: Council minutes, 26 October 1860; 5 December 1862; 2 October 1863; 28 January, 24 March 1874, and a letter in *PRHS*, vol. 2 (1862), p. 293. Bowman: 5 March, 7 May 1867. Elwes: 14 February-7 March 1877.

36. See Adrien René Franchet, *Plantae Davidianae* (1884-8), and *Plantae Delavayanae* (1888-90).

37. Council minutes: 24 February 1910 (Wilson); 16 December 1913, 22 March 1921 (Farrer). Wilson did at least publish a partial account of his first travels in *JRHS*: 'Wanderings in China', vol. 29 (1904-05), pp. 656-62. Vicary Gibbs presented a collection of Wilson seedlings to Wisley: Council minutes, 22 June 1910.

38. Council minutes, 1 August, 7 November, 19 December 1916; 29 January-12 February, 19 November-3 December 1918; 29 April, 29 July 1919; 10 February 1920; 19-26 January, 22 March 1932, and *passim* thereafter as the *Plantae Forrestianae* negotiations stumbled along. Similarly, Publications Committee minutes, 15 March 1937-28 March 1939 *passim*; 17 July 1949; 20 March 1951-12 February 1952 *passim*. The Wisley Herbarium holds a two-volume accession book of Forrest's plants received. Biographies: Scottish Rock Garden Club, *George Forrest* (1935); J. Macqueen Cowan, *The Journeys and Plant Introductions of George Forrest* (1954). The most comprehensive list of his plants was published as 'Plantae Chinenses Forrestianae' in *Notes from the Royal Botanic Garden Edinburgh*, vol. 7 (1912-13), pp. 1-411; vol. 14 (1924), pp. 75-393; vol. 17 (1929-30), pp. 1-406. The RHS published two volumes of his field notes: *Field Notes of Trees, Shrubs and Plants other than Rhododendrons Collected in Western China by Mr. George Forrest 1917-1919* (1929), and *Some Plants, Shrubs and Trees found by Mr. George Forrest in 1925*.

39. He started his career as Ward, Francis Kingdon; the hyphen first appeared on the spine of *About this Earth* (1946), though not on a title-page until *Commonsense Rock Gardening* (1948). Council minutes, 12-26 June, 21 August 1923 for the early refusal to finance; 12 February 1924; 26 January 1926; 20 November 1932; 4 June 1935; 27 October 1936; 12 January, 20 July 1937; 10 January 1939; 12 March 1946; 4 November 1947; 4 October 1949; 26 June, 25 September 1951; 22 July,

4 November 1952; 27 April 1954; 22 February 1955; 15-29 April 1958. Hitherto unpublished letters of Ward's are pasted into the minute book at 21 March 1950, 3 March, 7 July, and 8 September 1953, the last a tribute to the late Lord Aberconway. For a biography, see Charles Lyte, *Frank Kingdon-Ward* (1989), and for a bibliography, Ulrich Schweinfurth and Heidrun Schweinfurth-Marby, *Exploration in the Eastern Himalayas and the River Gorge Country of Southeastern Tibet* (1975); and, of course, his various books. For his plants, see his several volumes of published field notes.

40. Council minutes, 17 January 1933; 23 February 1938; 9 September 1947; 5 October 1948; 4 October 1949; 11 July 1950; 23 January 1951; 8 March 1955. Obituaries for both men appeared in *JRHS*: Sherriff, by Ludlow, vol. 93 (1968), pp. 11-19; Ludlow, by Sir George Taylor, vol. 97 (1972), pp. 416-17. H.R. Fletcher, *A Quest of Flowers* (1975), though Fletcher nowhere mentions RHS funding—every reference to the Society in the index refers to awards the Ludlow and Sherriff plants received. W.T. Stearn, 'Frank Ludlow (1885-1972) and the Ludlow-Sherriff expeditions to Bhutan and south-eastern Tibet of 1933-1950', *Bulletin of the British Museum (Natural History): Botany*, vol. 5 (1976), pp. 241-68.

41. For the negotiations over Rock's book, see Council minutes, 11 July 1950; 6 January, 3 March–14 April, 6 October 1953. Publications Committee minutes, 20 March 1951-8 October 1952 *passim*.

42. Council minutes, 23 February 1932; 9 January, 11 December 1934; 13 August 1935; 25 February 1936; 9 March 1937; 25 January, 9 August, 27 September 1938. The Society published an obituary: Joe Elliott, 'Edward Kent Balls', *The Garden (JRHS)*, vol. 110 (1985), pp. 234-6. Balls's only book was an ethnobotanic study of *Early Uses of Californian Plants* (1962), but he published two reports on his travels in *JRHS*: 'Expedition to the Andes, 1938-1939', vol. 65 (1940), pp. 289-95, and 'Two months' collecting in Morocco', vol. 69 (1944), pp. 357-65. For a handy account of his journeys see Coats, (1969), pp. 29-31, 36-7, 350-1, 376-7.

43. Council minutes, 22 February, 29 November, 13 December 1921. Report of Council for 1921, p. iv. For the plants sent back from this expedition, see *GC*, 10 December 1921, p. 296, and C.K. Howard-Bury, *Mount Everest: the Reconnaissance, 1921* (1922), pp. 346-50.

44. Council minutes, 26 April 1927 (Elliott); 24 March 1936 (Ingwersen); 1 September 1936; 23 March 1937, 25 January-22 February, 8 June 1938 (Hu); 13 September 1938, 3 January 1939 (Ratibor and Goodspeed)—see also T. Harper Goodspeed, *Plant Hunters in the Andes*, 2nd ed. (1961), pp. 11-12, 313-20.

45. Council minutes, 29 November 1938; 6 June 1939; 14 January 1947; 4 April 1950; 30 March 1954; 4 October 1955; 19 September 1956; 2 February 1965. Peter Davis, 'Through the Antilebanon', *JRHS*, vol. 69 (1944), pp. 7-13; 'Plants and experiences in the eastern Mediterranean', vol. 72 (1947), pp. 13-17; 'True colours', *ibid.*, p. 487; 'A journey in south-west Anatolia', vol. 74 (1949), pp. 104-15, 154-64; 'The spring flora of the Turkish riviera', vol. 83 (1957), pp. 65-73. Davis was later to become the compiler-in-chief of the *Flora of Turkey*.

46. Council minutes, 3 June, 15-29 July 1947; 1 January 1948, 31 July 1951. For the Admiralty, see 1 May, 12 June 1951; 23 September 1952. The order was Admiralty Fleet Order M.3623/51.

47. Not all the expeditions are well documented, but some resulted in reports published in *JRHS*. Here follows a list of these: Oleg Polunin, 'An expedition to Nepal', vol. 75 (1950), pp. 302-15; L.H.J. Williams, 'The 1952 expedition to western Nepal', vol. 78 (1953), pp. 323-37, and see also Annual report for 1952, p. ix; William Sykes, '1954 expedition to Nepal', vol. 80 (1955), pp. 538-44, vol. 81 (1956), pp. 6-14; Patrick M. Synge, 'A plant-collecting expedition to the mountains of north-eastern Turkey and western Iran', vol. 86 (1961), pp. 256-70; Polunin again, 'Plant hunting in the Karakoram', vol. 87 (1962), pp. 263-72; Paul Furse, 'Iran and Turkey, 1962', vol. 88 (1963), pp. 166-76, 199-211, 247-510, and 'Iran and Afghanistan, 1964', vol. 90 (1965), pp. 462-75, 504-9, vol. 91 (1966), pp. 18-26; Brian Mathew, 'Turkey and south-east Europe, 1965', vol. 91 (1966), pp. 334-44, 383-94; Polly and Paul Furse, 'Afghanistan 1966', vol. 93 (1968), pp. 20-30, 92-7, 114-24; T.F. Hewer, 'A botanical expedition to Iran and Afghanistan, 1969', vol. 96 (1971), pp. 403-12, 'A botanical expedition to Iran and Afghanistan, 1971', vol. 98 (1973), pp. 288-94, 341-8, and 'To Iran to find alpines', vol. 100 (1975), pp. 254-60. See also J.D.A. Stainton, *Forests of Nepal* (1972), pp. 1-2, 170, on the Williams and Sykes expeditions. At the 1951 AGM, Lord Aberconway said of Sykes, 'I hope he will follow the example of his well-known prototype and come back simply laden with loot': *JRHS*, vol. 76 (1951), pp. xliii-xliv. Thesiger's expedition was announced—see Council minutes, 11 July 1950; Annual report for 1950, p. xiv—but not his results, probably because they were disappointing: miscellaneous bulbs from Iraq that seem not to have done well. See, for general results, 'Survey of recently collected plants', *JRHS*, vol. 87 (1962), pp. 230-40, 273-82, 314-25, 410-23, 509-12; vol. 88 (1963), pp. 34-8.

48. Elmer D. Merrill, 'Metasequoia, a living relict of a fossil genus', *JRHS*, vol. 73 (1948), pp. 211-16 (reprinted with additional matter from *Arnoldia*); Albert Pam, 'Vegetative reproduction of Metasequoia', *ibid.*, vol. 75 (1950), p. 359. Council minutes, 17 February, 21 September 1948. See also *JRHS*, vol. 95 (1970), pp. 445-52; vol. 102 (1977), pp. 27-9; vol. 123 (1998), pp. 14-15. Annual report for 1952, p. iv, for Merrill's seed-laden arrival at the show.

49. Council minutes, 27 August 1824; 2 December 1825. Refusal for Bellenden Ker: Minutes of the Chiswick Board, 31 August 1829. The earliest ballot I can trace was for Botteri's 'chamaecyparis', for which see note 31 above. Ballots for seeds and plants: *PRHS*, vol. 2 (1862), pp. 123-8, 294-311, 483-90 (including a ballot for tree frogs, p. 490, an indication that collectors did not confine themselves to botanical collection only), 631-2; vol. 3 (1863), pp. 63-6, 150-4, 208-16, 272-9; vol. 4 (1864), pp. 88-9, 119-24, 145-51; vol. 5 (1865), pp. 114-20; vol. 1 n.s. (1866), pp. xxv-xxx, xli-lii, lxix-lxxix, cv-cx, cliii-clxv, clxxv-cxcvii, ccxiii-ccxxvi, cclxv-cclxxvi. Suspension of balloting, *GC*, 18 April 1874, p. 509; threatened discontinuation of buying-in stock, Council minutes, 7 December 1886. Council minutes, 29 July, 16 September 1958, on arrangements for seed distribution. *The Garden (JRHS)*, vol. 122 (1997), p. 841. 'Wisley's seeds on the move!', *Grassroots*, no. 76 (Oct/Nov 1999), p. 3. Henry Rimmer, 'Meet the seed collectors', *Garden News*, 2 January 2002, p. 12.

50. Council minutes, 24 March 1830.

51. For the 19th-century attrition, which helped fuel a myth of the wholesale loss of hardy plants during the heyday of the bedding system, see Elliott (1986), p. 160. For Taylor on the plight of *Primula sherriffae*, see his obituary for Sherriff cited in note 40 above. And for a general survey of plant introduction into British gardens, see Richard Gorer, *The Growth of Gardens* (1978).

52. Council minutes, 14 January–11 March 1919. *GC*, 15 February 1919, p. 76.

53. Council minutes, 9 July 1929 (efforts to protect Italian mountain flora). T. Vernon Wollaston, 'On the best means of preserving from extirpation some of the aboriginal plants of St. Helena', *JRHS*, vol. 5 (1879), pp. 31-3; George S. Boulger, 'The preservation of our wild plants', vol. 29 (1904-05), pp. 392-408—contrast this with H. Selfe Leonard, 'Rambles with a trowel', vol. 16 (1894), pp. 104-15. The Fauna and Flora Preservation Society was founded in 1903.

54. Sheila Pim, *The Wood and the Trees* (1966), pp. 97-100.

55. Thomas Cook: Council minutes, 13 March—3 April 1973. Turkish cyclamens: 9 January 1973. Max Walters, 'The role of botanic gardens in conservation', *JRHS*, vol. 98 (1973), pp. 311-15; Anthony Huxley, 'The ethics of plant collecting', vol. 99 (1974), pp. 242-9; John Codrington, 'Is a garden for beauty only?', vol. 104 (1979), pp. 66-7; Christopher Grey-Wilson, 'Trading at a loss', vol. 124 (1999), pp. 704-5. Deforestation: see Bob Mitchell, 'Habitat and ecology', in Postan (1996), esp. pp. 19-21. On re-introductions and seed banks, see Robert Burton, 'Sending plants home', *The Garden (JRHS)*, vol. 114 (1989), pp. 369-72; Hew Prendergast, 'Seeds for the future', *ibid.*, vol. 118 (1993), pp. 546-9; Trevor Wiltshire, 'Alpines of the Orient', vol. 120 (1995), pp. 219-21; Peter Brownless *et al.*, 'Monkey puzzle forests and beyond', vol. 122 (1997), pp. 50-3; and for a recent survey of endangered wild plants of horticultural importance, see Kerry Walter *et al.*, 'Counting our losses', vol. 123 (1998), pp. 573-7.

56. See Willem Wijnstekers, *The Evolution of CITES*, 3rd edition (1992).

57. For Azadehdel, see *HW*, 9 June 1989, p. 7; Ronald Payne, 'The case of the compulsive orchid hunter', *Telegraph Weekend Magazine*, 26 August 1989, pp. 20-3; Eric Hansen, *Orchid Fever* (2000), pp. 71-86, and be aware that the author has been accused by Kew of misrepresentation. Quite libellous documents on the case can be found on the internet, if one has a mind to do so. Memory tells me that the news of the conviction was greeted with satisfaction by the Orchid Committee, but this was not minuted.

58. Council minutes, 16 July, 13 August, 17 September 1991; 28 January 1992.

59. *HW*, 16 April 1993 p. 3; 21 May 1993, p. 15. Alasdair Morrison, 'The Society and conservation', *The Garden (JRHS)*, vol. 118 (1993), pp. 495-8, and 'Collective responsibility', *ibid.*, vol. 125 (2000), pp. 304-5; see also Roy Lancaster's letter in response, p. 785.

60. Michael Pollock, 'Conservation and the RHS', *The Garden (JRHS)*, vol. 120 (1995), esp. p. 86; Kerry Walter *et al.*, 'Counting our losses', vol. 123 (1998), pp. 573-7; Sara Oldfield, 'Collected wisdom', vol. 124 (1999), pp. 700-3, and see also advice to the public, p. 458. See also the earlier article by Sabina Knees, 'Plants from abroad', vol. 115 (1990), pp. 26-30. Successful projects: Turkey—Andy Byfield, 'Good for the bulbs, good for the people', vol. 119 (1994), pp. 512-15, and see also Abigail Entwistle *et al.*, 'Alternatives for the bulb trade from Turkey: a case study of indigenous bulb propagation', *Oryx*, vol. 36 (2002), pp. 333-41; Andrew Byfield, 'Reaping the rewards', *The Garden (JRHS)*, vol. 121 (1996), pp. 686-7. Hawai'i—Keith R. Woolliams, 'Conserving silverswords', vol. 120 (1995), pp. 668-71. Prairie habitat recreation—David K. Northington, 'Flowers for the future', *ibid.*, pp. 274-8; Virginia M. Kline, 'Resurrecting the great American prairie', vol. 121 (1996), pp. 580-5. Convention on Biological Diversity: see Simon Thornton-Wood, 'Rose of England? Not necessarily', *Times*, 27 August 2002.

61. Bowles travelling scholarship: Council minutes, 10 January 1956. Brian Mathew, 'The Bowles Scholarship botanical expedition to Iran, 1963', *JRHS*, vol. 90 (1965), pp. 5-18, 83-90. Queen Mother Bursary: *The Garden (JRHS)*, vol. 117 (1992), p. 552. Coke Trust: vol. 124 (1999), p. 73. The Coke Trust was founded in 1985 by Mr and Mrs Coke, to fund the future management of their garden at Jenkyn Place, Hampshire; when the garden was later sold, the purpose of the trust fund was altered to provide funds for work placements and travel. Merlin Trust: Joyce Stewart, 'The Merlin Trust', vol. 119 (1994), pp. 416-19, and see the issues of the *Merlin Newsletter*. At the time of writing, Christopher Brickell, Joyce Stewart, and the present author are Trustees. The full range of Merlin Trust reports is held in the Lindley Library, as are reports of students aided by RHS bursaries. See also Matt Bishop, 'Discovering plants in Romania', vol. 120 (1995), pp. 102-5, for a note on the Society's bursaries more generally.

62. Roy Lancaster, 'Ornamental plants from the wild', *The Garden (JRHS)*, vol. 115 (1990), pp. 10-18.

12 Horticultural Taxonomy and Registration, pp. 213-28

1. For the history of the Linnaean system, and its triumph in England, see Frans Stafleu, *Linnaeus and the Linnaeans* (1971); also, of course, Stearn's introduction to the facsimile edition of Linnaeus' *Species Plantarum* (1957-59), vol. 1, pp. 1-176. No modern history has yet been written of the natural classification movement that succeeded it, but a beginning has been made by Peter F. Stevens, *The Development of Biological Systematics* (1994), and see also Mabberley (1985), pp. 141-76. There is a tendency, intensely annoying to historians, among some modern polemicists for the reform of taxonomy to use the phrase 'Linnaean classification' for the existing system of phyla, classes, orders, families, genera and species, despite the facts that the use of classes and families predates Linnaeus, that the other higher-level categories postdate him, that we now use a different terminology from Linnaeus, and that his family names are now forgotten. See Marc Ereshefsky, *The Poverty of the Linnaean Hierarchy* (2001), for an example.

2. John Lindley, *Ladies' Botany*, 2nd edition (c.1835), pp. vi-viii.

3. For a handy summary of Lindley's various systems, see J. Reynolds-Green, *A History of Botany in the United Kingdom* (1914), pp. 336-53.

4. John Lindley, *Descriptive Botany* (1858). W.T. Stearn, *Botanical Latin* (1966, or any later edition), esp. p. 45. For a modern comment on euphony in plant names, see Wilfred Blunt, 'I name this plant "Colquhounia" ', *The Garden (JRHS)*, vol. (1977), pp. 157-8.

5. Alexandre-Henri de Cassini coined the name *Brachyscome* in 1816, but in 1825 amended it to *Brachycome*, the version that has been best known for the last century and three quarters. However, *Brachyscome* is a valid first publication, and we now have to adjust ourselves to adding the sibilant. (I can't help wondering whether *Brachyscome* was a typographical error ...)

6. For Lindley's early coinages, see the entries in *BR passim*; for his renunciation of them, *GC*, 16 July 1842, p. 467; for the crocus jibe, *ibid.*, 27 July 1850, p. 467. For orchid and conifer, see the *Oxford English Dictionary*. More generally, see Brent Elliott, 'Victorian gardeners and botanical nomenclature', *Botanical Journal of the Linnean Society*, vol. 109 (1992), pp. 473-83.

7. For a representative example, see Brent Elliott, 'The identity crisis of the Douglas fir', *New Plantsman*, vol. 1 (1994), pp. 20-8, which traces 21 different Latin names that have been given to the tree over the

course of two centuries.

8. Hibberd's paper was listed but not printed in the *Report* of the 1866 Conference. Hibberd published it in full in *FW*, 1866, pp. 278-81 ('On the naming of plants').

9. B. Daydon Jackson, 'The history of the compilation of *Index Kewensis*', *JRHS*, vol. 49 (1924), pp. 224-9. For Stearn's early articles, see 'Publications by William T. Stearn on bibliographical, botanical and horticultural subjects 1929-1976', *Biological Journal of the Linnean Society*, vol. 8 (1976), pp. 299-318. Frans Stafleu and R. S. Cowan, *Taxonomic Literature*, 2nd edition (1976-88).

10. The nomenclatural history of the redwood is fun. For Lindley's original description, see *GC*, 24 December 1853, pp.819-20, 823, and *BM*, tab. 4777-4778. For the changing perception and nomenclature of the tree by the 1880s, see Veitch, *A Manual of the Coniferae* (1881), pp. 204-11. The name *Sequoia gigantea* was first coined by Endlicher in 1847, but invalidly, because he used it for the tree already known as *S. sempervirens*; so it is Decaisne's 1854 use that is cited as correct. In 1939, Buchholz hived off *Sequoiadendron* as a distinct genus.

11. Sowerby had actually coined the name *Victoria amazonica* in 1850, but it was only after the 1905 Code that it became, shall we say, compulsory.

12. As an example of popular feeling on the question of Latin nomenclature, see Peter Seabrook, 'Am I a Latin lover?', *The Garden (JRHS)*, vol. 125 (2000), pp. 556-7, and the letters in response, p. 711.

13. Alice Coats, *GC*, 3 December 1960, p. 572. Publications Committee minutes, 24 September 1946, for a memo from Gilmour on the subject. Council minutes, 8 October 1946; 24 October 1950; 6 February 1951. One argument, that no one could remember whether a given epithet should be capitalised or not, could be dismissed by pointing out that all anyone need do was consult the *Index Kewensis*; a more ingenious argument was that it could often be ambiguous whether a given epithet was based on a personal or a geographical name. For an amusing version of this argument, see Nicholas Polunin, 'Specific and trivial decapitalization', *Bulletin of the Torrey Botanical Club*, vol. 77 (1950), pp. 214-221, esp. p. 218.

14. W.T. Stearn, 'Hookerianus or hookeranus?', *The Garden (JRHS)*, vol. 110 (1985), pp. 463-5. —And then there are little quibbles like the demand that *Buddleia* be spelled *Buddleja*, a demand that to the present author's mind merely reflects Otto Stapf's ignorance of the history of typography. Let us be thankful that the distinction between 'u' and 'v' had been sorted out by the time Linnaeus wrote.

15. *Times*, 20 May 1913, p. 9 d. Council minutes, 14 May 1913.

16. *GC*, 16 January 1915, p. 27 (announcement of sedum trial, for nomenclatural purposes). Council minutes, 4 November 1924 (iris standards).

17. Council minutes, 30 October, 13 November 1928; 7 May 1929; 28 January, 24 June 1930; 5-19 February, 16 April, 25 September 1935. For geographical names, see 6 December 1927; 7 January 1930. W. Dallimore, 'Reference list of conifers grown out of doors in the British Isles', in *Conifers in Cultivation* (1931), pp. 6-40, and esp. pp. 6-8 for a discussion of the nomenclatural problems. Campaign for stabilisation: Council minutes, 3 November 1942; 8 June 1943; 20 March 1945; 4-18 October 1955. John Gilmour, confidential report to Council on the Ninth International Botanical Congress, 1959. On the subsequent stabilisation programme, Council minutes, 26 January–20 April, 12 July 1960; 2-18 April 1963; 1 September 1964; and see G. Perry, 'Nomenclatural stability and the Botanical Code: a historical review', in D.L. Hawksworth, ed.,

Improving the Stability of Names: Needs and Options (1991), pp. 79-94; C.D. Brickell, 'Botany or gardening?', *JRHS*, vol. 95 (1970), pp. 480-1. For Gilmour, see W.T. Stearn, 'A tribute to John Gilmour (1906-1986)', *The Garden (JRHS)*, vol. 112 (1987), pp. 452-5.

18. Council minutes, 4 May 1965. W.T. Stearn, '*Viburnum farreri*, a new name for *Viburnum fragrans* Bunge', *Taxon*, vol. 15 (1966), pp. 22-3.

19. Council minutes, 4-18 April, 13 June, 1 August 1950; 22 July 1952; 1 December 1953; 2 February-2 March, 9 October 1954. For Dandy's original adoption of Buc'hoz's names, see 'The identity of *Lassonia* Buc'hoz', *Journal of Botany*, vol. 72 (1934), pp. 101-03; for his recantation, see 'Survey of the genus *Magnolia*', *Camellias and Magnolias* (1950), pp. 64-81. For later controversies, see Steven Spongberg, 'Magnoliaceae hardy in temperate North America', *Journal of the Arnold Arboretum*, vol. 57 (1976), pp. 250-312; Nigel Holman, '*Magnolia heptapeta* et alia?', *Plantsman*, vol. 1 (1979), pp. 56-61; Brent Elliott, 'In the absence of plants', *The Garden (JRHS)*, vol. 120 (1995), pp. 748-51.

20. The Cullen and Chamberlain revision was published in *Notes from the Royal Botanic Garden Edinburgh*, vols. 36-37 (1978-9), and the RHS *via media* announced in C.D. Brickell, 'Rhododendron cultivars: their nomenclature and international registration', *Rhododendrons 1978*, pp. 41-51. The reaction of the horticultural world to the Edinburgh reclassification yielded a lively little literature: Mavis Paton and E.M. Horwood-King, '*Rhododendron* species: the proposed new classification', *Rhododendrons 1981-2*, pp. 75-8, followed on pp. 78-81 by W.D. Davidson *et al.*, 'A revision of *Rhododendron*: a horticulturist's view'; Anne and Edward Boscawen, 'Re-listing the rhododendron collection at The High Beeches', *Rhododendrons 1982-3*, pp. 42-5; C. Jeffrey, 'Rhododendron and classification', *ibid.*, pp. 48-51, followed on pp. 51-2 by J.K. Hulme, 'The revision of *Rhododendron*'. See C.D. Brickell, foreword to the *Rhododendron Handbook* (1990); William and Melva Philipson, 'The taxonomy of the genus: a history', in Postan (1996), pp. 22-37.

21. The first appearance of *Dendranthema* in the Society's publications was in the *Proceedings* for 1983 (p. 4), where a plant was put forward as *Dendranthema erubescens*, 'supposed to be an ancestor of the florists' chrysanthemum'. See W.L. Tjaden, 'Regarding gender and number of generic names supposedly ending in –*anthema*', *Taxon*, vol. 44 (1995), pp. 213-16; Piers Trehane, 'Proposal to conserve *Chrysanthemum* L. with a conserved type (Compositae)', *ibid.*, pp. 439-41; R.K. Brummitt, '*Chrysanthemum* once again', *The Garden (JRHS)*, vol. 122 (1997), pp. 662-3; Tony Lord, 'The RHS Plant Finder', *ibid.*, vol. 123 (1998), p. 416.

22. William Herbert, 'Instructions for the treatment of the *Amaryllis Longifolia* as a hardy aquatic', *Transactions*, vol. 3 (1818), pp. 187-96; *Amaryllidaceae* (1837), pp. 31-3. Beaton describes his conversion to vernacular names in his autobiography, *CottGard*, vol. 13 (28 November 1854), pp. 153-8. The Society was already trying to enforce a clear distinction between species and varieties at exhibitions: Council minutes, 16 May 1865. Ferns: Peter Barnes, 'The horticultural nomenclature of ferns', *Pteridologist*, vol. 1 (1988), pp. 192-5. As late as 1942, though, Leslie Ahrendt was arguing that 'It is the custom to provide garden hybrids with "fancy names" which demand no botanical description, and which, as a consequence, are never defined; this seems an illogical proceeding, for no name, however informal, has any value unless there is a precise definition of the object to which that name applies'—*JRHS*, vol. 67 (1942), p. 129.

23. Council minutes, 5 January 1915 (proposal to change German names); 17 June 1947 (proposal to rename a plant named after a Nazi); 28 March 1911 (renaming of well-known plants); 13 June 1945 (proposal to replace foreign names). For interim names, see *GC*, 20 August 1887, p. 228, and 9 July 1892, p. 44. Maxwell T. Masters, 'On the nomenclature of garden plants', *JRHS*, vol. 5 (1879), pp. 126-35; G.W. Bulman, 'Garden nomenclature', vol. 32 (1907), pp. 25-36.

24. Daffodils: *GC*, 22 November 1884, p. 650; 5 May 1886, pp. 586-7; 22 May 1886, p. 650. F.W. Burbidge, 'Classification of *Narcissus*', *JHort*, 10 September 1903, pp. 233-4. Note that Baker published the first version of his classification of Narcissus in Burbidge's *The Narcissus* (1875). Orchids: *GC*, 8 March 1890, p. 296; 24 May 1890, p. 648; 10 May 1896, p. 614. *OR*, vol. 4 (1896), pp. 83, 94, 133-5.

25. Council minutes, 6 July 1948; 14-28 June 1949; 2 May-11 July, 12 September 1950. 21 January 1958: RHS to distribute Code. Stearn's correspondence on the incipient Code, much of it with the American taxonomist Wendell Holmes Camp, is held in the Lindley Library. For the announcement of the Code in the Society's *Journal*, see *JRHS*, vol. 77 (1952), pp. 157-73; John Gilmour, 'The new code for the naming of cultivated plants', vol. 79 (1954), pp. 12-21.

26. Arthur Simmonds, Memorandum on the use of the terms 'variety' and 'cultivar', Council minutes, 4 October 1955.

27. Council minutes, 11 March 1884; 10-24 March 1885; 27 April 1886. The account in Fletcher (1969) of the origin of this Committee is incorrect, Fletcher having confused the Narcissus Committee with the Scientific Committee's Subcommittee on Narcissus, which ran from 1884 to 1890.

28. Council minutes, 28 April, 21 July 1908; 6 April 1909. *List of Daffodil Names* (1908), p. 4. Scrase-Dickins, 'The work of the Narcissus Committee', *JRHS*, vol. 27 (1902-3), pp. 186-9, esp. p. 187.

29. Council minutes, 23 March 1886 [cancelled draft], 8 June 1886; 29 June, 13 August 1889; 21 April 1891; 12 July 1892. 'Report on the orchid nomenclature conference, June 1886', *JRHS*, vol. 7 (1886), pp. 297-312. For Reichenbach, and his quarrel with Rolfe, see Brent Elliott, 'Heinrich Reichenbach', *The Garden* (*JRHS*), vol. 119 (1994), pp. 440-41. For the debates over multigeneric hybrid nomenclature, see the *OR*, and more particularly the column 'Dies orchidiani' by 'Argus' (probably Rolfe), *passim* through the first decade or so of the 20th century—especially vol. 13 (1905), pp. 257-60; vol. 15 (1907), pp. 33-6, 97-100; vol. 16 (1908), pp. 340, 351-2; vol 17 (1909), pp. 65-8, 102-3; vol. 18 (1910), pp. 67-8. For *—ara*, see *JRHS*, vol. 35 (1909), p. xxxii; vol. 37 (1911), p. 151; and *OR*, vol. 17 (1909), p. 63; vol. 19 (1911), p. 98; vol. 20 (1912), pp. 258-9. 'Nomenclature of multigeneric orchid hybrids', *JRHS*, vol. 36 (1910-11), pp. 405-8.

30. Reactions to the *Stud-book*: Council minutes, 23 March, 6 April 1909; 14 March-11 April 1911; 8 October 1912. The abortive orchid hybrid register: 9 September-16 December 1913; 2-9 February, 20 July-17 August, 12 October 1915; 7-21 November 1917.

31. Council minutes, 6 September 1949; 31 January, 13 June, 9 August-13 September 1960. For Sander's life, see Arthur Swinson, *Frederick Sander: the Orchid King* (1970). See also 'Senex', '"Chelsea" Show in 1950', *GI*, 8 June 1929, p. 398, for a joke about the progress of orchid registration.

32. Tulip checklist: *Report of the Tulip Nomenclature Committee*, 1914-15. Council minutes, 17 January-14 February 1928; 15 January 1929; 29 September, 13 December 1938; 13 November 1956. Daniel Hall, 'Classification of garden tulips: a suggestion', *JRHS*,

vol. 62 (1937), pp. 78-80. Gladiolus: 7 September, 5 October 1926. Gentians: 13 October 1936. Chrysanthemums: 30 November 1954; 4 January, 22 March, 9 August 1955; 24 January 1956.

33. Council minutes, 2-30 November 1948; 11 January 1949; 13 June, 29 August, 12 September, 5 December 1950; 3-17 April 1951; 20 January, 23 June, 22 September, 20 October 1953; 3 May, 15 November 1955; 1 May, 13 November 1956; 4 June 1957; 1-29 July 1958.

34. International bureau: *Garden*, 13 September 1913, p. 468. HTA proposals: Council minutes, 14 December 1920; 14 May, 18 June, 10 September 1946. Rhododendron register: Rhododendron Year Book Committee minutes, 22 April 1952. Council minutes, 11 March 1952; 16 March 1954; 22 February—8 March 1955. C.D. Brickell, 'Rhododendron cultivars', *op. cit.*

35. Council minutes, 23 May 1972; 8 August 1978. For reports on the general progress of registration, see Alan Leslie, 'RHS—international agent', *The Garden* (*JRHS*), vol. 115 (1990), pp. 240-3; 'All present and correct', vol. 121 (1996), pp. 186-7. See *Grassroots*, no. 23 (January 1995), p. 3: 'Our secret army', for notes on the registrars at that date. International co-operation: in 2002 the American Daffodil Society awarded Sally Kington its Medal—a signal recognition, especially in view of the rather fraught relations that existed between the two organisations a couple of decades earlier.

36. For general background on colour theory and its relations to horticulture, see Brent Elliott, 'A spectrum of colour theories', *The Garden* (*JRHS*), vol. 118 (1993), pp. 573-5.

37. Council minutes, 9, 23 June, 21 July 1908. For a survey of the production of early colour charts, see C. Harman Payne, 'Colour charts', *GC*, 2 January 1915, p. 12; 23 January 1915, p. 42.

38. Council minutes, 14 August 1934; 26 November 1935; 24 November 1936; 12 January-9 February 1937. Minutes of the Horticultural Colour Chart Committee, *passim*. Miss M.E. Bunyard, 'Standardization in colour descriptions of flowers', *JRHS*, vol. 60 (1935), pp. 342-53; 'Horticultural colour chart', vol. 64 (1939), pp. 214-17.

39. Council minutes, 3 May 1955; 5 March 1963; 23 November 1965; 14 June 1966—18 July 1967 *passim*; 24 September 1968. Colour Chart minutes *passim*. 'The RHS colour chart', *JRHS*, vol. 91 (1966), pp. 433-8; Elspeth Napier, 'The RHS Colour Chart', vol. 96 (1971), pp. 563-4.

40. Brent Elliott, 'Match maker', *The Garden* (*JRHS*), vol. 126 (2001), pp. 344-5. The use of the Colour Chart is not confined to horticulture: because of its high colour range, organisations ranging from St Ivel Foods, to the African Love Bird Society of California, to Pinewood Studios have given testimonies to its utility. It has even been used for measuring the colour of monkeys' noses: see *Grassroots* no. 62 (May 1998), p. 6.

41. Council minutes, 27 October, 10 November 1964. Simon Thornton-Wood, 'A clearer view', *The Garden* (*JRHS*), vol. 121 (1996), pp. 644-5; Diana Miller, 'Pressing concerns', vol. 123 (1998), pp. 588-9.

42. Anon. (1829), pp. 5-6; see also his letter (signed 'B.') to *The Times*, 15 January 1830, p. 2 c, in which he says further that Sabine's attention to cultivars was 'at once the ridicule of every scientific man in London, and the disgrace of the Transactions'.

43. Diana M. Miller, 'Standard specimens for cultivated plants', *Acta Horticulturae* 413 (1995), Taxonomy of cultivated plants II, pp. 35-9; 'Raising standards', *The Garden* (*JRHS*), vol. 124 (1999), pp. 282-3; Miller and Susan R. Grayer, 'Standard portfolios in the Herbarium of the Royal Horticultural Society', in

Susyn Andrews *et al.*, eds., *Taxonomy of Cultivated Plants* (1999), pp. 397-9.

44. 'Computerisation of the orchid register', *OR*, vol. 98 (1990), pp. 31-2. *BG-Base*™: *The Garden (JRHS)*, vol. 122 (1997), p. 128. *BG-Base*™ was set up by the Arnold Arboretum and the World Conservation Monitoring Centre in Cambridge; read all about it at www.rbge.org.uk/bgbase. RHS Horticultural Database, vol. 123 (1998), pp. 763-4.

45. Tony Lord, '*The RHS Plant Finder*', *The Garden (JRHS)*, vol. 122 (1997), pp. 424-7; 'Trends and temptations', vol. 126 (2001), pp. 474-7. Jez Abbott, 'Setting the standard', *HW*, 23 January 2003, pp. 21-2.

46. Council minutes, 25 October 1853 (national tulip bed); 9 March 1937 (montbretias); 21 October 1947, 17 February 1948, 5 February 1957 (national collections scheme); 18 February 1958 (camellias and irises); 28 August 1962 (aquatics); 30 March 1965 (dwarf conifers).

47. C.D. Brickell, 'Conserving cultivated plants', *The Garden (JRHS)*, vol. 102 (1977), pp. 197-201; Elizabeth Coxhead, 'Amateurs to the rescue', vol. 103 (1978), pp. 96-9. For a proposal that the RHS should set up a scheme for plants like the Survival Service Commission for animals, see R. Melville, 'Plant conservation in relation to horticulture', *JRHS*, vol. 95 (1970), pp. 473-80.

48. C.D. Brickell, 'The RHS Conservation Conference', *The Garden (JRHS)*, vol. 104 (1979), pp. 161-71. C.D. Brickell and Fay Sharman, *The Vanishing Garden* (1986).

49. See the *NCCPG Newsletters*, later retitled *Plant Heritage*, *passim*; John Simmons' quotation will be found in *Plant Heritage*, vol. 4 no. 2 (1997), p. 4. G.A. Pattison, 'The National Council for the Conservation of Plants and Gardens', *ProfHort*, vol. 3 (1989), pp. 124-7.

50. Kay Sanecki, 'What is a pink sheet plant?', *The Garden (JRHS)*, vol. 111 (1986), pp. 36-9; Francesca Greenoak, 'Lost and found', vol. 124 (1999), pp. 194-7.

51. Graham Stuart Thomas, 'Treasures from the past', *The Garden (JRHS)*, vol. 114 (1989), pp. 378-84; Francesca Greenoak, 'Preserving our garden heritage', vol. 119 (1994), pp. 212-15. On national collections in RHS gardens, see Diana Miller, 'In safe hands', vol. 122 (1997), pp. 772-7.

13 Horticultural Science, pp. 229-50

1. *GC*, 7 March 1868, p. 235. Council minutes, 21 April, 5 May 1868; 20 April 1870.

2. For the conference advertisement, see *PRHS*, vol. 4 (1864), p. 79. Abstracts of the conference papers were published in *GC*, 26 May 1866, pp. 488-91; 2 June 1866, pp. 513-17; 9 June 1866, p. 539; 16 June 1866, p. 564; 25 June 1866, p. 588; 30 June 1866, pp. 611-12, in addition to the main volume of conference proceedings.

3. For the history of the revolution in glasshouses, see Elliott (1986), pp. 28-32, 65-6; and for general technical background, see E.W.B. van den Muijzenberg, *A History of Greenhouses* (1980).

4. Sir George Mackenzie, 'On the form which the glass of a forcing-house ought to have, in order to receive the greatest possible quantity of rays from the sun', *Transactions*, vol. 2 (1817), pp. 171-7; T.A. Knight, 'Suggestions for the improvement of Sir George Stuart Mackenzie's plan for forcing-houses', *ibid.*, pp. 350-3.

5. *QR*, vol. 112 (1862), p. 180. *GC*, 1845, *passim*, for Lindley's glass campaign; for the effect on price, 30 October 1847, p. 717, and 20 November 1847, p. 766; 1849 *passim* for Hartley's patent.

6. The literature is scattered through the ten volumes of *Transactions* and subsequent *Journals*, and is too large to footnote here. But see especially William Whale, 'An account of a plan of heating stoves by means of hot water, employed in the garden of Anthony Bacon', *Transactions*, vol. 7 (1830), pp. 203-8; R.B. Rogers, 'Note on electric heating', *JRHS*, vol. 29 (1904-05), p. 134; R.G.B. Evison, 'Some problems in greenhouse heating and ventilation', vol. 82 (1957), pp. 333-8; George Sheard, 'Heating a greenhouse', vol. 100 (1975), pp. 460-6, and 'Glasshouse heating 1977', vol. 102 (1977), p. 431; K.E. Morgan, 'Energy systems in greenhouses', vol. 104 (1979), pp. 298-9.

7. Council minutes, 30 October 1851; 8 November 1853; 17 January 1862.

8. Council minutes, 12 February, 26 March, 10 December 1889; 14 January 1890; 23 October 1894. W.J.C. Lawrence, 'Glasshouse design and management' *JRHS*, vol. 80 (1955), pp. 358-65.

9. Sir Joseph Banks, 'Some hints respecting the proper mode of inuring tender plants to our climate', *Transactions*, vol. 1 (1804-12), pp. 21-5; Abraham Hawkins, 'On some exotics, which endure the open air in Devonshire', *ibid.*, pp. 175-7, 242-3. Lindley's first frost report was published in vol. 6 (1826), pp. 493-500. Further major frost reports were published in 2nd series, vol. 2 (1835-41), pp. 225-316; *JHS*, vol. 8 (1853), pp. 207-48; *JRHS* vol. 8 (1887), entire volume. *The Plantsman* eventually followed suit in the 1980s.

10. For the meteorological equipment, see *Transactions*, vol. 7 (1830), pp. 97-101. Booth's and Thompson's observations were published in *Transactions*, ibid., pp. 102-29; throughout each volume of the second series, and vols. 6-9 of *JHS*. James Glaisher, 'Reduction of the meteorological observations made at the Royal Horticultural Garden, Chiswick, in the years 1826-1869', supplement to *JRHS*, vol. 2 (1870). After a long hiatus, publication resumed in vol. 25 (1900-01), and carried on until vol. 31 (1907), successively written by Edward Mawley and R.H. Curtis. Thompson also published 'Tables of temperature, for the use of gardeners', *JHS*, vol. 4 (1849), pp. 117-71. See *GC*, 28 May 1870, pp. 731-2 for meteorology at Chiswick.

11. Lindley, 'A notice of Simmons's patent hygrometer', *JHS*, vol. 1 (1846), pp. 127-30. Glaisher, 'On a thermometer for taking temperature at the roots of plants', *JRHS*, vol. 4 (1877), pp. 25-6, followed by 'On a dry and wet bulb thermometer', pp. 26-7. Council minutes, 5 January, 18 May 1870. For a note on Glaisher's career and activities with the RHS, see Brent Elliott, 'Above the clouds and beneath the soil', *The Garden (JRHS)*, vol. 117 (1992), pp. 528-31.

12. For relations with the Met Office, see Council minutes, 2 June 1874; 19 January 1875; 27 November 1894; 7 November 1905; 4 November 1947. See R.H. Curtis, 'The relation of meteorology to horticulture', *JRHS*, vol. 33 (1908), pp. 12-19. For the new station at Wisley, see *JRHS*, vol. 29 (1904-05), p. 645, and vol. 31 (1906), p. 74.

13. E.G. Gilbert, 'A tornado at Wisley', *JRHS*, vol. 91 (1966), pp. 101-3.

14. Council minutes, 2 February 1882; 11 November 1890; 23 June 1891; 15 November 1892. F.W. Oliver, 'On the effects of urban fog upon cultivated plants', *JRHS*, vol. 13 (1891), pp. 139-51, and 16 (1894), pp. 1-59; see also George Henslow, 'Injuries to plants by London fog, and by engine smoke', vol. 26 (1901-02), pp. 310-13, and C. Crowther, 'Town smoke and plant growth', vol. 38 (1912-13), pp. 461-8.

15. Donald Beaton, 'Stove plants in the open air', *CottGard*, vol. 8 (12 August 1852), pp. 305-6; see Banks, 'On the forcing-houses of the Romans', *Transactions*, vol. 1 (1809), esp. p. 151.

16. J. Weeks, 'A short account of the cultivation of the Victoria water lily in an open heated pond', *JHS*, vol. 6 (1851), p. 224; Trevor Clarke, 'Account of an experiment made upon heating a bed of earth in the open air', *PRHS*, vol. 2 (1862), pp. 182-9. For further accounts of Welton Place, see *JHort*, 22 December 1863, pp. 493-5, and 26 September 1865, p. 257. Geothermal border at Chiswick: Minutes of the Chiswick Board, 20 March, 7 August 1865.

17. Knight, 'Upon the supposed changes of the climate of England', *Transactions*, vol. 7 (1830), pp. 563-7.

18. S.W. Burrage, 'The microclimate of the garden', *The Garden (JRHS)*, vol. 101 (1976), pp. 91-5; Tom Wright, 'Microclimate and plant selection', *ibid.*, pp. 234-41.

19. See D.F. Cutler and I.B.K. Richardson, *Tree Roots and Buildings* (two editions, 1981, 1991); Hal Moggridge, 'A case without foundation' *The Garden (JRHS)*, vol. 103 (1978), pp. 244-5; Nigel Dunnett and Mohamed Qasim, 'Adapting to drought', vol. 121 (1996), pp. 418-20; Geoff Stebbings, 'A decade of drought?' vol. 123 (1998), pp. 162-5.

20. Nigel Hepper, 'The flower monitor', *The Garden (JRHS)*, vol. 122 (1997), pp. 48-9; Bill Burroughs, 'Degrees of damage', vol. 123 (1998), pp. 249-51; McKenzie Hedger and Anna Dourado, 'Climate change and the gardener', vol. 125 (2000), pp. 692-3; Phil Gates and Jon Ardle, 'Climate change ... coming soon to a garden near you?', vol. 127 (2002), pp. 912-17. Hellyer's once indispensable *Your Garden Week by Week* was first published in 1936, and reached a fourth edition in 1977; any future editions will have to have to be fitted with charts to allow the reader to revise the dates.

21. Knight on pots, *Transactions*, vol. 3 (1820), pp. 389-91; John Read's new tobacco fumigator, vol. 6 (1826), pp. 140-1; Glendinning on the pickfork, *JHS*, vol. 4 (1849), pp. 242-3; Forsyth's new level, vol. 7 (1852), pp. 198-200; Thompson on a new sulphurator, vol. 8 (1853), pp. 36-7. For the general history of garden tools, see my series of 12 articles in *The Garden (JRHS)*, vols. 120-1 (1995-6), odd-numbered months.

22. Exhibition of horticultural implements, June-July 1862, *PRHS*, vol. 2 (1862), pp. 263-5; further exhibition, vol. 5 (1865), pp. 106-7. Council minutes, 18 April 1944; 16 October 1945; 2 July, 19 July, 13 August, 5 November 1946; 14 January, 29 April 1947; 6 July, 10 August, 7 September 1948; 1 March 1949; 12-26 February, 23 June 1952. Second Horticultural Machinery Demo, *JRHS*, vol. 74 (1949), pp. 340-2, followed by E.R. Hoare, 'The engineer helps horticulture', pp. 342-6.

23. Sir Charles Monck, 'A plan for transplanting large forest trees in parks', *Transactions*, vol. 7 (1830), pp. 294-8; Robert Glendinning, 'On transplanting large evergreen trees and shrubs', *JHS*, vol. 4 (1849), pp. 41-4. For later treatments of the same issue, see T.H. Crasp, 'Lifting large trees', *JRHS*, vol. 19 (1896), pp. 24-9, and W.G. Ayres, 'Transplanting 60-year-old trees', vol. 81 (1956), pp. 174-7. For M'Glashan, see Council minutes, 25 January 1853; *GC*, 13 August 1857, p. 535; *Illustrated London News*, 12 March 1853, pp. 200-01. For a short history of tree transplanting systems, see Brent Elliott, 'Moving assets', *The Garden (JRHS)*, vol. 120 (1995), pp. 692-4.

24. Council minutes, 24 September 1912 (inception); 10 January 1950 (final cessation). Reports of the sundries awards were published annually in Proceedings, beginning with *JRHS*, vol. 39 (1913-14), pp. v-vi. *GC* 6 June 1925, p. 402 (mowers); 30 May 1936, pp. 343-4 (sprinklers). For the 1852 path surfaces trial, see *GC*, 31 July 1852, pp. 486-7, and more generally Brent Elliott, 'Paths', in Woudstra (2000), pp. 77-88.

25. Council minutes, 20 June 1838. Knight (1841).

26. For the subjects cited, see Lindley on double flowers,

Transactions, vol. 6 (1826), pp. 309-16; on growth rates at different times of day, *ibid.*, 2nd series, vol. 3, pp. 103-14, 247-64; J.B. Lawes [of Rothamsted fame, but here carrying out researches at Lindley's request] on evaporation, *JHS*, vol. 5 (1850), pp. 38-63, and vol. 6 (1851), pp. 227-42; Peter Mackenzie, 'Observations on inverted growth', *ibid.*, pp. 154-9; Edward Solly, 'On the influence of electricity on vegetables', vol. 1 (1846), pp. 91-109, and vol. 2 (1847), pp. 42-5.

27. *BM*, tab. 438 (1799). William Hedges, 'Account of experiments upon the production of blue instead of red flowers on the Hydrangea Hortensis', *Transactions*, vol. 3 (1820), pp. 173-7. Joseph Busch, note in *Transactions*, vol. 4 (1822), p. 568. James Donald, memorandum in *JHS*, vol. 1 (1846), p. 160. E.M. Chenery, 'The problem of the blue hydrangea', *JRHS*, vol. 62 (1937), pp. 304-20.

28. Masters, 'Notes on root-hairs and root growth', *JRHS*, vol. 5 (1879), pp. 173-86. For the institution of the Masters Memorial Lectures, see Council minutes, 31 March 1908; 12 August 1913.

29. *Gardening Which?*, November 1991, pp. 374-6. Horticultural Trades Association, *Code of Recommended Retail Practice Relating to the Labelling of Potentially Harmful Plants* (1994); Guidance Note 010, *The Display and Sale of Potentially Harmful Plants* (1994).

30. Council minutes, 28 May 1841; 24 March 1842; 25 April 1843; 17 March, 7 July 1846.

31. Knight, 'On the application of manure in a liquid form to plants in pots', *Transactions*, vol. 2 (1817), pp. 127-9.

32. Edward Solly, 'Experiments on the inorganic constituents of plants', *Transactions*, 2nd series, vol. 3 (1843-8), pp. 35-92; Garden Committee, 'The result of some experiments ... on the action of fertilizing agents upon the lawn', pp. 93-102; Solly, 'On the exhaustion of soils', pp. 189-96. Robert Thompson, 'Experimental enquiry into the comparative effect of various manures upon kitchen garden crops', *JHS*, vol. 1 (1846), pp. 264-9; Solly, 'Memorandum of an experiment on the continued cultivation of wheat', vol. 3 (1848), pp. 18-21; W.H. Pepys, 'Experiments on the growth of plants in the pure earths', vol. 4 (1849), pp. 57-60.

33. Karl Heinrich Schulz-Schultzenstein, 'On the nutritive constituents of water', *JRHS*, vol. 1 (1865), pp. 113-34, and Lindley's first comment on it, in *GC*, 14 January 1854, pp. 19-20. Masters, 'Report on various manures at Chiswick', vol. 3 (1872), pp. 19-79, 124-58. For Lawes's work at Rothamsted, see A.D. Hall, ed., *The Book of the Rothamsted Experiments* (1905).

34. Council minutes, 23 March 1909; 3 November 1914; 26 October 1915; 12-26 March 1918. *GC*, 16 April 1910, p. 248, and see *JRHS*, vol. 35 (1909-10), p. 391. Chittenden, 'Experiments with bacterized peat or humogen', *JRHS*, vol. 41 (1915-16), pp. 305-26. Potash permanganate: Council minutes, 9 February, 6 July 1937; soil sterilisation, 21 March 1944; refusals, 6 January 1942, 5 December 1972. 'Soil studies at Wisley', *JRHS*, vol 68 (1943), pp. 201-4, 239-42, 271-5. Note that Sir Frederick Keeble, the former Director of Wisley, undertook fertiliser research for ICI in the 1930s.

35. Solly, 'On seed-steeping', *Transactions*, 2nd series, vol. 3 (1843-48), pp. 197-20. Francis Henry Bickes, 'Report on experiments ... with seeds ...', *JHS*, vol. 2 (1847), pp. 35-9. Mummy wheat: *GC*, 11 November 1843, pp. 787-8; and for a recent summary of claims and counter-claims over a century and a half, see David A. Priestley, *Seed Aging* (1986), pp. 105-24. Dormancy: for the general wisdom in recent times, see E.H. Roberts, ed., *Viability of Seeds* (1972), pp. 321-

59; for the challenge, see Peter Thompson, 'Dormancy in seeds: fact or fiction?', *The Garden (JRHS)*, vol. 120 (1995), pp. 640-3.

36. For food adulteration, see Arthur H. Hassall, *Food and its Adulteration* (1855), and Henry W. Letheby, *On Food, its Varieties &c.* (1870), lecture 4. Lindley's manuscript report on coffee adulteration forms volume 1 of his bound series of Botanical Tracts in the Lindley Library.

37. Council minutes, 17 March, 16 June, 4 August, 23 October, 15 December 1868; 15 June, 6 July 1869. Report on the adulteration of seeds, *JRHS*, vol. 2 (1870), pp. 30-40. *GC*, 3 October 1868, p. 1042; 31 October 1868, pp. 1137-8; 7 November 1868, p. 1165; 14 November 1868, pp. 1188-9; 28 November 1868, p. 1233; 12 December 1868, pp. 1289-90; 26 December 1868, p. 1340; 2 January 1869, p. 8; 9 January 1869, p. 27; 23 January 1869, pp. 77-8; 6 February 1869, pp. 133-4; 20 February 1869, p. 193; 6 March 1869, p. 247; 12 June 1869, pp. 637-8; 19 June 1869, p. 661; 26 June 1869, p. 685; 4 September 1869, pp. 939-40; 11 September 1869, p. 968; 1 January 1870, p. 6.

38. *JRHS*, vol. 94 (1969), p. 121. G.C. Taylor and F.P. Knight, *The Propagation of Hardy Trees and Shrubs* (1927). For Bause, see *JHort*, 31 October 1895, p. 413.

39. Francis Hanger and J. Ravenscroft, 'Air layering experiments at Wisley', *JRHS*, vol. 79 (1954), pp. 111-16; David Hide, 'Taking the straight and narrow' [hardwood cuttings], vol. 122 (1997), pp. 38-40, and 'Simple but effective', vol. 123 (1998), pp. 731-3.

40. J.H. Priestley, 'Problems of vegetative propagation', *JRHS*, vol. 51 (1926), pp. 1-16; Tincker, 'The relation of growth-substances, or hormones, to agricultural practice', vol. 61 (1936), pp. 380-97; R.H. Stoughton, 'Soilless cultivation of plants', vol. 66 (1941), pp. 17-23; John Bleasdale, 'Better crops, fewer problems', part 2, vol. 117 (1992), pp. 360-1. Council minutes, 27 October 1936, for experiments on growth hormones, and 9 January 1958, for the use of MacPennys mist propagation equipment at Wisley.

41. W.J.C. Lawrence and J. Newell, *Seed and Potting Composts* (1st edition, 1939). Lawrence, on JI composts, *JRHS*, vol. 67 (1942), pp. 86-91; Michael Pollock, 'Peat and the gardener', vol. 116 (1991), pp. 13-15; David Hide, 'A fresh look at propagation composts', vol. 122 (1997), pp. 268-70; 'Improving on nature', vol. 123 (1998), pp. 188-90; Tony Kendle and Kate Lloyd-Bostock, 'Brickbats for bouquets', vol. 125 (2000), pp. 377-81, from which the quotation is taken.

42. William Herbert, 'Instructions for the treatment of the Amaryllis longifolia ...', *Transactions*, vol. 3 (1820), pp. 187-96; 'On the production of hybrid vegetables', vol. 4 (1822), pp. 15-50; 'On the cultivation of the Guernsey lily, and other bulbs ...', *ibid.*, pp. 176-84; 'Notice of certain seedling varieties of Amaryllis presented ...', vol. 5 (1824), pp. 337-40. For Rollisson's Cape heaths, see *GM*, vol. 1 (1826), pp. 366-74. Conway Zirkle, *The Beginnings of Plant Hybridization* (1935), esp. pp. 107-14 for Fairchild's Mule.

43. John Goss, 'On the variation in the colour of peas, occasioned by cross impregnation', *Transactions*, vol. 5 (1824), pp. 234-6, followed by a note on Alexander Seton's work, pp. 236-7; also Knight, 'Some remarks on the supposed influence of the pollen in cross breeding', *ibid.*, pp. 377-80.

44. For the most important theoretical articles in the *Transactions*, beside those in the last note, see William Herbert, 'On the production of hybrid vegetables', vol. 4 (1822), pp. 15-50; Knight, 'Observations on hybrids', *ibid.*, pp. 367-73; Herbert, 'On hybridization amongst vegetables', *JHS*, vol. 2 (1847), pp. 1-28, 81-107; Michel-Eugène Chevreul, 'General remarks on

the variations of the individuals ...', vol. 6 (1851), pp. 61-110. And, as a reminder that peas continued to be the subject of important experiments, see Thomas Laxton, 'Notes on some changes and variations in the offspring of cross-fertilized peas', *JRHS*, vol. 3 (1872), pp. 10-14. For Darwin's contributions to *GC*, see *The Collected Papers of Charles Darwin* (1977), *passim*.

45. Shirley Hibberd, 'The horticulture of fifty years', *GardMag*, 7 April 1883, pp. 163-4. See Council minutes, 6 January 1871, for his offer of a prize for hybridisation, which Council did not take up.

46. This is not the place for a Henslow bibliography, but even a listing of his most important papers in the *Journal* tends to take up space: 'On the origin of species in nature, and suggestions for experiments to induce varieties to arise under cultivation', *JRHS*, vol. 22 (1898-99), pp. 261-8; 'On protoplasm', vol. 25 (1900-01), pp. 81-4; 'Phenomena of germination', *ibid.*, pp. 91-4; 'Classification by evolution', vol. 27 (1902-03), pp. 132-41; 'Natural selection versus adaptation; or, Darwinism and evolution', vol. 28 (1903-04), pp. 71-83; 'On the heredity of acquired characteristics in plants', vol. 29 (1904-05), pp. 77-81; 'The true Darwinism', vol. 33 (1908), pp. 1-7; 'The mutation theory: a criticism', vol. 36 (1910-11), pp. 144-8; 'Life a director of force in development and evolution', *ibid.*, pp. 534-8; review of Wallace's *World of life*, *ibid.*, pp. 640-5; 'Darwin as ecologist', vol. 38 (1912-13), pp. 27-33; 'The passing of Darwinism', vol. 41 (1915-16), pp. 47-53; 'Darwin's alternative explanation of evolution', *ibid.*, pp. 54-63. See also G.F. Scott-Elliot, 'On the waning of Weismannism', vol. 35 (1909-10), pp. 327-9, just to show that Henslow was not alone.

47. Letter to W. Spiers, 1896; quoted, like all the examples of the Hurst and Wilks correspondence, from Hurst (1949). For the announcement of the Evolution Committee and the call for information, *GC*, 19 February 1898, p. 119.

48. Council minutes, 11 October 1898; 13 June 1899. The Hybrid Conference report was published as *JRHS*, vol. 24 (1900).

49. The standard account of the (re)discovery of Mendel is Olby (1967), which has superseded Sirks (1955). William Bateson, 'Problems of heredity as a subject for horticultural investigation', vol. 25 (1900-01), pp. 54-61 (and two papers by De Vries appeared in the same volume); Gregor Mendel, 'Experiments in plant hybridisation', vol. 26 (1901-02), pp. 1-32. This means, incidentally, that the RHS still holds the copyright on the English translation of Mendel's paper—publishers take note.

50. Council minutes, 13-27 August 1901; 14 February, 7 November 1905; 3 April, 14-28 August 1906. Hurst, 'Mendel's "law" applied to orchid hybrids', *JRHS*, vol. 26 (1901-02), pp. 688-97; 'Mendel's theory and orchid hybrids', vol. 27 (1902-03), pp. 614-24; 'Mendel's theory and wheat hybrids', *ibid.*, pp. 876-93; 'Experiments in the heredity of peas', vol. 28 (1903-04), pp. 483-94; report on the 1902 conference, vol. 29 (1904-05), pp. 417-33; 'Mendel's law of heredity', vol. 32 (1907), pp. 227-9; 'Mendel's law of heredity and its application to horticulture', vol. 36 (1910-11), pp. 22-52. The proceedings of the third conference were published in an edition of 3,000 copies, not as part of the *Journal*.

51. Hurst, 'Notes on the origin and evolution of our garden roses', *JRHS*, vol. 66 (1941), pp. 73-82, 242-50, 282-9. For Hurst's rose species, see Council minutes, 24 July, 9 October, 6 November 1934; 2 April 1935. Wisley as the place to improve plants: 12 October 1915. Salaman, 'Hereditary characters in the potato', *JRHS*, vol. 38 (1912-13), pp. 34-9; A.J. Bliss, 'Mendelian

characters in bearded irises', vol. 45 (1919-20), pp. 289-92); B. Buxton, 'Genetics of the Wisley Blue primrose', vol. 51 (1926), pp. 305-10.

52. Janaki Ammal: Council minutes, 16-30 July, 30 August 1946; 4 February 1947; 16 March, 4 May 1948. Ammal, 'Origin of the black mulberry', *JRHS*, vol. 73 (1948), pp. 117-19; 'Chromosomes and the evolution of garden *Philadelphus*', vol. 76 (1951), pp. 269-75; 'Chromosome numbers in hybrid nerines', *ibid.*, pp. 372-5; Ammal and Richard Seligman, 'Chromosomes in *Dianthus monspessulanus*', vol. 77 (1952), pp. 221-36.

53. J.K.A. Bleasdale, 'Better crops, fewer problems', *The Garden (JRHS)*, vol. 117 (1992), pp. 312-15; Sarah Ball and Anne-Louise Limm, 'Looking for the invisible', vol. 122 (1997), pp. 54-5; *ibid.*, p. 128, and vol. 124 (1999), p. 405, on the taxonomic use of DNA fingerprinting. Edward Cocking, 'Plant genetic engineering', vol. 116 (1991), pp. 606-9; David Ingram, 'Engineering the future', vol. 124 (1999), pp. 544-5, and p. 787 for correspondence; John MacLeod, 'On an equal footing', vol. 125 (2000), pp. 850-1, on the continued role of the amateur breeder. For the Quest project, see vol. 122 (1997), p. 128, and R.A. Clery *et al.*, 'An investigation into the scent of carnations', *Journal of Essential Oil Research*, vol. 11 (1999), pp. 355-9.

54. William Forsyth, *Observations on the Diseases, Defects, and Injuries in all Kinds of Fruit Trees* (1791); *Treatise on the Culture and Management of Fruit Trees* (seven editions, 1802-24). First edition, p. 250, for the lime-sulphur recipe. Meynell (1979).

55. Cats: Peter Kendall, 'On the employment of cats in the preservation of fruit from birds', *Transactions*, 2nd series vol. 1 (1831-35), pp. 390-1—a proposal, incidentally, revived by George Fergusson Wilson, which gave temporary fame to his cat Fat Tommy (*GC*, 23 November 1872, p. 1556). See also John Wilmot, 'On destroying slugs in gardens', *Transactions*, vol. 2 (1817), pp. 22-4; T.A. Knight, 'Upon the preservation of fruits from wasps', vol. 3 (1820), pp. 259-62; Sir Thomas Frankland, 'On the means of destroying wasps', vol. 4 (1822), pp. 107-8; Maxwell-Lefroy, 'The Wisley turnip fly trap', *JRHS*, vol. 40 (1914-15), pp. 269-71; G. Fox Wilson, 'A flea beetle trap' vol. 68 (1943), pp. 106-7.

56. *JRHS*, vol. 71 (1946), p. 336.

57. Council minutes, 29 August 1916; 8 May 1917; 16 July 1918. J.K. Ramsbottom, 'Investigations on the narcissus disease', *JRHS*, vol. 43 (1918-19), pp. 51-64; 'Experiments on the control of narcissus eelworm in the field', vol. 44 (1919), pp. 68-71 (reprinted in *GC*, 24 April-1 May 1920); report of the Daffodil Conference, vol. 52 (1927), pp. 60-8; G.W. Gibson, 'Some observations on the hot-water treatment of narcissus bulbs', *ibid.*, pp. 215-17; N.K. Gould, 'The hot-water treatment of narcissus bulbs', vol. 59 (1934), pp. 78-81. *GC*, 14 August 1920, pp. 79-80; 4 September 1920, p. 116.

58. William Spence, 'On an insect which is occasionally very injurious to fruit-trees [Tortrix moth]', *Transactions*, vol. 2 (1817), pp. 25-34; Banks, 'Notes relative to the first appearance of the Aphis Lanigera, or the apple tree insect, in this country', *ibid.*, pp. 162-70; Sir Oswald Mosley, 'On the Aphis lanigera, or American blight', vol. 3 (1820), pp. 54-61, with a note by Alexander Seton, p. 62; Mosley, 'Description of, and observations on, the Coccus laricis, or mealy insect, which infests the larch', *ibid.*, pp. 170-2.

59. *GC*, 23 August 1845, p. 575; 30 August, p. 591; 6 September, p. 607; 13 September, p. 623; and too much more to annotate here. Miles J. Berkeley, 'Observations, botanical and physiological, on the potato murrain', *JHS*, vol. 1 (1845-6), pp. 9-34; Edward Solly, 'Chemical observations on the cause of the potato murrain', *ibid.*, pp. 35-42; George John

Towers, 'Facts connected with the potato disease', vol. 2 (1847), pp. 31-4; Robert Thompson, 'A return of the proportion per acre of diseased and sound tubers in the Society's collection of potatoes', *ibid.*, pp. 45-9; Berkeley, 'Observations on the propagation of bunt ...', pp. 107-14; Thompson, 'Observations and experiments made in the garden ... in 1846 relative to the potato disease', pp. 179-82; Towers, 'The potato, its condition in 1847', vol. 3 (1848), pp. 22-6; Berkeley, 'On a form of scab in potatoes', *ibid.*, pp. 37-41; Thompson, 'Account of experiments made in the Garden ... in 1847', pp. 46-65; Thompson, 'Account of experiments ... 1848', vol. 4 (1849), pp. 62-74. Accounts of the potato blight abound, but from the horticultural point of view the story has never been told better than by Large (1940); supplement that for general purposes with G.C. Ainsworth, *Introduction to the History of Plant Pathology* (1981), and *Introduction to the History of Mycology* (1976). But see also E.C. Nelson, 'David Moore, Miles J. Berkeley and scientific studies of potato blight in Ireland, 1845-1847', *Archives of Natural History*, vol. 11 (1983), pp. 233-47.

60. Miles J. Berkeley, 'Vegetable pathology', *GC*, 4 January 1854, p. 4, continuing for 173 articles until 1857. Berkeley, 'On a peculiar form of mildew in onions', *JHS*, vol. 3 (1848), pp. 91-8; 'On the white rust of cabbages', *ibid.*, pp. 265-71; 'On a parasitic fungus which causes spot in orchids', *JRHS*, vol. 1 (1865), pp. 25-8; 'On the mildew of hollyhocks', vol. 4 (1877), pp. 149-53; plus several other articles, including translations.

61. For Smith's 'discovery', see *GC*, 1875, 10 July, pp. 35-6; 17 July, pp. 68-70; 24 July, p. 101; 31 July, pp. 130-1; comments thereon, 10 July, pp. 44-5; 24 July, p. 111; 2 October, p. 433. A. de Bary, 'Researches into the nature of the potato-fungus, Phytophthora infestans', *Journal of Botany*, 14 (1876), pp. 105-26, 149-54 [reprinted from the *Journal of the Royal Society of Agriculture*]. For press reaction, see *GC*, 1876, 12 February p. 209, 15 April pp. 506-7, 22 April p. 536, 20 May p. 661.

62. John Read, 'Description of a newly invented instrument for effectually applying tobacco fumigation to plants', *Transactions*, vol. 6 (1826), pp. 140-1. Tobacco petition: Council minutes, 6-20 November 1866; *GC*, 3 November 1866, p. 1042; 10 November 1866, p. 1065; 17 November 1866, pp. 1091-2; 1 December 1866, p. 1141. For fumigation on the verge of the 20th century, see H. H. Cousins, 'Fumigation with hydrocyanic acid gas', *JRHS*, vol. 21 (1897-8), pp. 303-6; R. Newstead, 'The results of some experiments with insecticides ...', vol. 26 (1901-02), pp. 745-54; George E. Williams, 'Nicotine in horticulture', vol. 27 (1902-03), pp. 50-4.

63. 'Proprietary products for the control of plant pests and diseases', *Agriculture*, vol. 50 (1943), pp. 331-4. H. Martin and R.L. Wain, 'DDT: its properties and possible uses', *JRHS*, vol. 69 (1944), pp. 366-9; M. Cohen and W. Steer, 'The control of leatherjackets with DDT', vol. 71 (1946), pp. 130-3; Tincker, 'Tests made at Wisley with a selective weedkiller: methoxone', *ibid.*, pp. 141-7; Fox Wilson, 'Recent developments in garden pest control', *ibid.*, pp. 334-43. See Janet Peach, 'A century of agrochemicals', vol. 108 (1983), pp. 281-4, for an overview, and John Sheail, *Nature Conservation in Britain: the Formative Years* (1998), pp. 108-12, for other early responses to DDT.

64. Edward R. Speyer, 'The greenhouse white-fly', *JRHS*, vol. 54 (1929), pp. 181-92; vol. 60 (1935), Proceedings, p. civ for the terms of purchase by Fellows; vol. 99 (1974), p. 160, for continued availability. Council minutes, 21 March 1933; 11 February 1936; 14 June, 26 July, 9 August 1955.

65. Sue Jupe, 'Tipping the balance of nature', *The Garden* (*JRHS*), vol. 119 (1994), pp. 222-4; 'Live and let live', vol. 120 (1995), pp. 428-31; Sarah Case, 'Disease diagnosis at Wisley', vol. 121 (1996), pp. 154-5; Chris Prior, 'Fireblight: a manageable disease', vol. 122 (1997), pp. 242-3; Andrew Halstead, 'The garden's little helpers', pp. 430-3; Sarah Ball, 'Something in the air', pp. 782-5; Debra Whitehead and Ana Pérez Sierra, 'Danger underground', pp. 790-2; Andrew Halstead, 'Preying on the enemy', vol. 124 (1999), pp. 360-3.

66. For the Poisons Bill amendment, see *Times*, 15 May 1931, p. 12 c (NFU supporting bill), 19 May 12 e (pharmacists opposing), 3 July 9 b (report on debate). Council minutes, 2-16 June 1931; 9-23 October 1934. Registration of contents: 1 August 1933.

67. Hormone sprays: Council minutes, 28 August, 2 October 1956; 30 April, 30 July 1957; 14 April 1959. Paul Bracey, 'The place of residual herbicides in the garden and nursery', *JRHS*, vol. 20 (1959), pp. 133-44; letter by E.H.M. Cox, pp. 280-1; note on p. 302 warning about spray drift damage.

68. Richard Trow-Smith, 'Chemical clearout', *The Garden* (*JRHS*), vol. 126 (2001), pp. 255-7.

69. Berkeley as botanical adviser (after failure of negotiations with Thompson): Council minutes, 22 July 1864; 6-24 January 1865. Dyer's appointment and resignation: 6 December 1871; 17 January 1872; 2-16 June 1874; 23 June, 21 July 1875.

70. Henslow: Council minutes, 11 May 1880; 22 March 1881; 9 May 1882; 14 December 1897. His floral demonstrations were published intermittently in the *Journal* from vol. 19 (1896) to vol. 26 (1902). Rendle: 17 January, 9 September 1919; 13 July 1920. On Ingram and his appointment, see *The Garden* (*JRHS*), vol. 121 (1996), pp. 240-3.

71. *JHort*, 21 May 1914, pp. 463-8. Council minutes, 11 December 1923; 13 May, 8 July, 16 December 1924; 27 January 1925; 6 December 1927; 3 December 1929; 30 December 1930. The anonymous pamphlet: Anon. (1916), esp. p. 23, which also misleadingly claimed that the experimental work was 'done on land not their own, lent to them by the late Sir Thomas Hanbury for purely garden work'. For Maxwell-Lefroy's terrifying lectures, see *GC*, 13 February 1915, p. 88; 29 May 1915, pp. 292-3.

72. Council minutes, 28 July 1931; 8 March 1932; 20 July 1937; 9 November 1937; 4 January 1938. For the history of the expansion of government agricultural and horticultural advisory services, see Susan Foreman, *Loaves and Fishes: an Illustrated History of the Ministry of Agriculture, Fisheries and Food 1889-1989* (1989); the story of their subsequent reduction has not yet been summarised in book form. See Fred W. Shepherd, 'Experimental horticulture', *ProfHort*, vol. 3 (1989), pp. 106-10. J.D. Bernal's proposals: Council minutes, 20 April, 4 May 1948; *Nature*, 15 May 1948, pp. 771-2; 22 May 1948, p. 799. See Maurice Goldsmith, *Sage: a Life of J.D. Bernal* (1980), pp. 149-50, for Bernal's earlier clash with the Advisory Council on Science Policy, to which this later controversy can be regarded as a footnote.

73. Council minutes, 3 July 1945; 13 December 1949; 18 April 1950; 6 March 1951; 8 January 1952; 30 October 1956; 10 September 1957. ISHS: 7 April, 7 July 1959; 9 February, 20 April 1960.

74. Council minutes, 27 October 1964; 8-22 March 1966.

75. Voelcker: Council minutes, 12 June 1894; 14 December 1897; 11 January 1898; 23 March, 13 April, 11 May 1920. Chelsea Information Bureau: *GC*, 4 June 1932, p. 430. David Pycraft, 'Wisley, where nothing is out of the question!', *The Garden* (*JRHS*), vol. 115 (1990), pp. 653-6; Barbara Abbs, 'At your service', vol. 120 (1995), pp. 47-9. For Gardencall, see vol. 114 (1989), p. 414.

76. Fred W. Shepherd, 'Experimental horticulture', *ProfHort*, vol. 3 (1989), pp. 106-10. Rosewarne: *The Garden* (*JRHS*), vol. 114 (1989), pp. 523-4. *HW*, 24 March 1989, p. 3; 14 April 1989, p. 3. East Malling: 'Horticulture pioneers left to wither', *Guardian*, 22 April 2003, p. 7.

77. H.R. Fletcher, 'Challenges and opportunities', *JRHS*, vol. 92 (1967), pp. 108-16, esp. p. 109.

78. Prizes for botanical collections, *PRHS*, vol. 4 (1864), pp. 90-5; vol. 5 (1865), pp. 47, 52. Council minutes, 15 April 1864; 6 January, 7 March 1865; 18 June 1867; 4 August 1868. See also Brent Elliott, 'Pressing matters for Council', *The Garden* (*JRHS*), vol. 129 (2004), p. 42.

79. George S. Boulger, 'The preservation of our wild plants', *JRHS*, vol. 29 (1904-05), pp. 392-48. Council minutes, 10 March 1914; 18 May, 15 June 1926; 3 November 1931; 13 August 1946; 8 July 1952; 3-31 March 1953. For background on nature conservation, see John Ranlett, 'Checking nature's desecration: late Victorian environmental organisation', *Victorian Studies*, vol. 26 (1983), pp. 197-222, and Sheail, *op. cit.*

80. A.D. Middleton, 'The grey squirrel in Britain', *Journal of the Ministry of Agriculture*, vol. 37 (1931), pp. 1069-78; *Field*, 21 February 1931, p. 239 (and of the ensuing correspondence see especially 28 March 1931, p. 437, on grey squirrels as food); *Times*, 21 February 1931 p. 9 c; also 22 May 1931 p. 8 c. Council minutes, 10 February, 10 March, 5 May, 16 June, 30 June, 11 August 1931. Compare two articles in *JRHS*: L. Swainson, 'The grey squirrel: the pros and cons of the question', vol. 63 (1938), pp. 489-90, and H.G. Lloyd, 'The grey squirrel', vol. 99 (1974), pp. 125-7. Swainson went on to administer the National Anti-grey Squirrel Campaign from his house in Boxmoor. See Hilda Kean, 'Imagining rabbits and squirrels in the English countryside', *Society & Animals*, vol. 9 (2001), pp.163-76.

81. Council minutes, 16 October 1945; 18 June 1946. For further concerns about pesticides during the 1960s, see 19 March 1963; 6 February 1968.

82. Council minutes, 9 October 1928. Eric Robinson, 'Keep off the pavement', *The Garden* (*JRHS*), vol. 119 (1994), pp. 210-11. See vol. 122 (1997), p. 77, for Plantlife's rescue of 26 hectares of limestone pavement in the Yorkshire Dales.

83. Council minutes, 1 December 1959. Graham Howell, *Gardening without Peat* (1991); Suki Pryce, *The Peat Alternatives Manual* (1991), and see also her 'Alternatives to peat', *ProfHort*, vol. 5 (1991), pp. 101-6; Neil Bragg, *Peat and its Alternatives* (1991). Peter Atkins and Michael Pollock, 'Peat and the gardener', *The Garden* (*JRHS*), vol. 116 (1991), pp. 10-15; Pollock, 'Peat and the gardener—an update', vol. 118 (1993), pp. 454-7; Bryan Wheeler *et al.*, 'Raising razed bogs', vol. 119 (1994), pp. 432-4; Pollock, 'The Society and conservation', vol. 120 (1995), pp. 86-9; Jon Pickering, 'Low-peat performers', vol. 125 (2000), pp. 676-8; Phil Gates, 'Peat, gardeners and conservation', vol. 127 (2002), pp. 200-3. See Catherine Caufield, *Thorne Moors* (1991), for an account of the early fight for peatland conservation and the beginnings of the anti-peat campaign.

84. Kenneth Gray and Anthony Biddlestone, 'The garden compost heap', *The Garden* (*JRHS*), vol. 101 (1976), pp. 540-5, 594-8. Jon Pickering, 'Waste not, want not', vol. 125 (2000), pp. 106-9.

85. Christopher Bailes, 'Havens for orchids', *The Garden* (*JRHS*), vol. 119 (1994), pp. 425-7; Franklyn Perring, 'The silent invasion', vol. 121 (1996), pp. 360-3; 'Gardening for the future', followed by Jennifer Owen, 'Watching the wildlife', vol. 127 (2002), pp. 844-9.

14 The Orchard and Kitchen Garden, pp. 251-68

1. Knight (1805), p. 5.

2. Knight, 'Observations on the grafting of trees' in Knight (1841), pp. 81-4. Knight's major theoretical papers on the subject in the *Transactions* are: 'Observations on the method of producing new and early fruits', vol. 1 (1804), pp. 30-40; 'On the want of permanence of character in varieties of fruit, when propagated by grafts and buds', vol. 2 (1817), pp. 160-1; 'Observations upon the effects of age upon fruit trees of different kinds', vol. 5 (1824), pp. 384-9; 'On the means of prolonging the duration of valuable varieties of fruits', 2nd series, vol. 1 (1831-5), pp. 147-50. For Alexander Hunter, see his *Georgical Essays* (1777 edition), pp. 350-1. For modern comments on Knight's hypothesis, see H.V. Taylor, *The Apples of England*, 3rd edition (1948), pp. 8-9; Joan Morgan and Alison Richards, *New Book of Apples* (2002), pp. 151-3.

3. For Knight's cherries, see *Transactions*, vol. 2 (1817), pp. 137-9, 208-11, 301-3; vol. 3 (1820), pp. 211-13, and see also N.H. Grubb, *Cherries* (1949), pp. 126-7; Council minutes, 5 August 1817, for the despatch of the cherries to Her Majesty. For his apples and pears, see *Transactions*, vol. 1 (1809-12), pp. 145-6, 178-83, 197-8, 226-9; vol. 2 (1817), pp. 1-2; 2nd series, vol. 1 (1831-5), pp. 103-10. For his plums, vol. 3 (1820), pp. 214-6; vol. 5 (1824), pp. 381-3; 2nd series, vol. 1 (1831-5), pp. 53-5. For his peaches, vol. 1 (1809), pp. 165-70; vol. 2 (1817), pp. 140-3, 214-16. For his currants, vol. 3 (1820), pp. 86-90. For his strawberries, *ibid.*, pp. 207-10, 396-8; vol. 4 (1822), pp. 197-9. For his grapes, vol. 1 (1812), pp. 258-60.

4. For 'Keens' Seedling', see *Transactions*, vol. 2 (1817), pp. 101-2. For 'Williams' Bon Chrétien', see *ibid.*, pp. 250-1; see also G. Wynne Thomas, 'The Williams' pear', *JRHS*, vol. 92 (1967), pp. 28-31. The list of prizes offered for new cultivars was published as an appendix to vol. 1.

5. Council minutes: 4, 16 May, 1 August 1815; 23 July 1819; 21 August, 28 October, 4 December 1822; 19 February, 21 August 1823; 17 May 1827. A list of the Hooker drawings was drawn up by E.A. Bunyard on their re-acquisition in 1927, and published in the Society's *Journal*, vol. 52 (1927), pp. 218-34. (In addition to Hooker's 138, there are 28 by C.J. Robertson, eight by Barbara Cotton, 13 by Mrs Withers, and 30 unsigned.) For reproductions of 50 of Hooker's drawings, see *Hooker's Finest Fruits*, ed. by F.A. Roach (1989), esp. pp. 19-21 for a note on Hooker's life. There are mysteries about Hooker's illness: the minute for 4 December 1822, noting that Hooker had guaranteed Galloway's expenses, remarks that he was quite sane at the time.

6. For receipts and distributions of fruit trees, see Council minutes, 3 October 1815; 18 June, 3 December 1816; 7-21 January, 4 March, 3 June, 2-16 September, 4 November 1817; 3-17 February, 15 December 1818; 5 January 1819; 8 March, 5 April 1820; 29 January 1821. David Hosack on the Seckle pear, *Transactions*, vol. 3 (1820), pp. 256-8; Council minutes, 15 December 1818; 5 January 1819.

7. *Catalogue of Fruits Cultivated in the Garden of the Horticultural Society ... at Chiswick* (1826, and subsequent editions of 1831 and 1842); supplement to the 3rd edition, *JHS*, vol. 8 (1853), pp. 243-69. The new (4th) edition of the 1860s was published in installments in *PRHS*, vol. 2 (1862), pp. 491-2, 596-610; 658-70; vol. 3 (1863), pp. 40-2, 120-39, 165-78, 246-52, 352-61; vol. 4 (1864), pp. 58-63, 101-2; vol. 5 (1865), pp. 98-102. See Council minutes, 27 December 1861, for the decision to publish in that form. See also Joseph Sabine, 'Observations on the formation of a select collection of apple-trees', *Transactions*, vol. 3 (1820), pp. '263'-71. Thompson's original MS is held in the

Archives. Thompson's appointment: Council minutes, 7 April 1826. *GM*, vol. 4 (1828), pp. 168-9; vol. 6 (1830), pp. 730-1; vol. 7 (1831), pp. 252-3. *FM*, vol. 5 (1840), pp. 155-6. *Annals of Horticulture*, 1847, pp. 97-8. *Florist*, 1859, pp. 115, for the quotation about the soil. On gooseberries, see R.A. Redfern, *Gooseberry Shows of Old* (1973), a reprinting of two historical articles published in the *North Cheshire Herald* in 1944.

8. Council minutes, 25 April 1823; 18 April 1825.

9. Council minutes, 6 February, 20 July 1822. John Lindley, 'A sketch of the principal tropical fruits which are likely to be worth cultivating in England for the dessert', *Transactions*, vol. 5 (1824), pp. 79-126. Sabine and Don, 'Some account of the edible fruits of Sierra Leone', vol. 5 (1824), pp. 439-66. Lindley, 'An account of ten varieties of Persian melons', vol. 6 (1826), pp. 553-62. Knight, 'On the degeneracy of the larger and finer varieties of Persian melon, in the climate of England', vol. 7 (1830), pp. 584-90; 'Upon the cultivation of the Persian varieties of the melon', 2nd series, vol. 1 (1831-5), pp. 85-90. For Knight on the mango and cherimoya, see 'Suggestions respecting the culture of the mango and cherimoyer', vol. 7, pp. 254-8. For the building of the peach houses and pineapple pits at Chiswick, see Council minutes, 20 July 1822; 3 September 1823; 9 April, 27 August 1824; 23 July, 3 December 1825.

10. Robert Fortune, 'Observations on the kumquat', *JRHS*, vol. 2 (1870), pp. 46-50.

11. John Giles, *Ananas* (1767), and Adam Taylor, *A Treatise on the Ananas or Pine Apple* (1769), were the first two English manuals. Report of the Garden Committee (1825), p.5; Donald Munro, pineapple varieties at Chiswick, *Transactions*, 2nd series, vol. 1 (1831-5), pp.1-34; seven other articles on pineapple culture appeared in *Transactions* and *JHS*. *GM*, vol. 1 (1826), p. 345; vol. 14 (1838), pp. 444-5.

12. Robert Schomburgk, 'West Indian fruits and esculents that may be advantageously introduced into cultivation in England', *JHS*, vol. 2 (1847), pp. 148-55. James Bateman, 'Particulars respecting the mode of cultivation &c. of the *Averrhoa carambola*', *Transactions*, 2nd series, vol. 2 (1835-41), pp. 30-1; 'On the cultivation of the dwarf banana (Musa Cavendishii)', *PRHS*, vol. 4 (1864), pp. 98-9.

13. *CottGard*, vol. 19 (9 March 1858), p. 347. *Florist*, 1859, pp. 114-16.

14. Council minutes, 19 May, 17 June, 18 August, 23 September 1856, for Thompson's problems; 3 December 1856 for Spencer's report and reorganisation; 10 July, 24 September 1857, for the Pomological Committee. *CottGard*, vol. 12 (1 June 1854), pp. 151-2; vol. 21 (23 November 1858), pp. 111-12. *Florist*, 1859, pp. 114-16. Council minutes, 7 January, 25 February, 16 March, 15 April, 7 May, 21 May, 4 June, 15 July 1858 for Harcourt and events leading up to the formation of the Committee; 1 October, 5 November 1858, 11 February 1859, 20 January 1860 for first changes. *GC*, 1858, pp. 171-2, 193, 216, 219.

15. For Archer Clive, see Eric Partridge's introduction to the 1928 Scholartis Press republication of Mrs Clive's *IX Poems by V.*; for Blackmore, see Brent Elliott, 'A novelist in the fruit garden', *The Garden (JRHS)*, vol. 117 (1992), pp. 488-91.

16. Council minutes, 20 January 1860; 19 February, 18 May 1864; 1 May 1906; 2-30 August 1910. For the plagiarism suit against Scott, see *JHort*, 7 May 1874, pp. 364-5, and *GC*, 9 May 1874, p. 610. Robert Hogg, *The Fruit Manual* (five editions: 1860, 1862, 1866, 1875, 1884). E.A. Bunyard, *A Handbook of Hardy Fruits*, 2 vols. (1920-5).

17. 'Report on some of the varieties of grapes in the large conservatory at Chiswick', *PRHS*, vol. 1 (1861), pp.

104-10. Grape management: *GC*, 7 July 1883, p. 16; 6 October 1883, pp. 423-6; *JRHS*, vol. 65 (1940), p. 396. Three tomatoes bred under Barron's supervision received awards: 'Chiswick Red' (FCC 1883), 'Chiswick Dessert' (AM 1896), and 'Chiswick Peach' (FCC 1899); Council minutes, 17 September 1889, for negotiations with Sutton's Seeds. Barron, *Vines and Vine-culture* (five editions, 1883, 1887, 1892, 1900, 1912); French translation 1893.

18. For the fruit shows of the 1850s, see Council minutes, 11 February 1851; 28 August, 23 September 1856; 17 November 1857; 5 November 1858; 7 October 1859. *GC*, 31 October 1857, pp. 739-40, 741-3; 23 October 1858, pp. 779-80; 20 November 1858, pp. 843-4. Potato shows: Council minutes, 7 April, 10 November 1875; 6 February, 21 March 1877. *GC*, 2 October 1875, p. 430; 6 October 1877, p. 432; 13 October 1877, p. 468; 20 October 1877, p. 500; 27 October 1877, p. 532; 3 November 1877, pp. 564-5; 10 November 1877, p. 595.

19. The proceedings of the great fruit conferences were published as follows: National Apple Conference 1883—published separately as *British Apples* (1884). National Pear Conference 1885, *JRHS*, vol. 9 (1887). Apple and Pear Conference 1888, vol. 10 (1888). Vegetable Conference 1889, vol. 12 (1890), pp. 2-105. Grape Conference 1890, vol. 13 (1891), pp. 40-63. Small Hardy Fruits Conference, 1891, *ibid.*, pp. 340-63. Apricot and Plum Conference, vol. 15 (1893), pp. 200-11. British-grown Fruit Conferences 1894-7, vols. 18 (1895), pp. 98-192; 19 (1896), pp. 228-340; 20 (1896-7), pp. 128-212; 21 (1897-8), pp. 343-412. Fruit Conference 1905, vol. 30 (1906). Fruit Spraying Conference 1908, vol. 34 (1908-9), pp. 305-60. For some selected reports on the conferences and their accompanying shows, see *JHort*, 15 May 1879, pp. 358-9; new series vol. 2 (1881), pp. 207-8, 352-3, 528-9; vol. 17 (1888), pp. 351-2; *GardMag*, 27 September 1890, pp. 586-90. See Morgan and Richards, *op. cit.*, pp. 115-20, on the Apple Conference.

20. Proposed International Fruit Shows: Council minutes, 27 October 1891; 13-27 March 1894. Colonial Fruit Shows: 28 March—11 April 1905; 13 February 1906; 17 September 1907; 29 September, 15-27 October 1908; 6 December 1910.

21. Fruit Growing Conference 1919, proceedings published in *JRHS*, vol. 45 (1919-20), pp. 60-80. International Potato Conference 1921, proceedings published separately in 1922; and see *GC*, 26 November 1921, pp. 280-1. Apple and Pear Conference 1934 (proceedings published 1935 as *Apples and Pears*). Cherry and Soft Fruit Conference 1935 (*Cherries and Soft Fruits*, 1935). Centenary Apple and Pear Conference, 1983 (*Apples and Pears*, 1983).

22. Council minutes, 8 December 1885; 12 August 1890; 10 November, 8 December 1891; 12 January, 3 May 1892; 23 October 1894; 13 October 1896; 21 September 1897; 22 February 1898.

23. Smith and his melon: Council minutes, 22 November 1910. Outdoor vineyard: Council minutes, 17 August 1905. Exhibits: 29 September 1908; 31 August 1909. H.M. Tod: 21 December 1909; 8 February, 27 September 1910; 12 September 1911. H.M. Tod, *Vine-growing in England* (1911), esp. pp. 57-8, 110-11; the photographs were taken in the Wisley vineyard. Hugh Barty-King, *A Tradition of English Wine* (1977), esp. pp. 124-42 for Castell Coch and Andrew Pettigrew, and 149-51 for Brock; Pettigrew, 'Lord Bute's vineyards in South Wales', *JRHS*, vol. 17 (1895), pp. 95-104.

24. *Transactions*, 2nd series, vol. 1 (1835), pp. 369-73 (beans), 374-87 (peas).

25. William Morgan, 'Account of the species and varieties of the beets ...', *Transactions*, vol. 3 (1820), pp. 272-86; Joseph Sabine, 'On the love apple or tomato', *ibid.*, pp. 342-54; Charles Strachan, 'Account and description of the different varieties of the onion', *ibid.*, pp. 369-79; Strachan, 'Account and description of the varieties of spring radish', 436-46; William Christie, 'Account and description of the varieties of autumn and winter radish', vol. 4 (1822), pp. 10-14; Christie, 'Description and account of the different varieties of the garden carrot', pp. 383-8. Christie's potato survey and resignation: Council minutes, 15 December 1824; 19 January 1825.

26. Andrew Mathews, 'Description of the different varieties of endives', *Transactions*, vol. 6 (1826), pp. 133-9; 'Description of the different varieties of parsneps', pp. 302-6; 'On the varieties of cardoon', vol. 7 (1830), pp. 9-15. See also vol. 6 pp. 563-86 for a general account of esculent vegetables at Chiswick.

27. Council minutes, 7 January 1817. Thomas Hare, 'On the advantages of blanching garden rhubarb for culinary purposes', *Transactions*, vol. 2 (1817), p. 258. For follow-ups see Daniel Judd, 'On a method of forcing garden rhubarb', vol. 3 (1820), pp. 143-5, and Knight, 'On a method of forcing rhubarb in pots', pp. 154-6.

28. Isaac Oldaker [more usually Oldacre], 'Account of the method of growing mushrooms in houses', *Transactions*, vol. 2 (1817), pp. 336-46; see *GM*, vol. 1 (1826), p. 215, and William Robinson, *Mushroom Culture* (1870), pp. 10-12. Council minutes, 20 January 1834.

29. Council minutes, 24 March 1842.

30. Decision to hold vegetable trials: Council minutes, 11 February 1859. See F.G. Potter, 'Vegetable cavalcade', *JRHS*, vol. 93 (1978), pp. 30-8, for a general survey of developments, but contrast his statements about the small number of cultivars available *c*.1850 with the trials reports in the *Proceedings* ten years later.

31. Vilmorin, 'On the improvement of the wild carrot', *Transactions*, 2nd series, vol. 2 (1835-41), pp. 348-56. Lindley on maize: *JHS*, vol. 1 (1846), pp. 114-17. Banks, 'An attempt to ascertain the time when the potatoe (Solanum Tuberosum) was first introduced into the United Kingdom', *Transactions*, vol. 1 (1804), pp. 8-12; Sabine, 'On the native country of the wild potatoe', vol. 5 (1824), pp. 249-59. Eleven or more articles on potato varieties and culture were published in the *Transactions*, depending on how many articles you count Lindley's potato experiments as. Ascension and St Helena: Council minutes, 22 January 1830; 21 May 1844. On the history of the question of the potato's introduction, see T.E.H.W. Krichauff, 'The tercentenary of the introduction of potatos into England', *JRHS*, vol. 19 (1896), pp. 224-7; and Redcliffe N. Salaman, 'The potato in its early home and its introduction into Europe', vol. 62 (1937), pp. 61-77, 112-23, 153-62, 253-66, the first version of his eventual book *The Introduction and Social History of the Potato* (1949).

32. Lindley, 'Notes on the wild potato', *JHS*, vol. 3 (1848), pp. 65-72. Large (1940), pp. 442-7. See, among much else, George Hemsley, 'The native country of the potato', *JRHS*, vol. 5 (1879), pp. 123-5; J.S. Gordon, 'Experiments in potato-growing', vol. 23 (1899-1900), pp. 283-98; Walter P. Wright, 'The ideal potato', vol. 31 (1906), pp. 97-101; Salaman, 'Hereditary characters in the potato', vol. 38 (1912-13), pp. 34-9.

33. Council minutes, 16 February, 26 October 1915; 5 December 1916; 2-13 February, 22 May, 3 July, 9 October 1917; 9-23 April, 28 May, 18 June 1918. *GC*, 17 July 1915, p. 40; 9 October 1915, p. 238; 13 October 1917, p. 145; 23 February 1918, pp. 81-3; 20 July 1918, p. 24.

34. *GC*, 16 February 1918, p. 69; 9 March 1918, p. 103; 7 September 1918, pp. 100-1; 21 September 1918, p. 121;

12 October 1918, p. 151; 28 February 1920, p. 100; 17 April 1920, p. 187; 10 July 1920, p. 14. Council minutes, 2 February 1917; 20 January, 26 February 1918; 11 February, 11 March, 17 June 1919; 27 January, 27 April 1920. Minutes of the Sugar for Jam Committee.

35. Bunyard: Council minutes, 13 December 1938. Hay (1946), p. 13; and see pp. 10-11 for the origin of the phrase 'Dig for victory'. Allotments and other work: Council minutes, 12 September 1939; 5 March, 4 June, 13 August, 12 November, 10 December 1940; 7 January-25 March 1941; 17 February, 15 September 1942.

36. Council minutes, 1 October, 12 November 1940; 17 June, 15 July, 16 September 1941; 17 February, 19 May, 16 June, 14 July 1942; 16 March, 18 May 1943; 15 February, 18 April, 20 June 1944. See the historical note in the 1992 edition. Translation: 12 March 1946; it appeared was published by the Paul Georg Hopfer Verlag in Norden under the title *Frisches Gemüse im Ganzen Jahr* (1947). To appreciate the state of German malnutrition at the time, see Victor Gollancz, *In Darkest Germany* (1947), pp. 23-52, and it wouldn't hurt to glance at W.G. Sebald, *On the Natural History of Destruction* (2003).

37. E.A. Bunyard *et al.*, *The Epicure's Companion* (1937), p. 69. See E.T. Cook, 'The advantages and evils of size in flowers, fruits, and vegetables', *JRHS*, vol. 28 (1903-04), pp. 407-19; also 'Size in fruit and vegetables', *JHort*, 5 December 1901, pp. 503-4. Veitch: Council minutes, 11 February 1896.

38. Herman Senn, 'Cooking of vegetables', *JRHS*, vol. 36 (1910-11), pp. 587-95; 'The cooking of roots and tubers', vol. 38 (1912-13), pp. 540-4; 'The cooking of vegetables', vol. 39 (1913-14), pp. 523-9; 'Leaf vegetables and how to cook them', vol. 41 (1915-16), pp. 436-44; 'Cooking of vegetables, fruits, &c.', vol. 42 (1916-17), pp. 253-9. Senn had offered a prize for the best essay on the continuous cropping of vegetables in 1912, and was to offer prizes again; see Council minutes, 18 June 1912; 9 September 1924. He was not the first writer in the *Journal* on cooking, however: that honour goes to the biologist Emmanuel Bonavia, 'Cooking vegetables', vol. 22 (1898-9), pp. 55-65.

39. Council minutes, 21 September, 5 October 1920; 11 January-8 March 1921. *GC*, 12 February 1921, pp. 73-4; 19 February 1921, p. 35; 26 February 1921, p. 97; 5 March 1921, pp. 118-19. Brent Elliott, 'A political family', *The Garden* (*JRHS*), vol. 117 (1992), pp. 37-9.

40. 'Quality in early vegetables: a symposium', *JRHS*, vol. 59 (1934), pp. 330-45. Council minutes, 10 March, 21 April, 30 June 1931; 10 March, 21 April, 23 June, 7-21 July 1959 (Harben). For a slightly earlier press discussion on the subject, in which the *Horticultural Show Handbook* was invoked to resolve the debate, see *Times*, 2 September 1955, p. 9 g; 5 September, p. 9 d; 7 September, p. 9 d; 8 September, p. 14 f. Tomato trial: Michael Pollock, 'Focus on tomatoes', *The Garden* (*JRHS*), vol. 116 (1991), pp. 113-17.

41. *GC*, 14 September 1895, p 302; 28 September 1895, p. 370.

42. *Gardeners' Magazine* special commissioners, *The Wasted Orchards of England* ([1896]). See also Owen Thomas, 'Wasted opportunities of fruit-growing in English villages', *JRHS*, vol. 27 (1902-03), pp. 960-7, and W.W. Tyler, 'The utilisation of railway embankments', vol. 15 (1893), pp. 57-61, esp. p. 60, on the emigration of lavender.

43. Hogg, *Fruit Manual*, 5th edition (1884), pears *passim*. *JHort*, 25 January 1900, p. 72. See also Elliott on Blackmore, *op. cit.*

44. Federation proposal: 14 January, 25 February 1902. Report of the committee on the fruit industry, *JRHS*,

45. Council minutes, 13 December 1921; 31 January, 14 March, 11 April, 5 September 1922; 26 June 1923.

46. J.M.S. Potter, 'The National Fruit Trials', *JRHS*, vol. 85 (1960), pp. 174-84. 'The National Fruit Trials (1922-72): a brief history', in *Fruit Present and Future*, vol. 2 (1973), pp. 8-13. Several reports on the commercial fruit trials were published in *JRHS* in the 1930s.

47. Council minutes, 9 November 1943; 16 October 1945; 22 January-12 March, 10 September, 5 November 1946; 17 June 1947; 21 September 1948; 18 November 1952; 30 March 1954. See Anon. (1916), p. 23, for the prophetic complaint about Wisley, 'The land is not suitable for fruit culture... If a garden is wanted for such work it should be in the best land in Kent'.

48. *The Garden* (*JRHS*), vol. 114 (1989), pp. 357, 471; vol. 115 (1990), p. 105. For some gems from the press coverage of Brogdale, see Audrey Wise, 'Ungrateful Government snubs carers', *Lancashire Evening Post*, 18 October 1989; James Erlichman, 'Shaken to the core', *Guardian*, 13 May 1989; Robert Pearson, 'Will a rescue plan bear fruit?', *Sunday Telegraph*, 5 November 1989; Maurice Weaver, 'Charles: another campaign bears fruit', *Daily Telegraph*, 15 January 1990; Natasha Edwards, 'When it comes to the crunch for apples', *Evening Standard*, 24 January 1990; Francesca Greenoak, 'The apple of a British eye', *Times*, 12 October 1991.

49. Sir James Mount, '25 years of fruit growing', *The Garden* (*JRHS*), vol. 107 (1982), pp. 75-8. Compare with Hatton, 'Modern commercial fruit planting', *JRHS*, vol. 59 (1934), pp. 18-36. Proposals for postwar restriction of varieties: *GI*, 1943. p. 172, and see pp. 208-9 for similar thoughts about ornamental plants. *Grower*, 8 September 1983, p. 31. 'Polish up your English': *Top Fruit Times*, no. 2 (October 1980), p. 1. The campaign's logo was an *echt*-American boy, looking as though he had stepped out of the pages of *Li'l Abner* but wearing a Union Jack t-shirt, on which he was polishing an apple.

50. Council minutes, 20 October 1931, for the reduction in glasshouse fruits. 7 May 1918, for the walnut bequest. 14 August, 11 September 1928; 1 January, 16 July, 13 August, 19 November 1929, for walnut activities. E.A. Bunyard, 'Cobnuts and filberts', *JRHS*, vol. 45 (1919-20), pp. 224-32; H.V. Taylor, 'An investigation of English walnuts', vol. 54 (1929), pp. 410-11; Howard Spence, 'Walnuts', vol. 55 (1930), pp. 244-56; A.W. Witt, 'Further observations on walnut growing in England', pp. 257-65. Spence's work was first described in his 'Inquiry into the quality of English-grown walnuts', *Journal of Pomology*, vol. 5 (1925-6), pp. 223-40. For the beginnings of the current revival of interest in cobnuts and filberts, see Meg Game, 'Nuts in autumn', *The Garden* (*JRHS*), vol. 115 (1990), pp. 568-71.

51. Michael Pollock, 'Potatoes on trial', *The Garden* (*JRHS*), vol. 119 (1994), pp. 574-7; Alan Toogood, 'Trialled and tested', vol. 123 (1998), pp. 710-12, and see p. 766 for the potato display at the Malvern Autumn Show; vol. 126 (2001), p. 4.

52. Gilbert (1953); Bultitude (1947).

53. J.M.S. Potter, 'Recent developments in fruit culture at Wisley: the new fruit collections', *JRHS*, vol. 77 (1953), pp. 408-13.

54. Council minutes, 8 February, 8 March 1921 for the institution of the award.

55. Joint Vegetable proposal: Council minutes, 16 February 1965. Elspeth Napier, 'Space tests for vegetables', *JRHS*, vol. 93 (1968), pp. 78-81.

56. For the HDRA scheme, see Sue Phillips, 'Vintage vegetables', *The Garden* (*JRHS*), vol. 117 (1992), pp. 507-11. On the vegetable plot competitions, see Alan

Toogood, 'Planning for bumper crops', vol. 122 (1997), pp. 253-5; 'The model plot', vol. 124 (1999), pp. 802-4. Old orchards: vol. 124 (1999), p. 886. Vegetable seeds: Bob Sherman, 'Vanishing heritage', vol. 125 (2000), 192-5; for increased sales, see vol. 126 (2001), p. 157. Charles Lyte, 'Digging for victory', vol. 116 (1991), pp. 146-8. Guy Barter, 'Off to a flying start', vol. 119 (1994), pp. 25-7.

57. *JRHS*, vol. 70 (1945), p. 220.
58. Council minutes, 16 April, 4 June 1957. Justin Brooke, *Peach Orchards in England* (1947). 'The Fruit Group', in *Fruit Present and Future*, vol. 2 (1973), pp. 102-4.

15 Garden Design, pp. 269-82

1. Thomas Gery Cullum, 'On the construction of piers and copings of garden walls', *Transactions*, vol. 4 (1822), pp. 269-73; Joseph Sabine, 'An account of some remarkable holly hedges and trees in Scotland', vol. 7 (1830), pp. 194-202; Sir Charles Monck, 'A plan for transplanting large forest trees in parks', pp. 294-8.
2. John Sales, 'Garden maintenance: an untenable term?', *The Garden (JRHS)*, vol. 121 (1997), pp. 514-15. Mark Laird, *The Flowering of the Landscape Garden* (1999).
3. Loudon's remark: *GM*, vol. 6 (1830), pp. 506-7. Lindley's history of the landscape garden started with *GC*, 6 February 1847, p. 83, and continued weekly in the leader column until 1 July 1848, p. 435. For a discussion of Lindley's influence as a critic of garden style, see Elliott (1986), pp. 99-102 *passim*.
4. John Lindley, 'On the arrangement of gardens and pleasure-grounds in the Elizabethan age', *JHS*, vol. 3 (1848), pp. 1-15. For a discussion of the background to this article, see Elliott (1986), pp. 66-70.
5. Robert Errington, 'On clumping out flowers', *JHS*, vol. 3 (1848), pp. 304-7; Robert Glendinning, 'On transplanting large evergreen trees and shrubs', vol. 4 (1849), pp. 41-4; James Duncan, 'Edgings of narrow turf as a substitute for box', *ibid.*, pp. 190-1; Peter Mackenzie, 'Mural gardening', vol. 5 (1850), pp. 126-8; Glendinning, 'On the introduction of new coniferous trees into park scenery', pp. 173-5; Thomas Moore, 'On the scenic "effect" of certain "common" plants possessing remarkable foliage', vol. 6 (1851), pp. 115-17; Errington, 'On style and expression in certain trees and shrubs', vol. 7 (1852), pp. 193-8; Glendinning, 'On garden walks', pp. 201-4; Robert Hogg, 'A new kind of garden edging', pp. 228-9; Glendinning, 'On edgings for garden walks and flower beds', vol. 8 (1853), pp. 270-3.
6. George Eyles, 'Bedding vs herbaceous plants', *F&P* (1883), pp. 145-6. On Eyles's bedding at Kensington, see *GC*, 21 September 1861, p. 850; 22 July 1865, p. 676; 10 October 1868, pp. 1069-70; also *JHort*, 15 October 1874, pp. 344-6. For the history of bedding schemes and colour theory during the 19th century, see Elliott, *op. cit.*, *passim*, but esp. pp. 48-51, 87-90, 123-40, 148-62.
7. William Wilks, 'A method of winter gardening', *JRHS*, vol. 12 (1890), pp. 233-43; William Ingram, 'Spring flower gardening', *ibid.*, pp. 273-87. See also Alexander Dean, 'Winter and spring bedding in flower gardens', vol. 21 (1897-8), pp. 65-77, and W.H. Divers (Ingram's successor at Belvoir Castle), 'The spring flower garden', vol. 39 (1913-14), pp. 17-28, and 'Spring flowers for small gardens', vol. 52 (1927), pp. 189-93.
8. Lindley on Chevreul: *GC*, 8 May 1841, p. 291; 16 October 1841, p. 685; 15 December 1849, pp. 787-8; 22 December 1849, pp. 803-5; 29 December 1849, p. 819; 5 January 1850, pp. 4-5; 19 January 1850, p. 36; 23 February 1850, pp. 116-17; 16 March 1850, p. 165; 23 March 1850, p. 181. Some of Lindley's discussion

was reprinted in *FC*, vol. 18 (1850), pp. 7-12, 58-60. The floral showdown: *CottGard*, vol. 21 (12 October 1858), pp. 17-19; 22 March 1859, p. 377. Lindley's subsequent endorsement of Gardner Wilkinson: *GC*, 12 March 1859, p. 216.
9. Murray (1863), p. 171; 'Ribbon beds versus gardens', *GC*, 27 December 1862, pp. 1218-19. The Lindley Library holds Murray's own volume of his assembled magazine articles, in which this pseudonymous piece is included.
10. Samuel Reynolds Hole, *The Memories of Dean Hole* (1892), p. 240, and 'Garden craft', *JRHS*, 20 (1896-7), pp. 89-100. For Robinson's changes of opinion, see Brent Elliott, 'Some sceptical thoughts about William Robinson', *The Garden (JRHS)*, 110 (1985), pp. 214-17, and for background of the stylistic swing of the 1870s, see Elliott (1986), pp. 166-174.
11. Brian Halliwell, 'Bedding schemes for gardens', *The Garden (JRHS)*, vol. 98 (1973), pp. 254-9, 405-12, 534-41. Richard Fulcher, 'A new approach to bedding', vol. 113 (1988), pp. 18-21. David Welch, 'That's entertainment!', vol. 118 (1993), pp. 364-7.
12. Gertrude Jekyll, 'Colour in the flower garden', *Garden*, 26 August 1882, p. 177; reprinted in William Robinson, *The English Flower Garden* (1883), pp. cx-cxii. Jekyll, 'The picturesque use of hardy perennial summer plants', *JRHS*, vol. 13 (1891), pp. 324-9; Jekyll and Selfe-Leonard, 'Hardy-plant borders', vol. 21 (1897-8), pp. 433-41. See Elliott (1986), pp. 203-9, for Jekyll's colour theories and their background.
13. George Bunyard, 'Hints on herbaceous borders', *JRHS*, vol. 39 (1913-14), pp. 351-62; B. Crisp, 'Autumn flower borders', *ibid.*, pp. 530-4; John Dickson, 'The herbaceous border', vol. 43 (1918-19), pp. 1-4; Mrs W.J. Muller, 'Herbaceous borders', vol. 54 (1929), pp. 379-86; and for a late example, see Ursula Buchan, 'Late summer splendour', vol. 120 (1995), pp. 530-3.
14. Robert James, 'Mixed shrub and herbaceous borders', *JRHS*, vol. 78 (1953), pp. 268-73.
15. For the history of the rock garden, see Elliott (1986), pp. 46-8, 94-9, 176-8, 187-92, and Graham Stuart Thomas, *The Rock Garden and its Plants* (1989).
16. Henri Correvon, 'Alpine plants and their treatment', *JRHS*, vol. 16 (1894), pp. 116-28; H. Selfe-Leonard, 'A few notes on rock gardens', vol. 19 (1896), pp. 446-60; F.W. Meyer, 'Rock gardens and streamlets', vol. 23 (1899-1900), pp. 78-95; R.L. Praeger, 'Rock gardens, natural and artificial', vol. 35 (1909-10), pp. 163-5; Arthur Clutton-Brock, 'Some lessons from the observation of alpine plants', *ibid.*, pp. 166-73; Clutton-Brock, 'How to build a small rock garden', vol. 36 (1910-11), pp. 331-8; R.R.C. Nevill, 'Alpine plants in their native haunts', vol.37 (1911-12), pp. 65-79; Correvon, 'Alpine gardens', *ibid.*, pp. 80-7; D. Sarsons (first superintendent of the Wisley rock garden), 'Notes on a rock garden', vol. 41 (1915-16), pp. 415-25; F.J. Hanbury, 'A Sussex rock-garden', vol. 42 (1916-17), pp. 271-80. On the Wisley rock garden, see James Pulham, 'The Wisley rock and water garden', vol. 38 (1912-13), pp. 225-33.
17. For a discussion of the Crisp affair, see Brent Elliott, 'Farrer and the Victorian rock garden', in John Illingworth and Jane Routh, eds., *Reginald Farrer: Dalesman, Planthunter, Gardener* (1991), pp. 27-35. The Farrer quotation comes from E.A. Bowles, *My Garden in Spring* (1914), pp. vii-viii. Crisp's article 'A new parable of the Pharisee and the publican' was published in *GI*, Supplement to 23 May 1914. For Willmott, see Le Lievre (1980), pp. 159-61. The letter from Jacob is in the E.A. Bowles papers, in the Lindley Library.
18. Selfe-Leonard, 'A few notes on rock gardens', *JRHS*, vol. 19 (1896), pp. 446-60, esp. p. 454; Murray

Hornibrook, 'Notes on so-called "moraine" gardens', vol. 56 (1931), pp. 61-4; L. de Rothschild, 'The rhododendron rock garden at Exbury', vol. 59 (1934), pp. 325-9; Roy Hay, 'Colour in rock and woodland gardens', vol. 64 (1939), pp. 175-9. *GC*, 1 June 1929, p. 407. Limestone: Council minutes, 9 October 1928. B.H.B. Symons-Jeune, *Natural Rock Gardening* (3 editions, 1932, 1936, 1955).

19. Valerie Finnis, 'Raised beds for rock plants', *JRHS*, 98 (1973), pp. 249-54. Lionel Bacon, 'Rock gardening—a dying art?', vol. 105 (1980), pp.94-8.

20. Paul first published his ideas in the *Gardeners' Chronicle* in 1864; the series was republished in his anthology, *Contributions to the Literature of Horticulture* (1892), pp. 219-79. Bateman's lecture: *GC*, 1 July 1865, pp. 605-6; Paul's 1870 lecture: *GC*, 30 July 1870, pp. 1025-6. On autumn colour, see Harry J. Veitch, 'Autumnal tints', *JRHS*, vol. 15 (1893), pp. 46-57; Vicary Gibbs, 'Planting for autumn & winter effect', vol. 29 (1904-05), pp. 170-81; W.J. Mitchell, 'Autumn colouring and berries at Westonbirt', vol. 58 (1933), pp. 372-9; Arthur Soames, 'Autumn colours at Sheffield Park', vol. 59 (1934), pp. 97-106; David Wright, 'Some neglected aspects of autumn colour', vol. 94 (1969), pp. 33-8.

21. For the wild and woodland garden, see Elliott (1986), pp. 194-6, and 'Rhododendrons in British gardens: a short history', in Postan (1996), esp. pp. 172-80. For early literature on the subject in *JRHS*, see William Robinson, 'Wild gardening in summer meadow grass', vol. 13 (1891), pp. 310-14; Selfe-Leonard, 'Some talk about wild gardens, vol. 26 (1901-02), pp. 47-67; Osgood Mackenzie, 'Shrub gardening on the west coast of Ross-shire', vol. 29 (1904-05), pp. 182-5; James Hudson, 'Informal and wild gardening', vol. 40 (1914-15), pp. 361-71.

22. Kenkichi Okubo, 'The garden of artificial hills', *JRHS*, vol. 29 (1904-05), pp. 82-5, and 'Trees in a Japanese garden', vol. 31 (1906), pp. 40-41; Reginald Farrer, 'Japanese plants and gardens', *ibid.*, pp. 12-17; N. Hayashi, 'Japanese horticulture' ibid., pp. 18- 28; James Hudson, 'A Japanese garden in England', vol. 32 (1907), pp. 1-10. Japanese ambassador's remark: Cecil Roth, *The Magnificent Rothschilds* (1939), p. 211. For the background to the Japanese garden, see Elliott (1986), pp. 199-202.

23. Charles Eley, 'Roadside planting', *JRHS*, vol. 51 (1926), pp. 271-5; Francis Le Sueur, 'Roadside planting', vol. 54 (1929), pp. 412-26; Wilfrid Fox, 'Roadside planting', vol. 69 (1944), pp. 231-8. Council minutes, 3-17 July, 30 October 1928; 6 June 1939; 29 July, 12 August, 7 October 1947; 12 November 1955. For what came after, see Madeline Spitta, 'A quarter of a century of highway planting', *JRHS*, vol. 77 (1952), pp. 4-11; Lanning Roper, 'Landscaping of motorways', vol. 92 (1967), pp. 302-8; Miles Hadfield, 'Colour in our forests', *Quarterly Journal of Forestry*, vol. 61 (1967), pp. 131-3.

24. William Wilks, On the construction of a verandah', *JRHS*, 26 (1901-02), pp. 130-5; Jekyll, 'Pergolas in England', vol. 27 (1902-03), pp. 93-7; Hugh Maule, 'Design in the suburban garden', vol. 29 (1904-05), pp. 68-76; Walter P. Wright, 'Arches, pillars, and pergolas', vol. 33 (1908), pp. 49-52; Thomas Mawson, 'Garden design', vol. 34 (1908-09), pp. 361-83; Edward White, 'Pergolas', vol. 43 (1918-19), pp. 291-9.

25. Edward White, 'The profession of landcape gardening', *JRHS*, vol. 34 (1908-09), pp. 32-9; Mawson, 'The practice of garden design', *ibid.*, pp. 384-93; White, 'Garden design', vol. 39 (1913-14), pp. 559-80. For his firm's career, see Imogen Wedd Leigh, 'Milner White and Partners', *LD*, no. 156 (August 1985), pp. 9-13. The proceedings of the Garden Design

conference were published in *JRHS*, vol. 54 (1929), pp. 256-378. Mawson was alleged to have said, when first canvassed about the idea of an Institute, that there was no need for one—his firm and Milner White could handle the country's garden design between them.

26. Examination Board minutes, 13 October 1968; 4 August 1970.

27. Council minutes, 13 June 1961. R.S. Lynch, 'Gardens of easy maintenance', *JRHS*, vol. 62 (1937), pp. 377 82; Brenda Colvin, 'Garden design in relation to reduction of labour and maintenance costs', vol. 82 (1957), pp. 294-302; A.D. Hodgson, 'The maintenance of fine lawns', vol. 89 (1964), pp. 332-8—contrast this with Ian Hodgson, 'Evolving the lawn', vol. 120 (1995), pp. 472-4, to see how far the manicured lawn had ceased to be an ideal. For 'Emerald Velvet', see Council minutes, 29 July, 12 August, 16 September 1958; 5-20 April, 4 October 1960; *GC*, 22 February 1958, p. 114; 11 November 1958, p. 264; 29 November 1958, p. 327. It was introduced into Britain by Matt Templeton and G.B. Rawinsky; see the latter's trade circular of September 1957. See also W.F.W. Harding, 'Clover lawns', *JRHS*, vol. 77 (1952), pp. 377-80, and *GC*, 15 November 1952, p. 191.

28. For a nice sequence of articles, which encapsulates the successive revivalist fashions of the 20th century, see Thomas Mawson, 'Renaissance gardens', *JRHS*, vol. 35 (1909-10), pp. 335-41; H. Avray Tipping, 'English garden making under the early Stuarts', vol. 55 (1930), pp. 212-22; Eleanour Sinclair Rohde, 'English gardens in medieval, Tudor and Stuart times', vol. 59 (1934), pp. 37-49; Geoffrey Taylor, 'Eighteenth-century flower gardening', vol. 77 (1952), pp. 130-4; F.B. Watson, 'The English landscape garden of the 18th century', vol. 82 (1957), pp. 75-87.

29. To trace the development of the Trust's attitude towards period restoration, see Graham Stuart Thomas, 'The gardens of the National Trust', *JRHS*, vol. 85 (1960), pp. 338-55; 'The National Trust: a further account of its gardens', vol. 96 (1971), pp. 207-22; 'The restoration of Claremont landscape garden', vol. 104 (1979), pp. 181-5; John Sales, 'The evolution of our garden heritage', vol. 114 (1989), pp. 373-7.

30. C.D. Brickell, 'Notes from Wisley', *JRHS*, vol. 95 (1970), pp. 284-5.

31. Any amount of literature promoting the trends, not much analysing them historically. See *GH*, vol. 28 no. 1 (2000), for a special issue on 'Reviewing the twentieth-century landscape': a beginning. For Bradley-Hole's Latin Garden, see *The Garden (JRHS)*, vol. 122 (1997), p. 467; for Balston's, vol. 124 (1999), p. 489. For some critical responses, see correspondence in vol. 125 (2000), p. 635.

32. See Susan Beattie, *The New Sculpture* (1983), for a survey of the work of the elder figures represented in the exhibition, though the 20th-century move of their work into garden settings does not feature as an issue. There has as yet been no survey of the unnamed but effectively Art Deco movement that grew up in the 1920s to succeed it. Reynolds-Stephens assembled an album of photographs of the exhibition and its sculptures, now in the Lindley Library.

33. *Times*, 19 October 1928, p. 5 f; 20 October 1928, p. 9 c (Bayes); 23 October p. 17 e (Gleichen); 25 October p. 12 d (Mrs M.I. Illingworth of Roads for Remembrance). *GC*, 27 October 1928, p. 338. *GI*, 1928, p. 681. Fletcher (1969), p. 323. For Henry Moore at Wisley, see *The Garden (JRHS)*, vol. 125 (2000), p. 733.

34. For the origins of the garden gnome, see Brent Elliott, 'Gnomenclature', *The Garden (JRHS)*, vol. 117 (1992), pp. 172-5 (an April issue, naturally). There has

not yet been a history of garden gnomes in the 20th century, despite the appearance of a couple of whimsical books on the subject.

35. Maxwell T. Masters, 'Trees and shrubs for large towns', *JRHS*, vol. 13 (1891), pp. 71-98; see also Lewis Castle, 'Trees for towns', vol. 31 (1906), pp. 84-9; C. Crowther, 'Town smoke and plant growth', vol. 38 (1912-13), pp. 461-8. Angus D. Webster, *Town Planting* (1910) and *London Trees* (1920). For the effects of air pollution on park planting in the worst areas of Manchester, see W.W. Pettigrew's lectures to the Smoke Abatement League, 'The influence of air pollution on vegetation', *GC*, 13 October 1928, p. 292; 20 October 1928, pp. 308-9; 27 October 1928, p. 335. Council minutes, 7 December 1915, for a proposed Town Gardening Committee.

36. For the troubled history of parks in the post-war years, see Brent Elliott, 'From people's parks to green deserts', *LD*, no. 171 (February 1988), pp. 13-15, and the various essays in Woudstra (2001). Robin Herbert and the Royal Parks: *HW*, 24 January 1992, p. 13; 13 March 1992, pp. 20-1. Moggridge's review: *The Garden (JRHS)*, vol. 126 (2001), p. 305. David Welch, 'The price of revitalising parks', vol. 121 (1996), pp. 374-5. Privatisation and parks: HW, 21 February 1986, p. 3; 18 July 1986, p. 4; 26 February 1988, p. 3; 18 November 1988, pp. 1, 24-5. Municipal horticulture exhibition: Council minutes, 13 November 1945; 22 January 1946.

37. Window-gardening: Council minutes, 7 February 1865. Prizes for window-gardening: *PRHS*, vol. 5 (1865), pp. 27-30, 104, 135-6. Window boxes at shows: Council minutes, 5 March 1957; 18 February 1958; 9 February 1960. Lia Leendertz, 'Off the wall', *The Garden (JRHS)*, vol. 127 (2002), pp. 261-3. Allotments: Charles Lyte, 'Digging for victory', vol. 116 (1991), pp. 146-8. Thorpe report: *Report of the Departmental Committee of Inquiry into Allotments*, presented to Parliament by the Minister of Housing and Local Government and the Secretary of State for Wales by Command of Her Majesty, October 1969.

38. Eyles: *JHort*, 28 August 1866, p. 167. Wright: Council minutes, 7 November 1899; *GC*, 11 May 1912, p. 322. Fielder as Garden Inspector: Council minutes, 19 March, 2 April, 30 April 1912; 9 March, 22 June, 23 November 1915; 5 December 1916; 29 January 1924. For his life, see *GC*, 21 July 1923, p. 34, and 18 January 1947, p. 35.

39. Vine and Penton: Council minutes, 11 March, 8 April 1924; 20 October 1925; 8 June 1927; 13 October 1936; 25 October 1938; 4 April 1939. Wilson: 20 June 1939; 30 April 1946; 18 February 1947; 14 February 1956; 18 June 1957. Tuffin: 13 August, 24 September 1957; 14 July 1970; 2 February 1971; Tuffin, garden adviser, VMM presentation: *JRHS*, vol. 96 (1971), pp. 161-2.

40. For Geoffrey Coombs's ideas of garden design, see 'Perspective planting in a small garden', *JRHS*, vol. 98 (1973), pp. 260-6, and his Wisley Handbooks on *Plans for small gardens* (1975; revised in two volumes, 1985-7). Only from Nelmes's time as Garden Adviser is there a collection of plans in the RHS archives.

41. Lord Rothschild is sometimes cited as the lecturer, but no such passage appears in his articles in the *RHS Journal*. I suspect that the source of this rumour might have been H. Selfe-Leonard's 'Some talk about wild gardens', vol. 26 (1901-2), pp. 47-67, in which he refers to the conversion of 'a thin eight acre wood' into a wild garden. (Admittedly, he goes on to consider the making of wild gardens 'on a *small* scale', but within a few paragraphs he remarks that 'the zone of planting should be wide enough, say 100 feet in its narrowest part ...') The ha-ha: Geoffrey Coombs, *Plans for Small Gardens 2* (1987), pp. 42-4. Jill Billington, *Really Small Gardens* (1998), p. 9.

16 Ornamental Garden Plants, pp. 283-304

1. Floral Committee regulations: *GC*, 13 August 1859, pp. 672-3. In 1872, W. Wilson Saunders proposed the creation of a Botanical Committee which would advise on First- and Second-Class Certificates, but as the intended membership was entirely derived from the Scientific Committee, it is likely that these certificates would have been for botanical interest only, and that this suggestion was an anticipation of the later Botanical Certificate. Council minutes, 17 January 1872.

2. Council minutes, 10 November 1891. The occasion was a conference on Hardy Summer-flowering Perennials, reported in *JRHS*, vol. 13 (1891), pp. 310-39, and including (pp. 330-9) a list of hardy perennials; the question was probably related to the compilation of the list.

3. Division between Floral A & B: Council minutes, 1 November 1921; 13-27 November 1923; 2 November 1926. 27 January 1931; 7 June, 5 July 1932; 26 November 1935; 7 July 1964; 27 June 1967.

4. Council minutes, 14 January, 5 May 1964; 2 February, 30 March 1965; 7 February 1967.

5. Council minutes, 28 November 1922; 21 February 1933, for complaints about the accuracy of the paintings; 1 March 1949; 6 March 1951. Photography: 9 October 1906. The miscellaneous award paintings are now in the Wisley Herbarium, the orchid paintings in London where they are held for the Orchid Committee's use.

6. Botanical Certificates: Council minutes, 11 March 1890; 11 April 1911. Tensions over awards: 14 March 1905 (interested growers on committees); 18 November 1924 (three similar chrysanthemums); 27 January, 8 April 1931 (never give a CPC and a Gold Medal at the same time). In 1949, E.H.M. Cox protested against the number of awards given (Floral A made 42 awards in 1948): Council minutes, 29 November 1949. Certificates of Preliminary Commendation: Council minutes, 20 July, 15 August 1915; 27 May 1919; *JRHS*, vol. 41 (1916), p. 470.

7. Council minutes, 25 November 1930; 27 January, 8 September, 24 November-15 December 1931; 9-30 November 1937; 20 October 1953. See *GC*, 14 February 1953, p. 55, for a discussion of the role of specialist societies, *à propos* the founding of the Hardy Plant Society (not a partner in a joint committee).

8. R. Perryman, 'Wisley trials', *The Garden (JRHS)*, vol. 115 (1990), pp. 486-90; Michael Pollock, 'The quest for excellence', vol. 118 (1993), pp. 564-7; Michael Pollock and Jeff Brande, 'Always on trial', vol. 121 (1996), pp. 428-31.

9. Trial by numbers: Council minutes, 11 February 1908; 5 April 1921; 12 September-10 October 1950. Commercial availability: 10 August 1948. Simultaneous trials: see *GC*, 13 September 1924, p. 176, and Council minutes, 24 June 1924; 16 March, 5 October 1948. Changes in rules and procedures: 25 April, 29 August 1933; 6 February 1968; *GC*, 12 March 1932, pp. 206-7; 2 April 1932, p. 265; 9 December 1933, p. 427. Comment by critic: *Garden*, 12 July 1919, pp. 328-9.

10. Council minutes, 12 September 1939; 12 August 1952 (in which Fletcher's letter of 8 August 1952 is pasted).

11. National reference collections: 21 October 1947; 17 February, 16 March 1948; 5 February 1957. The John Innes Research Institute assumed responsibility for roses; see Gordon Rowley, 'The national rose species collection', *JRHS*, vol. 79 (1954), pp. 382-9. All Britain Flower Seed Trials: *GC*, 26 September 1964, p. 315; Council minutes, 6 February 1962; 7 July, 13 October, 24 November 1964; 12 January 1965; 8-31 August 1967.

12. HTA protection bill: Council minutes, 9 June 1936; 4 May 1937. Trademarks and patents: 8 April 1952; 3 March-28 April 1953. Proposal for extending the 1920

Seed Act to ornamental plants: 17 April 1956. Plant Variety Rights: 22 January, 2 April 1957; 9 January 1958; 27 September 1960; 9 January, 3 April 1962; 22 January-19 February, 24 September, 22 October 1963; 21 April, 9 June 1964; 25 May, 13 July 1965; 8-22 March 1966; 5 January 1971; 23 May 1972. For a recent summary of the legislation and practices, see Elizabeth Scott, 'Profitable selections', *The Garden* (*JRHS*), vol. 124 (1999), pp. 844-7; Geoff Stebbings, 'Keeping them crossed', vol. 125 (2000), pp. 824-7.

13. Announcement of the AGM: *JRHS*, vol. 47 (1922), pp. 189-91. *Some Good Garden Plants*: editions of 1938, 1946, 1950, 1962. For its history, see Publications Committee minutes, 20 October 1936; 7 December 1937; 12 July 1938; 9 January, 3 July 1945; 12 July 1949; 15 March, 7 November 1961; 6 June 1962. *New Plants of the Year*: 1948-50; see Council minutes, 5 October 1948 and 7 November 1950 for its beginning and its end. For the revisions of the AGM, see Alan Leslie, 'Plants of distinction', *The Garden* (*JRHS*), vol. 118 (1993), pp. 356-7, and vol. 127 (2002), pp. 6-7.

14. For Sabine, see Council minutes, 2 June 1818; 22 March 1820; 10 December 1831. Spring bedding: John Fleming, *Spring and Winter Gardening* (1864), esp. pp. 88-9. For Peter Barr, see Kate Donald, 'Peter Barr (1826-1909)', *The Garden* (*JRHS*), vol. 109 (1984), pp. 401-5.

15. The account in Fletcher (1969) of the origin of this Committee is incorrect, Fletcher having confused the Narcissus Committee with the Scientific Committee's Subcommittee on Narcissus, which ran from 1884 to 1890. For more on the Nomenclature Committee, see the chapter on Taxonomy. Council minutes, 27 April 1886; 12 March 1889; 28 April 1908; 29 April, 17 June, 4 November 1913; 15 April 1914. C.R. Scrase-Dickins, 'The work of the Narcissus Committee', *JRHS*, vol. 27 (1902-03), pp. 186-9.

16. For the story of the daffodil shows, see Council minutes, 2 April, 30 April 1912; 15 April 1913; 28 July 1914; 11 April, 16 May, 6 June, 18 July, 1 August, 19 December 1916; 10 May 1921; 21 April 1925.

17. The 1911 proposal: *JHort*, 2 February 1911, pp. 95-6; 16 February 1911, p. 136. Jacob's proposal: Council minutes, 17 January 1922; *GC*, 24 January 1922, p. 109; 18 March 1922, p. 122 (Jacob couldn't attend his own meeting, and the proposal seems to have died). There is a file of correspondence relating to both proposals in the E.A. Bowles papers in the Lindley Library. For the centenary of the Midland Daffodil Society, see *The Garden* (*JRHS*), vol. 123 (1998), pp. 228, 392. Joint committee: Council minutes, 21 February 1939; 2 April 1968. Kirton: 26 April, 10 May, 5 July, 9 August 1932; 7 June 1933. Herbert R. Barr, 'A review of the daffodil trials at Wisley', *JRHS*, vol. 78 (1953), pp. 132-6. Rosewarne: see the Rosewarne reports. Transfer of Rosewarne daffodils: *The Garden* (*JRHS*), vol. 123 (1998), p. 75.

18. Edwards: Council minutes, 25 October 1853. For Archibald Henderson's abortive proposal for a one-man tulip show, see 22 July 1864. Tulip trials at Chiswick: *JRHS*, vol. 25 (1900-01), pp. 178-93. Tulip nomenclature and trials: Council minutes, 24 February 1910; 7 October, 16 December 1913; 15 April 1914; 2 March 1915.

19. See Merle Reinikka, *A History of the Orchid*, 2nd ed. (1995), for general background. For the transition from parasites to epiphytes, see William Herbert, 'On the treatment of the Dendrobia, Aerides, and other parasitical plants', *Transactions*, vol. 4 (1822), pp. 241-3; Lindley, 'Upon the cultivation of epiphytes of the Orchis tribe', 2nd series vol. 1 (1831-35), pp. 42-50; George Gordon, 'Notes on the proper treatment of epiphytal orchids', *JHS*, vol. 4 (1849), pp. 9-31. J.D. Llewellyn, 'Some account of an orchideous house,

constructed at Penllergare, South Wales', *JHS*, vol. 1 (1846), pp. 5-8. Veitch's reminiscence of Lindley: 'Hybridisation of orchids', lecture at the 1885 Orchid Conference, *JRHS*, vol. 7 (1886), pp. 22-36, esp. pp. 28-9.

20. *GC*, 1 January 1848, pp. 7-8; 19 August 1848, pp. 559-60; 16 December 1848, p. 827; 17 March 1849, p. 167; 20 October 1849, p. 663; 21 February 1852, p. 119. Council minutes, 25 January, 21 June, 19 July 1853; 19 December 1865; 23 January, 17 April 1866. For a review of Lindley's activities, see H.J. Veitch, 'Orchid culture past and present', *JRHS*, vol. 11 (1889), pp. 115-30.

21. The reports of both the original Orchid Conference and the Orchid Nomenclature Conference were published in *JRHS*, vol. 7 (1886); the 1885 papers were also published in *GC*, 16 May 1885, pp. 627-35. For the founding of the Committees, see Council minutes, 10 March 1885; 23 March 1886 [cancelled draft]; 8 June 1886; 12 March, 25 June, 13 August 1889. Morgenstern: 19 March, 2-18 April, 11 June-9 July, 3 September 1963. Prince Shimadzu (or Shimazu as it would be rendered now): 10 May 1921; 8 April 1931. For an account of Ballantine and the Schröder family's orchids, see *GC*, 18 May 1963, pp. 350-5.

22. Council minutes, 10 November, 15 December 1896; 6 March 1906. The 1982 volume of the *Orchid Review* was dedicated to Iris Humphreys; Gillian Young published a book, *Orchids in Line* (1975), as did David Leigh, *Orchids: their Care and Cultivation* (1990); for Cherry-Ann Lavrih, see *OR*, vol. 58 (1990), pp. 277-81. Several of their paintings have been reproduced in Mark Griffiths, *Orchids* (2002).

23. Alasdair Morrison, 'The R.H.S. Orchid Committee's 100th birthday', *OR*, vol. 97 (1989), pp. 88-91, 95. For the Eric Young Orchid Scholarship, see *JRHS*, vol. 100 (1975), pp. 79-80.

24. John Braddick, 'On the treatment of the cactus Opuntia, or prickly pear', *Transactions*, vol. 2 (1817), pp. 238-40; Donald Beaton, 'On the cultivation and management of the cactus tribe', *Transactions*, 2nd series, vol.2 (1835-41), pp. 459-70. Loudon: *Green-house Companion* (1824), vol. 1, p. 102. For Wilson Saunders and his garden at Hillfield, Reigate, see *GC*, 23 November 1872, pp. 1557-9, and, more especially for the succulents, 7 December 1872, pp. 1621-2. Succulent gifts: Council minutes, 2 October 1863; 7-21 February 1865. E.A. Bowles, 'Hardy cacti and other succulents', *JRHS*, vol. 34 (1908), pp. 24-31.

25. Council minutes, 24 July 1894; 4-18 October 1921. W.L. Tjaden, 'Amateurs at the Hall', *The Garden* (*JRHS*), vol. 112 (1987), pp. 213-15 .

26. R.A. Salisbury, 'Observations on the different species of Dahlia, and the best method of cultivating them in Britain', *Transactions*, vol. 1 (1804-12), pp. 84-98; John Wedgwood's reply, pp. 113-15; Joseph Sabine, 'Observations on, and account of the species and varieties, of the genus Dahlia', vol. 3 (1820), pp. 217-43; Sabine, 'Account and description of the varieties of Chinese chrysanthemums', *Transactions*, vol. 4 (1822), pp. 326-62; Joseph Wells, 'On the cultivation of Chinese chrysanthemums', *ibid.*, pp. 571-3; Sabine, 'Further account of Chinese chrysanthemums', vol. 5 (1824), pp. 149-62, and 'Account of several new Chinese and Indian chrysanthemums', vol. 6 (1826), pp. 322-59; Donald Munro, 'Notes upon the Chinese chrysanthemums', 2nd series, vol. 1 (1831-5), pp. 392-4. See also Brent Elliott, 'Treasures from the east', *CL*, 5 September 2002, pp. 128-31.

27. *GM*, vol. 2 (1827), p. 105, for chrysanthemums at Chiswick, and see also *CottGard*, vol. 9 (18 November 1852), p. 122. Pompon dahlia trials: *PRHS*, vol. 3 (1863), pp. 78-80; *JRHS*, vol. 23 (1899-1900), pp. 175-83. Cactus dahlia trials: vol. 25 (1900-01), pp. 390-401; vol. 28 (1903-

04), pp. 562-7. Chrysanthemum trials: vol. 23 (1899-1900), pp. 313-27. Abortive chrysanthemum conference: Council minutes, 22 March, 10 May 1887.

28. For the National Dahlia Show, see *GC*, 25 August 1883, p. 240; 8 September 1883, pp. 310-11. For the Dyffryn trials (and, yes, there are two different spellings of the name): *GC*, 27 September 1913, p. 221; 29 November 1913, p. 385; 13 December 1913, pp. 418-19; 12 December 1914, pp. 379-81; 2 January 1915, p. 11. Council minutes, 21 January, 4 February, 7 October, 4 November 1913; 3 November 1914. Cory Cup amendments: 12 December 1922; 30 January, 13 February 1923.

29. Sequence of names: Stoke Newington Chrysanthemum Society 1846; Stoke Newington and Hackney Chrysanthemum Society 1874; Borough of Hackney Chrysanthemum Society 1875; National Chrysanthemum Society 1884. Show report: *CottGard*, vol. 19 (24 November 1857), pp. 110-12.

30. Arrangements with Chrysanthemum Society: Council minutes, 18 November 1919; 6 November 1934. Joint committee: 22 February 1938. Conflict and resolution: 17 April, 23 October, 20 November 1951; 29 January, 26 February, 7-21 October 1952.

31. Ray Waite, 'Cascades of colour: chrysanthemums at Wisley', *JRHS*, vol. 122 (1996), pp. 682-5. Ogg, ibid., vol. 73 (1948), p. 219. Woodsman [John Street], 'Decline and fall', *GC&HTJ*, 7 October 1983, p. 17.

32. A quick guide to the early articles: T.A. Knight on nerines, *Transactions*, vol. 3 (1820), pp. 399-402; William Williamson *ditto*, pp. 447-51; Herbert on nerines, vol. 4 (1822), pp. 186-84, and on gladioli, pp. 153-5; James Verrel on crinums, *ibid.*, pp. 419-25; J.R. Gowen on hybridising amaryllis, *ibid.*, pp. 498-503, and vol. 5 (1824), pp. 361-4, 390-2; Lindley, an account of Herbert's amaryllis, vol. 5 (1824), pp. 337-40; John Spencer on amaryllids, *JHS* 1 (1846), pp. 178-80; James Duncan on gladioli, vol. 3 (1848), 259-60; Donald Beaton on amaryllids, vol. 5 (1850), pp. 132-6. On the history of the Gandavensis hybrids, see James Kelway, 'Gladiolus Gandavensis', *JRHS*, vol. 12 (1890), pp. 564-75; the same volume contains an article by Lemoine on hardy gladioli, pp. 549-64. Council minutes, 8 March 1881, for the distribution of Vilmorin's gladioli.

33. Council minutes, 1 August 1911; 24 September 1912; 12 August 1913. The correspondence was published in full in the Gladiolus Society's *Autumn Handbook* for 1913, pp. 27-32. Later revivals of the proposal: Council minutes, 10-24 February, 25 August, 23 September, 15 December 1931; 21 September 1948; 15 March 1949; 22 January 1963.

34. Foster was preparing a book before his death, which Ellen Willmott offered to finance: see Council minutes, 3-17 August 1909. Relations with the Iris Society and Joint Committee: 4 November 1924; 5 June 1928; 27 January 1931; 6 June 1937.

35. Donations accepted or rejected: Council minutes, 17 June 1947; 14 February 1961; 15 June 1965. Geoff Stebbings, 'Hovering in the wings', *The Garden* (*JRHS*), vol. 123 (1998), pp. 408-13.

36. Sabine, 'Notes on, and description of, varieties of the Magnolia glauca', *Transactions*, vol. 3 (1820), pp. 201-6; William Beattie Booth, 'History and description of the species of Camellia and Thea', vol. 7 (1830), pp. 519-62; Lindley, 'A notice of some species of Rhododendron inhabiting Borneo', *Transactions*, 2nd series, vol. 3 (1848), pp. 81-91; Standish and Noble, 'A chapter in the history of hybrid rhododendrons', *JHS*, vol. 5 (1850), pp. 271-5. For the history of rhododendrons generally, see Postan (1997). For the distribution of Hooker rhododendrons, see Mary Forrest, 'Hooker's rhododendrons: their distribution and survival', *ibid.*, pp. 55-70.

37. Cynthia Postan, 'Rhododendron lovers in the British Isles', in Postan (1997), pp. 187-200. Trials and Joint Committee: Council minutes, 4 May 1926; 10 December 1929; 29 April 1930; 27 January 1931; 11 April, 20 June 1933; 9 January, 2 February 1934. N.K. Gould, 'The trials of hardy hybrid rhododendrons', *Rhododendron Year Book* 1946, pp. 60-3.

38. Council minutes, 20 March, 1 May, 11 September, 2 October 1945; 1 May 1951; 11 August 1953; 27 April 1954. Waley Medal: *GC*, 25 June 1938, p. 441. Initiation of the Loder Rhododendron Cup: Council minutes, 15 November 1921; 25 April 1922.

39. Dan E. Mayers, 'Rhododendrons in the British Isles—an irreverent approach', privately circulated [*c*.1975]. *Private Eye*, 3 March 1978, p. 8 (this column abridged for publication in Greer's book *The Revolting Garden*).

40. For Ralph S. Peer's activities with the Society (sending American camellias, arranging for Chinese camellias to be sent, financing camellia publications), see Council minutes, 20 September 1949; 29 August 1950; 21 October, 18 November 1952; 23 June 1953; 16 February 1954; 22 February, 3 May 1955; 1 May 1956; 26 January 1960 (announcement of death).

41. Postan (1997), pp. 199-200.

42. See Brent Elliott, 'Rhododendrons in British gardens', in Postan (1997), pp. 180-2. *GC*, 23 January 1841, p. 52; 6 February 1841, p. 85. For an account of the early efforts at extirpating *Rh. ponticum*, see Paul Simons, 'The day of the rhododendron', *New Scientist*, 7 July 1988, pp. 50-5. *Rh. yakushimanum*: *JRHS*, vol. 72 (1947), pp. 341-4. Jim Gardiner, *Magnolias* (1989); *Magnolias: a Gardener's Guide* (2000).

43. Council minutes, 2 June, 4 August 1818. Samuel Brookes, 'Notice relative to the flowering of Lilium japonicum', *Transactions*, vol. 4 (1822), pp. 551-4. J.G. Baker, 'A classified synonymic list of all the known lilies', *JRHS*, vol. 4 (1877), pp. 39-48; vol. 26 (1901-02), pp. 332-427 for the proceedings of the lily conference.

44. Council minutes, 24 November 1931; 26 January, 5 July 1932. *GC*, 18 February 1933, pp. 109-10; 18 March 1933, p. 183; 5 August 1933, pp. 92-3.

45. Brent Elliott and Anthony Hayward, 'A brief history of the Lily Committee', *Lilies and Related Plants* 1992-3, pp. 10-18. North American Lily Society address: *JRHS*, vol. 94 (1969), pp. 464-6. Smithers lilies: *The Garden* (*JRHS*), vol. 122 (1997), p. 767. Jan de Graaff and Edward Hyams, *Lilies* (1967), p. 26.

46. For the conference, see *JRHS*, vol. 13 (1891), pp. 310-39. On the background to the use of hardy perennials in the 19th century, see Elliott (1986), pp. 134, 159-62, 230-2.

47. Council minutes, 10 May, 11 October 1932; 22 July, 7 October 1952; 30 March–13 April 1954. *Delphinium Society's Year Book*, 1930, p.3; 1932, pp. 73-5. For the first trials, see *GC*, 22 January 1916, pp. 48-9.

48. Council minutes, 27 June 1961. For the high hopes of the programme, see Legro in *JRHS*, vol. 88 (1963), pp. 13-19, and *GC*, 13 June 1964, p. 578. Legro's obituary: *The Garden* (*JRHS*), vol. 122 (1997), p. 544.

49. Walter P. Wright, *The Perfect Garden* (1908), pp. 4-5. Complaint: Council minutes, 9 October 1900. The winner of the *Daily Mail* prize was the Revd D. Denholm Fraser, who forthwith published a book, *Sweet Peas: how to Grow the Perfect Flower* (1911).

50. Council minutes, 23 September, 1 December 1931; 2 October 1945; 9 August 1949. For the Harlow Carr trials, see *JRHS*, vol. 126 (2001), p. 821.

51. Lindley: *GC*, 26 June 1847, p. 419. See also *FM*, vol. 5 (1840), pp. 56-7 on the tricks of pelargonium display. For Paul, see *JHort*, vol. 18 (1870), pp. 220, 261, 277, 291.

52. *GC*, 9 June 1906, p. 370. Council minutes, 7 November 1905; 28 August, 25 September 1906.

53. Joint Perpetual-Flowering Carnation Committee:

Council minutes, 20 February 1934. Joint Border Carnation Committee: 12 June 1934. Joint Dianthus Committee: 16 October, 11 December 1945; 22 January 1946. Allwood cups: 15 November 1921; 17 January 1922. *Carnation Year Book*, 1935, pp. 13-16, including a photograph of the first Joint Committee.

54. Dombrain: Council minutes, 24 February 1874. Hyacinth show, 7 April 1875. Polyanthus trial: 16-30 April 1957.

55. For the early history of alpines, see Richard Gorer and John Harvey, 'Early rockeries and alpine plants', *GH*, vol. 7 no. 2 (1979), pp. 69-81. For gentians, see Council minutes, 23 September 1931; 13 October 1936. For saxifrages, see 21 April 1914; 1 November 1921; and Murray Hornibrook, 'Hybrid saxifrages', *JRHS*, vol. 51 (1926), pp. 49-58.

56. Sir Stuart Hogg's proposal for an Alpine Committee: Council minutes, 18 March 1913. Negotiations witih the AGS: 7-14 January 1930; 1 December 1931; 10 March, 21 April, 5 May 1936; 4 May 1937; 2 July 1946.

57. Council minutes, 28 June 1949; 13 April, 15 June, 22 September, 5-19 October 1954; 22 March 1955.

58. Council minutes, [9 April, 26 May], 29 September 1964. For a summary of the disputes over the Sewell Medal, see the memorandum attached to the minutes for 23 June 1952.

59. Sabine, 'An account of the Rosa Banksiae', *Transactions*, vol. 4 (1822), pp. 170-5; Sabine, 'Description and account of the varieties of double Scotch roses', *ibid.*, pp. 281-305. Sabine's arrangement of roses: Council minutes, 4 November 1831. George Paul, 'Standard roses', *Rosarian's Yearbook*, 1888, pp. 73-7; and for evidence of the way in which roses were treated as florists' flowers, see his 'On too-much-alike roses', *ibid.*, 1879, pp. 58-64; 'The survival of the fittest', *ibid.*, 1880, pp. 26-9; and his contribution to 'A symposium on judging', *ibid.*, 1889, pp. 8-11. There are several histories of roses, of which I need only mention Graham Stuart Thomas's three volumes, and works by Charles Quest-Ritson and Peter Harkness which will have appeared by the time this book is published. See Richard Gorer, 'The puzzle of Repton's roses', *Country Life*, 11 March 1982, pp. 654-6, for the status of the rose garden at the time the Society was founded.

60. For a report of an early rose show, see *FM*, vol. 5 (1840), pp. 60-2. For the first National Rose Show, see *GC*, 3 July 1858, p. 527. For the 1865 Great Rose Show, see *PRHS*, vol. 5 (1865), pp. 133-4. Council minutes, 4 January, 16 July 1861; 3 March, 7 November 1862; 6 November 1877; 6 August 1878; 24 May, 11 October 1881; 11 November 1890; 15 October 1907; 8 December 1908; 28 September 1909; 6 November-4 December 1917; 5 November 1918; 9 May-7 June, 17 October 1922.

61. The proceedings of the National Rose Conference were published in *JRHS*, vol. 11 (1889), pp. 162-303. Rose trials: Council minutes, 4 November 1919; 27 June 1922; 25 January–22 February 1927; 20 October 1931; 7 June 1932. *GC*, 5 December 1925, p. 456; 5 March 1927, p. 166; 25 January 1930, p. 70; 1 March 1930, p. 173. For a later fuss, over Harry Wheatcroft's trial roses being labelled with his name, see Council minutes, 11 August-8 September 1953. Joint Rose Committee: 11 August 1959; 23 July, 13 August 1963; 4 February, 10-24 March 1964. *JRHS*, vol. 90 (1964), pp. 182-3 for announcement about rose awards. Hurst's rose species: Council minutes, 24 July, 23 October-6 November 1934; 2 April 1935; 18 April 1939. Miss J. Ferguson, 'A botanical study of rose stocks', *JRHS*, vol. 58 (1933), pp. 344-71. For Hyde Hall, see Lia Leendertz, 'Give it plenty of swagger', *The Garden (JRHS)*, vol. 127 (2002), pp. 31-5, and p. 330 for Rosemoor.

62. Robert James, 'Old garden roses', *JRHS*, vol. 62 (1937), pp. 190-4; E.A. Bunyard, 'Old roses', vol. 63

(1938), pp. 411-21. See also Arthur Hellyer, 'A new classification for garden roses', vol. 104 (1979), pp. 296-8. Old rose group: Council minutes, 23 September 1947.

63. George Gordon, 'Upon raising coniferous plants from seed', *Transactions*, 2nd series, vol. 2 (1835-41), pp. 344-7; 'Some account of the Cryptomeria Japonica, or Japan cedar', *JHS*, vol. 1 (1846), pp. 57-60; 'Notes upon some newly-introduced conifers collected by Mr. Hartweg in Upper California', vol. 4 (1849), pp. 211-20; 'A catalogue of coniferous plants, with their synonyms', vol. 5 (1850), pp. 199-228. Andrew Murray, 'On the synonymy of various conifers', *PRHS*, vol. 3 (1863), pp. 140-50, 202-7, 308-25.

64. The proceedings of the 1891 conference were published as *JRHS*, vol. 14 (1892); those of the 1931 conference as *Conifers in Cultivation* (1932); those of the 1970 conference as *Conifers in the British Isles*. For the announcement of that conference, see *JRHS*, vol. 95 (1970), pp. 289-91, and for a report of the show, vol. 96 (1971), pp. 8-14. The proceedings of the 1999 conference were published as *Acta Horticulturae*, no. 615 (2003). Masters, 'Hybrid conifers', *JRHS*, vol. 26 (1901-2), pp. 97-110; the quote is from his inaugural address to the 1891 conference, vol. 14, p. 10.

65. Council minutes, 1 March 1949 (Ashburton); 22 February, 14 June, 29 November 1955; 10 January, 14 August 1956; 19 February, 19 November, 3 December 1957; 24 November, 15 December 1964 (Nisbet); 30 March 1965 (national collection). See Hornibrook, 'The future of dwarf conifers', *JRHS*, vol. 67 (1942), pp. 81-2. A. Osborn, 'An interesting hybrid conifer: *Cupressocyparis Leylandii*', vol. 66 (1941), pp. 54-71; this plant was first identified (as *Cupressus leylandii*) in *Kew Bulletin*, 1926, pp. 113-15.

66. Council minutes, 16 May 1862; 19 October 1874; 17 March, 7 April 1875.

67. *GC*, 11 April 1868, pp. 376-7; 25 April 1868, p. 432; 21 November 1868, p. 1210; 12 December 1868, p. 1286. For the nomenclatural repercussions, see 18 April 1868, p. 406; 25 April 1868, p. 434; 2 May 1868, p. 462; 9 May 1868, p. 490. For the recent revival of interest in coleus, see Ralph Gould, 'Notes on Coleus at Wisley', *The Garden (JRHS)*, vol. 112 (1987), pp. 486-7; Ian Cooke, 'Fashionable "weeds"', vol. 116 (1991), pp. 660-5.

68. Thomas Hay, 'Gardening in London', *JRHS*, vol. 56 (1931), pp. 207-16; *Plants for the Connoisseur* (1938). *GC*, 31 August 1935, p. 164.

69. The proceedings of the Begonia Conference were published in *JRHS*, vol. 15 (1893), pp. 153-99. Joint Committee proposal: Council minutes, 31 January, 7 March 1950. For Maurice Mason and *Begonia rex*, see *JRHS*, vol. 77 (1952), p. 291, and vol. 83 (1958), pp. 357-8.

70. Wisley collection: *GC*, 24 September 1927, p. 250; Ray Waite, 'Greenhouse fuchsias', *JRHS*, vol. 109 (1984), pp. 372-4; Waite and Ron Gilkerson, 'File on Wisley: the fuchsia collection', vol. 117 (1992), pp. 232-5. Founding of Fuchsia Society: Council minutes, 7 February 1939. Joint Fuchsia proposal: 14 October 1958.

71. The conference proceedings were published as *Ornamental Flowering Trees and Shrubs* (1938). By 1940 the print-run was exhausted, and a further 500 copies printed—unheard-of figures for conference reports: Council minutes, 2 January 1940. For a list of cultivars in the cherry garden, see *ibid.*, 15 July 1947, and for reports, see 3 June, 12 August 1947, 16 April 1957. Peonies: Council minutes, 2 October 1945 (Stern's donation); 7 February 1939, 24 July 1945, 10 August 1948. For *Cornus* 'Eddie's White Wonder', see Bruce Macdonald, 'Two noteworthy Cornus introductions', *JRHS*, vol. 109 (1874), pp. 151-3, and John Bond,

'Some North American dogwoods at Windsor', pp. 154-5. Dan E. Mayers, *op. cit.*, p. 14, complained of the awards going not to the Eddies for raising, but to the Crown Estate for displaying, the tree, and made public what the *Journal* had glossed over, that the Cory Cup was transferred to the Eddies after its first award to Windsor.

72. Lindley, 'A short account of the more evergreen berberries cultivated in the gardens of Great Britain', *JHS*, vol. 5 (1850), pp. 1-21; Robert Fortune, 'Chinese pinnated berberries', vol. 7 (1852), pp. 225-6. *GC*, 9 October 1920, p. 177; 6 October 1923, pp. 208-9; 20 October 1923, pp. 235-6; 29 August 1925, p. 168; 16 November 1929, pp. 387-8. W. J. Bean, 'Barberries at Wisley', *JRHS*, vol. 59 (1934), pp. 433-43; Leslie Ahrendt, 'An analysis of the Wisley hybrid berberis', vol. 67 (1942), pp. 129-42.

73. For Wilks's account of the breeding of the Shirley poppies, see *GC*, 17 March 1923, p. 149.

74. *GC*, 12 June 1937, p. 414. Ronald Parrett, *The Russell Lupin* (1959).

17 Floral Arts, pp. 305-12

1. Schedule of opening of the RHS Garden, Kensington. *GC*, 26 January 1861, p. 73; 8 June 1861, p. 527; 22 June 1861, p. 577; 13 July 1861, pp. 646-7, 649.

2. *GC*, 13 July 1861, p. 646; 28 September 1861, pp. 865-6. *FW*, 1862, pp. 169-71. T.C. March, *Flower and Fruit Decoration* (1862); Donald Beaton in *JHort*, 23 December 1862, pp. 757-9. ('Epergne' had previously been a term for a pickle or sauce dish without any implication of height, but elevated glass stands had become fashionable after the Great Exhibition of 1851.)

3. E.A. Maling, *Flowers for Ornament and Decoration* (1862). Miss Maling had published a book on house plants, *Flowers and Foliage for Indoor Plant Cases*, the previous year, so perhaps deserves priority over March. Annie Hassard's *Floral Arrangements for Dwelling Houses* (1875) and F.W. Burbidge's *Domestic Floriculture* (1873) were the two leading works of the 1870s. For table settings, see the books by the head gardeners John Perkins, *Floral Designs for the Table* (1877), and William Low, *Table Decoration* (1887). The return of cut flowers: R.P. Brotherston, *The Book of Cut Flowers* (1906).

4. *PRHS*, vol. 4 (1864), p. 118. See *GC*, 15 August 1868, pp. 865-6, and 12 September 1868, pp. 969-70, for complaints about table decorations at the Leicester Show, with Richard Dean's interesting remark that judges ought to look at cut flower exhibits first because of their tendency to go off. Gaslight competition: *GC*, 11 May 1872, p. 638; *JHort*, vol. 22 (1872), p. 520. Miss H.C. Philbrick, 'On table decoration for exhibition and the house', *JRHS*, vol. 29 (1904-5), pp. 493-7. Council minutes, 9 January 1906; 17 October 1922.

5. John Wills, 'Plants for house decoration', *JRHS*, vol. 15 (1893), pp. 84-8. For his career, see *GC*, 20 July 1895, p. 78, and *GardMag*, 20 July 1895, p. 436. Shirley Hibberd, 'Mr. Wills's decorative groups', *GardMag*, 20 July 1878, pp. 359-60. Constance Spry, *Flower Decoration* (1934), pp. v-vi, preface by Sir William Lawrence. Council minutes, 24 October 1905 (Bouquet Show Schedule Committee—a committee whose minutes do not survive).

6. Council minutes, 11 March 1924. H. Jolis, 'Flower decorations', *JRHS*, vol. 57 (1932), pp. 293-303; vol. 62 (1937), pp. cliv-clv, for the announcement—with no subsequent report—of a flower arrangement competition for amateurs; Captain H. Stevens, 'Flower decoration', vol. 63 (1938), pp. 439-43.

7. Council minutes, 13 December 1932; 7 June 1933; 8 January 1952; 11 August 1953; 2 February 1954.

8. Constance Spry, 'Flower decoration in war-time', *JRHS*, vol. 68 (1943), pp. 191-2. *GC*, 31 August 1946, p. 98. Council minutes, 9 January, 24 July, 11 September 1945; 13 August 1946; 1 July 1947; 2 March 1948; 9 September 1952; 3 March, 7 July 1953; 26 July 1954; 20 September 1955; 9 January 1962; 19 February, 11 June 1963; 28 September 1976. Constance Spry, *Favourite Flowers* (1959), p. 20.

9. *JRHS*, vol. 77 (1952), p. 234, and pp. 268-74 for Constance Spry, 'Flower arrangement'. *GC*, 26 July 1952, p. 31; 9 August 1952, p. 57; 16 August 1952, p. 68. *Flower Arranger*, vol. 2 (1962), pp. 49-50: 'The first flower academy 1952'; also vol. 17 (1977), pp. 88-91 for Mary Pope's 'Memories through a quarter of a century'.

10. *British Delphinium Society's Year Book*, 1953 pp. 8-13; 1954 pp. 38-47 (Mary Pope on the 1953 delphinium show, followed by a cartoon of 'The Gambols' on the theme of the rivalry between border and vase); 1955 pp. 25-42; 1956 pp. 58-64; 1957 pp. 51-9. *National Chrysanthemum Society Year Book*, 1953 pp. 95-9; 1954, pp. 62-72. *GC*, 25 July 1953, p. 32 (Mason); 5 December 1953, p. 217; 27 November 1954, p. 211; 15 January 1955, pp. 23-4; 27 July 1957, p. 64 (Ingwersen); 31 August 1957, p. 155 (Lucas Phillips); 12 October 1957, p. 273. Galsworthy: *GI* (1954), pp. 237, 262. Council minutes, 26 August 1952.

11. Council minutes, 2-16 November 1954; 19 April 1955; 19 March 1957. Mary Pope, 'Memories through a quarter of a century', *op. cit.* Michael Upward, 'Looking back', *Flower Arranger*, vol. 21 (1981), pp. 9-10. *GC*, 15 October 1955, p. 148; 29 October 1955, pp. 167-8. For the Festival of Flower Decoration, see *ibid.*, 25 July 1959, p. 35; 8 August 1959, p. 67; 5 September 1959, p. 123; 26 September 1959, p. 167.

12. Iris Webb, 'Silver jubilation', *Flower Arranger*, vol. 24 (1984), pp. 102-12. Several NAFAS Chelsea exhibits were described and illustrated in *The Flower Arranger* in later years, but see especially Carolyn Claussen, 'Going for gold—Chelsea 1988', vol. 28 (1988), pp. 310-12, for an account of the work involved in preparing an exhibit.

13. See the leader 'Art or arrangement?' in *GC*, 3 July 1954, p. 1, and the resulting correspondence, 24 July 1954, p. 38; 9 October 1954, p. 148 (argument about medal cards); 30 October 1954, p. 178; 27 November 1954, p. 211; 25 December 1954, p. 254; 8 January 1955, p. 16; 15 January 1955, pp. 23-4; 29 January 1955, p. 45. Estelle Norman, 'A challenge to horticultural societies', *National Chrysanthemum Society Year Book* 1954, pp. 64-72. Council minutes, 26 July 1954. For the Hambly Parker fuss, see *GC*, 12 July 1958, p. 18; 26 July 1958, p. 57; 2 August 1958, p. 73; 9 August 1958, p. 89; 16 August 1958, p. 101; 30 August 1958, p. 132; 6 September 1958, p. 145; 13 September 1958, p. 159; 27 September 1958, p. 193; 11 October 1958, p. 225; 1 November 1958, p. 269; 15 November 1958, p. 297.

14. John Livingstone, 'On the method of dwarfing trees and shrubs, as practised by the Chinese', *Transactions*, vol. 4 (1820), pp. 24-31; John Lindley, *Theory of Horticulture* (1840), pp. 262-4; Robert Fortune, *Three Years' Wanderings in Northern China* (1847), pp. 90-4; *GC*, 9 August 1845, p. 547; *FC*, vol. 16 (1848), p. 308; *JHort*, vol. 1 (18 June 1861), p. 224; *GC*, 3 September 1870, p. 1191; 10 September 1870, p. 1218; *Florist's Journal*, 1840, pp. 25-6. Reginald Farrer, *The Garden of Asia* (1904), pp. 17-19.

15. *CottGard*, vol. 23 (8 November 1859), pp. 84-6. *JHort*, 20 June 1872, pp. 501-3; 21 July 1892, p. 50.

16. *GC*, 19 October 1872, p. 1386. The specimen dwarfed trees had probably been imported to England rather than trained there, but I have found no data on this point.

17. See Brent Elliott, 'Mixed reactions', *The Garden (JRHS)*, vol. 123 (1998), pp. 334-6.

18. *GardMag*, 25 May 1901, pp. 322, 328; 2 January 1904, p. 29; 29 May 1909, p. 424; 5 June 1909, p. 439. *GC*, 1 June 1901, p. 350. Albert Maumerné [*sic*], 'The Japanese dwarf trees: their cultivation in Japan and their use and treatment in Europe', *JRHS*, vol. 33 (1908), pp. 53-70. Mrs Hart's ships and flamingos were probably of Chinese rather than Japanese origin, but Japan was more fashionable at the time, and distinctions were elided.

19. Cory's bonsai collection was depicted by Edith Helena Adie in a painting in the early 1920s (now in the Lindley Library). For the Dalrymple/Anley collection, see Gwendolyn Anley, 'Japanese plants and gardens', *JRHS*, vol. 71 (1946), pp. 291-6, esp. p. 294; and Lanning Roper's description of her garden in 'The smaller garden: St George's [Woking]', *ibid.*, vol. 81 (1956), pp. 84-93, esp. pp. 92-3.

20. Many publications give 1960 as the date of the Japan Society's first exhibit at Chelsea, but it first appears in the Chelsea catalogue, and the awards list, for 1961. The 1987 catalogue lists ten stands specialising in bonsai; the estimate of 13 comes from the *British Bonsai Association Bulletin*, Summer 1987, p. 5.

21. Robert Burgess, 'The Japanese art of bonsai', *JRHS*, vol. 93 (1968), pp. 288-93; Alan Roger, 'Bonsai: the story and development of the dwarfed tree', vol. 96 (1971), pp. 249-53, and see pp. 294-5, for his bonsai garden at Dundonnell House; Alan Roger, '*Bonsai*: a short guide to appreciation and judgment', vol. 97 (1972), pp. 447-9; and see also Colin Ellis, 'Bonsai: art and horticulture', vol. 114 (1989), pp. 232-7.

18 Amateur and Professional, pp. 313-36

1. For Queen Charlotte, see Council minutes, 16 January-6 February 1816; subsequent royal patronages will usually be found in the relevant Coronation year.

2. Council minutes, 19 March 1816; 3 June 1817. Joseph Knight was the author of a treatise on Proteaceae, and the proprietor of the Exotic Nursery, Chelsea, later taken over by James Veitch.

3. Associate status: Council minutes, 28 February, 6 March 1888; 10 February 1903; 2 October 1945.

4. Knight: 'Upon the cultivation of the pine apple without bark, or other hot-bed', *Transactions*, vol. 4 (1822), pp. 72-8, esp. p. 77. Loudon's quip appeared in his anonymous *Different Modes of Cultivating the Pineapple* (1822), p. 159. His unanonymous squib on Knight appeared in *GM*, vol. 5 (1829), pp. 86-7, and see more generally pp. 86-9 for the controversy. Beaton: *CottGard*, vol. 3 (21 February 1850), p. 276.

5. Council minutes: Report relative to the Garden at Chiswick ... January 1822.

6. Curtis (1940), p. 394. Working man's wage: so cited in David Davies, *The Case of Labourers in Husbandry Stated and Considered* (1795).

7. *GM*, vol. 1 (1826), pp. 314-16.

8. 'Hortulanus' in *ibid.*, pp. 146-50, and same author, vol. 2 (1827), pp. 105-6.

9. Council minutes, 4 May 1826 for the ruling; Sckell's departure is noted on 4 October 1826, but not his arrival in the first place. See Jan Woudstra, 'The Sckell family in England (1770-1830)', *Gartenkunst*, vol. 14 (2002), pp. 211-20.

10. Council minutes, 22 February 1827; 21 August, 9 December 1828; 5 February 1830. The most famous of the early gardeners' associations, the West London Gardeners' Association for Mutual Instruction, founded by Robert Fish and John Caie, only got going in the mid-1830s.

11. *GM*, vol. 12 (1836), pp. 610-12, 613-6.

12. Lindley, *Theory of Horticulture* (1840); 2nd ed., *Theory and Practice of Horticulture* (1855). Cramb's homage is in his memoir, in *GC*, 5 June 1875, pp. 719-20.

13. J.C. Loudon, *Self-instruction for Young Gardeners* (1845). Fish's anguish was recorded in his memoir, again in *GC*, 22 May 1875, pp. 655-6.

14. Council minutes, 19 February 1864. *GC*, 27 February 1864, pp. 195-6, and see 19 March 1864, pp. 270, 271 for the resulting correspondence.

15. Council minutes, 23 February 1864; 24 January, 21 November 1865. *GC*, 2 December 1865, pp. 1129-30. *JHort*, 28 March 1865, pp. 244-6. Brent Elliott, 'Top marks for James Hudson', *The Garden* (*JRHS*), vol. 117 (1992), pp. 118-19. F.W. Burbidge was another early achiever: Council minutes, 17 November 1868.

16. Indian Forestry: Council minutes, 30 July, 16 November, 14 December 1869; 2 March, 18 May, 8 June, 15 July 1870. Part of the debate concerned prevailing theories of forest management, and the contrast between English and German methods, but part of it concerned educational provision and professional qualification.

17. *GC*, 18 February 1888, p. 214 (Sir Trevor Lawrence, speaking at the Annual General Meeting). For renewed demands for a School of Horticulture, see Council minutes, 23 July 1889, and Henry Cannell's similar call in *GardMag*, 21 September 1895, p. 599.

18. Council minutes, 22 September, 24 November 1891; 22 March, 17 May, 20 September, 18 October, 1 November 1892; 14 February, 28 March, 11-25 April, 11 July, 10 October 1893.

19. *GC*, 17 February 1906, pp. 106-7; 24 February 1906, p. 124; 3 March 1906, pp. 141-2; 10 March 1906, p. 155; 17 March 1906, pp. 168-9.

20. The teachers' examination: Council minutes, 1 September 1903. The parks examination, 20 June 1905, 13 February 1906, 14 January 1908; the quotation comes from *GC*, 17 March 1906, p. 168.

21. *JRHS*, vol. 36 (1910-11), p. 459, for the teachers' exam, and vol. 39 (1913-14), pp. 228-9 for the parks exam.

22. Council minutes, 5 December 1911; 2 April 1912; 4 February 1913; 2 March, 11 May, 8-22 June 1915. *GC*, 30 August 1913, pp. 156-7; *Garden*, 6 September 1913, p. 443. H.V. Taylor, 'The National Diploma in Horticulture', *JRHS*, vol. 88 (1963), pp. 381-7.

23. Council minutes, 21 June, 18 October 1921; 27 June, 25 July 1922.

24. F.W. Shepherd and E.J. Lamont, 'The National Diploma in Horticulture (Hons)', *The Garden* (*JRHS*), vol. 108 (1983), pp. 160-1.

25. Council minutes, 15 September 1942, 1 May 1945; Examination Board minutes, 9 July 1942.

26. With something of a time-lag, in part because the early campaigns for state provision of technical education centred on the mining and manufacturing industries. Speaking as one who went through the Canadian educational system, and has had to learn about the British system at second hand, I must complain about the absence of a history of British education comparable with Lawrence Cremin's survey of American. Even the best historical works tend, as they approach the present day, to slide into ideological propaganda; and the history of technical education tends to be written (as here) from the standpoint of some particular industry. Some books that I have found particularly useful are George A.N. Lowndes, *The Silent Social Revolution*, 2nd edition (1969), still the best book on the subject; Brian Simon's series of *Studies in the History of Education*; Bernard Cronin, *Technology, Industrial Conflict and the Development of Technical Education in 19th-century England* (2001); and Stuart Maclure, *The Inspectors' Calling: HMI and the Shaping of Educational Policy 1945-1992* (2000), a much more useful book than its meagre index would suggest. It may be pertinent, if only to show the author's bias, for me to quote with approval Lowndes's comment: 'the infinitely diverse

needs of modern civilization can never be met by one system of schools unified under rigid public control, still less by a system at the mercy of successive party machines.'

27. Examinations Board minutes, 5 February 1942; 16 April, 3 June 1949. Council minutes, 17 March 1942; 8 June 1948; 12 June 1951; 10 January 1956. President's address to the Jubilee meeting of the NDH, *JRHS*, vol. 88 (1963), pp. 516-18. British Boys: Robert Pearson, 'First steps in gardening', *GC*, 1 December 1962, pp. 390-1, and a file in the RHS archive.

28. Memorandum in file of documents on Pilkington report, RHS archives. At the 1966 AGM, Lord Aberconway joked that the RHS 'can set up our own Pilkington Committee, and publish our own Pilkington Report, and I would back our Geoffrey against their Harry'—referring to the iris grower Geoffrey Pilkington, an active Council member. *JRHS*, vol. 91 (1966), pp. 140-1; also pp. 53-4. The Technical Education Council was subsumed into BTEC in 1983. For some surveys of horticultural education during these years, see A.J. Cooper, 'Horticultural education—future policy', *GC*, 23 October 1965, pp. 388, 406; V. Fowler, 'Horticultural education to university level', *ibid.*, 22 December 1972, pp. 18-19, 22.

29. *JRHS*, vol. 92 (1967), p. 53; see also Lord Aberconway's AGM speech, pp. 141-2. It is worth noting that the structure created by Pilkington was already being unravelled by the Haselgrave report in 1972.

30. For the negotiations with the IPRA over the parks examination, see Council minutes, 13 November 1945; 10 September 1946; Examinations Board minutes, 26 July, 23 November 1945; 13 September 1946.

31. Teachers' Diploma: *JRHS*, vol. 91 (1966), p. 58. Examinations Board minutes, 23 October 1967; 19 October 1970; 29 July 1971.

32. Examinations Board minutes, 12 January—9 May 1967; 13 May, 15 October 1968; 6 May, 4 August 1969.

33. The NCVQ argued that the M.Hort. should be considered as an equivalent to the 'Meister' award in agriculture, introduced in Germany in 1958 and subsequently adopted throughout the German-speaking states. In 1988 the National Farmers' Union proposed creating a Meister or Master award, which the RHS and the Arboricultural Association campaigned against for fear it would cause confusion.

34. Council minutes, 11 January 1921. Examinations Board minutes, 5 March 1942, 3 February 1944, 4 July 1947. David S. Ingram *et al.*, eds. *Science and the Garden* (2002).

35. P.K. Willmott, 'Assessing practical skills in horticulture', *ProfHort*, vol. 1 (1987), pp. 54-60; Peter R. Thoday, 'Higher education and professional qualifications in horticulture: a personal point of view', *ibid.*, vol. 2 (1988), pp. 15-18; Jeff Moorby, 'Challenges to the curriculum', *Horticulturist*, vol. 9 no. 3 (summer 2000), pp. 2-5; Institute of Horticulture Position Paper, 'Educational provision for horticulture', *ibid.*, vol. 10 no. 4 (autumn 2001), pp. 13-16.

36. For the history of school gardening, see Brent Elliott, 'Gardening in the classroom', *The Garden (JRHS)*, vol. 118 (1993), pp. 526-8. Textbooks: see A.C. Hilton, *Rural Science and School Gardening* (1959), esp. p. 224 for recommended examinations, and F.J. Bolger, *Rural Studies* (1965), esp. pp. 17-24 for the four-year syllabus for secondary schools, and the recommended examinations. For the situation in the 1970s, see Faith Whiten, 'The tender years', *GC&HTJ*, 28 September 1979, pp. 15-16; and a decade later, J.B.E. Simmons, 'Projecting the image of horticulture to children', *Professional Horticulture*, vol. 2 (1988), pp. 10-14.

37. *The Garden (JRHS)*, vol. 122 (1997), pp. 839, 878; vol. 123 (1998), p. 307.

38. *JRHS*, vol. 34 (1908-09), pp. 303-4. *GC*, 27 July 1907, pp. 64-5.

39. Council minutes, 19 July, 2 August 1910; 9 May 1911; 23 January 1912; 20 July 1915; 20 June 1916; 2 February, 13 March 1917; 13 November 1923. Nicholson and Hudson prizes: Council minutes, 27 October-22 December 1908. A similar prize was established by the Lensbury Horticultural Society in the 1960s: see 30 March, 29 June 1965.

40. Council minutes, 12 February, 21 October 1952; 17 February, 28 April 1953; 19 January, 16 March, 13 April, 25 May 1954. Opening ceremony: *JRHS*, vol. 79 (1954), pp. 432-5. *GC*, 28 February 1953, p. 75.

41. Council minutes, 13 May 1924; 30 December 1930; 28 July, 29 October, 17 November 1931.

42. *JRHS*, vol. 93 (1968), p. 63; vol. 96 (1971), pp. 148-9; vol. 97 (1972), p. 52. See Gordon Hayward, 'Trained at Wisley', *Horticulture*, August 1982, pp. 31-7.

43. Council minutes, 2 June-20 July 1830.

44. For Mrs Marryat's garden, see *GM*, vol. 10 (1834), pp. 337-46. For Louisa Lawrence's garden at Drayton Green, see *ibid.*, vol. 14 (1838), pp. 305-22. For instances of her crossing swords with Council and/or Lindley, see Council minutes, 7 June 1837; 2 June 1838; 21 April 1849; 25 January, 19 July 1853; 14 March 1854.

45. On the history of horticultural education for women, see Dawn Macleod, *Down-to-earth Women* (1982), and Peter King, *Women Rule the Plot* (1999); for background on their earlier technical education, see Helen Sillitoe, *A History of the Teaching of Domestic Subjects* (1933). For Swanley, see Moira A. Savonius, 'The advent of the lady gardener', *Field*, 21 January 1939, pp. 114-15; Elsa Morrow, 'A history of Swanley Horticultural College', *Wye*, vol. 12 no. 3 (1984-5), pp. 59-142. For Studley, see Kay N. Sanecki, *A Short History of Studley College* (1990). For the WFGU, see Peter King, *op. cit.*; Rory Stuart, 'Women of a growing concern', *The Garden (JRHS)*, vol.123 (1998), pp. 634-7, and correspondence vol. 124 (1999), p. 203. For Glynde, see Sally Festing, 'Viscountess Wolseley and her College for Lady Gardeners', *ibid.*, vol. 106 (1981), pp. 404-6. For Bedford College, see 'The study of botany and horticulture at the Bedford College', *Illustrated London News*, 14 March 1914, Ladies' supplement, p. iii.

46. Glynde: Council minutes, 12 February 1907. Studley: 16 July 1914; 4 July 1916. Thatcham: 8 June 1915. Greenway Court: 19 January 1915. Swanley: 13-27 January 1925; 21 March, 16 May 1944; 29 May, 16 June 1945; 26 March 1946.

47. See Sanecki, *op. cit.*, p. 31: 'Studley College was closed just 70 years after it had been founded, and for the same reason; *it was a College for the training of Women.*' Council minutes, 31 July, 11 September 1962; 7 February 1967; 3 February 1970. For Waterperry, see Ursula Maddy, *Waterperry: a Dream Fulfilled* (1990); Council minutes, 15 July, 12 August 1969; 15 January, 16 March, 4 May 1971. Emmie Clough Scholarship: 8 March 1960; 13 March, 13-27 June 1961; 19 October 1965; 13 December 1966.

48. On the position of women in horticulture, see Elizabeth Hess, 'Where are the women?', *GC*, 20 April 1963, p. 273, and ensuing correspondence, 25 May 1963, p. 371; 8 June 1963, p. 411; 15 June 1963, p. 429; 22 June 1963, p. 447; 29 June 1963, p. 463; Hess, 'Opportunities for women in horticulture', *JRHS*, vol. 89 (1964), pp. 286-94; Sue Gregory, 'A man's world, is it!', *GC&HTJ*, 18 June 1982, pp. 21-23.

49. *JRHS*, vol. 92 (1967), pp. 147, 326-8. *Times*, 21 April 1967, p. 9 g; 25 April p. 9 d. Frances Perry's election: *JRHS*, vol. 93 (1968), p. 149.

50. For the salaries cited, see Council minutes,

25 February, 18 April, 20 May, 19 June 1822. Glenny: *GardGaz*, vol. 2 (1838), p. 441, and see p. 345 for gardeners' wages generally. Head gardener for Chiswick: Donald Beaton, *CottGard*, vol. 17 (27 January 1857), pp. 290-1, pointing out that 'My own first situation, when I was hardly a fourth-rate gardener, was worth £150 a year', and urging the Society to offer a minimum of £200; *ibid.*, p. 321, for M'Ewen's salary. M'Ewen's letter: Council minutes, 12 January 1858. To illustrate the stability of 30s. p.w. over a 70-year period, see Council minutes, 25 July 1865 (Dick, chief clerk—pay raised to 35s. the next year); 19 January 1892 (severance pay rate for Barry, Chiswick clerk); 13 March 1894 (pay before increase of Humphreys, Assistant Superintendent); 16 July 1918, 2 June 1919 (Wisley wages). Barron and Thiselton-Dyer: Council minutes, 6 January, 6 December 1871. Wilks: 7 June 1892. For comparative wages in this later period, see E. H. Hunt, *Regional Wage Variations in Britain 1850-1914*.

51. Dykes: Council minutes, 17 January 1922. Cashier's department: 27 September 1927. Simmonds and Pavey: 13 November 1945. Gilmour and Fletcher: 18 April, 21 November-5 December 1950.

52. Lindley and two gardeners received a total of £40 p.a. in lieu of house rent while looking for accommodation: Council minutes, 19 June 1822. Medical: 8 April 1825; 31 January 1860. Kensington dismissal: 6 March 1888. Pensions: in 1863 the 77-year-old George Turner, 31 years on the Chiswick staff, received a pension of 6s. p.w. (20 March 1863); in 1896 a 68-year-old staff member, 20 years at Chiswick, got 10s. (10 March 1896); in 1922 the pension granted to S. T. Wright, the Superintendent of Wisley, was £1,028 p.a. (25 July 1922). Pension scheme: 2-30 August 1910; 29 July 1919; 22 March 1921; 27 March 1923; 17 June 1947; 9 January 1951. Unemployment insurance: 11 January-8 March 1921, 16 January 1923. Retirement age: 25 March 1952. Office hours: 7 July 1959.

53. John Gilmour, 'The Lindley Society', *RHS Garden Club Journal*, no. 41 (1948), pp. 7-8. Donald E. Green, 'Mr. J.S.L. Gimour: an appreciation', no. 44 (1951), pp. 8-9. David Mulford, 'Evolution of a garden', part 5, *Grassroots*, no. 45 (November 1996), p. 4.

54. *CottGard*, vol. 15 (29 January 1856), p. 309.

55. *GC*, 15 February 1873, p. 221.

56. Woodbridge: *GC*, 28 January 1888, p. 118; 4 February 1888, p. 150; 11 February 1888, p. 181.

57. *GardGaz*, vol. 3 (1839), p. 392. Dean: *GC*, 26 January 1901, p. 63. Council minutes, 15 April 1859; 29 December 1875; 5 January 1876; 22 May 1888; 12 February 1895; 18 December 1900; 23 February 1909.

58. See Elliott (1986), pp. 13-16, and pp. 214-16 for the backlash. Barnes vs Rolle: *GC*, 18 December 1869, p. 1305; and see 1 January 1870, p. 7, for the continuation of the quarrel under Barnes's successor. See also Malcolm Dunn, 'Relations between gardeners and their employers', *JRHS*, vol. 17 (1895), pp. 86-95. For a French view of the status of gardeners in England at the turn of the century, see Maurice Lecoufle, 'As others see us—English horticulture in 1907', *OR*, vol. III (2003), pp. 226-9.

59. *GC*, 29 May 1875, p. 697. For Williams vs Leslie, see 13 November 1875, pp. 620, 624; 27 November 1875, p. 684.

60. *GC*, 2 March 1901, p. 147; 9 March 1901, pp. 160-1.

61. *GC*, 25 January 1919, p. 43; 15 February 1919, p. 76; 8 March 1919, pp. 115, 117-8; 15 March 1919, pp. 128-9; 22 March 1919, p. 144 (Elwes); 29 March 1919, p. 157; 5 April 1919, pp. 169-70; 12 April 1919, p. 183 (call for RHS to form committee); 19 April 1919, p. 196 (Dykes); 26 April 1919, p. 209; 10 May 1919, pp. 230-1; 24 May 1919, p. 251; 31 May 1919, p. 271; 7 June 1919, p. 286. Council minutes, 17 December 1918; 21 October

1919.

62. Council minutes, 25 April, 7 June, 31 October, 28 November 1922; 16 January 1923; 13 December 1932. The Bribery and Secret Commissions Prevention League issued regular news-sheets reporting prosecutions for bribery in a wide range of trades.

63. Roy Hay, *Gardening the Modern Way* (1962), pp. 17-18. J.B.E. Simmons, 'Projecting the image of horticulture to children', *ProfHort*, vol. 2 (1988), p. 10.

64. *The Garden* (*JRHS*), vol. 109 (1984), pp. 82, 273-4. *GC&HTJ*, 28 September 1984, p. 4; 26 October 1984, p. 5; 1 November 1985, p. 6; 10 January 1986, p. 17; 21 February 1986, p. 7; 12 June 1987, p. 15. *HW*, 13 April 1995, p. 16; 13 July 1995, p. 7; 18 April 1996, p. 4; 28 November 1996, pp. 20-1. Despite the remark about the umbilical cord, it should be noted that the RHS was once represented on the board of the Society for Industrial Chemistry: see Council minutes, 6 April 1948.

65. Pollock: *The Garden* (*JRHS*), vol. 127 (2002), p. 8. The major polemical articles on education have already been listed above in note 33, but see also 'Learning to Succeed: a new framework for post-16 learning (June 1999, Cm 4392): response by the IOH', *Horticulturist*, vol. 9 no. 1 (winter 2000), p. 13. For the Institute's evidence to the House of Lords Select Committee on Science & Technology re research and development, see *ProfHort*, vol. 1 (1987), pp. 4-6. I cannot help remarking on the curiosity of the promotion of training in business management on the part of an Institute so concerned with the decline in practical training: I venture to predict that the increasing emphasis on training in an allegedly autonomous discipline of management will prove to be as great a problem for the future of practical training as the current emphasis on academic degree courses has been. As early as 31 July 1973 the Examinations Board was remarking that the increasing proportion of managers and decreasing number of craftsmen in commercial horticulture had limited the demand for the NDH.

66. Council minutes, 12 January, 29 June-29 July, 10 August, 7-21 September 1897. *JRHS*, vol. 21 (1897-98), pp. 1-4, 571-81.

67. Sutton: Council minutes, 11 January 1898. Cannell: 22 July 1902. Increase in number: 26 February 1901. In 1997 a commemorative booklet was published to celebrate the award's centennial.

68. *GC*, 18 September 1869, p. 990, for Veitch's obituary. For the Veitch Memorial: *GC*, 9 October 1869, p. 1062; 16 October 1869, p. 1084; 23 October 1869, pp. 1110, 1112; 30 October 1869, p. 1134; 4 December 1869, p. 1252 (subscribers' list); 25 December 1869, p. 1330; 15 October 1870, p. 1373; 29 October 1870, pp. 1438, 1439-40. Council minutes, 9 August 1921; 31 October, 14-28 November 1922; 16 July 1929.

69. Council minutes, 5 November, 19 November, 10 December 1929; 14 January, 25 February, 25 March, 23 April, 4 November 1930. At the time the Associateship of Honour was created, 'Associate' was still an RHS reduced-rate membership category for practical gardeners, but no one seems to have commented on the resemblance of title.

70. Council minutes, 14-28 June, 12 July 1949; 3 December 1957; 15-29 April, 5 June, 12 August, 30 September, 14-28 October, 25 November 1958; 13-27 January, 21 April 1959.

71. Council minutes, 24 October-28 November 1893; 27 May 1919; 21 April 1931. For the role of the gardening press in the rise of the professional gardener, see Elliott (1986), esp. pp. 11-13.

72. *GC*, 3 January 1925, p. 2. For the history of broadcasting generally, see Asa Briggs, *History of Broadcasting in the United Kingdom*, especially the first

volume, *The Birth of Broadcasting* (revised ed., 1995).

73. Council minutes, 10 February—24 March 1931. Broadcast bulletins: texts are held in RHS archives. Northern bulletin: Council minutes, 4 November, 2 December 1924. For C.H. Middleton's impact as a broadcaster, see Briggs, *op. cit.*, volume 3: *The War of Words* (revised ed., 1995), pp. 199-200, 503-4.

74. For various aspects of the RHS's vexed relations with the BBC, see Council minutes, 9 March 1926; 13 August 1929; 24 February 1931; 10 May 1932; 31 January 1933; 20 February 1934; 1 December 1953; 19 October 1954; 24 March 1959. For Streeter's career, see Geoffrey Eley, *And Here is Mr. Streeter* (1950); Frank Hennig, *'Cheerio Frank Cheerio Everybody': the Gardening World of Fred Streeter* (1976). Streeter was originally Middleton's deputy, and chosen over Billitt to succeed him (Streeter was awarded the VMH in 1945, when he was still Middleton's deputy, but it was for his work at Petworth, and as an exhibitor—his radio work was not mentioned). For *GQT*, see Council minutes, 21 September 1971. For Hellyer's resolution, see *JRHS*, vol. 95 (1970), pp. 150-2.

75. Correspondence with the Pilkington Committee: file in RHS archives. See Asa Briggs, *History of Broadcasting*, vol. 5: Competition (1995), pp. 257-308.

76. For Billitt's career, see Arthur Billitt, *The Story of Clack's Farm* (1981); for Thrower's, Percy Thrower and Ronald Webber, *My Lifetime of Gardening* (1977), and Timothy O'Sullivan, *Percy Thrower: a Biography* (1989); for Hamilton's, Gay Search and Tony Hamilton, *Geoff Hamilton: a Man and his Garden* (1998), and Tony Hamilton, *My Brother Geoff: the People's Gardener* (2001). See also Marc Rosenberg, '35 years of *Gardeners' World*', *Amateur Gardening*, 8 March 2003, pp. 22-5.

77. *The Garden* (*JRHS*), vol. 125 (2000), p. 805; vol. 127 (2002), p. 242.

78. Mary Keen, 'Makeover madness', *The Garden* (*JRHS*), vol. 125 (2000), pp. 398-9, and correspondence, p. 561; Pattie Barron, 'Producing addiction', vol. 126 (2001), pp. 296-7. For Titchmarsh's career, see Alan Titchmarsh, *Trowel and Error* (2002).

19 National and International, pp. 337-58

1. Council minutes, 30 March, 21 April 1852 (Foreign Members); 14 July 1848 (Corresponding Members).

2. Council minutes, 15 December 1818.

3. Council minutes, 2 February 1820; 19 January 1825; and see 6 March 1888 for a later, abortive proposal for local RHS secretaries.

4. There are many references in Council minutes to the distribution of medals; here I will cite only those which include some discussion of the principles involved: 7 October 1826; 22 February 1827; 26 November 1830; 4 February 1832; 17 June 1845.

5. Council minutes, 25 February, 16 March, 15 April, 7 May, 1 October, 5 November 1858; 20 March 1866. *PRHS*, vol. 5 (1865), p. 27.

6. Council minutes, 14 February, 21 March 1877. Unfortunately, the names of affiliated societies stopped being recorded in the minutes of Council after 1881, by which point only three more had been recorded since Churchill's proposal.

7. Council minutes, 14 January 1890; 27 September 1910.

8. Affiliated Societies' Cup and other awards: Council minutes, 9 April, 24 September 1901; 20 December 1910; 24 October 1911; 5 November-3 December 1912; 8 January, 19 March 1939. Library proposals: 24 October 1911; 27 August 1935. Mutual Improvement Societies: 1 October 1907. Allotment proposals: 29 January, 23 April, 28 May, 5-19 November 1918; 21 September 1920. Ruhleben: Elliott (1988). Two tiers: 14 March, 31 October 1922; 27 October 1936. Tylerstown and District Horticultural Society

expenses: 27 November 1928.

9. Council minutes, 14 June 1861.

10. For the Bury Show, see Council minutes, 25 July, 6-20 November 1866. *GC*, 13 July 1867, pp. 733, 737; 20 July 1867, pp. 757, 761-3 (show report), 765, 767-71 (agricultural show report); 27 July 1867, pp. 781 (receipts), 784-5; 3 August 1867, pp. 807-8 (prize complaints); 9 November 1867, p. 1142. For Fish's Life Fellowship, see Council minutes, 5 November 1866, and *GC*, 20 July 1867, p. 757.

11. Council minutes, 16 April, 5-29 November 1867; 2 June, 7-16 July, 4 August 1868. *GC*, 18 July 1868, p. 765; 25 July 1868, pp. 791-3 (reports); 1 August 1868, p. 814; 15 August 1868, p. 865; 12 September 1868, p. 969. See also pp. 682 and 717 for two announcements about the inaugural dinner, with different organisers named: some entertaining story of local politics doubtless underlies the change. For the Life Fellowship awards, see Council minutes, 16 July, 4 August 1868: William Penn Cox, Thomas Charlesworth, and John Buck of the Leicester and Rutland Asylum, who raised the guarantee.

12. For the negotiations and advance controversy, see Council minutes, 15 January, 9-16 February, 16 March, 20 April, 4 May, 28 June, 6 July 1867. *GC*, 15 May 1869, p. 528; 22 May 1869, p. 557; 29 May 1869, pp. 585-6; 5 June 1869, p. 612; 24 July 1869, p. 785. For the show itself, see *ibid.*, pp. 790-3; 31 July 1869, pp. 818 (report), 817. Council minutes, 20-21 July 1869, and 10 August 1869 for Henry Whitworth's 40-guinea Fellowship.

13. See Council minutes, 10 August, 16 November 1869; 20 April, 29 June 1870; 6 January 1871. *GC*, 25 June 1870, pp. 859-60; 16 July 1870, p. 953; 23 July 1870, pp. 985, 992-6 (report); 30 July 1870, pp. 1021, 1026-7; 6 August 1870, pp. 1058, 1061-2 (report on implements).

14. Council minutes, 7 September 1870; 7-21 June 1871; 17 January 1872. *GC*, 4 March 1871, pp. 272, 273-4; 29 April 1871, p. 546; 13 May 1871, p. 610; 3 June 1871, pp. 707-8; 17 June 1871, pp. 769-70, 773; 1 July 1871, pp. 835, 839-43 (report); 8 July 1871, pp. 869, 876; 20 April 1872, p. 538 for the Gold Medals.

15. Council minutes, 14 February, 20 March, 17 April, 3 July 1872. *JHort*, vol. 22 (1872), pp. 517-20. *GC*, 27 January 1872, p. 107; 23 March 1872, p. 391; 13 April 1872, p. 509; 27 April 1872, p. 574; 11 May 1872, p. 638; 1 June 1872, pp. 729-30; 15 June 1872, pp. 797-8; 22 June 1872, pp. 830-1; 29 June 1872, pp. 863, 866-71 (report), 873-4 (Rose Show report); 6 July 1872, p. 909; 23 November 1872, p. 1554; 30 November 1872, p. 1586.

16. *GC*, 24 February 1872, p. 255 (Ayres' proposal); 6 April 1872, p. 466; 13 April 1872, p. 504; 20 April 1872, pp. 538, 543-4; 27 April 1872, pp. 574, 575; 11 May 1872, p. 639; 29 June 1872, pp. 870-71; for horticultural buildings, 18 May 1872, pp. 666, 671; 25 May 1872, p. 703; for the boiler trials and resulting controversy, 13 April 1872, p. 509; 4 May 1872, p. 606; 11 May 1872, p. 639; 1 June 1872, p. 735; 20 July 1872, p. 968; 27 July 1872, p. 1003; 3 August 1872, pp. 1034-5; 10 August 1872, p. 1066; 17 August 1872, p. 1098; 31 August 1872, p. 1160; 7 September 1872, p. 1192.

17. Council minutes, 6 November 1872; 4-30 June 1873. *GC*, 17 May 1873, pp. 680-1, 683; 21 June 1873, pp. 841-2; 28 June 1873, pp. 875, 880-4 (report, incl. rose show); 5 July 1873, pp. 913-14, 918; 20 December 1873, p. 1700; and see 4 January 1873, pp. 9-11 for Rendle's pavilions.

18. For these abortive shows, see Council minutes, 16 April 1867 (Derby and others); 18 February 1868, 11 December 1874 (Maidstone); 24-31 March, 21 April 1874 (Brighton); 28 April, 5-26 May 1874 (Wigan); 19 October 1874, 14 February, 21 March 1877 (Sheffield); 10 November 1874 (Leeds).

19. Council minutes, 16 June 1874; 5 June, 3 July, 4 September, 6 November 1877; 19 March, 2-12 April,

7-8 May, 4-11 June, 2 July 1878. *GC*, 9 February 1878, p. 179; 13 April 1878, p. 470; 27 April 1878, pp. 536-7; 4 May 1878, p. 568; 11 May 1878, p. 599; 18 May 1878, p. 630; 29 June 1878, p. 825.

20. Council minutes, 23 July 1878; 14 January, 11 March, 22 April, 21-28 October 1879. *GC*, 13 July 1878, pp. 54-8; 20 July 1878, p. 86; 3 August 1878, p. 154; 28 September 1878, p. 408; 5 October 1878, pp. 441-2. The protestors against Bull's award were Benjamin S. Williams and William Rollisson.

21. Rejected offers: Council minutes, 6 August, 15 October, 7 November 1878; 14 January, 11 March 1879; 13 March 1883.

22. Council minutes, 10 November 1885; 9 February, 9 March, 11-25 May, 13 July, 12 October 1886; 22 February 1887. *GC*, 13 March 1886, pp. 338-9; 20 March 1886, p. 368; 27 March 1886, p. 402; 22 May 1886, p. 656; 26 June 1886, p. 820 and supplementary sheet; 3 July 1886, pp. 16, 21-27 (report); 10 July 1886, pp. 48, 50; 14 August 1886, p. 208; 21 August 1886, pp. 242-3.

23. Council minutes, 25 November 1890 (Torquay); 12 January 1892 (Lowe); 14 January, 10 March, 14 July 1896 (Chester); 9 February 1897 (Shrewsbury); and on and on in the 20th century.

24. Council minutes, 10 February-13 July 1920 *passim. GC*, 12 June 1920, pp. 289-90; 3 July 1920, p. 2; 10 July 1920, pp. 26-8. Though Birmingham tried to secure a provincial show the next year-see Council minutes, 13 January 1920.

25. Council minutes, 12 November 1835, for Lindley's appointment. For the history of his activities at Chelsea, see F.G.D. Drewitt, *The Romance of the Apothecaries' Garden at Chelsea* (1922), pp. 80-3; Penelope Hunting, *A History of the Society of Apothecaries* (1998), pp. 141-4; and more substantially, Sue Minter, *The Apothecaries' Garden* (2000), pp. 67-86. *GardGaz*, vol. 2 (1838), p. 329.

26. Council minutes, 8-15 May 1838; 13-25 February 1840. Beaton: *CottGard*, vol. 15 (10 October 1855), p. 35. Desmond (1995), pp. 143-9. Susan Campbell, 'The genesis of Queen Victoria's great new kitchen garden', *GH*, vol. 12 no. 2 (1984), pp. 100-19. Joseph Hume is a well-known radical politician; less well known is the fact that in younger days he had collected plants in Cyprus: see Robert Walpole, *Memoirs relating to European and Asiatic Turkey* (2nd ed., 1818), pp. 253-4.

27. Council minutes, 17 July 1872. *GC*, 3 August 1872, p. 1034; 10 August 1872, p. 1066. Admission fee: Council minutes, 21 December 1915; 12 September 1916.

28. Council minutes, 14 January 1902; 8 June, 3 August, 28 September, 12 October, 9-23 November, 21 December 1909; 8 August, 27 November 1923; 15-29 January 1924; 21 April, 24 November-15 December 1931.

29. *Times*, 9 October 1923, p. 15 e; 12 October 1923, p. 8 c; 15 October 1923, p. 8 c; 16 October 1923, p. 13 e; 19 October 1923, p. 13 e; 21 November 1923, p. 13 e. Council minutes, 16 October 1923. The correspondence was started by Beatrice Kew Clark, whose garden at Waxwell Farm, Pinner, while not well known through the gardening press, was visually familiar to a gardening audience through Beatrice Parsons's paintings of it, published in E.T. Cook's *Gardens of England* (1910).

30. For the Hampton Court limes, see *Times*, 28 August 1978, p. 9 g; 16 September, p. 13 g; 18 September p. 15 e-f; 20 September p. 15 f-g; 25 September, p. 15 g; 27 September, p. 15 g; 4 October, p. 17 g; 3 November, p. 19 a-b; 11 November, p. 15 a-c. The correspondence this time was started by Nancy-Mary Goodall, a member of the Garden History Society.

31. Council minutes, 27 May, 29 July 1919. *GC*, 1 March 1919 pp. 98-9; 24 May 1919, p. 254; 30 August 1919, p.

120; 6 September 1919, pp. 131-2. Ernest Law, *The Flower-lover's Guide to the Gardens of Hampton Court* (1923). Department of the Environment, *Royal Parks Historical Survey: Hampton Court and Bushy Park*, vol. 1 (1982), pp. 70-74.

32. Council minutes, 18 April-6 June, 12 September 1944; 30 April 1946.

33. Council minutes, 17 June, 4 November, 2 December 1947; 1 January-2 March, 6 April, 4 May, 22 June 1948; 5 December 1950; 19 October 1954. *JRHS*, vol. 74 (1949), p. 85, for Aberconway's letter. *Times*, 28 June 1948, p. 5 c-d; 7 January 1949, p. 5 f-g. For early articles in *JRHS* on the National Trust gardens, and the Joint Committee, see Lord Rosse, 'The National Trust gardens', *JRHS*, vol. 74 (1949), pp. 432-9; Sir David Bowes Lyon, 'The gardens of the National Trust', vol. 82 (1957), pp. 6-11; Rosse, 'The preservation of our gardens', vol. 94 (1969), pp. 426-35, 466-70. For the history of the Joint Committee seen from the Trust's point of view, see John Gaze, *Figures in a Landscape: a History of the National Trust* (1988), pp. 165-73; Jennifer Jenkins and Patrick James, *From Acorn to Oak Tree: the Growth of the National Trust 1895-1994* (1994), pp. 157-60, 206-13; Anna Pavord, 'Gardens', in Howard Newby, ed., *The National Trust: the Next Hundred Years* (1995), pp. 135-49.

34. Council minutes, 25 August, 29 September 1925; 7 September 1926; 30 October 1928; 24 October 1933.

35. Council minutes, 2 March, 4 May, 8 June, 30 November 1948. *GC&HTJ*, 22 August 1980, pp. 11-13.

36. Westonbirt: Council minutes, 7 October 1952. Tower Court: 1 August 1950; 3 April 1951; 10 October 1961. Borde Hill: 4 May 1965. Brodick Castle: 1 April 1958. Branklyn: 15 January, 25 February 1969.

37. Council minutes, 5 October 1965.

38. Council minutes, 28 March, 11 April 1916; 9 April, 8-22 October 1918; 10 February, 11 May 1920. Brookwood: 21 January, 18 March 1958. War Graves Commission at Chelsea: 20 September 1966. See Philip Longworth, *The Unending Vigil: a History of the Commonwealth War Graves Commission 1917-1967* (1967).

39. Guildford: Council minutes, 24 February 1959; 26 January 1960. Westminster: 28 June, 26 July 1960.

40. Windlesham Trophy—*The Garden (JRHS)*, vol. 118 (1993), p. 486. *Prisons Handbook* (2002), p. 650. Esther Addley, 'Prisons: the best and worst', *Guardian*, 30 January 2001. Whatton Board of Prison Visitors, Annual Report 2000 (website), p. 4. Sir David Ramsbotham, inspection report on HM Prison Kingston, November 1997 (website). The RHS had provided seeds for prison gardens at least as far back as 1921: see Council minutes, 29 November 1921 (seeds for Newport prison). Paula Deitz, 'Free to grow bluebells in England', in the *New York Times*, 16 July 1998. The film *Greenfingers* (2001) was made by Joel Hershman and Travis Swords.

41. *RHS West Midlands Regional Centre at Pershore Newsletters. HW*, 2 September 1988, p. 6. Report of Council for 1988, p. i.

42. *The Garden (JRHS)*, vol. 107 (1982), pp. 172, 302.

43. *GC&HTJ*: 4 February 1983, p. 4; 11 July 1983, p. 11; 9 September 1983, p. 4; 11 November 1983, pp. 14-32; 3 February 1984, pp. 19-20; 13 April 1984, p. 3, 6; 4 May 1984, pp. 11-16; 15 June 1984, p. 4; 20 July 1984, p. 4; 19 October 1984, p. 4; 26 October 1984, pp. 17-29; 25 January 1985, p. 6; 29 March 1985, p. 7; 17 October 1986, p. 3. Allan Smith, 'Muddles on the Mersey', *LD*, no. 151 (October 1984), pp. 16-18; Rodney Beaumont, 'The city that walked tall', no. 160 (April 1986), pp. 25-6; David Parker and Tony Bradshaw, 'Another look at Liverpool', no. 161 (June 1986), pp. 32-5; Richard Cass, 'Liverpool's legacy', no. 173 (June 1988), pp. 53-4.

44. *GC&HTJ*, 11 November 1983, pp. 27-9; 26 October

1984, pp. 32-3; 9 August 1985, p. 3; 18 October 1985, p. 14; 31 January 1986, pp. 19-37; 25 July 1986, p. 3; 19 September 1986, pp. 3, 14; 24 October 1986, p. 3. Joe Samworth, 'NFG 86 Stoke-on-Trent', *LD*, no. 151 (October 1984), pp. 25-8; Roger Butler *et al.*, 'From furnaces to festival', no. 157 (October 1985), pp. 13-25; Stoke Festival special issue, no. 160 (1986), pp. 30-89; Joe Samworth, 'Festival gardens', no. 163 (October 1986), pp. 14-17; 'Stoke—after the Festival', no. 173 (June 1988), pp. 58-9.

45. *GC&HTJ*, 18 October 1985, p. 3; *HW*, 3 January 1986, p. 3; 31 January 1986, p. 39; 14 February 1986, p. 8; 16 January 1987, pp. 19, 24-5; 10 June 1988, p. 7; 22 April 1988, pp. 15-25; 27 May 1988, p. 7; 29 July 1988, pp. 26-7; 30 September 1988, pp. 1-4 *passim*; 14 October 1988, p. 5; 20 January 1989, p. 3. Glasgow Festival special issue, *LD*, no. 173 (June 1988), pp. 13-51; Joe Samworth, 'Getting over Glasgow', no. 176 (December 1988), pp. 31-4; David Skinner, 'Roots in the future', *ibid.*, p. 35.

46. *HW*, 31 January 1986, p. 39; 23 January 1987, pp. 25-6; 22 April 1988, pp. 31-2; 14 October 1988, pp. 1-3; 4 November 1988, p. 1; 26 January 1990, pp. 20-31; 25 May 1990, pp. 3, 14-16; 2 November 1990, p. 13. Gateshead Festival special issue, *LD*, no. 192 (July/August 1990), pp. 28-45.

47. *HW*, 22 April 1988, pp. 27-8; 14 February 1992, pp. 28-31; 1 May 1992, pp. 19-24; 14 August 1992, pp. 26-8; 2 October 1992, p. 3; 16 October 1992, pp. 28-30. Jane Porter, 'Enter Ebbw Vale', *LD*, no. 192 (July/August 1990), pp. 46-8; Jon E. Lewis, 'How green is my valley', no. 212 (July/August 1992), pp. 11-17.

48. Peter Bareham, 'A brief history', *LD*, no. 160 (April 1986), pp. 14-16; Allan Smith, 'Creating a sense of place', *ibid.*, pp. 20-1; Jane Porter, 'The future of festivals', no. 192 (July/August 1990), pp. 49-50; Rodney Beaumont, 'Focus on the festivals', no. 212 (July/August 1992), pp. 18-20. *HW*, 2 October 1987, p. 3 (no further after '92); 5 October 1990, p. 3; 19 October 1990, p. 5 (Heseltine pushing for decision); 2 November 1990, pp. 10-13; 16 October 1992, p. 30; 8 October 1993, p. 24. J. Robert Bent, 'Garden festivals', *ProfHort*, vol. 1 (1987), pp. 104-5; Jim Wilson, 'Glasgow holds the key to future garden festivals', vol. 2 (1988), pp. 27-31.

49. J. D. Boocock, 'Southport Flower Show', *The Garden (JRHS)*, vol. 112 (1987), pp. 323-4. *HW*, 13 February 1987 p. 7; 10 July 1987 p. 7.

50. Council minutes, 8 January-5 February, 11 June 1963. *GC,* 24 November 1962, p. 365; 26 October 1963, pp. 298-9, 305. David Welch, 'Britain in Bloom', *The Garden (JRHS)*, vol. 118 (1993), pp. 124-7; Graham Ashworth, 'Keeping Britain in Bloom', *ibid.*, vol. 121 (1996), pp. 784-5. The English press consistently attributed the Fleurissement de France to De Gaulle, though French sources credit Robert Buron, the Ministre pour Travaux Publiques at the time.

51. *HW*: 'Britain no longer in Bloom', 20 May 1983 p. 5; 'Britain in Bloom is saved', 8 July 1983, p. 5; 'RHS embraces Britain in Bloom', 5 October 2000, p. 5. *The Garden (JRHS)*, vol. 125 (2000), p. 803; vol. 127 (2002), pp. 292-5.

52. Council minutes, 22 January 1830; 21 May 1844.

53. Council minutes, 20 March 1863. J. B. Hurlbert, 'On the horticultural possibilities of Canada', *PRHS*, vol. 3 (1863), pp. 12-16.

54. *JRHS*, vol. 82 (1957), pp. 366-7.

55. Council minutes, 16 October 1945; 30 July 1946. Peace Garden: 21 October-4 November 1947; 7 September 1948.

56. Council minutes, 13 January 1925, for Cecil Hanbury's sending citrus fruits to the Society. Michael Lear, 'Plants in flower at La Mortola on 1 January 1985', *The Garden (JRHS)*, vol. 110 (1985), pp. 278-82; Fred Whitsey, 'La Mortola looks good', vol. 117 (1992), pp. 24-9. For the history of La Mortola, see Cecil Hanbury *et al.*, *La Mortola Garden* (1938), and Francesca Mazzino, *An Earthly Paradise: the Hanbury Gardens at La Mortola* (1997).

57. The best history so far of the international exhibitions is John Allwood, *The Great Exhibitions* (1977), though it seldom discusses their horticultural aspects: that is a book remaining to be written. Council minutes in the 19th century seldom record more than the setting in motion of plans for participation in foreign shows. For coverage of the horticulture of the international shows, see *JHort*, 9 May 1867, pp. 327-9 (Paris), and 21 May 1874, pp. 403-6 (Florence). For Dilke's death, see *GC*, 15 May 1869, pp. 527, 533; for coverage of the St Petersburg exhibition, at which Robert Warner and the Veitch nursery were major exhibitors, *see ibid.*, pp. 609-10, and Audrey Le Lievre, 'St Petersburg 1869', *The Garden (JRHS)*, vol. 113 (1988), pp. 222-6.

58. Council minutes, 16-30 January 1923; 10 May, 7 June, 30 September, 4 October 1932; 23 February, 9-23 March, 22-29 June 1926. *GC*, 10 July 1926, p. 23.

59. Council minutes, 5 May 1936 (Horticultural Society of South Australia centenary show); 10 November 1936 (Massachusetts); 6 April 1937 (President's American tour); 15 February 1949 (cup for Royal Horticultural Society of Victoria); 27 August 1951 (Rhodesia); 21 May, 14 August 1962 (Kirstenbosch, and see also *GC*, 19 January 1963, pp. 44-6).

60. Council minutes, 20 May, 2 July, 24 September 1957, 9 January, 4 February, 3 June, 1 July 1958, 10 March, 24 March 1959; 11 November 1958, 30 May 1961; 10 October 1961, 1 May 1962. Paris Floralies: *GC*, 9 May 1959, pp. 287-9. Bowes Lyon: 30 May 1959, p. 353. Valenciennes, 12 May 1962, pp. 343, 352-4.

61. Council minutes, 1 September 1959 (stated desirability of sending exhibits overseas each year). Hamburg: 3-31 July, 23 October 1962, 8-22 January, 30 April, 24 September 1963 (and see *GC*, 11 May 1963, pp. 325, 328-9). Paris Floralies: 5 February, 5 March 1963, 14 January 1964. Ghent Floralies: 21 May, 9 July 1968. Quoted rule: 17 March 1970.

62. Munich: *GC&HTJ*, 29 April 1983, pp. 27-8; 21 October 1983, p. 4; 11 November 1983, pp. 24-5. Osaka: Alan Tate and Brian Clouston, 'From Liverpool to Osaka—with flowers', *LD*, no. 158 (December 1985), pp. 30-3. *HW*, 14 July 1989, p. 5; 25 August 1989, pp. 3, 14-15; 3 August 1990, p. 6; 10 August 1990, pp. 31-3. Floriade: *HW*, 3 April 1992, p. 17; 3 July 1992, p. 6; 17 July 1992, pp. 26-7; 16 October 1992, p. 5. Stuttgart: *HW*, 8 October 1993, pp. 21-27; *The Garden (JRHS)*, vol. 118 (1993), p. 485.

63. Patti Hagan, 'Chelseagate: the flower-show flap', *Wall Street Journal*, 10 February 1993 (or 12 February, in the European edition). Dulci Mahar, 'One big disappointment', *Oregonian*, 12 February 1993.

64. Council minutes, 12 September—24 October 1950.

65. Brief biographical notices of some of the first officials were published in *The Garden (JRHS)*, vol. 115 (1990): pp. 448 (Arai), 505 (Suzuki), 562 (Iida), 622 (Arimasa).

66. *The Garden (JRHS)*, vol. 122 (1997), p. 3. For a noteworthy example of the literature of the English gardening boom, see *Kei Yamada no igirissu gadden bokku* [Kei Yamada's English garden book] (1996), by a garden designer who later created two gardens at Chelsea. Kazuko Yahiro published a guidebook to English gardens for Japanese visitors: *Akogare no igirissu gadden / Gardens in England, Scotland & Wales* (1997).

67. Council minutes, 24 November 1903; 23 February 1904. Fletcher (1969), pp. 366-83.

Bibliography

(1) Periodicals cited in the notes by abbreviations. Note that weekly gardening periodicals are cited by date, and volume numbers are only added when the volumes are not in synchrony with calendar years. Attributions of authorship of anonymous articles in the *Quarterly Review* are based on the Wellesley Index of Victorian Periodicals; in the *Athenaeum*, on the annotations in the editor's marked file of that magazine, now held in the City University Library. In the *Gardeners' Chronicle* and other gardening magazines, unsigned leaders are attributed to the editors unless evidence is presented otherwise; other attributions are explained in the relevant notes.

BM	*Botanical Magazine*
BR	*Botanical Register*
CL	*Country Life*
CottGard	*Cottage Gardener*. 1848-1861, continued as *J.Hort*.
F&P	*Florist & Pomologist*
FC	*Floricultural Cabinet*
FM	*Floricultural Magazine*
FW	*Floral World*
Garden (JRHS)	*The Garden* (title since 1975 of *JRHS*)
GC	*Gardeners' Chronicle*. 1841- , continued as *GC&HTJ*, then as *HW*.
GC&HTJ	*Gardeners' Chronicle & Horticultural Trades Journal*, continued as *HW*.
GardGaz	*Gardeners' Gazette*.
GFA	*Gardener, Florist, & Agriculturist*
GI	*Gardening Illustrated*
GM	*Gardener's Magazine*. 1826-1843.
GMB	*Gardener's Magazine of Botany*. 1850-1851.
GardMag	*Gardeners' Magazine*. 1865-1916.
GH	*Garden History*
GW	*Gardening World*
HW	*Horticulture Week*
JHS	*Journal of the Horticultural Society of London*. Vols. 1-9 (1846-54).
JHort	*Journal of Horticulture*. 1861-1915.
JRHS	*Journal of the Royal Horticultural Society*. Vols. 1- (1866-), continued from 1975 as *Garden (JRHS)*.
LD	*Landscape Design*
NG	*Northern Gardener*
OR	*Orchid Review*
PRHS	*Proceedings of the Royal Horticultural Society*
ProfHort	*Professional Horticulture*
QR	*Quarterly Review*
Transactions	*Transactions of the Horticultural Society of London*
Trans. Linn. Soc.	*Transactions of the Linnean Society*.

(2) Select bibliography of books and articles

ALTICK, RICHARD D. (1978). *The Shows of London*. Cambridge, MA: Harvard University Press.

ANON. (1829). *A Letter to Thomas Andrew Knight, Esq., Pres. Hort. Soc., on the Management of the Garden and Funds of the Horticultural Society*. London: Baldwin and Cradock.

ANON. (1916). *The Royal Horticultural Society's True Work. By a Life Fellow of the Society*. London: Simpkin, Marshall.

BABBAGE, CHARLES (1830). *Reflections on the Decline of Science in England, and on Some of its Causes*. London: B. Fellowes.

BANKS, R.E.R. *et al.* (1994). *Sir Joseph Banks: a Global Perspective*.

BRETSCHNEIDER, E. (1898). *European Botanical Exploration in China*. London: Sampson Low.

BROWN, MALCOLM (1996). 'William Atkinson, F.G.S., F.H.S.: a versatile architect', *Archives of Natural History*, vol. 23, pp. 429-35.

BULTITUDE, J.W. (1947). 'Model fruit gardens at Wisley', *Fruit Year Book*, pp. 43-9.

CHADWICK, GEORGE F. (1961). *The Works of Sir Joseph Paxton*. London: Architectural Press.

CHITTENDEN, F.J. (1933). 'The Royal Horticultural Society's gardens at Wisley: the first twenty-five years', *JRHS*, vol. 58, pp. 258-87.

COATS, ALICE M. (1969). *The Quest for Plants*. London: Studio Vista.

CORY, REGINALD (1914). *The Horticultural Record* (1914). London: J. & A. Churchill.

COX, E.H.M. (1945). *Plant Hunting in China*. London: Collins.

COX, E.H.M. (1955). 'The plant collectors employed by the Royal Horticultural Society, 1804-1846', *JRHS*, vol. 80, pp. 264-80.

CURTIS, C.H. (1940). 'Chiswick Garden', *JRHS*, vol. 65, pp. 391-8.

DESMOND, RAY (1995). *Kew: the History of the Royal Botanic Gardens*. London: Harvill Press.

ELLIOTT, BRENT (1986). *Victorian Gardens*. London: B.T. Batsford.

ELLIOTT, BRENT (1988). 'Behind barbed wire', *The Garden (JRHS)*, vol. 113, pp. 530-4.

ELLIOTT, BRENT (1992). 'The South Kensington connection', *The Garden (JRHS)*, vol. 117, pp. 210-13.

ELLIOTT, BRENT (2001). 'Flower shows in nineteenth-century England', *GH*, vol. 29, pp. 171-84.

FLETCHER, H.R. (1969). *The Story of the Royal Horticultural Society*. London: Oxford University Press.

FLETCHER, H.R. (1970). *The Royal Botanic Garden Edinburgh 1670-1970*. Edinburgh: HMSO.

GEDDES-BROWN, LESLIE (2000). *Chelsea: the Greatest Flower Show on Earth*. London: Dorling Kindersley.

GILBERT, E.G. (1953). 'The development of the model fruit gardens at Wisley', *JRHS* vol. 77, pp. 344-9.

GOULD, N.K. (1946). 'The Wisley gardens and their development', *JRHS*, vol. 71, pp. 215-24.

GREGORY, JAMES [pseud. = Edward Beck] (1841). *A Packet of Seeds Saved by an Old Gardener*, 2nd ed. London: Chapman & Hall.

HAY, ROY (1946). *Gardener's Chance*. London: Putnam & Co. [actually published 21 April 1947].

HENREY, BLANCE (1975). *British Botanical and Horticultural Literature Before 1800*. Oxford: Clarendon Press.

HOBHOUSE, HERMIONE (2002). *The Crystal Palace and the Great Exhibition ... A History of the Royal Commission for the Exhibition of 1851*. London: Athlone Press.

HURST, RONA (1949). 'The R.H.S. and the birth of genetics', *JRHS*, vol. 74, pp. 377-89.

KNIGHT, THOMAS ANDREW (1805). 'Introductory remarks relative to the objects which the Horticultural Society have in view', *Transactions*, vol. 1, pp. 1-7.

KNIGHT, THOMAS ANDREW (1841). *A Selection of the Physiological and Horticultural Papers ... by Thomas Andrew Knight*. London: Longman, Orme, Brown, Green, and Longmans.

LARGE, E.C. (1940). *The Advance of the Fungi*. London: Jonathan Cape.

LE LIEVRE, AUDREY (1980). *Miss Willmott of Warley Place*. London: Faber & Faber.

LEMMON, KENNETH (1968). *The Golden Age of Plant Hunters*. London: Phoenix House.

MABBERLEY, D.J. (1985). *Jupiter Botanicus: Robert Brown and the British Museum*. Braunschweig: J. Cramer.

MARSDEN-SMEDLEY, HESTER (1975). *The Chelsea Flower Show*. London: Constable.

MEYNELL, GUY (1979). 'The personal issue underlying T.A. Knight's controversy with William Forsyth', *Journal of the Society for the Bibliography of Natural History*, vol. 9, pp. 281-7.

MEYNELL, GUY (1980). 'The Royal Botanic Society's Garden, Regent's Park', *London Journal*, vol. 6, pp. 135-46.

MORELAND, JOHN (2000). *Chelsea Gold*. London: Cassell.

MURRAY, ANDREW (1863). *The Book of the Royal Horticultural Society*. London: Bradbury & Evans.

MYLECHREEST, MURRAY (1984). 'Thomas Andrew Knight and the founding of the Royal Horticultural Society', *Garden History*, vol. 12, pp. 132-7.

OLBY, ROBERT (1966). *Origins of Mendelism*. London: Constable.

POSTAN, CYNTHIA, ed. (1996). *The Rhododendron Story*. London: Royal Horticultural Society.

RHS (1864). *The Official Handbook to the Royal Horticultural Gardens*. London: Royal Horticultural Society.

RHS (1978). *Wisley: the First Hundred Years*. London: Royal Horticultural Society.

RIX, MARTYN and ALISON (1989). *Wisley: the Royal Horticultural Society's Garden*. Baltonsborough, Somerset: Julian Holland.

SIMMONDS, ARTHUR (1941a). 'The founders: William Forsyth', *JRHS*, vol. 66, pp. 319-24.

SIMMONDS, ARTHUR (1941b). 'William Forsyth: a parliamentary grant and its sequel', vol. 66, pp. 374-81.

SIMMONDS, ARTHUR (1944a). 'The founders: Richard Anthony Salisbury', *JRHS*, vol. 69, pp. 95-100.

SIMMONDS, ARTHUR (1944b). 'A caricature of the Society', *JRHS*, vol. 69, pp. 324-32.

SIMMONDS, ARTHUR (1946). 'The Horticultural Fate', *JRHS*, vol. 71, pp. 43-4.

SIMMONDS, ARTHUR (1948). 'The Society's gardens behind the Royal Albert Hall', *JRHS*, vol. 73, pp. 70-3.

SIRKS, M.J. (1955). 'The Royal Horticultural Society and the science of genetics', *JRHS*, vol. 80, pp. 214-19.

STEARN, W.T., ed. (1999). *John Lindley 1799-1865: Gardener, Botanist, and Pioneer Orchidologist*. Woodbridge: Antique Collectors' Club.

TJADEN, W.L. (1974). *A History of the Horticultural Club 1875-1974*. Privately printed.

TJADEN, W.L. (1983). 'The Gardeners Gazette 1837-1847 and its rivals', *Garden History*, vol. 11, pp. 70-8.

TJADEN, W.L. (1986). 'George Glenny: horticultural hornet', *The Garden (JRHS)*, vol. 111, pp. 318-323.

TJADEN, W.L. (1987). 'The loss of a library', *The Garden (JRHS)*, vol. 112, pp. 386-8.

TJADEN, W.L. (1993). 'The Lindley Library of the Royal Horticultural Society, 1866-1926', *Archives of Natural History*, vol. 20, pp. 93-128.

TJADEN, W.L. (1994). 'The medals of the Royal Horticultural Society', *Archives of Natural History*, vol. 21, pp. 77-112.

WHITEN, FAITH and GEOFF (1982). *The Chelsea Flower Show*. London: Elm Tree Books. [Second edition, 1988] London, Cassell.

WILSON, GEORGE FERGUSSON (1874). *The Royal Horticultural Society, as it is and as it might be*. London: Gilbert.

WOUDSTRA, JAN and FIELDHOUSE, KEN, eds. (2000). *The Regeneration of Public Parks*. London: E. & F.N. Spon.

Index

Page numbers in *italics* refer to captions